Lecture Notes in Computer Science 13330

More information about this series at https://link.springer.com/bookseries/558

Qin Gao · Jia Zhou (Eds.)

Human Aspects of IT for the Aged Population

Design, Interaction and Technology Acceptance

8th International Conference, ITAP 2022
Held as Part of the 24th HCI International Conference, HCII 2022
Virtual Event, June 26 – July 1, 2022
Proceedings, Part I

Springer

Editors
Qin Gao
Tsinghua University
Beijing, China

Jia Zhou
Chongqing University
Chongqing, China

ISSN 0302-9743   ISSN 1611-3349 (electronic)
Lecture Notes in Computer Science
ISBN 978-3-031-05580-5   ISBN 978-3-031-05581-2 (eBook)
https://doi.org/10.1007/978-3-031-05581-2

Foreword

Human-computer interaction (HCI) is acquiring an ever-increasing scientific and industrial importance, as well as having more impact on people's everyday life, as an ever-growing number of human activities are progressively moving from the physical to the digital world. This process, which has been ongoing for some time now, has been dramatically accelerated by the COVID-19 pandemic. The HCI International (HCII) conference series, held yearly, aims to respond to the compelling need to advance the exchange of knowledge and research and development efforts on the human aspects of design and use of computing systems.

The 24th International Conference on Human-Computer Interaction, HCI International 2022 (HCII 2022), was planned to be held at the Gothia Towers Hotel and Swedish Exhibition & Congress Centre, Göteborg, Sweden, during June 26 to July 1, 2022. Due to the COVID-19 pandemic and with everyone's health and safety in mind, HCII 2022 was organized and run as a virtual conference. It incorporated the 21 thematic areas and affiliated conferences listed on the following page.

A total of 5583 individuals from academia, research institutes, industry, and governmental agencies from 88 countries submitted contributions, and 1276 papers and 275 posters were included in the proceedings to appear just before the start of the conference. The contributions thoroughly cover the entire field of human-computer interaction, addressing major advances in knowledge and effective use of computers in a variety of application areas. These papers provide academics, researchers, engineers, scientists, practitioners, and students with state-of-the-art information on the most recent advances in HCI. The volumes constituting the set of proceedings to appear before the start of the conference are listed in the following pages.

The HCI International (HCII) conference also offers the option of 'Late Breaking Work' which applies both for papers and posters, and the corresponding volume(s) of the proceedings will appear after the conference. Full papers will be included in the 'HCII 2022 - Late Breaking Papers' volumes of the proceedings to be published in the Springer LNCS series, while 'Poster Extended Abstracts' will be included as short research papers in the 'HCII 2022 - Late Breaking Posters' volumes to be published in the Springer CCIS series.

I would like to thank the Program Board Chairs and the members of the Program Boards of all thematic areas and affiliated conferences for their contribution and support towards the highest scientific quality and overall success of the HCI International 2022 conference; they have helped in so many ways, including session organization, paper reviewing (single-blind review process, with a minimum of two reviews per submission) and, more generally, acting as goodwill ambassadors for the HCII conference.

This conference would not have been possible without the continuous and unwavering support and advice of Gavriel Salvendy, founder, General Chair Emeritus, and Scientific Advisor. For his outstanding efforts, I would like to express my appreciation to Abbas Moallem, Communications Chair and Editor of HCI International News.

June 2022   Constantine Stephanidis

HCI International 2022 Thematic Areas and Affiliated Conferences

Thematic Areas

- HCI: Human-Computer Interaction
- HIMI: Human Interface and the Management of Information

Affiliated Conferences

- EPCE: 19th International Conference on Engineering Psychology and Cognitive Ergonomics
- AC: 16th International Conference on Augmented Cognition
- UAHCI: 16th International Conference on Universal Access in Human-Computer Interaction
- CCD: 14th International Conference on Cross-Cultural Design
- SCSM: 14th International Conference on Social Computing and Social Media
- VAMR: 14th International Conference on Virtual, Augmented and Mixed Reality
- DHM: 13th International Conference on Digital Human Modeling and Applications in Health, Safety, Ergonomics and Risk Management
- DUXU: 11th International Conference on Design, User Experience and Usability
- C&C: 10th International Conference on Culture and Computing
- DAPI: 10th International Conference on Distributed, Ambient and Pervasive Interactions
- HCIBGO: 9th International Conference on HCI in Business, Government and Organizations
- LCT: 9th International Conference on Learning and Collaboration Technologies
- ITAP: 8th International Conference on Human Aspects of IT for the Aged Population
- AIS: 4th International Conference on Adaptive Instructional Systems
- HCI-CPT: 4th International Conference on HCI for Cybersecurity, Privacy and Trust
- HCI-Games: 4th International Conference on HCI in Games
- MobiTAS: 4th International Conference on HCI in Mobility, Transport and Automotive Systems
- AI-HCI: 3rd International Conference on Artificial Intelligence in HCI
- MOBILE: 3rd International Conference on Design, Operation and Evaluation of Mobile Communications

List of Conference Proceedings Volumes Appearing Before the Conference

1. LNCS 13302, Human-Computer Interaction: Theoretical Approaches and Design Methods (Part I), edited by Masaaki Kurosu
2. LNCS 13303, Human-Computer Interaction: Technological Innovation (Part II), edited by Masaaki Kurosu
3. LNCS 13304, Human-Computer Interaction: User Experience and Behavior (Part III), edited by Masaaki Kurosu
4. LNCS 13305, Human Interface and the Management of Information: Visual and Information Design (Part I), edited by Sakae Yamamoto and Hirohiko Mori
5. LNCS 13306, Human Interface and the Management of Information: Applications in Complex Technological Environments (Part II), edited by Sakae Yamamoto and Hirohiko Mori
6. LNAI 13307, Engineering Psychology and Cognitive Ergonomics, edited by Don Harris and Wen-Chin Li
7. LNCS 13308, Universal Access in Human-Computer Interaction: Novel Design Approaches and Technologies (Part I), edited by Margherita Antona and Constantine Stephanidis
8. LNCS 13309, Universal Access in Human-Computer Interaction: User and Context Diversity (Part II), edited by Margherita Antona and Constantine Stephanidis
9. LNAI 13310, Augmented Cognition, edited by Dylan D. Schmorrow and Cali M. Fidopiastis
10. LNCS 13311, Cross-Cultural Design: Interaction Design Across Cultures (Part I), edited by Pei-Luen Patrick Rau
11. LNCS 13312, Cross-Cultural Design: Applications in Learning, Arts, Cultural Heritage, Creative Industries, and Virtual Reality (Part II), edited by Pei-Luen Patrick Rau
12. LNCS 13313, Cross-Cultural Design: Applications in Business, Communication, Health, Well-being, and Inclusiveness (Part III), edited by Pei-Luen Patrick Rau
13. LNCS 13314, Cross-Cultural Design: Product and Service Design, Mobility and Automotive Design, Cities, Urban Areas, and Intelligent Environments Design (Part IV), edited by Pei-Luen Patrick Rau
14. LNCS 13315, Social Computing and Social Media: Design, User Experience and Impact (Part I), edited by Gabriele Meiselwitz
15. LNCS 13316, Social Computing and Social Media: Applications in Education and Commerce (Part II), edited by Gabriele Meiselwitz
16. LNCS 13317, Virtual, Augmented and Mixed Reality: Design and Development (Part I), edited by Jessie Y. C. Chen and Gino Fragomeni
17. LNCS 13318, Virtual, Augmented and Mixed Reality: Applications in Education, Aviation and Industry (Part II), edited by Jessie Y. C. Chen and Gino Fragomeni

http://2022.hci.international/proceedings

Preface

The 8th International Conference on Human Aspects of IT for the Aged Population (ITAP 2022) was part of HCI International 2022. The ITAP conference addresses the design, adaptation, and use of IT technologies targeted to older people in order to counterbalance ability changes due to age, support cognitive, physical, and social activities, and maintain independent living and quality of life.

A strong and unique theme of this year's proceedings is the role and impact of information technologies in older people's life during the COVID-19 pandemic. Researchers from all over the world shared their findings on how older people accepted new technologies, including those applications specific to this special period, how they used new technologies to stay informed and connected during lockdown, and what the experience of this intense term reveals for the design and development of technologies to provide more reliable and resilient support for older people. Another emerging research area concerns innovative ways to involve older people in the design process to ensure that their needs and requirements are adequately elicited and properly addressed. Researchers continue to experiment on innovation and design of smart homes, robots, and VR/AR applications for older people, and the design of voice-based AI has received notable research attention. In addition to supporting older people's health and safety, enhancing social connections, and facilitating daily life activities, this years' proceedings also discuss how technologies can help older people to expand their life experience by bridging the gap between virtual and physical worlds, and how the wide adoption of information technologies has influenced intergenerational dynamics, which brings about further cultural and societal impact.

Two volumes of the HCII 2022 proceedings are dedicated to this year's edition of the ITAP conference, entitled Human Aspects of IT for the Aged Population: Design, Interaction, and Technology Acceptance (Part I) and Human Aspects of IT for the Aged Population: Technology in Everyday Living (Part II). The first focuses on topics related to design and gamification for aging; mobile, wearable and multimodal interaction for aging; and social media use and digital literacy of the elderly, as well as technology acceptance and adoption and related barriers and facilitators for older adults, while the second focuses on topics related to intelligent environments for daily activities support, health and wellbeing technologies for the elderly, and communication and social interaction for older adults.

Papers of these volumes are included for publication after a minimum of two single-blind reviews from the members of the ITAP Program Board or, in some cases, from members of the Program Boards of other affiliated conferences. We would like to thank all of them for their invaluable contribution, support, and efforts.

June 2022

Qin Gao
Jia Zhou

8th International Conference on Human Aspects of IT for the Aged Population (ITAP 2022)

Program Board Chairs: **Qin Gao**, Tsinghua University, China and **Jia Zhou**, Chongqing University, China

- Inês Amaral, University of Coimbra, Portugal
- Ning An, Hefei University of Technology, China
- Maria José Brites, Lusófona University, Portugal
- Alan H. S. Chan, City University of Hong Kong, Hong Kong
- Honglin Chen, Eastern Finland University, Finland
- Hongtu Chen, Harvard Medical School, USA
- Loredana Ivan, National University of Political Studies and Public Administration, Romania
- Chaiwoo Lee, MIT, USA
- Hai-Ning Liang, Xi'an Jiaotong-Liverpool University, China
- Chi Hung Lo, Tunghai University, Taiwan
- Eugene Loos, Utrecht University, The Netherlands
- Xinggang Luo, Hangzhou Dianzi University, China
- Yan Luximon, Hong Kong Polytechnic University, Hong Kong
- Lourdes Moreno Lopez, Universidad Carlos III de Madrid, Spain
- Simone Mulargia, Lumsa University, Italy
- Karen Renaud, University of Strathclyde, UK
- Wang-Chin Tsai, National Yunlin University of Science and Technology, Taiwan
- Ana Isabel Veloso, University of Aveiro, Portugal
- Nadine Vigouroux, University of Toulouse, France
- Konstantinos Votis, CERTH/ITI, Greece
- Yuxiang (Chris) Zhao, Nanjing University of Science and Technology, China

The full list with the Program Board Chairs and the members of the Program Boards of all thematic areas and affiliated conferences is available online at

http://www.hci.international/board-members-2022.php

HCI International 2023

The 25th International Conference on Human-Computer Interaction, HCI International 2023, will be held jointly with the affiliated conferences at the AC Bella Sky Hotel and Bella Center, Copenhagen, Denmark, 23–28 July 2023. It will cover a broad spectrum of themes related to human-computer interaction, including theoretical issues, methods, tools, processes, and case studies in HCI design, as well as novel interaction techniques, interfaces, and applications. The proceedings will be published by Springer. More information will be available on the conference website: http://2023.hci.international/.

General Chair
Constantine Stephanidis
University of Crete and ICS-FORTH
Heraklion, Crete, Greece
Email: general_chair@hcii2023.org

http://2023.hci.international/

Contents – Part I

Mobile, Wearable and Multimodal Interaction for Aging

Aging, Social Media and Digital Literacy

Technology Acceptance and Adoption: Barriers and Facilitators for Older Adults

Contents – Part II

Health and Wellbeing Technologies for the Elderly

Aging, Communication and Social Interaction

Aging, Design and Gamification

Contribution Participatory Methodologies and Generational Research

Maria José Brites[1]($\boxtimes$) , Teresa Sofia Castro[2,3] , Ana Filipa Oliveira[3] ,
and Inês Amaral[4,5]

[1] Lusófona University, CICANT, Porto, Portugal
mariajosebrites@ulp.pt
[2] Nova University of Lisbon, ICNOVA, Lisboa, Portugal
[3] Lusófona University, Porto, Portugal
{teresasofiacastro,p6764}@ulp.pt
[4] Faculty of Arts and Humanities, University of Coimbra, Coimbra, Portugal
ines.amaral@uc.pt
[5] Communication and Society Research Centre of the University of Minho, Braga, Portugal

Abstract. This paper debates and describes how the use of participatory methodologies were useful and flexible to engage and access the digital attitudes and practices of different generations of participants - from young people to older people - involved in two research projects in Portugal: DiCi-Educa and SMaRT-EU. The paper also describes the methodological decisions and how these impacted in participants involvement as how they adjusted to different contexts, including disconnecting settings and COVID-19 and its digital challenges, in DiCi-Educa. Both projects used workshops as an active and participatory methodology to engage the different generations with transformations during COVID-19 pandemic context. Despite the unpredictable difficulties, the use of the online environment also promoted positive ways of better engaging with the participants, namely in the SMaRT-EU project. Both experiences were very enriching to prepare a third project we present in the final part of the paper: YouNDigital.

1 Introduction

This paper discusses the use of participatory methodologies to engage and access the digital attitudes and practices of different generations of participants involved in two research projects: DiCi-Educa (cofinanced by Calouste Gulbenkian Foundation, General Directorate of Reintegration and Prisons - DGRSP and Lusófona University) and SMaRT-EU (European Commission, LC-01563446). These methodologies prove to be a useful and flexible approach with different generational groups contexts: young people, adults and older people. DiCi-Educa is an action research project with young people institutionalized in juvenile delinquency educational centres (from now on designated as ECs), and SMaRT-EU – Social Media Resilience Toolkit involves intergenerational groups of participants. The two projects followed similar approaches where participatory workshops were privileged to engage participants in thematic sections and reflections on issues of digital citizenship, media education, and information literacy. Since both projects were designed and planned in pre-COVID times, this paper will discuss both the challenges, obstacles, good practices, and the lessons learned in the field, and the work the two research teams developed with the participants. We will discuss offline and online settings since both projects had to adjust to the pandemic and the context of doing research digitally by default.

Finally, taking advantage of these experiences in the final part of the article we present a third project designed and recently approved during the COVID pandemic - which means its methodological approach was designed to consider this strong digitalisation of fieldwork: YouNDigital (Portuguese Foundation for Science and Technology, PTDC/COM-OUT/0243/2021). The project will run from 2022 to 2024, and it will add a multidimensional element with the inclusion of a digital newsroom, which will have a participatory focus involving young people to explore their *prosuming* relations with the news.

In the first part of the article, we will engage with the existing literature, establishing connections with the three research projects presented here. In the following sections, we will detail the methodology and research questions, followed by each projects' main results.

2 Literature Review

The participatory culture context [1] amplified by always-on digital environments led to an increased emergence of core (digital) skills and new forms of (digital) civic and political engagement and forms of expressing and participating digitally with responsibility [2] that need to be deeply understood.

The United Nations Convention on the Rights of the Child (UNCRC) was a crucial document with an impact on children's status in both domains: in society and in research. From this moment on, children, as every person aged under 18 years old, became recognised as social actors worthy of being studied in their own right [3], and their experiences and perspectives about life became valued to understand this social group. This shift rescued this demographic group from the previous social invisibility [4]. Children and young people were no longer seen as a homogeneous group; instead, they became recognised by researchers as respected and competent informants capable of making active decisions and critically describing their lived experiences [5]. In this line of thought, recognising children as 'agentic' implies recognising they can and do "influence their lives, the lives of their peers and that of the wider community around them" [6]. From passive and invisible beings, relegated to the social context of family and home, the UNCRC earned for children the active participants role empowered by the recognition of their right of freedom of thought and expression, capable of contributing in decisions regarding matters that affect them [7].

This important upsurge in empirical interest in children/young people for the past decades, and their recognition as participants in research raised new ethical discussions, dilemmas, concerns, and responsibilities for researchers.

Children and young people's participation in research is inspired in the 'ladder of participation' proposed by Hart [8], which by its turn is inspired in Arnestein's citizenship ladder, "a beginning typology to think about children's participation in projects" [8], and better perceive the different levels of children's active enrolment, and their power (agency) in decision-making processes. Nevertheless, there are some pitfalls in participatory projects, as Thomas [9] alerts by distinguishing between 'participation' and 'consultation'. Participation projects are child-centred when they give children more power to see their engagement translated into a real social contribution; when it enables children to be heard and actively involved in decision-making processes about issues that are part of and affect their lives, whether individually or collectively. Consultation, on the other hand, as the word suggests, operates by asking for children's and young people's opinions, which by the way may or may not be considered, and this approach does not even require hearing the children directly. The risk in consultation is that children's voices may be reduced to just a glimpse of their views. Interestingly the same ladder can be inspiring when putting to test or when considering the level of participation of other demographic groups in research.

James and James reason children's and young people's participation as the opportunity "to take part in and contribute actively to a situation, an event, a process or an outcome" [10].

In line with this, the ethical framework that guided the projects mentioned previously, endorsed the consequentialist model elaborated from the feminist ethic of care [11] and 'ethical symmetry' [12]. To avoid undesirable and instrumental pitfalls, hence, consideration of ethics was a reflexive exercise that happened "before, after and during the research" [13].

Corroborating Woodhead and Faulkner's observation: "significant knowledge gains result when children's active participation in the research process is deliberately solicited and when their perspectives, views and feelings are accepted as genuine, valid evidence" [14].

Thus, departing from a robust ethical preoccupation in the field of children rights we move to an intergenerational perspective. We privileged participatory and experimental methodologies based on dialogue [15] and Freire's principle that "teaching is not about transferring knowledge; it is about creating possibilities for its production" [16]. In DiCi-Educa we mostly worked with young people, while, in parallel, considering the needs of the staff, and in SMaRT-EU we closely approached an intergenerational perspective.

Recently, COVID-19 pandemic and the turn to the digital, raised other challenges related with methodological and ethical concerns and pressures that needed careful thought and reflexivity [17, 18]. For all this, ethical requirements take a crucial place in the three projects, which follow the standard of Portuguese and European procedures and good practices to ensure participants safety, anonymity, and data confidentiality, along with the gathering, analysis, exploitation and dissemination of the data.

3   Methodology

DiCi-Educa focuses on young offenders institutionalized in Educational Centers (ECs), with whom we took a non-formal education approach and training to support them develop competencies on media literacy and digital citizenship, based on dialogical reflexive and critical thinking strategies, with a particular focus on key skills namely, communication, critical and reflexive thinking, which ultimately translate in their active and civic participation in the surrounding world and in an increasingly mediatized society. The training with the institutionalized young people (aged 12–18) was based on situations that offered rich discussion and reflection. The goal was to empower these participants with a clear lack of awareness about their social role as citizens and make them reflect on the impact of their decisions and actions participating in their community, in their relationships and their (digital) health. Hence, the fieldwork developed in two dimensions: i) workshops based on a thematic toolkit approaching topics on digital media literacy and citizenship taking in consideration participants' views, and life experiences (e.g. digital rights/duties, competencies for the XXI century). Nevertheless, it is important to add that the DiCi institutions - the ECs - do not grant internet access to the youngsters (for security reasons), which means that these very digitally entangled issues had to be reflected and discussed in a disconnected setting, relying on participants' memories of their digital experiences. The intergenerational factor in this project was envisaged by the active participation of ECs staff in the training reflecting with the group based on their views and personal life experiences. After March 2020, the training was conducted via video chatting platforms.

The European project SMaRT-EU - Social Media Resilience Toolkit was cofunded by the European Commission (LC-01563446) and had as the main objective to provide tools, suggestions, and resources to train young people, old people and educators to be more resilient and critical in the face of misinformation and fake news in an intergenerational perspective. Considering the potential of holding participatory workshops to actively engage the research team and the project's participants, as well as to promote discussions in contexts where it is not usual to talk about specific subjects or to promote interaction between groups that often do not interact - such as different generations [19] -, in the scope of SMaRT-EU intergenerational participatory workshops were conducted to focus on pressing issues related to fake news, critical perspective towards social networks and digital footprint. Due to the pandemic context, the workshops took place in a digital environment, relying on Zoom to gather and reach participants from different backgrounds and sociodemographic contexts.

After initial brainstorming, the research team decided to address six different subjects in the workshops, all associated with the confluence of media education, digital citizenship and disinformation challenges. The original template was created by the Croatian team members, in English. Afterwards, the materials were translated and adapted by the national teams to each country's specificities, such as language, target groups and contexts (http://smart-toolkit.eu/participatory-workshops/). The sessions were carefully designed, seeking to achieve a balance between the provision of information and the promotion of a learning context that valued the participants' interventions and opinions.

Lastly, and considering the lessons and the knowledge built from the two previous projects and the new landscape of digital challenges that emerged with the sanitary crisis, YouNDigital aims to understand the attitudes and practices that young people have concerning news and digital citizenship. The project builds from establishing connections between the younger generations and their relations with the news while at the same time considering the role influential adults have in the building of their news consumption behaviours and habits. It is expected to get a better understanding of their news interests and needs, socialisation processes for news consumption either in the family, school, peer group context, and their experiences as "produsers" of news. This project is anchored in a participatory action-research approach combined with an initial online survey and a central focus on qualitative methods.

For this paper we will ground our contribution reflecting on three research questions: (RQ1) what were the most challenging parts of the participatory dimensions of the projects? (RQ2) What extra challenges were added due to COVID-19? (RQ3) What were the critical ethical dimensions of these research projects?

4 Results

The first research project, DiCi-Educa, was conceived to be a participatory project with the objective of offering subjective thinking using an informal and ludic experiences and approaches to work with institutionalized young people and the staff (e.g., educators, psychologists, social assistants) that work with them in the ECs. We decided to promote very hands-on, thematic and reflexive workshops. In the technical (but offline context) workshops, we used an equipment kit with computers, web and photo cameras, audio recorders, 360° cameras, and sound editing software. The thematic part of the workshops was a moment to present and discuss issues around participation, digital citizenship and otherness. During these moments of the training, they were able to express and bring what they discussed in the thematic workshop into a digital product (photovoice, 360° videos, radio shows – podcast, songs). This combination of the theory with the digital making allowed young people to improve their creativity, communication and critical perspectives as well as technical and literacy skills, while promoting negotiation and collaborative work, dimensions quite important in the process of future reintegration in society.

We can evaluate the level of reflexivity that the participants reached based on the discussions and the multimodal digital outputs they develop during the training. These outputs expressed their own views and voices, on how they see the surrounding world and their own lives (family, friends, past/future lives). Along the project, we were able to notice signs of positive transformation and maturity of youngsters' views, and critical thinking on matters that were very grounded in very conservative, patriarchal and narrow views.

Although the training was centred on institutionalized young people needs, we adopted strategies and contents to take into consideration the educational project, rules and schedules of each EC (with the assent of the DGRSP, partner in the project) as well as the characteristics of each group, and interests as much as possible. The training involved also the staff working in the ECs, so they can continue this work after the end of the project. ECs staff work with a lot of constraints (including lack of professionals, overload of paperwork and bureaucracies, lack of digital skills and updated digital resources), so we were expecting to have professionals more dedicated to absorbing the DiCi-Educa approach and ensuring its future sustainability, but this was not straightforward. For the future, we consider that it is fundamental to conceive a training working package for professionals of the ECs and other professionals that work with institutionalised children and young people.

We clarified from the beginning that we wanted to create possibilities for them to open up and reflect not only in the perspective of their lives but also, and mostly, to prospective their future after finishing the tutelary measure. After the workshops, they shared a richer standpoint in critically evaluating the social appropriation of digital and demonstrated to have gained a safer consideration of their online behaviour, and of enlarging the view they had on what participation is.

At the beginning of the workshops, they had a very narrow idea of this concept and what it entails, and about forms of participation either at a micro or macro level (unaware of how they could actively participate, for instance in their close communities: neighbourhood, school, etc.). Later, when asked on how workshops can help them to prepare a better self and for a better future, some pointed to using digital media to express emotions through video, to teach others and to use them in their future jobs: "I want to be a plumber and I can take advantage of digital to photograph damaged pipes, for example" and "safeguard my privacy, by not sharing personal data and intimate photos". In addition, three of these young people started attending courses in multimedia and sound, an experience that was heavily stimulated by the project.

We believe that DiCi-Educa methodology promotes this philosophy. The methodology and approach to the youngsters were prepared to ensure a bottom-up and participatory approach, both when bringing to discussion more thematic critical thinking topics or when involving them in more practical and technical moments. We also revised and validated our strategies by making a dialogic and reflexive evaluation involving the research team, to weigh what went well and in which way we needed to make improvements or use different strategies. At the same time, was granted a more active and reflexive role from the perspective of young people. From the 3rd group onwards, we involved youngsters who already were in the project as ambassadors, not just to give them recognition, but also to make them feel part of the project, and to have them acting and ensuring a peer-to-peer education approach. Some of these young people repeated on their own accord up to 3 times these blocks of workshops. This clearly demonstrates the engagement and the positive impact the experience of this project had in their lives.

Working at an EC is a twofold challenge, on the one hand, because we are working with marginalized, stigmatised young people and, on the other hand, because we have to obey high-security protocols. To keep youngsters motivated and involved we had to be very committed, but also creative, and flexible enough to perceive and address their needs and interests.

The challenges were reinforced by the emergency of COVID-19. Further to the situation in itself, the project had been prepared completely within a face-to-face paradigm. For security reasons, from the beginning, we knew that we would need to implement the project about digital citizenship in a disconnection setting. The lockdowns situation completely changed the paradigm, without putting at risk the security aspects. ECs were among the first institutions to lockdown in Portugal, in March 2020, and they had for the first time to give in and to reconsider the access to the internet. During the lockdown, the DGRSP and the ECs decided to give the youngsters' access to the internet to enable video calls to keep closely in touch with their families. Also, classes moved to online learning. To face these unexpected ordeals the ethical needs to be an ongoing exercise due to the nature and the target of the project. We found some resistance and narrow views in relation to racism and women/men roles as we highlighted before. During the training sessions (thematic, practical and reflexive) we adopted the position of not looking on the other side when we identified some of these situations or when we were questioned about these subjects with situations on pluralism and diversity. We tried to open up their perspectives by bringing to the table diverse examples, but we will rely on one example to illustrate. In between groups, there was a small mutiny in an EC we were working on. When we were allowed to return there, during the discussion on participation, they questioned if a mutiny was a form of participation. This was a very enriching opportunity by that time to reflect with them on the basis of positive and negative forms of participation and also in relation to citizenship and the common good.

Regarding SMaRT-EU's results, we can highlight several aspects related to the online participatory approach. Firstly, the use of online platforms provided a way to reach both young and old people, locations and groups, something that would have been extremely difficult if the project was conducted in the offline world. By switching to an online model, it was possible to meet the purpose of promoting dialogue and enriching moments of co-cooperation and co-learning, while giving the opportunity to people with digital competencies and others with low literacy levels to explore not only new tools and environments but also new subjects, through learning-by-doing and the exchange of experiences. As to the research team, the use of online platforms presented itself as a solution to pursue the research surpassing time and space constraints resulting from the pandemic, and it allowed the researchers to contact people from different backgrounds and age groups in the same space. Furthermore, by relying on the online platforms as a way to conduct research, it was possible to have a closer look into the participants' routines, habits, and experiences, and to learn from them – aspects that we consider extremely rewarding and not always possible in research projects conducted in the offline world.

However, challenges were also identified in the transition to the online training environment, mainly related to age (digital) gaps. Some of the older participants found it strange to talk to people on the other side of the screen and participants aged over 90 reported to have never used the internet before and did not know how to use it - although some of them had used tools such as Skype and WhatsApp to communicate with their families during lockdown periods. In addition, it was also noticed that while older people missed physical contact and seeing people in person during the sessions, youngsters were used to the reality of online contact and online education and did not find it strange to meet new people and learn through digital tools and platforms.

The research team also had to deal with a number of challenges. First off, by moving to the online environment the recruitment of participants and scheduling of the sessions proved to be more difficult than if the sessions were to be conducted face to face. Namely, recruiting older participants and finding viable dates and times to gather all participant groups was a demanding task. Then, it was not possible to avoid technical challenges and issues such as bad internet connection, lack of availability of devices, and demanding technical conditions, constraints that were constant in the sessions. Finally, issues related to the digital divide also emerged. By working with diverse groups, some of them with marked economic and social inequalities and with low levels of access, use or knowledge of ICTs, it was difficult to address some subjects. The research team encountered several difficulties related, for example, to the language and terminologies used.

4.1 YouNDigital: Intergenerational Approach, Departing from the Point of View of Young People

The lessons learned in the two previous research projects will feed YouNDigital (Portuguese Foundation for Science and Technology, PTDC/COM-OUT/0243/2021), particularly the newsroom approach with young people. Digital newsrooms allow to bring together young people worldwide. We aim to capture their interest to participate actively in the project. This stage is very relevant because it will allow them to participate by expressing their interests in a learning-by-doing manner. For sure, this part of the project will benefit from intergenerational experiences where we listen in semi-structured interviews and media diaries that will gather together young people and adults, some of their family members in the discussion about news and digital citizenship options and influences.

Promoting knowledge transference and societal impact - the creation of the digital newsroom and of two training courses aimed at youth, educators, journalists and decision-makers that will be available to the international community. These two tasks are especially relevant to promote and solidify the transference of knowledge at the national and international level, - corresponding and seeking to overcome societal challenges - and promote knowledge through a sustainable education perspective.

YouNDigital expects to show valuable results that can underline better understanding about young people's attitudes and practices towards news with an international perspective and deepen our understanding on the processes related to digital citizenship (expectations, action, competencies) that can be fostered by a participatory approach and with learning-by-doing approach. Learning about news processes, their dynamics, to better understand how to deal with news and surpass challenges, like fake news and disinformation. Another important aspect is to collect participants' own reflections about the research process in co-collaboration, reinforcing citizen science dimensions. Lastly, with the training courses, we aim to create awareness about news, digital citizenship and news literacy.

5 Final Notes and Future Perspectives

These past and in progress projects and the transition to pandemic times evidenced increasing challenges in being digitally inclusive, and in addressing and ensuring participatory dimensions of the research, in particularly, when older people and young people institutionalized. The same happens regarding the ethical dimensions. The digital context will reinforce these and other unforeseen situations we need to take care of, not only for tackling those that are always being left behind, but also more operational aspects related with cybersecurity reasons, and to cover participants' (digital) rights, including participation and protection of personal rights.

References

1. Jenkins, H., Clinton, K., Purushotma, R., Robison, A.J., Weigel, M.: Confronting the Challenges of Participatory Culture: Media Education for the 21st Century. MacArthur Foundation, Chicago (2009)
2. Frau-Meigs, D., O'Neill, B., Soriani, A., Tomé, V.: Digital Citizenship Education: Overview and New Perspectives (vol. 1). Council of Europe, Strasbourg (2017)
3. Hill, M., Davis, J., Prout, A., Tisdall, K.: Moving the participation agenda forward. Child. Soc. **18**(2), 77–96 (2004)
4. James, A., Prout, A.: Introduction. In: James, A., Prout, A. (eds.) Constructing and reconstructing childhood. Contemporary issues in the sociological study of childhood, 2nd edn. Falmer Press, UK (2005)
5. Montgomery, H.: Childhood an anthropological approach. In: Kehily, M.J. (ed.) Understanding childhood: a cross-disciplinary approach, pp. 163–209. The Policy Press, UK (2013)
6. Waller, T.: Modern Childhoods: contemporary theories and children's lives. In: Waller, T., Davis, G. (eds.), An Introduction to Early Childhood. 3rd end., pp. 27–46. SAGE, NY (2012)
7. Balen, R.: Involving children in health and social research: 'human becomings' or 'active beings'? Childhood **13**(1), 29–48 (2006)
8. Hart, R.: Children's Participation: From Tokenism to Citizenship. Innocenti Essay no.4 (1992)
9. Thomas, N.: Towards a theory of children's participation. Int. J. Children's Rights **15**(2), 199–218 (2007)
10. James, A., James, A.: Keys Concepts in Childhood Studies. SAGE Publications Ltd., NY (2009)
11. Denzin, N., Lincoln, Y. (eds.): Handbook of qualitative research. SAGE, California (1994)
12. Christensen, P., Prout, A.: Working with ethical symmetry in social research with children. Childhood **9**(4), 477–497 (2002)
13. Boyden, J., Ennew, J.: Children in Focus: A Manual for Participatory Research with Children. Radda Barnen, Stockholm (1997)
14. Woodhead, M., Faulkner, D.: Subjects, objects or participants? dilemmas of psychological research with children. In: Christensen, P., James, A. (eds.) Research with children. Perspectives and Practices, pp. 9–3. Routledge Falmer, UK (2003)
15. Freire, P.: A educação como prática da liberdade. Editora Paz e Terra, São Paulo (1967)
16. Freire, P.: Pedagogia da autonomia: saberes necessários à prática educativa. Editora Paz e Terra (1996/2010)
17. Castro, T.: Research, children and ethics: an ongoing dialogue. Revista EDaPECI – Educação a Distância e Práticas Educativas Comunicacionais e Interculturais, dossiê: Ética em Pesquisa em Contextos Educativos. **17**(2), 81–92 (2017)
18. Castro, T.: Overcoming pandemic social distancing challenges in research in Portugal and England. J. Child. Media **15**(1), 130–133 (2021)
19. Lamas, R., Burnett, G., Cobb, S., Harvey, C.: Please Let me in: A Participatory Workshop Approach to the Design of a Driver-to-driver Communication Device. Procedia Manufacturing. **3**, 3309–3316 (2015)

Safety and Ethical Considerations When Designing a Virtual Reality Study with Older Adult Participants

Julie A. Brown[1]([✉]) [iD], An T. Dinh[2] [iD], and Chorong Oh[1] [iD]

[1] Ohio University, Athens, OH 45701, USA
{brownj14,ohc}@ohio.edu
[2] The University of Toledo, Toledo, OH 43606, USA
an.dinh@utoledo.edu

Abstract. Research focusing on virtual reality (VR) has increased in recent years as multiple mobile systems have become available to the mass consumer market. In particular, there has been greater attention to how VR may serve as a tool to benefit, promote, and assess health-related and wellbeing aspects for older adults. However, there are potential risks that researchers need to be aware of when designing such a study. This manuscript provides an overview of select usability factors that merit consideration to ensure the safety of potential older adult participants. This includes cybersickness, balance and falls, vision, hearing, arthritis, and cognitive limitations. Although not all older adults are at risk for harm when using VR, researchers need to be aware of potential issues for screening purposes and ensure safety throughout the study. In addition, older adults need to be adequately informed about risk factors before agreeing to participate and what forms of support will be in place to ensure safety.

Keywords: Virtual reality · Older adults · Safety

1 Introduction

Virtual Reality (VR) research has spanned multiple disciplines and areas of study, from medicine [1] to hospitality and tourism [2]. More so, research in this area has gained traction since the advent of VR provided on head-mounted displays (also known as HDMs), including those that use a smartphone. As VR technology has continued to advance, researchers have been exploring ways that it may serve as a tool to promote or measure health and aspects of wellbeing. In particular, there has been increasing interest in VR application and use among select older adult populations [e.g., 3–17].

When considering the design of a VR study and the diversity of functional abilities and needs within the older adult population, safety considerations must be taken into account. Not doing so has the potential to put some older adult participants at risk for harm. In addition, ethical considerations need to be given when exploring potential VR use among older adult participants, as it cannot be assumed that it would be an enjoyable experience and of benefit to each person. This manuscript was designed to provide an

© The Author(s), under exclusive license to Springer Nature Switzerland AG 2022
Q. Gao and J. Zhou (Eds.): HCII 2022, LNCS 13330, pp. 12–26, 2022.
https://doi.org/10.1007/978-3-031-05581-2_2

overview of such considerations. More specifically, the aims of this study were 1) to identify health-related aspects that may influence VR engagement, 2) to investigate safe options and workarounds for VR use, and 3) to explore ethical considerations for VR use, among older adult users.

Research Aims:

1) To identify health-related aspects among older adults that may influence VR engagement.
2) To explore safe options and workarounds for VR use among older adult users.
3) To explore ethical considerations for VR use among older adult users.

2 Background

About six years ago, Samsung's introduction of Gear VR opened the door for researchers to explore how VR could be used and applied in varied settings. This was followed by the mass marketing of newer VR products, such as Oculus Quest. As increasingly affordable VR systems continue to advance in ways that offer unique experiences, it is reasonable to suggest that its appeal will continue to grow among tech-savvy consumers. Yet, will this trend be reflected among older adult consumers?

Consumers in modernized societies typically adopt newer modes of digital technology as they are available to the mass market and this rate is reflected in technology adoption and use among older populations (those age 65 +). For example, a market report indicated that the proportion of older Americans who use smartphones more than doubled between 2012 and 2017 and tablet computer ownership also increased to roughly one-third of the older population [18]. Moreover, a more recent study indicated that 77% of older adults owned a smartphone by 2020 [19]. These findings indicate a shift in older adult consumer characteristics as more tech-savvy Baby Boomers transition into older adulthood.

The origin of this manuscript stems from a pilot study and then primary study that explored VR usability and potential application among community-dwelling older adults [20]. In the primary study 10 older adults were asked to view a series of self-selected videos on a mobile HDM VR device and navigate through the program with a handheld remote. Participants were then interviewed to glean insight on their experience. This was then followed with two focus groups to capture collective perspectives that surfaced from a guided discussion. Overall, the aim of the study was to identify usability issues with the participants use of the VR system, preferences for video content, and potential applications for older adults.

A notable observation and topic of discussion was the number of safety factors that emerged over the course of both the pilot study and the primary study. Although no participants were harmed in either, individual interviews and focus group discussions highlighted concern about how VR could be an uncomfortable – or unsafe- experience for some older adults, especially those who may be identified as vulnerable.

The key points discussed in this manuscript are a direct reflection of the observations and findings of the studies described above [20]. In addition, supportive material was identified by reviewing related studies that reflected comparable findings (e.g., cyber-sickness, balance, etc.) Google Scholar and PubMed were used as the primary search engines.

3 Functional Ability and Health Considerations for Safe VR Use

When technologies are introduced to the mass market, it is only natural for researchers to think creatively about how the technology could be of use to help or enhance some aspects of a person's life. This may include those who explore potential technology applications among older adults with specific needs. However, some of these older adults may be regarded as vulnerable, either due to physical or cognitive decline that influences their ability to be fully independent.

Yet before a researcher assesses older individual use of a technology like VR, they must first have an appropriate level of understanding of their participants' health status in relation to the study. For example, a researcher who is assessing the potential benefits of an app on a smartphone may first need to know that a participant can clearly see and know how to use the app. So, if the potential participant had significant vision loss and/or severe arthritis in the hands that would prevent them from holding or using a smartphone, this may exclude them from the study.

In addition, it is critical for researchers to consider potential safety issues before assessing the use or application of a specific technology with an older adult participant, especially those who may be classified as vulnerable. A key component to this is an adult's range of functional ability and potential limitations that are a result of age-related or pathological changes. Naturally, the functional ability of older adults cannot (and must not) be lumped into one general category based on chronological age because older adults are the most heterogeneous population in terms of functional ability.

Many of the age-related changes that tend to occur with persons as they age are normative – meaning, these are changes that are typical of advancing age. This can include a decline in visual acuity and reaction time. Whereas, other physical changes that can occur in older adulthood can be traced to a pathological source (i.e., a disease) and can be chronic in nature. For example, this would include macular degeneration or osteoporosis.

An adult's functional ability is also influenced by life course factors that shapes their health over time. For example, an individual who had a long and physically demanding career with low-wages and/or health insurance is in a position to experience health issues in older adulthood due to potential strain on the body over time and limited access to healthcare to address health-related needs. Whereas, this may not be the case as much for someone whose job was physically accommodating and allowed them to have easy access to quality health-related services and forms of self-care.

So, although age can serve as a general indicator, when considering the functional status and health of older adult participants in a study, one cannot use "age" alone as criteria to participate. For example, it is possible for a 67-year-old to have mobility issues and severe hearing loss, yet also for a 84-year old to be independent and active. However, in either case, a researcher may not be aware of their experience and proficiency with digital technologies unless it is specifically asked as part of the screening process. These are important components to keep in mind when designing a study with older adults and their current or potential use of digital technologies.

Some aspects of health and functional ability may not be apparent in the screening process of a VR study but can put a participant at risk for harming themselves. It is these aspects that merit further consideration before employing a study. This may influence the formulation of inclusion and exclusion criteria or things to be aware of during the study to minimize harm to the participant.

3.1 Cybersickness

One of the first considerations that may come to mind when designing a VR study is cybersickness. Cybersickness is similar to motion sickness. However, they are not the same, as motion sickness tends to involve stimulation of the vestibular system and that alone can cause symptoms [21]. Yet, visual stimulation can also contribute to motion sickness [22]. Contrary, cybersickness can be induced from just visual stimulation alone.

Cybersickness affects persons differently and can be dependent upon the visual stimuli [23]. Symptoms may include the following: eye strain, headache, pallor, sweating, dryness of mouth, fullness of stomach, disorientation, vertigo, ataxia, nausea, and vomiting.

Although cybersickness has been a focus of some VR studies, reports among the older adult participants have been found to be of minimal [24, 25]. Nonetheless, it is important for researchers to be aware of it as a potential side effect among study participants, include appropriate information in the consent form, and closely monitor the participants for symptoms.

Symptoms do not always occur during use of the VR system but emerge in the hours following [23]. Participants – and in some cases, caregivers – would need to know what to be aware of should symptoms of cybersickness appear in the hours following the study. In particular, cybersickness could be potentially dangerous to those who are already managing notable health issues (i.e., residents of a skilled nursing care facility or nursing home). Similarly, community dwelling adults need to be aware of this possibility and considerations, such as driving after the study, need to be taken into account.

One way to help minimize the enrollment of older adults who may be at risk for cybersickness is to incorporate a question that asks about a history of motion sickness in the inclusion/exclusion criteria. In addition, it may be advantageous to utilize a VR environment where the older adult participant controls the simulation rather than being a passive observer [26]. For example, this would be like comparing a VR gaming environment where the user controls their virtual actions and movement to a user who is watching a recorded video and take on a more observational, passive role. If employing a video in the study, the quality of the video would need to be taken into account. Videos that include movement and are recorded without a stabilization mechanism are likely to produce footage that includes shaking, which may induce cybersickness.

Finally, to help minimize harm that may be due to cybersickness after the study, it would be advantageous for the older adult participant to remain at the location where the study took place. This is especially important for those who intend to drive afterward. For some studies, this would be an appropriate time to conduct a follow-up interview or to provide them with a comfortable environment where they can relax for an hour before leaving. And, of course, it would appropriate for a research team member to check with the adult to verify that they are feeling okay before leaving.

3.2 Balance and Falls

Falls are the single leading cause of injury among older persons. Approximately 30% of older adults experience falls every year [27], often causing premature mortality, loss of independence, and placement in assisted living facilities among them [28]. They can be caused by intrinsic factors – i.e., age-related physiologic changes – and extrinsic factors – i.e., environmental barriers or hazards. Intrinsic components that influence balance includes considerations such as increased postural sway, slowed reflexes, gait speed, reduced peripheral sensation, weakened lower limb strength, [29–31] and changes in cognition particularly in domains of executive function and working memory [32–35]. Although falls area associated with adults who have increased risk factors, such as a chronic health condition, they also occur among those who are regarded as functionally healthy.

To help decrease – or even eliminate – the opportunity of a fall when using VR, there are several precautions that can be employed by researchers. An increasing number of VR games and videos are becoming available where the user is encouraged to stand as a means to engage. If aspects of balance and standing are being assessed, a stable support can be made available, like a grab bar, for the user to hold onto. The benefit of standing in this kind of situation is that it may allow the user to better observe and explore the visual field of the VR system. In other words, they are better positioned to look in full range of directions that may enhance the experience.

However, if standing is not being assessed, then the researcher may want to consider a seated option. Assuming the adult does not have notable balance concerns, a chair that swivels could be used so that the adult participant could rotate 360 degrees if they wished. However, it is suggested that such a chair should have any rocking feature locked or disabled to help provide a greater level of stability. In addition, it would be ideal for the chair to have secured arms. This would not only help prevent falling off a chair if disorientation were to occur, but it may also provide a sense of security. If using a chair, an added measure of safety could also include a research team member to help facilitate this component of the study. This would be an individual who is immediately next to the older adult participant to monitor their behavior and provide physical support if the participant became disoriented or starts to fall off the chair when rotating.

There may be instances when it may not be realistic, appropriate, or advised for an older adult to use a swivel chair. In these situations, a traditional chair may be best. Similar to the swivel chair, it would be advised for the chair to have sturdy arm rests and a dedicated member of the research team to monitor. Although a non-rotating chair provides more stability, it can limit the visual field within a VR environment. Thus, the user may try to turn their bodies while seated or extend their head and necks more than usual so that they may see the VR environment "behind" them. For some, this has the potential to be dangerous, as this movement may influence the user's sense of balance and could result in a fall. This is because sensory manipulation that influences head position and vision can negatively affect balance [36–40].

Similar to concerns related to cybersickness, to help minimize feelings of imbalance and reduce a risk for falling after VR use, the researcher would want to consider having the older adult remain seated after the VR headset is removed. This may be an opportunity to ask the participant follow-up questions about their experience and to ensure that they feel stable. If a community-dwelling older adult is participating in a study at a remote location, it may be advantageous to suggest in the consent form that they have a ride home or at least follow-up with a phone call later that same day to confirm that there were no balance-related effects.

If the older adult in the study resides in a facility, additional support may be required to ensure their safety when being seated and standing. This would also need to be discussed with the facility ahead of time, as they may want to be involved with this process as part of required protocol. This may also be an issue if the older adult participant has greater levels of immobility and are in seated or reclined in a specialized chair, mobility device, or bed. Although this may present greater challenges to visually engage and immerse oneself in the VR environment, it does not mean that the VR experience would not merit exploration. Indeed, an argument could be made that persons who are more vulnerable may be in a unique position to value the opportunity to virtually explore environments that would otherwise be out of reach. Nonetheless, the researcher will want to consider how this limitation (i.e., not being able to see the full range of the VR environment) might influence the user's engagement.

3.3 Vision

A core component to being immersed in a virtual environment is based on the user being able to adequately see the environment. Visual acuity is a sensory element that tends to decline in old age [41] and vision impairment among older adults has been related to challenges with activities of daily living and instrumental activities of daily living [42–44]. In addition, visual acuity is associated with factors that influence older adult user experience with digital platforms that employ certain types of technology such as eye-tracking [see 45 for an overview].

Some VR headsets allow for adjustments that account for interpupillary distance, "the distance between the center of the pupils in your eyes" [46]. Although this can help sharpen focus, it cannot adjust so much as to meet the needs of all users. To help account for this, the researcher may want to incorporate something related to visual acuity in the inclusion/exclusion criteria of the study's design. However, it is possible that an older adult participant may report no visual issues prior to trying the VR headset but soon discover concerns that cannot be fixed with headset adjustments alone.

To help with this process, it may be beneficial to the older adult participant if they are shown the components of the selected headset at the start of the study so that they become familiar with how to make such adjustments. In addition, for VR headsets that incorporate a mobile phone, the researcher may want to check before use that the phone is in the secured *and accurate* position. It is possible for a phone to be locked in but not centered. This can produce a visual effect of "double vision" for the user.

For those older adult participants who wear glasses, the researcher will need to ensure that the glasses will fit inside the headset without risk of scratching the lenses. This may be done before the VR headset is placed on the head of the user. In addition, if the headset has straps that can be adjusted, it may be helpful to make them loose before the it is placed on the head and then sufficiently secured after the headset is in place. Depending on the VR video that is to be used in the study, it may also be helpful to determine if bifocal glasses could be worn or if wearing them could detract from the experience or cause headaches.

Just as the researcher may show the VR headset and its features to the older adult participant before it is used, this should also be the case for those systems that incorporate a handheld device (i.e., handheld controller). Although this cannot be physically seen when wearing the headset, seeing the controller ahead of time is likely to help when trying to use it while navigating the VR environment.

Older adults who have had a stroke may also have visual neglect on the contralesional side of the body [47]. Visual neglect is an attention disorder, not necessarily vision per se. Individuals with visual neglect fail to attend to visual stimuli from one side of their body or visual field despite typical visual acuity. When working with older adults who have had a stroke, researchers might need to consider providing extra instructions or exclude the individuals from the study unless the study is designed to promote awareness on the impaired side. For instance, stroke survivors who have acquired visual neglect can attend to visual stimuli with simple explicit instructions such as "turn your head to the left".

3.4 Arthritis

In general terms, arthritis is identified by joint inflammation and can be caused by "wear and tear" or be pathological in nature (i.e., a disease, such as rheumatoid arthritis). A common part of the body where arthritis is found on older adults is the hand area and can include the wrist and joints in the fingers. This health condition is associated with varying degrees of stiffness and pain, both of which influences movement, strength, and control.

Although VR use is largely a visual experience, navigating the system is typically achieved by use of a handheld device or by manipulating the headset – such as tapping a touchpad. Handheld controllers have become increasingly common with VR systems, so this is an important navigational element to consider. Similar to how a researcher may want to check for or verify sufficient visual acuity, this may also be appropriate when considering the prevalence of arthritis among older adults. For those who cannot grip a controller very well - or sufficiently feel the buttons of a controller – a research team member can hold it instead and ask the adult participant when they are ready to select a button on the controller. However, this may cause increased confusion or be a point of frustration for the participant. In addition, the VR may be set up to play a game and this back-and-forth may be counterproductive.

For those who have been diagnosed with some form of arthritis, it can be manageable and may not significantly influence daily activities. However, symptoms can fluctuate over the course of a day and be painful. For others, symptoms may be so severe that it precludes them from even holding a controller – or at least doing so comfortably for an extended period of time. This does not mean that persons with arthritis are to be automatically excluded from a study, but the researcher should consider if or how older adults with significant arthritis in their hands could still participate in the study.

3.5 Hearing

Although engaging with a VR system depends largely on the user's ability to adequately view virtual content, the element of sound can greatly lend to the experience. In addition to offering a sense of realism for a more immersive experience, sound can also provide audible cues and signals – such as those that may be embedded in a virtual game. Hearing loss is prevalent in older adults: approximately 80% of functionally significant hearing loss cases occur in older adults [48]. The prevalence of hearing loss tends to steadily increase with age [49]. Presbycusis, or age-induced hearing loss, is a prevalent cause of hearing loss in adulthood across the world. Presbycusis particularly affects the ability to recognize high frequencies components of sound. In terms of speech sounds, voiceless consonants such as p and s are greatly affected [50].

When involving an older participant in a VR study, it is critical to screen the individual's hearing acuity – or at least confirm they are able to hear adequately – to provide a safer VR experience. Based on the screening results, high frequency sounds could be reduced or the auditory stimuli from the VR environment may be amplified.

In addition, VR systems tailored for individuals using hearing aids are necessary. It is estimated that over 80% of the old-old population (those ages over 85) have hearing loss, although degrees vary [51]. A particular concern is that some VR devices, such as mobile devices that include head-mounted-displays, use and/or adjust the radio frequency and may interfere with hearing aids [52]. When an older participant cannot hear well due to the distraction to the hearing aids, the person may face an increased risk of injury.

Similar to visual neglect, individuals who acquired stroke experience auditory neglect at times. In case of auditory neglect, the individual demonstrates inability to localize sound in a sound field, often contralateral to the lesion, despite the normal peripheral hearing. Given that older adults are as perceptive of audio elements as of visual elements of VR [53], auditory neglect is a condition to be considered when designing accessible and inclusive VR experiences.

3.6 Cognitive Impairment

As the life expectancy increases, more older adults experience cognitive impairment [54]. Cognitive impairment in older adults arises from different causes including but not limited to side effects of medication, stroke, depression, and Alzheimer's disease. Over the past decade, VR intervention has shown significant improvement in different cognitive domains such as memory [55–57], attention [5], and orientation [58] among older adults with cognitive impairments. More importantly, VR experiences were found to improve socio-emotional wellbeing of the individuals [59–61]. Despite the advantages that VR provides to older adults with cognitive impairments, these individuals may face challenges in adopting and accepting VR technology.

When conducting a VR study, researchers need to consider if the adults with cognitive impairments preserve the capability of making a final decision regarding whether or not to try or adopt the new technology being introduced. In many cases, a legal guardian or primary caregiver of an individual with cognitive impairment makes a decision on the individual's behalf. However, it is critical to provide the older adult with sufficient and proper information and to ensure that his/her decision should be respected. Some individuals with cognitive impairments may be competent to make reasonable decisions. However, 'competence', as Rivera-Mindt [62] asserted, is multidimensional and the degree of competence varies.

For example, an individual who sustained a stroke in the right hemisphere may preserve decision-making skills, but his/her reasoning skills may be impaired. Even if an individual made a solid and sound decision on the use of VR technology, the issue could arise at any point. In one study [60], people with dementia reported a higher level of fear and anxiety regarding their VR experience. In case of any discomforting moments, people with cognitive impairments should be able to communicate about their wants and needs to cease their participation. If the individuals are incapable, serious ethical implications around the safety of the user will be raised [63].

In addition, given the varying levels of cognitive impairments and accompanying symptoms, VR technology should be personalized to the extent possible for each respective user. With respect to this notion, researchers should consider the strengths, and not just weaknesses, of an individual with cognitive impairments. These individuals could offer meaningful information regarding which senses to be used and what VR environments to implement. This positions the adult with cognitive impairment as the active participant and provide a person-centered experience.

Another concern that is often raised in VR research among cognitively impaired users, particularly those diagnosed with a dementia, is the possibility of the adult being 'hooked up' to the VR system [64]. When this issue occurs, the VR system may replace the individual's social interactions. Meanwhile, some older VR users with cognitive impairments may gain a misperception that the virtual worlds being introduced to them are real [65]. In order to prevent this issue, Hodge and colleagues suggested positioning the person with dementia as an active participant by blending the old with the new, which enables the person to revisit meaningful experiences as the focal point [66]. Given that the use of VR for people with cognitive impairments is a relatively new area of research, more discussions on safety and ethical considerations are warranted.

4 Ethical Considerations

A final point to consider is ethical considerations when assessing VR use among older adult participants. Depending upon the nature of the VR content, it may be psychologically harmful to the adult. This aspect was discussed in-depth among the participants of the first author's primary VR study mentioned in the "Background" section of this manuscript. Although it seems largely believed that VR can be beneficial for older adult users, this must not be assumed. Not everyone has circumstances (or a mindset) that positions them to take advantage of this digital tool.

For example, an immobile older adult who lives in nursing home (with few or no visitors) may be at risk of clinical depression because of their situation. Yet, it is noted that this is not the case for everyone in this situation. If a researcher offered them the opportunity to virtually explore (i.e., tour) a location, such as the streets of Paris or even the adult's hometown, it may be viewed by the adult with enthusiasm. However, it is also possible that the older adult will feel further isolated, lonely, or functionally limited – reminded that they are no longer able to walk the streets of their town or travel to destinations beyond their residential facility. This experience may reinforce the realities of their unwelcomed situation which may, in turn, result in the aforementioned 'hooked up' issue among older adult VR users. Although it may be challenging for a researcher to be aware of this potential for a participant in this circumstance, they should be aware of its possibility and take measures to address this concern. This may include follow-up appointments with the adult to ask about their wellbeing and checking with caregivers who monitor their overall status.

5 Conclusion

This manuscript aimed to answer three research questions, and each was addressed. The following is a summary.

1) *To identify health-related aspects among older adults that may influence VR engagement.*

A number of health-related aspects were identified and discussed. This included cybersickness, balance, vision, arthritis, hearing, and cognitive impairment. Naturally, these may not affect every older adult who may use VR, but these considerations should be taken into account when designing a study that includes older adults.

2) *To explore safe options and workarounds for VR use among older adult users.*

Not every health-related or functional limitation that may influence VR use has a workaround option to ensure participant safety. However, there are numerous measures that can be taken by researchers to enhance safety measures and appropriate use of the VR system by older adult participants. For example, researchers could screen study candidates by asking about their history of motion sickness. Another example includes providing a chair with arms for older adult participants with balance concerns or are at risk for falling.

3) *To explore ethical considerations for VR use among older adult users.*

Not everyone who engages with a VR system may find it beneficial. It is critical that researchers of such studies consider possible circumstances or mental health factors that may influence recruitment efforts or participant eligibility.

As VR continues to become more sophisticated and available to the mass market, it is likely that VR research among older adults will also continue. In addition, as more is learned about its potential benefit, researchers will likely continue to explore new applications to promote health and wellbeing among select older adult populations. Nonetheless, it will be important for researchers to carefully consider potential risks and screening considerations when participants are asked to use VR in a study. This is especially critical for those researchers who may be unfamiliar with normative and pathological changes associated with aging and how they may influence VR use or pose a risk to the older adult participant.

Aspects discussed in this manuscript include a range of functional ability factors: cybersickness, balance and falls, vision, arthritis, and cognitive impairment. The older adult population is considerably heterogenous and every older adult participant – or potential participant – may (or may not) represent each of these factors. For functionally health older adults, there may be no issues when using VR. However, it is not out of the realm of possibility, especially as health-related concerns arise. In addition, most VR studies at this point that incorporate older adults are those that include older adults with cognitive limitations. (This is followed by studies that assess balance and falls.) As VR continues to be examined within aging research, greater attention will be needed to determine how VR can best be studied while taking into account the safety of the older adult participants and how to minimize potential risk.

References

1. Li, L., et al.: Application of virtual reality technology in clinical medicine. Am. J. Transl. Res. **9**(9), 3867–3880 (2017)
2. Nayyar, A., Mahapatra, B., Le, D., Suseendran, G.: Virtual Reality (VR) and Augmented Reality (AR) technology for tourism and hospitality industry. Int. J. Eng. Technol. **7**(2.21), 156–160 (2018). https://doi.org/10.14419/ijet.v7i2.21.11858
3. Riaz, W., Khan, Z.Y., Jawaid, A., Shahid, S.: Virtual reality (VR)-based environmental enrichment in older adults with mild cognitive impairment (MCI) and mild dementia. Brain Sci. **11**(8), 1103 (2021). https://doi.org/10.3390/brainsci11081103
4. Man, D.W., Chung, J.C., Lee, G.Y.: Evaluation of a virtual reality-based memory training programme for Hong Kong Chinese older adults with questionable dementia: a pilot study. Int. J. Geriatr. Pscyhiatry. **27**(5), 513–520 (2011). https://doi.org/10.1002/gps.2746
5. Manera, V., Chapoulie, E., Bourgeois, J., Guerchouche, R., David, R., Ondrej, J., Drettakis, G., Robert, P.: A feasibility study with image-based rendered virtual reality in patients with mild cognitive impairment and dementia. PLoS ONE **11**(3), e0151487 (2016). https://doi.org/10.1371/journal.pone.0151487
6. Serino, S., Pedroli, E., Tuena, C., De Leo, G., Stramba-Badiale, M., Goulene, K., Mariotti, N.G., Riva, G.: A novel virtual reality-based training protocol for the enhancement of the "mental frame syncing" in individuals with Alzheimer's disease: a development-of-concept trial. Front. Aging Neurosci. **9** (2017) https://doi.org/10.3389/fnagi.2017.00240
7. Liao, Y.-Y., Chen, I.-H., Lin, Y.-J., Chen, Y., Hsu, W.-C.: Effects of virtual reality-based physical and cognitive training on executive function and dual-task gait performance in older adults with mild cognitive impairment: a randomized control trial. Front. Aging Neurosci. **11** (2019) https://doi.org/10.3389/fnagi.2019.00162
8. Appel, L., Kisonas, E., Appel, E., Klein, J., Bartlett, D., Rosenberg, J., Smith, C.: Introducing virtual reality therapy for inpatients with dementia admitted to an acute care hospital: learnings from a pilot to pave the way to a randomized controlled trial. Pilot Feasibility Stud. **6**(1) (2020) https://doi.org/10.1186/s40814-020-00708-9
9. Coelho, T., et al.: Promoting reminiscences with virtual reality headsets: a pilot study with people with dementia. Int. J. Environ. Res. **17**(24), 9301 (2020). https://doi.org/10.3390/ijerph17249301
10. Yousefi Babadi, S., Daneshmandi, H.: Effects of virtual reality versus conventional balance training on balance of the elderly. Exp. Gerontol. **153**, 111498 (2021). https://doi.org/10.1016/j.exger.2021.111498

11. Zahedian-Nasab, N., Jaberi, A., Shirazi, F., Kavousipor, S.: Effect of virtual reality exercises on balance and fall in elderly people with fall risk: a randomized controlled trial. BMC Geriatr. **21**(1) (2021) https://doi.org/10.1186/s12877-021-02462-w

12. Donath, L., Rössler, R., Faude, O.: Effects of virtual reality training (exergaming) compared to alternative exercise training and passive control on standing balance and functional mobility in healthy community-dwelling seniors: a meta-analytical review. Sports Med. **46**(9), 1293–1309 (2016). https://doi.org/10.1007/s40279-016-0485-1

13. White, P.J.F., Moussavi, Z.: Neurocognitive treatment for a patient with Alzheimer's disease using a virtual reality navigational environment. J. Exp. Neurosci. **10**, JEN.S40827 (2016). https://doi.org/10.4137/JEN.S40827

14. Plancher, G., Tirard, A., Gyselinck, V., Nicolas, S., Piolino, P.: Using virtual reality to characterize episodic memory profiles in amnestic mild cognitive impairment and Alzheimer's disease: influence of active and passive encoding. Neuropsychologia **50**(5), 592–602 (2012). https://doi.org/10.1016/j.neuropsychologia.2011.12.013

15. Mirelman, A., Maidan, I., Herman, T., Deutsch, J.E., Giladi, N., Hausdorff, J.M.: Virtual reality for gait training: Can it induce motor learning to enhance complex walking and reduce fall risk in patients with Parkinson's disease? J. Gerontol. A Biol. Sci. Med. Sci. **66A**(2), 234–240 (2010). https://doi.org/10.1093/gerona/glq201

16. Mrakic-Sposta, S., Di Santo, S.G., Franchini, F., Arlati, S., Zangiacomi, A., Greci, L., Moretti, S., Jesuthasan, N., Marzorati, M., Rizzo, G., Sacco, M., Vezzoli, A.: Effects of combined physical and cognitive virtual reality-based training on cognitive impairment and oxidative stress in MCI patients: a pilot study. Front. Aging Neurosci. **10** (2018) https://doi.org/10.3389/fnagi.2018.00282

17. Muhla, F., et al.: Impact of using immersive virtual reality over time and steps in the timed up and go test in elderly people. PLoS ONE **15**(3), 1–16 (2020). https://doi.org/10.1371/journal.pone.0229594

18. Anderson, M., Perrin, A.: Tech adoption climbs among older adults. Pew Research Center: Internet, Science & Technology. (2017) http://www.pewinternet.org/2017/05/17/tech-adoption-climbs-among-older-adults/. Accessed 22 Nov 2021

19. Kakulla, B.N.: Tech Trends of the 50+. AARP Research (2020). https://doi.org/10.26419/res.00329.001

20. Brown, J.A.: An exploration of virtual reality use and application among older adult populations. Gerontol. Geriatr. Med. **5**, 2333721419885287 (2019). https://doi.org/10.1177/2333721419885287

21. Money, K.E.: Motion sickness. Psychol. Rev. **50**(1), 1–39 (1970)

22. Kennedy, R.S., Hettinger, L.J., Lilienthal. M.G.: Simulator Sickness. In: Crampton, G.H. (Ed.) Motion and Space Sickness, pp. 317–341. CRC Press, Boca Raton, FL (1988)

23. LaViola, J.J.: A discussion of cybersickness in virtual environments. ACM SIGCHI Bulletin. **32**(1), 47–56 (2000). https://doi.org/10.1145/333329.333344

24. Dilanchian, A.T., Andringa, R., Boot, W.R.: A pilot study exploring age differences in presence, workload, and cybersickness in the experience of immersive virtual reality environments. Front. Virtual Real. **2**, 1–11 (2021). https://doi.org/10.3389/frvir.2021.736793

25. Huygelier, H., Schraepen, B., van Ee, R., Vanden Abeele, V., Gillebert, C.R.: Acceptance of immersive head-mounted virtual reality in older adults. Sci. Rep. **9**, 1–12 (2019). https://doi.org/10.1038/s41598-019-41200-6

26. Lackner, J.: Human orientation, adaptation, and movement control. In: Lackner, J. (ed.) Motion sickness, visual displays, and armored vehicle design, pp. 28–50. Ballistic Research Laboratory, Washington DC (1990)

27. Bergen, G., Stevens, M., Burns, E.: Falls and fall injuries among adults aged≥ 65 years—United States, 2014. MMWR Morb Mortal Wkly Rep. **65**(37), 993–998 (2016). https://doi.org/10.15585/mmwr.mm6537a2

28. Gazibara, T., et al.: Falls, risk factors and fear of falling among persons older than 65 years of age. Psychogeriatr. **17**, 215–223 (2017). https://doi.org/10.1111/psyg.12217
29. Cho, K.H., Bok, S.K., Kim, Y.J., Hwang, S.L.: Effect of lower limb strength on falls and balance of the elderly. Ann Rehabil Med. **36**(3), 386–393 (2012). https://doi.org/10.5535/arm.2012.36.3.386
30. Rubenstein, L.Z.: Falls in older people: Epidemiology, risk factors and strategies for prevention. Age Ageing **35**(Suppl. 2), 37–41 (2006). https://doi.org/10.1093/ageing/afl084
31. Tinetti, M.E., Kumar, C.: The patient who falls: "It's always a trade-off." J Am Med Assoc. **303**(3), 258–266 (2010). https://doi.org/10.1001/jama.2009.2024
32. Kearney, F.C., Harwood, R.H., Gladman, J.R.F., Lincoln, N., Masud, T.: The relationship between executive function and falls and gait abnormalities in older adults: a systematic review. Dement Geriatr Cogn Disord. **34**(1–2), 20–35 (2013). https://doi.org/10.1159/000350031
33. Welmer, A.-K., Rizzuto, D., Laukka, E.J., Johnell, K., Fratiglioni, L.: Cognitive and physical function in relations to the risk of injurious falls in older adults: a population-based study. J. Gerontol. A Biol. Sci. Med. Sci. **72**(5), 669-675 (2016) https://doi.org/10.1093/gerona/glw141
34. Liu-Ambrose, T., Ahamed, Y., Graf, P., Feldman, F., Robinovitch, S.N.: Older fallers with poor working memory overestimate their postural limits. Arch Phys Med Rehabil. **89**(7), 1335–1340 (2008). https://doi.org/10.1016/j.apmr.2007.11.052
35. Davis, J.C., et al.: Slow processing speed predicts falls in older adults with a falls history: 1-year prospective cohort study. J Am Geriatr Soc **69**, 916–923 (2017). https://doi.org/10.1111/jgs.14830
36. Hsieh, K.L., Roach, K.L., Wajda, D.A., Sosnoff, J.J.: Smartphone technology can measure postural stability and discriminate fall risk in older adults. Gait Posture. **67**, 160–165 (2019). https://doi.org/10.1016/j.gaitpost.2018.10.005
37. Johnson, M.B., Van Emmerik, R.E.A.: Effect of head orientation on postural control during upright stance and forward lean. Mot. Control **16**(1), 81–93 (2012). https://doi.org/10.1123/mcj.16.1.81
38. Anson, E., Bigelow, R.T., Studenski, S., Deshpande, N., Agrawal, Y.: Failure on the foam eyes closed test of standing balance associated with reduced semicircular canal function in healthy older adults. Ear Hear. **40**(2), 340–344 (2019). https://doi.org/10.1097/AUD.0000000000000619
39. Razavi, H.: A comparison between static and dynamic stability in postural sway and fall risks. J Ergon. **7**(1), 1–7 (2017). https://doi.org/10.4172/2165-7556.1000186
40. Hasson, C.J., Van Emmerik, R.E., Caldwell, G.E.: Predicting dynamic postural instability using center of mass time-to-contact information. J Biomech. **41**(10), 2121–2129 (2008). https://doi.org/10.1016/j.jbiomech.2008.04.031
41. Congdon, N., et al.: Causes and prevalence of visual impairment among adults in the United States. Arch Ophthalmol. **122**(4), 477–485 (2004). https://doi.org/10.1001/archopht.122.4.477
42. Cacciatore, F., Abete, P., Maggi, S., Luchetti, G., Calabrese, C., Viati, L., Leosco, D., Ferrara, N., Vitale, D.F., Rengo, F.: Disability and 6-year mortality in elderly population. role of visual impairment. Aging Clin. Exp. Res. **16**(5), 382–388 (2004). https://doi.org/10.1007/BF03324568
43. Guralnik, J., LaCroix, A.Z.: Assessing physical function in older populations. In: Wallace, R.B., Woolson, R.F. (eds.) The Epidemiologic Study of the Elderly, pp. 159–181. Oxford University Press, New York (1992)
44. Hochberg, C., et al.: Association of vision loss in glaucoma and age-related macular degeneration with IADL disability. Invest Ophthalmol Vis Sci. **53**(6), 3201–3206 (2012). https://doi.org/10.1167/iovs.12-9469

45. Loos, E.F., Romano Bergstrom, J.: Older adults. In: Romano Bergstrom, J., Schall, A.J. (eds.) Eye Tracking in User Experience Design, pp. 313–329. Elsevier, Amsterdam (2014)
46. Adjusting the IPD on the headset. VIVE: (2021). https://www.vive.com/us/support/vive-focus/category_howto/adjusting-the-ipd-on-the-headset.html Accessed 7 Dec 2021
47. Ting, D.S., et al.: Visual neglect following stroke: current concepts and future focus. Surv. Ophthalmol. 56(2), 114–134 (2011). https://doi.org/10.1016/j.survophthal.2010.08.001
48. Davis, A.C.: Epidemiological profile of hearing impairments: the scale and nature of the problem with special reference to the elderly. Acta Otolaryngol Suppl. 111(476), 23–31 (1990). https://doi.org/10.3109/00016489109127252
49. Nash, S.D., et al.: The prevalence of hearing impairment and associated risk factors: the Beaver Dam Offspring Study. Arch Otolaryngol Head Neck Surg. 137(5), 432–439 (2011). https://doi.org/10.1001/archoto.2011.15
50. Gates, G.A., Mills, J.H.: Presbycusis. Lancet 366(9491), 1111–1120 (2005). https://doi.org/10.1016/S0140-6736(05)67423-5
51. Feder, K., Michaud, D., Ramage-Morin, P., McNamee, J., Beauregard, Y.: Prevalence of hearing loss among Canadians aged 20 to 79: audiometric results from the 2012/2013 Canadian health measures survey. PLoS ONE 26(7), 18–25 (2015)
52. Appel, L., et al.: Older adults with cognitive and/or physical impairments can benefit from immersive virtual reality experiences: a feasibility study. Front. Med. (2020). https://doi.org/10.3389/fmed.2019.00329
53. Vanden Abeele, V., Schraepen, B., Huygelier, H., Gillebert, C., Gerling, K., Van Ee, R.: Immersive virtual reality for older adults: empirically grounded design guidelines. ACM Trans. Access. Comput. 14(3), 1–30 (2021). https://doi.org/10.1145/3470743
54. Pais, R., Ruano, L., Carvalho, O.R., Barros, H.: Global cognitive impairment prevalence and incidence in community dwelling older adults – a systematic review. Geriatrics 5(4), 84 (2020). https://doi.org/10.3390/geriatrics5040084
55. Kim, B.R., Chun, M.H., Kim, L.S., Park, J.Y.: Effect of virtual reality on cognition in stroke patients. Ann Rehabil Med. 35, 450–459 (2011). https://doi.org/10.5535/arm.2011.35.4.450
56. Man, D.W., Chung, J.C., Lee, G.Y.: Evaluation of a virtual reality-based memory training programme for Hong Kong Chinese older adults with questionable dementia: a pilot study. Int J Geriatr Psychiatry 27(5), 513–520 (2012). https://doi.org/10.1002/gps.2746
57. Optale, G., et al.: Controlling memory impairment in elderly adults using virtual reality memory training: a randomized controlled pilot study. Neurorehabil Neural Repair 24(4), 348–357 (2010). https://doi.org/10.1177/1545968309353328
58. Hofmann, M., et al.: Interactive computer-training as a therapeutic tool in Alzheimer's disease. Compr Psychiatry 44(3), 213–219 (2003). https://doi.org/10.1016/S0010-440X(03)00006-3
59. Mendez, M.F., Joshi, A., Jimenez, E.: Virtual reality for the assessment of frontotemporal dementia, a feasibility study. Disabil Rehabil Assist Technol. 10(2), 160–164 (2015). https://doi.org/10.3109/17483107.2014.889230
60. Moyle, W., Jones, C., Dwan, T., Petrovich, T.: Effectiveness of a virtual reality forest on people with dementia: a mixed methods pilot study. Gerontologist 58(3), 478–487 (2018). https://doi.org/10.1093/geront/gnw270
61. Siriaraya, P., Ang, C.S.: Recreating living experiences from past memories through virtual worlds for people with dementia. In: Jones, M., Palanque, P. (eds.) CHI '14: CHI Conference on Human Factors in Computing Systems, pp. 3977–3986. Association for Computing Machinery, New York (2014)
62. Rivera-Mindt, M.: Ethical decision making and capacity to consent in neurocognitively impaired vulnerable patient populations. In: Paper Presented at the 40th Meeting of the International Neuropsychological Society, Montreal, QC , Canada, 18 Feb 2012

63. Rose, V.R., Stewart, I., Jenkins, K., Ang, C.S., Matsangidou, M.: A scoping review exploring the feasibility of virtual reality technology use with individuals living with dementia. In: Proceedings of the 28th International Conference on Artificial Reality and Telexistence (ICAT) / 23rd Eurographics Symposium on Virtual Environments (EGVE), Limassol, Cyprus, (2018)
64. Pringle, R.: Virtual reality is still too isolating to be 'the next big thing' in tech. CBC. (2017) https://www.cbc.ca/news/opinion/vr-isolation-1.3980539 Accessed 7 Dec 2021
65. D'Cunha, N.M., et al.: A mini-review of virtual reality-based interventions to promote well-being for people living with dementia and mild cognitive impairment. Gerontology **65**, 430–440 (2019). https://doi.org/10.1159/000500040
66. Hodge, J., et al.: Exploring the design of tailored virtual reality experiences for people with dementia. In: Mandryk, R., Hancock, M. (eds.) CHI '18: CHI Conference on Human Factors in Computing Systems, pp. 1–13. Association for Computing Machinery, New York (2018)

A Study on the Recognition and Memory of Shapes for the Elderly

Ku-Hsi Chu[1]($\boxtimes$), Jui-Che Tu[1], and Chang-Franw Lee[2]

[1] Graduate School of Design, National Yunlin University of Science and Technology, Douliu, Yunlin 640, Taiwan
eason79@gmail.com
[2] Department of Industrial Design, National Yunlin University of Science and Technology, Douliu, Yunlin 640, Taiwan

Abstract. This research is mainly aimed at exploring the recognition and memory ability of basic geometric shapes in the elderly, in order to understand the status of recognition and memory ability of shapes of different complexity in the elderly. It is mainly carried out through the experimental method. The experimental method is carried out with 12 shape test samples, and the accuracy of shape recognition and different time differences are discussed. The subjects were divided into 10 elderly people in the experimental group and 10 college students over the age of 20 in the control group. The results show that there is a gap in the accuracy of shape recognition among the elderly. The more complex the shape, the lower the recognition ability. In addition, both groups of subjects made errors in recognizing the obliquely angled figures. The time difference between 5 s and 30 s between shape F (original hexagon) and shape I (hexagon with rounded corners) is significantly different, and shape I obtains the lowest recognition accuracy rate at a 5-s interval for the elderly. The experimental results also show that the front and back positions of the shape images in the sequence have an impact on the memory ability.

Keywords: Elderly · Shape recognition · Memory ability · Visual cognition

1 Introduction

1.1 Research Background and Motives

As countries around the world have entered an aging society, the demand for product design for the elderly is also increasing. In particular, in today's Internet society, the graphical user interface (GUI) design of many information products is becoming more and more complex due to the variety of functions, and the aging population is prone to operational obstacles and difficulties due to the gradual deterioration of physiological functions. Secondly, the deterioration of the relevant cognitive and memory abilities of the elderly will also lead to errors in the judgment of the appearance and shape of some products in daily life. As for the research on vision in shape recognition and memory, there have been many related studies accumulated in the past. In the research on shape cognition of different levels of complexity, the research are different orientation, including: the influence of symmetrical shape on visual cog-nitive attention (Olivers and Van Der Helm 1998), the discussion of object cognition and memory description (Biederman 1987; Pentland 1986; Liu et al. 1995), and the difference in attention to the upper and lower parts of the object shape (Chambers et al. 1999). However, from the perspective of shape, because most of us perceive the shape of many different products in our daily life through vision, we need to rely on vision to identify information such as product operation functions and graphic inter-faces with judgment.

1.2 Research Purpose

This research mainly explores the changes in the recognition and memory of basic geometric shapes among the elderly, and through the research results obtained from this research survey, it can help designers when designing products with various shapes or visual designs such as graphic interfaces can have reference. Secondly, the results of this study can also be used as a reference for relevant academic researchers who are engaged in design research on the elderly. Therefore, it is hoped that the results of this study can serve as the basis for the continued advancement of research on the design of the elderly. Based on the research expectations and pursuits proposed above, this research has the following two purposes:

1. Understand the accuracy and extent of the effects of different complex shapes on visual shape recognition and memory in the elderly.
2. Understand the influence of different time differences on visual shape recognition and memory of the elderly.

2 Related Research

2.1 Physiological Characteristics of the Elderly

Aging is an inevitable physiological process. From a biological point of view, aging is the process by which the functioning of cells, tissues, organs and systems in the body gradually declines over time until it ceases completely (Aguiar and Macário 2017; Haci-hasanoglu et al. 2012). Aging causes the decline of physiological functions in the elderly, such as low motor control ability, poor body flexibility and coordination, decreased muscle strength, and the gradual decline of vision, hearing, taste, touch and other abilities (Huang et al. 2011). Human beings receive more than 70% of external information, which is received and processed by the visual system. Therefore, many scholars have also mentioned that with the increase of age, the visual function of the elderly will have great changes (Haigh 1993; Toshimoto, 1994; Morris 1994; Yoshida 1994; Lee et al. 1998; Hawthorn 2000).

2.2 Cognitive Aging Phenomenon

The aging of cognitive function of the elderly directly affects the daily activities and problem solving of the elderly. Aging causes cognitive decline, which mainly occurs in the process of information encoding and retrieval. If information retrieval fails, it cannot be recalled. When the environment contains irrelevant information, recall performance declines even when individuals make efforts to extract event details (Wais et al. 2010). The cognitive function of the elderly gradually declines, including information processing speed, attention, episodic memory, spatial ability, executive function, etc. (Park et al. 2002). Cognitive aging leads to the decline of various abilities in the elderly, such as often complaining of poor memory, inattention, decreased judgment, and even significant changes in personality and behavior (Demir et al. 2017), when performing tasks related to memory, compared to young adults with longer reaction times and lower response accuracy (Goffaux et al. 2008). Aging deteriorates the short-term memory of the elderly, especially the ability to update memory, which seriously affects the cognitive function of the elderly.

2.3 Shape Recognition Cognition

Biederman (1987) has indicated that when the observer observes and recognizes the shape, the elements in the shape (including structure, secondary shape, and details of parts, etc.) will affect the observer's identification, and then produce different cognitive subjective judgments. Baxter (1995) has shown that the processing of human visual information can be analyzed in two distinct stages. The first stage is a rapid scan of the overall visual image to obtain patterns and shapes. The process in this stage is quite fast and does not require It takes a lot of effort. The second stage is the processing of the overall visual imagery, which involves attention to the detailed visual components. However, attention acts like a filter, limiting the amount of information that can be recognized at one time, followed by pattern recognition. The selection stage is that all information is recognized, and only some important information is noticed and processed further, and the next stage of memory is entered. This part will be divided into short-term memory or long-term memory. Therefore, the pattern recognition stage is an important stage in the information processing mode, and recognizing the shape of various objects is one of the important primitive instincts of human beings.

3 Research Method

3.1 Research Objects and Tools

A total of 20 subjects were tested in this study, including 10 elderly subjects as subjects in the experimental group, and 10 subjects in the control group from university students over the age of 20. And all the subjects have normal vision, or the visual acuity of 0.5 or more can be tested after correction. Regarding the gender of the 20 subjects, the elderly subjects were selected by random sampling, with a total of 7 females and 3 males. As for the students who were tested, five male and five female students were selected by intentional sampling. In terms of experimental tool samples, 12 shape test samples extended from the four basic shapes used are shown in in Fig. 1.

Among the features of these 12 shapes, the figure features in the longitudinal axis direction are gradually increased in the number of sides, consisting of three, four, five, and

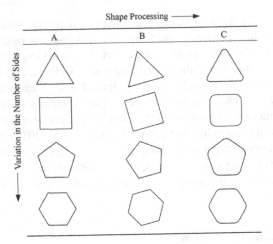

Fig. 1. 12 shape test samples

six, these four different basic shapes. The graphic features in the horizontal axis direction are mainly in the shape and angle, and the shape image is changed in different processing methods, and the requirements for the number of shape sides are maintained. First, in column A, there are four basic shapes, ranging from the minimum number of sides to six sides, which have the same shape characteristics as line thickness, left-right symmetry, etc.; in column B, the graph in column A is rotated 15 degrees counterclockwise; the graphics in column C retain the characteristics of the graphics in column A, but are processed with rounded corners in shape processing. The setting of these 12 shape test samples is mainly used to explore the relationship between subjects' shape recognition and memory of different complexity.

3.2   Experimental Design and Steps

In order to understand the influence of the subjects on the recognition and memory ability of shape features under different time differences, the experimental investigation design was carried out through three different time differences. Each image sample was viewed by the subjects for 5 s, 10 s and 30 s, and disappeared immediately after viewing (Fig. 2. A.). Then play a video of 12 shape stimulus images (as shown in Fig. 2. B., there are 12 sculpts in total, including 1 original viewing image sample and 11 interference stimulus shape images), and the 12 shapes are numbered according to English letters. Including: A (square inclined at 15 degrees), B (pentagon inclined at 15 degrees), C (triangle inclined at 15 degrees), D (original square), E (pentagon with rounded corners), F (original hexagon), G (original triangle), H (square with rounded corners), I (hexagon with rounded corners), J (triangle with rounded corners), K (original pentagon) and L (hexagon inclined 15 degrees). This provides the subject with a selection of image samples that he personally considers to be the original viewing. After each time difference test, the subjects were allowed to rest for ten seconds before proceeding to the next test.

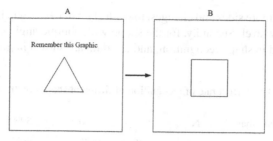

Fig. 2. A. Original viewing image sample and B. 12 shape stimulus images

At the same time as the 12 images of the shape stimulus are played, the time will also be recorded, so when the subject thinks that the original viewed image sample has been found, he will stop and record the time spent. In order to ensure the consistency of the experimental conditions, the random sequence of the images of the shape stimuli played by each image sample after each time difference is the same (the interval between the images of the shape stimuli is 1 s). And each subject conducted a total of 12 sets of experiments. The overall experiment will repeat the above steps until the 12 groups of experimental stimuli are finished.

3.3 Data Analysis Process

There are two experimental sites in this research, the first place is to arrange elderly subjects at local community centers. Second place is to arrange students in the re-search room on campus. In terms of experimental tools, the stimuli were displayed on an Apple notebook with a 15.4-inch screen and a resolution of 2880 x 1800 pixels. The stimulus lines on the screen display are black and the background is white. The viewing distance from the subject's eyes to the screen is maintained at 50 cm. In addition, the experimental stimuli were presented in two forms. First, the image was viewed through the computer's built-in preview program. Then, the computer to play a sample video in mp4 format for the sub-jects to watch. The research method of this research is to use the notebook computer screen to display the experimental samples, combined with the paper record method. Through the statistical software SPSS, data analysis of relevant experimental results was carried out.

4 Result and Discussion

4.1 Different Shape Recognition Accuracy

According results, this study sorted out the correct rate of shape recognition obtained by the experimental group and the control group in three different time tests. First, the elderly group had the lowest recognition accuracy rate at 5-s intervals for the shape I (40%). The lowest identification accuracy rate (50%) in the interval of 10 s is the shape B, shape D and shape L. The lowest recognition accuracy rate (60%) at the interval of 30 s is the shape A and shape I. Among the 12 shapes, only the shape C has a correct recognition rate of 100% after an interval of 30 s. From this result, it can be found that for the shapes with more sides and changes, the elderly will have a gap in the recognition ability and memory level. Secondly, for the shape with oblique angles, it seems that the elderly are troubled in shape recognition, and the data are shown in Table 1.

Table 1. The correct rate of recognition of different shapes by the elderly.

Shape Number	N	5 s	10 s	30 s
A	10	50%	70%	60%
B	10	60%	50%	70%
C	10	90%	90%	100%
D	10	50%	50%	70%
E	10	90%	90%	80%
F	10	70%	70%	80%
G	10	60%	70%	80%
H	10	60%	80%	80%
I	10	40%	70%	60%
J	10	80%	80%	90%
K	10	60%	60%	80%
L	10	70%	50%	70%

The student's group had the lowest recognition accuracy rate at 5-s intervals for the shape D (70%). And in the interval of 10 s, the identification accuracy rate is the lowest (80%) for the shape C. The lowest recognition accuracy rate (80%) at the interval of 30 s is also the shape C. Although the subjects in this group were the control group, there would still be errors in the identification of the sample. The shape with oblique angles are troubled by the same with elderly group, and there is a situation of misidentification. However, the identification status of most subjects is better than that of the elderly group, and the data are shown in Table 2.

Table 2. The correct rate of recognition of different shapes by students.

Shape Number	N	5 s	10 s	30 s
A	10	80%	100%	100%
B	10	100%	100%	100%
C	10	100%	80%	80%
D	10	70%	100%	100%

(continued)

Table 2. (*continued*)

Shape Number	N	5 s	10 s	30 s
E	10	100%	100%	100%
F	10	90%	100%	100%
G	10	90%	100%	100%
H	10	100%	100%	90%
I	10	90%	100%	100%
J	10	100%	90%	90%
K	10	90%	100%	100%
L	10	90%	100%	100%

4.2 Comparison of Recognition and Memory of Different Time

According to the experimental data of images recognition performed at three different time differences, the time difference between the experimental group and the control group was compared, as shown in Tables 3, 4, 5, 6, 7 and 8. First, from Table 3 that the average number of seconds between the three time differences in the control group is smaller than that in the experimental group, and there is a big difference in the average number of seconds between the two experimental groups of shape A when the interval is 5 s. The gap is fine, but it can also reflect the impact of recognition accuracy. In the shape B experiment, the average number of seconds in the experimental group was less than that in the control group only at intervals of 5 s, but in the subsequent experiments at intervals of 10 s and 30 s, the average number of seconds in the control group was smaller than that in the experimental group. The shape B was randomly arranged at the position of sequence 7, so it can be found that the longer the time difference, the better the memory ability of the control group than the experimental group for the stimulus objects placed at the back of the sequence.

Table 3. Comparison of recognition time of shape A&B under different time.

Shape	Sec	Group	N	M	SD
A	5 s	Elderly	10	11.24	10.40
		Young	10	4.83	0.94
	10 s	Elderly	10	6.23	5.33
		Young	10	4.79	0.41
	30 s	Elderly	10	6.23	4.78
		Young	10	4.28	1.26

(*continued*)

Table 3. (*continued*)

Shape	Sec	Group	N	M	SD
B	5 s	Elderly	10	6.54	2.46
		Young	10	7.18	0.94
	10 s	Elderly	10	7.89	3.64
		Young	10	6.85	1.21
	30 s	Elderly	10	7.17	2.43
		Young	10	6.87	1.15

From Table 4, it can be seen that in the shape C of the experimental group, in the experiments with an interval of 5 s and 10 s, the average number of seconds in the experimental group is greater than that in the control group, but the average number of seconds in the 30-s interval is smaller than that in the control group. In the recognition accuracy rate of the shape C, the experimental group was slightly better than the control group. The average number of seconds in the three different time of the experimental group in the shape D experiment is smaller than that of the control group, but from the recognition accuracy rate that the experimental group has poor recognition ability in the shape D. In contrast, the average number of seconds between 10 and 30 s in the control group was a relatively normal number of seconds. The shape D is randomly arranged at the position of sequence 10, so it can be found that the longer the time difference is, the better the memory ability of the control group is than that of the experimental group for the stimulus objects placed at the back of the sequence.

Table 4. Comparison of recognition time of shape C&D under different time.

Shape	Sec	Group	N	M	SD
C	5 s	Elderly	10	5.35	0.71
		Young	10	4.84	0.14
	10 s	Elderly	10	5.16	0.52
		Young	10	4.97	0.40
	30 s	Elderly	10	5.10	0.71
		Young	10	5.32	0.88
D	5 s	Elderly	10	7.66	2.15
		Young	10	8.86	1.66
	10 s	Elderly	10	8.82	2.57
		Young	10	9.72	0.32
	30 s	Elderly	10	8.85	2.48
		Young	10	9.64	0.52

From Table 5, in the shape E experiment, the average number of seconds in the experimental group was only smaller than that in the control group at an interval of 10 s, but in the experiments with an interval of 5 s and 30 s, the average number of seconds in the control group was smaller than that in the experimental group. The average number of seconds in the three different time differences of the control group in the shape F experiment was smaller than that of the experimental group, and the difference was huge. The factors that cause the huge difference in average seconds may be related to the complexity of the shape F. It can be seen from the identification accuracy rate that the experimental group has poor identification ability in the shape F experiment.

Table 5. Comparison of recognition time of shape E&F under different time.

Shape	Sec	Group	N	M	SD
E	5 s	Elderly	10	7.97	1.80
		Young	10	7.91	0.42
	10 s	Elderly	10	7.76	1.79
		Young	10	7.91	0.38
	30 s	Elderly	10	8.66	3.65
		Young	10	7.88	0.24
F	5 s	Elderly	10	9.41	7.52
		Young	10	3.60	2.16
	10 s	Elderly	10	8.10	5.30
		Young	10	2.83	0.34
	30 s	Elderly	10	6.91	5.96
		Young	10	2.60	0.40

From Table 6, the average number of seconds in the three different time of the experimental group in the shape G experiment is smaller than that of the control group. From the identification accuracy rate, the experimental group has poor identification ability in the shape G experiment. In contrast, the average number of seconds in the control group at three different times was relatively normal. The average number of seconds in the three different time differences in the shape H experiment of the control group was smaller than that of the experimental group. The shape G is randomly arranged at the position of sequence 12, and the shape H is arranged at the position of sequence 10. Therefore, it can be found that the longer the time difference, the more the memory of the control group is better than the experiment group.

From Table 7, the average number of seconds in the three different time differences in the shape I experiment of the control group is smaller than that of the experimental group, and the difference is extremely large. The factors that cause the huge difference in average seconds may be related to the complexity of the shape I. From the identification accuracy rate, it can be known that the identification ability of the experimental group in the shape I experiment is not good. The average number of seconds in the three different

Table 6. Comparison of recognition time of shape G&H under different time.

Shape	Sec	Group	N	M	SD
G	5 s	Elderly	10	9.88	3.33
		Young	10	11.13	2.63
	10 s	Elderly	10	10.51	2.92
		Young	10	11.98	0.34
	30 s	Elderly	10	11.44	1.06
		Young	10	11.82	0.19
H	5 s	Elderly	10	10.78	5.08
		Young	10	9.90	0.51
	10 s	Elderly	10	10.49	3.93
		Young	10	9.80	0.30
	30 s	Elderly	10	11.77	8.10
		Young	10	10.49	1.89

time differences in the shape J experiment of the control group was smaller than that of the experimental group. From the identification accuracy rate, it can be known that the identification ability of the experimental group in the shape J experiment is not good.

Table 7. Comparison of recognition time of shape I&J under different time.

Shape	Sec	Group	N	M	SD
I	5 s	Elderly	10	9.87	8.11
		Young	10	2.49	1.02
	10 s	Elderly	10	7.64	8.56
		Young	10	1.94	0.30
	30 s	Elderly	10	10.16	9.10
		Young	10	1.86	0.19
J	5 s	Elderly	10	8.12	4.62
		Young	10	6.69	0.29
	10 s	Elderly	10	9.27	5.87
		Young	10	6.66	0.44
	30 s	Elderly	10	6.97	1.39
		Young	10	6.63	0.48

From Table 8, in the shape K experiment, the average number of seconds in the experimental group was only smaller than that in the control group at an interval of 30 s, but in the experiments with an interval of 5 s and 10 s, the average number of seconds in the control group was smaller than that in the experimental group. From the identification accuracy rate, it can be seen that the identification ability of the experimental group in the shape K experiment is not good. In the control group, the average number of seconds in the interval of 5 s was smaller than the number of seconds in the other two time differences. The average number of seconds in the three different time differences of the control group in the shape L experiment was smaller than that of the experimental group, and the difference was not small. The factors that cause the difference in the average seconds may be related to the shape L complexity. From the identification accuracy rate, it is known that the experimental group has poor identification ability in the shape L experiment.

Table 8. Comparison of recognition time of shape K&L under different time.

Shape	Sec	Group	N	M	SD
K	5 s	Elderly	10	7.62	3.13
		Young	10	7.61	0.96
	10 s	Elderly	10	9.56	5.16
		Young	10	7.90	0.39
	30 s	Elderly	10	7.60	1.03
		Young	10	7.79	0.12
L	5 s	Elderly	10	5.27	3.22
		Young	10	3.02	0.21
	10 s	Elderly	10	9.04	9.20
		Young	10	2.83	0.17
	30 s	Elderly	10	7.28	7.61
		Young	10	2.90	0.39

4.3 T-test for Shape Recognition Under Different Time

This research conducted an independent sample T test for the two groups of ethnic groups to find out whether there were significant differences between the two groups in the recognition of shapes of different complexity. The test results show that the recognition of different shapes between the two groups only occurs in the three time differences of shape F (original hexagon) and the 5-s and 30-s time differences of shape I (hexagon with rounded corners), as shown in the Table 9, while the rest of the shapes were not significantly different.

Table 9. T-test for the identification of shape by different groups.

Shape	Sec	df	t	p	(d)
F	5s	10.473	2.346	.040	−1.05
	10s	9.072	3.141	.012	−1.40
	30s	9.080	2.283	.048	−1.02
I	5s	9.285	2.855	.018	−1.28
	30s	9.008	2.883	.018	−1.29

p < 0.05.

5 Conclusion

This research investigates the changes in the recognition and memory of basic geometric shapes in the elderly. Through the comparison between the experimental group and the control group, the related research was carried out. According to the experimental results, there is a gap in the accuracy of shape recognition among the elderly, especially the more complicated the shape, the lower the recognition ability. Wang (2017) also pointed out that the elderly people are not good at recognizing image symbols that are too abstract and complicated. In this study, the control group had a higher overall recognition accuracy rate than the experimental group, but the subjects in both groups had errors in recognition of the sample graphics with oblique angles, which involved people's cognitive mode of graphics judgment. In addition, the experimental results show that there are significant differences between the three time differences of shape F (original hexagon) and the 5-s and 30-s time differences of shape I (hexagon with rounded corners) under three time differences, and The difference in average seconds between the two groups is very large. And shape I is the lowest recognition accuracy rate in the 5-s interval experiment for the elderly. Finally, the experimental results of the 12 shape test samples are also consistent with Bernbach's (1975) research results on sequence effects, that is, the timing of stimulus object presentation affects the accuracy of subjects' recall of stimulus sequence locations. In the end, the research results obtained by this research can not only help designers to have reference and application in product design or graphic interface, but also provide the basis for the follow-up research of scholars and experts engaged in the design research of the elderly.

References

Olivers, C.N., Van Der Helm, P.A.: Symmetry and selective attention: A dissociation between effortless perception and serial search. Percept. Psychophys. **60**(7), 1101–1116 (1998)

Biederman, I.: Recognition by components: a theory of image understanding. Psychol. Rev. **94**(2), 115–147 (1987)

Pentland, A.: Perceptual organization and the representation of natural form. Artifical Intelligence **28**, 293–331 (1986)

Liu, Z., Knill, D.C., Kersten, D.: Object classification for human and ideal observers. Vision. Res. **35**(4), 549–568 (1995)

Chambers, K.W., McBeath, M.K., Schiano, D.J., Metz, E.G.: Tops are more salient than bottoms. Percept. Psychophys. **61**(4), 625–635 (1999)

Aguiar, B., Macário, R.: The need for an elderly centred mobility policy. Transpo. Res. Procedia **25**, 4355–4369 (2017)

Hacihasanoglu, E., Simga-Mugan, F.N.C., Soytas, U.: Do global risk perceptions play a role in emerging market equity return volatilities? Emerg. Mark. Financ. Trade **48**(4), 67–78 (2012)

Huang, M.B., Lin, J.D., Chen, L.M.: Falling of elderly people living alone at Sanchong District, New Taipei City. Taiwan J. Gerontological Health Res. **7**(2), 135–156 (2011)

Haigh, R.: The aging process: a challenge for design. Appl. Ergon. **24**(1), 9–14 (1993)

Toshimoto, M.: Architectural Environment for the Elderly. *Architectural Society of Japan* (ed.), Shokokusha, Tokyo, 87–95 (1994)

Morris, J.M.: User interface design for older adults. Interact. Comput. **6**(4), 373–393 (1994)

Yoshida: Architectural Environment for the Elderly. Architectural Society of Japan (ed.), Shokokusha, Tokyo, pp. 96–106 (1994)

Lee, C.F., Chu, Z.M., Lin, R.L., Lin, L.Y.: To explore the effect of different age groups on the trompe Illusion amount of the muller-lyer. In: Collection of Academic Research Achievements of the 3rd Design Society (Volume 1), pp. 75–78 (1998)

Hawthorn, R.: Possible implications of aging for interface designers. Inter. Comput. **12**, 507–528 (2000)

Wais, P.E., Rubens, M.T., Boccanfuso, J., Gazzaley, A.: Neural mechanisms underlying the impact of visual distraction on retrieval of long-term memory. J. Neurosci. **30**(25), 8541–8550 (2010)

Park, D.C., Lautenschlager, G., Hedden, T., Davidson, N.S., Smith, A.D., Smith, P.K.: Models of visuospatial and verbal memory across the adult life span. Psychol. Aging **17**(2), 299–320 (2002)

Demir, E., Köseoğlu, E., Sokullu, R., Şeker, B.: Smart home assistant for ambient assisted living of elderly people with dementia. Procedia Computer Science **113**, 609–614 (2017)

Goffaux, P., Phillips, N.A., Sinai, M., Pushkar, D.: Neurophysiological measures of task-set switching: effects of working memory and aging. J. Gerontol. B Psychol. Sci. Soc. Sci. **63**(2), 57–66 (2008)

Baxter, M.R.: Product Design: Practical Methods for the Systematic Development of New Products. Chapman & Hall, New York (1995)

Wang, C.: Intuitive Icon Design for Elderly People. (Master's Thesis). Fu Jen Catholic University, Taipei, Taiwan (2017)

Bernbach, H.A.: Rate of presentation in free recall: a problem for two-stage memory theories. J. Exp. Psychol. Human Learn. Memory **1**(1), 18 (1975)

E-Focus Groups as a Conceptual Tool for Co-creation of Products and Services for the Elderly

Maria Lilian de Araújo Barbosa[(✉)] [ID] and Maria Lucia Leite Ribeiro Okimoto[ID]

Federal University of Paraná, Curitiba, Brazil
{maria.lilian,lucia.demec}@ufpr.br

Abstract. The context, this article aims to present the study on the behavior profile of the elderly in relation to digital technologies and to survey the opportunities for the introduction of new digital technological solutions for the elderly. The method used in this study, was the application of conceptual online tools, in the format of questionnaires, with structured questions for completion, for a data collection with the elderly, over 60 years old and with different educational profiles. A convenience sample was defined, with a total sample size of 50 elderly people, 25 females and 25 males. The present study was conducted in a community of elderly people in the city of Curitiba, Brazil. The results of this step assisted the researchers for new strategies, refinement, and configuration of e-focus groups for interactions with seniors, and new opportunities for both research and product development. Thus, this article highlights the results obtained, the method employed, the opportunities for the insertion of Human Centered Design that involve different dimensions and complexities of science, technology, innovation, but also address, the inclusion of people with different profiles, such as the elderly, so that they have access to social welfare in different contexts, including digital.

Keywords: E-Focus groups · Aging and DUXU · Digital technologies

1 Introduction - Research Context

1.1 Senior Audience Growth

The increase in life expectancy over the next few decades is a worldwide phenomenon, and is based on projections from the United Nations (UN), [1] the World Bank (WB), [2] and Euromonitor International (EI) [3]. The UN presents a projection of 1.5 billion elderly people by 2050 [1] and Euromonitor International (EI) states in its latest annual report that the global population over 60 will increase by 65% from 2021 to 2040, reaching over two billion people [3].

To minimize the impact of population aging, the UN declared the Decade of Healthy Aging for the period 2020–2030, through UN Resolution 75/131, to encourage actions that benefit this age group of the world population [4]. In Brazil, in 2017, the elderly population was estimated at 30.2 million [5]. Aligned with the UN recommendations for the decade of healthy aging, Brazil created the program "Estratégia Brasil Amigo da Pessoa Idosa" (EBAPI) in 2021. This program aims to encourage actions for active, healthy, and sustainable aging for this profile of the population, through Decree No. 10,604, of January 20, 2021 [6].

1.2 The Elderly and the Use of Technologies in the Pandemic Period

It is estimated that more than three billion people were isolated during the Covid-19 pandemic period, and in this context, digital interactions have changed dramatically, imposing new behaviors in the use of these technologies. While it has become a convenience for some, for others it has become essential, being necessary to learn and handle digital technologies in a short period of time [7].

In this pandemic period, the elderly public, for the most part had little or no knowledge of the use of these technologies, but were forced to use the digital resources of the WEB, while the world became isolated [1].

The elderly to minimize the imposed isolation needed to: assimilate knowledge and become familiar with technology, obtain digital access services to perform consultations, online shopping, and interact socially [8]. In this way a greater dependence on this technology occurred, becoming in some cases, the only means of supplying their daily needs and social interaction.

In this context, this article aims to present a study on the perception of the elderly about the use of digital technologies in activities of daily living and perception of use of social networks in the period of the pandemic, through a questionnaire and the E-Focus Group Technique for interaction and co-creation of solutions and opportunities for the introduction of new digital technological solutions for the elderly with the participation of the elderly.

2 The E-Focus Groups Technique and Its Potential for the Creation of Products and Services for the Elderly

The behavioral changes of the elderly are transforming and impacting companies around the world, thus highlighting new demands for product and service solutions, interaction challenges and elderly user experiences with these technologies [1].

Therefore, it is a challenge to investigate the appropriate strategies for the development of products and services for the elderly public. In this sense, design is a connection point between professionals and users for the co-creation of innovations.

Design centered on the human being, places the user at the center of the process, to understand their needs and thus propose solutions for the development of products, systems, services, and experiences, using methods and tools to solve problems [9].

A conceptual design tool for generating ideas and solutions in the interaction with users is the Focus Group technique, created by Robert Merton in 1946, in the academic environment and applied initially in qualitative research in the area of social sciences and later, incorporated into other areas [12].

2.1 Human Centered Design (HCD)

Placing the human being at the center of the product or service development process involves identifying user demands in specific contexts, the restrictions of each solution and thus establishing which priorities should be developed.

The Human-Centered Design (HCD) proposes three pillars: The first pillar is the user's desire, his need and what makes sense to him. For each type of user, the product makes sense or not, according to their values and life context.

The second pillar is practicality, that is, what is technically and organizationally possible and the last pillar is the financial feasibility for execution, as the best proposal may not be viable, as it does not have the necessary resources to implement the proposed solution [10].

For Norman, the principles of HCD are people-centered, and seek to assess not the symptoms of a problem, but the cause of them. The assessment of the cause leads to the basic and fundamental problem. From the understanding of what the priority problem is, the best solution is sought, in terms of technical and feasibility aspects, to meet the user's needs [11].

2.2 E-Focus Groups as a Creative Design Tool

The technique is based on an in-depth interview carried out in groups containing, normally, six to 10 people, lasting 90 min [13, 14].

During the worldwide pandemic, research, data collection, project validation, etc., had to reinvent themselves, and new protocols, conceptual design tools, and platforms for online access were used for interactions with users at a distance [15].

In this context, the Focus Group technique was adapted to the online format, being called E-Focus Group (electronic focus groups) that allows conducting virtual interviews with the help of tools such as e-mail, chats, and video calls, replacing total or partially face-to-face interactions by synchronous or asynchronous online interactions [16].

In this online format, virtual materials are used, such as slides, videos, images, articles, and other textual and visual materials that can support the contextualization of the research problem using free online platforms, therefore, with low operating costs [12–14].

Conducting the E-focus Group requires more planning, requiring detailed use of time, and technological resources. The technique can be used alone or in conjunction with other methods to stimulate the decision-making process of a group of users [13, 14].

Another benefit of using the E-focus Group is a greater geographical coverage, as people from different regions of the country can participate, allowing greater participation without distinction of social class or gender, as it is more affordable, since the person participates home, without the need for transportation costs, which allows for a more "homogeneous" data collection [13, 14].

In the behavioral aspect, the participants' initial reactions and opinions tend to be more spontaneous, which can give researchers more reliable results, as shy participants feel more comfortable expressing their opinion on some subjects that they might not feel comfortable with in person. give an opinion [13, 14].

However, there are some disadvantages, such as not knowing to what extent collective opinion would equal individual opinion. The comments must be analyzed within the context in which they were said, and therefore, it is up to the researcher to assess which opinions are relevant to the research. [13, 14].

3 Research Methods and Procedures

This is an exploratory and descriptive study, with an experience report in conducting an online focus group with elderly people, carried out in the initial prospection stage in the Doctorate in Design of the postgraduate program in Design at the Federal University of Paraná, with the objective of identifying the perception of the elderly about the use of digital technologies in activities of daily living and perception of use of social networks during the pandemic period.

3.1 Human Centered Design

To conduct the study, the HCD Strategy was defined with the acronyms of the words, H = Hear, C = Create, and D = Deliver [10]. The strategy has as its main focus, putting the user at the center of the whole process, as illustrated in Fig. 1.

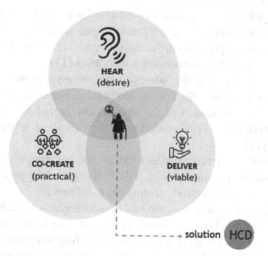

Fig. 1. Human Centered Design (HCD). Adapted IDEO (2009).

The hear phase corresponds to listening to the user, collecting information to understand their pain and needs. In the context of this study, this step was performed using the online questionnaire to collect information. The Create phase in this study was called CO-Create, as the objective was to show the possibilities of co-creation with users, in an E-Focus Group. The last phase corresponds to Deliver, which is the phase where opportunities are identified and solutions are delivered, which in this study corresponded to the solution proposals generated by E-Focus Group.

3.2 Participants and Questionnaires

A convenience sample was defined, with a total sample of 50 elderly people, with 25 female and 25 male participants, for asynchronous completion of an online questionnaire. Elderly with over 60 years old and with different educational and professional profiles, from an online community of elderly people who meet in Curitiba, Brazil. However, this group includes people from different other Brazilian states.

The electronic questionnaire was prepared on the Google form platform and a link was generated with the invitation to send it to the WhatsApp groups of communities that deal with topics related to the elderly, such as LAB 60 +, CIS LAB60 and Grupo de elders of Agape Church Curitiba. Access to the questionnaire was programmed to be released only after reading and accepting the Free and Informed Consent Term. (FICT).

Questionnaires are one of the resources used for extracting information and in qualitative research. Researchers use this tool to communicate with the target audience of their research. They are prepared with open, closed or mixed questions. When preparing the questions, one should take into account the level of knowledge, attitude, and preferences of the respondents, to maximize the response rate, considering the purpose of collecting information for the research [17].

The closed questions were designed in the single-answer model with options of yes, no, perhaps, which limited the respondent to the set of alternatives offered. However, they offer more accurate data. The open questions were prepared in the format of justifications for the answers to the closed questions.

Open questions allow the respondent to express their opinion without being influenced by the researcher. But they have disadvantages due to the need for coding the researcher's subjective interpretation in the analysis stage, in addition to requiring greater cognitive effort and time for the respondent's responses [17].

Considering the user's profile, the online format, and asynchronous access, 15 closed questions were defined for the collection of information. For each question, a space was made available for the justification of the answer, configured as optional, so that the respondent could express their opinion and justify their choice in relation to the question, as suggested by Reja [17].

The questions were designed in order to know the perception of the elderly about the use of digital technologies in activities of daily living and the perception of isolation or not, from the use of social networks during the pandemic.

The results of the questionnaires were analyzed and synthesized in order to identify the main demands identified by the 50 elderly people. The justifications and opinions of the elderly were grouped in an Affinity table according to similarity, proximity, and affinity, adding N = number of repetitions of the same idea or argument. [18].

The affinity board is a conceptual tool that organizes ideas and data, also called the KJ Method, in allusion to the name of its creator, Kawakita Jiro, who developed it in the 1960s. It is a creative process to organize and consolidate information from complex problems, describing data without quantifying them [19].

3.3 Conducting the E-focus Group for Co-design with Seniors

Only one online meeting was held, which was recorded, for the realization of the E-focus Group, using the free online platform of Google Meet and the Jamboard tool, which is a digital whiteboard of G Suite, accessed for free from an account from Gmail. Jamboard has a playful and intuitive appearance, with sticky note features, such as colorful virtual post-its, which can be used to organize ideas in an interactive and collaborative way, and can be accessed in online format from anywhere, by different devices such as smartphones, tablet or desktop.

For this second phase, 5 female and 5 male participants were selected. Whereas the E-focus Group technique is based on an in-depth interview carried out in groups containing from six to 10 people [12–14].

The criteria for sending the invitations to the 10 participants for the E-focus Group were: Expression of the desire to participate in this phase, in one of the answers to the questionnaire, the respondent has the google email (Gmail) to facilitate access to the platform from Google meet and Jamboard.

The invitation was sent via WhatsApp, which is the means of communication used by 99% of the participants, according to the responses to the questionnaire. A presentation in PDF format was also sent, explaining the conduct of the study (Fig. 2).

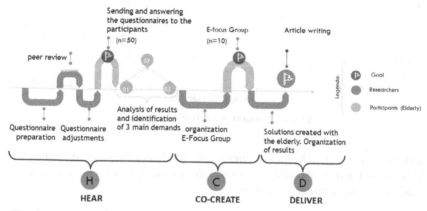

Fig. 2. Synthesis conducts of the study and moments of participation of the elderly.

3.4 Practical and Viable Idea Generation

The synchronous online meeting for the E-FOCUS GROUP was structured based on the HCD, divided into four moments: Moment 1: Presentation to the group of participants, the problems classified according to the answers to the questionnaires. Time was made available for each participant to present their doubts regarding the conduct of the dynamics or comments about the results presented.

Moment 2: Reading the arguments of each demand. Voting to choose only one demand/problem for the next moment. 10 min were available for the activity. Moment 3: After the vote, the group considered the problem of digital literacy as a priority and, in sequence, the participants presented proposals for solutions to this problem prioritized by them.

Moment 4: After voting, the Prioritization Matrix [18] was introduced, where instructions were given on its use, to identify the best proposal, considering the criteria "impact x ease of implementation" (Fig. 3) at the discretion of the participants. 5 min were allotted for this activity.

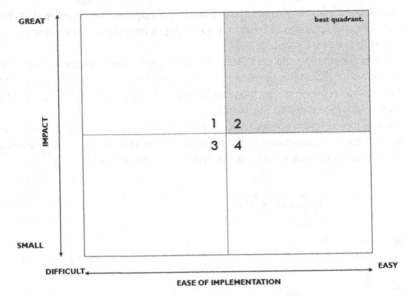

Fig. 3. Proposal prioritization matrix.

Regarding the impact, the largest number of elderly people reached by the solution should be considered. In the criterion ease of deployment, it was considered which of the solutions would be easier to implement.

4   Resulted

In the data collection stage, to know the perception of the elderly about the use of digital technologies in activities of daily living, during the pandemic, the answers to the closed questions (P1 to P8), are organized with their respective results in Table 1. Regarding the perception of the elderly about isolation and the use of social networks, the closed questions (P9 to P15) are organized with their respective results in Table 2.

Table 1. Perception of the elderly on the use of digital technologies in activities of daily living

QUESTIONS	ANSWERS
P1. How old are you?	Of the 50 elderly people who participated in this study, 68% reported being between 60 and 69 years old. 30% between 70 and 79 years old and 2% between 80 and 89 years old

(*continued*)

Table 1. (*continued*)

QUESTIONS	ANSWERS
P2. Have you retired?	Regarding their professional life, 80% responded that they were retired and 20% were still working
P3. During the pandemic period, did you use digital technologies for medical appointments?	36% of the elderly reported that they never used digital technologies for medical appointments. 48% sometimes, and only 16% made frequent medical appointments during the pandemic period
P4. During this period of the pandemic, have you used digital technologies for online purchases of medicines, food, and essential items, in supermarkets, stores, etc.?	24% of the elderly reported that they have never used digital technologies to purchase medicines, food and essential items online, in supermarkets, stores, etc
P5. Were you able to successfully complete these activities?	76% declared that they were able to successfully complete online purchase activities, although they are afraid of the security of their bank details, preferring to generate payment slips for online purchases
P6. Did you feel safe to make online purchases/payments?	72% said they feel safe and buy online because they trust the supplier or because their children helped
P7. What equipment did you use the most to carry out these activities?	Regarding equipment, 58% use their smartphones for online purchases and interactions. 26% use a notebook, and only 16% use a desktop
P8. Do you think the use of digital technologies makes your day to day easier?	98% of the elderly said that technology facilitates their daily lives

With the answers, the problems most cited by the elderly were identified, which were classified into 3 categories, namely: Equipment and Infrastructure; Digital literacy and Ageism in the digital divide, drawing up the affinities table (Table 3), with the opinions

Table 2. Perception of the elderly about isolation and the use of social networks

QUESTIONS	ANSWERS
P9. Has social media reduced your social isolation during the pandemic?	78% of the elderly reported that social networks reduced the feeling of isolation, as they connected with friends and family, in addition to looking for news and fun

(*continued*)

Table 2. (*continued*)

QUESTIONS	ANSWERS
P10. Which social network did you use the most?	46% of the elderly use Facebook for these activities. 30% use Instagram and 20% report that they do not use social networks
P11. Which social network for sending messages did you use the most during this period?	98% use WhatsApp to communicate with family and friends and 2% use telegram to send messages
P12. Did you attend or participate in online meetings (lives, meetings) during the pandemic?	94% reported having participated in online meetings during the pandemic period
P13. If yes, did you have difficulty using these online platforms for meetings/lives?	28% reported having little difficulty with the platforms and 10% reported having many difficulties. the biggest problem being the connection issue
P14. If you had difficulties, who helped you?	54% reported that family or friends taught them how to use the platforms and 42% reported that they had to learn on their own
P15. Do you think there is a digital exclusion of elderly people (over 60 years old)?	46% reported that there is a digital exclusion of the elderly. 34% think that maybe there is this digital exclusion, and 20% answered that there is no exclusion

and arguments of the elderly, made available in the questionnaires, as suggested by Viana et al. [18] and Cesar [19].

The Number of occurrences (*N) of the same idea or argument were organized by affinities, according to the criteria, similarity, proximity and affinity [18, 19].

The participants, from the E-Focus Group, defined the need for digital literacy for the elderly as the main problem. For them, this is the central problem, as technology and infrastructure are useless if the elderly do not know how to use them, and digital ageism would be minimized when the greatest number of elderly people are using digital technologies deftly in everyday life.

The proposed solutions were: Encourage daily practice in the use of technologies, as repetition generates skill. Creation of free online courses for people over 50 years old, with didactics suitable for this age group. Family members develop the habit of teaching their parents about the use of digital technologies that impact their daily lives, citing as an example, APPS for parking, scheduling appointments, health monitoring, and services available in the community, among others.

All participants present at the meeting considered that the proposed solutions are of great impact, but difficult to implement, as they depend on the community and policies. All proposed solutions were grouped in quadrant 1. The proposals that were in quadrant 2, with low impact and difficult implementation, were discarded.

Table 3. Proposals organized according to criteria, similarity, proximity and affinity

	A.Equipment and B.Infrastructure	C.Digital Literacy	D.Ageísm and digital E.exclusion
1	"Weak internet. Every tool has another way to access it"	"The biggest problem is when you have participants who don't know how to use the tool causing turmoil in live"	"It is a path where there are several situations: the biggest, in my view, is that of the elderly who self-exclude or block themselves, as an example. I quote my family members who say "I will never learn to use this iphone" or… this WhatsApp"
2	Bad internet connection	Who invited me, used an unknown platform, and didn't guide me and I couldn't enter. I was very frustrated!	Many times, we exclude ourselves, for not having much knowledge
3	The link didn't work. I always had to ask for help with connections!	I have a lot of limitations with technology	"I believe that the elderly are often invisible. Those who can participate face difficulties because they have "inherited devices""
4	Connection, no signal	The vast majority of the elderly population does not have access to these technologies, and they would need to be taught how to use them well. It is known that rare relatives lend themselves to help	Because people still think that the elderly cannot learn the use of technologies and treat us as if we were mentally retarded
5	The internet that fails a lot	Due to the difficulty in learning and lack of patience of those who teach	Because we are only elderly and not useless, we are capable and still have a lot of intelligence
6	Internet signal oscillation… equipment incompatibilities	For lack of adequate didactics for our age	
7	Not having access to devices and the internet for this - or due to technical, financial, family problems, etc	Some people have blocks. Difficulty learning and understanding this sequence of steps, programs, links	
	F.Equipment and G.Infrastructure	H.Digital Literacy	I.Ageísm and digital J.exclusion

(continued)

Table 3. (*continued*)

	A.Equipment and B.Infrastructure	C.Digital Literacy	D.Ageísm and digital E.exclusion
8	Not everyone can afford a cell phone	For young family members, it all seems obvious. So, they do and don't demonstrate it step by step. You don't have time with those who are slower to learn this technology. Even a certain arrogance in the attitude when "teaching" causes the elderly to give up	
9	Not everyone has access to or financial conditions to acquire any technology service	Difficulty finding people who have detachment, patience	
10	Lack of money, fast internet, technology lag	Language nomenclature	
11	Because many do not have access to good internet, the expensive price makes it unfeasible	Learn, and also who teaches, because of this they are isolated	
	*N = 11 occurrences	***N = 11 occurrences**	***N = 05 occurrences**

5 Final Thoughts

The E-Focus Group was conducted, seeking to select the priority problem, not only looking at the identified demand, but also presenting the arguments and opinions of the 50 elderly people who responded to the questionnaire. The arguments help to identify the cause of the problem and not its symptoms. We reflect the true essence of Human Centered Design, as defended by Norman [11].

Regarding the perception of the elderly about the use of digital technologies in activities of daily living, during the pandemic, the answers to the questionnaire show that the elderly, for the most part, were protagonists and had an overcoming to absorb knowledge and master the use of digital technologies in a short period of time and in an adverse canary of social isolation.

It is necessary to understand that this is a great overcoming, when one takes into account the available resources, such as the internet and obsolete equipment, in addition to the learning challenge of interacting with other people in a short space of time and in some contexts, completely isolated.

98% of the elderly declare that technology facilitates their daily lives, which demonstrates a high rate of acceptance by this population profile, however, they feel frustrated by the lack of skill and dexterity in its use and would like people and courses with appropriate didactics for this age group that help them in digital literacy.

The elderly argue that there are digital inequalities for the elderly population, as their retiree income is restrictive to paying for internet access and appropriate equipment, with up-to-date technology, such as smartphones, notebooks, or desktops.

The collection of information through a questionnaire made it possible to understand the behavior profile of the elderly in the use of digital technologies during the pandemic period and to map opportunities for the introduction of new digital solutions for and with the elderly.

It is concluded, therefore, that the elderly accept and understand the benefits of technology. But they need to understand its use and need solutions for teaching appropriate to their context with didactics and content aimed at the profile of seniors, which corroborates the choice of the priority problem defined in the E-Focus Group, which is digital literacy.

The growth projections of this user profile can be observed, which will promote an impact on the consumption of goods and services, challenging companies and service providers from different segments to align their language to meet the expectations and needs of the elderly, with solutions for digital literacy.

It is noteworthy that the conduct of the E-Focus Group, structured on the pillars of the HCD, contributes to the research area in Design for the elderly. The results of this study contributed to the understanding of the perceptions of the elderly in the use of technologies to adjust strategies and conduct a next stage of research.

References

1. United Nations (UN). World Population Ageing, (ST/ESA/SER.A/444). Department of Economic and Social Affairs, Population Division: (2019). https://www.un.org/en/develo pment/desa/population/publications/pdf/ageing/WorldPopulationAgeing2019-Report.pdf, Accessed 16 Dec 2021
2. Rofman, R., Apella, I.: When We're Sixty-Four: Opportunities and Challenges for Public Policies in a Population-Aging Context in Latin America. International Development in Focus. World Bank, Washington, DC. (2020) https://doi.org/10.1596/978-1-4648-1605-5
3. Angus, A., Westbrook, G.: Top 10 Global Consumer Trends 2022. Euromonitor International. (2022) https://go.euromonitor.com/white-paper-EC-2022-Top-10-Global-Consumer-TrendsPG.html?utm_source=website&utm_medium=website&utm_campaign=CT_22_01_18_WP_Top_10_GCT_2022_PG, Accessed 19 Jan 2022
4. United Nations (UN): UN Resolution 75/131: United Nations Decade of Healthy Ageing (2021–2030) (2020) https://undocs.org/en/A/RES/75/131 Accessed 16 Dec 2021
5. Instituto Brasileiro de Geografia e Estatística (IBGE): Projeções da População do Brasil e Unidades da Federação por sexo e idade: 2010–2060. (2018) https://agenciadenoticias.ibge. gov.br/agencia-detalhe-de-midia.html?view=mediaibge&catid=2103&id=2188 Accessed 16 Oct 2021
6. Brasil: Decreto n° 10.604, de 20 de janeiro de 2021. Dispõe sobre Política Nacional do Idoso. (2021) https://www.in.gov.br/en/web/dou/-/decreto-n-10.604-de-20-de-janeiro-de-2021-299 973647 Accessed 16 Nov 2021
7. Beaunoyer, E., Dupéré, S., Guitton, M.: COVID-19 and digital inequalities: reciprocal impacts and mitigation strategies. Comput. Human Behavior 111, 106424 (2020). https://doi.org/10. 1016/j.chb.2020.106424

8. Rodrigues, Rosalina Aparecida Partezani (Org.); Fhon, Jack Roberto Silva; Lima Fabia Maria de. O cuidado ao idoso na atenção primária à saúde em tempos de COVID-19. Ribeirão Preto, SP: Centro de Apoio Editorial da Escola de Enfermagem de Ribeirão Preto, (2021)
9. World Design Organization (WDO)®: https://wdo.org/about/definition/, Accessed 14 Nov 2021
10. Ideo - The Field Guide to Human-Centered Design: HCD Toolkit Homepage, (2009) https://www.ideo.com/post/design-kit
11. Norman, D.: Principles of Human-Centered Design. (2018) https://www.nngroup.com/videos/principles-human-centered-design-don-norman/, Accessed 16 Nov 2021
12. Morgan, D.: Robert Merton and the History of Focus Groups: Standing on the Shoulders of a Giant? The American Sociologist. (2021) https://doi.org/10.1007/s12108-021-09500-5. Accessed 14 Nov 2021
13. Duque, R., Bringas, S., Montaña, J.L.: Active learning based on electronic focus groups and participatory design during the COVID-19 period. In: Ninth International Conference on Technological Ecosystems for Enhancing Multiculturality (TEEM'21). Association for Computing Machinery, New York, NY, USA. pp. 67–71, (2021) https://doi.org/10.1145/3486011.3486421, Accessed 15 Dec 2021
14. Schröeder, C.D.S., Klerin, L.R.: On-line focus group: uma possibilidade para a pesquisa qualitativa em administração. Cadernos EBAPE.BR [online]. vol. 7, no. 2 pp. 332–348. (2009) https://doi.org/10.1590/S1679-39512009000200010, Accessed 14 Dec 2021
15. Zacar, C.R.H. et al.: Atividade de Aprendizado Integradora do curso de Design de Produto da UFPR: proposta de ensino-pesquisa-extensão em resposta à pandemia de COVID-19. Extensão em Foco, [S.l.], n. 23, jun. (2021). http://dx.doi.org/https://doi.org/10.5380/ef.v0i23.79232. Accessed 14 Dec 2021
16. Oringderff, J.: "My way": piloting an on-line focus group. International Journal of Qualitative Methods, Edmonton, Alberta, Canada, vol. 3, no. 3, Sept. (2004).s <http://www.ualberta.ca/~iiqm/backissues/3_3/html/oringderff.html>. Accessed 14 Dec 2021
17. Reja, U., Manfreda, K.L., Hlebec, V., Vehovar, V.: Open-ended vs. close-ended questions in web questionnaires. Dev. Appl. Stat. **19**(1), 159–177 (2003)
18. Vianna, M., et al.: Design Thinking: Inovação em negócios. MJV Press, Rio de Janeiro (2011)
19. César, F.I.G.: Ferramentas Básicas da Qualidade. Biblioteca24horas. São Paulo (2011)

The Role of Information and Communication Technologies in Researching Older People During the Covid-19 Pandemic

The Case of the Italian Longitudinal Study on Older People's Quality of Life During the Covid-19 Pandemic (ILQA-19)

Giulia Melis[1]([✉]), Emanuela Sala[2], and Daniele Zaccaria[3]

[1] University of Cagliari, 09123 Cagliari, CA, Italy
giulia.melis10@unica.it
[2] University of Milano Bicocca, 20126 Milan, MI, Italy
[3] University of Applied Sciences and Arts of Southern Switzerland, 6928 Manno, CH, Switzerland

Abstract. The Longitudinal Study on Older People's Quality of Life during the Covid-19 pandemic (ILQA-19) is a qualitative study carried out during the 2020 lockdown on 40 older men and women living in the ten villages in northern Italy subject to the first lockdown in Europe. This study focuses on older people's lives and the role of digital technologies during the pandemic, and it has been carried out fully remotely. Despite the need to research the social consequence of pandemics for older people, there is a shortage of studies that provide guidelines on how to successfully involve this population in online qualitative studies. This paper contributes to fill this gap by discussing the use of Information and Communication Technology (ICT) in implementing the different stages of ILQA-19 research. The best practices of qualitative studies conducted through ICTs are discussed, along with the strategies we enacted to enhance participation in the study. Specifically, panel engagement, tailoring procedures and building positive and trustworthy interactions with study members are crucial when researching older people through online methods.

Keywords: COVID 19 · Qualitative research · ICT · Older people · Online methods

1 Introduction

The Covid-19 pandemic has radically changed people's lives, posing serious challenges to their well-being. Specifically, the containment measures that the government adopted to contrast the effects of the pandemic had a dramatic impact on the old age population. There is therefore an urgent need to explore the social consequences of Covid-19 in old age. With this respect, qualitative research methods are powerful tools to investigate the changes brought about by Covid-19. However, conducting qualitative research during pandemics poses a number of challenges because of the mobility restrictions and the need to avoid close physical contacts. In these circumstances, qualitative research methods that fully exploit the potential of Innovation and Communication Technologies (ICTs) are a feasible alternative to face-to-face based research methods. This work describes the procedures we adopted to conduct the Longitudinal Study on Older People's Quality of Life during the Covid-19 pandemic (ILQA-19). Specifically, it describes the strategies we enacted to research older people through qualitative methods of online data collection, with the view to identify best practices. ILQA-19 is a qualitative study that was carried out during the first lockdown (March 2020); it explores the social consequences of the pandemic on older people's well-being and everyday life. ILQA-19 is conducted on a panel of 40 older men and women living in ten villages located in a rural province South of Milan (in the Italian Lombardy region) subject to the first lockdown in Europe.

2 ICT Use in Doing Qualitative Research on Older People in Pandemic Times

There is still a shortage of knowledge on older people's recruitment and interviewing for qualitative studies during pandemics (Guha-Sapir et al. 2015). However, research conducted in the field of sociology of disasters has provided useful guidelines with this respect (Phillips 2014; Rodríguez et al. 2007). Scholars in this field have acknowledged the importance of early recognition and involvement of community leaders, who can provide key support in participant recruitment (Cheung et al. 2003; Johnson and Vindrola-Padros 2017) and encourage reluctant individuals' participation (Henderson et al. 2009), thus indirectly reducing selection bias. As for the interview process, they have stressed the importance of minimizing participants and interviewers' discomfort and emotional burden (Lavin et al. 2012; Parkes 2011). Despite their relevance, these studies have not provided any specific indications for situations in which in-person interviews are not feasible, as during pandemics when face-to-face social interactions are very limited or even forbidden.

Research on online synchronous interviewing methods has shown the relevance of ICT use in conducting social research, providing useful suggestions that can also be applied when carrying out qualitative studies in pandemic times. For example, Lo Iacono et al. (2016) have documented the feasibility of doing online qualitative research, especially when using technologies that allow for interviewer-interviewee visual interactions, such as video-call apps on computers and mobile devices. Specifically, the authors contribute with some practical suggestions that can be adopted when conducting qualitative interviews remotely, including in-depth investigation of participants' ability and willingness to use video-interviews, sending advance preliminary instructions (e.g., shutting down other applications, silencing phones, choosing a quiet place), and contacting participants several times before the interview to establish trust. The authors also recommended paying attention to ethical issues, such as gaining participants' informed consent and warranting data security. Specifically, the choice of the platform for video-interviewing participants depends mainly on data security evaluations (Lobe et al. 2020).

More recently, some scholars have discussed their research experience when shifting planned research from in-person interviews to online techniques of data collection.

Conducting virtual qualitative studies makes participants' recruitment more challenging, especially when recruiting populations at risk of social exclusion, due to their limited or inconsistent access to virtual tools (Saberi 2020; Sy et al. 2020). Indeed, researchers may need to undertake additional, creative, and purposive efforts to reach their target population, e.g., using digital technologies and social media, such as Facebook and Instagram, (Kobakhidze et al. 2021), or extending the study timeline to reach the established number of participants (Roberts et al. 2021). Also, dealing with ethical issues, such as obtaining consent virtually, may become a complex task. On the one hand, some scholars argue that only minor amendments to the process of obtaining informed consent are needed (Dodds & Hess, 2020), on the other, some researchers claim that gaining informed consent, along with the entire online research process, poses new challenges (Roberts et al. 2021). Obtaining consent via email is the most common way of replacing in-person consent procedures (Lobe et al. 2020); however, this procedure does not allow for the two-way conversation necessary for researchers to explain and, whenever necessary, negotiate the terms of the consent form. For this reason, Roberts and colleagues (2021) preferred a two-way interaction in real time with a digital signature, when collecting informed consent for their study. In addition, there are also mixed research experiences when focusing on remote interviewing. Indeed, there is preliminary evidence suggesting that participants benefited from feeling comfortable and more relaxed whereas researchers felt less intrusive and safer not going into people's homes (Dodds & Hess, 2020). However, transcriptions became more difficult and sometimes conversations were interrupted due to poor connectivity (Kobakhidze et al. 2021; Roberts et al. 2021). Also, online interviewing increased the workload of researchers because they needed to attend to technology-related tasks and raised participants' fatigue due to the time spent in front of a computer or holding a smartphone. For these reasons, some suggest that the interview duration should be limited to 30 min (Kobakhidyze et al., 2021).

Research that we mentioned so far acknowledges the challenges of "going online" when researching populations at risk of vulnerability (mainly referring to homeless persons or alcohol consumers). However, these studies did not focus specifically on the older population, which may pose different (or additional) challenges. More often, older people are deemed not suitable for online research because of the extra effort it requires in terms of research design and recruitment process (Newman et al. 2021). A recent study by Richardson et al. (2020) contributed to fill in the literature about researching older people online. The authors stress that, when researching older people, tailoring is the key principle that should drive the design of the recruiting and interviewing procedures. Indeed, the interview mode and interview protocol should meet older people's preferences and skills, e.g., offering those who are familiar with technology the opportunity to collect interviews using video calls, reducing respondent burden. To reach this goal the interview guide should be short and flexible, interviews should be scheduled at a time of the day most convenient for participants, the intensity of data collection should be reduced at specific points of the pandemic (i.e., during the epidemiologic peaks), as also suggested by Vindrola-Padros et al. (2020). Richardson and colleagues (2020) also acknowledge the complexity of collecting informed consent when interviewing older people remotely, because the consent form cannot be discussed in person with the interviewers, a procedure that usually enhances study participation, by facilitating trust. Despite the relevance of Richardson et al. (2020)'s study, their contribution does not address specifically the methodological issues that arise when conducting qualitative research on older people remotely. This paper contributes to fill this gap by discussing the use of ICT in implementing the different stages of the Longitudinal Study on Older People's Quality of Life during the Covid-19 pandemic (ILQA-19), a study that is carried out fully remotely. Specifically, this work addresses the following research questions:

i)   what are the strategies that need to be implemented when researching older people through online qualitative methods?
ii) which online strategies are most suitable for qualitative longitudinal research?
iii) to what extent does ICT use play a role in interviewer-interviewee interactions?

In the attempt to answer our research questions, in the next sections we will illustrate in detail our research design and discuss the specific choices we made during each stage of the data collection process.

3 The ILQA-19 Study

ILQA-19 is a qualitative longitudinal study conducted on a purposive sample of 40 men and women aged between 65 and 80, living in ten villages located in the rural area of the Lodi province (in the Lombardy region) and belonging to Europe's first Covid-19 'Red Zone'. The study aims to explore the consequences of the social distancing measures introduced to contrast the Covid-19 outbreak on older people's well-being and everyday life. In addition, it also intends to longitudinally explore the consequences of the COVID-19 outbreak on older people's everyday life practices, exploring the resources enacted to react to the challenges brought about by the health emergency.

The first wave of the data collection was conducted in spring 2020, during the lock-down, using semi-structured video-interviews. The interview guide covered the following topics: changes occurred in everyday life, role of social relationships and ICT, and impact of the different containment measures on well-being. The second wave started in spring 2021 and the interview guide was updated to adapt to the changing context of the pandemic situation and the related institutional response (e.g., social distancing measures and vaccination programs). While the research design was planned jointly by the three authors, Giulia Melis carried out all interviews.

4 ILQA-19 Data Collection Stages and ICT Use

When discussing the use of ICT in the different stages of the ILQA-19 data collection, we focus on the recruitment (study advertising and participant recruitment), interviewing, and panel maintenance stages. Figure 1 provides an overview of the data collection process.

Stage	Date	ICT use
1. Recruitment	April-July-2020	
- Study advertising	April 2020	email to mayors
- Participant recruitment	May – July 2020	email to local organisations; SNS use
2. Interviewing		
-Wave 1	May-July 2020	Video-calls (i.e. WhatsApp, Google Meet, Zoom, Skype)
-Wave 2	May - October 2021	Video-calls
3. Panel maintenance		
-Wave 1	August 2020 - April 2021	Youtube videos; online seminars
-Wave 2	November 2021 - ongoing	Youtube videos

Fig. 1. Overview of the data collection process

5 Recruiting

In Spring 2020, when the data collection started, Italy was in lockdown. Therefore, in order to remotely recruit older people, we developed a two-step procedure, i.e., study advertising and participant recruitment. The protocol is described in detail in Melis, Sala and Zaccaria (2021a); here, we provide a brief overview of the steps undertaken to recruit study participants.

5.1 Study Advertising

During the study advertising phase, we informed the general population and the local authorities about the beginning of the study, published several articles in the local newspapers, and contacted by email or telephone call the mayors of the ten villages where the study was conducted, inviting them to advertise the study amongst the local community (e.g., using the city council website). This strategy proved to be successful; considering that the majors had to deal with the challenges posed by an unprecedented health emergency, six (out of ten) advertised the study on the city council website or using more traditional communication media (e.g., bulletin boards) and provided the contact details of the local stakeholders, e.g., AUSER, the most important Italian voluntary association in the field of active aging.

5.2 Participant Recruitment

The participant recruitment phase is grounded on community engagement. Specifically, to start the snowball sample, we contacted the local organizations by email, providing them with the study description and inviting them to identify, amongst their members, older people potentially interested in taking part in the study. In addition, we also activated our weak ties, facilitated by the fact that one of the team members had connections in the area where the study is based. To recruit further study participants, we fully exploited the potential of social networking sites (SNS), posting the call to action on the local Facebook pages. All in all, either through snowballing or through spontaneous responses to our study advertisement, we managed to recruit 40 participants.

6 Interviewing

ICT played a pivotal role in contacting and interviewing study participants. During the first wave of data collection, each interview was preceded by a preliminary contact by telephone. This first call aimed to provide a general overview of the case study, present the team members, and anticipate the details of the interview process (e.g., the online nature of data collection). In addition, it also intended to establish a common ground of trust among the participants and contrast any potential barrier to participation, i.e., oppositions due to the fear of scams (Melis et al. 2021a) and unwillingness to conduct a video-call for personal discretion or lack of basic digital literacy. We responded to participants' reluctance by highlighting the advantages of video-interviews in terms of trust and informality (as also mentioned in Howlett 2021), describing them as a useful solution to implement during the lockdown. To enhance participation among the less digitally savvy, we also developed a protocol aimed at enabling each potential participant to take part in the study regardless of their ICT skills (Melis et al. 2021a). Sometimes, potential participants contacted us directly to volunteer for the study and ask for further information. In these cases, obtaining participants' cooperation was easier. In general, mentioning the support of local institutions and stakeholders, together with the study advertisement available on local newspapers and on our own Department webpage were key to provide a clear and concrete guarantee about the academic nature of the study. All in all, the contact phase was extremely important to enhance online participation, assess participants' digital skills, and present fieldwork documents. For example, the request for a clear expression of consent was anticipated in this preliminary call and the consent module was forwarded through text message or email before the date of the interview.

As previously mentioned, the interviews were carried out remotely, using video-interviews. Once the video-call was started, we ensured participants had access to a clear internet connection and a place where they could speak freely - e.g., without the presence of third parties. In addition, we reviewed together the study procedure, asked for their consent and permission to audio-record (participants' consent was also audio-recorded). In contrast to the informality described by Howlett (2021), some participants showed both eagerness and anxiety for their video-interview: whereas some called in before the interview to properly arrange their laptops and video-call software, others introduced themselves dressed up and seemed to privilege the choice of a nice room instead of the one with better signal. With this respect, whereas for some participants taking part in research might have been an unprecedented experience, we are unsure whether ICT use and specifically the use of a webcam (as a medium for the video-interview) might have played a role in inducing some forms of the so-called *observer effect* (Gregory 2020), where the presence of a webcam increased participants' attention to their performance and visual aesthetics.

In our review of the literature, the main issues about online research with older people are related to difficulties in online interaction (Newman et al. 2021). However, wave

1 interviews were conducted during the first lockdown: along with technical problems, the interviewer also had to safeguard participants' mental health in such a challenging time. Should any sign of emotional distress arise during the interviews, through verbal or nonverbal clues, the interviewer was prepared to pause the interview or shift to less intrusive contents. In the case of significant traumatic experiences, we pointed to the psychological helpline that was also provided within the research consent module. The empathic role of the interviewer (as in Lo and Fan 2021) was crucial in dealing with participants' perceived vulnerabilities and in making them feel listened to. In this case, as some studies suggest (Lo Iacono et al. 2016), the medium of online technologies should be put into perspective: as in face-to-face qualitative data collection techniques, interviewer's efforts in building a positive and trustworthy relationship with the interviewee might be more important than the choice of the medium. A few days after the interview, each participant was called back to ask whether any distress (interview-related) emerged.

In general, wave 2 interviews were more fluent and richer than the ones conducted during wave 1: due to their follow up nature, most participants anticipated the topics of our interests and provided clear and exhaustive accounts. Compared to the first data collection (in 2020), the interviewer encountered fewer technical issues ascribed to participants' poor ICT skills. Although older people auto-assessed few changes in their digital literacy, it was quite clear that after a year most of them gained more familiarity with digital technologies and online interactions within their daily lives compared to Wave 1 (as is also documented in Melis et al. 2021b).

7 Data Analysis

As we closed the fieldwork for wave 1, we integrally transcribed the interviews' audio recordings and conducted the analyses through CAQDAS software (Nvivo 12 Pro). First, every interview file has been divided into segments, where each chunk of text corresponds to a meaning unit - e.g., representations, actions, interactions, etc. We then coded each text segment using a preliminary coding frame, which has been developed through sensitizing concepts (Blumer 1954; Charmaz 2003) identified in the literature review and adjusted when new meanings emerged from the data through a recursive process (Saldaña 2012). We drew on Boyatzis' (1998) inclusion/exclusion principles to label each text segment with a code, then we clustered each group of codes to a main family-code belonging to the same semantic field. In doing so, we collectively discussed the analysis between research team members, adopting an iterative approach: the analysis report was defined when intersubjective agreement amongst researchers was reached. In the end, the following macro-themes (each corresponding to a family of codes) emerges from the analysis: practices of ICT use, social interactions, experience of time, sense of self.

Wave 2 data analysis is still at its beginning. To perform it we shall adopt specific longitudinal data analysis techniques. Drawing on Grossoehme and Lipstein (2016) we plan to adopt the following steps: first, we shall conduct recurrent cross-sectional analysis, to identify themes and dimensions that are specific to each single wave; in addition, we shall perform trajectory data analysis to disentangle changes in older people's representations and experiences over time.

8 Panel Maintenance

Panel maintenance is key for the success of a longitudinal study. To enhance study participation over time, we developed a specific plan that was implemented between data collection waves, consisting of sending study participants Christmas greetings and inviting them to dissemination events (see Fig. 2). This plan, which fully exploits the potentialities of ICTs, was developed after an evaluation of panel members' digital skills.

Content & date	Description	Link	Participants' feedbacks
Christmas greetings (22/12/2020 and 23/12/2021)	WhatsApp message with a link to pre-recorded YouTube videos	2020 video: https://youtu.be/liFwZ Z2-Vg0	9/40
		2021 video: https://www.youtube.c om/watch?v=eHbaEQb YRTc	25/38
Invitation to Milano Digital Week Seminar (15/03/2021)	WhatsApp message with the leaflet of the seminar	2021 video: https://www.youtube.c om/watch?v=uzhzR0C PWqM	13/40

Fig. 2. Between-waves panel maintenance strategy

Specifically, for Christmas, we sent WhatsApp (WA) messages with a link to pre-recorded YouTube videos in which we thanked panel members for their collaboration, updated them on our scientific activities, and sent them our Christmas greetings. Study participants seem to have appreciated our messages. Indeed, the 2020 Christmas greeting video registered 106 visualizations (on 29/11/2021); given that the link to the YouTube video was private, this suggests that study participants must have forwarded the link to their family and friends. In addition, we received several messages in reply to our Christmas greetings videos; panel members congratulated us for the study, reciprocated the greetings, and offered cooperation for further waves of the study, expressing gratitude and joy for having contributed to the research as documented in the following messages[1].

«Congratulations on your interesting work. I heartily reciprocate. Happy Holidays, in high esteem» (Woman, 67).

«Dear Giulia, thank you for the nice Christmas present! I am glad to know that my small contribution was useful for your research. Merry Christmas and a (hopefully) better 2021!» (Woman, 68)

---

[1] There is debate in the literature on how to transcribe qualitative interviews. We have opted for the literal transcription of the interviews, maintaining typos, use of capital letters, etc.

«Thank you Giulia for your message. While hoping that I can still help with your work, I wish you a happy Christmas. Till next time» (Man, 67)

«I am HONORED for having contributed even to a small extent to your research, and I take the opportunity to offer to all of you my best GREETINGS» (Man, 72)

On March 19th, 2021, we organised an online seminar in the context of the *Milano Digital Week*, i.e., one of the cultural events organised by the Milan City Council. On March 15th, we sent a WA message with a link to a pre-recorded YouTube video inviting study participants to the seminar and informing them of the upcoming second wave of data collection. Similar to the Christmas greeting videos, study participants appreciated the invitation; 13 panel members replied to our messages, thanking us for the invitation, apologising for not being able to attend, or confirming the attendance to the seminar (five panel members). Interestingly, as some of these messages clearly show, several participants asked for technical advice on how to participate in the online event, documenting the challenges that they face when using advanced functions of video-calling applications (e.g., Meet).

«Good evening Giulia, thank you for involving me. About Friday's event, unfortunately, I won't be able to participate because of a previous commitment. I remain available for future initiatives. Kind regards with the hope that everything is going well» (M, 65)

«Thank you for your message. I would love to attend the event, hoping that I'm able to log on (my ICT skills are limited). About the possibility of a future interview, I am always available. Till next time» (M, 67)

«Good morning Giulia .i have seen your video, on my smartphone ,because „on my laptop it was unavailable,Anyway I would like to attend the conference ,please explain to me what I should do ,thank you» (F, 66)

It is worth noticing that study members' involvement in the actions envisaged in our panel maintenance plan is key for granting study participation over time. Indeed, those who participated in wave 2 were more likely to reply to our messages than those who did not (means: 1,3 and 0,9). Given the small sample size, these findings need to be interpreted with care.

9 Wave 2 Participation

In wave 2, we managed to re-interview 32 participants. As illustrated in the previous section, when wave 2 recruitment started, a few participants had already shown availability for a second interview. Participants were contacted in groups of ten people, to schedule each interview without overlap. Specifically, the interviewer contacted participants by text message or phone call in chronological order, from the more distant to the more recent date from the first interview, before moving to the following group from the list. Surprisingly, obtaining participants' cooperation was more difficult than we expected. Most causes of reluctance were ascribed to shortage of time; with the easing of government restrictions, older people resumed their daily routines with family and friends, as well as volunteering and caregiving activities. For this reason, we had to increase our efforts in convincing people to take part in the second interview. Many participants reported less time-availability for our study because of their busy schedule, so we extended the recruitment phase accordingly. As we introduced wave 2 data collection as a follow up on our first encounter, we also had to reassure participants that believed to have little to add to their first interview.

10   Engaging with Participants Through ICTs: The Interviewer Account

ICT use poses some specific challenges to humane interactions when it comes to researching older people. In our case study, generational differences in ICT use added up to the traits of participants within our case study: a rural community with a long-standing habit of face-to-face encounters with family members, friends, and acquaintances, wherein the use of digital technologies was unneeded. For that reason, the first issue the interviewer had to overcome was introducing the necessity to use video-call apps. Until then, as reported, most participants were only passive-recipients of video-calls. Whereas a few of them, for reasons related to their life course, had previously learned the basic functions of most devices, some of them, instead, were not familiar at all with technologies. As previously mentioned, against the risk that digital technologies could jeopardize study participation, the interviewer strengthened the efforts to build a positive relationship with each member of the panel. This effort of trust-building came to help when dealing with various issues experienced during the interview, of technical and emotional nature: in the first place, the interviewer assisted study participants with ICT issues related to the interview. The positive outcome of this exchange was shown by some participants who felt at ease in asking technical assistance unrelated to our interview. E.g., one lady asked for help with her laptop, after the interview, because she wanted to connect her smartphone and upload her pictures; another one, while showing appreciation for the step-by-step procedure that guided her through the video-interview, asked the interviewer to teach her the procedure for starting a video-call on her own; finally, the same sense of ease in asking for technical assistance was shown during the panel engagement activities, as previously illustrated in some of the excerpts. In the second place, video-interviews did not constitute an issue when the interviewer had to deal with emotional distress: the relationship between the interviewer and interviewees overcame limits of remote interviewing, thanks to preliminary communication, ice breaking chit chats and more relaxed communication after the interview. Overall, our study participants felt at ease expressing emotions and the traumatic experiences related to the sudden changes in their everyday life through online interaction with the interviewer. An emphatic position was also maintained in each interaction during the panel engagement process, wherein the interviewer made use of dissemination activities to also display a more informal interest about participants' everyday life, health, etc. Our video-messages of festivity greetings were perceived as a sign of proximity and care, and were met with an affectionate response. This was also shown by our dissemination activities: when invited to conferences and seminars, some of the participants asked for technical assistance, thus showing positive outcomes both in terms of trust and of the effectiveness of our protocol for ICT assistance.

During wave 2 data collection, different challenges were documented. On one hand, as previously mentioned, in 2021 study participants had generally more chances to spend time with their family and friends, which eventually led to less time to dedicate to our research. On the other hand, because the pandemic and its corresponding government measures were extended another year, our study participants had the chance to experiment with online interactions and appeared more confident with ICT use.

Compared to wave 1 recruitment, the interviewer had to dedicate much more time with text messages and telephone calls, in the hope to grant their participation for a second interview. Whenever study participants proposed to withdraw because they were busy with caregiving activities, medical conditions or on holiday, the interviewer had to dedicate numerous attempts to adapt to their agenda and wait for weeks, sometimes months, until they felt more comfortable with rescheduling a second interview. Discussing the extra efforts we went through in this process, we wonder whether this effort during wave 2 recruitment was to be expected in longitudinal research or it was due to the online research design: the impossibility of face-to-face connections might have loosen participants' remembrance of previous encounter with the interviewer, along with the feeling of belonging they initially showed to our research. This dynamic was experienced on both sides: in fact, the loss of memory about wave 1, also affected the research team. However, whereas the interviewer was able to gather all the information collected about each participant, either through fieldwork notes or through interviews' transcripts, the same resource was not available for our panel members.

With regard to ICT use during the second interview, as anticipated, wave 2 participants surprised us with more familiarity with online technologies. Covid-19 played a significant role in this process, as it pushed most of them to experiment with new technologies and gain more familiarity. When arranging a date for the interview, many of the participants expressed their preference to WhatsApp, as they increased the habit of using this app for text messages as well as video-calls in many activities - e.g., one participant scheduled the interview during his holidays and started the video-call from the hotel balcony. From wave 1 to wave 2 they experienced multiple occasions to strengthen their ICT skills and were eager to take the challenge: in one case, one interviewee proposed to shift from Google Meet to Zoom because of technical difficulties, and the interviewer let her lead the process autonomously and successfully. About ICT use, one last interview is worth of notice: the participant was a 73-year-old man who, in wave 1, claimed to be so many worlds apart from ICT use that, he declared, not only he used his smartphone for telephone calls only, but our interview was the first video-call he experienced in his entire life. When we met again for wave 2, he seemed more familiar with his device, he also contacted us a few hours after our interview to send us some pictures through WhatsApp that documented some events he previously mentioned.

As discussed before, some participants withdrew from all communication during the phase of panel engagement. When the interviewer started the recruitment for wave 2 interviews, some dropped out of the study without verbally informing us of their intention to stop participating. With this respect, although online interactions between the interviewer and study participants were positive in both waves, we wonder whether ICT might have played a role in engendering weaker connections between study participants and research team members that affected their participation in wave 2.

11   Conclusions, Limitations, and Implications for Future Research

This paper described waves 1 and 2 of the ILQA study, an exploratory case study about the social consequences of the pandemic for the older people living in the ten villages that constituted the first area subject to lockdown (i.e., "Red Zone") in Europe. It outlines the processes of remote recruitment, data collection, and panel engagement while looking deeper at the role of ICTs in remote qualitative research with the older population. Specifically, we addressed the following research questions: i) what are the strategies that need to be implemented when researching older people through online qualitative methods?, ii) which online strategies are most suitable for qualitative longitudinal research?, iii) to what extent does ICT use play a role in interviewer-interviewee interactions? We will summarize the main results and then discuss more in detail the pros and cons of ICT use in qualitative online research with older people that emerged during our case study.

First, we found that community engagement, building a positive and trusting relationship between study participants and research team members, and developing a tailored approach to ICT use are key factors to recruiting and interviewing older people using qualitative online. Second, we documented that planning a panel maintenance procedure, entailing study participants' active participation and the production of video-materials is effective in boosting study participation over time. Third, as previously mentioned, a positive, trustworthy, and ongoing interaction between study participants and the interviewer was most crucial in conducting online qualitative research. Indeed, a positive interviewer-interviewees' relationship was successful in mitigating the technical difficulties, e.g., related to study participants' poor ICT-skills, to the new procedures concerning gaining informed consent, or more in general to poor internet connection. To our experience, all these strategies proved effective and are to be taken as good practices of online research with older people. The efforts in relationship building and the panel engagement, in particular, allowed us to overcome the limits of online technologies and successfully research a population that is usually deemed hard-to-reach or with low ICT skills.

Moving forward, while discussing the specific challenges and strategies enacted along our research process, this study also contributes to the literature by highlighting the pros and cons about online research with older people.

The first advantage we gained through ICT use was in terms of cost-reduction: to this respect, our data collection strategy proved effective, as the research was easily conducted from home. However, the time we saved from reaching each participant for a traditional face-to-face interview was dedicated to other steps of the process. Whereas remote research is easier to start, participants' engagement might need some extra efforts during the first recruitment and in-between waves. New and creative solutions are needed in order to face the challenges represented by ICT use in social research. For example, we dedicated most of the months between wave 1 and 2 to the implementation of the panel maintenance activities. To maintain between-waves participation, we developed a systematic panel engagement protocol that proved effective and obtained a solid response rate.

The positive outcome of the panel engagement activities has to be put into perspective when considering the extra effort it sometimes took to reschedule the interview in wave 2: compared to face-to-face interactions, study participants are more difficult to catch through online communications and it was not always easy to reconfirm their participation. To this respect, further research is needed to better discern between the influence of Covid-19 and the role of ICT use in engendering more detached interactions.

In our opinion, the ICTs might have played a more important role during wave 1 of data collection: on one hand, the establishing of trust between study participants and the research team members was at its beginning, and, on the other hand, more technical difficulties were experienced in 2020. By contrast, in wave 2 ICTs appeared to have been gradually embedded within participants' habits and daily routines. As anticipated, it is unclear whether remote video-interviewing could engender a more relaxed and informal setting, as some literature suggests (Howlett 2021), or instead create the conditions for an ICT-related observer effect (Gregory 2020).

Online research with older people also presents some pros and cons regarding ethics issues. In our experience, no significant online-related difficulties were found when dealing with traumatic experiences: as long as trust was established, the interviewer was able to reassure study participants and go on with the interview. Regarding the consent module procedures, tailoring our documents to participants' needs was key, as also recent evidence suggests: e.g., asking our participants where they preferred to receive our study documents, along with pivoting to verbal consent, allowed our panel members to read them in advance and store them in their preferred device.

Regarding informed consent, another positive outcome of online social research is worth mentioning. In our experience, online technologies provided the possibility to drop out of the study without any further explanation (by declining to respond to calls and text messages, as did some of our participants). While observing once again the role that ICT might have played for some of the participants in allowing more detached interactions, we cannot help but compare participants from wave 1 that abruptly drop out of the study with the ones that instead accepted to take part in wave 2. As online interactions grant the possibility to withdraw from communication, avoiding any further explanation as well as our attempts to prolong their participation, we might presume that by responding to our calls wave 2 participants actively chose to express their consent. Ironically, the downside of ICTs on one side might also become a sign of a more solid informed consent on the other.

In this dynamic, however, it is necessary that study participants are able to trust research team members and especially the one/s that will conduct the online fieldwork. In order to establish a trusting interaction, it is crucial that study participants receive clear and trustworthy communication by the research team members. As already noted, the interviewer-interviewees interaction is the key aspect to consider when researching older people through ICTs. When technical issues were encountered, the interviewer had a crucial role in mitigating the negative effects of remote research, thus balancing this intermediation by establishing trust and seeking contacts whenever possible. In our opinion, drawing on Lo Iacono and colleagues' suggestion (2016), the effort in building a basis for human interaction is far more important than dealing with the effects of online technologies. This has been shown by the excerpts and the fieldnotes we previously discussed.

11.1 Limitations

Although this work provides useful suggestions on how to successfully involve the old age population in online qualitative studies, it has two main limitations. The first limitation can be brought back to the context in which ILQA-19 is set, i.e. a rural area of the Lombardy region characterised by very strong interpersonal social connections. Such "strong ties" (Granovetter 1973) may have facilitated the remote recruiting of study participants. However, researching older people living in different contexts may pose additional challenges to the recruitment process, because of the greater fragmentation of social connections (e.g., in urban areas). In such cases, a different remote recruiting strategy may therefore be developed. The second limitation concerns the characteristics of the study participants. Although we adopted an inclusive approach, aimed at interviewing older people with different levels of ICT proficiency, older people with no familiarity with ICTs (e.g., those who do not own a smartphone) were excluded from our study. It is currently unclear what strategies need to be implemented to remotely recruit and interview this specific group of older people, who are very likely to be excluded from social research.

11.2 Implications for Future Research

Overall, our study has shown the performative potential of ICTs in researching older people: from a segment of the population that is excluded, more often than not out of mere prejudice, from online techniques of data collection, our research has shown that it is still possible to engage older people during social distancing periods and, additionally, to profit from online qualitative research as a medium to spark their interest in ICTs. However, a segment of the older population is still excluded from ICT use and ICT-related social research, as more recent literature documents (Sala & Gaia 2019). Given that there is a group of older people with no ICT skills, there is an urgent need to develop specific remote recruiting and interviewing protocols targeted specifically to this sub-population and ensure that their views and opinions are reported in social research.

References

Blumer, H.: What is wrong with social theory? Am. Sociol. Rev. **19**(1), 3–10 (1954)

Boyatzis, R.E.: Transforming Qualitative Information. Sage, Thousand Oaks (1998)

Charmaz, K.: Grounded theory: Objectivist and constructivist methods. In: Denzin, N.K., Lincoln, Y.S. (eds.) Strategies for Qualitative Inquiry, pp. 249–291. Sage, Thousand Oaks (2003)

Cheung, E., Mutahar, R., Assefa, F., Ververs, M.T., Nasiri, S.M., Borrel, A., Salama, P.: An epidemic of scurvy in Afghanistan: assessment and response. Food Nutr. Bull. **24**(3), 247–255 (2003). https://doi.org/10.1177/156482650302400303

Dodds, S., Hess, A.C.: Adapting research methodology during COVID-19: lessons for transformative service research. J. Serv. Manage. ahead-of-print (ahead-of-print). (2020) https://doi.org/10.1108/JOSM-05-2020-0153

Granovetter, M.S.: The strength of weak ties. Am. J. Sociol. **78**(6), 1360–1380 (1973)

Gregory, K.: The video camera spoiled by ethnography: a critical approach. Int. J. Qual. Methods **19**, 1–9 (2020). https://doi.org/10.1177/1609406920963761

Grossoehme, D., Lipstein, E.: Analyzing longitudinal qualitative data: the application of trajectory and recurrent cross-sectional approaches. BMC. Res. Notes **9**(1), 1–5 (2016)

Guha-Sapir, D., Hoyois, P., Below, R.: Annual disaster statistical review 2014: The numbers and trends. CRED (2015)

Henderson, T.L., Sirois, M., Chen, A.C.C., Airriess, C., Swanson, D.A., Banks, D.: After a disaster: lessons in survey methodology from Hurricane Katrina. Popul. Res. Policy Rev. **28**(1), 67–92 (2009) https://doi.org/10.1007/s11113-008-9114-5

Howlett, M.: Looking at the 'field' through a Zoom lens: Methodological reflections on conducting online research during a global pandemic. Qual. Res. 1468794120985691 (2021)

Johnson, G.A., Vindrola-Padros, C.: Rapid qualitative research methods during complex health emergencies: a systematic review of the literature. Soc. Sci. Med. **189**, 63–75 (2017). https://doi.org/10.1016/j.socscimed.2017.07.029

Kobakhidze, M.N., Hui, J., Chui, J., González, A.: Research disruptions, new opportunities: re-imagining qualitative interview study during the COVID-19 pandemic. Int. J. Qual. Methods **20**, 16094069211051576 (2021). https://doi.org/10.1177/16094069211051576

Lavin, R.P., Schemmel-Rettenmeier, L., Frommelt-Kuhle, M.: Conducting research during disasters. Annu. Rev. Nurs. Res. **30**(1), 1–19 (2012). https://doi.org/10.1891/0739-6686.30.1

Lo, M.C.M., Fan, Y.: How narratives of disaster impact survivors' emotionality: the case of Typhoon Morakot. Poetics, 101579 (2021)

Lo Iacono, V.L., Symonds, P., Brown, D.H.: Skype as a tool for qualitative research interviews. Sociol. Res. Online **21**(2), 1–12 (2016). https://doi.org/10.5153/sro.3952

Lobe, B., Morgan, D., Hoffman, K.A.: Qualitative data collection in an era of social distancing. Int. J. Qual. Methods **19**, 160940692093787 (2020). https://doi.org/10.1177/1609406920937875

Melis, G., Sala, E., Zaccaria, D.: Remote recruiting and video-interviewing older people: a research note on a qualitative case study carried out in the first Covid-19 Red Zone in Europe. Int. J. Soc. Res. Methodol. (2021a). https://doi.org/10.1080/13645579.2021.1913921

Melis, G., Sala, E., Zaccaria, D.: «I turned to Facebook to know when they would open the cemetery» Results from a qualitative case study on older people's social media use during COVID-19 lockdown in Italy. RASSEGNA ITALIANA DI SOCIOLOGIA, LXII(2), 431–457, (2021b). https://doi.org/10.1423/101851

Newman, P.A., Guta, A., Black, T.: Ethical considerations for qualitative research methods during the COVID-19 pandemic and other emergency situations: navigating the virtual field. Int. J Qual. Methods **20**, 16094069211047824 (2021)

Parkes, E.: 'Wait! I'm not a journalist': conducting qualitative field research in post-disaster situations. Graduate J. Asia-Pacific Stud. **7**(2), 30–46 (2011)

Phillips, B.D.: Qualitative disaster research. In: Leavy, P. (ed.) The Oxford Handbook of Qualitative Research, pp. 533–556. Oxford University Press (2014)

Richardson, S.J., et al.: Research with older people in a world with COVID-19: Identification of current and future priorities, challenges and opportunities. Age Ageing **49**(6), 901–906 (2020). https://doi.org/10.1093/ageing/afaa149

Roberts, J.K., Pavlakis, A.E., Richards, M.P.: It's more complicated than it seems: virtual qualitative research in the COVID-19 era. Int J Qual Methods **20**, 16094069211002960 (2021). https://doi.org/10.1177/16094069211002959

Rodríguez, H., Quarantelli, E.L., Dynes, R.R. (eds.) Handbook of Disaster Research. vol. 643. New York, Springer (2007). http://eprints.ukh.ac.id/id/eprint/294/1/2007_Book_HandbookOfDisasterResearch.pdf

Saberi, P.: Research in the time of coronavirus: continuing ongoing studies in the midst of the COVID-19 pandemic. AIDS Behav. **24**(8), 2232–2235 (2020)

Saldaña, J.: The Coding Manual for Qualitative Research. Sage, Thousand Oak (2012)

Sy, M., O'Leary, N., Nagraj, S., El-Awaisi, A., O'Carroll, V., Xyrichis, A.: Doing interprofessional research in the COVID-19 era: a discussion paper. J. Interprof. Care **34**(5), 600–606 (2020)

Vindrola-Padros, C., et al.: Carrying out rapid qualitative research during a pandemic: emerging lessons from COVID-19. Qual. Health Res. **30**(14), 2192–2204 (2020). https://doi.org/10.1177/1049732320951526104973230951526

Senior Citizens as Storytellers: Contribution to Gamified Contexts

Cláudia Ortet(✉) , Ana Isabel Veloso , and Liliana Vale Costa

DigiMedia, Department of Communication and Art, University of Aveiro, Aveiro, Portugal
{claudiaortet,aiv,lilianavale}@ua.pt

Abstract. A global demographic turn is observed with senior citizens increasing in number, resulting on wellbeing concerns. That culminates into challenges and opportunities for creating tools, such as digital storytelling and gamification, to promote senior citizens' interest and motivation to certain activities. While digital storytelling involves the narrative's potential to facilitate the construction of meaning and sharing experiences with information and communication technologies' languages, gamification elements can trigger senior citizens' motivations. However, so far, little attention has been paid to the potential of digital storytelling in gamification. In this context, an iterative approach involving storytelling narratives and gamification should be designed to enhance cyclotourism experiences. The aim of this position paper is to discuss the senior citizens' digital storytelling applied to gamified cyclotourism to foster participatory strategies and inclusion, exploring their life story while connecting them with others. In specific, it proposes the delivery of a storytelling sessions model to senior citizens integrated with gamification aspects in the cyclotourism context.

Keywords: Senior citizens · Digital storytelling · Gamification · Cyclotourism

1 Introduction

The rise in longevity enables the incessant ageing of the world population. According to World Health Organization [1], the proportion of the world's population over 60 years old will double between 2000 and 2050. Owing to that, concerns about an active and healthy ageing are acquiring significant importance in scientific, academic, and politic studies. Active ageing can be defined as "(…) the process of optimizing opportunities for health, participation and security in order to enhance quality of life as people age." [2, p.2]. Being active refers not only to the functional capability of being physically active, but also embodies the individuals' willingness to participate in other activities (*i.e.* social, economic, cultural, spiritual and civic matters).

Research into senior citizens' participation in civic matters has increased noticeably over the last 55 years [3], as also practices and policy initiatives aimed at promoting active ageing. This growing interest often relies on the assumption of mutual beneficial for both individuals and their communities in a participatory culture. It unites individuals and communities who feel a certain degree of social connection with each other in a culture with relatively low barriers to artistic expression and civic engagement, strong support for creation and shared creations of each, and some type of informal orientation, in which what is known by the most experienced is passed on to beginners [4]. The flow of information through multiple media and the fact that the media industries are interested in exploring a wide range of sectors, also contributed to the emergence of new ways of telling stories.

The narrative consists of the account of real or imaginary events, supported by human capacities of imagination and empathy, operating in the process of representation and elaboration of reality, helping to understand the most varied topics. Reminiscing and storytelling are significant human processes related to wellbeing, since individuals can make sense of who they are, build their identities, create, and transmit culture and support social cohesion [5]. Specifically, narrative gerontology is a practice where senior citizens tell their life story. It occurs between the storyteller and the story collector, through informal learning for both parties and provide a strategy for active ageing [6].

Stories form a valuable part of people's identity and communication, providing a chance to explore the self, the culture, and others [7]. Moreover, the act of sharing and reflecting upon life narratives may contribute to increased self-knowledge and self-actualization, and consequently to a sense of wellbeing. Following that practice, digital storytelling can provide senior citizens with an opportunity to become digital producers, interlink with others through their story, explore their memories and imagination of life, and feel treasured.

According to Maslow [8], the fundamental levels of the hierarchy of human needs (*i.e.* love and belonging, esteem and self-actualization) are considered as motivational factors, being the most challenging and needed to achieve. Senior citizens may have a great deal of interest in intangible goods, such as respect and status, and these forms of motivation are the same principles that are part of the basic concept of gamification [9].

While observing the use of storytelling and gamification approaches in a range of sectors, such as tourism, in parallel there is also noticed a tendency of preference to the cycling activity [10]. With that, cyclotourism emerges, as it combines tourism and physical exercise, two sectors linked to motivation and active ageing. Cyclotourism epitomizes a niche market associated to strong mobility practices and changes in social practices connected with rising debates around quality of life, participation, and senior citizens' motivation [11].

Little has been published on the use of digital storytelling with senior citizens. While there is literature about its application in educational and tourism settings, and potential therapeutic implications, there is a lack of understanding about the use of digital storytelling with gamification to foster active ageing. Therefore, the aim of this position paper is to explore the benefits of digital storytelling in senior citizens and the use of narratives in gamification strategies, in order to apply it to the context of cyclotourism. Also, an iterative process of storytelling to senior cyclotourism is given by addressing on how digital storytelling and gamification can contribute to senior citizens' participation and sharing of cyclotourism.

This position paper is structured as follows: Sect. 1 is introductory and exposes the problem of an ageing population and the importance of their participation; Sect. 2 addresses the storytelling impact on senior citizens' wellbeing; Sect. 3 presents the use of narrative strategies in gamification; Sect. 4 establishes the use of storytelling narratives and gamification in senior cyclotourism context; and Sect. 5 reflects on possible limitations and contributions.

2 Digital Storytelling and Senior Citizens

Storytelling is an intrinsic part of humankind and can be declared as one of the oldest habits of social life, communication, motivation, teaching and learning. Some of the advantages of storytelling are that it promotes the use of imagination, creativity, and teamwork [12]. Since the act of narrating implies revealing stories and experiences through memories, as well as organizing them so that they make sense and transmit information, narrative and experience are, therefore, two concepts that are related [13]. It is possible to consider it event-centered and experience-centered, since the storyteller connect story with experience, in order to provide meaning.

Digital storytelling recovers the idea of the storyteller to assembled audiences, no longer on the verge of bonfires, but rather around electrical systems, forming virtual tribes. Thus, one of the specificities of the term is the importance of the digital medium and how it can help to involve and attract more public attention. It conveys life experiences, offer therapeutic and emotional opportunities, bear witness to one's life, and foster social support within communities [14].

Digital storytelling is the method of introducing a story based on a combination of different digital media (*e.g.* texts, images, sounds), that often starts with a narration that is further converted and expanded using digital elements. The final product can be easily read by others, allowing storytellers to share their stories with a wide audience [15]. Currently, digital storytelling, is studied and considered to be an innovative and creative tool to bring ideas and knowledge to people.

Life stories gathered during narrative gerontology can be transcribed to digital forms of storytelling, thus technology and storytelling are beneficial for senior citizens' wellbeing. By telling their stories, they may gain from the possibility for emotional expression, the ability to express their identity, and the experience of being listened to [16]. Participating in digital storytelling may contribute to an individual's capability to prosper by providing experiences to support their emotional, psychological, and social wellbeing [17].

Digital storytelling may be used with senior citizens as a tool to enhance mood, improve memory, increase social connectedness, and encourage intergenerational learning [15]. Guillemot and Urien [13] consider 6 motivations for narrative gerontology: (i) flattering ego, (ii) fixing the ego, (iii) not being forgotten, (iv) sharing, (v) spreading, and (iv) bearing witness. It contributes to the storytellers' life quality, but also to the community's health improvement, through the exchange of the narrative with the collector (*i.e.* listener). This happens because the work of narrating, recollecting, creating, and sharing not only promotes a sense of wellbeing for the storyteller but also to the listener and future audiences, who may introspect into their own emotional responses and empathize with the storyteller.

Cybulski [18] identifies the narrative as a linguistic practice capable of making the speeches clearer, contextualizing the information in order to be closer to the participants' reality, making it easier to reinterpret the data and create more understandable analogies. But narratives can also be used as approaches in health and social care of senior citizens. Care can be conceptualized as a narrative endeavor, since it can be an effective, interactive, vibrant, and dialogic co-creation of experiences. Thus, it entails playfulness and world travelling, that acknowledges not only the empathy for the perception of the story told by others, but the creation of new stories to live by, whereas curiosity, attentiveness, and relations are the key factors [19].

In fact, the narrative work of storytelling is often linked to toughness and healthy ageing promotion, since it "aids the development of personal resilience and provides opportunities to celebrate the hardiness of participants who recount their stories of difficulty and adversity" [14, p.17]. Getting to know others' stories frequently encourages the development of greater understanding and sympathy by delivering a wider context to understand oneself's life experiences.

When personal stories are shared, they can provide meaning, consciousness, and understanding, which develop resilience in the listener and storyteller. Through communicating stories, senior citizens can express their identity, personal story, beliefs, and interests, which inspire a feeling of connection with each other. It may also lead to the development of a social network through the sharing of stories in groups, reducing feelings of loneliness or isolation.

While creating a digital story, senior citizens have the opportunity to rewrite their story (i.e. how they perceive it now). Pecorini and Duplaa [6] suggest that narrative gerontology paired with digital storytelling could have some powerful benefits for well-being in late adulthood, as already proven in both narrative work with senior citizens and digital storytelling results. This position paper defends that gamification, combined with these, may improve the intended goal of motivating towards an activity, participation, inclusion, and active ageing.

3 Narratives in Gamification

A narrative is a form of communication that improves self-development and implies a sense of cultural and self-identity, since individuals may produce meaning by expressing and reconstructing their memory. It is part of the process of getting to know people, getting to know communities, beliefs, values, and knowledge, all through stories that are collectively and individually constructed, being sources of studies with great value.

When the narrative begins to be produced in digital environments, its characteristics are transformed into multiform plots, in which interactors start to develop actions and build stories, within a navigable space, in the most varied environments and times. Since the narrative is a phenomenon of cognitive construction, its relevance in the digital environment is reflected on the openness to new readings that this medium suggests. A media will be considered relevant in narrative terms if it has an impact on the story, the speech or the social or personal use of the narrative [20]. For Ryan [20, 21], digital (versus analogue) has the following properties that can favor narrative discourse: (i) the interactive and reactive nature; (ii) the multimedia competence; (iii) the ability to network; (iv) the volatility of digital images; and (v) the characteristic of reproduction, combination and transformation of objects (i.e. modularity).

The discussion about narratology, and even ludology, no longer dominates the main arenas of game studies, but one cannot underestimate the potential that stories have in the strengthen of engagement, motivation, and commitment effectiveness of users. Although there is a scarcity of articles that cite the narrative elements in gamification, there are some studies that intend to combine storytelling and gamification, often within the education sector (e.g. [12, 22]). Based on the results from these studies, it is believed that similar results can be obtained in the matter of this paper.

Gamification can be defined as the use of game design elements and techniques in the non-games' context, to motivate users to carry out a serious activity [23]. Werbach and Hunter [9] proposed a game element hierarchy for gamification (i.e. DMC Pyramid), divided into three levels in which an evolution principle is applied: (i) Components are the basis of gamification elements (e.g. achievements, badges, unlocking content, rankings, and points); (ii) Mechanics are the rules' set and techniques to gamify something and motivate the user (e.g. challenges, cooperation and competition, feedback, and rewards); and (iii) Dynamics are based on the users' behaviors (e.g. relationships, emotions, constraints, and progression).

McGonigal [24] lists four intrinsic rewards of games, transponible in gamification, that would help to build users' happiness: (i) the rewarding work, (ii) the experience or hope of being successful, (iii) the search for social connection, and (iv) the chance to be part of something bigger than themselves. The use of game design elements in contexts external to games can make gamification valuable for changing routines, by making activities more fun, motivating, and engaging [23].

Gamification is a technique used in different domains, from the entertainment industry, education, tourism, or health. Based on the premise that everything that exists has the potential to be fun, gamifying a product or service does not mean simply offering virtual badges each time the user performs a certain action [25]. Gamifying means drawing up a plan in order to motivate the players to take a set of tasks with pleasure, seducing them to a certain quantifiable objective.

It is perceived that the main purpose of gamification is to reproduce experiences lived in games and portray them to real contexts, in order to promote powerful emotions. It can be assumed that, through the extensive practice of these activities, even negative emotions become positive, or that users will develop personal qualities that will transcend the game, such as persistence, creativity, and resilience [24].

Even though the narrative is part of a game element that can be used in gamification, is not often mentioned in the literature. Nevertheless, it is known that narratives have the potential to be motivational, as it can arousing interest, increasing engagement and improving participants' satisfaction towards specific activities [26].

Salen and Zimmerman [27] define narrative for digital games in one of the most complex ways, distinguishing two types of narrative (i.e. embedded and emergent). The authors considered it as a composition of rules that are experienced through play, in order to facilitate the player interaction within the possibility of actions, enabling them to explore and work together with the game's universe. The embedded narrative is presented as a pre-generated content, aiming to give a meaningful stake or motivation to the player through the storyline, which provide a dramatic plot to the player's interactions and journey [27]. Whereas the emergent narrative is generated from the interactive experience of the player (*i.e.* organic consequence of the player's autonomy) [27].

Sattoe and colleagues [28] cite narrative as an element of gamification that allude to personification (*i.e.* roleplaying), as it is a feature that is commonly used and can be understood as the process in which the users construct their own experience through a certain content, employing their autonomy of choice in a certain space and time, delimited by the logic of the gamified system [22]. This can favor participation in order to allow the proposed objectives of an activity to be fulfilled. The combination of gamification with narrative, and possible personification, is an example of an activity that can be used in therapeutic contexts to encourage behavior change and improve self-regulation conditions in individuals with chronic illnesses [28].

Furthermore, narrative engines can also engage users to participate with greater commitment in tasks [29], so when properly designed, narratives in gamified contexts are likely to make users feel a greater sense of immersion. In fact, using narratives or storytelling helps to provide coherence and can have a big impact on the other elements of the entire gamified experience [29].

Contradistinguishing, Toda and colleagues [30] define narrative and storytelling, highlighting that a narrative targets at users' motivation and storytelling stimulate users' engagement. The authors describe the narrative element as an "Order of events where they happen in a game. These are choices influenced by the players' actions" [31, p. 87], conversely, storytelling "(…) is the way the story of the game is told (as a script). It is told within the game, through text, voice, or sensorial resources" [30, p. 87].

Narratives in a digital media (*i.e.* digital storytelling) are naturally attached to the system from which it derives. Since both storytelling and gamification depends on the user experience (UX), it is important to consider the Human-Computer Interaction (HCI) and playcentric approaches of testing and evaluation [31], concepts inherent to a participatory culture, as it provides a proper distribution of roles between users and technology.

In order to be able to use narrative as an element for the design of gamified projects, it is essential to cover the following features: (i) the presence of the actor (*i.e.* the user/senior citizen), (ii) the element of choice, (iii) interactivity (*i.e.* the system must be responsive), (iv) sequence of events (*i.e.* logical chain of actions), (v) space (*i.e.* the gamified space), and (vi) information [22].

Even though there is still little work about the combination of gamification and narratives, probably because the terms 'narrative' and 'story' blend together and are often confused, for this paper it will be considered that the narratives accrue from stories and storytelling. Therefore, the use of these two tools (gamification and storytelling) can be a combined strategy to enhance and improve specific contexts, as demonstrated in the following section.

4   Senior Citizens' Stories in Gamified Cyclotourism

Cyclotourism is an unexploited sector with great potential for health promotion, participation, and social inclusion [11]. Hence, the senior citizens' motivations for cyclotourism indicate physical and mental health, economic impact, ease and convenience of transportation, physical exercise, relationships formed, pleasure inherent to cycling and the surroundings [32, 33]. Also, Ortet and colleagues [32, 33] found that gamification elements are important and can motivate senior citizens to cyclotourism, highlighting competition and challenges, feedback, rewards, and social sharing. The same authors also stated that a future work of their research would be the inclusion of narratives in this gamified context, being the exploration purpose of this paper.

A specific or supported model for the creation of digital stories does not exist, since the steps to be followed in the construction of digital storytelling will depend on who does it, the author from whom the research is sustained or the technique that is intended to be used. The ability to map and control the user experience, in order to guide the senior citizen through the content, is considered as one of the pathways on the usage narrative as an element for gamified cyclotourism.

Since there are almost non-existent studies or reports that cover the case of gamification in cyclotourism, storytelling in gamification, and storytelling in gamified cyclotourism (specifically when addressed to senior citizens), it is important to acknowledge that this process should be iterative, following a participatory approach. Therefore, this process should follow a cyclic or spiral course, by embodying analysis, design, evaluation, and revision activities, which are iterated until a satisfying balance between ideals and realization is achieved.

In order to provide a sharing environment, focus groups sessions or storytelling courses must be used to gather senior citizens and collect their stories. As Hausknecht and colleagues [34] have designed and tested digital storytelling workshops with senior citizens successfully, some guidelines must be taken into consideration when reproducing to the cyclotourism context. As the authors suggested, the process should be divided into two phases: (i) story creation and (ii) digital production, so that participants have a full story to work with, and to understand it as a digital story script and not just a story. Even so, for this paper, other phases should be considered, such as the phase of the previous cyclotourism experience that senior citizens wish to tell (*i.e.* phase zero, since is not mandatory), and the ICT learning phase taken before the digital production phase.

During the first sessions, participants should (ideally) have already practice cyclotourism, learn about story creation, and share ideas and drafts of their stories. After brainstorming and peer feedback from story creation, participants should digitize their work by merging voice, images, music, and sounds to explain their narrative. Most of these components can be taken from the cyclotourism experience and use of apps like Jizo or Strava [32].

Participants must think on an occasion or moment in their lives that stood out, related or not to cyclotourism, that can be used in this context. In cases where participants do not have something relevant to add to a story, elements of intertextuality or even imaginative events can be considered. Digital stories must be, typically, 2 to 3 min in length, and though short, must efficiently communicate compelling narratives that inform the user on a specific issue, concept or practice related to cyclotourism.

The point of using narratives in a gamified context is not only to provide a richer experience, but also to foster a participatory culture in senior citizens. Using the Jizo app [32] as example, it may contain stories from senior citizens related to: (i) choosing a route; (ii) exploring tips on how to take care of the bicycle; (iii) absorbing knowledge on how to prepare for a ride; (iv) selecting days of the calendar for riding planning; (v) following friends; (vi) exploring nearby conveniences; among others.

An addon proposal, being the main contribute from this study, is to try to incorporate senior citizens' storytelling to points of interest (POI) in the moment of cyclotourism practice. Hence, when senior citizens are using the app and stop at a local (*e.g.* restaurant, monument, street), emergent narratives arise. These narratives may be stories from users' experience, curiosities of the POI, suggestions on directions, and calls to action. Here, gamification elements such as rewards and social interaction must be included. Strategies of augmented and virtual reality, and mechanisms of artificial intelligence may be also useful to incorporate with the created narratives.

In fact, the app may also be a bridge between the activity and the storytelling sessions through challenges, adding points for the ones who join and complete the task. Also, linked to that, a social media or website for sharing stories or sessions events may be created to promote participation, inclusion, and community. Rankings and leaderboards could also be included to motivate content generation.

Therefore, gamification with narratives becomes an excellent mechanism in this task, as it transforms the gamified cyclotourism environment conducive to providing enthusiasm, fun, protagonism, cooperation and innovation. Also, these two approaches may contribute to senior citizens' participation and sharing of cyclotourism.

5   Final Considerations

Technology and communication are tools that can improve the senior citizens' wellbeing, offering the opportunity for creative expression and sharing experiences. Digital storytelling could inspire senior citizens to communicate their stories, become digital producers, express creativity, and improve digital literacy. Stories may evoke in all involving participants unforeseen emotions, ideas and ultimately, unexpected selves. It is through stories that experiences gain meaning, and through reflection and interpretation such meaning is transformed into knowledge, changing perspectives on comprehension, constructing and deconstructing understanding.

Since it was found that gamified cyclotourism tend to be a motivating activity, it is believed that storytellers, while narrating it, would feel important, appreciated, valued, and active, which would reinforce their resilience, confidence, motivation, and self-esteem, and therefore their wellbeing. It is expected that by increasing the senior citizens' motivation, a favorable environment occurs and may improve the active ageing process.

Even if there are still few, and somehow scattered, research on these topics, this position papers supports the following of an iterative process when using senior citizens storytelling in gamified cyclotourism. To do that, it is important to delve into user experience concepts and cross them with gamification interaction. Not forgetting that the engaging capability is, amongst other things, precisely connected to the experience and satisfaction resulting from the interaction process.

However, a few limitations should be considered for this study. Firstly, this research is innovative and the aforementioned topics are not found altogether in the literature, being a position paper based on replication or adaptation from other similar studies. Secondly, specific skills essential for the narration collection (*e.g.* interviewing techniques, sound recording, attitudes for a secure sharing environment) should be acquired before starting the process. Thirdly, in terms of feasibility, due to the context of COVID-19 pandemic, this research seems very needed, but also arises concerns of senior citizens' safety. Following the last point, it is worth noting that the pandemic has been extremely impactful in the future of tourism, whereas the senior citizens' feeling of loneliness and marginalization has also been noticeable.

Despite this, it is considered that this work should have a high potential impact on senior citizens' inclusion and, accordingly, participatory culture. It may contribute to the promotion of active ageing, especially with a focus on the pillars of health and participation. It may also open the door to develop similar strategies for different subjects (other than education), thereby improving the experience significantly. This research may also contribute to the field of gerontechnology by providing a deeper understanding of senior citizens relation with storytelling and technology, and the benefits and challenges this provides. It also offers insights into the experiences senior citizens may have within digital storytelling sessions and examines the way in which storytelling and multimedia can play a role in cyclotourism.

Acknowledgments. This work was supported by FCT – Foundation for Science and Technology (Fundação para a Ciência e Tecnologia), I.P. nr. 2020.04815.BD, DigiMedia Research Center, under the project UIDB/05460/2020, and the project SEDUCE 2.0 - Use of Communication and Information in the miOne online community by senior citizens, funded by FCT – Fundação para a Ciência e a Tecnologia, I.P., COMPETE 2020, Portugal 2020 and European Union, under the European Regional Development Fund, POCI-01-0145-FEDER-031696 SEDUCE 2.0.

References

1. World Health Organization: Facts About Ageing. World Health Organization, Switzerland (2014)
2. World Health Organization: Active Ageing: A Policy Framework. A Contribution of World Health Organization to the Second United Nations World Assembly of Ageing, Madrid, Spain (2002). https://doi.org/10.1080/713604647
3. Serrat, R., Scharf, T., Villar, F., Gómez, C.: Fifty-five years of research into older people's civic participation: Recent trends, future directions. Gerontologist **60**(1), e38–e51 (2020). https://doi.org/10.1093/geront/gnz021
4. Jenkins, H., Ito, M., Boyd, D.: Participatory Culture in a Networked Era: A Conversation on Youth, Learning, Commerce and Politics. Polity Press (2016)
5. Alexandrakis, D., Chorianopoulos, K., Tselios, N.: Older adults and Web 2.0 storytelling technologies: probing the technology acceptance model through an age-related perspective. Int. J. Hum. Comput. Interact. **36**(17), 1623–1635 (2020). https://doi.org/10.1080/10447318. 2020.1768673
6. Pecorini, B.C., Duplaa, E.: Narrative gerontology and digital storytelling: what benefits for elders? MOJ Public Health **6**(6), 451–454 (2017). https://doi.org/10.15406/mojph.2017.06. 00192
7. Hibbin, R.: The psychosocial benefits of oral storytelling in school: developing identity and empathy through narrative. Pastoral Educ. **34**(4), 218–231 (2016)
8. Maslow, A.H.: Motivation and Personality. Harper & Row, New York (1954)

9. Werbach, K., Hunter, D.: For the Win: How Game Thinking Can Revolutionize Your Business. Wharton Digital Press, Philadelphia (2012)
10. Fundação Portuguesa de Ciclismo (FPC): Ciclismo e Dinamização da Atividade Turística. Retrieved February 2021. http://business.turismodeportugal.pt/pt/Conhecer/estrategia-turismo/programasiniciativas/Paginas/programaportuguese-trails.aspx. Accessed 18 Dec 2021
11. Ortet, C., Veloso, A.I., Costa, L.V.: Fostering senior community-based cyclotourism using transmedia: a proposal. In: Gao, Q., Zhou, J. (eds.) HCII 2021. LNCS, vol. 12787, pp. 124–134. Springer, Cham (2021). https://doi.org/10.1007/978-3-030-78111-8_8
12. Ibarra-Herrera, C.C., Carrizosa, A., Yunes-Rojas, J.A., Mata-Gómez, M.A.: Design of an app based on gamification and storytelling as a tool for biology courses. Int. J. Interact. Des. Manuf. (IJIDeM) 13(4), 1271–1282 (2019). https://doi.org/10.1007/s12008-019-00600-8
13. Guillemot, S., Urien, B.: Legacy writing among the elderly: conceptual bases, dimensioning and a proposed scale for measuring motivations. Recherche et Applications En Marketing (English Edition) 25(4), 25–43 (2010). https://doi.org/10.1177/205157071002500402
14. East, L., Jackson, D., O'Brien, L., Peters, K.: Storytelling: an approach that can help to develop resilience. Nurse Res. 17(3), 17–25 (2010)
15. Hausknecht, S., Vanchu-Orosco, M., Kaufman, D.: Digitising the wisdom of our elders: Connectedness through digital storytelling. Ageing Soc. 39(12), 2714–2734 (2019). https://doi.org/10.1017/S0144686X18000739
16. Fiddian-Green, A., Kim, S., Gubrium, A.C., Larkey, L.K., Peterson, J.C.: Restor(y)ing health: a conceptual model of the effects of digital storytelling. Health Promot. Pract. 20(4), 502–512 (2019)
17. Tay, L., Pawelski, J.O., Keith, M.: The role of the arts and humanities in human flourishing: a conceptual model. J. Posit. Psychol. 13(3), 215–225 (2018). https://doi.org/10.1080/17439760.2017.1279207
18. Cybulski, J.L., Keller, S., Nguyen, L., Saundage, D.: Creative problem solving in digital space using visual analytics. Comput. Hum. Behav. 42, 20–35 (2015). https://doi.org/10.1016/j.chb.2013.10.061
19. Blix, B.H., Berendonk, C., Clandinin, D.J., Caine, V.: The necessity and possibilities of playfulness in narrative care with older adults. Nursing Inquiry 28(1) (2020). https://doi.org/10.1111/nin.12373
20. Ryan, M.L.: Narrative and Digitality: Learning to Think With the Medium. A Companion to Narrative Theory. Blackwell Publishing, Edit. James Phelan and Peter Rabinowitz, Hamilton College, pp. 515–528. ISBN: 9781405184380. (2005)
21. Ryan, M.L.: Narrative Across Media: The Languages of Storytelling. University of Nebraska Press: Board of Regents of the University of Nebraska. ISBN: 0803289936 (2004)
22. Palomino, P.T., Toda, A.M., Oliveira, W., Cristea, A.I., Isotani, S.: Narrative for gamification in education: why should you care?. In: IEEE 19th International Conference on Advanced Learning Technologies (ICALT), Maceió, Brazil, 2019, pp. 97–99. https://doi.org/10.1109/ICALT.2019.00035
23. Deterding, S., Sicart, M., Nacke, L., Ohara, K., Dixon, D.: Gamification: using game- design elements in non-gaming contexts. In: Proceedings of the 2011 Annual Conference Extended Abstracts on Human Factors in Computing Systems – CHI EA 11 (2011). https://doi.org/10.1145/1979742.1979575
24. McGonigal, J.: Reality is Broken: Why Games Make us Better and How They Can Change the World. Jonathan Cape, London (2011)
25. Zichermann, G., Cunningham, C.: Gamification by Design: Implementing Game Mechanics in Web and Mobile Apps, Sebastopol, California 95472. OReilly Media (2011)
26. González, C.S., et al.: Learning healthy lifestyles through active videogames, motor games and the gamification of educational activities. Comput. Hum. Behav. 55, 529–551 (2016) https://doi.org/10.1016/j.chb.2015.08.052

27. Salen, K., Zimmerman, E.: Rules of Play: Game Design Fundamentals. MIT press, Massachusetts (2004)
28. Sattoe, J.N.T., Bal, M.I., Roelofs, P.D.D.M., Bal, R., Miedema, H.S., Van Staa, A.: Self-management interventions for young people with chronic conditions: A systematic overview. Patient Educ. Couns. **98**(6), 704–715 (2015). https://doi.org/10.1016/j.pec.2015.03.004
29. Grobelny, J., Smierzchalska, J., Czapkowski, K.: Narrative gamification as a method of increasing sales performance: a field experimental study. Int. J. Acad. Res. Bus. Soc. Sci. **8**(3), 430–447 (2018)
30. Toda, A.M., et al.: A taxonomy of game elements for gamification in educational contexts: proposal and evaluation. In: 2019 IEEE 19th International Conference on Advanced Learning Technologies (ICALT), pp. 84–88 (2019). https://doi.org/10.1109/ICALT.2019.00028
31. Fullerton, T.: Game Design Workshop: A Playcentric Approach to Creating Innovative Games, 3rd edn. Taylor & Francis Group (2014)
32. Ortet, C.P., Costa, L.V., Veloso, A.I.: Jizo: a gamified digital app for senior cyclo-tourism in the miOne community. In: Zagalo, N., Veloso, A.I., Costa, L., Mealha, Ó. (eds.) VJ 2019. CCIS, vol. 1164, pp. 195–207. Springer, Cham (2019). https://doi.org/10.1007/978-3-030-37983-4_15
33. Ortet, C., Veloso, A.I., Costa, L.V.: Gamified app to promote senior cyclo-tourism: a pilot study. In: 21st annual European GAMEON® Conference (GAME-ON®'2020) on Simulation and AI in Computer Games, pp. 71–78 (2020)
34. Hausknecht, S., Vanchu-Orosco, M., Kaufman, D.: Sharing life stories: design and evaluation of a digital storytelling workshop for older adults. In: Costagliola, G., Uhomoibhi, J., Zvacek, S., McLaren, B.M. (eds.) CSEDU 2016. CCIS, vol. 739, pp. 497–512. Springer, Cham (2017). https://doi.org/10.1007/978-3-319-63184-4_26

Senior-Centered Gamification: An Approach for Cyclotourism

Cláudia Ortet[✉] ⓘ, Liliana Vale Costaⓘ, and Ana Isabel Velosoⓘ

DigiMedia, Department of Communication and Art, University of Aveiro, Aveiro, Portugal
{claudiaortet,lilianavale,aiv}@ua.pt

Abstract. There has been an increasing interest in gerontechnology due to the growth of an ageing population and subsequent challenges in interface design development. Methods of user-centered design and gamification have demonstrated to be powerful, leading to an excellent user experience, and also motivating and changing senior citizens' behaviors. Applying user-centered design and gamification is starting to gain its importance in the design field, but there is still a lack of studies regarding the use of these concepts with senior citizens and/or applied to the cyclotourism context. The goal of this paper is to provide a state-of-the-art review on user-centered design, user experience and gamification, to outline and propose an approach for senior cyclotourism. The approach is based on user-centered design to senior citizens, followed by gamification design guidelines to the development and testing of products or prototypes. It is recommended that the method should be iterative, unequivocal, and inclusive, performed by a multidisciplinary team and should followed phases of requirement gathering and analysis, design, implementation, and evaluation with subsequent design guidelines. This study may also deliver maneuverable and adaptable guides on how to conduct a method of user-centered design and user experience with gamification for senior citizens applied to other contexts.

Keywords: User-centered design · User experience · Gamification · Senior citizens · Cyclotourism

1 Introduction

Declining fertility rates and growing longevity will ensure the continued ageing of people. According to United Nations' World Population Ageing Report [1], the global population aged 60 years or older has registered a total of 962 million people in 2017 and this number is expected to double by 2050. As the ageing population continues to grow, there has been an increasing interest in the subject of gerontechnology, since encouraging senior citizens to use information and communication technologies (ICT) may stimulate their cognitive abilities, autonomy and engagement in interpersonal relations and productive activity in performing everyday tasks [2].

Gerontechnology is the transdisciplinary study of ageing (*i.e.* social science: gerontology) and technology [3] – to adapt the environments in which senior citizens live and

© The Author(s), under exclusive license to Springer Nature Switzerland AG 2022
Q. Gao and J. Zhou (Eds.): HCII 2022, LNCS 13330, pp. 80–92, 2022.
https://doi.org/10.1007/978-3-031-05581-2_7

work so they can have their independence and be able to participate and contribute to the society, as well as working better with health, comfort and safety –, aiming to respond to the challenges of a digital society with an aged population [4]. Hence, gerontechnology represents a concept that includes research, development and conception of new technologies aimed at improving the quality of life of the senior citizens. It presents a wide scope for action from health and safety, assistance with mobility, to communication and stimulation [5]. Consequently, it has brought age-related challenges in product development and interface design.

The various changes in ICT come with the relationships between people, products, and services. Seeking this understanding, interaction design allows for the structuring of tasks, making it possible to design the interaction to support the users' goals. In this scenario, the user can be placed at the center of the design process for the development of products and artifacts. Thus, Human-Centered Design (HCD) is usually defined by: (i) the active participation of users, in order to have a clear understanding of user and task requirements; (ii) a proper distribution of roles between users and technology; (iii) an iteration of design and evaluation processes; and (iv) a multidisciplinary approach [6].

Derived from HCD, User-Centered Design (UCD) emerge, being a more attentive and concise version with greater analysis of the target audience, highlighting that the primary purpose of a system should be helping the user, rather than the technology. As example, it is possible to mention the emotional design [7], based on the visceral (*i.e.* product's appearance that rely on rapid judgements and human's senses), behavioral (*i.e.* pleasure and experience of use) and reflective (*i.e.* acts at a conscious level and expresses through self-image, personal satisfaction and memories) dimensions, which intertwine simultaneously with emotions and cognitions in design.

Following that, the term meaningful gamification arises with the integration of UCD and game design elements into non-game contexts. It suggests that is feasible to design game elements that are meaningful to users through information interaction between users and designers [8].

The purpose of this paper is to provide an overview on the state-of-the-art review of user-centered design, user experience and gamification, in order to apply some of the methods and techniques into the cyclotourism for senior citizens' active and healthy ageing. On the one hand, gamification is considered a persuasive strategy that can influence changes in user behavior through the stimulation of motivation by elements and techniques of game design [9]; and, on the other hand, active and healthy ageing is the process of optimizing health, participation, and safety opportunities, in order to improve the quality of life and the functional capability as people age [10]. Furthermore, cyclotourism, enhanced with gamification techniques, may foster an active and healthy ageing.

This paper is organized as follows: Sect. 2 gives an overview of user-centered design, user experience and gamification, also exploring its potential when applied to senior citizens; Sect. 3 contextualizes the ageing paradigm and importance of cyclotourism for an active and healthy ageing; Sect. 4 presents a method of user-centered design methods applied to gamified cyclotourism for senior citizens, by proposing an UCD approach with gamification guidelines; and Sect. 5 shares some concerns and limitations, while highlighting the contributions of this paper.

2 State-of-the-Art Review

One of the major concerns in an increasingly ageing society is the overdependence in ICT and the subsequent challenges faced by senior citizens, owing to the limitations of the Human ageing process [2]. Furthermore, ICT still represents a major challenge for senior citizens, as many are fearful and anxious of damaging hardware and/or software, are unaware or have aversion of digital languages, and there is also an unavailability of equipment adapted to this audience [11]. According to Fisk and colleagues [12], UCD helps designers to create a balance between demands imposed by products on users and the mental and physical resources of the (older) users.

Brox and colleagues [13], have proved the success of UCD aimed at the use of game elements with particular focus onto this target audience, especially when dedicating time in order to gain senior citizens' trust so that communication can be easier, and users' opinions can be documented. Following this point of view, playing digital games has become increasingly popular amongst senior citizens [2], and considering that their age group is becoming one of the biggest consumers, it is important to understand which and how game elements can motivate them to adhere to activities. Beyond individual's extrinsic motivations (*e.g.* rewards), intrinsic motivations (*e.g.* respect and status) play an important role in changes in behavior and characterize the concept of gamification.

Hence, some methods such as user-centered design, user experience and gamification can be considered suitable when applying to this target audience. These methods rely on the human-focused design principle and are often concerned with the users' characteristics and needs, in order to provided them a valuable experience and shaping behaviors. The following sub-sections provide an overview on UCD and UX, as well on gamification.

2.1 User-Centered Design and User Experience

Norman and Draper [14] presented the philosophy of user-centered design, changing the way people think of the interaction between humans and computers, being a process framework in which the usability goals, user characteristics, environment, tasks, and workflow of a product, service, or process receive extensive attention at every stage of the design process. In other words, UCD is an iterative design process that allows for direct end-user engagement and participation, arguing that the interaction has a relationship between the system and the context, in order to understand the users' needs and expectations in relation to a given product or service [15–17]. It considers the social, physical, and cognitive aspects of the audience, and uses an approach that does not impose preferences and solutions [15, 16]. In contrast to product-centered design, it reflects and translates the public's desire, in addition to encouraging them to understand their own needs through the final solution of the project.

The relevance of including users into the project, or product/service development, lies in the fact that designers are not always able to understand the reality of users, which makes their participation fundamental [15–17]. The level of user involvement in the project can vary according to each team or methodology chosen, but typically, participants will be involved both in the initial stage – when designers need to understand the requirements – and in the final stages of usability testing. According to [16], not always the same users should be involved in all phases of the project, since someone who has been part of developing a solution may not be the best user to test it out because they probably know what to expect as a result.

The ISO standard [6] provided six key principles for UCD to follow: (i) the design should be based upon an explicit understanding of users, tasks, and environments; (ii) users should be involved in the entire design development process; (iii) the design should be driven and refined through user-focused evaluations; (iv) the process should be iterative; (v) the design should address the whole user experience (UX); and (vi) the design team should have multidisciplinary skills.

Therefore, UCD is considered a process to achieve a whole and good (UX). While UCD implies the process or approach employed to engineer experiences, UX addresses specific experience users have with the product or service they use, being much more than just assessing product's usability and utility. Also, all "(…) instance of human-object interaction has an associated user experience, but, in general, UX practitioners are interested in the relationship between human users and computers and computer-based products" [18: p.5]. It is worth mentioned that is only possible to design for a user experience, rather than the user experience itself, since it is crucial to understand the users' needs and values beforehand in order to design and evaluate a prototype or validate the proposals, and given that:

"(…) it is about how people feel about a product and their pleasure and satisfaction when using it, looking at it, holding it, and opening or closing it. It includes their overall impression of how good it is to use, right down to the sensual effect small details have on them, such as how smoothly a switch rotates or the sound of a click and the touch of a button when pressing it" [19: p.25].

User experience is also considered to be the key concern in the heart of product development [20], because it brings a much more humanistic approach by relating the hedonic level of personal Human needs and values, which motivate people to use a set of products and help managers set UX targets for product development.

Morville [21] emphasizes seven factors – based on the balance between user, context and content – to be considered when designing UX, as they will be vital to dictating the success or failure of a product: (i) Useful: concerns about not only the degree of utility, but also non-practical benefits (e.g. fun aesthetic appeal). If the product is purposeless, it is unlikely to be able to compete with other meaningful and useful offerings.; (ii) Usable: allows users to easily, effectively and efficiently achieve the ultimate goal that led them to use the product; (iii) Desirable: involves the user's emotional elements, usually transmitted through branding, image, identity and aesthetics; (iv) Findable: refers to the users' ability to find what they needs, namely, the product or service's features; (v) Credible: is closely related to the user's ability to trust the product or service, not only for design reasons, but also for the fidelity of the content it presents; (vi) Accessible: the experience offered must serve a wide and diverse range of users, so that anyone can access or interact with the product, regardless of their condition (*e.g.* visual, hearing, motor or learning disability); and (vii) Valuable: the product must translate into a bilateral value (*i.e.* both for the product's sponsors/creators and for the user who buys it and uses it).

The concept of UX is commonly confused with the term usability. While the latter is simply a study technique and a contribution that validates the usage and better understands the UX, the UX, despite needing usability, exceeds it, in the sense that it focuses on more facets. The user experience reaches the individual before, during and after performing a task. Thus, it is concerned with the users' emotional responses when they interact with a certain product or service, considering the user's perception and subjectivity. However, there is a clear interdependence between the two terms, since usability is a quality attribute that evaluates the user-friendliness of a user interface, and it also refers to the methods used during the design process that aim to improve the ease of use of a product [22].

2.2 Gamification

According to Maslow [23], people may have interest in intangible goods, such as respect and status, and these forms of motivation are the same principles that are part of the basic concept of gamification [24]. Gamification is often defined as the use of game design elements and techniques in a non-game context, attempting to motivate and engage the user to carry out a mundane activity [9], increasing specific behaviors, social interaction, and the quality and productivity of their actions.

Although its popularity, gamifying something does not mean simply giving badges and insignias for an action performance, involving a plan to persuade the user to perform a set of tasks with enjoyment and seducing them to a specific measurable goal [25]. Ultimately, gamification explores the individual's empathy to meet their intrinsic and extrinsic motivations.

McGonigal [26] identifies the following use of games elements on intrinsic motivation: (i) increase in user satisfaction (*i.e.* the end-user's progress results from attainable personal goals and immediate feedback, giving a perceived sense of high individual performance); (ii) conveyance of optimism (*i.e.* gamification enables self-determination and the feeling of accomplishment); (iii) facilitation of social interaction (*i.e.* gamification enables social exchange and/or competition because, normally, the user enters to a community); and (iv) provision of meaning (*i.e.* gamification fosters daily life challenges, helping to overcome individual's limitations). In terms of extrinsic motivation, gamification has also an important role by encouraging changes on behaviors through points, badges, leaderboards (*i.e.* PBL triad) and other formal game elements that, when used correctly, are considered powerful, practical, and relevant.

Werbach and Hunter [24] proposed a game element hierarchy for gamification (*i.e.* DMC Pyramid) – based on the origins of the MDA framework (*i.e.* Mechanics, Dynamics and Aesthetics) [27], that form the core of a gamified design and the playful experience, both from the point of view of the designer and the end-user. – which covers different categories of game elements. The pyramid is divided into three levels, in which an evolution principle is applied: (i) Components that include achievements, avatars, badges, boss fights, collections, combat, unlocking content, gifting, rankings, levels, points, quests, social chart, teams and virtual goods; (ii) Mechanics that encompasses challenges, chances, cooperation and competition, feedback, acquisition of resources, rewards, transactions, turns and win states; and (iii) Dynamics which embody narrative, relationships, emotions, constraints and progression.

In this context, the potential of gamification is now being studied to deliver more effective and personalized services to senior citizens and to encourage and persuade them to undertake physical, cognitive, and social activities according to their individual capabilities and needs, thus contributing to their overall wellbeing and to motivate to pursuit more active and healthy lifestyles [28].

In order to build a gamified system, it is important to have a gameful thinking to apply motivation techniques [24], since it will deal with potential problems, enabling the inclusion of the right game elements and having in account users' behaviors and motivation in the proposed context. In fact, gamification can be categorized as Gamification of Behavioral Change [24], as it seeks to generate and motivate new habits beneficial to the population in order to produce desirable results in society, such as active and healthy ageing.

3 Ageing Context and Cyclotourism as a Solution

The rise in longevity enables the incessant ageing of the world population, obvious through the inverted European demographic pyramid, where the senior citizen represents a vulnerable group for social and digital marginalization, sedentary routine and subsequent mobility limitations, health deficiencies and mortality [29, 30]. According to World Health Organization [31], the proportion of the world's population over 60 years old will double between 2000 and 2050. Owing to that, concerns about an active and healthy ageing are acquiring significant importance in scientific, academic, and politic studies.

Moreover, the phenomenon of active and healthy ageing in the information and communication society and the use of digital platforms have been the main topics of interest for gerontechnology. This new info-communicational era, characterized by interconnections, flows and networks [32], highlights the digital inclusion or exclusion in the social appropriation of ICT. Thus, gerontechnology adjusts and/or creates the technological environments in which senior citizens live and work so they can be active contributors to the society, while their quality of life and wellbeing is being improved [4, 5]. In fact, research into senior citizens' participation in civic matters has increased noticeably over the last 55 years [33], as also practices and policy initiatives aimed at promoting active and healthy ageing. This growing interest often relies on the assumption of mutual beneficial for both individuals and their communities in a participatory and inclusive culture.

When thinking of an activity that may influence senior citizen's motivations for continuation and attendance, improving physical and mental health, cyclotourism arises – by combining cycling and tourism – as it tends to be enjoyable and may contribute to active and healthy ageing. As a physical health activity, it has several benefits and can act as a disease preventor, muscle toner and joints strengthener. Furthermore, it is an unexploited sector with great potential for participation and social inclusion [34]. According to Cavill

[35] cyclotourism encourage sociocultural exchange and the culture of communities. In addition, maintaining social contacts contributes to mental health, wellbeing, and quality of life, and is particularly important for senior citizens and vulnerable populations. It also contributes to the humanization of cities and promotes the exercise of citizenship, and participation in public life, reducing inequalities, increasing the sense of community, and individual and collective wellbeing [36].

Cyclotourism has also been through a digital growth, noticeable not only in ICT solutions, but also in the evolution of the bicycle itself and related equipment. On the one hand, regarding ICT, the use of bicycles boosts websites, social networks, and virtual discussion groups, adding the value of sharing experiences, their motivations, problems encountered, facilities and difficulties on a certain route or infrastructure [36, 37]. Also the dissemination of applications and mobile devices for localization and monitoring of activities in real time is a trend that is growing, with technical improvements being required to meet the new demands and expectations of practitioners. On the other hand, regarding the bicycle evolution, beyond bicycle types (*e.g.* road, gravel, mountain, city), its buildings resort to a variety of materials (*e.g.* steel, aluminum, carbon, titanium) that can be used in different parts of the bicycle, being adapted to the users' preference and financial capacity.

Likewise, strategies for active and healthy ageing [38], and cyclable mobility [39, 40] have common ground with the goals of gerontechnology, UCD and UX – in the inclusion, appreciation, understanding and enhancement of the senior citizen as a user – by wanting to maximize the health benefits of citizens, providing them with healthier lifestyle habits, and also by promoting cooperation and intersectoriality.

4   An Approach to Senior Cyclotourism

Based on the results obtained by Ortet and colleagues [36, 37], the senior citizen's motivations for cyclotourism refer to physical and mental health, economic impact, ease and convenience of transportation, physical exercise, relationships, cycling pleasure and the surrounding scenery. Also, in this study was possible to observe the appreciation of senior citizens' opinion in co-design techniques and usability tests for the participatory creation of a gamified app prototype. Findings suggest that gamification elements, divided into pre-, in loco and post-cyclotourism experience, can trigger senior citizens' motivations towards the activity, highlighting social relationships, progression, challenges, competition, feedback and rewards [36].

Considering the pertinence and relevance of Brox and colleagues [13] study on UCD for senior citizens, and Chen [41] study on UCD in gamification, it was possible to cross and adapt some relevant guidelines explained in the following sub-section.

The selection of these authors went through a search of published papers from the last 5 years, due to being more recent in the matter, in Scopus and Web of Science databases, on the main keywords of this paper (*i.e.* User-Centered Design, User Experience, Gamification, Senior Citizens). The criteria fall on peer-reviewed publications that have these keywords or related topics in title, keywords and body, with the logical conjunctions of "and" and/or "or". From 13 papers, only these two were considered relevant, providing feasible, validated, and tested protocols and guidelines.

4.1 Method

Based on the aforementioned authors, an adaptation of UCD for senior citizens approach [13] and design guidelines for using UCD in gamification development [41] is proposed in this paper.

For ensuring the success of the experiment, the participants recruitment must include different profiles of senior citizens, not only to expand the sample, but also to be more inclusive and adapted to the users' reality of life. That is, senior citizens (i) interested in ICT and/or cycling or cyclotourism; (ii) not involved/interested in ICT and/or cycling or cyclotourism; (iii) physically and mentally healthy; and (iv) with physical and mental impairments.

Since this approach benefits from an experimental research design, a set of ethical concerns must be anticipated for the participants' protection and assure the integrity of this research: (i) participants or their caregivers' consent and understanding to take part in the research project; (ii) protect participants' identity and treat them with respect; (iii) explain the purpose, procedures and the duration of the investigation and included group discussion, interviews and testing sessions; (iv) assure the quality of the content; and (v) ask for permission for data gathering, coding, analysis and publication of the results.

Considering ISO [6] and the authors in which the proposed approach is based on [2, 8, 13, 20, 36, 37, 41], it should be iterative, explicit, and inclusive, performed by a multidisciplinary team and following these phases with subsequent design guidelines:

i. **Requirement gathering and analysis** – The goal is to gather requirements for an initial design by collecting basic needs of the end users, as well as requirements for the gamified product to be developed. Hence, it is important to have a multi-disciplinary team that can conduct a literature review, apply users' characterization questionnaires, and organize group discussions about the cyclotourism context and playability of gamification elements.

   Some design guidelines must be used in this phase, for instance it is important to understand the main goals regarding which problems to solve and which users' behaviors to change towards ICT and/or cyclotourism; briefing on the gamification goals and solutions for short term and quick wins, to get approval before further development; design progress pointers according to the available budget and time, and long-term/short-term goals; and explore what motivators factors have already been successful.

ii. **Design** – the initial design of the gamified context should give users a real opportunity to give feedback and, therefore, influence the outcome. Techniques such as direct observation, semi-structured interviews and focus groups should be applied.

   Establish a collaborative environment for co-design with users and gamification design decisions on dynamics, mechanics, and components should be made; create the narrative and aesthetic elements that can enhance users' motivation; map the users' interests to the researchers' interests; and attempt to learn users' intrinsic motivations through their participation in the design process.

iii. **Implementation** – Aspects of the design may need to be adjusted. Such aspects may be discovered through observation in focus groups and interviews.

   Create levels and progress to observe how users grow in the experience; keep the design interesting and innovative by constantly introducing new challenges and renewal elements; and offer users meaningful choices and purposes to explore their hidden potential within the ICT and/or cyclotourism context.

iv. **Evaluation** – Test and evaluation of the final prototype. Common approaches may include pilot tests, although smaller new user groups can also give significant contribution. It is important to evaluate UX rather than only usability.

Test the prototype iteratively throughout the protocol with small pilot groups before making it available to all users; perform lab and real context testing; supervise stepwise cognitive walkthrough with users; measure user usage and satisfaction; and consider users' reasoning and motivations behind their actions.

Having in mind the aforementioned recommendations, it is also important to acknowledge what should not be included when designing to this target audience. Visual, auditory, cognitive, haptic and motor skills need to be taken into consideration and, according to several authors [12, 42, 43], the designer should avoid: (i) elements that obliges high levels of physical agility; (ii) time or speed limits to perform a task; (iii) an overload of menus: (iv) large quantity of disorganized and complex information; (v) serif fonts without scalable text; (vi) non-familiar icons without identifiable text; (vii) sound as the only feedback; (viii) technical or specific terms; (ix) pastel colors; (x) not using back and undo tasks, among others.

4.2 Suppositions

In this paper, a method of user-centered gamified cyclotourism for senior citizens is given. The principle of design by users and for users may provide better results and higher success than only relying on the designer's role. Nevertheless, it is important to acknowledge that senior citizens have some difficulties dealing with digital devices and technologies, which may compromise the establish approach.

According to the state-of-the-art review and the results of co-designing a cyclo-tourism app prototype with and for senior citizens [36, 37], it is expected that user-centered design can motivate senior citizens to the co-design of a gamified solution, whereas user experience of gamification can be a promising tool for cyclotourism motivation and adherence.

Regarding the sample collection, involving senior citizens as end users is essential and it will allow for a more inclusive process. Thus, it may result in a gamified app designed for all profiles of senior citizens, enabling to explore the solutions' fragilities and strong points aimed at such wide audience.

Adopting UCD will allow the development of more effective, efficient, and safe senior cyclotourism gamified solution, since it aims to actively involve different profiles of senior citizens at every stage of the design process. Hence, for the researcher's perspective can be the success or failure of the solution, as it saves time, cuts cost and improves satisfaction. If a product results from this process, it will make a great contribution to science and especially to the life, adaptation and inclusion of a socially and digitally excluded group.

5 Final Considerations

As the ageing population continues to grow, it is important to focus on the role of gamification to senior citizens' wellbeing and meet their needs and preferences. Also, it is imperative to recognize that senior citizens have some problems dealing with digital devices and technologies, therefore, human-centered design approaches may help to overcome some of the difficulties.

Design is not only a reflective activity, but also an emotional and intuitive process. Thus, user experience is the main aspect in the heart of product or service development, since it brings a much more humanistic approach by relating the hedonic level of personal humans' needs and values, which motivate people to use a set of products. This means that user-centered design is still the key to design for a good UX, because it is crucial to understand the users' requirements and values beforehand, in order to design and evaluate a prototype or validate proposals.

It is noteworthy that most of the gamification design frameworks are based on UCD methods [44]. A meaningful gamification is believed to motivate engagement to an activity, helping users to find individual connections to it. For designing a gamified solution, understanding motivation is also essential to interlink the end-user's behavior with persuasive design. Gamification designs are effective in increasing engagement and modifying behaviors, but that success depends on a good implementation. Therefore, applying UCD with gamification elements, having in consideration the UX, appears to be a recipe for success. Yet, there is still a lack of research on these three topics.

As Ortet and colleagues [36, 37] have demonstrated, the co-design process and the gamification elements selected by the users' expectations on the cyclotourism activity can contribute to the prototype success. Even so, this paper proposes an approach to cyclo-tourism, following an adaptation of UCD protocol to senior citizens and gamification design guidelines, to try to offer a good UX. That experience is expected to be meaningful and pleasant, since such plan is created to incorporate the users' requirements, but also to motivate them to the process and, ultimately the activity (*i.e.* cyclotourism). It is important to remember that the process must be cyclic or spiral until a satisfactory balance between ideals and development is achieved.

However, a number of limitations should be considered for this research. Firstly, the context of gamified cyclotourism for senior citizens is an unexplored topic, therefore this research is innovative and not a replication, rather an adaptation from other studies. Secondly, the proposed approach and design guidelines were not tested in the gamified senior cyclotourism context, which may result in some adjustments throughout the development and testing phases. Thirdly, recruiting the suggested sample may be an incomplete process, since it is more difficult to engage people who are not interested in the studied context. Finally, as a participatory scenario usually requires a safe environment for participation and sharing, participants' trust must be gain, which may lead to biased results.

Regardless such constraints, this cogitation of methods is expected to be a scientific contribution that can have a high impact while promoting senior citizens' digital inclusion and their participation in the info-communicational era, therefore, promoting an active and healthy ageing. It may offer a reflection prior to the creation of gamified solutions and open the door to develop similar strategies for different subjects and contexts, thereby improving the experience significantly.

Acknowledgments. The study reported in this publication was supported by FCT – Foundation for Science and Technology (Fundação para a Ciência e Tecnologia), I.P. nr. 2020.04815.BD, DigiMedia Research Center, under the project UIDB/05460/2020, and the project SEDUCE 2.0 - Use of Communication and Information in the miOne online community by senior citizens, funded by FCT – Fundação para a Ciência e a Tecnologia, I.P., COMPETE 2020, Portugal 2020 and European Union, under the European Regional Development Fund, POCI-01–0145-FEDER-031696 SEDUCE 2.0.

References

1. UN World population ageing 2017 report: (2017) https://www.un.org/en/development/desa/population/theme/ageing/WPA2017.asp, Accessed 29 Nov 2021
2. Zheng, R.Z., Hill, R.D., Gardner, M.K.: Engaging older adults with modern technology: Internet use and information access needs. Information Science Reference, Hershey, Pa (2013)
3. Kort, H.S.M., Woolrych, R., van Bronswijk, J.E.M.H.: Applying the gerontechnology matrix for research involving ageing adults. In: Pecchia, L., Chen, L.L., Nugent, C., Bravo, J. (eds.) IWAAL 2014. LNCS, vol. 8868, pp. 328–331. Springer, Cham (2014). https://doi.org/10.1007/978-3-319-13105-4_47
4. Bouma, H., Fozard, J.L., Bronswijk, J.E.M.H.V.: Gerontechnology as a field of endeavour. Gerontechnology 8(2), 68–75 (2009). https://doi.org/10.4017/gt.2009.08.02.004.00
5. Le Deist, F., Latouille, M.: Acceptability conditions for telemonitoring gerontechnology in the elderly. IRBM 37(5–6), 284–288 (2016). https://doi.org/10.1016/j.irbm.2015.12.002
6. ISO: Ergonomics of human-system interaction - Part 210: Human-centred design for interactive systems - ISO 9241–210:2010 (2010)
7. Norman, D.A.: Emotional Design: Why We Love (or Hate) Everyday Things. Basic Books, New York, NY (2004)
8. Nicholson, S.: A user-centered theoretical framework for meaningful gamification. In: Proceedings of Games+Learning+Society 8.0, pp. 223–229 (2012)
9. Deterding, S.: Gamification: designing for motivation. Interactions 19(4), 14–17 (2012). https://doi.org/10.1145/2212877.2212883
10. World Health Organization: Global Report on Ageism. World Health Organization, Geneva (2021)
11. Veloso, A.I.: SEDUCE – utilização da comunicação e da informação em ecologias web pelo cidadão sénior. Afrontamento, Portugal. p. 274 (2014)
12. Fisk, A.D., Rogers, W.A., Charness, N., Czaja, S.J., Sharit, J.: Designing for Older Adults - Principles and Creative Humane Factors Approaches (Second ed.). Taylor & Francis, London. (2009) https://doi.org/10.4324/9780203485729
13. Brox, E., Konstantinidis, S.T., Evertsen, G.: User-Centered design of serious games for older adults following 3 years of experience with exergames for seniors: a study design. JMIR Serious Games. 5(1), e2 (2017). https://doi.org/10.2196/games.6254.PMID:28077348;PMCID:PMC5266825
14. Norman, D.A., Draper, S.W.: User-Centered System Design: New perspectives on Human Computer Interaction. Lawrence Erlbaum, Hillsdale, NJ (1986)
15. Baxter, K., Courage, C., Caine, K.: Understanding Your Users: A Practical Guide to User Research Methods. Morgan Kaufmann, Elsivier, Waltham (2015)

16. Ladner, R.E.: Design for user empowerment. Interactions **22**(2), 24–29 (2015). https://doi. org/10.1145/2723869
17. Still, B., Crane, K.: Fundamentals of User-Centered Design: A Practical Approach (1st ed.). CRC Press, Boca Raton (2017) https://doi.org/10.4324/9781315200927
18. Soegaard, M.: The basics of user experience design. A UX Design Book by the Interaction Design Foundation (2018)
19. Sharp, H., Rogers, Y., Preece, J.: Interaction Design: Beyond Human-Computer Interaction. John Wiley & Sons,Ltd., Indianapolis, IN (2019)
20. Väänänen-Vainio-Mattila, K., Roto, V., Hassenzahl, M.: Towards practical user experience evaluation methods. In: Law, E.L.-C. (Ed.), Proceedings of the International Workshop on Meaningful Measures: Valid Useful User Experience Measurement (VUUM) 2008, Reykjavik, Iceland, pp. 19–22 (2008)
21. Morville, P.: The 7 Factors that Influence User Experience. Interaction Design Foundation. (2020) https://www.interaction-design.org/literature/article/the-7-factors-that-influence-user-experience, Accessed 29 Nov 2021
22. Nielsen, J.: Usability 101: Introduction to usability. Nielsen Norman Group. (2012) https://www.nngroup.com/articles/usability-101-introduction-to-usability/, Accessed 20 Nov 2021
23. Maslow, A.H.: A theory of human motivation. Psychol. Rev. **50**(4), 370–396 (1943)
24. Werbach, K., Hunter, D.: For the Win: How Game Thinking Can Revolutionize Your Business. Wharton Digital Press, Philadelphia, USA (2012)
25. Zichermann, G., Cunningham, C.: Gamification by Design: Implementing Game Mechanics in Web and Mobile Apps. OReilly Media, Sebastopol, CA (2011)
26. McGonigal, J.: Reality is Broken: Why Games Make us Better and How They Can Change the World. Vintage, London (2012)
27. Hunicke, R., Leblanc, M., Zubec, R.: MDA: a formal approach to game design and game research. In: Proceedings of the Association for the Advancement of Artificial Intelligence Workshop on Challenges in Game AI. San Jose, California (2004)
28. Kostopoulos, P., Kyritsis, A.I., Ricard, V., Deriaz, M., Konstantas, D.: Enhance daily live and health of elderly people. Proceedings Comp. Sci. **130**, 967–972 (2018)
29. D'cruz, M., Banerjee, D.: 'An invisible human rights crisis': the marginalization of older adults during the COVID-19 pandemic – an advocacy review. Psychiatry Res. **292**, 113369 (2020). https://doi.org/10.1016/j.psychres.2020.113369
30. Rezende, L.F., Rey-López, J.P., Matsudo, V.K., Luiz, O.: Sedentary behavior and health outcomes among older adults: a systematic review. BMC Public Health, 14(1) (2014) https://doi.org/10.1186/1471-2458-14-333
31. World Health Organization: Facts about ageing. World Health Organization, Switzerland (2014)
32. Castells, M.: The Information age: Economy, Society and Culture. Wiley-Blackwell, Chichester, West Sussex (2010)
33. Serrat, R., Scharf, T., Villar, F., Gómez, C.: Fifty-five years of research into older people's civic participation: recent trends, future directions. Gerontologist **60**(1), 38–51 (2020). https://doi.org/10.1093/geront/gnz021
34. Ortet, C., Veloso, A.I., Costa, L.V.: Fostering senior community-based cyclotourism using transmedia: a proposal. In: Gao, Q., Zhou, J. (eds.) HCII 2021. LNCS, vol. 12787, pp. 124–134. Springer, Cham (2021). https://doi.org/10.1007/978-3-030-78111-8_8
35. Cavill, N.: The potential of non-motorised transport for promoting health. In: Sustainable Transport-Planning for Walking and Cycling in Urban Environments. (Ed.) Rodney Tolley, Cavill Associates, UK. pp. 144-158 (2003)
36. Ortet, C.P., Costa, L.V., Veloso, A.I.: Jizo: a gamified digital app for senior cyclo-tourism in the mione community. In: Zagalo, N., Veloso, A.I., Costa, L., Mealha, Ó. (eds.) VJ 2019.

CCIS, vol. 1164, pp. 195–207. Springer, Cham (2019). https://doi.org/10.1007/978-3-030-37983-4_15

37. Ortet, C., Veloso, A.I., Costa, L.: A gamified app to promote senior cyclo-tourism. In: A Pilot Study. 21st International Conference on Intelligent Games and Simulation, GAME-ON 2020, pp. 71-78 (2020)

38. World Health Organization: Global Strategy and Action Plan on Ageing and Health. World Health Organization, Geneva (2017)

39. Sagaris, L.: Lessons from 40 years of planning for cycle-inclusion: reflections from Santiago. Chile. Natural Res. Forum **39**(1), 64–81 (2015). https://doi.org/10.1111/1477-8947.12062

40. Scorza, F., Fortunato, G.: Cyclable cities: Building feasible scenario through urban space morphology assessment. J. Urban Plann. Dev. **147**(4), 05021039 (2021). https://doi.org/10.1061/(asce)up.1943-5444.0000713

41. Chen, Y.: Exploring design guidelines of using user-centered design in gamification development: a delphi study. Int. J. Human-Comput. Interact. **35**(13), 1170–1181 (2019). https://doi.org/10.1080/10447318.2018.1514823

42. Cunha, B.C.R., Rodrigues, K.R.H., Pimentel, M.G.C.: Synthesizing guidelines for facilitating elderly-smartphone interaction. In: Proceedings of the 25th Brazilian Symposium on Multimedia and the Web (WebMedia'19). Association for Computing Machinery, New York, NY, USA, pp. 37–44 (2019) https://doi.org/10.1145/3323503.3349563

43. Ortet, C., Costa, L., Veloso, A.I.: Gamification design patterns and touchscreen interactions in mobile apps for senior citizens: In: An Overview. 22nd annual European GAMEON® Conference (GAME-ON®'2021) on Simulation and AI in Computer Games, pp. 113–119 (2021)

44. Mora, A., Riera, D., Gonzalez, C., Arnedomoreno, J.: A literature review of gamification design frameworks. In: 7th International Conference on Games and Virtual Worlds for Serious Applications (VS-Games), Skovde, 2015, pp. 1-8 (2015) https://doi.org/10.1109/VS-GAMES.2015.7295760

A Study of the Effects of Interactive AI Image Processing Functions on Children's Painting Education

Jie Sun[1], Chao Gu[1(✉)], Jiangjie Chen[2], Wei Wei[3], Chun Yang[2], and Qianling Jiang[2]

[1] Honam University, Gwangju 62399, Korea
{20208429,cguamoy}@my.honam.ac.kr
[2] Jiangnan University, Wuxi 214013, China
{chenjiangjie,8202201014,jiangqianling}@jiangnan.edu.cn,
doublewei@cslg.edu.cn
[3] Changshu Institute of Technology, Changshu 215500, China
doublewei@cslg.edu.cn

Abstract. Digital media technologies have been gradually integrated into teaching activities over the past few years, providing teachers with more possibilities for teaching. This study examines the teaching effects of an interactive AI based image-processing platform in assisting as a teaching aid for children painting education. In this study, we compared the learning interest, learning attitude, and continuous learning intention of 96 children aged 5 to 13 in the process of painting education. The subjects were divided into two groups: the experimental group used AI image processing for painting education, and the control group utilized traditional teaching methods for painting learning. Results showed that the use of AI image-processing tools in painting education reduces girls' learning attitudes and continuous learning intention, while stimulating boys' learning interest.

Keywords: AI-art · Learning interest · Learning attitude · Continuous learning intention · Painting education

1 Introduction

Painting is a way for children to learn about the world and to explore it as they grow up. Children may engage in the process of painting by using their observational skills, their critical thinking abilities, and their ability to make decisions concerning the composition, colors, etc. of their paintings. With the help of graphic representations, children develop a greater capacity for cognitive development and improve their skills in visual thinking, as well as their ability to use painting as a method of communication to solve problems [1].

A positive learning attitude towards art is not only important to artists, teachers, designers, and other professionals involved in the field of art, it is also important for students to participate in art activities as adults, because art is important in everyday life as an alternative way of demonstrating intelligence [2]. Laura Chapman emphasizes

Q. Gao and J. Zhou (Eds.): HCII 2022, LNCS 13330, pp. 93–108, 2022.
https://doi.org/10.1007/978-3-031-05581-2_8

that in the three responsibilities of children's art education that drawing should promote students' personal fulfillment and creative development [3]. In the digital age, high-tech products are rapidly transforming children's way of life and cognitive abilities. Meanwhile, the digital transformation is also having a significant impact on education. In the context of the development of digital technology in the modern era, it is essential to integrate art education in a manner that is more conducive to children.

A study by Cutcher and Wilks (2012) suggests that adopting new methods or new technologies in the teaching process can strengthen the teaching and learning effect [4]. With the development of computer vision technology, AR, VR, real-time positioning, etc. have brought new experiences to all aspects of people's lives. A growing number of scholars are also integrating it with education [5, 6]. In contrast to the fields of science and language education, there is little research that has been conducted on the children's art education. In computer vision, artificial intelligence is easier to implement and promote because it requires relatively low-cost equipment. Actually, Artificial intelligence has been widely applied in the field of education. With the development of the adversarial network gradually becoming more mature and user-friendly, users can utilize the trained style or online training machine to generate their own style without programming. If it is applied to the field of art education, students will be influenced by machines while creating artwork, and the large student group will also add new nutrients to machine learning, thus, both human and machine learning can be mutually improved.

Thus, this study explores the use of an interactive AI image processing platform as a teaching tool for children's art. A study is conducted to examine its effects on learning interest, learning attitude, and continuous learning intention of different genders toward painting education. It is difficult for teachers to pay attention to each student's learning in traditional art class instruction. With the collaboration between AI and educators, students are exposed to new visual stimuli, more personalized learning experience. Currently, AI image processing functions are primarily utilized by artists. This study also provides a reference for AI image processing function designers to apply it in the field of education.

2 Literature Review

2.1 AI-art

The concept of artificial intelligence refers to the human-like function of reasoning, interacting, and learning [7]. AI in education (AIed) can be traced back to the 1980s, marked by the first publication of the International Journal of Artificial Intelligence in Education in 1989 and the establishment of the International Association for Artificial Intelligence in Education (IAIED) in 1993 [8]. There are two main categories of artificial intelligence in education: first, AI-based tools for class instruction; second, using AI to understand, measure, and improve students' performance [9]. Computer science and social sciences account for 56% of AI education in Scopus, while arts and humanities constitute only 1% [10]. Therefore, there is still considerable room for advancing AI education in the humanities and arts.

In the late 1960s, AI art was still regarded as traditional algorithmic art whose aesthetic rules depended on coding. A typical example is Harold Cohen's AARON art program [11]. New algorithms for visual generation have been developed with the advancement of technology, such as: Fractal Flame [12, 13], Computational Aesthetics [14], hybrid methods [15], neural style transfer [16], and deep learning-powered adver-sarial evolution [17]. At present, the most widely used platform is the Generative Adversarial Network (GAN) launched by Goodfellow in 2014 [18].

This study utilized the Playform, which was specifically designed for the creation of visual arts. The platform solves the problem that GAN needs to learn a great deal of images over a long period of time. The user has the option of using the generated style, or training the machine to generate a specific style image. The process of drawing can be assisted by artificial intelligence (AI), which allows children to process images and receive a variety of visual stimuli.

2.2 Learning Interest

Interests consist of situational and individual interests [19]: situational interest includes trigger interest and maintenance interest [20–23]; individual interests include emerging individual interest and well-developed individual interests [24]. Situational interest can directly enhance learning by increasing attention and engagement. Thus, interest is often used as a traditional measure of educational success [25].

According to Reininger and Hidi, the basic measures of intervention in contextual interest in education are known as "triggers for interest" [26]. Organizing learning activities that capture the student's attention is one way to stimulate interest. Berkeley identified a number of collative variables that are capable of influencing and arousing attention [27]. He found, in his series of studies that varying the novelty, complexity, surpriseness, and incongruity of visual stimuli cause attention, arousal, and interest to increase. In the stage of children's painting learning, the AI image processing platform is used to change objects. The different images provided by AI will expose students to new visual stimulations, which may enhance students' situational interest.

Based on a four-stage model of interest development (trigger situational interest; sustain situational interest; develop individual interest; well-developed individual interest), situational interest is triggered by specific situations, and situational interest develops over time so as to become a more enduring individual interest [19, 28] . Engaging in meaningful activities can maintain situational interest [23, 29–33]. The use of the AI image processing platform in the painting teaching process will help maintain student situational interest and may further stimulate individual interest, by allowing them to interact with the machine according to their subjective preferences. When situational interests become individual interests, students are more likely to have deep learning [34]. In other words, in order to maximize students' in-depth learning, the teacher should turn students' situational interests into the individual interests.

2.3 Learning Attitude

Attitude refers to a mental and emotional entity, which is either inherent in a person or characterized by that individual [35]. It can be used to interpret emotional reactions [36]. Some scholars argue that attitude and satisfaction are essentially synonymous. The only difference between them lies in the measurement time, attitude is part of the pre-acceptance dimension, and satisfaction is part of the post-acceptance dimension [37].

Some studies speculate that as a direct determinant of continuous intention, attitude is similar to satisfaction in the technology acceptance model (TAM) and expectation-confirmation model (ECM) mode [38]. Nevertheless, there are many researchers who consider attitudes and satisfaction as conceptually separate variables [36, 39]. The attitude is future-oriented (i.e. the sense of future use). A person's satisfaction is related to previous experiences, but the benefits of the past are not sufficient to explain the future. A future-oriented approach is more evocative than looking back [39, 40]. Furthermore, attitudes are emotional reactions to specific behaviors that improve the accuracy of intent-predicted behavior, as opposed to satisfaction based on past experiences.

In the field of arts education, attitudes toward learning are often neglected. There are some theoretical models of teaching art believed that knowing the abilities of students will facilitate effective teaching, and the focus is on students' learning abilities [41, 42]. Most textbooks on the teaching of the arts make an indirect reference to attitudes when considering how to promote students' understanding [43, 44]. In order to promote learning, it is important to understand students. It is vital to understand students not only by considering their developmental levels, abilities, and learning strategies, but also by considering their motivations, prior knowledge, and attitudes toward the subjects they are studying [2, 45].

According to technology acceptance model, attitudes directly affect continuous use intentions. Thus, in this study, different gender students were used in the experimental group and the control group to explore the impact of the AI image processing function on their attitude towards learning to paint, as well as assess its effect on continuous learning intention. Meanwhile, it can also test the students' expectations for future use of the interactive AI image processing platform as a painting tool.

2.4 Continuous Learning Intention

The concept of continuous learning refers to individuals continually acquiring knowledge, skills, and competence in response to changing demands within their professional lives [46, 47]. The learner's continuous learning intention refers to their specific desire to learn.

Research in the field of digital teaching methods indicates that students' willingness to learn is affected by a variety of factors, including the content of the course, the system quality, and the services students receive etc. [48–50]. However, interactive experience has been identified as a key factor in the willingness to continue learning [51, 52]. In general, student learning motivation theory states that learning motivation is affected by learning intentions, as well as a direct relationship between motivation and attitude. According to the TAM, students' perceptions of the ease of use and utility of technology determine their behavior and use intentions. It is possible to predict students' continuous intention to learn from their learning attitudes [53, 54]. Perceived ease of use may influence behavior intentions of students, which might be moderated by perceived usefulness [55].

According to TAM, attitudes directly affect continuous use intentions. Thus, in this study, through the use of AI image processing functions, the psychological changes in student attitudes towards painting learning were utilized to further analyze students' continuous learning intentions.

3 Research Design and Method

In this study, Playform [56] was used as the interactive AI image processing platform. As an AI Art studio, Playform allows artists to experiment and explore the use of generative AI in their creative process without the need for coding. For GANs, huge amounts of images (tens of thousands) and long hours of training are required, whereas Playform has developed optimized versions of GANs that can be trained with tens of images and can provide reasonable results in one or two hours. Furthermore, it is user friendly, as the users do not have to be familiar with programming languages or the terminology of the AI libraries. A variety of creative projects and artists use Palyform, including HBO, Christie's, SCOPE and NYU. It is possible to train Playform to obtain a particular style, or to simply use the trained style. We use the trained style in this study to process images, as a tool to assist children in learning to paint. The function is shown in Fig. 1. After experiencing the function in painting learning, the subjects were asked to complete a questionnaire.

Fig. 1. The interactive AI image processing functions of *Playform*

3.1 Questionnaire Design

In this study, we adjusted and optimized the final questionnaire, which based on the established scales that have been verified in relevant literature, in accordance with the characteristics of interactive AI image processing. Study subjects were divided into two groups: the experimental group using the AI image processing platform for painting learning and the control group using traditional teaching methods for painting learning. Each group of questionnaires is divided into two parts, the first part collecting the basic information of users, and the second part measuring the behavior of the subjects. In this study, a Likert five-point scale was used to measure the constructs, with 1 representing strongly disagree and 5 representing strongly agree. The questions are shown in Table 2.

3.2 Data Collection

Based on the psychological theory proposed by Colin Martindale, the Art and Artificial Intelligence Laboratory of Rutger University developed AICAN, which focused on the process of creation and the evolution of artists from the standpoint of perception and cognition [57]. Playform for visual creators, developed by the Art and Artificial Intelligence Laboratory at Rutger University, is used in this study to access AICAN technology without the need of coding.

AICAN used by Playform differs from GAN, which requires long training periods and tens of thousands of image for training. The algorithm of this system only requires less than 100 photographs, which means that it can be trained to create its own style within one or two hours. Creative Adversarial Networks (CAN) mimics the way artists draw from previous works and then develop new styles [58]. Novelty is achieved through "stylistic ambiguity". The machine is trained between two opposing forces: one forces the machine to follow the aesthetics of the art being shown (reducing deviations from the distribution of art), and the other that forces the machine do not to imitate a currently existing style (maximizing style ambiguity). The "least effort" principle of Martindale suggests that too much novelty is not easily accepted by the audience. The novel aspects of the art produced are ensured by the opposing forces and without straying too far from acceptable aesthetic standards. The algorithm utilizes 80K images spanning from five centuries of Western art history, simulating the growth and learning process of an artist, without focusing on any particular style. In contrast to general AI art, the process of CAN generating art works is a creative process [58].

Images generated by AI art could provide children new visual stimuli and promote their learning interest. This study examines the possibility of using an AI image processing platform as a teaching tool for teaching children to paint. The target population is children aged 5–13 years old. This study was conducted with 96 children in an art training facility in Xiamen, Fujian, China in January 2022. Comparing the changes in learners' learning interest, learning attitude and continuous learning intention when utilize the AI image processing function as a teaching tool in experiment and control groups. The subjects, after participating in an interactive AI image processing platform and a painting lesson, fill out an online questionnaire immediately. The questionnaire is phonetized verbatim, based on the subjects' age and literacy level, and a teacher explains the content of the questionnaire to the subjects, in order to ensure the questionnaire's efficiency (Table 1).

Table 1. Basic data of the respondents.

Sample	Category	Number	Percentage
Gender	Male	34	35.42
	Female	62	64.58
Education background	Pre-school	12	12.50
	Elementary school	84	87.50

Table 2. Measurement scale.

Latent variable	Coding	Item	Source
Attitude	AT1	It is a good idea to learn to paint (with AI)	Jiangjie Chen, Yen Hsu, Weiwei, Chun Yang (2021)
	AT2	The idea of (using artificial intelligence to help students) learn to paint appeals to me	
	AT3	It is enjoyable to learn to paint (using AI as a tool)	
Continuance Intention	CI1	I plan to continue to (use AI as a tool in) painting learning in the future	Yen Hsu, Jiangjie Chen, Chao Gu, Weilong Wu (2021)
	CI2	I plan to (use AI as a tool in) painting learning often in the future	
	CI3	Generally speaking, I intend to continue to (use AI as a tool in) painting learning	
Learning Interest	LI1	I am more interested in painting learning than (I was) previously (since using AI as a teaching aid)	Chu, H. C., Hwang, G. J., & Tsai, C. C. (2010)
	LI2	I have been more interested in painting learning (since taking the AI as a teaching tool)	
	LI3	Learning to paint (with the aid of AI) will make the learning process (more) enjoyable	
	LI4	I (am impressed with this innovative method of learning and) am interested in learning more about painting method	
	LI5	(Using the AI tool to learn) painting stimulates my painting learning motivation	

4 Results

The results show that Mean $= 4.19$, SD $= .54$, Cronbach's $\alpha = .62$ in the construct of LI. In the AT construct, Mean $= 4.21$, SD $= .67$, Cronbach's $\alpha = .61$ and in the CI construct Mean $= 3.83$, SD $= .72$, Cronbach's $\alpha = .63$. For all constructs, the Cronbach's alpha is greater than 0.6 indicating that the items have reliability [59]. This result is consistent with the normal distribution hypothesis [60] as the absolute value of the skewness coefficient for each item is less than 2 and the absolute value of the kurtosis coefficient is less than 7. The correlation test results are shown in Table 3. Results of the Pearson correlation test indicate that a significant pairwise correlation exists between the constructs, with a coefficient of $r > .60$, $p < .05$. In addition, the correlation coefficient of $r < .90$ indicates that there is no multivariate collinearity between the constructs. Thus, the data are assumed to follow a linear distribution [61].

Table 3. Results of Pearson's correlation test.

	AT	CI	LI
AT	–		
CI	.418**	–	
LI	.592**	.538**	–

Note.*$p = .05$,**$p = .001$.All tests were two-tailed

Table 4 presents the results of the data distribution test. The Box' Test result shows that $F = 1.70$, $p = .03$. Box' Test, however, is sensitive to the number of samples, so its significance standard should be relaxed to a more relaxed level [62]. Accordingly, $p > .01$ is meant to represent the assumption that the covariance matrix is equal [63]. Further, the results of the interaction between the teaching method and gender showed that $F < 1.96$ and $p < .05$ were not significant in all three constructs. In other words, teaching method and gender have a fixed impact on the learning of painting and will not be affected by the change on the other side.

Table 4. Distribution test results.

Constructs	Box' test			Interaction TM*G	
	Box'M	F	Sig.	F	Sig.
AT	33.12	1.70	.03	1.21	.27
CI				.08	.78
LI				3.03	.09

The paired comparison results are shown in Table 5 and Table 6. The results of the Pairwise comparison indicate a significant difference between male and female students' LI ($p < 0.5$, Mean Difference $= .46$), after the use of AI to participate in painting teaching. The results between the experimental group and the control group of male students ($p < 0.5$, Mean Difference $= .42$) indicate that The use of artificial intelligence in painting teaching has greatly increased boys' interest in painting. In contrast, female students in the experimental group and the controls did not demonstrate effective engagement in learning ($p < 0.5$, Mean Difference $= .00$), suggesting that artificial intelligence in this experiment is not attractive to girls.

There was also a significant difference between the boys and girls in the two groups in terms of their painting learning attitude (p*0.5, Mean Difference = .41). These results indicate that the girls' AT (p < 0.5, Mean Difference = −.37) have decreased in their learning attitude towards drawing after using AI as a teaching tool. Boys did not demonstrate a significant change in their attitude toward painting learning (p < 0.5, Mean Difference = −.05).

In terms of continuous learning intention, there were slight differences between boys and girls in two groups. Results of the experimental and control groups (p < 0.5, Mean Difference = −.45; p < 0.5, Mean Difference = −.37) suggest that using artificial intelligence to support painting instruction in children reduces female students' continue learning intention.

Table 5. Pairwise comparison1.

Dependent variable	Group	(I)gender	(J)gender	Mean difference(I-J)	Std.error	Sig.b	Cohen's d	Effect size
AT	1	1	2	.41	.21	.06	.77	.36
	2	1	2	.09	.20	.66	.14	.07
CI	1	1	2	.11	.23	.62	.20	.10
	2	1	2	.03	.22	.90	.03	.02
LI	1	1	2	.46*	.17	.01	.19	.51
	2	1	2	.04	.17	.80	.07	.03

Table 6. Pairwise comparison2

Dependent variable	Gender	(I)group	(J)group	Mean Difference(I-J)	Std.Error	Sig.b	Cohen's d	Effect size
AT	1	1	2	−.05	.24	.84	−.10	−.05
	2	1	2	−.37*	.17	.03	−.55	−.26
CI	1	1	2	−.37	.26	.16	−.46	−.22
	2	1	2	−.45*	.18	.02	−.69	−.33
LI	1	1	2	.42*	.20	.04	.91	.41
	2	1	2	−.00	.14	.99	−.00	−.00

5 Discussion

In this study, we examined students' perceptions of using AI image processing functions as an art learning tool by evaluating three constructs: learning interest, learning attitude, and continuous learning intention.

For the student's learning interest (LI). Using AI image processing to teach painting significantly improved boys' interest in painting learning, but did not have a similar effect on girls' interest. The results of this experiment contrast with other studies in which girls were found to be more interested in using new technology than boys [64]. According to contemporary theories, personal and situational interests are interrelated in the development of learning interests, and individual interests are promoted by situational interests [19]. Situational interest is generated when the learner interacts with the learning environment. Furthermore, the key factors that influence this interaction are the learning content and learning environment [65–67]. In other words, male painting learners can interact with AI graphics processing functions to generate new learning content, thus stimulating students' situational interests through machine-generated images and nurturing them into individual interests. Additionally, if this instructional device is used with female students, it is imperative to pay attention to the direct experiences that female students have while painting, and to adapt the environment and related learning content accordingly.

In terms of the student's learning attitude (AT). The use of interactive AI image processing functions during the instruction of children's painting has a negative effect on the learning attitudes of female students, but have no significant impact on male students. Based on social psychology and gender roles, the results could be explained by gender differences in behavior. Social psychology indicates that men are more pragmatic, task-oriented, and result-oriented than women [68]. As well, the literature on gender roles has indicated that men possess the traits of greater self-confidence, a greater sense of adventure, and a greater willingness to take risks. As opposed to men, females prefer light and routine tasks and dislike taking risks [69]. According to this theory, the new learning experience of using AI image processing to assist painting learning could be compared to an adventure that leaps out of the comfortable zone of usual painting environment. Therefore, most female students hold a more negative attitude than male students.

For students continuous learning intention (CI), the use of AI image processing as a teaching aid participating in children's painting instruction, negatively affect the continuous learning intention of the female students.

A widely used technology acceptance model states that behavior is determined by the intention to perform it, while the intention could be predicted by attitude [70, 71]. According to this experiment, using the AI image processing function to assist teaching, the girls had a negative attitude towards painting learning. A t the same time, their continuous learning intention weakened, which was consistent with the prediction of attitudes and intentions in the TAM. In the technology acceptance model, the user's acceptance of a technology is determined by the perceived usefulness and ease of use of the technology. Research has shown that technical characteristics and individual characteristics are the most influential external factors in the learning process [72]. Using this approach, experiments can be conducted at the level of perceived usefulness and perceived ease of use in order to examine the factors that influence males and females. We can take full advantage of the beneficial effects of technology, and explore the practical application of artificial intelligence in children art education if we could understand and control these factors.

6 Managerial Implications

This study indicates that students of different genders have different reactions to the use of AI interactive image processing to participate in the teaching of painting. It increases the interest of boys in painting learning, however, it reduces the interest of girls in painting learning and students' continue learning intention.

To use artificial intelligence image processing as a universally applicable teaching tool to assist painting learning, developers should pay particular attention to the female students. Adjusting the factors that affect perceived usefulness and perceived ease of use leads to improving students' attitudes toward learning and strengthening their intentions for continuous learning. Adapting the program to the characteristics of students of different genders is needed. The role of artificial intelligence for image processing can be explored in terms of delivering differentiated and individualized of art education. Furthermore, in traditional school classrooms, the teacher cannot give attention to and guide all students at the same time. However, when using artificial intelligence's functions to collaborate with the teacher, the AI can be tailored according to the needs of different students, and is more suitable for the adaptation of teaching activities for each student. The student may select the style in which they wish to express themselves, and may use images generated by the computer for inspiration. At the same time, when the interactive AI image processing functions are applied to painting teaching, the machine will also be continuously trained, so the processes of human learning and machine learning will complement each other.

7 Theoretical Contribution

This study uses interactive AI image processing as an auxiliary teaching tool in painting teaching, and explores the changes in students' learning interest, learning attitude and continuous learning intention. The results of this study provide a theoretical foundation for the integration of AI technology and the teaching of art disciplines. Specifically, this study examines the differences in social psychology and gender roles in human behavior, as well as the academic hypothesis in technological acceptance models that through behavioral attitudes could predict the intention to perform. Academically, this research advances the practical application of AI technology in art teaching. Meanwhile, it also provides a reference for the developers of interactive AI graphics functions for the purposes of designing interactive systems for the field of art education.

8 Conclusion

In the midst of technological advancement, education is embracing the digital transformation. The challenge of integrating new technology into teaching, building a cooperative relationship between humans and machines in the field of education, and fostering the personalization of education are challenges faced by educators in various disciplines.

The implications of this study are significant for AI education. The use of artificial intelligence (AI) technology in education is becoming increasingly prevalent, however, there is little study on its application to humanities and arts, and in particular to children's painting education. On the other hand, interactive AI image processing that utilizes generative adversarial networks has attracted significant attention from art practitioners, and has been applied to the production of art works in various scenarios and styles. In spite of this, there has been little investigation of applying this function to the teaching of children's art.

Electronic products such as robots, story machines, drones, and children's smart watches are changing the lives of modern children as technology develops. In some ways, the interaction between humans and machines is influencing the way we perceive traditional things in the post-human era. Education is exploring new paths for digital transformation by incorporating AR, VR, AI and other technologies, and artificial intelligence plays an important role in it. According to a report on artificial intelligence in the US education market, the number of AI in education has increased by about 50% from 2017 to 2021. However, there are fewer cases of AI being utilized in the teaching of humanities and arts. In this study, we have explored the possibility of AI applications in art education, and have provided a reference for the interactive AI image processing platform for its use in art education.

The study results indicate that the use of artificial intelligence (AI) image processing tools to participate in the teaching of painting has a negative impact on female students' learning attitude and continuance learning intention. In contrast, it significantly stimulates boys' interest in painting.

There are still certain limitations remain in this study. This study was limited in size by the fact that it was conducted among students of a training class in art; all participants came from Fujian, a relatively small region. In this case, there is a wide margin of error. In the following experiments, the number and size of the selected samples should be increased. Students are grouped according to content rather than age in experimental art training classes. As the class is used as the unit of experimentation, this leads to a different age distribution in the sample, affecting the comprehensiveness of the data. Future experiments should consider grouping test subjects according to their age range. Moreover, the subjects of this study are children. Although the questionnaire has been reworded and the testers have provided assistance in interpretation, some young children may still have difficulty understanding the content of the questionnaire, which will also affect the accuracy of the study. When subjects are grouped by age, it is possible to tailor the questionnaire expression to match the cognitive abilities of children in different age groups for more effective communication. In addition, the amount of experimental equipment is limited, which may adversely affect the user experience when interacting with AI image processing platform. The number of lab equipment can be increased in the future to enhance the students' user experience.

The findings of this study demonstrate that the use of AI image processing tools to participate in teaching painting reduces female students' intention to continue learning painting and negatively affects their learning attitudes. However, it has significantly influenced boys' interest in learning to paint. So, new research can be conducted from the perspective of gender differences in technology acceptance models. Analyze what factors affect both male and female students' continuous learning intentions on painting learning when utilizing AI image processing tools. Adjusting these variables will allow the development of a more differentiated and personalized method of teaching painting and explore the possibility of incorporating interactive AI image processing functions to art education. At the same time, since the existing AI image processing platform is not specifically designed and developed for the field of art education, this study also provides new development ideas for the designer and developer of AI image processing platforms.

References

1. Grant Cooke, D.G.: Maureen Cox, Teaching Young Children to Draw. (2005)
2. Pavlou, V., Kambouri, M.: Pupils'attitudes towards art teaching in primary school: an evaluation tool. Stud. Educ. Eval. **33**(3–4), 282–301 (2007)
3. Nikoltsos, C.: The Art of Teaching Art in Early Childhood Education. (2000)
4. Snyder, L., Klos, P., Grey-Hawkins, L.: Transforming teaching through arts integration: AI implementation results: middle school reform through effective arts integration professional development. J. Learn. Arts **10**(1), n1 (2014)
5. Jiang, Q., et al.: The impact of perceived interactivity and intrinsic value on users' continuance intention in using mobile augmented reality virtual shoe-try-on function. Systems **10**(1), 3 (2022)
6. Lin, J.-C., Hsieh, C.-C.: A Real-time Posture Recognition System using YOLACT++ and ResNet18. In: 2021 IEEE International Conference on Consumer Electronics-Taiwan (ICCE-TW). IEEE (2021)
7. Rai, A., Constantinides, P., Sarker, S.: Next generation digital platforms: toward human-AI hybrids. MIS Q. **43**(1), iii–ix (2019)
8. Williamson, B., Eynon, R., Potter, J.: Pandemic Politics, Pedagogies and Practices: Digital Technologies and Distance Education During the Coronavirus Emergency. Taylor & Francis. pp. 107–114 (2020)
9. Holmes, W., Bialik, M., Fadel, C.: Artificial Intelligence in Education. Center for Curriculum Redesign, Boston pp. 1–35 (2019)
10. Bozkurt, A., et al.: Artificial intelligence and reflections from educational landscape: a review of AI studies in half a century. Sustainability **13**(2), 800 (2021)
11. Boden, M.A.: Creativity and artificial intelligence. Artif. Intell. **103**(1–2), 347–356 (1998)
12. Draves, S.: The electric sheep screen-saver: a case study in aesthetic evolution. In: Workshops on Applications of Evolutionary Computation, Springer (2005)
13. Draves, S., Reckase, E.: The Fractal Flame Algorithm. Citeseerx. Recuperado de http://citeserx.ist.psu.edu/viewdoc/summary (2008)
14. Machado, P., Romero, J., Manaris, B.: Experiments in computational aesthetics. In: Romero, J., Machado, P. (eds.) The art of artificial evolution, pp. 381–415. Springer Berlin Heidelberg, Berlin, Heidelberg (2008). https://doi.org/10.1007/978-3-540-72877-1_18
15. Colton, S.: The painting fool: stories from building an automated painter. In: McCormack, J., d'Inverno, M. (eds.) Computers and creativity, pp. 3–38. Springer Berlin Heidelberg, Berlin, Heidelberg (2012). https://doi.org/10.1007/978-3-642-31727-9_1
16. Gatys, L.A., Ecker, A.S., Bethge, M.: Image style transfer using convolutional neural networks. In: Proceedings of the IEEE Conference on Computer Vision and Pattern Recognition (2016)
17. Blair, A.: Adversarial evolution and deep learning–how does an artist play with our visual system? In: International Conference on Computational Intelligence in Music, Sound, Art and Design (Part of EvoStar). Springer (2019)
18. Goodfellow, I., et al.: Generative adversarial nets. Adv. Neural Inf. Process. Syst. **27** (2014)

19. Hidi, S., Renninger, K.A.: The four-phase model of interest development. Educ. Psychol. **41**(2), 111–127 (2006)
20. Harackiewicz, J.M., et al.: Short-term and long-term consequences of achievement goals: predicting interest and performance over time. J. Educ. Psychol. **92**(2), 316 (2000)
21. Pugh, K.J., Bergin, D.A.: Motivational influences on transfer. Educ. Psychol. **41**(3), 147–160 (2006)
22. Hidi, S.: An Interest Researcher's Perspective: The Effects of Extrinsic and Intrinsic Factors on Motivation. In: Intrinsic and extrinsic motivation, pp. 309–339. Elsevier (2000)
23. Mitchell, M.: Situational interest: its multifaceted structure in the secondary school mathematics classroom. J. Educ. Psychol. **85**(3), 424 (1993)
24. Renninger, K.A.: Individual Interest and its Implications for Understanding Intrinsic Motivation. In: Intrinsic and extrinsic motivation, pp. 373–404. Elsevier (2000)
25. Harackiewicz, J.M., Smith, J.L., Priniski, S.J.: Interest matters: the importance of promoting interest in education. Policy Insights Behav. Brain Sci. **3**(2), 220–227 (2016)
26. Renninger, K.A., Bachrach, J.E., Hidi, S.E.: Triggering and maintaining interest in early phases of interest development. Learn. Cult. Soc. Interact. **23**, 100260 (2019)
27. Berlyne, D.E.: Novelty, complexity, and hedonic value. Percept. Psychophys. **8**(5), 279–286 (1970)
28. Renninger, K.A., Hidi, S.E.: The Power of Interest for Motivation and Engagement. Routledge (2015)
29. Hidi, S.: Interest, reading, and learning: theoretical and practical considerations. Educ. Psychol. Rev. **13**(3), 191–209 (2001)
30. Häussler, P., Hoffmann, L.: An intervention study to enhance girls' interest, self-concept, and achievement in physics classes. J. Res. Sci. Teach. **39**(9), 870–888 (2002)
31. Renninger, L.A., Wade, T.J., Grammer, K.: Getting that female glance: patterns and consequences of male nonverbal behavior in courtship contexts. Evol. Hum. Behav. **25**(6), 416–431 (2004)
32. Schraw, G., Dennison, R.S.: Assessing metacognitive awareness. Contemp. Educ. Psychol. **19**(4), 460–475 (1994)
33. Davidson, J.W., Sloboda, J.A., Howe, M.J.: The role of parents and teachers in the success and failure of instrumental learners. Bulletin Council Res. Music Educ. 40–44 (1995)
34. Harackiewicz, J.M., et al.: The role of achievement goals in the development of interest: reciprocal relations between achievement goals, interest, and performance. J. Educ. Psychol. **100**(1), 105 (2008)
35. Perloff, R.M.: The Dynamics of Persuasion: Communication and Attitudes in the Twenty-First Century (2016)
36. Wixom, B.H., Todd, P.A.: A theoretical integration of user satisfaction and technology acceptance. Inf. Syst. Res. **16**(1), 85–102 (2005)
37. LaTour, S.A., Peat, N.C.: Conceptual and methodological issues in consumer satisfaction research. ACR North American Advances, (1979)
38. Bhattacherjee, A.: Understanding information systems continuance: an expectation-confirmation model. MIS quarterly 351–370 (2001)
39. Oliver, R.L.: A cognitive model of the antecedents and consequences of satisfaction decisions. J. Mark. Res. **17**(4), 460–469 (1980)
40. Seddon, P.B.: A respecification and extension of the DeLone and McLean model of IS success. Inf. Syst. Res. **8**(3), 240–253 (1997)
41. Gentle, K.: Children and art teaching. Routledge (1990)
42. Stankiewicz, M.A.: Discipline and the future of art education. Stud. Art Educ. **41**(4), 301–313 (2000)
43. Herne, S.: Art in the Primary School. Policy and Guidelines for the Art National Curriculum. London Borough of Tower Hamlets Inspection and Advisory Services, London (1994)

44. Meager, N.A.: Teaching art at Key Stage 2. Corsham, Wiltshire: National Society for Education in Art&Design. VIsual Impact Publications (1995)
45. Cochran, K.F., DeRuiter, J.A., King, R.A.: Pedagogical content knowing: an integrative model for teacher preparation. J. Teach. Educ. **44**(4), 263–272 (1993)
46. Molloy, J.C., Noe, R.A.: Learning a living: Continuous learning for survival in today's talent market. Learn., Train., Dev. Organ. **333**, 361 (2010)
47. Grant, D.M., Malloy, A.D., Murphy, M.C.: A comparison of student perceptions of their computer skills to their actual abilities. J. Inf. Technol. Educ. Res. **8**(1), 141–160 (2009)
48. Jin, L., et al.: Understanding user behavior in online social networks: a survey. IEEE Commun. Mag. **51**(9), 144–150 (2013)
49. Mohammadi, H.: Investigating users' perspectives on e-learning: an integration of TAM and IS success model. Comput. Hum. Behav. **45**, 359–374 (2015)
50. Dağhan, G., Akkoyunlu, B.: Modeling the continuance usage intention of online learning environments. Comput. Hum. Behav. **60**, 198–211 (2016)
51. Guo, Z., et al.: Promoting online learners' continuance intention: an integrated flow framework. Inf. Manage. **53**(2), 279–295 (2016)
52. Huang, L., Zhang, J., Liu, Y.: Antecedents of student MOOC revisit intention: moderation effect of course difficulty. Int. J. Inf. Manage. **37**(2), 84–91 (2017)
53. Tarhini, A., Hone, K., Liu, X.: A cross-cultural examination of the impact of social, organisational and individual factors on educational technology acceptance between British and Lebanese university students. Br. J. Edu. Technol. **46**(4), 739–755 (2015)
54. Too, T., Noyes, J.: An assessment of the influence of perceived enjoyment and attitude on the intention to use technology among pre-service teachers: a structural equation modeling approach. Comput. Educ. **57**(2), 1645–1653 (2011)
55. Li, Y., et al.: An empirical study on behavioural intention to reuse e-learning systems in rural China. Br. J. Edu. Technol. **43**(6), 933–948 (2012)
56. *Playform:* Available from: https://www.playform.io/
57. Martindale, C.: The Clockwork Muse: The Predictability of Artistic Change. Basic Books (1990)
58. Elgammal, A., et al.: Can: Creative Adversarial Networks, Generating "Art" by Learning about Styles and Deviating from Style Norms. arXiv preprint arXiv:1706.07068 (2017)
59. Setbon, M., Raude, J.: Factors in vaccination intention against the pandemic influenza A/H1N1. Eur. J. Pub. Health **20**(5), 490–494 (2010)
60. Kline, R.B.: Principles and Practice of Structural Equation Modeling. Guilford publications (2015)
61. Al-Refaie, A., Ghnaimat, O., Ko, J.-H.: The effects of quality management practices on customer satisfaction and innovation: a perspective from Jordan. Int. J. Prod. Quality Manage. **8**(4), 398–415 (2011)
62. Cohen, B.H.: Explaining psychological statistics. John Wiley & Sons (2008)
63. Hahs-Vaughn, D.L.: Applied multivariate statistical concepts. Routledge (2016)
64. Dirin, A., Alamäki, A., Suomala, J.: Gender Differences in Perceptions of Conventional Video, Virtual Reality and Augmented Reality. pp. 93-103 (2019)
65. Knogler, M., et al.: How situational is situational interest? investigating the longitudinal structure of situational interest. Contemp. Educ. Psychol. **43**, 39–50 (2015)
66. Linnenbrink-Garcia, L., Patall, E.A., Messersmith, E.E.: Antecedents and consequences of situational interest. Br. J. Educ. Psychol. **83**(4), 591–614 (2013)
67. Tsai, Y.-M., et al.: What makes lessons interesting? the role of situational and individual factors in three school subjects. J. Educ. Psychol. **100**(2), 460 (2008)
68. Ramkissoon, H., Nunkoo, R.: More than just biological sex differences: examining the structural relationship between gender identity and information search behavior. J. Hospitality Tourism Res. **36**(2), 191–215 (2012)

69. Lynott, P.P., McCandless, N.J.: The impact of age vs. life experience on the gender role attitudes of women in different cohorts. J. Women Aging, **12**(1–2), 5-21 (2000)
70. Davis, F.D., Bagozzi, R.P., Warshaw, P.R.: User acceptance of computer technology: a comparison of two theoretical models. Manage. Sci. **35**(8), 982–1003 (1989)
71. Ajzen, I.: The theory of planned behavior. Organ. Behav. Hum. Decis. Process. **50**(2), 179–211 (1991)
72. Park, C., et al.: Adoption of multimedia technology for learning and gender difference. Comput. Hum. Behav. **92**, 288–296 (2019)

Environmental Boundaries and Road Regularity in Virtual Reality: Examining Their Effects on Navigation Performance and Spatial Cognition

Liu Tang[1], Yanling Zuo[2], and Jia Zhou[2(✉)]

[1] Department of Industrial Engineering, Chongqing University, Chongqing, China
[2] School of Management Science and Real Estate, Chongqing University, Chongqing, China
zhoujia07@gmail.com

Abstract. This study investigated how environmental boundaries and road regularity influence people navigating through Virtual Reality (VR) and constructing cognitive maps. Thirty-six younger adults participated in the VR experiment, where they navigated in two different roads (a regular road and an irregular road) on three types of environmental boundaries (no boundary, square boundary, and trapezoidal boundary) to learn virtual environments and locate a reward. The results of the experiment showed that environmental boundaries and participants' spatial ability had significant influences on cognitive map construction. In regular road environments, participants constructed worse cognitive maps when navigating in the trapezoidal boundary than in the square boundary. In addition, the better spatial ability the participants had, the better cognitive map they constructed. These results give insights into researches on how older adults use spatial geometric cues including environmental boundaries and road regularity when navigating.

Keywords: Environmental boundary · Road regularity · Cognitive map · Navigation · Virtual reality

1 Introduction

Head-mounted display virtual reality (VR) applications offer a 3D viewing experience, and many of them, such as game applications and traveling applications, allow users to navigate in immersive environments. Despite the unrivaled experience, a problem has arisen with VR spatial disorientation [1–4]. Users do not acquire spatial knowledge in VR as well as they do in the real world [5–7]. When navigating in the real world, humans adopt visuospatial perception and path integration which is related to physical movement, proprioceptive, and vestibular inputs [8] to obtain navigation information [9, 10]. Various attempts have been made to mimic real-world navigation in terms of the sense of presence [11–13], ways of teleportation [1, 3], and the presentation of landmarks or routes [14, 15]. However, directly transferring spatial navigation in the real world to VR is challenging, because VR changes the interaction between humans and the environment and thus

© The Author(s), under exclusive license to Springer Nature Switzerland AG 2022
Q. Gao and J. Zhou (Eds.): HCII 2022, LNCS 13330, pp. 109–126, 2022.
https://doi.org/10.1007/978-3-031-05581-2_9

the role of navigation information (e.g., vestibular information, [16])and the use of navigation strategies [17, 18]. The dynamic changes during interaction call for an in-depth understanding of spatial cognition to provide a relatively stable stepping stone to intervention.

Neuroscience research on spatial cognition unveils how the brain's GPS works and might throw light on the disorientation problem. The discovery of place cells, grid cells, border cells, and other navigation cells opened up a new era of research in the field of navigation in cognitive and behavioral neurobiology (for a review, see [19]). In these studies, environment boundaries have been shown to affect the firing fields of navigation cells [20–23]. These studies concentrated on how environmental boundaries affected animals' ability to locate targets in the real world, and only a few studies considered how environmental boundaries influence people navigating in a virtual environment. It is possible that environmental boundaries could be a fixed reference frame in egocentric navigation [24]. Participants have better navigation performance in a VR environment with a square boundary than an environment with a trapezoidal boundary, and the dis-tortion of their spatial memory is related to grid cell activity [25]. However, navigation usually involves travel within environments with various boundaries and roads. It is still not clear whether the regularity of roads would influence people's experiences of navi-gating environments with various boundaries. Therefore, this study aims to investigate how environmental boundaries and road regularity affected people navigating in virtual environments.

2   Literature Review

2.1   Effects of Environmental Boundaries on Navigation

Behavior Studies of the Effects of Environmental Boundaries on Navigation.
Environmental boundaries influence how species navigate in environments. Certain species could use environmental boundaries as a visual cue to help them reorient in certain environments, for example, ants could use the panoramic skyline to orient them-selves in deserts [26], and humans could locate a target more accurate when the target was located near environmental boundaries than when the location of the target was far from environmental boundaries [27] and their reorientation performance gradually decreased with the increase of the rotational symmetry of the environmental boundary geometry [28, 29]. Hartley et al. [30] explored the influence of expanding and compress-ing the virtual environment on spatial memory. The results show that the participants tend to maintain a fixed distance from a nearby wall when the environment is expanded, and when the environment is compressed, the participants tend to maintain a fixed pro-portional distance from the wall [30], which indicates that the environmental boundary might be used to help spatial memory. These studies have shown that environmental boundaries have a positive effect on animal navigation in space. However, recent stud-ies have shown that the geometry of environmental boundaries affected people's spatial memory of the location of an object. People located a target in a trapezoidal environ-ment more inaccurately than in a square environment, especially in the more polarized parts [25], which suggested that the polarized geometry of environmental boundaries

might distort cognitive mapping. However, another study showed that participants oriented a target as well in square rooms as in trapezoidal and rectangular rooms [28]. Although both studies were testing people's spatial memory of the target's position, the former required a higher accuracy of the object's position and focused on the offset of the object's position, while in the latter, the participant was given several positions to choose from, which might have led to their different results.

Neural Bases of Navigation Related to Environmental Boundaries. The influence of environmental boundaries on spatial navigation and spatial memory are related to the neural mechanism in the brain. A number of studies showed that environmental boundaries would influence the firing field of place cells, boundary cells, and grid cells. Extending the geometry of environmental boundaries would stretch or split the firing field of place cells in the extended direction [31]. Studies also showed that the hexagonal firing fields of grid cells would be distorted, and the firing field of boundary cells and place cells would be shifted in polarized enclosures [21, 22], which might lead to the inaccurate memory of the locations of objects. However, the environmental boundary has the effect of stabilizing the firing field of the grid cell. Studies have shown that the coding errors of grid cells with regular firing fields will accumulate with the increase of travel time and distance, and the environmental boundary could help correct coding errors [20]. In addition, the closer animals are to the environmental boundary, the more precise the egocentric boundary representation of egocentric boundary cells is, and the firing fields of the egocentric boundary cells were not affected by the environmental boundary's visual appearance, a change in the size of the environment, and the rotation of boundaries [24]. Neural activity related to the boundary distance has also been found in the human subiculum [27].

2.2 Road regularity's Effect on Navigation

In a new environment, people first learn about distinguishable landmarks; then, they connect different landmarks to form a route and finally construct a cognitive map of the environment in their minds [32, 33]. Navigators could acquire information about the location and route after visiting them. Road patterns affect people's navigation and wayfinding. The complexity of straight roads was considered to be lower than that of curved roads, and participants tend to select straight roads to minimize complexity during navigation [34–36]. However, if only the aesthetics are considered, participants preferred curved roads to straight roads [37]. Additionally, the type of irregular road could provide navigation clues for navigators. A study suggested that participants spent more time processing information and paid more attention when they navigated on irregular roads, rather than on regular roads, during the orientation and shorter route selection tasks [38].

Thus, in this study, our hypotheses are as follows:

1. Participants have higher spatial navigation performance in regular road environments compared to irregular road environments, and they have more difficulty in generating a cognitive map in irregular road environments than in regular road environments.

2. Participants have better spatial navigation performance in a trapezoidal environment than in no boundary and square boundary environments, but they could generate better cognitive maps more easily in the square and no boundary environments than in the trapezoidal boundary environments.

3 Materials and Methods

3.1 Tasks

The tasks were based on research involving the virtual Morris Water Maze (vMWM), which required subjects to repetitively learn an environment and was widely used to test participants' spatial memory and ability to construct a cognitive map [39, 40]. In our experiment, participants wore a VR helmet and used a gamepad to navigate in virtual environments and were asked to quickly and precisely locate a hidden reward. When the reward was found, participants had 15 s to observe the surrounding environment. Six trials were conducted in this experiment. In each of the trials, the location of the reward was fixed, while the location of the starting point changed. After six trials, participants needed to draw an overview map of the virtual environment they navigated.

3.2 Variables

In this study, we conducted a mixed factorial experiment. The independent variables were environmental boundaries (the between-subject factor) and road regularity (the within-subject factor), as shown in Table 1. Environmental boundaries had three levels: no boundary, square boundary, and trapezoidal boundary. Road regularity had two levels: regular road and irregular road. A regular road was defined as a road with orthogonal intersections and linear shapes, and an irregular road was defined as a road with non-orthogonal intersections and curves [38].

The dependent variables were reciprocal speed and cognitive map construction. Since the total lengths between the regular road and irregular road conditions varied in the virtual environment, we used the reciprocal speed which was calculated by taking the total time (the sum of the times of the six learning trials) divided by the road's total length as the dependent variable, (see Eq. (1)). We divided the road net into 10 roads (see Fig. 1). The accuracy of cognitive map construction was calculated by the following criteria: (1) If both the placement of the road relative to the reward and the shape of the road were correct, add 1 point; otherwise, add 0 points. (2) If the participants draw an extra road, 1 point will be deducted. The maximum score is 10 points.

$$reciprocal\ speed\ =\ total\ time/road\ length \tag{1}$$

Since spatial ability and spatial memory might affect participants' performance, spatial ability and spatial memory were included as covariates. Computer experience which was the experience of participants in using VR, using gamepads, and playing 3D games was also included as a covariate.

Table 1. Design of the experiment

Environmental boundaries	Road regularity	
	Regular road	Irregular road
No boundary	P1-P12	P1-P12
Square boundary	P13-P24	P13-P24
Trapezoidal boundary	P25-P36	P25-P36

Note: P represents participant

3.3 Participants

Thirty-six participants (M = 23.64, SD = 1.175, ages ranged from 20 to 26) who came from Chongqing University were recruited. Sex was counterbalanced in this experiment. Volunteers who had nausea and dizziness were excluded from this study.

3.4 Procedure

The experiment was conducted on two consecutive days. On the first day, the experiment required approximately 60 min. First, participants needed to complete a background information questionnaire, and then, their spatial memory and spatial ability were tested. Second, participants practiced in a smaller virtual environment that was similar to formal environments to familiarize themselves with the VR environment and the use of the gamepad, and to allow us to exclude participants who had 3D vertigo. Third, participants began the formal experiment of learning the environment and locating the reward six times. Participants stood up during the experiment. During the experiment, we recorded the time participants spent on each trial. Participants were allowed to take a break every three trials. After six trials, participants needed to draw an overview map of the environment. The next day, participants did the second experiment, which required approximately 40 min. Participants did six trials in which the environment was different from the previous experiment. After six trials, they drew a sketch map of the environment that they learned. Finally, we recorded the amount of time participants used the gamepad to navigate on a road in the virtual environment, in order to test how participants used gamepads.

3.5 Apparatus

Software. Six prototypes (i.e., two levels of road regularity × three levels of environmental boundaries) were designed in this study, as presented in Fig. 1. We used Unity 3D to develop VR environments. The area of the square enclosure was the same as that of the trapezoid enclosure. The number of intersections was the same between regular road environments and irregular road environments. There was a reward, which was hidden, and it was always in the same place in the virtual environment. When the participants were close to the reward, the reward was visible. An example of experimental virtual environment is shown in Fig. 2(a, b).

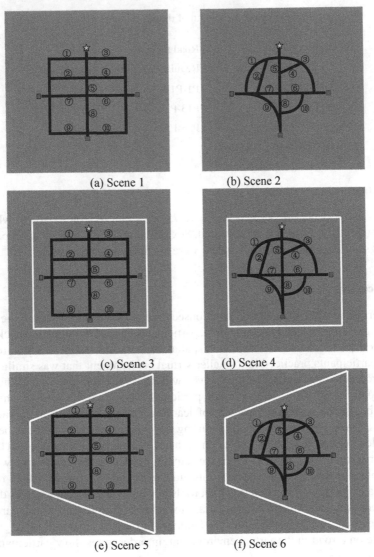

(a) Scene 1   (b) Scene 2

(c) Scene 3   (d) Scene 4

(e) Scene 5   (f) Scene 6

Fig. 1. The star symbol represents the reward. The white lines are the environmental boundaries and the black lines are roads. The prototypes in this experiment: (a) Scene 1 (S1)—no boundary and irregular roads environment; (b) Scene 2 (S2) —no boundary and regular roads environment; (c) Scene 3 (S3) —square boundary and irregular roads environment; (d) Scene 4 (S4) —square boundary and regular roads environment; (e) Scene 5 (S5) —trapezoidal boundary and irregular roads environment; (f) Scene 6 (S6) —trapezoidal boundary and regular roads environment.

Equipment. This experiment was conducted in the HCI Lab of Chongqing University. A paper folding test was used to test participants' spatial ability [41]. In the paper folding test, participants were asked to imagine the folding and unfolding of pieces of paper. The test included two parts. Participants were given 3 min to complete each part of the test. Spatial memory was tested by the KJ-I spatial location memory span tester which had 16 (4 x 4) buttons with LEDs. Participants needed to correctly remember the order in which 2–7 buttons randomly lit up. Then, they were required to press the buttons according to the order in which buttons were illuminated. The step was repeated, and the number of lit buttons increased. A higher score meant that a participant had better spatial memory. We used HTC Vive (consumer version), which had a head-mounted display (HMD), two single-hand gamepads, and a positioning system (lighthouse) that tracks both the monitor and the controller in space, to run the VR software. HTC Vive had an effective resolution of 1200 x 1080 for one eye, a combined resolution of 2160 x 1200 for both eyes, and a refresh rate of 90 Hz. The experimental scenario is shown in Fig. 2(b).

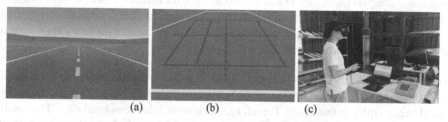

(a)   (b)   (c)

Fig. 2. (a) One virtual environment in which participants navigated with first-person vision; (b) a top view of one virtual environment; (c) participants navigating in the virtual environment.

4 Results

4.1 Background Information

The demographic information of the participants is shown in Table 2. The spatial ability of the participants ranged from 9 to 20 (M = 15.22, SD = 2.674). The spatial memory of the participants was in the range from 3.66 to 5.00 (M = 4.496, SD = 0.36). Three of the participants reported they had mild vertigo in the later stage of the experiments.

Table 2. Demographic information

Variable	Category	num	%
Education	Bachelor's	2	5.6%
	Master's	34	94.4%
Experience using VR	With	20	55.6%
	Without	16	44.4%

(continued)

Table 2. (*continued*)

Variable	Category	num	%
Experience using gamepad	With	19	52.8%
	Without	17	47.2%
Experience playing 3D games	With	29	80.6%
	Without	7	19.4%

4.2 Performance

Covariance analysis (ANCONA) was used to analyze the effects of independent variables (environmental boundaries and road regularity) on the reciprocal speed and construction of a cognitive map. The spatial ability, spatial memory, and computer experience of participants were included in the analysis model.

Reciprocal Speed. Except for one participant who had been navigating in an environment for too long and could not locate the reward, all other participants could locate the reward successfully in this study. Therefore, we removed this abnormal data. The results of the covariance analysis showed that environmental boundaries and road regularity had no significant effect on the reciprocal speed. Spatial ability, spatial memory, and the computer experience of participants also had no significant effect on the reciprocal speed. There was a learning effect in this experiment (see Fig. 3). We observed that in trials 1–3, participants randomly searched for the reward while observing their surroundings and remembering the shapes of roads. After getting familiar with the environment, in trials 4–6, most of the participants were able to locate the position of the reward according to the environmental boundaries and road shapes.

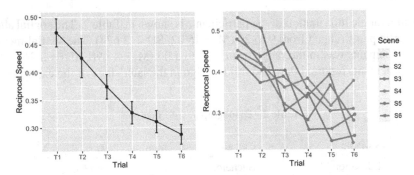

Fig. 3. Participants learned the environment in six trials.

Cognitive Map Construction. In this study, we invited two other experts on human-computer interaction to grade the sketch maps of the participants and calculated the consistency of the scores. Kendall's coefficient of concordance (W) was used to analyze the consistency. Kendall's W coefficient was equal to 0.957, which indicated that there was a high level of consistency in grading the cognitive map scores and that the data were reliable.

Accuracy of cognitive map construction. The data were analyzed by using ANCONA and Turkey's HSD. The covariates were spatial ability, spatial memory, and computer experience. The results have shown that environmental boundaries had a significant main effect on the accuracy of cognitive map construction ($F(2, 62) = 5.4786$, $p < 0.01$, partial $\eta2 = 0.16$), and there were significantly different performances between square boundaries and trapezoidal boundaries in regular road environments (diff = -2.88, $p < 0.01$), as shown in Fig. 4(a). Spatial ability had a significant effect on the accuracy of cognitive map construction ($F(1, 62) = 7.5157$, $p < 0.01$, $r = 0.35$). We divided the spatial ability into two levels (low and high) by using the median of the tested scores of the spatial ability. The results showed that participants with higher spatial ability drew more accurate cognitive maps than those with lower spatial ability ($F(1, 69) = 5.519$, $p < 0.05$), as shown in Fig. 4(b).

List of Drawing Errors on Sketch Maps. We checked participants' sketch maps and found that 66.2% of sketch maps were drawn well (the cognitive map construction score is 8–10 points), 23.9% of sketch maps were medium (the cognitive map construction score is 5–7 points), and 0.1% of sketch maps were bad (the cognitive map construction score is 0–4 points). In order to analyze the factors that make it difficult for participants to construct cognitive maps, we counted the reasons for the errors in drawing sketch maps from four aspects: the shape of the road drawn by the participant is incorrect, extra roads are drawn, the roads drawn are in incorrect locations, or there are missing or incomplete roads on the map. In the collected sketch maps, 21 (29.6%) of sketch maps were completely consistent with the environments. In incorrect sketch maps, 29 (40.8%) of sketch maps had incomplete roads or missing roads, 27 (38%) of sketch maps had incorrect road shapes, 8 (11.3%) of sketch maps had some roads that were incorrectly positioned relative to the reward, and 4 (5.6%) of sketch maps had extra roads. The frequency of errors per participant was computed from the total frequency divided by the number of participants who made a unique error in a sketch map (as shown in Table 3). In addition, because there was a significant difference between the trapezoidal boundary and the square boundary on the accuracy of cognitive map construction in regular road environments, we counted the frequency of the four types of errors under different environmental boundary conditions in the regular road environment (as shown in Table 4).

Environmental boundary effects. In this study, we found that participants seldom noticed environmental boundaries. The statistics data showed that only 10 (41.7%) participants who navigated in the square and trapezoidal boundary environment (24 participants) drew 16 environmental boundaries (34%) in their sketch maps, as shown in Fig. 5(a, b). Additionally, only 5 participants drew 6 correct environmental boundary shapes (37.5%) in the square and trapezoidal boundary condition experiments. In the trapezoidal environment, participants drew the environmental boundary into other shapes, such as a square and a non-isosceles trapezoid, as shown in Fig. 6. After the experiment, we interviewed participants. Participants said that they seldom pay attention to the environmental boundaries or said that they thought the shape of the environmental boundary was square, which could not help them navigate, so they did not use the environmental boundary to locate the reward. Instead of taking the environmental boundary as a whole, some participants (5 participants) located the reward based on the far one side of the environmental boundary (the trapezoidal side) from the end of the road.

We analyzed the data to discover whether drawing environmental boundaries could help people navigate in environments. The results showed that participants who drew environmental boundaries took significantly less time than participants who did not draw environmental boundaries $(F(1, 45) = 5.4082, p < 0.05)$, and the time to locate the reward was reduced by 15.2%, as shown in Fig. 4(c). However, there was no difference in the accuracy of cognitive map construction. We also explored whether the correctness of the environmental boundary drawn by the participants would affect their performance. The results showed there was no significant effect of the correctness of environmental boundary shape on the time they spent to locate the reward and the construction of the cognitive map.

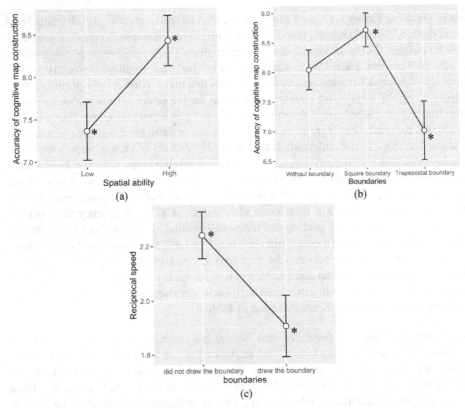

Fig. 4. (a) The main effects of environmental boundaries on cognitive map construction; (b) the effect of spatial ability on cognitive map construction;(c) the effectiveness of drawing an environmental boundary based on the reciprocal speed.

Table 3. List of drawing errors on sketch maps with different environmental boundaries

Environmental boundaries	Incorrect shape		Incorrect position		Drew extra roads		Missing or incomplete roads		Total	
	T.Num (P.Num)	Ave	T.Num (P.Num)	Ave	T.Num (P.Num)	Ave	T.Num (P.Num)	Ave	T.Num (P.Num)	Ave
No boundary	18 (11)	1.64	5 (3)	1.67	0	0	18 (10)	1.8	41 (24)	1.71
Square boundary	9 (7)	1.29	3 (2)	1.5	4 (2)	2	13 (9)	1.44	29 (20)	1.45
Trapezoidal boundary	18 (9)	2	4 (3)	1.33	4 (2)	2	43 (11)	3.91	69 (25)	2.76
Total	45 (27)	1.67	12 (8)	1.5	8 (4)	2	74 (29)	2.55	139 (69)	2.01

Table 4. List of drawing errors on sketch maps with regular road environments

Environmental boundaries	Incorrect shape		Incorrect position		Drew extra roads		Missing or incomplete roads		Total	
	T.Num (P.Num)	Ave	T.Num (P.Num)	Ave	T.Num (P.Num)	Ave	T.Num (P.Num)	Ave	T.Num (P.Num)	Ave
No boundary	4 (1)	4	2 (1)	2	0	0	9 (5)	1.8	15 (7)	2.14
Square boundary	0	0	2 (1)	2	2 (1)	2	4 (2)	2	8 (4)	2
Trapezoidal boundary	8 (3)	2.67	0	0	2 (1)	2	29 (6)	4.83	39 (10)	3.9
Total	12 (4)	3	4 (2)	2	4 (2)	2	42 (13)	3.23	62 (21)	2.95

Note: T.Num: Total number; P.Num: number of participants; Ave: average number

Relationship between accuracy of cognitive map construction and reciprocal speed.
We did a linear regression analysis to verify whether the time spent in the environment would affect the construction of cognitive maps. The results showed that there was no significant influence of total time on the construction of cognitive maps ($t = -0.574$, $p = 0.568$).

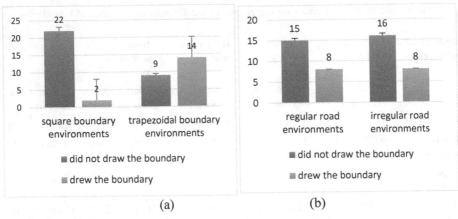

Fig. 5. (a) The number of participants who drew the environmental boundary and did not draw the environmental boundary on their sketch map in square boundary environments and trapezoidal boundary environments, respectively; (b) the number of participants who drew the environmental boundary and did not draw the environmental boundary on their sketch map in regular road environments and irregular road environments, respectively.

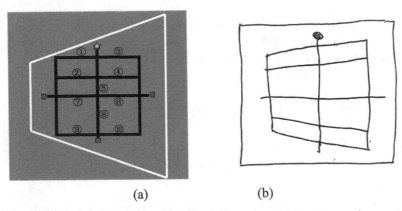

Fig. 6. (a) The overview map of the regular road with trapezoidal boundary environment, where the environmental boundary shape is isosceles trapezoid. (b) The cognitive map perceived by participant 27, who navigated in the regular road conditions with a trapezoidal boundary environment. In (b), the participant perceived the environmental boundary shape as a square shape, and roads ①,②,③,④,⑨,⑩ were distorted according to the environmental boundary shape.

5   Discussion

Environmental boundaries and participants' spatial ability affected their performance in constructing cognitive maps. Adding an environmental boundary is not necessarily helpful for navigation, but it is useful for spatial cognition; participants constructed more accurate cognitive maps and had fewer drawing errors in their sketch maps in square boundary environments than in no boundary environments. However, the effects were influenced by the geometry of the environmental boundaries. Participants constructed worse cognitive maps and had more errors in their sketch maps while navigating in trapezoidal environments with regular roads than in square boundary and no boundary environments, which might indicate that participants in the regular road environment had a better spatial cognition of the roads in the square boundary environment than in the trapezoidal boundary environment. One possible reason might be that participants had to remember roads to locate the reward in the regular road environments with the square boundary, where there were fewer cues to help participants determine the direction of the reward. However, in the trapezoidal boundary environment, participants could rely on the geometry of the environmental boundary for orientation, so that they did not have to deliberately remember all roads. Our data also shows that 60.9% of participants who navigated in the trapezoidal boundary environment drew the environmental boundary in their sketch maps, while only 8.3% of participants who navigated in the square boundary environment drew the environmental boundary in their sketch maps, as shown in Fig. 5(a).

The shape of the environmental boundaries did not affect the navigation time needed to locate the reward, while other studies indicated that mobile animals (such as rats, birds, fishes) tended to use the geometry of environmental boundaries to help them navigate [29, 42]. We thought that the result might be related to the perception of the environmental boundary. Participants seldom noticed the environmental boundary during the experiment and had difficulty perceiving the shape of environmental boundaries. There are three reasons that might account for these results. First, participants did not have good recall of environmental boundaries, because there were no other cues (such as different colors) on environmental boundaries. Second, the color of the environmental boundaries was similar to the sky color, which might cause the environmental boundaries to be less noticeable. In addition, because all sides of the environmental boundary were a blue color, geometric edges and corners were not salient in square and trapezoidal boundaries, which might make it difficult for participants to distinguish the geometric shapes of the environmental boundary. The third reason is that possibly the scale of the environment was too large for the participants to notice the boundaries. Studies have shown that in large enclosures, participants rely more on feature information than geometric information [43, 44]. Possibly, the walls were too long for participants to see the entire wall, and thus, they had difficulty perceiving the geometry of the environmental boundary. Two participants in our study said they only noticed on the side of the environmental boundary around the reward and took it as a cue to locate the position of the reward.

In this study, road regularity did not influence the time that took for participants to locate the reward and construct a cognitive map. This might be because there were not too many landmark cues, which made it was easier for the participants to find the corresponding geometric clues to help them locate the reward.

This study gives insights into researches on how older adults use spatial geometric cues including environmental boundaries and road regularity when navigating. In previous studies, landmark cues, rather than geometric cues, were generally considered to be the most helpful environmental factors for older adults to navigate [45–47]. This was mainly because aging led to processing defects of spatial and self-localization representations in the entorhinal cortex [48] and hippocampus [49–51]. Thus, the transformation of spatial information processing structure from hippocampus to caudate nucleus during aging was promoted [52]. However, some researchers suggested that geometric cues were the key cues older adults use to self-orient and navigate in environments. A recent study found that when geometric cues were conflict with landmark cues, older adults relied more on geometric cues to locate the target objects [53]. Besides, when older adults were trained to locate objects, they learned to integrate geometric cues around the object, rather than landmarks [54]. According to the above researches, how older adults use the geometric cues in the environment when navigating is still not clear. Therefore, subsequent studies should be considered to focus on the geometric environmental cues used by older adults. Since spatial ability declines with age [55], reciprocal of speed and accuracy of cognitive map construction could be inferred to get worse with age.

Furthermore, older adults' use of geometric cues in space may be affected by the size of environments. A screen-based virtual reality study showed that older adults had difficulty in redirecting using marker cues [56]. Conversely, another study based on virtual reality found that older participants were hindered in learning the location of objects using environmental boundaries, that is, they had difficulty navigating using geometric cues [57]. It should be noted that the former study conducted experiments at a room scale, while the latter study at a larger spatial scale. Therefore, subsequent studies on older adults should be considered to include the independent variable of environmental scale.

There are several limitations that should be noted. One limitation of our study is that the irregular road environments included regular roads, which might cause participants to select linear roads rather than curvy roads for orientation [58]. Second, the height and color of the environmental boundaries are fixed, and they are not taken into consideration in the experiment. Third, in the experiment, participants were standing up without walking, which was different from navigating in a real environment, where animals could rely on locomotion and accompanying activation to orient and navigate [8, 16]. In addition, we only tested one type of trapezoidal boundary. In the future, more geometric shapes of environmental boundaries need to be tested.

6 Conclusions

In this study, we examined how environmental boundaries and road regularity influenced people navigating in a virtual environment and constructing a cognitive map. With respect to navigation performance, we found that environmental boundaries and road regularity did not influence the time participants took to locate the reward, but there was a learning effect: as the number of trials the participants navigated in the virtual environment increases, the time for them to find the reward decreases. For cognitive construction, the results showed that when participants navigated in trapezoidal boundary environments, they constructed worse cognitive maps and made more errors, i.e., not being able to recall the roads, than when they navigated in no boundary and square boundary environments. What is more, we also found that participants seldom noticed the environmental boundary, but participants who drew environmental boundaries in their sketch maps took significantly less time than participants who did not draw environmental boundaries. However, participants could not correctly perceive the shape of the environmental boundary; that is, some participants drew the environmental boundary in an incorrect shape.

References

1. Bhandari, J., MacNeilage, P., Folmer, E.: Teleportation without spatial disorientation using optical flow cues. Presented at the, Toronto, Ontario, Canada (2018). https://doi.org/10.20380/gi2018.22

2. Forte, J.L.B., Vela, F.L.G., Rodríguez, P.P.: User experience problems in immersive virtual environments. Presented at the, Donostia Gipuzkoa Spain June 25 (2019). https://doi.org/10.1145/3335595.3336288

3. Sayyad, E., Sra, M., Hollerer, T.: Walking and teleportation in wide-area virtual reality experiences. Presented at the , Recife/Porto de Galinhas November (2020). https://doi.org/10.1109/ISMAR50242.2020.00088

4. Wallet, G., Sauzéon, H., Pala, P.A., Larrue, F., Zheng, X., N'Kaoua, B.: Virtual/real transfer of spatial knowledge: benefit from visual fidelity provided in a virtual environment and impact of active navigation. Cyberpsychol. Behav. Soc. Netw. **14**, 417–423 (2011). https://doi.org/10.1089/cyber.2009.0187

5. Richardson, A.E., Powers, M.E., Bousquet, L.G.: Video game experience predicts virtual, but not real navigation performance. Comput. Hum. Behav. **27**, 552–560 (2011). https://doi.org/10.1016/j.chb.2010.10.003

6. Richardson, A.E., Montello, D.R., Hegarty, M.: Spatial knowledge acquisition from maps and from navigation in real and virtual environments. Mem. Cognit. **27**, 741–750 (1999). https://doi.org/10.3758/BF03211566

7. Waller, D., Hunt, E., Knapp, D.: The transfer of spatial knowledge in virtual environment training. Presence: Teleoperators Virtual Environ. **7**(2), 129-143 (1998). https://doi.org/10.1162/105474698565631

8. Taube, J.S., Valerio, S., Yoder, R.M.: Is navigation in virtual reality with fMRI really navigation? J. Cogn. Neurosci. **25**, 1008–1019 (2013). https://doi.org/10.1162/jocn_a_00386

9. Ekstrom, A.D.: Why vision is important to how we navigate: human spatial navigation and vision. Hippocampus **25**, 731–735 (2015). https://doi.org/10.1002/hipo.22449

10. Ekstrom, A.D., Spiers, H.J., Bohbot, V.D., Rosenbaum, R.S.: Human Spatial Navigation. Princeton University Press (2018)

11. Lorenz, M., Busch, M., Rentzos, L., Tscheligi, M., Klimant, P., Frohlich, P.: I'm There! The influence of virtual reality and mixed reality environments combined with two different navigation methods on presence. Presented at the , Arles, Camargue, Provence, France 2015–3 (2015). https://doi.org/10.1109/VR.2015.7223376

12. Clemente, M., Rodríguez, A., Rey, B., Alcañiz, M.: Assessment of the influence of navigation control and screen size on the sense of presence in virtual reality using EEG. Expert Syst. Appl. **41**, 1584–1592 (2014). https://doi.org/10.1016/j.eswa.2013.08.055

13. Brade, J., Lorenz, M., Busch, M., Hammer, N., Tscheligi, M., Klimant, P.: Being there again – presence in real and virtual environments and its relation to usability and user experience using a mobile navigation task. Int. J. Hum Comput Stud. **101**, 76–87 (2017). https://doi.org/10.1016/j.ijhcs.2017.01.004

14. Cliburn, D., Winlock, T., Rilea, S., Van Donsel, M.: Dynamic landmark placement as a navigation aid in virtual worlds. Presented at the , Newport Beach, California (2007). https://doi.org/10.1145/1315184.1315225

15. Ruddle, R.A.: The effect of trails on first-time and subsequent navigation in a virtual environment. Presented at the , Bonn, Germany (2005). https://doi.org/10.1109/VR.2005.1492761

16. Chrastil, E.R., Warren, W.H.: Active and passive spatial learning in human navigation: acquisition of survey knowledge. J. Exp. Psychol. Learn. Mem. Cogn. **39**, 1520–1537 (2013). https://doi.org/10.1037/a0032382

17. Fabroyir, H., Teng, W.-C.: Navigation in virtual environments using head-mounted displays: Allocentric vs. egocentric behaviors. Comput. Human Behav. **80**, 331-343 (2018). https://doi.org/10.1016/j.chb.2017.11.033

18. Walkowiak, S., Foulsham, T., Eardley, A.F.: Individual differences and personality correlates of navigational performance in the virtual route learning task. Comput. Hum. Behav. **45**, 402–410 (2015). https://doi.org/10.1016/j.chb.2014.12.041

19. Moser, E.I., Moser, M.-B., McNaughton, B.L.: Spatial representation in the hippocampal formation: a history. Nat. Neurosci. **20**, 1448–1464 (2017). https://doi.org/10.1038/nn.4653

20. Hardcastle, K., Ganguli, S., Giocomo, L.M.: Environmental boundaries as an error correction mechanism for grid cells. Neuron **86**, 827–839 (2015). https://doi.org/10.1016/j.neuron.2015.03.039

21. Krupic, J., Bauza, M., Burton, S., Barry, C., O'Keefe, J.: Grid cell symmetry is shaped by environmental geometry. Nature **518**, 232–235 (2015). https://doi.org/10.1038/nature14153

22. Krupic, J., Bauza, M., Burton, S., O'Keefe, J.: Local transformations of the hippocampal cognitive map. Science **359**, 1143–1146 (2018). https://doi.org/10.1126/science.aao4960

23. Keinath, A.T., Epstein, R.A., Balasubramanian, V.: Environmental deformations dynamically shift the grid cell spatial metric. eLife. **7**, e38169 (2018). https://doi.org/10.7554/eLife.38169

24. Hinman, J.R., Chapman, G.W., Hasselmo, M.E.: Neuronal representation of environmental boundaries in egocentric coordinates. Nat Commun. **10**, 2772 (2019). https://doi.org/10.1038/s41467-019-10722-y

25. Bellmund, J.L.S., de Cothi, W., Ruiter, T.A., Nau, M., Barry, C., Doeller, C.F.: Deforming the metric of cognitive maps distorts memory. Nat Hum Behav. **4**, 177–188 (2020). https://doi.org/10.1038/s41562-019-0767-3

26. Graham, P., Cheng, K.: Ants use the panoramic skyline as a visual cue during navigation. Curr. Biol. **19**, R935–R937 (2009). https://doi.org/10.1016/j.cub.2009.08.015

27. Lee, S.A., et al.: Electrophysiological signatures of spatial boundaries in the human subiculum. J. Neurosci. **38**, 3265–3272 (2018). https://doi.org/10.1523/JNEUROSCI.3216-17.2018

28. Kelly, J.W., McNamara, T.P., Bodenheimer, B., Carr, T.H., Rieser, J.J.: The shape of human navigation: How environmental geometry is used in maintenance of spatial orientation. Cognition **109**, 281–286 (2008). https://doi.org/10.1016/j.cognition.2008.09.001

29. Cheng, K., Newcombe, N.S.: Is there a geometric module for spatial orientation? squaring theory and evidence. Psychon. Bull. Rev. **12**, 1–23 (2005). https://doi.org/10.3758/BF03196346

30. Hartley, T., Trinkler, I., Burgess, N.: Geometric determinants of human spatial memory. Cognition **94**, 39–75 (2004). https://doi.org/10.1016/j.cognition.2003.12.001

31. O'Keefe, J., Burgess, N.: Geometric determinants of the place fields of hippocampal neurons. Nature **381**(6581), 425–428 (1996). https://doi.org/10.1038/381425a0

32. Sjölinder, M., Höök, K., Nilsson, L.-G., Andersson, G.: Age differences and the acquisition of spatial knowledge in a three-dimensional environment: evaluating the use of an overview map as a navigation aid. Int. J. Hum Comput Stud. **63**, 537–564 (2005). https://doi.org/10.1016/j.ijhcs.2005.04.024

33. Siegel, A.W., White, S.H.: The development of spatial representations of large-scale environments. In: Advances in Child Development and Behavior, pp. 9–55. Elsevier (1975)

34. Dalton, R.C.: The secret is to follow your nose: route path selection and angularity. Environ. Behav. **35**, 107–131 (2003). https://doi.org/10.1177/0013916502238867

35. Zacharias, J.: Pedestrian behavior and perception in urban walking environments. J. Plan. Lit. **16**, 3–18 (2001). https://doi.org/10.1177/08854120122093249

36. Sadalla, E.K., Montello, D.R.: Remembering changes in direction. Environ. Behav. **21**, 346–363 (1989). https://doi.org/10.1177/0013916589213006
37. D'Acci, L.: Aesthetical cognitive perceptions of urban street form. Pedestrian preferences towards straight or curvy route shapes. J. Urban Des. **24**(6), 896–912 (2019). https://doi.org/10.1080/13574809.2018.1554994
38. Liu, B., Dong, W., Zhan, Z., Wang, S., Meng, L.: Differences in the gaze behaviours of pedestrians navigating between regular and irregular road patterns. ISPRS Int. J. Geo Inf. **9**, 45 (2020). https://doi.org/10.3390/ijgi9010045
39. Moffat, S.D., Zonderman, A.B., Resnick, S.M.: Age differences in spatial memory in a virtual environment navigation task. Neurobiol. Aging **22**, 787–796 (2001). https://doi.org/10.1016/S0197-4580(01)00251-2
40. Moffat, S.D., Resnick, S.M.: Effects of age on virtual environment place navigation and allocentric cognitive mapping. Behav. Neurosci. **116**, 851–859 (2002). https://doi.org/10.1037//0735-7044.116.5.851
41. Ekstrom, R.B., French, J.W., Harman, H.H.: Kit of factor-referenced cognitive tests. Presented at the (1976)
42. Lee, S.A., Spelke, E.S.: Two systems of spatial representation underlying navigation. Exp. Brain Res. **206**, 179–188 (2010). https://doi.org/10.1007/s00221-010-2349-5
43. Sturz, B.R., Forloines, M.R., Bodily, K.D.: Enclosure size and the use of local and global geometric cues for reorientation. Psychon. Bull. Rev. **19**, 270–276 (2012). https://doi.org/10.3758/s13423-011-0195-5
44. Miller, N.: Modeling the effects of enclosure size on geometry learning. Behav. Proc. **80**, 306–313 (2009). https://doi.org/10.1016/j.beproc.2008.12.011
45. Anacta, V.J.A., Schwering, A., Li, R., Muenzer, S.: Orientation information in wayfinding instructions: evidences from human verbal and visual instructions. GeoJournal **82**(3), 567–583 (2016). https://doi.org/10.1007/s10708-016-9703-5
46. Goodman, J., Gray, P., Khammampad, K., Brewster, S.: Using landmarks to support older people in navigation. In: Brewster, S., Dunlop, M. (eds.) Mobile HCI 2004. LNCS, vol. 3160, pp. 38–48. Springer, Heidelberg (2004). https://doi.org/10.1007/978-3-540-28637-0_4
47. Goodman-Deane, J., Brewster, S., Gray, P.: How can we best use landmarks to support older people in navigation? Behav. Inf. Technol. (2005). https://doi.org/10.1080/01449290512331319021
48. Stangl, M., Achtzehn, J., Huber, K., Dietrich, C., Tempelmann, C., Wolbers, T.: Compromised grid-cell-like representations in old age as a key mechanism to explain age-related navigational deficits. Curr. Biol. **28**, 1108-1115.e6 (2018). https://doi.org/10.1016/j.cub.2018.02.038
49. Lithfous, S., Dufour, A., Després, O.: Spatial navigation in normal aging and the prodromal stage of Alzheimer's disease: insights from imaging and behavioral studies. Ageing Res. Rev. **12**, 201–213 (2013). https://doi.org/10.1016/j.arr.2012.04.007
50. Moffat, S.D., Elkins, W., Resnick, S.M.: Age differences in the neural systems supporting human allocentric spatial navigation. Neurobiol. Aging **27**, 965–972 (2006). https://doi.org/10.1016/j.neurobiolaging.2005.05.011
51. Yassa, M.A., Mattfeld, A.T., Stark, S.M., Stark, C.E.L.: Age-related memory deficits linked to circuit-specific disruptions in the hippocampus. Proc. Natl. Acad. Sci. U.S.A. **108**, 8873–8878 (2011). https://doi.org/10.1073/pnas.1101567108
52. Konishi, K., Etchamendy, N., Roy, S., Marighetto, A., Rajah, N., Bohbot, V.D.: Decreased functional magnetic resonance imaging activity in the hippocampus in favor of the caudate nucleus in older adults tested in a virtual navigation task. Hippocampus **23**, 1005–1014 (2013). https://doi.org/10.1002/hipo.22181
53. Bécu, M., et al.: Age-related preference for geometric spatial cues during real-world navigation. Nat Hum Behav. **4**, 88–99 (2020). https://doi.org/10.1038/s41562-019-0718-z

54. Kimura, K., Moussavi, Z.: Do older and young adults learn to integrate geometry while navigating in an environment of a serious game? J Exp Neurosci. **16**, 263310552098886 (2021). https://doi.org/10.1177/2633105520988861
55. Iaria, G., Palermo, L., Committeri, G., Barton, J.J.S.: Age differences in the formation and use of cognitive maps. Behav. Brain Res. **196**, 187–191 (2009). https://doi.org/10.1016/j.bbr.2008.08.040
56. Picucci, L., Caffo, A.O., Bosco, A.: Age and sex differences in a virtual version of the reorientation task. Cogn. Process. **10**, 272–275 (2009). https://doi.org/10.1007/s10339-009-0321-8
57. Schuck, N.W., Doeller, C.F., Polk, T.A., Lindenberger, U., Li, S.-C.: Human aging alters the neural computation and representation of space. Neuroimage **117**, 141–150 (2015). https://doi.org/10.1016/j.neuroimage.2015.05.031
58. Ishikawa, T., Fujiwara, H., Imai, O., Okabe, A.: Wayfinding with a GPS-based mobile navigation system: a comparison with maps and direct experience. J. Environ. Psychol. **28**, 74–82 (2008). https://doi.org/10.1016/j.jenvp.2007.09.002

A Pilot Study on Synesthesia Between Color Senses and Musical Scales in Chinese Musical Instrument "Guqin"

Cheng-Min Tsai[1]([✉]), Ya-Ting Chang[2], and Wang-Chin Tsai[3]

[1] Department of Visual Arts and Design, Nanhua University, Chiayi, Taiwan, R.O.C.
ansel.tsai@gmail.com
[2] Department of Ethnomusicology, Nanhua University, Chiayi, Taiwan, R.O.C.
[3] Department of Creative Design, National Yunlin University of Science and Technology, Yunlin, Taiwan, R.O.C.

Abstract. This study aims to understand the synesthesia phenomenon between color senses and different musical scales of the Chinese musical instrument "Guqin", the research method is a quasi-experiment design method. Twenty-one observers were invited to join the assessment of the experiment in synesthesia between the color and musical scales of Guqin by using convenient sampling. Three tasks should be finished on each observer. These include increasing the lightness task, decreasing the lightness task, and selecting the target color when hearing the eight musical scales of Guqin.

This study analyzes the difference between the observers who have music training backgrounds or do not, using the independent-sample T-test. It is also to understand the synesthesia between the musical scales of Guqin and the lightness/color. The study results show no significant difference between music and arts backgrounds observers in the lightness adjustment task. Result also shows a positive correlation between lightness and musical scales. The saturation of color is no significant correlation with musical scales, the pilot study figures out the robust results, which provide the next stage in experiment design.

Keywords: Color synesthesia · Lightness · Saturation · Music scales of Guqin

1 Introduction

Based on Tsai's research points, the high-level's information processing should be considered the "semantic understanding" in the information process system (IPS) and the "task-oriented" in the cognition processing system (CPS) for visual assessment tasks (Tsai et al. 2018). Synesthesia has related two senses and a high-level process in humans' cognitive activity. Lynn Kaye Goode (2010) points out that synesthesia is a peculiar neurological phenomenon when two senses combine. Thus, the people who experience these two sensations are called "synesthetes." Such as, when people hear a high musical tone or see the bright colors and then feel the lightness are types of synesthesia. According to Tsai's model of perceptual image quality assessment. The top-level shows that visual or

Q. Gao and J. Zhou (Eds.): HCII 2022, LNCS 13330, pp. 127–135, 2022.
https://doi.org/10.1007/978-3-031-05581-2_10

image assessment considers complex cognition issues. It is directly related to semantic understanding and the task-oriented concept (Tsai et al. 2016; Tsai et al. 2018). The research papers also point out the critical assessment items for visual assessment at the high level of cognition when assessing brightness, colorfulness, etc. This study is to understand the human's feeling in brightness and color when they hear the different musical scales. This pilot study focuses on a uniform color patch, not a complex image.

2   Literature Review

2.1   Synesthesia Phenomenon

Synesthesia is when an individual experiences a neurological sensation in which some of the usual senses are not separate but seem to be cross-wired (Hanlon 1991). Many research papers discuss the grapheme-color synesthesia phenomenon. For example, the experiment task asks observers to describe or speak the color of the ink for certain words where the single word shows a different color (see Fig. 1). Ward (2008) argues "that sensory mixing is the norm even though only a few of us cross the barrier into the realms of synesthesia." Synesthesia is meant to stimulate one of the human senses and several other senses. In other words, the feeling of visual and sound may be commingled or the taste and the touch.

| Green | Red | Blue | Yellow |

Fig. 1.   The example of a study on the grapheme-color synesthesia phenomenon.

2.2   The Synesthesia Between Color Feeling and the Music Scales

Many studies have discussed synesthesia phenomena about 64% in grapheme-color synesthesia in past years. Achromatic letters or digits automatically trigger a distinctive color perceptual experience (e.g., the letter 'm' induces blue color percepts). Substantial advances have been made in the understanding of synesthesia, and hence more globally in the comprehension of perception and consciousness (Safran and Sanda 2015). To understand the synesthesia phenomenon between color senses and different musical scales. A pilot study focuses on the relationship between color feeling and the Music scales. The "Guqin" is a Chinese culture-historical and typical musical instrument.

2.3   The Guqin

Guqin is one of the oldest musical instruments in Chinese culture. According to Chinese historical records, it was created more than 3000 years ago. The appearance of the modern Guqin dates back to 1500 years ago during the "Wei, Jin, Southern and Northern Dynasties."

The most common tuning of Guqin's seven strings are 5 6 1 2 3 5 6 in relative pitch, and the absolute pitch is about C D F G A c d. Guqin has three basic tones according to the ways of playing: "San" (Open String), "Fan" (Harmonics), and "An" (Stopped string). Through different playing methods, the players can obtain a range of four octaves, and most listeners feel that the Guqin has a calm tone, giving people a sense of tranquility.

3 Research Method

3.1 Experimental Instrument "Guqin"

The experiment material of sound is made from the typical Guqin in which the entire length is 122.5 cm, and the effect of the scale length is 112 cm. The Guqin's strings were made of modern nylon-flat wound steel strings. The tuning standard set as the A is equal to 440, according to the standard pitch to locate the string position. The play method of the right hand is to hook the string of Guqin[1], which records the timbre. The right-hand position is also located between the 1st Hui and Yue Shan, about 8 cm from the Yue Shan. To get the uniform timbre of each sound, all the sounds were played with the press method. Table 1 shows the position of each string and its scale length had set in the musical scale of Guqin.

Table 1. The position of each string and its scale length.

Tuning	Left thumb position	Scale Length
C	position 10 of the forth string	84
D	position 9 of the forth string	74.5
E	position 7.9 of the forth string	67
F	position 7.6 of the forth string	63
G	position 7 of the forth string	56
A	position 6.5 of the forth string	50
B	position 6 of the forth string	45
c	position 5.6 of the forth string	42

3.2 Observers

A quasi-experiment design method has been set in this study. The 21 observers with normal color vision were invited to join the assessment of the experiment in synesthesia between the color and musical scales of Guqin by using convenient sampling. There were six males and 15 females. Twelve observers had been recruited from the department of visual arts and design; 9 observers had been recruited from the Department of Ethnomusicology. All students who join the experiment and their major for more than two years in the bachelor program at Nanhua University.

---

[1] Use the middle finger of the right hand to pluck the string inward.

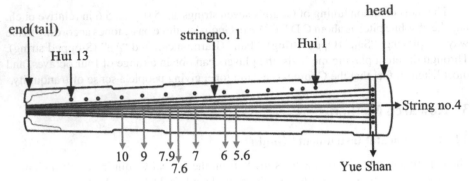

Fig. 2. An example of the left fingers' position is related to playing the Guqin.

3.3 CIE*Lab* Color Space

The International Commission on Illumination (CIE) defined the CIE*Lab* 1976 color space, which describes the three dimensions, including X, Y, and Z, which are the tristimulus values of the stimulus, and X_n, Y_n, and Z_n, which are the tristimulus values of the reference white point (CIE 1986; Fairchild 2005). The CIE*Lab* color space sets up the color as three dimensions of the CIE L^* for lightness from zero (black) to one hundred (white) and the CIE a^* and CIE b^* for the hue and chroma. The CIE*Lab* color space was also designed as a "perceptually uniform or uniform color space," which means that "the same amount of numerical color value change corresponds to roughly the same amount of visually color perceived change" (CIE 1986; Brainard 2003). This study displays the RGB color patch translated from the CIE*Lab* value (Tsai 2019). The color judgment includes the hue and chroma dimension. The CIE L^* value was calculated in tasks 1 and 2, increasing and decreasing the lightness judgment. The CIE a^* and CIE b^* values had calculated in task 3, which judgment the color when hearing the musical scale of Guqin.

3.4 Experiment Setting and Analysis Method

The eight sounds had created by the professional musician of Guqin. Each sound was recorded separated into a single mp3 format file with 256 Kbps. The experiment interfaces were designed by using the Visual Basic Program. The duration time of judgment, the CIE*L* value on tasks I & II, and the CIE*Lab* value on task III were collected.

In task III, the calculated values of distances were reported in terms of delta E_{ab} using the CIE*Lab* color difference formula (see Eq. 1). Figure 2 shows that the delta E_{ab} was calculated the distance between each target E_{ab} value and the center area which the L_m^* is equal to 50, the a_m^*, and b_m^* are equal to zero. The target L_n^*, a_n^*, and b_n^* values will be generated from each observer selecting the current color on the monitor by using the mouse arrow and clicking the left key when they hear the single sound of Guqin (see Fig. 3).

To analyze the difference between the observers who have music training backgrounds or not by using the independent-sample T-test. It is also to understand the synesthesia phenomenon in which the lightness/color is affected by the different Guqin musical scales.

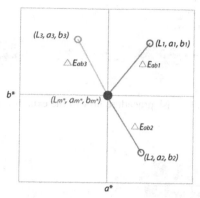

Fig. 3. Hints of the distance (delta E_{ab}) calculation between median value and all L_n*, a_n*, and b_n* in the CIE*Lab* color space.

$$\Delta E_{ab}* = \sqrt{(L_m - L_n)^2 + (a_m - a_n)^2 + (b_m - b_n)^2} \qquad (1)$$

where the delta E_{ab} is the distance between each pixel and the center area of the CIE*Lab* color space and each color.

3.5 Experiment Procedure

Three tasks should be finished on each observer. These include increasing the lightness task (a task I), decreasing the lightness task (task II), and selecting the target color when hearing the eight randomly musical scales of Guqin (task III). These three tasks were randomly shown to each observer. Figure 4 shows the procedure of the experiment in this study. After the observer reads the introduction of the experiment, then do two or more exercises of an experiment for understanding the procedure and its operation. Usually, below the 15 min to finish all the tasks. For example, observers judge the lightness increase from black to white when hearing a randomly single sound in task I. 8 sounds were randomly played in task I. Figure 5 shows the procedure of the task; the observers adjust the lightness/color on the monitor through the mouse arrow after hearing the sound. They could replay the sound one more time by themselves if needed. The random noise image will show after the observer clicks the confirmation button to avoid the after image effect (Fig. 6).

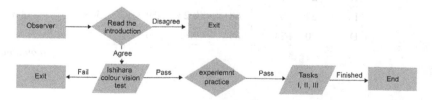

Fig. 4. The flow chart of the experimental procedure.

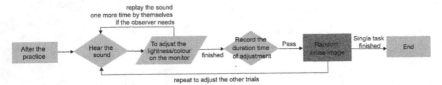

Fig. 5. Task procedure flow in the experiment.

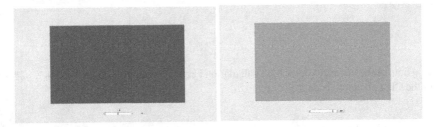

Fig. 6. Experiment screen in tasks I, II (left image), and task III (right image).

4 Data Analysis

The results show that the significant difference between the two tasks (tasks I and II) is increasing and decreasing the lightness judgment. Generally speaking, the decreasing lightness's average CIE*L* value of the decreasing lightness is significantly large than the increasing lightness. Thus, the follow-up analysis should be merged those CIE*L* values from two tasks to balance the difference between the two tasks. On the other hand, the different major has no significance in each sound of musical scales (see. Table 3). Results also show that the marginal mean distribution of the lightness is significantly affected by the different Guqin musical scales. (Unit: CIE*L* value). Figure 7 shows the lightness sensation growly based on the different pitches of musical scales from the item as "Do" (tunning C) to the item as hDo (tunning c) (Table 2).

Table 2. The results of independent-sample T-Test in between the different tasks (Unit: CIE*L* value)

Musical scales	Task	N	Min	Max	Mean	S.D	*Levene test*	*Sig*
Do	I	22	0	82	28.14	19.31	.569	.085
	D	20	11	84	38.90	20.235		
Re	I	22	0	68	30.23	19.31	.563	.003*
	D	20	24	83	49.85	20.37		

(continued)

Table 2. *(continued)*

Musical scales	Task	N	Min	Max	Mean	S.D	Levene test	Sig
Mi	I	22	21	86	55.30	19.35	.792	.001*
	D	20	5	73	32.86	19.211		
Fa	I	22	10	84	42.64	20.60	.706	.003*
	D	20	33	100	61.90	19.04		
So	I	22	18	90	51.14	19.04	.470	.001*
	D	20	38	100	69.35	14.90		
La	I	22	12	89	52.59	19.44	.937	.003*
	D	20	30	100	71.60	19.28		
Si	I	22	12	96	62.27	21.78	.165	.012*
	D	20	32	98	77.80	15.58		
hDo	I	22	43	97	63.50	16.36	.649	.001*
	D	20	29	100	80.90	16.27		

Note: the I task is to increase the lightness from black to white; the D task is to decrease the lightness from white to black. * p < .05

Table 3. The results of the independent-sample T-test between the majors. (Unit: CIEL value)

Musical scales	Major	N	Min	Max	Mean	S.D	Levene test	Sig
Do	M	18	0	71	30.28	20.71	.690	.418
	A	24	4	84	35.50	20.54		
Re	M	18	0	76	37.44	21.95	.745	.592
	A	24	2	83	41.17	22.28		
Mi	M	18	10	86	45.78	23.59	.768	.570
	A	24	5	84	41.79	21.34		
Fa	M	18	10	100	49.67	25.11	.261	.603
	A	24	14	84	53.42	19.59		
So	M	18	18	100	61.00	24.23	.010	.751
	A	24	19	86	58.92	15.1		
La	M	18	36	100	65.22	21.91	.773	.354
	A	24	12	89	58.96	21.07		
Si	M	18	12	98	67.22	25.79	.019	.539
	A	24	36	95	71.50	15.60		
hDo	M	18	29	100	69.72	22.38	.035	.558
	A	24	43	97	73.33	14.99		

Note: the M is major in Ethnomusicology the A is major in art and design

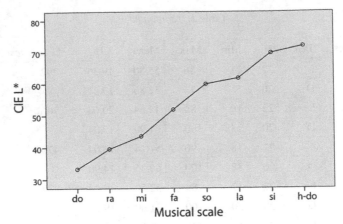

Fig. 7. The marginal mean distribution of the lightness is significantly affected by the different Guqin musical scales. (Unit: CIEL value)

5   Results and Discussion

The study results show no significant difference between music and arts backgrounds observers in the lightness adjustment task. The result also shows a positive correlation between lightness and musical scales, and the saturation of color is no significant correlation with musical scales. This study also to understand the synesthesia phenomenon between color senses and musical scales. Many studies have discussed synesthesia phenomena in grapheme-color synesthesia in past years. This pilot study focuses on the relationship between color feeling and the Music scales, which figures out the robust results. It could provide the basis of experiment design in the following study.

Acknowledgement. The author would like to thank the participants for supporting this research and providing insightful comments. The author would also like to thank Miss Ting-Yu Chen, who assisted in this study to smoothly execute the experiment, and all participants who joined the color adjustment experiment.

References

Goode, L.K.: Synesthesia: a sixth sense or a sensation: a research project based upon interviewing persons with color synesthesia, Master's Thesis, Smith College, Northampton, MA. (2010) https://scholarworks.smith.edu/theses/1126

Tsai, C.-M., Guan, S.-S., Tsai, W.-C., Zhang, Z.-H.: Semantic understanding and task-oriented for image assessment. Lect. Notes Comput. Sci. **10296**, 392–400 (2018)

Tsai, C.-M., Guan, S.-S., Tsai, W.-C.: Eye movements on assessing perceptual image quality. In: Zhou, J., Salvendy, G. (eds.) ITAP 2016. LNCS, vol. 9754, pp. 378–388. Springer, Cham (2016). https://doi.org/10.1007/978-3-319-39943-0_37

Hanlon, R.E. (ed.): Cognitive Microgenesis; A neuropsychological Perspective. Basic Books, New York (1991)

Murray, R.: A review of synesthesia: historical and current perspectives. UWL J. Undergraduate Res. **24** (2021)

Ward, J.: The Frog who Croaked Blue: Synesthesia and The Mixing of The Senses. Routledge, Taylor & Francis Group (2008)

Fairchild, M.D.: Color Appearance Models. The John Wiley & Sons (2005)

CIE: Colorimetry, Commission Internationale de l'Eclairage (CIE) Publication, 15.2, Vienna (1986)

Brainard, D.H.: Color appearance and color difference specification. In: Elsevier Science (Eds.), The Science of Color (2nd Edition) pp. 191-216. Elsevier Science, Amsterdam, Netherlands (2003)

Tsai, C.-M.: Using CIELAB color space in analyzing the colors of Van Gogh's paintings. In: Proceeding of 2019 International Academic Conference and Exhibition on Visual Arts and Design, Nanhua University, Chiayi, Taiwan, (2019)

Safran, A., Sanda, N.: Color synesthesia. insight into perception, emotion, and consciousness. Current Opin. Neurol.. **28**(1), 36–44 (2015). https://doi.org/10.1097/WCO.0000000000000169

Mobile, Wearable and Multimodal Interaction for Aging

Pandemic-Driven Mobile Technology in Saudi Arabia: Experience of the Elderly Pilgrims and Visitors During COVID-19

Asmaa S. Alayed[✉]

Faculty of Computer and Information Science, Umm Al-Qura University, Makkah, Saudi Arabia
asayed@uqu.edu.sa

Abstract. With the spread of COVID-19, Saudi Arabia implemented a policy to keep people physically distanced. Mandatory pandemic-driven mobile technologies have been utilized in the country to limit the spread of the coronavirus. The current study aimed to explore and understand the experience of Arab elderly people with the pandemic-driven mobile app Eatmarna. We conducted a task-based usability test, followed by a satisfaction questionnaire and interview with Arab elderly between 65 and 85 years old. This study has provided an insight into the challenges that were faced by older adults when using pandemic-driven apps. Identification of these challenges contributes to a better understanding of the situation and can lead to appropriate solutions and plans to improve such apps.

Keywords: COVID-19 · Pandemic-driven mobile technology · Mobile apps · Saudi Arabia · Elderly · Pilgrims · Eatmarna · User experience

1 Introduction

When the COVID-19 coronavirus outbreak spread worldwide, the World Health Organization (WHO) announced COVID-19 as a global pandemic in March 2020 [1]. Almost all aspects of our lives were suspended, and lockdown was regulated in several countries. Saudi Arabia is one of the countries that was greatly affected by the worldwide pandemic since a large number of Muslims from around the world visit Saudi Arabia for Umrah and Hajj—the two biggest mass gatherings in the world. Umrah and normal daily mass prayers in all mosques including the two holy mosques were suspended [2, 3].

During the pandemic, mobile technologies including mobile health solutions have been utilized in the country to control the spread of the coronavirus [4, 5]. Coronavirus-related mobile apps have several functionalities, such as COVID tracing, self-assessments of symptoms, and enforcing social distancing, which are used to help limit the spread of the virus. One of the major apps that was launched by the Saudi Data and Artificial Intelligence Authority (SDAIA) was Tawakkalna [6]. It is considered the kingdom's national health app during the pandemic. It was used to manage electronic permits during the curfew period. It is also used for infection tracing and exposure control. It is a mandatory application that must be used by every adult in order to enter or engage in any social activity (e.g., going to grocery stores, universities, shopping malls, etc.) to help prevent the spread of the coronavirus. It displays the health status of its users through colored QR codes.

The mosques in Saudi Arabia were reopened towards the end of 2020, but with COVID-19 restrictions. Eventually, entry to the grand mosques in Makkah and Madinah was allowed only for immune people (vaccinated with two doses) who obtained electronic permits through the Eatmarna app [2, 7]. The Eatmarna app was launched by the Ministry of Hajj and Umrah to enable immune pilgrims to book appointments to perform Umrah or to visit the two grand mosques. The Eatmarna app issues electronic permits according to the capacity approved by the concerned authorities to ensure the provision of a protected and safe environment that satisfies health precautionary measures and controls. Additionally, the Tawakkalna app was used by the health inspectors at the grand mosques' entrances to verify and confirm the health status of the permit user (immune, incomplete vaccination, nonimmune, ...).

According to recent statistics, as of 2019, elderly individuals who are 65 years of age or older represented almost 4.2% of the total population in Saudi Arabia [8]. Several aging-related changes occur for the elderly, including changes in vision, hearing and motor skills. Moreover, as people reach old age, in general, their cognitive skills deteriorate, which may affect their learning capabilities [8]. Because of enforced social isolation and quarantine, loneliness and mental health issues of the elderly increased during the pandemic [10, 11].

During the pandemic, older people in Saudi Arabia were overwhelmed by the urgent and unplanned adoption of mobile technology. They were urged to learn and use certain apps in a short period of time in order to engage in any social or religious activity, such as visiting the grand mosques for prayers or umrah, which could have negatively affected their physical and mental well-being [9]. For individuals, especially the elderly who live in Saudi Arabia, religion and religious practices are an integral part of life and existence [12]. One form of religious practices is visiting the grand mosques for prayers or Umrah.

Previous studies show that understanding older users' experiences would help in designing better technology and increase the use of it [9, 11, 12]. However, previous studies have not paid enough attention to them, especially when it comes to the use of mandatory pandemic-driven apps [10]. Therefore, in this study, the aim was to examine and understand the experience of elderly Arab people in using the obligatory pandemic-related mobile app Eatmarna.

In this paper, related work is discussed in Sect. 2. Research methodology is presented in Sect. 3. Section 4 discusses the results. Section 5 concludes with a summary of the paper and recommendations.

2   Related Work

In Saudi Arabia, innovative mobile technology-based solutions have been adopted during the COVID-19 pandemic to help fight the virus and reduce its spread [2, 3, 5, 14]. Examples of pandemic-driven mobile technology, include Tawakkalna [6], Tabaud [15], Sehhaty, Tataman in the healthcare sector, Madrasati, Rawdhatii in the educational sector, Eatmarna in the Islamic affairs sector [7].

Studies investigating those technologies and their use are increasing [10, 14, 16–18]. Experience of older adults with mobile apps was investigated in [10]. Research conducted in [14] assessed the performance of three COVID-19 mobile apps related to the health sector. The results showed the effectiveness and high performance of those apps. Public attitude toward health applications used during the COVID-19 pandemic was explored in [16]. Citizens' satisfaction with the e-government services and health care applications during the COVID-19 pandemic in Al-Madinah region was measured in [17]. The study conducted by [18] aimed to measure the user experience of Tawakkalna by collecting data from the intended users in Saudi Arabia using the User Experience Questionnaire. Although the results showed a good user experience, the study recommended improvements in the user interface.

As noticed, previous studies focused primarily on mobile health technologies introduced in Saudi Arabia during the pandemic. The user experience with pandemic-driven mobile apps that serve other purposes, such as Hajj and Umrah have not been investigated in the literature.

There have been many studies in the literature investigating the use of mobile technology among Arab elderly people [19–21]. However, there appears to have been little effort to understand the elderly Arab experience with mobile technology adopted during the COVID-19 pandemic [10]. Religious practices are crucial for the elderly who live in Saudi Arabia [12], however, seniors' experience with pandemic-driven apps, such as Eatamarna have not been addressed in previous studies. Therefore, the current study aims to fill this gap by exploring and deeply understanding the experience of older users of such applications.

3   Research Methodology

The study was conducted in the period between August 2021 and October 2021. The data gathering process is comprised of a number of steps, as explained in the sections below:

3.1   Recruiting Participants

A total of 25 (12 males, 13 females) Arab elderly - between 65 and 85 years old - participated in this study. All of the participants have used Eatamrna before. The participants were recruited by using a mixture of purposeful and snowball sampling techniques. The purposeful sampling technique is the most common sampling technique [22]. In this technique, the researcher actively selects the most suitable sample for the study. In this research, senior citizens were sought through social media platforms (Twitter and WhatsApp). In the snowball sampling technique, the current participants were used to recruit further participants [22]. The profile of all participants is shown in Table 1.

Table 1. Profile of the Arab elderly participated in the study

#	Age	Gender	Education level	Career domain (if any)	Experience with smart phone apps	Difficulties in vision/hearing/movement
P1	65	Female	Bachelor Degree	Retired teacher	Yes	No
P2	67	Female	Master's Degree	Retired teacher	Yes	Vision
P3	66	Male	Bachelor Degree	Retired engineer	Yes	No
P4	65	Female	Bachelor Degree	Retired teacher	Yes	No
P5	69	Male	Bachelor Degree	Retired teacher	Yes	No
P6	71	Male	PhD	University Professor	Yes	No
P7	65	Female	Bachelor Degree	Retired teacher	Yes	Vision
P8	65	Male	PhD	University Professor	Yes	No
P9	66	Male	High School	Retired Soldier	Yes	No
P10	72	Female	PhD	Lawyer	Yes	Vision
P11	71	Male	PhD	Retired university professor	Yes	No
P12	85	Male	Intermediate School	Retired real estate agent	To some extent	Vision
P13	71	Female	Bachelor Degree	Retired teacher	Yes	Vision
P14	66	Female	High School	Housewife	Yes	Vision
P15	68	Female	Intermediate School	Housewife	Yes	Vision
P16	65	Female	Bachelor Degree	Retired teacher	Yes	No
P17	68	Male	Nephrology Professor	Nephrology consultant	Yes	Vision
P18	66	Female	Bachelor Degree	Retired teacher	Yes	No

(*continued*)

Table 1. (*continued*)

#	Age	Gender	Education level	Career domain (if any)	Experience with smart phone apps	Difficulties in vision/hearing/movement
P19	83	Male	Intermediate School	Businessman	To some extent	No
P20	80	Male	High School	Retired Soldier	To some extent	No
P21	73	Female	High School	Housewife	Yes	No
P22	70	Male	Master's Degree	Retired University Lecturer	Yes	Vision
P23	69	Male	PhD	Retired University Professor	Yes	No
P24	78	Female	Intermediate School	Housewife	Yes	No
P25	76	Female	High School	Housewife	Yes	No

As noticed from the table above, all the participants are literate and their education levels vary between PhD (24%), Master's degree (8%), Bachelor degree (32%), High School (20%) and Intermediate School (16%). Most of them (88%) have good experience with mobile apps, while 12% of them had less experience. School teaching was the career for 32% of the participants, working in academia was represented by 16%, whereas 20% of the participants are housewives. Around 8% used to work as soldiers, other jobs such as engineer, lawyer, real estate agent, businessman, nephrology consultant are represented by 4% each. Among the participants, 36% have vision defects and wear prescription glasses.

3.2 Pilot Study

Two HCI researchers were invited to pilot the materials presented in the study and the interview questions. This was to gather comments and recommendations regarding the questions. Each was met individually, and comments were made. Some questions were recommended to be deleted, and the phrasing of some questions was found to be unclear. By the end of the pilot study, the interview questions and other materials were ready to be presented to the participants as shown in the next sections.

3.3 Procedure

The testing session was conducted with each participant individually. In each session, the participant was given a brief explanation of the study and its purpose. After that, demographic data (Table 2) was collected.

Table 2. Demographic data

Gender	
Age	
Education Level	
Career Domain (if any)	
Any difficulties in vision, hearing or movement. If any clarify how it would affect you in using the app	
Experience with smart phone apps (Yes, To some extent, No experience)	
How did you get to know Eatmarna?	

Usability evaluation entails three elements: Efficiency (time on task), Effectiveness (task success and number of errors) and Satisfaction (participant's opinion). The participants were given a number of general tasks (1 & 7) and core tasks (2 - 6) to perform on Eatmarna (Table 3) and their performance was observed. No support was provided to them while carrying out these tasks. During the task, the participant's interaction with the app was observed and the time it took to do each task was recorded. The number of times the participant made errors until the task was completed was also counted.

Table 3. Usability Test Task List

Task#	Task List
Task1	Log in Eatmarna
Task2	Request permit for Umrah
Task3	Request permit for Praying in the Grand Mosque
Task4	Request permit for Tawaf with companion
Task5	Check your previous permits
Task6	Cancel one of your active permits
Task7	Change your login password

After that, participants were asked to rate their satisfaction using the System Usability Scale (SUS) [23]. This scale was chosen because it is a very easy scale to administer to participants, it can be used on small sample sizes with reliable results and is valid which means it can effectively differentiate between usable and unusable apps [24, 25]. It was adapted by replacing the word "system" in every question with "app". Each question is a statement and a rating on a five-point scale of Strongly Disagree to Strongly Agree, as follows: [23].

(1)   *I think that I would like to use this app frequently.*
(2)   *I found the app unnecessarily complex.*

(3) *I thought the app was easy to use.*
(4) *I think that I would need the support of a technical person to be able to use this app.*
(5) *I found the various functions in this app were well integrated.*
(6) *I thought there was too much inconsistency in this app.*
(7) *I would imagine that most people would learn to use this website very quickly.*
(8) *I found the app very cumbersome to use.*
(9) *I felt very confident using the app.*
(10) *I needed to learn a lot of things before I could get going with this app.*

In addition to SUS, the participants were interviewed to help understand their experience more deeply and to discuss any issues related to challenges or barriers in the app, Eatmarna. The open-ended questions were asked as shown in Table 4.

Table 4. Interview questions

Question#	Question list
Q1	How would you describe your experience with the app?
Q2	What kind of issues and barriers did you face when using the app (if any)?
Q3	Based on your experience, do you have any suggestion for the app?
Q4	Do you recommend this app to others? Why?

The study was conducted in Arabic and the interviews were audio recorded after obtaining participants' permission.

4 Results and Discussion

Table 5 summarizes the results obtained after performing the tasks listed in Table 3; the results are presented as averages for both the time and error rate. We can notice that the efficiency time of the tasks were in the range between 15.7 to 121.8 s. The tasks that took longer time to accomplish (1, 4 and 7) involved typing or entering information. Effectiveness of the app was measured using task success and number of errors. In terms of task success, all tasks were completed easily expect Task 4 (Request permit for Tawaf with companion) and Task 7 (Change your login password) where at least four participants failed to complete the task. In terms of number of errors, participants encountered errors while performing Tasks 1, 2, 4 and 7, yet the error rate was less than 0.5 for all of them except Task 7, which indicates that the tasks were successfully accomplished.

The results of responses to SUS were calculated as suggested in [23]. The average SUS score for all participating users was 77.8 -higher than the threshold 68- which was categorized as good and could be improved [23]. As can be seen from Fig. 1, the scores for all participants are above the threshold except P12, P19 and P20 who have less experience with mobile apps.

Table 5. Usability (effeciency and effectivenesss) evaluation results

Task#	Task description	Efficiency (time in seconds)	Effectiveness	
			Task success	Number of errors
1	Log in Eatmarna	91.3	Completed easily	0.16 (4 of 25)
2	Request permit for Umrah	64.5	Completed easily	0.12 (3 of 25)
3	Request permit for Praying in the Grand Mosque	59	Completed easily	0
4	Request permit for Tawaf with companion	121.8	Completed with difficulty	0.2 (5 of 25)
5	Check your previous permits	15.7	Completed easily	0
6	Cancel one of your active permits	53.5	Completed easily	0
7	Change your login password	114	Completed with difficulty	0.6 (15 of 25)

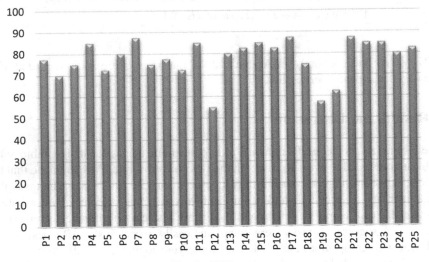

Fig. 1. SUS scores

To analyze participants' responses to the interview questions, the interviews were transcribed and saved into NVivo. NVivo is a software tool used to manage and understand textual data, and make the most of it. Participants' responses were tagged using NVivo according to analysis themes and components, collected together into groups, then synthesized. A thematic analysis approach was followed [26], looking for similar themes and patterns among the collected data.

The answer to the first interview question (Table 4) revealed that 84% of the participants had enjoyed using the app and had a satisfying experience. However, 16% did not enjoy the experience and stated that they would prefer it if a family member used it for them.

In response to the second interview question (Table 4), the participants mentioned a number of issues and barriers that hindered their interaction with the app and caused them to make mistakes. One of these issues was related to **the presentation of time and date**. Around 60% of the participants pointed out that the 24h time format was confusing, and that they were not used to it in their daily lives. Date format in the app was another issue mentioned by 44% of the participants. Participant P12 emphasized this issue by saying: *"We have been using Hijri date format in all our life occasions, so when I try to issue a permit, I have to change the default date presentation from Gregorian to Hijri which is unnecessary effort if the Hijri format was the default"*.

The cultural background of users is considered one of the attributes that might affect users' performance and satisfaction while interacting with the interface. As suggested in [27], one way to achieve surface level of localization is by providing the users with a familiar date and time format.

Log in and verification code was another issue mentioned by 40% of the participants. They justified that by the need to look at the sent code as fast as they can or they have to go to the messages to retrieve it, memorize it and then write it in the app for verification purposes. Participant P21 explains *"We are used to the idea of verification codes, and we see it in all government-based apps, but I think it is exhausting in terms of the need to be quick and focused to remember the code and write it down in the app to allow us to log in"*. Participant P20 pointed out that he sometimes asks for help to retrieve the code as it takes him a long time to do it.

Another challenge that was reported by 52% of the participants is **the need to enter information that might not available on-hand**, such as missing or lost information. Issuing a companion's permit in Task 4 required entering the ID number and the date of birth for the companion, which explains why this task took a long time to accomplish. In this matter, participant P4 stated *"When I tried to add a companion, the app asked me for information I didn't have at that moment. Even if I had it, it would've taken me time to enter and check their validity"*. More than half of the participants struggled with login information (Id and password), as sometimes they could not remember the password. P24 referred that to the number of apps they are mandate to use during the pandemic and the amount of login information they have to remember. P25 explained how to overcome this issue, *"I write down the login information for all apps I use in the Notes app on my iPhone. I used to ask my children to keep the information safe for me, but now I rely on myself to do it"*.

Difficulty reading small text was a challenge for 56% of the participants. They complained that the text was relatively small especially when they tried to pick a date for prayer or Umrah. Participant P6 suggested adding an option to the app to allow the users to enlarge the font size whenever it is needed. Difficulty reading text was also pointed out as a challenge faced by the Arab elderly when they use pandemic-driven apps [10]. This issue needs careful design consideration in order to provide readable text with the option to enlarge the text size.

The last challenge faced by 60% of the participants was **invisibility of constraining instructions**. To change the password, the app asked them to enter the old password once and new password twice for confirmation. However, they received error messages because the password must be more than 7 characters containing upper case and lower-case letters. The constraining instructions to change the password should be clear and visible as commented by participant P7: *"The instructions for password change should be visible and clear before we have the first attempt to change it. Appearance of error messages would bother me and lower my confidence in using the apps"*. Both visibility and constraints were promoted to be design principles that would be used by interaction designers to aid their thinking when designing for the user experience [28], since they prevent the user from incorrect actions and thereby reduce the chance of making a mistake.

When the participants were asked about their suggestions to improve the app (third interview question), their responses were around resolving the difficulties they had when using the app as clarified above. Suggested improvements include, making the instructions clear and visible for the user, giving more time to enter information especially if it needs typing or remembering, providing readable text size, and presenting date and time in a format the user is familiar with.

In response to the fourth interview question, 76% of the participants reported that they would recommend the app to family and friends. The participants who have less experience with mobile apps (12%) admitted that they would prefer to have someone use the app for them if they planned to make Umrah or visit one of the grand mosques. They also admitted that the need for using new pandemic-driven apps during the COVID-19 lockdown had forced them to use the technology and decrease the need for help from others. As a result, the fear of technology decreased, and their confidence and self-esteem increased.

Task observations revealed some issues that were not stated clearly by the participants in the interviews. It was observed that the small screen size was an issue experienced by the elderly where accidental taps of buttons adjacent to the target buttons occurred for almost 40%. This issue was corroborated by the results of a study conducted by [29], where the authors suggested providing better feedback through both audio and visual when a key is pressed.

Around 16% of the participants showed slow response and hesitance when carrying out the tasks. They were expecting assistance, but they were told the tasks should be performed independently in order to measure their performance accurately.

As a result of facing such challenges, elderly people would ask for help from others in using the app. Doing so in public places would raise their chances of virus infection as they might violate the social distancing restrictions. Therefore, pandemic-driven apps should be improved by taking into consideration the challenges and barriers faced by older adults.

5   Conclusion

The results from the current exploratory study indicated the good user experience the Arab elderly had with one pandemic-driven mobile app used in Saudi Arabia (Eatamarna). Nevertheless, several challenges and barriers faced by the elderly were observed and reported. To overcome those challenges, different aspects of Eatamarna would be improved in order to enhance the experience of the Arab elderly. Following the design principles for interaction designers, such as visibility and constraints is one aspect that would make the instructions clear and visible for the user. Giving more time to enter information especially if it needs typing or remembering is another aspect to improve according to Web Content Accessibility Guidelines (WCAG) [30]. Providing readable text size and ability to resize the text was also recommended by [30]. Localization should be emphasized by presenting date and time in a format the user is familiar with. Making such improvements would not just enhance the elderly experience, but it would also enhance the experience of other categories of Eatamarna users as well.

It is worth mentioning that mandatory pandemic-driven mobile apps have had a positive impact on the Arab elderly in decreasing the need for help from others as they get to know how to use them. As a result, the fear of technology decreased, and their independence, confidence and self-esteem increased.

Engaging elderly people in all phases of the mobile app design process would contribute to designing more accessible and usable apps. Conducting several usability and accessibility studies on different pandemic-driven apps to evaluate them was planned to be future work.

References

1. WHO, WHO | World Health Organization: https://www.who.int/, Accessed 9 Feb 2022
2. Basahel, S., Alsabban, A., Yamin, M.: Hajj and Umrah management during COVID-19. Int. J. Inf. Technol. **13**(6), 2491–2495 (2021). https://doi.org/10.1007/s41870-021-00812-w
3. Orfali, R., Perveen, S., Aati, H.Y., Al-Taweel, A.M.: nCOVID-19 outcomes on curfews and lockdown: precautionary decisions in Saudi Arabia. Health Policy Technol. **10**(3), 100538 (2021)
4. Adeniyi, E.A., Bamidele Awotunde, J., Ogundokun, R.O., Kolawole, P.O., Kazeem Abiodun, M., Adeniyi, A.A.: Mobile health application and Covid-19: opportunities and challenges. J. Critical Rev. **7**(15), 3481–3488 (2020)
5. Khan, A., et al.: The role of digital technology in responding to COVID-19 pandemic: Saudi Arabia's experience. Risk Manag. Healthcare Policy **21**(14), 3923–3934 (2021)
6. The Saudi Data and Artificial Intelligence Authority (SDAIA): Tawakkalna. https://ta.sdaia.gov.sa/en/index, Accessed 8 Feb 2022
7. Unified National Platform: List of Government Applications. https://www.my.gov.sa/wps/portal/snp/content/appslist, Accessed 8 Feb 2022
8. Authority of Stat. 2019: Results of the Elderly Survey 2019. https://www.stats.gov.sa/sites/default/files/elderly_survey_2017en.pdf
9. Van De Watering, M.: The Impact of Computer Technology on the Elderly. In Human Computer Interaction (2005)
10. Alharbi, R., Altayyari, F., Alamri, F., Alharthi, S.: Pandemic-driven technology during COVID-19: experiences of older adults. In: Companion of the 2021 ACM CSCW Conference on Computer Supported Cooperative Work and Social Computing, October 23–27, 2021, Virtual. ACM, (2021)
11. van Tilburg, T.G., Steinmetz, S., Stolte, E., van der Roest, H., de Vries, D.H.: Loneliness and mental health during the COVID-19 pandemic: a study among dutch older adults. J. gerontol.. Series B Psychol. Sci. Soc. Sci. **76**(7), e249-e255 (2021)

12. Karlin, N.J., Weil, J., Felmban, W.: Aging in Saudi Arabia: an exploratory study of contemporary older persons' views about daily life, health, and the experience of aging. Gerontol. Geriatr. Med. **2**, 2333721415623911 (2016)
13. Rolanda, K., Markusb, M.: COVID-19 pandemic: palliative care for elderly and frail patients at home and in residential and nursing homes. Swiss Med. Weekly 150(1314) (2020)
14. Hidayat-ur-Rehman, I., Ahmad, A., Ahmed, M., Alam, A.: Mobile applications to fight against COVID-19 pandemic: the case of Saudi Arabia. TEM Journal **10**(1), 69–77 (2021)
15. The Saudi Data and Artificial Intelligence Authority (SDAIA): Tabaud. https://tabaud.sdaia. gov.sa/IndexEn, Accessed 7 Feb 2022.
16. Bamufleh, D., Alshmari, A.S., Alsobhi, A.S., Ezzi, H.H., Alruhaili, W.S.: Exploring public attitudes toward e-government health applications used during the COVID-19 pandemic: evidence from Saudi Arabia. Comput. Inf. Sci. **14**(3), 1 (2021)
17. Allam, A.A., AbuAli, A.N., Ghabban, F.M., Ameerbakhsh, O., Alfadli, I.M., Alraddadi, A.S.: Citizens satisfaction with E-Government mobile services and M-Health application during the COVID-19 pandemic in Al-Madinah Region. J. Serv. Sci. Manag. **14**(06), 636–650 (2021)
18. AlGothami, S.S., Saeed, S.: Digital Transformation and Usability: User Acceptance of Tawakkalna Application During Covid-19 in Saudi Arabia, pp. 95–109 (2021)
19. Al-Khalifa, H.S., Al-Twaim, M., Al-Mohsin, M., Al-Razgan, M.: Technologies developed for older adults: trends and directions. In: Stephanidis, C. (ed.) HCI 2014. CCIS, vol. 435, pp. 279–283. Springer, Cham (2014). https://doi.org/10.1007/978-3-319-07854-0_49
20. Al-Razgan, M., Al-Khalifa, H.S.: SAHL: A Touchscreen mobile launcher for arab elderly. J. Mobile Multimedia **13**(1&2), 075–099 (2017)
21. Nassir, S., Leong, T.W.: Traversing boundaries: understanding the experiences of Ageing Saudis. In: Proceedings of the 2017 CHI Conference on Human Factors in Computing Systems, pp. 6386–6397 (2017)
22. Marshal, M.N.: Sampling for qualitative research. Fam. Pract. **13**(6), 522–526 (1996)
23. Brooke, J.: SUS-a quick and dirty usability scale. Usability Eval. Ind. **189**(194), 4–7 (1996)
24. Sauro, J., James, R.L.: When designing usability questionnaires, does it hurt to be positive?. In: Proceedings of the SIGCHI conference on human factors in computing systems, pp. 2215–2224 (2011)
25. Tullis, T.S., Jacqueline, N.S.: A comparison of questionnaires for assessing website usability. In: Usability Professional Association Conference, vol.1 (2004)
26. Braun, V., Clarke, V.: Using thematic analysis in psychology. Qual. Res. Psychol. **3**(2), 77–101 (2006)
27. Kim, I.: Cultural Impacts on Web: An Empirical Comparison of Interactivity in Websites of South Korea and the United Kingdom. PhD Thesis, Brunel University (2013)
28. Sharp, H., Preece, J., Rogers, Y.: Interaction Design: Beyond Human-Computer Interaction, 5th ed. Wiley (2019)
29. Schlögl, S., Chollet, G., Garschall, M., Tscheligi, M., Legouverneur, G.: Exploring voice user interfaces for seniors. In: Proceedings of the 6th International Conference on Pervasive Technologies Related to Assistive Environments, pp. 52:1–52:2. New York, NY, USA (2013)
30. W3C, Web Content Accessibility Guidelines (WCAG) 2.1: https://www.w3.org/TR/WCAG21/, Accessed 8 Feb 2022

The Impact of the Interface on the Perception of Trust of Older Adults Users When Using the Smartphone

Mayckel Barbosa de Oliveira Camargo[✉], Marcelo Valério Rino,
Paula da Cruz Landim, and Antônio Carlos Sementille

São Paulo State Univertisy, Bauru, São Paulo, Brazil
{mayckel.camargo,paula.cruz-landim}@unesp.br,
semente@fc.unesp.br

Abstract. The older adults, who were born and grew up in an analog era where digital technology was not part of their lives, look with some suspicion on currently existing digital artifacts, such as the smartphone. This damaged trust relationship not only refers to the technology itself, but also to the way these older adults users interact with it. Thus, in this scenario, the interface is highlighted as a gateway to interaction for being, in most cases, responsible for the presentation and translation of systemic elements into graphic results that will serve as a subsidy for the entire cognitive process of the user. Based on this context, through the case study carried out with three users from exploratory research and qualitative questionnaires. The present work identified that visual representation on the graphic interface of apps has a direct impact, being negative or positive, on the trust relationship of older adults users in the using of the smartphone depending on their characteristics of real-world representation and facility of use.

Keywords: Older adults · Smartphone · Trust · UX

1 Introduction

Inherent in the human condition, aging is both an inevitable and an expected process in the population. For the World Health Organization, the definition of older adults includes individuals aged 65 years or over in developed countries and 60 years or over in developing countries [1]. For this study, people aged 60 years or older will be understood as older adults.

According to the Brazilian Institute of Geography and Statistics, in 2018 the Brazilian population had about 13.5% of older adults people aged 60 years or older in its composition [2]. This represents approximately 28 million older adults citizens who end up experiencing various situations related to aging, such as reduced motor skills, vision problems, cognition and memory problems, and even problems with interpersonal interaction. These older adults belong to an analog generation, characterized by growing up in a time when digital technology was not directly present in their daily lives, which in

© The Author(s), under exclusive license to Springer Nature Switzerland AG 2022
Q. Gao and J. Zhou (Eds.): HCII 2022, LNCS 13330, pp. 151–159, 2022.
https://doi.org/10.1007/978-3-031-05581-2_12

many cases, ended up not keeping up with the evolution of technology and today they view the digital environment with suspicion.

Garrett [3] defines the user experience from the interface of a software or application as a set of five layers (strategy, scope, structure, skeleton, and surface), where the most external and primary to the user is the surface, that by your concrete and visual characteristics, behaves as the user's gateway to the interaction being proposed by the system architecture. It directly or indirectly represents all the elements necessary to carry out the proposed activities concretely and directionally for the user's understanding.

Based on this context, through the case study carried out with three users from exploratory research and qualitative questionnaires, the present study aims to verify the existence and reflect on the impact of the interface on the trust relationship of older adults users during smartphone usage.

2 Literature Review

Currently, the world population has almost seven billion eight hundred million inhabitants, and this number may reach 8 billion within 5 years and ten billion inhabitants by the year 2055 [4]. In Brazil, there are almost two hundred ten million inhabitants, with a percentage of 13.5% of older adults, which corresponds to something around 28 and a half million older people [2]. Burlá [5] highlights that the 21st century is the age of aging, emphasizing the considerable increase in the population aged over eighty years [2].

The statute of the older adults raises concerns about the importance of this part of the population to stay up to date with modern life, oriented lately by technologies. It is proposed the discussion about the interaction of the older adults with technological instruments to be able to work and enjoy the independence for their day-to-day activities when performing regular activities, taking as an example the use of common and everyday technological tools such as an ATM without the aid of an assistant [6].

Based on data released by the IBGE, in 2013 more than half of the older adults population in Brazil (51.6%) used and owned a smartphone. Ownership of devices such as these by the older adults is related to education level and family income, according to Anderson and Perrir [7]. In developed countries like the USA, the number was extremely higher, with a total of 81% with high family income and 27% for those with lower incomes.

With the arrival of older age, we can identify the occurrence of loss of cognitive, psychosocial and motor skills according to Nielsen [8]. Capacities such as hearing, vision and memory also begin to decline where, according to Veras [9], these older adults people have a greater burden of diseases and disabilities, that in themselves, characterize a phase of life that requires care. Despite information like this, the habits of individuals influence the entire aging process. According to Bizelli et al. [10], the changes caused by the improvement in quality of life are caused by an increase in cognitive stimuli, motor and muscle activities, and also by the good experiences of social, face-to-face and technological approximation, thus making it important to search for practices that can help to slow down these losses.

When thinking about applications for the older adults audience, the formal characteristics of the interface are of vital importance for their acceptance and good use, as can be seen in the study conducted by Carmien and Manzanares [11], about the needs and requirements of according to and for older adults users, related to mobile applications. A sequence of three different application designs was developed and tested with the older adults using the focus group technique. It was noticed that to serve this audience, smartphone applications must be easy to use, they must present only the most important tasks and use simplified words, where information must be short and instructions clear, with large buttons, in the least amount possible.

Based on Williams et al. [12], it can be identified that these devices help the users in their understanding and quality of life, being that the proper design is one of the most important considerations. An application can be both useful to a new user and to a problematic one, if the design presented is inadequate to understand how best to use it.

Reflecting on the difficulty of creating a relationship of trust between the older adults users and the smartphone, Phiriyapokanon [13] observes that much of this difficulty is related to the older adults user's distrust of technology, its use and contact with the equipment. Williams [12] relates that simplicity is key when designing visual displays for seniors - while visual displays for teens may need flash and bounce to catch their attention, too much color and action in an interface can cause confusion and even frustration for older adults users. Hunter [14] considers that the existence of problems related to memory impairment associated with age causes "a harmful effect on exploratory learning", where the ability to create mental models of a given task is significantly reduced and can be commonly perceived in the difficulty that seniors end up having a more significant role in navigation-based tasks.

From the interface, trust in the application is understood, where the older adults have fear and distrust of the unknown at high levels, in addition to difficulties to assimilate learning with new technologies. Thus, the applications need to adapt in order to allow access for those who live under different conditions and have different information absorption abilities [15].

3   Research Methods

In order to assess confidence while using the smartphone, the evaluation protocol was structured in two sections of activity constituted by a task and a questionnaire to evaluate the subjective aspects of the subject in relation to the newly performed task. In both activities, touchscreen smartphones with the Android operating system were used.

The initial hypothesis, based on the reviewed literature and the researchers' previous experience, is the idea that the more direct and correlated with the real world the graphical interface of the application, the greater the perception of trust of the older adults users, and that, consequently, a more abstract interface tends to require a higher level of both digital literacy and cognitive processes, making users feel less confident during activities. In this way it was observed, as a determining factor for the choice of applications, its interface. For the first activity, an application was selected that contained, in addition to large and easily accessible icons, also its graphic representation directly associated with elements of the physical world, such as a paint bucket for color selection. For the second activity, an application was selected that presented similar functions to the first, but that had its graphic representation in an abstract way, without a direct relationship with the real world.

In the first section, subjects were proposed to paint a previously selected drawing, using the application "Jogos para colorir: animais"[1] (Fig. 1a), free distribution through the Play Store. While in the second activity, it was proposed similarly to what happened in the first task, that the subjects colored the same drawing, but in this one, using a second application called "Ibis Paint X"[2] (Fig. 1b), also freely distributed through the Play Store. In both the first and second activities, the subjects had no time limit for their performance, just signaling to the applicator when they had finished the painting.

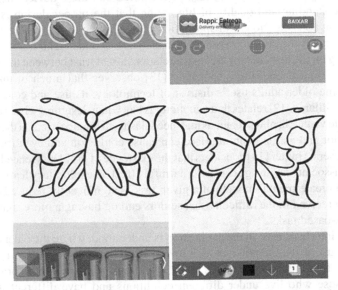

Fig. 1. Activity 1 screen on the left (a) and Activity 2 screen on the right (b)

The objective of the protocol was not the evaluation of items such as the usability, effectiveness or even efficiency of the applications, but the experience that users would have during their use. At the beginning of each activity it was explained, not only which task the subjects should perform it, but also how they would perform it, including where the tools were and how to use them in the application.

After completing each step, a questionnaire consisting of 3 closed questions was applied. Using a five-point scale, the first question was aimed at verifying whether the subject was lost or confident during the activity. The second, was aimed at verifying subjective aspects of the user's perception of the task, through the semantic differential technique, with 3 pairs of adjectives, observed in Fig. 2, and finally, the third question, intended to verify whether or not the subjects would repeat the activity at home with a five-point Likert scale. In the questionnaire, applied after activity 1, a question was added in order to directly verify whether the subjects thought it was safe or not to make purchases or payments over the internet, and in the questionnaire applied after activity

---

[1] https://play.google.com/store/apps/details?id=com.coloring.book.animals (11/02/2022).

[2] https://play.google.com/store/apps/details?id=jp.ne.ibis.ibispaintx.app (11/02/2022).

2, a question was added to identify in which of the two activities the subjects felt more confident.

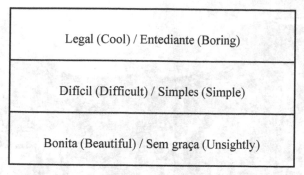

Fig. 2. Adjective pairs used in the semantic differential

Yin [16] states that the protocol in a case study is more than an instrument. It contains the procedures and guidelines that must be followed throughout the experiment, being one of the main tools to increase the reliability of a case study. Thus, to ensure a greater chance of success in carrying out the study, the protocol was previously tested with two volunteers, not participating in the sample, for possible corrections of the procedure.

As volunteers for the research, former students of the "3rd Age Connected" course were invited, a digital inclusion project for the 3rd age, carried out by Assomary (Association of Residents of Mary Dota), a neighborhood in the city of Bauru, located in in the interior of the State of São Paulo, Brazil. As a requirement for participation in the study, volunteers should be 60 years of age or older and use a smartphone in their daily lives. The invitation was made through the communication application via "WhatsApp" messages, enabling sampling of 3 older adults people.

The protocol was applied in July 2019, collectively, at the association's building (Fig. 3), where the older adults routinely meet for recreational and educational activities. The application had three mediators to ensure its smooth running and control. The entire protocol was filmed with a camera positioned to capture the image of the entire room, providing better further analysis and control. For the entire procedure to be constituted transparently and adequately, the subjects read, agreed and signed the Free and Informed Consent Term (FICT) for participation in the research and authorization for the use of their image for exclusively academic purposes.

The protocol lasted approximately 20 min, with an uneventful performance. It is worth noting that, right at the beginning of the activity, it was clarified that at any time, if they had any doubts, the subjects could request help from the mediators. It is also important to emphasize that the completion of the post-activity questionnaires was monitored by the applicators, in order to guarantee the best possible degree of clarification regarding the questions and their correct forms of filling, always taking care not to influence the content of the answers of the subject.

In addition to collecting data through post-activity questionnaires, participant observation was also carried out. This has been used by researchers in recent years to collect

Fig. 3. Users during application of protocol

data and insights about facets of subjects that may not be as easily visualized using other methods, identify the results of specific processes, and document physiological events and psychological [17]. Thereby, facilitating the act of carefully observing the details, resulting in the insertion of the researcher as an integral part of the observed reality, so that he can understand the complexity of the psychosocial aspects, allowing a more efficient dialogue with the studied group [18].

4   Results and Discussion

The first activity was performed without intercurrences or even limit situations in relation to the use of the application. After the activity was explained, the painting process was practically instantaneous. The use of "paint buckets" for painting was quickly assimilated and their use ended up being intuitive. Even raising initial doubts of "how do I paint?" or "how do I get this color", it was observed that the questions raised were much more of a self-affirming nature than requests for help. At this point, a previous validation of the first part of the hypothesis can be observed, noting a high perception of trust when using the application with a concrete graphical interface and with a direct correlation to the real world. The room was buzzing, but there was no sign of tension. All subjects talked to each other, freely, while carrying out the activity in a concentrated manner. During the realization process, conversations about emotional and affective issues can clearly be observed, such as, for example, what color to use in each item of the drawing.

Similar to the first activity, after the initial explanation, the subjects started painting their drawings. Even with the interface graphically constructed in an abstract way, the activity took place without any overt signs of tension or concern. The main doubts raised were how to select the color and how to change the color of an already painted area. In this activity, some subjects asked more than once how these procedures were performed. As perceived by the applicators and later verified in the protocol recording, the room was slightly more agitated, with more parallel subjects and less concentration on the activity, with the subjects dispersing throughout the period.

It was not possible to observe, comparing the first and second activities, significant differences in tension, anxiety, or even concentration between the subjects. In both activities, the volunteers were comfortable talking about parallel subjects while they were doing it. It is possible to notice a greater number of requests for help when using Ibis Paint X, an application that contains an interface constructed in an abstract way to the physical world. Thus, suggesting that the simpler, more intuitive and objective the interface is, the easier for cognition and meaning will be for the user, directly impacting its use. It was not possible, however, from the performance of the second activity, to establish a relationship of lower perception of safety on the part of the subjects when using the abstract interface, thus not being possible to validate the second part of the initial hypothesis.

Analyzing the data collected in the post-activity evaluation questionnaires, the first question, which was intended to reveal how much the subjects felt lost or confident during the activities, it was observed that 66% of the subjects declared themselves fully confident and 34% partially confident. In the first activity while 100% of the volunteers declared themselves fully confident in activity 2, which demonstrates that despite having requested more interventions from the applicators in relation to how they should perform the task, the subjects did not have a perception of lack of confidence in what they were making.

The second question, aimed at verifying subjective aspects of the user's perception of the task, that had an absolutely identical answer in both activities, declaring the subjects to have found both activities to be fully beautiful, fully legal, and fully easy.

The last question to assess the subjects' preference between the two activities, 66% declared that they felt more comfortable and motivated in the second activity, preferring it, while only 1 volunteer preferred the first.

Observing the totality of perceptions raised via the questionnaire, the impact that the interface offers on the perception of trust on the activity that the subjects were performing is not clearly established, and a slight inclination of preference for the interface can even be observed. more abstract.

However, in an informal conversation after carrying out the protocol, the subjects ended up declaring the difficulty in knowing what the screen says and in assertively visualizing where to touch the display for the correct action to take place, as a fundamental point for knowing that what they are doing is right, and as a result, have confidence in their own action. This can be exemplified with the answer of one of the subjects to the third question of the questionnaire after activity 1, where he declares that he does not think it is safe to make payments or even purchases over the internet because he does not know how to "move" the application, because it cannot understand exactly what each "drawing" means and consequently what it will do. Along with these perceptions, concerns about security in general were also expressed, with the cloning of cards and with processes that transcend the interface layer in applications and materialize in concepts and processes overall interaction with the internet and technology.

5 Conclusion and Suggestions

It is clear and apparent the difficulty with which the older adults population assimilates technology, and consequently makes use of it. Mendes [19] says that people's desires and aspirations change along with technological means, which portrays the reality of this population niche. Now, the older adults want to use technology and take advantage of the facilities that the digital information age brings to their lives. But, being a generation that was born and raised in another era, where digital technology was not part of their daily lives, this Integration encounters several obstacles, especially when it comes to trust not only in the technology, but trust that they are handling it correctly, that they are playing in the right place and carrying out interactions properly. At this point, the interface is an important factor in building the relationship of trust between the older adults users and the technology.

Although, it cannot be clearly stated through the research carried out that the interface constructed with clear icons and objective representations of reality, for older users directly impacts the improve of their relationship of trust with the task to be performed. Thus, it was possible abstractly to identify this feeling not only throughout the protocol applied, but also in post-activity conversations.

As a caveat to the study carried out, the proximity of the subjects to the responsible researcher may have influenced their attitudes and responses during the protocol, and a discrepancy between the answers obtained in the questionnaire and the content of informal conversations after the activities could be noticed. It is also important to point out that this is a pilot study, and its reproduction and suitability for a significantly larger sample are referred to as referral, to extract more solidly and directly related to the influence that the interface has or does not have on the trust relationship in the use of smartphones by the older adults users.

Acknowledgement. This study was financed in part by the Coordenação de Aperfeiçoamento de Pessoal de Nível Superior - Brasil (CAPES) - Finance Code 001 and part by the Graduate Program in Design of the School of Architecture, Arts and Communication of Universidade Estadual Paulista "Júlio de Mesquita Filho".

References

1. OMS: The World Health Organization quality of life assessment (WHOQOL): position paper from the World Health Organization. Social Science and Medicine 10, 1403-1409 (1995)
2. IBGE: Projeção da população do Brasil e das unidades da federação (2022) http://www.ibge.gov.br/apps/populacao/projecao/
3. Garrett, J.J.: The Elements of User Experience: User-Centred Design for the Web and Beyond. Pearson Education, Berkeley (2011)
4. WORLDOMETERS: World Population projection (2022) https://www.worldometers.info/world-population/

5. Burlá, C., Py, L.: Cuidados paliativos: ciência e proteção ao fim da vida. Cad. Saúde Pública, Rio de Janeiro, **30**(6), 1–3 (2014) http://dx.doi.org/https://doi.org/10.1590/0102-311XPE 020614

6. Brasil: Estatuto do Idoso (2003) http://www.planalto.gov.br/ccivil_03/leis/2003/l10.741.htm

7. Anderson, M., Perrin, A.: Technology use Among Seniors (2017) http://www.pewinternet. org/2017/05/17/technology-use-among-seniors

8. Nielsen, J.: Seniors as web users. Nielsen Norman Group (2013) http://www.nngroup.com/ articles/usability-for-senior-citizens/

9. Veras, R.: Experiências e tendências internacionais de modelos de cuidado com o idoso. Ciência e Saúde Coletiva **17**, 231–238 (2012)

10. Bizelli, M.H.S.S., et al.: Informática para a Terceira idade: características de um curso bem sucedido. Revista Ciência em Extensão **5**(2), 4–14 (2009)

11. Carmien, S., Manzanares, A.G.: Elders using smartphones - a set of research based heuristic guidelines for designers. In: Stephanidis, Constantine; Antona, Margherita (Ed.). Universal access in human-computer interaction: universal access to information and knowledge. (Lecture notes in computer science, 8514). Cap. 3, pp. 26–37. Springer International Publishing, Heraklion (2014)

12. Williams, D., Ul Alam, M.A., Ahamed, S.I., Chu, W. Considerations in designing human-computer interfaces for elderly people. In: Proceedings of the International Symposium on the Physical and Failure Analysis of Integrated Circuits, IPFA, Najing, pp. 372-377 (2013) https://doi.org/10.1109/QSIC.2013.36

13. Phiriyapokanon, T.: Is a big button interface enough for elderly users? toward user interface guidelines for elderly users. Masters thesis, Comput. Eng., Mälardalen University, Västerås, Sweden (2011)

14. Hunter, A., Sayers, H., McDaid, L.: An Evolvable Computer Interface for Elderly Users. In: Proceeding of Supporting Human Memory with Interactive Systems Workshop at the 2007 British HCI Conference, Lancaster, UK, pp. 29–32 (2007)

15. Moller, F.: Uso do smartphone por pessoas da terceira idade: a utilização de apps para operações bancárias. Santa Catarina, p. 26 (2017)

16. Yin, R.K.: Estudo de Caso: Planejamento e Métodos. 2. ed. Bookman, Porto Alegre (2001)

17. Paterson, B.L., Bottorff, J.L., Hewat, R.: Blending observational methods: possibilities, strategies and challenges. Int J Qual Methods **2**(1), 29–38 (2003)

18. Zanelli, J.C.: Pesquisa qualitativa em estudos da gestão de pessoas. Estudos de Psicologia **7**, 79–88 (2002)

19. Mendes, C.F.: Paisagem Urbana: uma mídia redescoberta. Editora Senac São Paulo, São Paulo (2006)

Research on Wearable Smart Products for Elderly Users Based on Kano Model

Xin Chen[✉] and Shuyuan Li

Shenzhen University, Guangdong, China
xinchen@szu.edu.cn

Abstract. In 2021, the key indicators of the seventh national census released by the National Bureau of Statistics of China showed the deepening population aging. Nowadays, the Chinese government vigorously promotes a series of elderly care measures at home and encourages the development of smart wearable devices combined with Internet technology for monitoring elderly health. However, due to the complex functions and low aging suitability of smart devices, their acceptance by the elderly is very low. Therefore, this paper divides the elderly into three groups on the basis of age to study their basic health status. Based on the KANO model, the real needs of the elderly in different age groups for smart wearable devices are calculated, providing a reference for the development and design of smart wearable devices for the elderly. Moreover, it helps to settle the uneven distribution of resources caused by the wave of population aging.

Keywords: Smart wearable devices · Elderly users · Kano model

1 Introduction

1.1 Aging Population in China

On May 12, 2021, the National Bureau of Statistics of China released key indicators for the seventh national census. Compared with the data from the sixth national census (2010), the population in mainland China increased from 1.33972 billion to 1.41178 billion, with an average annual growth rate of 0.53% [1]. Meanwhile, the number of people aged 60 had overreached 264.02 million, accounting for 18.70% of the total population, and the number of people aged 65 had overreached 191 million, 13.50% of the total population. Compared with 2010, the percentage points respectively increased by 5.44 and 4.63. The old-age dependency ratio(ODR) reached 29.5%, that is, about 3.4 working-age population (16-59 years old) supported one older people (over 60 years old) [2]. Figure 1 suggests that China's aging population is extending, only one step away from deep aging. According to the China Development Report 2020— Trends and Policies of the Aging Population, the proportion of the Chinese population aged 65 and above will reach at 27.9% by 2050. Such a rapid wave of aging is both an opportunity and a challenge for China.

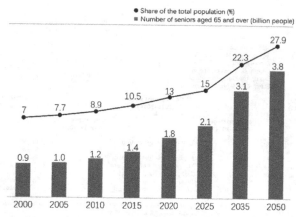

● Share of the total population (%)
■ Number of seniors aged 65 and over (billion people)

Fig. 1. The forecast of the changes and trend of China's elderly population (Data source: National Bureau of Statistics)

1.2 Aging Population in China

Influenced by Confucian culture, no matter what stage of history is, "filial piety" is an important criterion for the society. Under the traditional influence, family care is the first choice for most of the aged and their children compared with institutional care. Internationally, the developed countries and regions like the United Kingdom, the United States, Japan, and Singapore have gradually formed a "community integrated care" model for the elderly [3]. "Home care" is the trend for the aged in China and even human society.

According to foreign research, home care service was originated from the British "Community Care" which was defined as "community care for the elderly" by most scholars. It means that the elder live in their own families and enjoy the services provided by the community-related care institutions [4]. In China, home care means that the family undertakes the main responsibility and aspects of supporting the elderly, taking care of their lives, providing spiritual comfort, and helping and supporting the elderly [5]. In 2016, the 13th Five-Year Plan for the Development of Civil Affairs officially proposed to "completely build a multi-level elderly care service system at home by relying on communities, supplementing institutions, and combining medical care and nursing care". It is the first time that China's Guiding ideology clarified that pension is based on home care.

So far, China's home care mainly has five stages of development, specific time, and the corresponding policy support, as shown in Fig. 2 [6].

1.3 Aging Population in China

In recent years, dominated by the Internet of Things, information technology, big data and cloud computing, the fourth technological revolution has greatly promoted the development of elderly care services. Many emerging technologies are the driving force for home care progress, of which smart wearable devices are an important part [6]. The

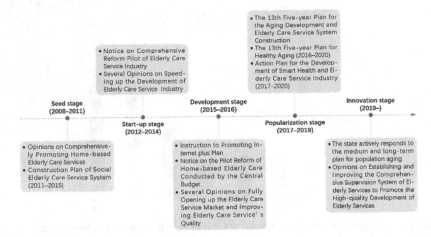

Fig. 2. Main policies of China's smart home for the elderly care

pervasive use of smart wearable devices could ease the social burden of the growing demand for health care and assistance for the elderly [7].

China had a strict policy of birth control since 1982, leading to severe population aging problems in the early stages of economic development. Compared with the "getting rich before getting old" in developed countries, China's dilemma of "getting old before getting rich" limits the development of comprehensive intelligent technology. The promotion of smart products is not in place, and competent elderly care is still in its infancy. In addition, smart medical devices for the elderly are policy-rather than demand-driven products. Therefore, many older people do not have a deep understanding towards it, and it is a bit hard to conceptually understand how to make smart technology facilitate lives [6]. A study shows that only 27% of China's elderly can properly understand smart elderly care [8].

The positive side is that the country's active policy promotion effectively expands the consumers of smart elderly care services, gradually transforming China's home-based model of elderly care into an intelligent and network model.

Therefore, it will be effective to ease the plight of China's rapidly aging population by following the trend of development and vigorous promotion of smart wearable devices suitable for the elderly under the situation of insufficient resources for the elderly.

2   Literature Review

2.1   CHARLS: A Survey of the Basic Health Status of the Elderly in China

The China Health and Retirement Longitudinal Study (CHARLS) project of Peking University is a longitudinal survey. It aims to collect a set of high-quality micro-data about the middle-aged and the elder aged 45 and above in China to analyze the problem of China's aging population so as to promote interdisciplinary research on aging issues. The CHARLS baseline survey covers 150 countries/regions and 450 villages/urban communities involving 17,708 people in 10,257 households, which is highly representative to reflect the basic situation of China's collective middle-aged and elderly population [9]. This paper uses the fourth issue of CHARLS (2018), officially published in September 2020, for theoretical analysis.

According to the international standard for the definition of the elderly, 60-74 years old are pre-elderly (Group A), 75-89 years old elderly (Group B), and 90 years old and above (Group C) long-lived elderly. As a consequence, this paper only analyzes 10,818 respondents (aged 60 and above) born in 1958 and before in the CHARLS 2018 data.

Self-report Health Status. Among the 10,818 respondents, excluding blank data, the effective samples of this questionnaire are 9,898. The total number of samples was 7958(80.40%) in Group A, 1907(19.27%) in Group B and 33(0.33%) in Group C (Table 1).

Table 1. Descriptive analysis of self-assessed health.

	Very good	Good	Fair	Poor	Very poor	Total
Group A	818 (10.28%)	909 (11.42%)	3856 (48.46%)	1836 (23.07%)	539 (6.77%)	7958
Group B	152 (7.97%)	207 (10.85%)	880 (46.15%)	513 (26.90%)	15 (8.13%)	1907
Group C	1 (3.03%)	5 (15.15%)	16 (48.49%)	10 (30.30%)	1 (3.03%)	33
Total	971 (9.81%)	1121 (11.33%)	4752 (48.01%)	2359 (23.83%)	695 (7.02%)	9898

Investigation of Basic Physical Condition. The CHARLS questionnaire asked respondents about their basic physical condition such as whether being physically disabled or having mental health problems, hearing problems, vision problems, or speech impediments [10].

Excluding the blank data, 2,141 of the 10,818 elderly respondents experienced these physical discomforts, among which, hearing problems was the immediate physical change faced by 750 (35.03%), following vision problems by 506 (23.63%), and mental retardation by 428(19.99%) (Fig. 3).

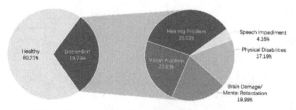

Fig. 3. Investigation of basic physical condition

Investigation of Chronic Diseases. By screening the CHARLS survey on chronic diseases of the elderly over 60 (Fig. 4), we found that the most common chronic diseases on top three were hypertension, dyslipidemia and heart attack in Group A, hypertension, stroke and dyslipidemia in Group B, and hypertension, memory-related disease and stroke in Group C. In summary, the three chronic diseases that have the greatest impact on the elderly over 60 are Hypertension, Dyslipidemia, and Heart Attack.

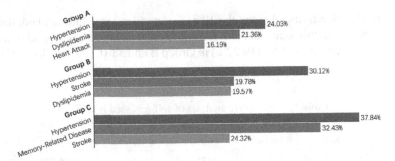

Fig. 4. Common chronic diseases and their proportions affecting the elderly in China

2.2 An Analysis on Existing Smart Wearable Devices for the Elderly

At present, whether at home care, community care, or institutional care, it is impossible to monitor the elderly 24 h a day in real time. The use of smart wearable devices has largely filled this gap.

As an emerging technology, the smart wearable device is a body with comprehensive performance which integrates such multiple functions as microprocessor-controlled embedded systems and computer network communications. It can provide a full range of efficient and multi-functional services for the elderly at home [11]. The existing smart wearable devices are mainly smart bracelets/watches. According to the research, from the perspective of user psychology, ease of use, and readability (Fig. 5), the wrist is the most suitable place to wear smart devices, then the neck, and the arm at last [12].

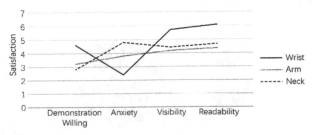

Fig. 5. Average satisfaction with wearable products for common body in three parts [12]

Smart Wearable Bracelets/watches. There are two main types of elderly smart bracelets/watches, one focuses on the functional comprehensiveness, the other focuses on the specificity of emergency prevention and control.

Part of emergencies may have serious consequences due to the decline of physical function in the elderly group. For example, fractures and strains from falls can lead to bedridden conditions. The resulting stasis pneumonia and lower extremity deep vein thrombosis are common causes of death in the elderly [13].The Everthere (Fig. 6-a), a wearable medical alarm device, launched by AT&T in 2013 focuses on detecting whether the wearer has fallen and automatically alarming when an accident occurs, so as to timely rescue the elderly who have fallen and reduce subsequent injuries. Compared with Everthere, the elderly smart bracelet (Fig. 6-b) released by Tempo in 2014 pays more attention to the functional comprehensiveness. The device has a variety of built-in sensors that can monitor physical data such as exercise, sleep, and heart rate.

At present, the functions of smart wearable bracelets/watches are gradually transforming into health management and entertainment. Besides the two bracelets above designed especially for the elderly, many smart wearable bracelets/watches for the general public in the Chinese market have adopted health management as their basic function. Taking the APPLE WATCH S7 launched by APPLE in 2021 as an example, the function of testing blood oxygen saturation has been added when compared with the APPLE WATCH S6.

Table 2 summarizes the common functions and services of several elderly smart wearable bracelets/watches that are sold well in the mainland market. There are mainly five categories, health management, safety, entertainment, basic parts, and outlook. The necessity of these functions will be continuously and deeply discussed in the following sections.

Table 2. Common features of wearable devices.

Function/service		
Health management	A1	Call for help by one-key SOS
	A2	Provide more professional and accurate measurement of heart rate, blood pressure, and other body data
	A3	Remind you to seek medical attention when abnormal data is detected
	A4	Share body data with family doctors online for chronic disease management
	A5	Possess voice memos, reminders for daily medicines, or other matters
	A6	Fall detection and notification of family members in critical moments

(continued)

Table 2. (*continued*)

Function/service		
Safety	B1	Share GPS location and real-time location with family
	B2	Set the range of activities, and notify family members if the area is exceeded (electronic fence)
	B3	Record daily activity track and time
	B4	Query location with one-click
Entertainment	C1	Possess music play, audiobooks, and other entertainment functions
	C2	Make video call
Basic parts	D1	Rely not on a cell phone that can be used independently
	D2	Bind your family's mobile phone for auxiliary use
	D3	Have long battery life
	D4	Have bigger screen, bigger volume
	D5	With color screen
	D6	With physical buttons
Outlook	E1	With personalized look and different color choices

Wearable Exoskeleton. In addition to such wrist wearable devices as watches and bracelets, exoskeleton support devices for the protection and assistance of other body parts have also successively come out.

Aurora Powered Suit (Fig. 6-c), an exoskeleton suit for the elderly with reduced mobility, mainly aims at supporting the core parts of the human body (spine, hip, and pelvis). The built-in exoskeleton can help the elderly sit still, stand, and walk. The Spring Loaded Technology Bionic Knee Brace (Fig. 6-d) focuses on improving knee pain. As for Steadiwear Anti-Shake Gloves (Fig. 6-e), a hand exoskeleton support product for Parkinson's patients, its anti-shock technology that is similar to buildings can effectively reduce hand tremors. Active Protective (Fig. 6-f) a body-worn airbag, can be quickly inflated to protect the hip bones of the elder when falling. Chronolife T-shirts (Fig. 6-g) add embedded sensors to the clothing to measure in real-time the six key factors without affecting daily life, namely electrocardiograms, chest lung, belly breathing, body temperature, and general physical activity.

Although these exoskeleton products have comprehensive functions and various forms, their popularity and user acceptance in mainland China are very low due to technology and cost limitations [14]. Therefore, this paper will conduct an in-depth analysis of smart wearable bracelets/watches with relatively high popularity and relatively mature technology.

Although these exoskeleton products have comprehensive functions and various forms, their popularity and user acceptance in mainland are very low on account of

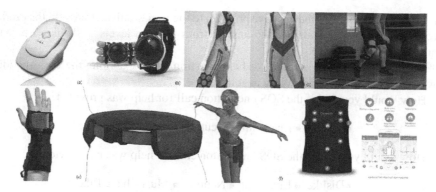

Fig. 6. Existing senior wearable devices

technology and cost limitations [14]. As a result, this paper will conduct an in-depth analysis of smart wearable bracelets/watches with relatively high popularity and mature technology.

2.3 Summary

This section uses data from CHARLS 2018 to find out the basic health status of the elderly in China, the most common changes in physical function, and the most far-reaching chronic diseases, by doing so, to provide a reference for the design of smart wearable devices for the elderly under the home-based care model in the future Chinese market.

Secondly, the existing wearable devices for the elderly are summarized as and divided into wearable bracelets/watches and wearable exoskeletons. This paper concentrates on the common functions of wearable bracelets/watches, based on which the follow-up research will further discuss the needs of the elderly at different ages for these functions.

3 Research Methods

This paper uses the KANO model to clarify the demand for smart wearable bracelets/watches of the elderly at different ages (Group A/B/C). The KANO model is an instrument for classifying and prioritizing user needs in the analysis of the nonlinear relationship between product performance and user satisfaction. The higher the user's satisfaction towards the product performance, the stronger the user's demand for this product function. This method consists of the following three steps, Kano questionnaire, Kano evaluation table, and Kano Results Assessment [15].

3.1 Kano Questionnaire

Each group contains positive and negative questions about a product attribute in the Kano questionnaire. The positive problem refers to the user's satisfaction with the product that has certain function, and the negative problem to the user's satisfaction with the product that has none. Respondents need to answer from the five levels of dislike, live with, neutral, must-be, and like.

Taking the SOS one-key call for help function as an example, the corresponding positive and negative problems are as follows.

How would you feel if the SOS one-button call for help was provided?

●Dislike ● Live with ● Neutral ● Must - be ● Like

How would you feel if the SOS one-button call for help was not provided?

●Dislike ● Live with ● Neutral ● Must - be ● Like

This KANO questionnaire is based on the functions and services summarized in Table 2 from five aspects of health management, safety, entertainment, basic parts, and outlook. There are 19 groups of questions are set to investigate the real needs of smart wearable bracelets/watches of the elderly at different ages.

3.2 Kano Results Assessment Method

According to the cross summary between the positive and negative items in the KANO questionnaire, six attributes can be obtained (Table 3).

Table 3. Kano evaluation table [16].

Functional	Dysfunctional				
	Like	Must-be	Neutral	Live with	Dislike
Like	Q	A	A	A	O
Must-be	R	I	I	I	M
Neutral	R	I	I	I	M
Live with	R	I	I	I	M
Dislike	R	R	R	R	Q

Note: A-Attractive; O-One dimensional; M-Must-be; I-Indifferent; R-Reverse; Q-Questionable

The user's sensitivity to function/service level changes can be determined by using the Better and Worse values. The calculation formulas of Better and Worse values are,

$$Better = (A + O)/(A + O + M + I),$$

$$Worse = -1 \times (O + M)/(A + O + M + I).$$

The Better value is between 0 and 1. The larger the value is, the higher the sensitivity and the priority will be. The Worse value is between -1 and 0. The smaller the value is, the higher the sensitivity and the priority are.

4 Findings

4.1 Analysis of KANO Questionnaire Results

This questionnaire adopts the method of on-the-spot research, showing some functions of APPLE WATCH SE and HUAWEI Band 6 to the respondents to establish the relative understanding of smart wearable bracelets/watches. 150 questionnaires were distributed, with 139 valid questionnaires, of which 72 questionnaires were returned by Group A, 50 by Group B, and 17 by Group C.

The results of the questionnaire were coded and analyzed by SPSSAU. Corresponding to the Kano evaluation table, the proportion of the six attributes is calculated on the basis of each problem and the final classification result (referring to the attribute corresponding to the highest proportion of the six). Furthermore, the formula is used to calculate the Better and Worse values.

In this survey's results, Table 4 shows the changes in the demand for various functions/services in different age groups, the corresponding attributes, and Better and Worse values.

Table 4. Better and Worse values.

Function/service	60–74 (Group A)			75–89 (Group B)			90 + (Group C)		
	Results	Better	Worse	Results	Better	Worse	Results	Better	Worse
A1	I	30.88%	−33.82%	M	28.26%	−58.70%	M	25.00%	−56.25%
A2	M	34.43%	−52.24%	M	28.27%	−48.98%	I	25.00%	−31.25%
A3	I	33.33%	−28.79%	I	28.57%	−19.05%	I	25.00%	−25.00%
A4	I	25.76%	−18.18%	I	23.08%	−25.64%	I	25.00%	−12.50%
A5	I	30.43%	−18.84%	I	26.19%	−28.57%	A	58.82%	−29.41%
A6	I	31.34%	−28.36%	M	29.17%	−54.17%	M	29.64%	−64.71%
B1	I	23.08%	−29.23%	M	25.53%	−46.81%	O	37.50%	−62.50%
B2	I	16.67%	−18.52%	I	29.17%	−18.75%	I	31.25%	−31.25%
B3	I	32.86%	−31.43%	I	28.89%	−20.00%	I	23.53%	−29.41%
B4	I	30.99%	−28.17%	I	28.26%	−34.78%	I	29.41%	−11.76%
C1	A	71.43%	−34.29%	A	38.64%	−27.27%	I	35.29%	−35.29%
C2	O	65.15%	−71.21%	O	65.12%	−65.12%	O	68.75%	−68.75%
D1	I	32.31%	−32.31%	I	26.67%	−31.11%	I	31.2%	−31.25%
D2	I	25.40%	−31.75%	I	28.57%	−32.65%	I	26.67%	−33.33%
D3	M	25.00%	−76.39%	M	28.00%	−68.00%	M	23.53%	−64.71%
D4	I	20.90%	−29.85%	M	22.00%	−58.00%	M	25.00%	−62.50%
D5	I	31.75%	−33.33%	I	26.53%	−16.33%	I	17.65%	−17.65%
D6	I	24.14%	−34.48%	I	28.57%	−36.73%	O	41.18%	−41.18%
E1	A	61.19%	−34.33%	I	20.00%	−33.33%	I	11.76%	−11.76%

The results in the table change into the Better-Worse scatter plot according to the coordinates, where the absolute value of the Worse is taken as the abscissa, the Better as the ordinate, and then the scatter plot is divided by the absolute value of the Better and the Worse, so the following four-quadrant diagram is obtained (Fig. 7).

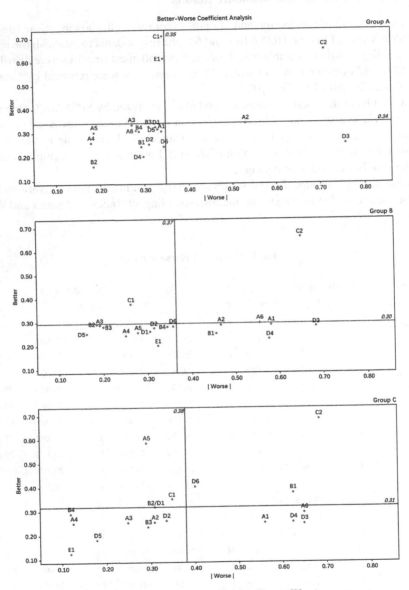

Fig. 7. A coefficient analysis on Better-Worse

The first quadrant is the One-dimensional Quality. If the Better value is high and the Worse value high in absolute value, it is necessary to satisfy this function/service first. The second quadrant is the Attractive Quality. If the Better value is high, but the Worse value low in absolute value, it is necessary to satisfy this function/service first. The third quadrant is the Indifference Quality. If the Better value is low, and the absolute value of Worse value low too, it is unnecessary to provide this function/service. The fourth quadrant is the Must-be Quality. If the Better value is low, but the Worse value high in absolute value, it is of necessity to fulfill this function/service.

4.2 Sensitivity Analysis

A sensitivity matrix can sort these requirements. Example in Group A (Fig. 8) can draw a circle with the origin O as the center and OP the radius. Within the circle, it is Indifference Quality, unhelpful to improve product satisfaction and generally not considered in the process of product design. Outside the circle, the farther the distance from the center O is, the higher the sensitivity and the impact on product satisfaction will be, and the more priority needs to be given. In addition, function/service provisioning priority is usually sorted sequentially by the level of Must-be Quality, One-dimensional Quality, Attractive Quality and Indifference Quality.

In SUM, the demand order of Group A is obtained, that is, D3 > A2 > C2 > C1 > E1.

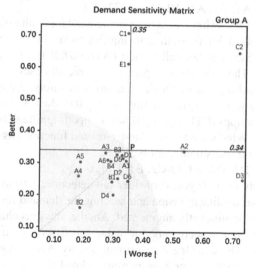

Fig. 8. Demand sensitivity matrix

In the same way, the demand order of Group B and C is obtained,
Group B: D3 > A1 > D4 > A6 > A2 > B1 > C2 > C1
Group C: A6 > D3 > D4 > A1 > C2 > B1 > D6 > A5

5 Analysis and Discussion

Figure 9 shows the demand for smart wearable bracelets/watches functions by the elderly in three different age groups.

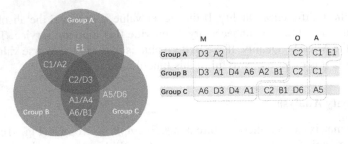

Fig. 9. Demand scenario

Group A: M-D3, A2; O-C2; A-C1, E1

Pre-elderly aged 60–74 have relatively good physical functions, requiring not much health management-related functions. However, due to chronic diseases such as hypertension, it is desirable to obtain accurate blood pressure and heart rate data (A2). At the same time, entertainment functions (C1, C2) can also increase its satisfaction. It is worth mentioning that among the three groups, only group A lists "Personalized look and different color choices" (E1) as an attractive quality.

Group B: M-D3, A1, D4, A6, A2, B1; O-C2; A-C1

Older people aged 75–89 have an increasing demand for health management. Owing to their declining physical functions, to settle injuries caused by emergencies has become a priority. Therefore, SOS one-key call for help (A1) and fall detection (A6) are classified as Must-be Quality. The long-term impact of chronic diseases makes physical data measurement (A2) still a Must-be Quality. In terms of safety, group B classifies GPS positioning (B1) as a less sensitive function among the Must-be Quality. The demand for entertainment functions (C1) of group B has dropped significantly, which belongs to Indifference Quality. What's more, such family-related functions as video call (C2) are still classified as One-dimensional Quality.

Group C: M-A6, D3, D4, A1; O-C2, B1, D6; A-A5

Long-lived elderly over 90 years consider fall detection (A6) as their top need. On account of the obvious decline in vision and hearing, the demand for bigger screens and volume (D4) has also significantly augmented. Another obvious change is that because these elderly people are not accustomed to using touch screens, it is the first time to have physical buttons (D6) as a One-dimensional Quality. According to CHARLS 2018, 32.43% of the elderly over 90 suffer from memory-related diseases, supported also by the data in the KANO questionnaire. Therefore, for the first time, the voice memo function (A5) is classified as Attractive quality.

The demand for video calls (C2) of the three groups tends to be the same with the complex operation of smartphones and low suitability for aging, resulting in the low popularity of the elderly group. Therefore, the elderly are eager to seek a simpler way than WeChat video call to maintain family relationships and meet their spiritual needs.

Another requirement that tends to be consistent is the long battery life (D3). It is because the way to wear the bracelet/watch and the lack of standardization of the charger that make charging process complicated for the elderly with poor memory.

During the survey, some elderly users who gave up using bracelets/watches present that long charging time and poor battery life are important factors.

6 Conclusion

By screening the survey data of CHARLS 2018, this paper obtained the record of the basic health status, main changes of physical function, and common chronic diseases of the elderly over 60 years old in the mainland, accordingly, a reference for future smart wearable devices designed for the elderly in China is provided.

Most of the existing wearable smart bracelets/watches for the elderly have numerous complex functions. However, many functions are not often used by the elderly, resulting in increased operational complexity and cost. This paper summarizes their common functions in recent years by using the KANO model to conduct a group study on the elderly over 60 years old, so as to discuss the changes in different needs of the elderly in three age groups. It should be noted that the research object in this paper is the elderly living in Shenzhen, China. Thus, the study results may have certain limitations with the changes in the region. The inconvenience of surveying the elderly over 90 also led to the small sample size of Group C. In addition, the conclusions may change over time if smart wearable devices are gradually transform into being aging-friendly and convenient, correspondingly the needs of the elderly may increase.

In general, the research and application of smart wearable devices in elderly care is a hot trend in the future development of China and even the world. For this reason, it is a topic worthy of in-depth study to improve the cost-effectiveness ratio and the suitability of elderly smart wearable devices, meet the individual needs of the elderly based on being safer, more convenient, and lower in cost.

Acknowledgments. We thank the Foundation for Young Talents in Higher Education of Guangdong, China [Project Batch No. 2020WQNCX061] for the research support.

References

1. Tu, W.J., Zeng, X., Liu, Q.: Aging tsunami coming: the main finding from China's seventh national population census. Aging Clin. Exp. Res. 1-5 (2021)
2. Fang, E.F., Scheibye-Knudsen, M., Jahn, H., et al.: A research agenda for aging in China in the 21st century. Ageing Res Rev **24**, 197–205 (2015)
3. Mira, J., Francois, B., Howard, B.: International experiments in integrated care for the elderly: a synthesis of the evidence. Special Issue: Issues and challenges in long term care – an international perspective **18**(3), 222–235 (2003)
4. Christine, M., Celia, R., Maggie, M.: Telecare and older people: who cares where? Soc. Sci. Med. **72**(3), 347–354 (2011)
5. Xia, Y., et al.: Rural–urban differences in home-based care willingness among older adults: a cross-sectional study in Shandong, China. Int. J. Qual. Health Care **32**(2), 126–134 (2020)
6. Zhang, Q., Li, M., Wu, Y.: Smart home for elderly care: development and challenges in China. BMC Geriatr **20**(1), 1–8 (2020)
7. Li, J., Ma, Q., Chan, A.H., Man, S.: Health monitoring through wearable technologies for older adults: smart wearables acceptance model. Appl. Ergon. **75**, 162–169 (2019)

8. Gao, L., Liu, D., Song, S., et al.: Analysis of influencing factors of community elderly's demand on smart home care. Health Vocat. Educ. **25**(12), 123–125 (2019)
9. Zhao, Y.H., et al.: China Health and Retirement Longitudinal Study Wave 4 User's Guide. Peking University, National School of Development (2020)
10. Zhao, Y.H., Hu, Y.S., James, P.S., John, S., Yang, G.H.: Cohort profile: the China Health and Retirement Longitudinal Study(CHARLS). Int. J. Epidemiol. **43**(1), 61–68 (2014)
11. Jia, Y., Yin, T.: Application of smart wearable devices in elderly care. In: Macintyre, J., Zhao, J., Ma, X. (eds.) SPIoT 2021. LNDECT, vol. 97, pp. 613–622. Springer, Cham (2022). https://doi.org/10.1007/978-3-030-89508-2_79
12. Fang, Y.M., Chang, C.C.: Users' psychological perception and perceived readability of wearable devices for elderly people. Behav. Inf. Technol. **35**(3), 225–232 (2016)
13. Jung, H.Y., et al.: Relating factors to severe injury from outdoor falls in older people. Geriatr Gerontol **18**(1), 80–87 (2018)
14. Li, J.D., Ma, Q., Alan, H.S., Chan, S.S.: Man, Health monitoring through wearable technologies for older adults: smart wearables acceptance model. Appl. Ergon. **75**, 162–169 (2019)
15. Wu, M., Wang, L.: A continuous fuzzy Kano's model for customer requirements analysis in product development. Proc. Inst. Mech. Eng. Part B J. Eng. Manuf **226**(3), 535-546 (2012)
16. Lin, Y., Pekkarinen, S.: QFD-based modular logistics service design. J. Bus. Ind. Mark **26**, 344–356 (2011)

Voice Controlled Devices and Older Adults – A Systematic Literature Review

Dietmar Jakob[✉] [iD]

Technology Campus Grafenau, Deggendorf Institute of Technology, Hauptstrasse 3,
94481 Grafenau, Germany
dietmar.jakob@th-deg.de

Abstract. For older adults Voice Controlled Devices (VCDs) could offer an easy way to access to digital services. This paper provides a systematic literature review (N = 60) of the state of research on learnability, usability, and use of VCDs and older adults. Furthermore, the paper highlight the predominant study methods used and identify positive and negative characteristics of VCDs. In addition, it presents reservations and barriers that prevent older adults from using VCDs. This work extends related work by conducting a literature review within the databases *Goolge Scholar, ACM Digital Library, IEEE Xplore*, and *ProQuest*. The structured literature review was conducted using the Preferred Reporting Items for Systematic Reviews and Meta-Analyses (PRISMA) proposed scheme.

The results show that as of 2018, the number of researches on VCDs and older adults is steadily increasing, and this population group is receiving increasing attention. Most of the studies (40%) used mixed methods for data collection and analysis. The literature review clearly shows that older adults have few problems learning and using VCDs. Older adults face problems caused by faulty speech recognition of commands or a non-existent display that visually shows input and output of commands. Obstacles are largely privacy and data protection concerns.

Keywords: Voice Controlled Devices · Voice User Interface · Voice Assistant · Intelligent Virtual Assistant · Human Computer Interaction · Learnability · Usability · Reservations · Older adults · Elderly

1 Introduction

Devices with interfaces controlled by natural language processing (NLP) [20] have been known for some time. Manufacturers of digital devices such as *Apple,*

This work was funded by the *Bavarian State Ministry of Family Affairs, Labor and Social Affairs.*

Supplementary Information The online version contains supplementary material available at https://doi.org/10.1007/978-3-031-05581-2_14.

Google, Amazon, Microsoft, Samsung, and *IBM* have recognized the market potential of voice interfaces and integrated them into their products as part of the operating system or as a stand-alone solution in loudspeakers known as smart speakers. These voice interfaces are also used in navigation devices, satellite receivers, vehicles, and other devices.

Interaction with Voice Controlled Devices (VCDs) is through natural speech input and output and is similar to human-to-human communication. Due to the similarity to human-to-human communication, it could be assumed that this form of interaction reduces the barriers to the use of digital technologies that exist mainly in the population of older adults [52], enables more straightforward operation of digital technologies, and easy access to digital services. Older adults, in particular, could profit from this type of human-machine interaction by easing their access to digital services. However, there is a lack of studies considering how older adults interact with VCDs. [83]

The essential motivation of this work was to provide an overview of the scientific literature of what research has been done on using VCDs and older adults. *Sayago et al.* [83] already criticized in their work the insufficient attention given to the population group of the older adults in scientific research related to voice interfaces. Literature reviews have already been conducted by *Stigall & Caine* [96], *Stigall et al.* [97], and *Sin & Munteanu* [90]. These works were limited to investigating the databases *ACM Digital Library*[1], *SAGE Publication*[2], and *American Association of Retired Persons*, known as *AARP*[3].

The formulation of the relevant research questions (RQ) is specified according to the *Patient/Population-Intervention-Comparison-Outcome (PICO)* scheme, which originated in evidence-based medicine but served as a template for other scientific disciplines [9]:

- *Population* The population of research interest is the group of older adults. The *United Nations (UN)* defines older adults as persons who have reached or exceeded the age of 60 years. [105]

  In this paper, however, the age limit was corrected to persons 55+, since specifically, the birth cohorts 1963 and 1964 were the cohorts with the highest birth rates in Germany. Their share of the total population in Germany in 2019 was 3%, and these cohorts were already 55 and 56 years old, respectively, at that time. The 55–59 age group is relevant because statistics show that the proportion of people in the labor force is already declining from the 55–59 age group onwards, which means they are no longer participating in the labor force. [94] *Huebner* [46] considers age phases from a sociological perspective from a life course perspective, in which normative phases are terminated or initiated by transitions and life events. *Huebner* lists the transition to retirement as a classic life event. [46]

---

[1] https://dl.acm.org.
[2] https://uk.sagepub.com.
[3] https://aarp.org.

According to official data, 69% of 50–54-year-olds in Germany are still employed, while the share in the 55–59 age group is only 62% and in the 60-65 age group only 45%. [94, 95]
- *Intervention* The main research interest lies in technical devices with integrated voice interfaces, intelligent assistance systems, and smart speaker that can be operated via voice.
- *Comparison* In connection with the learnability, operability, and use of the devices, possible barriers that prevent older adults from using them will also be investigated.
- *Output* The knowledge objective of the literature review focuses on a better understanding of how specifically the group of older adults perceives the use of VCDs, for what purposes they are used, and what reasons prevent them from using them.

The following research questions (RQ) are deduced from the specification of the research interest according to the PICO scheme:

RQ1 What is the state of research on the learnability, usability, and usage of VCDs among older adults?
RQ2 What are the predominant methods used for empirical findings in the context of VCDs and older adults?
RQ3 What positive and negative characteristics of VCDs and older adults have been identified?
RQ4 What reasons prevent older adults from using VCDs?

Based on the research questions, a structured literature review was conducted. The *Preferred Reporting Items for Systematic Reviews and Meta-Analyses (PRISMA)* scheme guided the description of the approach to selecting articles for analysis. [74]

This work provides a comprehensive overview and extends the work of *Stigall & Caine* [96], *Stigall et al.* [97], and *Sin & Munteanu* [90]. The findings should help further research understand how older adults interact with VCDs. This work will also help provide device developers and designers with insights into what older adults want when designing voice interfaces. In addition, the paper aims to provide an incentive to continue not forgetting older adults, as digitization accelerates, in research.

Section 2 presents the methodology, the databases used to select the literature, and the inclusion and exclusion criteria. It also explains which search terms and search strings were used, how many contributions were found by the search in total, and which contributions were irrelevant or removed in advance due to duplicates found. Section 3 presents preselection results by categorizing the contributions according to the year of publication, the language interfaces or devices used, the methods used, sample sizes, and the age groups studied. In addition, this section discusses the positive and negative characteristics of voice interfaces, as well as reasons and reservations that prevent older adults of their use. The limitations of the paper are described in Sect. 4, the findings and the inconsistencies in literature are discussed in Sect. 5. In the end, the whole paper is summarized in Sect. 6.

2   Methodology

For the selection of literature sources, the search was conducted in:

1. *Google Scholar*[4]: Database for a broad search of scholarly literature across many disciplines ad sources.
2. *ACM Digital Library*[5]: Database of full-text articles and bibliographic literature covering computing and information technology.
3. *IEEE Xplore Digital Library*[6]: Research database for discovery and access journal articles, conference proceedings, technical standards, and related materials on computer science, electrical engineering and electronics, and allied fields.
4. *ProQuest*[7]: Collection of many databases that provide access to thousands of journals, magazines, newspapers, dissertations, and other publications.

It should be noted that *Google Scholar* can only be searched in the document title or the full text. Therefore, the search was performed exclusively in the document title since a search in the full text would lead to results unrelated to the search terms. For example, a search for the terms 'smart speaker' and 'elderly' would show all results in which both search terms occur at least once without context in the text. Furthermore, *Google Scholar* searches excluded citations, and all databases omitted acronyms in the document title of voice-activated devices (e. g., 'VA' or 'VUI'). Because abbreviations for terms not in common use do not appear in the document title and should be introduced first. [22]

   All search results were printed and archived.

2.1   Inclusion Criteria

No temporal restrictions were applied to the search in the selected databases for a comprehensive overview of the available literature to answer the research questions. Regardless of publication date and type of article, any publication that met the search criteria was included in the selection.

2.2   Exclusion Criteria

No exclusion criteria were applied.

2.3   Search Terms

For searching the relevant databases, the terms generally referred to in literature for VCDs were used. In contrast to *Stigall & Caine* [96], *Stigall et al.* [97], and *Sin & Munteanu* [90], the names of the voice interfaces *Alexa, Siri,* or

---

[4] https://scholar.google.com.
[5] https://dl.acm.org.
[6] https://ieeexplore.ieee.org/.
[7] https://www.proquest.com.

Google Assistant were included in the search query. Furthermore, the term 'smart speaker' was included for the voice interfaces integrated into popular speakers. This terms complement and extend the work of *Stigall & Caine* [96], *Stigall et al.* [97], and *Sin & Munteanu* [90].

For searching in the selected databases, the commonly used terms for VCDs (including common acronyms) were combined with terms related to older adults as search terms, explained in Table 1.

Table 1. Search terms.

Search terms VCDs	Search terms older adults
Voice Assistants (VA)	Older adults
Voice Assistants	Elderly
Intelligent Virtual Assistant (IVA)	Older
Intelligent Personal Assistant (IPA)	Senior
Smart speaker	
Alexa	
Siri	
Google assistant	
Voice User Interface (VUI)	
Voice user interfaces	

A variety of terms and acronyms for VCDs are used in the related literature: Voice Assistant (VA), Intelligent Virtual Assistant (IVA), Virtual Personal Assistant (VPA), Voice-Activated Personal Assistant (VAPA), Natural User Interface (NUI), Intelligent Personal Assistant (IPA), Voice User Interface (VUI), to name a few. However, the most commonly used terms are Voice Assistant (VA), VAs, Voice User Interface (VUI), Intelligent Virtual Assistant (IVA), and Intelligent Personal Assistant (IPA), so the search was limited to these terms.

The search terms were entered into the databases on September 21, 2021.

2.4   Search Strings

The search in *Google Scholar* was done in two search cycles to avoid field length limitations in the input. As mentioned above, the search in *Google Scholar* was performed in the document title only. Two search cycles were started in the *ACM Digital Library* and *IEEE Xplore Digital Library* (search in the document title and search abstract). The acronyms used were also included in the search in the abstract. When searching the *ProQuest* database, the acronyms were omitted. Especially in this database, many acronyms are used in other contexts (e. g., medical abbreviations), and thus, many papers were irrelevant for the work.

The individual search strings used for searching in databases are explained as supplementary material to this paper.

No automated tools that filter results were used. Furthermore, the results were verified by an independent reviewer who checked the discovered datasets for completeness and relevance concerning the research questions.

2.5 Documents Retrieved

A total of 112 (n = 112) documents were identified via the search in the databases. In additional thirteen (n = 13) documents were added to the overall selection from cross references (N = 125).

Eight documents (n = 8) were removed from the preselection in the first review which are explained below. From the *ProQuest* results list, five papers [24,69,80,93] (n = 5) were removed due to the lack of reference to VCDs that were exclusively medical technical topics, or only a listing of reviewers by name [50]. Two papers (n = 2) were removed from the *IEEE Xplore* database because one was a commentary on Artificial Intelligence [75], and one was a personal portrait of a keynote speaker [48]. One (n = 1) entry was preliminary removed from the *ACM Digital Library* results from the search that described only a content summary of a conference keynote [1].

The initial screening also identified in summary sixteen duplicates (n = 16) of identical papers in two or more selected databases [23,56,66,71,77,78,83,96, 97,101,107,112] which were also removed from the preselection.

Thus, 101 (N = 101) records were included in the preselection. The abstracts of the preselected 101 records were reviewed in the next step.

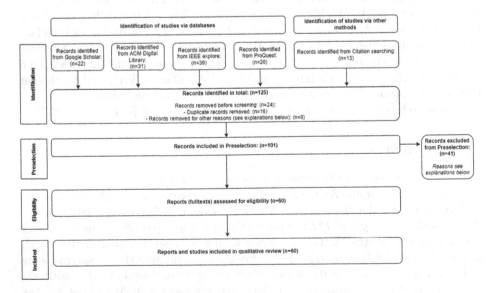

Fig. 1. Flow for systematic screening.

In the reviewed process, 33 (n = 33) articles had to be removed from the preselection that had no reference to VCDs or older adults [2, 4, 6, 7, 13, 14, 16, 21, 26, 29–32, 35, 37, 40, 43, 44, 51, 51, 54, 55, 57, 60, 61, 63, 73, 79, 80, 100, 102, 106, 108]. Five articles (n = 5) were identical in content (duplicates) [41, 87, 90, 92, 101], and three articles (n = 3) were not studies but exclusively product descriptions in which no more detailed statements were made about the use of VCDs [27, 28, 33]. The flow chart for systematic screening is shown in Fig. 1.

3   Results

A total of 60 (N = 60) documents were included in the full-text analysis and were categorized by author, year of publication, population group considered, sample size and, the methods used (see Table 2).

Table 2. Documents included in the full-text analysis.

Author	Year	Population	Sample size	Methods
Apergi, Lida Anna et al. [3]	2021	Mean age 55–56.5 y.	30	Questionnaire
Balsa, Joao et al. [5]	2020	67–80	11	SUS [8]
Blocker, Kenneth A. et al. [8]	2020	66–89	18	Interview
Bolaños, Manuel et al. [10]	2020	not stated	24	Interview
Bonila, K. & Martin-Hammond, A. [11]	2020	60+	7	Interview
Budd, B. [12]	2020	not stated	20	Interview
Chen, C. et al. [15]	2021	not stated	16	Interview
Cheng, Amy et al. [17]	2018	not stated	10	Questionnaire
Choi, Y. et al. [18]	2018	65+	19	Interview
Choi, Yong K. et al. [19]	2020	not stated	37	Mixed
Colombo-Ruano, Lorena et al. [23]	2021	62–79	9	Mixed
Conde-Caballero, David et al. [24]	2021	65+	34	Mixed
Cordasco, Gennaro et al. [25]	2014	not stated	42	Mixed
Gollasch, David & Weber, Gerhard [34]	2021	55+ (6)	6	Questionnaire
Graf, B. et al. [36]	2002	not stated	not stated	No Study
Gunathilaka, L. A. S. M. et al. [38]	2020	60–95	20	Mixed
Gusev, Marjan et al. [39]	2017	not stated	not stated	No Study
Hellwig, Andre et al. [42]	2018	60–95	20	Mixed
Huang, Jung-Tang et al. [45]	2021	not stated	not stated	Experiment
Huisingh-Scheetz, Megan et al. [47]	2020	not stated	5	Focus group
Ilievski, Andrej et al. [49]	2019	not stated	not stated	Proof of C.
Jaskulska, Anna et al. [53]	2020	mean age 73.14	9	Interview
Tan et al. [101]	2020	not stated	not stated	No study,
Kim, Sunyoung [56]	2021	74+	18	Interview

(*continued*)

Table 2. (*continued*)

Apergi, Lida Anna et al. [3]	2021	Mean age 55–56.5 y.	30	Questionnaire
Kowalski, Jaroslaw et al. [58]	2019	64–89	7	Mixed
Larsen, Alison [59]	2019	not stated	not stated	Interview
Luengo-Polo, Jeronimo et al. [62]	2021	65+	20	Mixed
McDowell, Saba B. et al. [65]	2020	50+	46	Survey
Meliones, Apostolos & Maidonis, Stavros [66]	2020	not stated	not stated	No study
Mirheidari, Bahman et al. [67]	2019	56–69	61	Experiment
Mizak, Aaron et al. [68]	2017	79–100	18	Mixed
Mtshali, Progress & Khubisa, Freedom [70]	2019	not stated	not stated	No study
Nallam, Phani et al. [71]	2020	60–76	10	Interview
O'Brien, K. et al. [72]	2021	not stated	not stated	Mixed
Peres, Karine et al. [76]	2021	60–83	53	Mixed
Pradhan, Alisha et al. [77]	2019	65+	7	Mixed
Pradhan, Alisha et al. [78]	2020	65+	7	Mixed
Reis, Arsenio et al. [81]	2018	not stated	not stated	No study
Sanders, Jamie & Martin-Hammond, Aqueasha [82]	2019	60–76	10	Mixed
Sayago, Sergio et al. [83]	2019	not stated	not stated	No study
Scherr, Simon André et al. [84]	2020	68–83	11	Mixed
Schlögl, S. et al. [85]	2013	mean age: 70.22	18	Focus group
Schlomann, Anna et al. [86]	2021	not stated	not stated	Mixed
Sengupta, Korok et al. [88]	2020	not stated	not stated	No study
Shalini, Shradha et al. [89]	2019	mean age: 80	23	Mixed
Sin, Jaisie & Munteanu, Cosmin [90]	2020	50+	5	Mixed
Sin, Jaisie & Munteanu, Cosmin [92]	2021	not stated	not stated	Literature review
Stigall, Brodrick & Caine, Kelly [96]	2020	not stated	not stated	Literature review
Stigall, Brodrick et al. [97]	2019	not stated	not stated	Literature review
Striegl, Julian et al. [98]	2021	70–85	9	Mixed
Sun, Ningjing [99]	2020	79–89	6	Experiment
Ting, Chawchen et al. [103]	2020	not stated	39	Mixed
Trajkova, Milka & Martin-Hammond, Aqueasha [104]	2020	67–97	38	Focus group
Valera Román, Adrián et al. [107]	2021	not stated	3	No study
West, A. J. [109]	2019	50+	53 &192	Mixed
Wulf, Linda et al. [110]	2014	65–83	10	Interview
Yamada, Satoshi et al. [111]	2018	65+	33	Mixed
Zeng, Zhiwei et al. [113]	2016	not stated	not stated	No study
Ziman, Randall & Walsh, Greg [114]	2018	65+	15	Mixed
Zubatiy, Tamara et al. [115]	2021	mean age: 78	20	Mixed

[8] European Portuguese System Usability Scale, [64]

When analyzing the publications, it can already be seen that many different terms are used for VCDs. The most commonly used terms are *voice/virtual assistant (VA)*, *Voice User Interface (VUI)*, and *intelligent voice/virtual assistant (IVA)*. However, the motivation for using them remains unclear and is not explained in detail.

Voice-based interfaces can be integrated into product developments to assistive robots, media technologies (i. e., smart TVs, TV receivers, smartphones, tablets, and PCs), or used as stand-alone systems in smart speakers. Since intelligent speakers, in particular, are referred to as assistants, it is not easy to differentiate between the devices. Therefore, based on the designation, the term VCD is used since it accurately describes all possible device groups.

3.1 Presentation of the Publications According to the Year of Publication

Most of the publications found for the older adults were from 2020 (n = 21). [5,8,10–12,19,38,47,53,65,66,71,78,84,88,90,96,99,101,103,104] In 2021, fifteen (n = 15) papers were identified by the cutoff date. [3,15,23,24,34,45,56,62, 72,76,86,92,98,107,115] Eleven (n = 11) papers from 2019 [49,58,59,67,70,77, 82,83,89,97,109] and six (n = 6) from 2018 [17,18,42,81,111,114]. In the period from 2002–2017, only a total of seven (n = 7) papers [25,36,39,68,85,110,113] were found on the topic, which means that interest in research on older adults and VCDs was shallow during this period, even though *Apple's Siri*, and *Google's Assistant* were already implemented in smartphones, tablets, and PCs. Only since 2018 has there been a steady increase in publications, which the rising popularity of smart speakers could explain. The survey corresponds exactly to the total number of 60 articles found (N = 60).

Table 3 shows the number of publications chronologically.

Table 3. Number of publications by year and type in chronological order.

Year of publication	Number of Journals	Number of Papers	Number of Books	Number of Grey Literature	Total
2021 (until 2021-09-21)	8	6	1	0	15
2020	7	9	3	2	21
2019	2	8	1	0	11
2018	1	4	0	1	6
2017	1	1	0	0	2
2016	0	1	0	0	1
2014	0	2	0	0	2
2013	0	1	0	0	1
2002	0	1	0	0	1
Total					60

The numbers illustrate that research on VCDs and older adults begun as of 2018 and indicates an increasing interest in research of this population.

The number of journal articles was nine-teen (n = 19) [3,5,8,18,19,24, 47,56,59,62,68,71,72,76–78,86,96,107], whereas five (n = 5) were book chapters [10,12,15,65,109]. The majority of publications were in conference papers (n = 33) [10,17,23,25,34,36,38,39,45,49,58,66,67,70,81–83,85,88–90,92,97–99,101,103,104,110,111,113–115]. Three (n = 3) contributions were unpublished publications (gray literature) [42,53,84].

3.2   Kind of VCDs Used

The VCDs used varied widely in the publications. Most studies predominantly focused on interfaces, or devices, from the *Amazon* , commonly known as *'Alexa'*. Smart speakers without a display from *Amazon* were found in sixteen publications (n = 16) [8,10,12,19,38,42,49,56,59,68,70,77,78,81,104,111]. Smart speakers with a display from the same company were dealt with in four (n = 4) papers [8,47,84,89], while three (n = 3) papers used the *Amazon* Voice Interface [3,18,23]. Ten (n = 10) papers used *Google Assistant* in their publications [15,38,42,45,49,53,58,89,107,115], while *Apples' Siri* and *Microsofts' Cortana* were used in only five (n = 5) papers [81,85,86,88,110]. In four (n = 4) papers, the voice interface used was not further defined [25,36,39,91].

3.3   Categorization of Publications by Research Methods Used

Of the total sixty (N = 60) publications selected, forty-one (n = 41) used qualitative or mixed methods. Seventeen works was conducted qualitative (n = 17) [3,8,10–12,15,17,18,34,47,53,56,59,71,85,104,110], and twenty-four studies uses mixed methods (n = 24) [19,23–25,38,42,58,62,68,72,76–78,82,84,86, 89,90,98,103,109,111,114,115].

For qualitative methods, data collection focus on interviews with participants (n = 11) [8,10–12,15,18,53,56,59,71,110], focus group meetings and interviews (n = 3) [47,85,104], and questionnaire surveys (n = 3) [3,17,34].

Mixed methods, interviews, questionnaires, participant observation, diaries, user logs, account-activity logs, 'Wizard of Oz' applications, or customer reviews are mainly used. A total of six (n = 6) contributions were also identified, which present the development of engaging, own applications using voice interfaces [5,45,49,65,67,99]. Three (n = 3) contributions present a literature review about older adults and voice interfaces [90,96,97].

3.4   Categorization of Publications by Age Group Studied

Three studies (n = 3) investigated people aged 50+ [65, 90, 109], a further three studies (n = 3) focus on people aged 55+ [3, 34, 67]. The 60+ age group was of interest in eight (n = 8) publications [11, 23, 38, 42, 58, 71, 76, 82], and twelve studies (n = 12) examined the 65+ age group [5, 8, 18, 24, 62, 77, 78, 84, 104, 110, 111, 114]. A further eight (n = 8) studies relate to people aged 70+ [53, 56, 68, 85, 89, 98, 99, 115]. Twenty-six authors (n = 26) did not specify the age group in their studies [10, 12, 15, 17, 19, 25, 36, 39, 45, 47, 49, 59, 66, 70, 72, 81, 83, 86, 88, 92, 96, 97, 101, 103, 107, 113].

3.5   Identified Positive Characteristics of VCDs

A total of thirty-five (n = 35) studies reported predominantly positive features of how participants perceived VCDs [5, 8, 10, 12, 17, 18, 23, 25, 38, 49, 53, 56, 58, 65, 67, 67, 68, 71, 72, 76–78, 82, 84–86, 89, 92, 97, 98, 104, 110, 111, 114, 115]. Among the positive aspects of using VCDs was the ease of learning the systems (n = 7) [25, 34, 53, 56, 58, 77, 114]. Thus, the simplicity of the systems was rated as high due to their voice-based use. However, it was noted in this context by three authors (n = 3) that older adults also encountered problems in the usage that could be solved by training or training courses as well as printed manuals on the devices [72, 85, 85].

Furthermore, seven authors (n = 7) particularly emphasized the devices' 'good' to 'very good' usability [5, 17, 56, 77, 84, 98, 110].

Thus, six authors (n = 6) see a potential of the systems for personal health management [18, 38], in home care [49], people living alone [38], people with cognitive impairments [76], and incipient dementia [98]. Four papers (n = 4) describe that the use of VCDs increases well-being and quality of life among older adults [12, 18, 38, 98].

Another positive aspect is the convenient control of heating thermostats and light sources (n = 2) [42, 68].

The older adults consider the devices not only as an assistant but in three (n = 3) contributions as a companion and even as a friend [38, 77, 84].

The participants found the usage options of VCDs provided primarily by smart speakers to be positive. The majority of participants used the devices at least once a day. The older adults used functions such as listening to music, checking weather reports, asking questions about general knowledge, current news or recipes, setting reminders or timers, making video calls, or creating shopping lists [12, 18, 38, 53, 56, 68, 78, 84, 104, 111, 115].

VCDs with an additional display were preferred by the participants in two publications (n = 2) because the visual output is possible in addition to voice output (e. g., *Google Assistant, Amazon Echo Show*) [8, 89].

3.6   Identified Negative Characteristics of VCDs

In addition to a large number of positive aspects about VCDs, five authors (n = 5) also expressed negative viewpoints in their contributions. For example, the participants have concerns about privacy and data protection. On the one hand, privacy statements are difficult to interpret, and, on the other hand, they are not fully read due to their length [11,15,23,25,34].

Frustrations among participants occurred because of the complexity of the technology [15], the sometimes faulty speech recognition [15,89,110], and discrepancies between the perceived and expected functions [15].

Some participants misunderstood how the devices worked by assuming that the participants themselves had to store the information in the device [56]. The studies also revealed that older adults prefer a slow step-by-step dialog [34,99], simple sets of commands [34,99], error feedback, and confirmatory feedback at the end of the interaction [99,114]. In addition, older adults have difficulties with functions that can only be activated roundabout and require technical affinity [115].

Other adverse facts about the non-use or lower acceptance of VCDs in the studies were a lack of interest in technological innovations [24], the lack of proactivity (system only interacts with the user when prompted) [107], and a lack of benefit [104], after which participants partially discontinued their activities with the VCDs. The authors disagree on the control of smartphone components.

Some participants appreciated the convenience of controlling heating systems, lights, or other sensors [68]. Others found the comfort rather negative, as it could give the impression that one is no longer active and dependent on support. [53]

Negative impressions were also left by the devices - predominantly models of smart speakers - that do not have a display and thus do not provide an additional visual representation of the answers. Here, models with displays are clearly favored by older adults [8].

4   Limitations

As a limitation of this work, it should be noted that the literature review refers primarily to older adults aged 55+, and the screening was conducted only in four selected databases. Quantitative studies across different age groups are not considered in the present work.

The acronyms in the *ProQuest* database were omitted, as the acronyms are also commonly used in medical contexts.

Another limitation in this work is the restriction of the search to the terms VA, VAs, VUI, VUIs, IVA, and IPAs.

Furthermore, as described in Sect. 2, the search terms were formulated and submitted to the databases exclusively in English. Therefore, this work focuses on English language published literature.

5   Discussion

In general, VCDs are perceived positively by older adults [97,111,115]. In their studies, the authors notes potential in VCDs for older adults as a conversational partner [111], as a counseling support device in health issues [71], in health management [18], or as a friend/companion [77,84]. The authors notes benefits of VCDs [23,53]. These benefits lie in the reduction of loneliness of the older adults [84] and in the efficiency in the use of the devices [56]. In addition, VCDs are noted as helpful for people with disabilities [58], or for people living alone [38]. High levels of acceptance and trust in the technology are also noted [17, 68,76,84,97]. Basically, VCDs are considered useful and interesting [10] and are even liked [8]. The focus of this paper refers specifically to how older adults assess learnability, usability, usage RQ1, the barriers, and reasons that prevent them from not using RQ4. Some of the literature has differing opinions on this. Which is outlined in the following sub-sections.

5.1   Learnability of VCDs

In four of the studies investigated (n = 4), older adults found VCDs to be basically easy to learn [25,58,78,114]. In contrast, one study (n = 1) states, that the VCD (investigated: Google Home) is difficult to learn for older adult [17].

In numerous studies, the independent learnability of VCDs is not investigated or not investigated neutrally. For example, some authors instructed study participants in advance on how to use the VCDs [8,56,77,78], provided manuals, or offered individual support [76,78,115], which bias the independent learnability.

Kowalski et al. [58] and *Peres et al.* [76] notes that less or no training is needed or just some support is required for older adults to learn how to use VCDs.

Regarding the learnability of VCDs, it can be summarized that, according to *Kowalski et al.* and *Peres et al.*, it is not necessary to provide support for learning to use VCDs. However, numerous study designs on VCDs are conceptualized in such a way that study participants nevertheless receive support in handling or learning VCDs in advance or during the study. This suggests a gap in research in the context of the independent learnability of VCDs.

5.2   Usability of VCDs

Literature particularly emphasized the ease of use of VCDs for older adults [12,25,78,110,111,114]. *Cheng et al.* [17], *Balsa et.* [5], *Striegl et al.* [98], and *Peres et al.* [76] also stated high usability of VCDs for older adults in their studies. VCDs also allow easy access to digital services [78], and older adults were aware of how VCDs works [115].

However, the otherwise positive usability is negatively impacted by the difficulty of setting up the devices, according to *Chen et al.* [15]. Difficulty formulating commands to VCDs was noted as another negative aspect by *Kim* [56] and *Sun* [99] added, that older adults requires more time for formulating the commands. Interaction with VCDs was also aborted if the action command [110,114] followed immediately after the wake-up word was uttered.

Further, criticized in relation to the usability of VCDs was the partly faulty speech recognition [15,110,114].

The complexity of VCDs and occurring technical glitches (e. g., Internet connection termination) also negatively affects usability [15]. *Kim* [56] found in her study that the functionality of VCDs was not understood by the older adults because the participants thought they had to first provide the system with information before they could use it.

According to *Peres et al.* [76], negative usability limitations arise specifically for people with cognitive impairments needing assistance in using VCDs.

Engaging in the context of usability is the fact that older adults prefer VCDs with a display for confirmatory feedback of successful command. They favor VCDs with a display opposite VCDs without a display [8,58,89,114].

Overall, there is a consensus in the literature on positive usability of VCDs, although some aspects (e. g., difficulty of setup, reliability of speech recognition) still need to be improved.

5.3   Usage and Usefulness of VCDs

The use of VCDs by older adults during participation in the studies varied between daily use [104,115] and regular use [12,68,82], indicating high willingness to use. A negative effect on willingness to use VCDs, according to *Kim* [56], is that there is a dismissive attitude among older adults because of the belief that one can no longer do things for oneself.

Basically, older adults see a benefit in VCDs [8,78] and are considered as helpful (e. g., with health issues or for health management) [71]. Reasons why VCDs are considered as less useful were identified by *Conde-Caballero et al.* [24] due to a lack of interest in technical innovations. *Trajkova & Martin-Hammond* [104] stated in their study that usage was also discontinued by participants due to lack of usefulness.

5.4   Reservations and Barriers to Use VCDs

The negative features described in Sect. 3.6 (e.g., privacy and data protection, faulty speech recognition) and Sect. 5.3 (e.g., lack of usefulness) also prevent older adults from using VCDs.

Older adults have the most reservations about their privacy and data protection [11,15,23,25,34]. They prevented from using VCDs by the difficulty of formulating command sentences [56,99] or misunderstanding how the VCDs works [56]. Lack of utility [104], usefulness [104], and the ability to ask the device to do something they can still do themselves are other barriers [56,104]. The participants want full control over who manages data (e. g., health data) and want to retain their autonomy about a VCDs [82].

However, engaging in this context is that the recording of conversational dialogues does not elicit any reservations [78].

6   Conclusion

This work provides a comprehensive systematic literature overview of VCDs concerning older adults and is consistent with the previous work by *Stigall & Cain* [96], *Stigall et al.* [97], and *Sin & Munteanu* [90]. However, additional databases and thus additional literature were used in this work, extending the previous reviews. The overall goal of this work was to identify the state of research on the learnability, usability, and usage of VCDs among older adults RQ1. Reviewing literature (N = 60) shows, that there is a gap in research in the context of the independent learnability of VCDs and older adults. Regarding to usability of VCDs it can be stated, that there is a consensus in the literature on positive usability of VCDs, although some (technical) aspects still need to be improved. Basically, the literature also shows that VCDs are considered useful for older adults and are perceived as useful by them.

A further goal was, to identify the predominant methods used for empirical findings in the context of VCDs in literature RQ2. It could be determined, that the majority of the studies used mixed methods and qualitative research methods.

It also aimed to determine what positive and negative characteristics older adults associate with VCDs RQ3. In literature, older adults rated the simplicity of VCDs as high due to their voice-based use. Negatively, the studies described privacy concerns by older adults and a faulty speech recognition of the systems.

Finally, to answer RQ4, we were investigated in the reasons that prevent older adults from using VCDs. Once again, mainly concerns and obstacles exist primarily due to privacy concerns.

This paper reveals that there has been an increase in research on VCDs and older adults in recent years. The review also shows that there are still gaps in the research, especially in terms of independent learnability, and should be investigated in more detail in future work.

Supplementary Material

Search strings used for searching in databases.

Database	Search in	Search string
Google Scholar, 1st search run	title	allintitle: ("Voice Assistant" OR "Voice Assistants" OR "Smart Speaker" OR "Alexa" OR "Siri" OR "Google Assistant" OR "Voice User Interface" OR "Voice User Interfaces") AND ("Elderly" OR "Older" OR "Older Adults" OR "Senior")
Google Scholar, 2st search run	title	allintitle: ("Intelligent Personal Assistant" OR "Intelligent Virtual Assistant") AND ("Elderly" OR "Older" OR "Older Adults" OR "Senior")
ACM, 1st advanced search run	title	("Voice Assistant" OR "Voice Assistants" OR "Smart Speaker" OR "Alexa" OR "Siri" OR "Google Assistant" OR "Voice User Interface" OR "Voice User Interfaces" OR "Intelligent Personal Assistant" OR "Intelligent Virtual Assistant") AND ("Elderly" OR "Older" OR "Older Adults" OR "Senior")
ACM, 2st advanced search run	abstract	("Voice Assistant" OR "Voice Assistants" OR "Smart Speaker" OR "Alexa" OR "Siri" OR "Google Assistant" OR "Voice User Interface" OR "Voice User Interfaces" OR "Intelligent Personal Assistant" OR "Intelligent Virtual Assistant" OR "VUI" OR "VA" OR "IPA" OR "IVA") AND ("Elderly" OR "Older" OR "Older Adults" OR "Senior")
IEEE Xplore, 1st advanced search run	document title	("Voice Assistant" OR "Voice Assistants" OR "Smart Speaker" OR "Alexa" OR "Siri" OR "Google Assistant" OR "Voice User Interface" OR "Voice User Interfaces" OR "Intelligent Personal Assistant" OR "Intelligent Virtual Assistant") AND ("Elderly" OR "Older" OR "Older Adults" OR "Senior")
IEEE Xplore, 2st advanced search run	abstract	("Voice Assistant" OR "Voice Assistants" OR "Smart Speaker" OR "Alexa" OR "Siri" OR "Google Assistant" OR "Voice User Interface" OR "Voice User Interfaces" OR "Intelligent Personal Assistant" OR "Intelligent Virtual Assistant" OR "VUI" OR "VA" OR "IPA" OR "IVA") AND ("Elderly" OR "Older" OR "Older Adults" OR "Senior")
ProQuest, 1st advanced search run	document title	("Voice Assistant" OR "Voice Assistants" OR "Smart Speaker" OR "Alexa" OR "Siri" OR "Google Assistant" OR "Voice User Interface" OR "Voice User Interfaces" OR "Intelligent Personal Assistant" OR "Intelligent Virtual Assistant") AND ("Elderly" OR "Older" OR "Older Adults" OR "Senior")
ProQuest, 2st advanced search run	abstract	ab("Voice Assistant" OR "Voice Assistants" OR "Smart Speaker" OR "Alexa" OR "Siri" OR "Google Assistant" OR "Voice User Interface" OR "Voice User Interfaces" OR "Intelligent Personal Assistant" OR "Intelligent Virtual Assistant" OR "VUI" OR "VA" OR "IPA" OR "IVA") AND ("Elderly" OR "Older" OR "Older Adults" OR "Senior")

References

1. IVA 2019: Proceedings of the 19th ACM International Conference on Intelligent Virtual Agents. Association for Computing Machinery, New York (2019)

2. Ahmadhon, K., Al-Absi, M.A., Jae Lee, H., Park, S.: Smart flying umbrella drone on internet of things: AVUS. In: 2019 21st International Conference on Advanced Communication Technology (ICACT), pp. 191–195. IEEE (2/17/2019–2/20/2019). https://doi.org/10.23919/ICACT.2019.8702024

3. Apergi, L.A., et al.: Voice interface technology adoption by patients with heart failure: pilot comparison study. JMIR mHealth uHealth 9(4) (2021). https://doi.org/10.2196/24646

4. Ashparie, Y.M., Bashorun, O.P., Koch, G.J., Siegel, G.R., Stoyanov, P.T.: Infrastructure analysis system (IAS). In: 2005 IEEE Design Symposium, Systems and Information Engineering, pp. 40–44. IEEE (5/1/2005–5/1/2005). https://doi.org/10.1109/SIEDS.2005.193236

5. Balsa, J., et al.: Usability of an intelligent virtual assistant for promoting behavior change and self-care in older people with type 2 diabetes. J. Med. Syst. 44(7), 1–12 (2020). https://doi.org/10.1007/s10916-020-01583-w

6. Benelli, G., Meoni, G., Fanucci, L.: A low power keyword spotting algorithm for memory constrained embedded systems. In: 2018 IFIP/IEEE International Conference on Very Large Scale Integration (VLSI-SoC), pp. 267–272. IEEE (10/8/2018–10/10/2018). https://doi.org/10.1109/VLSI-SoC.2018.8644728

7. Bhatnagar, H.V., Kumar, P., Rawat, S., Choudhury, T.: Implementation model of wi-fi based smart home system. In: 2018 International Conference on Advances in Computing and Communication Engineering (ICACCE), pp. 23–28. IEEE (6/22/2018–6/23/2018). https://doi.org/10.1109/ICACCE.2018.8441703

8. Blocker, K.A., Kadylak, T., Koon, L.M., Kovac, C.E., Rogers, W.A.: Digital home assistants and aging: initial perspectives from novice older adult users. In: Proceedings of the Human Factors and Ergonomics Society Annual Meeting, vol. 64, no. 1, pp. 1367–1371 (2020). https://doi.org/10.1177/1071181320641327

9. Blümle, A., et al.: Manual systematische recherche für evidenzsynthesen und leitlinien. https://doi.org/10.6094/UNIFR/174468

10. Bolaños, M., Collazos, C., Gutiérrez, F.: Adapting a virtual assistant device to support the interaction with elderly people. In: Proceedings of the 6th International Conference on Information and Communication Technologies for Ageing Well and e-Health, pp. 291–298. SCITEPRESS - Science and Technology Publications (5/3/2020–5/5/2020). https://doi.org/10.5220/0009840102910298

11. Bonila, K., Martin-Hammond, A.: Older adults' perceptions of intelligent voice assistant privacy, transparency, and online privacy guidelines. In: Sixteenth Symposium on Usable Privacy and Security (SOUPS 2020) (2020). https://www.usenix.org/system/files/soups2020_poster_bonilla.pdf

12. Budd, B.: Smart speaker use and psychological well-being among older adults (2020). http://fpciw.org/wp-content/uploads/sites/15/2020/11/updated_brennabudd_frontporch_dissertationfindings.pdf

13. Carroll, J.M., Rosson, M.B.: The neighborhood school in the global village. IEEE Technol. Soc. Mag. 17(4), 4–9 (1998). https://doi.org/10.1109/44.735855

14. Chan, Z.Y., Shum, P.: Smart office. In: Proceedings of the 2nd International Symposium on Computer Science and Intelligent Control. pp. 1–5. ACM, New York, 21 September 2018. https://doi.org/10.1145/3284557.3284712

15. Chen, C., Johnson, J., Charles, A., Lee, K.A., et al.: Understanding barriers and design opportunities to improve healthcare and QOL for older adults through voice assistants. In: The 23rd International ACM SIGACCESS Conference on Computers and Accessibility (2021). https://doi.org/10.1145/3441852.3471218, http://voli.ucsd.edu/pdfs/2021_assets_voli.pdf

16. Chen, S.: Toward ambient assistance: a spatially-aware virtual assistant enabled by object detection. In: 2020 International Conference on Computer Engineering and Application (ICCEA), pp. 494–501. IEEE (3/18/2020–3/20/2020). https://doi.org/10.1109/ICCEA50009.2020.00111

17. Cheng, A., Raghavaraju, V., Kanugo, J., Handrianto, Y.P., Shang, Y.: Development and evaluation of a healthy coping voice interface application using the google home for elderly patients with type 2 diabetes. In: 2018 15th IEEE Annual Consumer Communications & Networking Conference (CCNC), pp. 1–5. IEEE (1/12/2018–1/15/2018). https://doi.org/10.1109/CCNC.2018.8319283

18. Choi, Y., Demiris, G., Thompson, H.: Feasibility of smart speaker use to support aging in place. Innov. Aging **2**(suppl_1), 560 (2018). https://doi.org/10.1093/geroni/igy023.2073

19. Choi, Y.K., Thompson, H.J., Demiris, G.: Use of an Internet-of-Things smart home system for healthy aging in older adults in residential settings: pilot feasibility study. JMIR Aging **3**(2) (2020). https://doi.org/10.2196/21964

20. Chowdhury, G.G.: Natural language processing. Ann. Rev. Inf. Sci. Technol. **37**(1), 51–89 (2003). https://doi.org/10.1002/aris.1440370103

21. Chung, S., Woo, B.K.P.: Using consumer perceptions of a voice-activated speaker device as an educational tool. JMIR Med. Educ. **6**(1) (2020). https://doi.org/10.2196/17336

22. Cochrane Community: When to use abbreviations, acronyms and initialisms (12/21/2021). https://community.cochrane.org/style-manual/abbreviations-acronyms-and-initialisms/when-use-abbreviations-acronyms-and-initialisms

23. Colombo-Ruano, L., Rodríguez-Silva, C., Violant-Holz, V., González-González, C.S.: Technological acceptance of voice assistants in older adults. In: Molina-Tanco, L., Manresa-Yee, C., González-González, C., Montalvo-Gallego, B., Reyes-Lecuona, A. (eds.) Proceedings of the XXI International Conference on Human Computer Interaction, pp. 1–5. ACM, New York, 22 September 2021. https://doi.org/10.1145/3471391.3471432

24. Conde-Caballero, D., Rivero-Jiménez, B., Cipriano-Crespo, C., Jesus-Azabal, M., Garcia-Alonso, J., Mariano-Juárez, L.: Treatment adherence in chronic conditions during ageing: uses, functionalities, and cultural adaptation of the assistant on care and health offline (ACHO) in rural areas. J. Personal. Med. **11**(3), 173 (2021). https://doi.org/10.3390/jpm11030173

25. Cordasco, G., et al.: Assessing voice user interfaces: the vassist system prototype. In: 2014 5th IEEE Conference on Cognitive Infocommunications (CogInfoCom), pp. 91–96. IEEE (11/5/2014–11/7/2014). https://doi.org/10.1109/CogInfoCom.2014.7020425

26. Coskun-Setirek, A., Mardikyan, S.: Understanding the adoption of voice activated personal assistants. Int. J. E-Serv. Mob. Appl. **9**(3), 1–21 (2017). https://doi.org/10.4018/IJESMA.2017070101

27. Ding, W., Chang, W., Gan, H., Xiong, X.: Multi-functional intelligent bathing machine for the elderly. In: 2020 5th International Conference on Mechanical, Control and Computer Engineering (ICMCCE), pp. 966–969. IEEE (12/25/2020–12/27/2020). https://doi.org/10.1109/ICMCCE51767.2020.00211

28. Dojchinovski, D., Ilievski, A., Gusev, M.: Interactive home healthcare system with integrated voice assistant. In: 2019 42nd International Convention on Information and Communication Technology, Electronics and Microelectronics (MIPRO), pp. 284–288. IEEE (5/20/2019–5/24/2019). https://doi.org/10.23919/MIPRO.2019.8756983

29. Eldeeb, S.M., Abdelmoula, W.M., Shah, S.M., Fahmy, A.S.: Quantitative assessment of age-related macular degeneration using parametric modeling of the leakage transfer function: Preliminary results. In: 2012 Annual International Conference of the IEEE Engineering in Medicine and Biology Society, pp. 5967–5970. IEEE (8/28/2012–9/1/2012). https://doi.org/10.1109/EMBC.2012.6347353

30. Ennis, A., et al.: A smart cabinet and voice assistant to support independence in older adults. In: Ochoa, S.F., Singh, P., Bravo, J. (eds.) UCAmI 2017. LNCS, vol. 10586, pp. 466–472. Springer, Cham (2017). https://doi.org/10.1007/978-3-319-67585-5_47

31. Ezenwa, B., Burns, E., Wilson, C.: Multiple vibration intensities and frequencies for bone mineral density improvement. In: 2008 30th Annual International Conference of the IEEE Engineering in Medicine and Biology Society, pp. 4186–4189. IEEE (8/20/2008–8/25/2008). https://doi.org/10.1109/IEMBS.2008.4650132

32. Filipescu, A., Susnea, I., Minzu, V., Vasiliu, G., Filipescu, S.: Obstacle avoidance and path following control of a WMR used as personal robotic assistant. In: 18th Mediterranean Conference on Control and Automation, MED 2010, pp. 1555–1560. IEEE (6/23/2010–6/25/2010). https://doi.org/10.1109/MED.2010.5547828

33. Ganesh, D., Seshadri, G., Sokkanarayanan, S., Rajan, S., Sathiyanarayanan, M.: Iot-based google duplex artificial intelligence solution for elderly care. In: 2019 International Conference on contemporary Computing and Informatics (IC3I), pp. 234–240. IEEE (12/12/2019–12/14/2019). https://doi.org/10.1109/IC3I46837.2019.9055551

34. Gollasch, D., Weber, G.: Age-related differences in preferences for using voice assistants. In: Schneegass, S., Pfleging, B., Kern, D. (eds.) Mensch und Computer 2021, pp. 156–167. ACM, New York, 05 September 2021. https://doi.org/10.1145/3473856.3473889

35. Goto, Y., et al.: Alternating chemoradiotherapy in patients with nasopharyngeal cancer: prognostic factors and proposal for individualization of therapy. J. Radiat. Res. **54**(1), 98–107 (2013). https://doi.org/10.1093/jrr/rrs071

36. Graf, B., Hans, A., Kubacki, J., Schraft, R.D.: Robotic home assistant care-o-bot ii. In: Proceedings of the Second Joint 24th Annual Conference and the Annual Fall Meeting of the Biomedical Engineering Society] [Engineering in Medicine and Biology, vol. 3, pp. 2343–2344. IEEE (10/23/2002–10/26/2002). https://doi.org/10.1109/IEMBS.2002.1053313

37. Guerra, R.S., Amaral, T.F., Marques, E., Mota, J., Restivo, M.T.: Accuracy of SIRI and BROZEK equations in the percent body fat estimation in older adults. J. Nutrition Health Aging **14**(9), 744–748 (2010). https://doi.org/10.1007/s12603-010-0112-z

38. Gunathilaka, L.A.S.M., Weerasinghe, W.A.U.S., Wickramasinghe, I.N., Welgama, V., Weerasinghe, A.R.: The use of conversational interfaces in long term patient care. In: 2020 20th International Conference on Advances in ICT for Emerging Regions (ICTer), pp. 131–136. IEEE (11/4/2020–11/7/2020). https://doi.org/10.1109/ICTer51097.2020.9325473

39. Gusev, M., Tasic, J., Patel, S.: Architecture of a system for stimulating intellectual activity with adaptive environment smile. In: 2017 25th Telecommunication Forum (TELFOR), pp. 1–4. IEEE (11/21/2017–11/22/2017). https://doi.org/10.1109/TELFOR.2017.8249484

40. Habscheid, S., Hector, T.M., Hrncal, C., Waldecker, D.: Intelligente persönliche assistenten (IPA) mit voice user interfaces (VUI) als, beteiligte' in häuslicher alltagsinteraktion. welchen aufschluss geben die protokolldaten der assistenzsysteme? Journal für Medienlinguistik 4(1), 16–53 (2021). https://doi.org/10.21248/jfml. 2021.44

41. Hans, M., Graf, B., Schraft, R.D.: Robotic home assistant care-o-bot: past-present-future. In: Proceedings. 11th IEEE International Workshop on Robot and Human Interactive Communication, pp. 380–385. IEEE (9/27/2002–9/27/2002). https://doi.org/10.1109/ROMAN.2002.1045652

42. Hellwig, A., Schneider, C., Meister, S., Deiters, W.: Sprachassistenten in der pflege - potentiale und voraussetzungen zur unterstützung von senioren. https://doi.org/ 10.18420/muc2018-mci-0341

43. Herbert, D., Kang, B.: Comparative analysis of intelligent personal agent performance. In: Ohara, K., Bai, Q. (eds.) PKAW 2019. LNCS (LNAI), vol. 11669, pp. 127–141. Springer, Cham (2019). https://doi.org/10.1007/978-3-030-30639-7_11

44. Hirakawa, R., Kawano, H., Nakashi, K., Nakatoh, Y.: Study on watching system for door-to-door sales detection and risk determination. In: Tsuchida, K. (ed.) Proceedings of the 7th ACIS International Conference on Applied Computing and Information Technology, pp. 1–6. ACM, New York, 29 May 2019. https:// doi.org/10.1145/3325291.3325391

45. Huang, J.T., Chang, L.Y., Lin, H.C.: Implementation of IoT, wearable devices, Google assistant and google cloud platform for elderly home care system. In: Proceedings of the 7th International Conference on Information and Communication Technologies for Ageing Well and e-Health. SCITEPRESS - Science and Technology Publications (2021). https://doi.org/10.5220/0010473102030212

46. Hübner, I.-M.: Das Alter(n) – Eine Einführung. In: Subjektive Gesundheit und Wohlbefinden im Übergang in den Ruhestand, pp. 5–19. Springer, Wiesbaden (2017). https://doi.org/10.1007/978-3-658-16402-7_2

47. Huisingh-Scheetz, M., Nicholson, R., Smith, C., Shervani, S., Montoya, Y., Hawkley, L.: Engage via alexa for older adults and caregivers: Design, utilization, and impact of socially motivated exercise. Innov. Aging 4(Supplement_1), 645 (2020). https://doi.org/10.1093/geroni/igaa057.2219

48. Hussey, T.W.: Dr. Thomas W. Hussey (2009). https://ieeexplore.ieee.org/stamp/ stamp.jsp?tp=&arnumber=4816080

49. Ilievski, A., Dojchinovski, D., Gusev, M.: Interactive voice assisted home healthcare systems. In: Eleftherakis, G., Lazarova, M., Aleksieva-Petrova, A., Tasheva, A. (eds.) Proceedings of the 9th Balkan Conference on Informatics, pp. 1–5. ACM, New York, 26 September 2019. https://doi.org/10.1145/3351556.3351572

50. Imperiale, M.J.: Acknowledgment of ad hoc reviewers. mSphere 4(6) (2019). https://doi.org/10.1128/mSphere.00873-19

51. Isyanto, H., Arifin, A.S., Suryanegara, M.: Performance of smart personal assistant applications based on speech recognition technology using iot-based voice commands. In: 2020 International Conference on Information and Communication Technology Convergence (ICTC), pp. 640–645. IEEE (10/21/2020–10/23/2020). https://doi.org/10.1109/ICTC49870.2020.9289160

52. Jakob, D., Wilhelm, S., Gerl, A., Ahrens, D.: A quantitative study on awareness, usage and reservations of voice control interfaces by elderly people. In: Stephanidis, C., et al. (eds.) HCII 2021. LNCS, vol. 13096, pp. 237–257. Springer, Cham (2021). https://doi.org/10.1007/978-3-030-90328-2_15

53. Jaskulska, A., Skorupska, K., Karpowicz, B., Biele, C., Kowalski, J., Kopeć, W.: Exploration of voice user interfaces for older adults - a pilot study to address progressive vision loss. https://arxiv.org/pdf/2012.15853

54. Jenpoomjai, P., Wosri, P., Ruengittinun, S., Hu, C.L., Chootong, C.: VA algorithm for elderly's falling detection with 2d-pose-estimation. In: 2019 Twelfth International Conference on Ubi-Media Computing (Ubi-Media), pp. 236–240. IEEE (8/5/2019–8/8/2019). https://doi.org/10.1109/Ubi-Media.2019.00053

55. Khan, S.: Audiovisual interactive companionship; the next breakthrough in computers. In: 2020 IEEE International IOT, Electronics and Mechatronics Conference (IEMTRONICS), pp. 1–6. IEEE (9/9/2020–9/12/2020). https://doi.org/10.1109/IEMTRONICS51293.2020.9216341

56. Kim, S.: Exploring how older adults use a smart speaker-based voice assistant in their first interactions: qualitative study. JMIR mHealth uHealth 9(1) (2021). https://doi.org/10.2196/20427

57. Kitakoshi, D., Hirose, S., Yamashita, A., Suzuki, M., Suzuki, K.: Development of an intelligent dialogue agent for older adults: evaluation of functions to control spontaneous talk and coordinate speech content. In: 2019 International Conference on Technologies and Applications of Artificial Intelligence (TAAI), pp. 1–6. IEEE (11/21/2019–11/23/2019). https://doi.org/10.1109/TAAI48200.2019.8959870

58. Kowalski, J., et al.: Older adults and voice interaction. In: Brewster, S., Fitzpatrick, G., Cox, A., Kostakos, V. (eds.) Extended Abstracts of the 2019 CHI Conference on Human Factors in Computing Systems, pp. 1–6. ACM, New York, 02 May 2019. https://doi.org/10.1145/3290607.3312973

59. Larsen, A.: Voice user interfaces supporting older adults with differing physical and cognitive abilities complete daily activities. Maryland Shared Open Access Repository (2019). https://mdsoar.org/handle/11603/22887

60. Lee, E., Vesonder, G., Wendel, E.: Eldercare robotics - Alexa. In: 2020 11th IEEE Annual Ubiquitous Computing, Electronics & Mobile Communication Conference (UEMCON), pp. 0820–0825. IEEE (10/28/2020–10/31/2020). https://doi.org/10.1109/UEMCON51285.2020.9298147

61. Looije, R., Cnossen, F., Neerincx, M.: Incorporating guidelines for health assistance into a socially intelligent robot. In: ROMAN 2006 - The 15th IEEE International Symposium on Robot and Human Interactive Communication, pp. 515–520. IEEE (9/6/2006–9/8/2006). https://doi.org/10.1109/ROMAN.2006.314441

62. Luengo-Polo, J., Conde-Caballero, D., Rivero-Jiménez, B., Ballesteros-Yáñez, I., Castillo-Sarmiento, C.A., Mariano-Juárez, L.: Rationale and methods of evaluation for ACHO, a new virtual assistant to improve therapeutic adherence in rural elderly populations: a user-driven living lab. Int. J. Environ. Res. Public Health 18(15), 7904 (2021). https://doi.org/10.3390/ijerph18157904

63. Maarek, Y.: Alexa and her shopping journey. In: Cuzzocrea, A., et al. (eds.) Proceedings of the 27th ACM International Conference on Information and Knowledge Management, p. 1. ACM, New York, 17 October 2018. https://doi.org/10.1145/3269206.3272923

64. Martins, A.I., Rosa, A.F., Queirós, A., Silva, A., Rocha, N.P.: European Portuguese validation of the system usability scale (SUS). Procedia Comput. Sci. 67, 293–300 (2015). https://doi.org/10.1016/j.procs.2015.09.273

65. McDowell, S.B., Chung, Bennett, J.: Perceptions of using smart speaker technology for improving the health and wellness of older adults living in a low-income community (2020). https://scholarscompass.vcu.edu/gradposters/46/

66. Meliones, A., Maidonis, S.: Dalí. In: Makedon, F. (ed.) Proceedings of the 13th ACM International Conference on PErvasive Technologies Related to Assistive Environments, pp. 1–9. ACM, New York, 30 June 2020. https://doi.org/10.1145/3389189.3397972

67. Mirheidari, B., et al.: Computational cognitive assessment: Investigating the use of an intelligent virtual agent for the detection of early signs of dementia. In: ICASSP 2019–2019 IEEE International Conference on Acoustics, Speech and Signal Processing (ICASSP), pp. 2732–2736. IEEE (5/12/2019–5/17/2019). https://doi.org/10.1109/ICASSP.2019.8682423

68. Mizak, A., Park, M., Park, D., olson, K.: Amazon 'Alexa' pilot analysis report. Front Porch Center for Innovation and Wellbeing (2017). http://fpciw.org/wp-content/uploads/sites/15/2017/12/FINAL-DRAFT-Amazon-Alexa-Analysis-Report.pdf

69. Monaghan, T.M., Robins, A., Knox, A., Sewell, H.F., Mahida, Y.R.: Circulating antibody and memory b-cell responses to c. difficile toxins a and b in patients with c. difficile-associated diarrhoea, inflammatory bowel disease and cystic fibrosis. PLoS ONE 8(9), e74452 (2013). https://doi.org/10.1371/journal.pone.0074452

70. Mtshali, P., Khubisa, F.: A smart home appliance control system for physically disabled people. In: 2019 Conference on Information Communications Technology and Society (ICTAS), pp. 1–5. IEEE (3/6/2019–3/8/2019). https://doi.org/10.1109/ICTAS.2019.8703637

71. Nallam, P., Bhandari, S., Sanders, J.e.a.: A question of access: exploring the perceived benefits and barriers of intelligent voice assistants for improving access to consumer health resources among low-income older adults. Gerontology Geriatric Med. (2020). https://doi.org/10.1177/2333721420985975

72. O'Brien, K., Bradley, S., Weiner-light, S., Kwasny, M., Mohr, D., Lindquist, L.: Voice intelligent personal assistant for managing social isolation and depression in homebound older adults. J. Am. Geriatrics Soc. S108–S108 (2021). https://pesquisa.bvsalud.org/global-literature-on-novel-coronavirus-2019-ncov/resource/pt/covidwho-1214890

73. Ooster, J., Krueger, M., Bach, J.H., Wagener, K.C., Kollmeier, B., Meyer, B.T.: Speech audiometry at home: automated listening tests via smart speakers with normal-hearing and hearing-impaired listeners. Trends in Hearing 24, 2331216520970011 (2020). https://doi.org/10.1177/2331216520970011

74. Page, M.J., et al.: The PRISMA 2020 statement: an updated guideline for reporting systematic reviews. BMJ p. n71, March 2021. https://doi.org/10.1136/bmj.n71

75. Pedersen, I.: Home is where the AI heart is [commentary]. IEEE Technol. Soc. Mag. 35(4), 50–51 (2016). https://doi.org/10.1109/MTS.2016.2618680

76. Pérès, K., Zamudio-Rodriguez, A., Dartigues, J.F., Amieva, H., Lafitte, S.: Prospective pragmatic quasi-experimental study to assess the impact and effectiveness of an innovative large-scale public health intervention to foster healthy ageing in place: the sobeezy program protocol. BMJ Open 11(4), e043082 (2021). https://doi.org/10.1136/bmjopen-2020-043082

77. Pradhan, A., Findlater, L., Lazar, A.: 'phantom friend' or 'just a box with information'. Proc. ACM Human Comput. Interact. 3(CSCW), 1–21 (2019). https://doi.org/10.1145/3359316

78. Pradhan, A., Lazar, A., Findlater, L.: Use of intelligent voice assistants by older adults with low technology use. ACM Trans. Comput. Human Interact. 27(4), 1–27 (2020). https://doi.org/10.1145/3373759

79. Prlja, A., Anderson, J.B.: Reduced-complexity receivers for strongly narrow-band intersymbol interference introduced by faster-than-nyquist signaling. IEEE Trans. Commun. **60**(9), 2591–2601 (2012). https://doi.org/10.1109/TCOMM.2012.070912.110296

80. Prost, S., Kishen, R.E.B., Kluth, D.C., Bellamy, C.O.C.: Choice of illumination system & fluorophore for multiplex immunofluorescence on FFPE tissue sections. PLOS ONE **11**(9) (2016). https://doi.org/10.1371/journal.pone.0162419

81. Reis, A., et al.: Using intelligent personal assistants to assist the elderlies an evaluation of Amazon Alexa, Google assistant, Microsoft Cortana, and Apple Siri. In: 2018 2nd International Conference on Technology and Innovation in Sports, Health and Wellbeing (TISHW), pp. 1–5. IEEE (6/20/2018–6/22/2018). https://doi.org/10.1109/TISHW.2018.8559503

82. Sanders, J., Martin-Hammond, A.: Exploring autonomy in the design of an intelligent health assistant for older adults. In: Proceedings of the 24th International Conference on Intelligent User Interfaces: Companion, pp. 95–96. ACM, New York, 16 March 2019. https://doi.org/10.1145/3308557.3308713

83. Sayago, S., Neves, B.B., Cowan, B.R.: Voice assistants and older people. In: Cowan, B.R., Clark, L. (eds.) Proceedings of the 1st International Conference on Conversational User Interfaces - CUI 2019, pp. 1–3. ACM Press, New York (2019). https://doi.org/10.1145/3342775.3342803

84. Scherr, S.A., Meier, A., Cihan, S.: Alexa, tell me more - about new best friends, the advantage of hands-free operation and life-long learning. https://doi.org/10.18420/MUC2020-WS120-342

85. Schlögl, S., Chollet, G., Garschall, M., Tscheligi, M., Legouverneur, G.: Exploring voice user interfaces for seniors. In: Makedon, F., Betke, M., El-Nasr, M.S., Maglogiannis, I. (eds.) Proceedings of the 6th International Conference on PErvasive Technologies Related to Assistive Environments - PETRA 2013. pp. 1–2. ACM Press, New York (2013). https://doi.org/10.1145/2504335.2504391

86. Schlomann, A., et al.: Potential and pitfalls of digital voice assistants in older adults with and without intellectual disabilities: relevance of participatory design elements and ecologically valid field studies. Front. Psychol. **12** (2021). https://doi.org/10.3389/fpsyg.2021.684012

87. Schraft, R.D., Schaeffer, C., May, T.: Care-o-bot/sup tm/: the concept of a system for assisting elderly or disabled persons in home environments. In: IECON 1998. Proceedings of the 24th Annual Conference of the IEEE Industrial Electronics Society (Cat. No.98CH36200), pp. 2476–2481. IEEE (31 Aug–4 Sept 1998). https://doi.org/10.1109/IECON.1998.724115

88. Sengupta, K., et al.: Challenges and opportunities of leveraging intelligent conversational assistant to improve the well-being of older adults. In: Extended Abstracts of the 2020 CHI Conference on Human Factors in Computing Systems, pp. 1–4. ACM, New York, 25 April 2020. https://doi.org/10.1145/3334480.3381057

89. Shalini, S., Levins, T., Robinson, E.L., Lane, K., Park, G., Skubic, M.: Development and comparison of customized voice-assistant systems for independent living older adults. In: Zhou, J., Salvendy, G. (eds.) HCII 2019. LNCS, vol. 11593, pp. 464–479. Springer, Cham (2019). https://doi.org/10.1007/978-3-030-22015-0_36

90. Sin, J., Munteanu, C.: Whoever controls the media, controls the VUI. In: Torres, M.I., Schlögl, S., Clark, L., Porcheron, M. (eds.) Proceedings of the 2nd Conference on Conversational User Interfaces, pp. 1–3. ACM, New York, 22 July 2020. https://doi.org/10.1145/3405755.3406159

91. Sin, J., Munteanu, C.: An information behaviour-based approach to virtual doctor design. In: Proceedings of the 21st International Conference on Human-Computer Interaction with Mobile Devices and Services, pp. 1–6. ACM, New York, October 2019. https://doi.org/10.1145/3338286.3344391

92. Sin, J., Munteanu, C., Ramanand, N., Rong Tan, Y.: VUI influencers: How the media portrays voice user interfaces for older adults. In: CUI 2021–3rd Conference on Conversational User Interfaces, pp. 1–13. ACM, New York, 27 July2021. https://doi.org/10.1145/3469595.3469603

93. Staff, T.P.G.: Correction: genome-wide meta-analysis of homocysteine and methionine metabolism identifies five one carbon metabolism loci and a novel association of aldh1l1 with ischemic stroke. PLoS Genetics **10**(7) (2014). https://doi.org/10.1371/journal.pgen.1004571

94. Statista: Beschäftigtenanzahl nach alter und geschlecht 2019 — statista (12/21/2021). https://de.statista.com/statistik/daten/studie/1132916/umfrage/beschaeftigtenanzahl-nach-alter-und-geschlecht/

95. Statistisches Bundesamt: (destatis: 14. koordinierte bevölkerungsvorausberechnung für deutschland) (2019). https://service.destatis.de/bevoelkerungspyramide/#!a=55,60&g

96. Stigall, B., Caine, K.: A systematic review of human factors literature about voice user interfaces and older adults. In: Proceedings of the Human Factors and Ergonomics Society Annual Meeting, vol. 64, no. 1, pp. 13–17 (2020). https://doi.org/10.1177/1071181320641004

97. Stigall, B., Waycott, J., Baker, S., Caine, K.: Older adults' perception and use of voice user interfaces. In: Proceedings of the 31st Australian Conference on Human-Computer-Interaction. pp. 423–427. ACM, New York, 02December 2019. https://doi.org/10.1145/3369457.3369506

98. Striegl, J., Gollasch, D., Loitsch, C., Weber, G.: Designing VUIS for social assistance robots for people with dementia. In: Schneegass, S., Pfleging, B., Kern, D. (eds.) Mensch und Computer 2021, pp. 145–155. ACM, New York, 05 September 2021. https://doi.org/10.1145/3473856.3473887

99. Sun, N.: Carehub: smart screen VUI and home appliances control for older adults. In: Guerreiro, T., Nicolau, H., Moffatt, K. (eds.) The 22nd International ACM SIGACCESS Conference on Computers and Accessibility, pp. 1–4. ACM, New York, 26 October 2020. https://doi.org/10.1145/3373625.3418051

100. Tablado, A., Illarramendi, A., Bermudez, J., Goni, A.: Intelligent monitoring of elderly people. In: 4th International IEEE EMBS Special Topic Conference on Information Technology Applications in Biomedicine, 2003, pp. 78–81. IEEE, 24–26 April 2003. https://doi.org/10.1109/ITAB.2003.1222447

101. Tan, K., Sekhar, K., Wong, J., Holgado, J., Ameer, M., Vesonder, G.: Alexa eldercare toolbox: a smarthome solution for the elderly. In: 2020 11th IEEE Annual Ubiquitous Computing, Electronics & Mobile Communication Conference (UEMCON), pp. 0806–0812 (2020). https://doi.org/10.1109/UEMCON51285.2020.9298127

102. Tang, V., Choy, K.L., Siu, P.K., Lam, H.Y., Ho, G., Cheng, S.W.: An intelligent performance assessment system for enhancing the service quality of home care nursing staff in the healthcare industry. In: 2016 Portland International Conference on Management of Engineering and Technology (PICMET), pp. 576–584. IEEE (9/4/2016–9/8/2016). https://doi.org/10.1109/PICMET.2016.7806657

103. Ting, C., Li, Z., Zhang, Y.: Research on smart speaker speech interaction in the therapy of senior with early dementia. In: The eighth International Workshop of Chinese CHI. pp. 40–46. ACM, New York, 26 April 2020. https://doi.org/10.1145/3403676.3403681

104. Trajkova, M., Martin-Hammond, A.: Alexa is a toy: exploring older adults' reasons for using, limiting, and abandoning echo. In: Bernhaupt, R., et al. (eds.) Proceedings of the 2020 CHI Conference on Human Factors in Computing Systems, pp. 1–13. ACM, New York, 21 April 2020. https://doi.org/10.1145/3313831.3376760

105. UNO: Lebenserwartung hat weltweit um 20 jahre zugenommen. Vereinte Nationen (1/10/1998). https://unric.org/de/lebenserwartung-hat-weltweit-um-20-jahre-zugenommen-2/

106. Vacher, M., Aman, F., Rossato, S., Portet, F., Lecouteux, B.: Making emergency calls more accessible to older adults through a hands-free speech interface in the house. ACM Trans. Accessible Comput. 12(2), 1–25 (2019). https://doi.org/10.1145/3310132

107. Valera Román, A., Pato Martínez, D., Lozano Murciego, Á., Jiménez-Bravo, D.M., de Paz, J.F.: Voice assistant application for avoiding sedentarism in elderly people based on IoT technologies. Electronics 10(8), 980 (2021). https://doi.org/10.3390/electronics10080980

108. Wang, D., Subagdja, B., Kang, Y., Tan, A.H.: Silver assistants for aging-in-place. In: 2015 IEEE/WIC/ACM International Conference on Web Intelligence and Intelligent Agent Technology (WI-IAT), pp. 241–242. IEEE (12/6/2015–12/9/2015). https://doi.org/10.1109/WI-IAT.2015.183

109. West, A.J.: 'what's with what's her name? siri, call so and so... can't you use your own hands!?' older adult perspectives on the roles communication technology and physical activity play in their aging experiences (2019). https://digitalrepository.unm.edu/cj_etds/124/

110. Wulf, L., Garschall, M., Himmelsbach, J., Tscheligi, M.: Hands free - care free. In: Roto, V., Häkkilä, J., Väänänen-Vainio-Mattila, K., Juhlin, O., Olsson, T., Hvannberg, E. (eds.) Proceedings of the 8th Nordic Conference on Human-Computer Interaction: Fun, Fast, Foundational, pp. 203–206. ACM, New York, 26 October 2014. https://doi.org/10.1145/2639189.2639251

111. Yamada, S., Kitakoshi, D., Yamashita, A., Suzuki, K., Suzuki, M.: Development of an intelligent dialogue agent with smart devices for older adults: A preliminary study. In: 2018 Conference on Technologies and Applications of Artificial Intelligence (TAAI), pp. 50–53. IEEE (11/30/2018–12/2/2018). https://doi.org/10.1109/TAAI.2018.00020

112. Yamada, Y., et al.: Using speech data from interactions with a voice assistant to predict the risk of future accidents for older drivers: prospective cohort study. J. Med. Internet Res. 23(4) (2021). https://doi.org/10.2196/27667

113. Zeng, Z., Wang, D., Borjigin, A., Miao, C., Tan, A.H., Leung, C.: Human-centred design for silver assistants. In: 2016 IEEE International Conference on Agents (ICA), pp. 112–113. IEEE (9/28/2016–9/30/2016). https://doi.org/10.1109/ICA.2016.038

114. Ziman, R., Walsh, G.: Factors affecting seniors' perceptions of voice-enabled user interfaces. In: Mandryk, R., Hancock, M., Perry, M., Cox, A. (eds.) Extended Abstracts of the 2018 CHI Conference on Human Factors in Computing Systems, pp. 1–6. ACM, New York, 20 April 2018. https://doi.org/10.1145/3170427.3188575

115. Zubatiy, T., Vickers, K.L., Mathur, N., Mynatt, E.D.: Empowering dyads of older adults with mild cognitive impairment and their care partners using conversational agents. In: Kitamura, Y., Quigley, A., Isbister, K., Igarashi, T., Bjørn, P., Drucker, S. (eds.) Proceedings of the 2021 CHI Conference on Human Factors in Computing Systems, pp. 1–15. ACM, New York, 06 May 2021. https://doi.org/10.1145/3411764.3445124

A Data Collection and Annotation Tool for Asynchronous Multimodal Data During Human-Computer Interactions

Nibraas Khan[1]([✉]), Ritam Ghosh[1], Miroslava Migovich[1], Andrew Johnson[2], Austin Witherow[2], Curtis Taylor[2], Matt Schroder[2], Tyler Vongpanya[2], Medha Sarkar[2], and Nilanjan Sarkar[1]

[1] Vanderbilt University, Nashville, TN 37212, USA
nibraas.a.khan@vanderbilt.edu
[2] Middle Tennessee State University, Murfreesboro, TN 37132, USA

Abstract. Supervised Learning is a Machine Learning technique where a predictor is trained using a set of labeled data where each data point has a label associated with it. The technique can be used for Affective Computing where a person's physiological signals are measured and used in conjunction with labels to create a predictor for affective states. However, creating this labeled dataset is labor-intensive and prone to human errors. To alleviate some of the costs of manual labeling, a data annotation tool is needed to create labels that can eventually be combined with physiological data to create a fully labeled dataset. The goal of the tool is to streamline the steps from data collection and data annotation to creating an effective computing agent. A use case and initial development of this tool stems from a socially assistive robotics system setting with older adults who have cognitive impairment and dementia. However, the tool was further developed to be adaptive to the needs of any data annotation. In this paper, we present a data annotation tool that can be adapted to any domain for streamlining the process of data annotation.

Keywords: Data annotation · Supervised learning · Affective computing

1 Introduction

An estimated 14% of the older adult population above the age of 71 in the United States are diagnosed with dementia, with an estimated 5.8 million adults ages 65+ with Alzheimer's. The expected population of older adults (65+) is projected to rise by 32 million over the next 30 years [1]. This leads to a disparity in the number of both formal (paid) and informal caregivers for older adults and the number of older adults in need of caregivers [2]. For those with Alzheimer's and related dementias, apathy is an expected emergent behavior that leads to cognitive decline, social isolation, and reduced quality of life [3]. Current treatments promote the development and use of activities that foster social, physical, and cognitive skills [4]; however, they require the use of limited finite personnel resources [5].

© The Author(s), under exclusive license to Springer Nature Switzerland AG 2022
Q. Gao and J. Zhou (Eds.): HCII 2022, LNCS 13330, pp. 201–211, 2022.
https://doi.org/10.1007/978-3-031-05581-2_15

Due to limited personnel resources, several technological systems with Socially Assistive Robots (SAR) have been developed and explored. Yu et al. and Šabanovic et al. used a therapeutic baby robot seal PARO to foster social-engagement and improve overall mood [6, 7]; however, interventions such as these are passive and require the personnel or older adult to take the initiative and need a trained therapist to be effective. Other implementations of SARs for older adults include a fitness coach that demonstrates exercises to older adults and provides feedback based on their performance [8–10], a robot that assists older adults in a meal eating activity [11], and a robot that can recognize and synthesize voices, navigate, remember appointments, manage shopping lists, play music, and can be used as a video conference system for the care of older people [12]. While these systems are promising, many of them are built for very specific applications and are limited to the type and variety of tasks they can perform. In addition to SAR systems, the use of Virtual Reality (VR) has been proposed [13], but research shows that participants are likely to respond better to instructions from physical robots rather than from a VR system [14, 15]. To address the personnel limitations and lack of engagement with pure VR systems, a novel system was developed which combines social robotics with non-immersive VR to create activities for older adults that are both cognitively and physically engaging while encouraging social engagement [16]. This system needs to be sensitive to the affective states [17] experienced by the older adults during the activities, specifically stress [18–21] for a natural interaction. For example, if a user is feeling stressed while they are taking part in an activity, the system can observe this emotion and automatically adapt the difficulty to lower stress.

For the development of an adaptive system, multimodal data capturing information about the older adult's mood and feelings, needs to be collected and processed for affective computing. Physiological signals are a response to the Autonomic Nervous System (ANS) communicating and operating between the Central Nervous System (CNS) and the various organs or muscles. The ANS is composed of the Sympathetic (SNS) and Parasympathetic (PNS) nervous systems. The sympathetic nervous system prepares the body for emergency action, "fight or flight", by activating the adrenal glands [22]. This response leads to measurable physiological signal changes such as heart rate, blood flow, and increased muscle activation which can be mapped to affective states. On the other hand, the PNS helps sustain homeostasis during rest by decreasing and maintaining physiological signals in measurable ranges [23]. Since ANS activity is involuntarily, responses cannot be manipulated or masked by an individual. Therefore, physiological signals are a preferred modality in affective computing, especially for stress detection.

A collection of useful algorithms for affective computing come from the field of Machine Learning (ML). ML can be broadly defined as a collection of computational techniques which use past information to improve prediction performance [24]. Specifically, Supervised Learning (SL) algorithms are useful for the detection of affective states; however, they require a fully labeled dataset as each point of past data requires a label to be associated with it [25]. Creating a fully labeled dataset is expensive and labor intensive. To alleviate some of these constraints, this paper proposes an online and offline annotation and meta-data, such as time of experiment and experiment ID, collection tool to be used in conjunction with a data synchronization module to generate a fully annotated dataset.

Acquired unlabeled multimodal data needs to be annotated for supervised learning [26]. Previous studies have shown the use and effectiveness of an online annotation tool used by trained professionals [27]; however, they can be improved through offline data annotation, meta-data collection, and real time application adaptability. Our tool addresses the lack of offline annotation through a four-page tool design: (1) information of the activity and caregiver, (2) online tool to collect data (live annotation), (3) offline tool to collect data (recorded session annotation), and (4) summary of the session. The annotation tool is used to collect meta-data about the system through the trained professional such as the observed effectiveness of the system and social engagement and mental load of the older adults. Additionally, the users of this tool have the ability to modify it for their labeling needs such as increasing the number of labels by addition or deletion. Following the annotation step, a synchronization module is used to synchronize the multimodal data and annotations for a fully labeled dataset. With the annotation tool, we aim to streamline the steps from data collection and data annotation to creating an affective computing agent. Current techniques are labor intensive and require significant time, and this tool will alleviate limitations from older techniques. While the data annotation tool and data synchronization module were built in the context of SARs for older adults, it can be used with any multi-modal data, including physiological and other informative data, that needs annotation and synchronization.

The development of a SL affective computing agent requires a pipeline that begins with physiological data collection, data annotation, and data synchronization. This paper will follow the structure of the pipeline where we describe the tools used for physiological data collection, current state-of-the-art data annotation techniques, our more streamlined data annotation tool, and data synchronization.

2 Multi-modal Data Acquisition

For the SAR systems to be adaptive, several modalities of physiological data are collected such as Heart Rate and Skin Conductance along with other informative data such as Facial Expressions and Skeleton Information. The Empatica E4[1] watch is used to collect the physiological data, including blood volume pulse, electrodermal activity, and temperature, as well as acceleration data. A webcam is used to collect facial expression and a Tobii EyeX is used for eye tracking as a means of additional multi-modal information. The physiological data collected from users along with a labeling system is used to train SL algorithms for affective computing. The data collected from these sensors is individually saved with a timestamp associated with each sample and stored in common types including text, CSV, and JSON files. Figure 1 shows an example of what automatically generated EDA and BVP data from the E4 sensor looks like. Various data types have different timestamps and sampling rates associated with them.

---

[1] www.empatica.com.

1634151743	1634151743
4	64
0	0.01
0.096077	0.01
0.128102	0
0.128102	-0.03
0.131945	-0.05

Fig. 1. Example of EDA and BVP data, respectively, where the first row are Unix timestamps, second row are sampling rates, and the rest are samples.

To produce an effective SL algorithm for affective computing, the sensor data needs to be fused together using the generated files and combined with affective state labels for the algorithm to use for training. An example of different modalities and activity data that can be acquired during a human-computer interaction is presented in Fig. 2 along with the data annotation and synchronization steps which lead to a fully labeled dataset.

3 Data Annotation

This section will begin with the current state-of-the-art data annotations techniques for the generation of labels followed by a discussion of our data annotation tool for asynchronous multi-modal data leading to a more robust system. Finally, we will discuss the structure of the generated labels.

3.1 State-of-the-Art Data Annotation Techniques

While collecting physiological data from sensors is inexpensive, SL needs ground truth labels associated with the data for the learner to accurately classify affective states. In practice, there are several methods of data collection and annotation each with distinct advantages and disadvantages. Schmidt et al. created the Wearable Stress and Affect Detection (WESAD) dataset, which is one of the most widely used public dataset for affective computing [28]. It contains neutral, stress, and amusement affective states where stress was induced by asking participants to perform certain tasks. The E4 wrist sensor and RespiBAN chest sensor were used to collect Accelerometer (ACC), Electromyography (EMG), Respiration (RESP), Temperature (TEMP), Electrocardiogram (ECG), and Electrodermal Activity (EDA) from 15 subjects. The authors of the dataset provide four ground truth labels: Baseline, Stress, Amusement, and Meditation. These are considered ground truth based on what the participants were asked to do during the time when the labels were collected. For example, the participants were asked to perform a stressful task such as mental math and public speaking, and the time spent on the task was recorded as stress. However, ground truth extracted from this technique is not always reliable as a participant might not be stressed while performing mental math or not amused when presented with amusement stimuli. Another form of creating a labeled dataset involves a novel game-based emotion elicitation method designed to induce emotions while accounting for the particularities of individuals such as different perceptions and feelings of stress as developed by Bevilacqua et al. [29]. This method is also based on eliciting certain emotions from the users, but the expected emotion

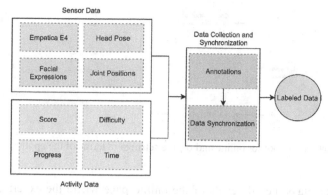

Fig. 2. Example of a pipeline from the collection of raw multi-modal data to a fully annotated and synchronized dataset

cannot always be guaranteed. While ground truth generation using emotion elicitation is inexact, it can be useful for certain tasks and is inexpensive to generate compared to exact ground truth.

On the other hand, high quality labels can be generated with an expensive process of manual observation and annotation by a trained therapist. Zheng et al. conducted an experiment where problem behaviors were elicited in children with autism spectrum disorder to train models that can detect these behaviors in the future [27]. For their data annotation, they built an application that allows for trained therapists to observe sessions in real time and generate labels of problem behaviors. While this application was useful, it was lacking robust meta-data collection, offline data annotation, and adaptability to modify the application in run time. Manual labeling can be labor intensive and prone to errors, but applications such as these aim to reduce the complexity of annotation and allow for experts to focus on subjects and therapy. Therefore, a robust and easy to use annotation tool is essential for high quality labels where the alternative is expert-based manual annotation. The tool developed in this paper is an improvement on previous annotation tools for meta-data collection, online and offline annotation, and real time modifiability.

3.2 Structure of the Data Annotation Tool

Our application consists of four pages that allow for robust and adaptive data annotation. The flow of use for the tool is presented in Fig. 3. In the first screen, the menu page, the experts or labelers who use the tool are prompted to enter the meta-data of the experiment they are running. Figure 4 shows the UI of the menu screen where the meta-data such as the name of the trained therapist can be entered, experiment code, session number, and patient ID. Additional fields can be added as needed during run time. The rest of the available fields are options that can be entered by the experts to modify the tool in real time for their labeling specificities. Following this page, the data annotation can be conducted in an online or offline manner. The online section of the tool allows for the experts to observe an experiment in real time and log their notions, and the offline portion allows the users to view recorded videos and annotate on past experiments.

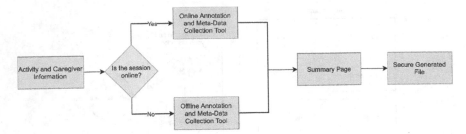

Fig. 3. Flow of the tool for online and offline settings in terms of the application pages

Figure 5 displays the UI details of the online page where the expert can observe and annotate. The buttons made available to the expert are generated based on the input provided in the menu page. For example, a use case is presented in Fig. 5 where the expert is observing an experiment for the stress sensitive SAR and VR system for older adults. In this labeling scheme, the expert can label any observation as high stress, medium stress, low stress, older adults helping each other, conversing with each other, being amused, and neutral. Each time a button is clicked, the timestamp, label information, and meta-data is stored in a JSON file for easy access and use for affective computing.

On the other hand, an online setting might not always be viable. In certain settings, getting an expert to come and observe the experiments in real time might not be possible, so an offline version of the data annotation tool was created. The functionality of the tool remains the same; however, the expert can view the experiment side by side to the labeling scheme. The recorded video can be viewed in the tool through an upload directly into the tool or a stream from a URL. Figure 6 highlights the offline functionalities of the tool in the same use case as the online setting. Once the labels have generated, a small summary page is displayed to the expert about the experiment they have run as shown in Fig. 7.

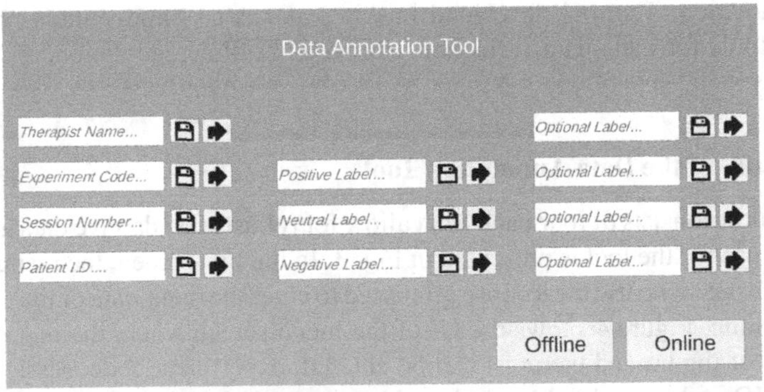

Fig. 4. The menu page of the annotation tools allows for experts to add meta-data and modify the application for their labeling needs

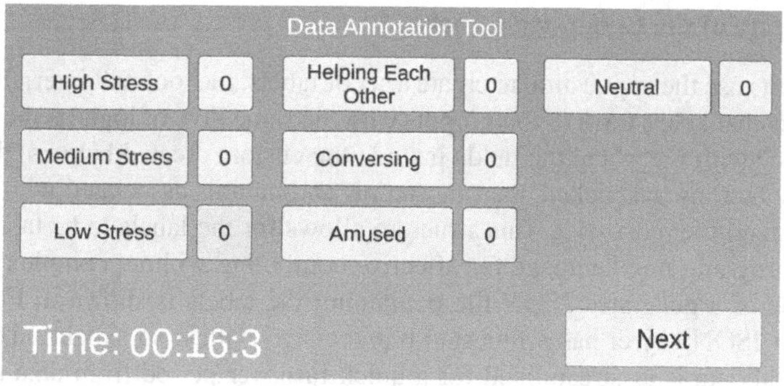

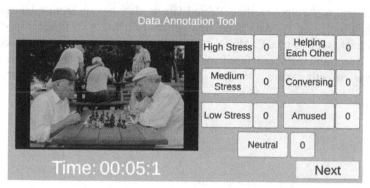

Fig. 5. Main online page of the tool where experts can observe a experiment in real time and generate labels

Fig. 6. Main offline page of the tool where experts can review a previous experiment and generate labels

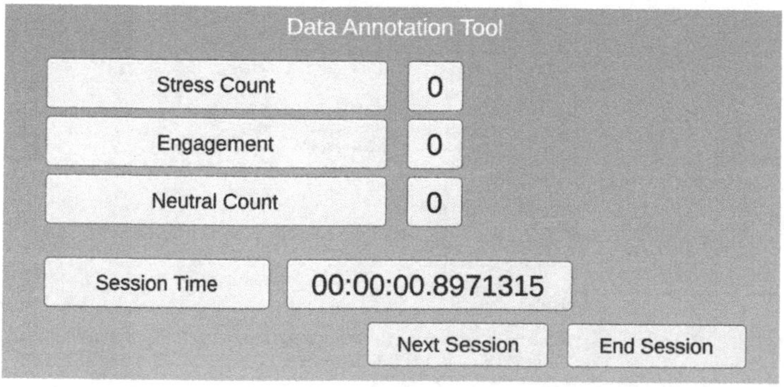

Fig. 7. Summary page of the tool where the expert can see information about their experiment labels

3.3 Structure of the Generated Labels

As the experts use the application to create a set of labels, the tool will internally create a JSON object that keeps track of their inputs with the same flow of logic as the users. The file is created with C# where the fields include the custom created buttons, the number of times the buttons are clicked, the timestamps and buttons associated with each click of a button, and the meta-data. This structure allows for the labels to be taken as input using any programming language for affective computing without complex processes. An example of a generated JSON file containing the labels is shown in Fig. 8. Each entry in the JSON object has a timestamp associated with it so synchronization with physiological data is as streamlined for a quick turnover period from data acquisition and data annotation to affective computing.

4 Multi-modal Data and Annotation Synchronization

In the final steps of the pipeline, the collected data needs to be synchronized the generated labels. Each tool used for data collection generates a file with timestamped data in various formats such as text, CSV, and JSON. The individual files need to be converted into the same framework and fused together for a more complete understanding of the subjects' affective states. Our data synchronization tool accepts any form of data

```
{
    "data": {
        "buttons": {
            "high": 1,
            "medium": 0,
            "low": 0,
            "helping": 1,
            "amused": 0,
            "conversing": 1,
            "neutral": 0
        },
        "times": [
            {
                "time": "2022-02-03T14:37:43.4655657-06:00",
                "timeClicked": "00:00:05.8777597",
                "buttonName": "High Stress"
            },
            {
                "time": "2022-02-03T14:37:43.8827488-06:00",
                "timeClicked": "00:00:06.2949428",
                "buttonName": "Helping Each Other"
            },
            {
                "time": "2022-02-03T14:37:44.4830553-06:00",
                "timeClicked": "00:00:06.8952493",
                "buttonName": "Conversing"
            }
        ],
        "name": "Expert Name",
        "code": "28131",
        "patientId": "A01",
        "type": "Online"
    },
    "metaData": {
        "StartTime": "2022-02-03T14:37:37.587806-06:00",
        "EndTime": "2022-02-03T14:38:05.0845466-06:00",
        "lengthOfSession": "00:00:27.4967406",
        "numberOfClicks": 11
    },
    "sessionId": 10
}
```

Fig. 8. Example of the generated JSON file from the data annotation tool

(following certain standard file structuring for physiological data) and fuses sensor data to create a synchronized dataset.

While the synchronized physiological data carries useful information, a SL agent will not be able to learn from this data without the addition of labels. The labels can be easily combined with the physiological data due to the structure of the JSON object. It should be noted that the final dataset is sparse with many empty data. This is due to the fact that many sensors have varying sampling rates. There are several techniques for handling the sparse nature of physiological data such as interpolating the mean between available data points. This detail is left open to interpretation to researchers who use this tool as the imputing technique is domain specific. Figure 9 displays an example of the final dataset created from collected data and labels.

	FaceID	FaceRectangle - top	FaceRectangle - left	FaceRectangle - width	FaceRectangle - height	Smile	HeadPitch	HeadRoll	HeadYaw	Anger	...
1900-01-01 14:23:22.586000	1.634152e+09	1.634152e+09	1.634152e+09	1.634152e+09	1.634152e+09	1.634152e+09	1.634152e+09	1.634152e+09	1.634152e+09	1.634152e+09	...
1900-01-01 14:23:22.587000	1.634152e+09	1.634152e+09	1.634152e+09	1.634152e+09	1.634152e+09	1.634152e+09	1.634152e+09	1.634152e+09	1.634152e+09	1.634152e+09	...
1900-01-01 14:23:22.593750	1.634152e+09	1.634152e+09	1.634152e+09	1.634152e+09	1.634152e+09	1.634152e+09	1.634152e+09	1.634152e+09	1.634152e+09	1.634152e+09	...
1900-01-01 14:23:22.609375	1.634152e+09	1.634152e+09	1.634152e+09	1.634152e+09	1.634152e+09	1.634152e+09	1.634152e+09	1.634152e+09	1.634152e+09	1.634152e+09	...
1900-01-01 14:23:22.610000	1.634152e+09	1.634152e+09	1.634152e+09	1.634152e+09	1.634152e+09	1.634152e+09	1.634152e+09	1.634152e+09	1.634152e+09	1.634152e+09	...
1900-01-01 14:23:22.611000	1.634152e+09	1.634152e+09	1.634152e+09	1.634152e+09	1.634152e+09	1.634152e+09	1.634152e+09	1.634152e+09	1.634152e+09	1.634152e+09	...
1900-01-01 14:23:22.612000	1.634152e+09	1.634152e+09	1.634152e+09	1.634152e+09	1.634152e+09	1.634152e+09	1.634152e+09	1.634152e+09	1.634152e+09	1.634152e+09	...
1900-01-01 14:23:22.623000	1.634152e+09	1.634152e+09	1.634152e+09	1.634152e+09	1.634152e+09	1.634152e+09	1.634152e+09	1.634152e+09	1.634152e+09	1.634152e+09	...

Fig. 9. Example of the fully generated dataset

5 Conclusion

There is a large disparity in the number of both formal (paid) and informal caregivers for older adults and the number of older adults in need of caregivers [2] due to the large number of older adults diagnosed with dementia and Alzheimer's. Those with Alzheimer's and related dementias are prone to apathy which is an expected emergent behavior that leads to cognitive decline, social isolation, and reduced quality of life [3]. The current treatments promote activities that foster social, physical, and cognitive skills [4]; however, they require the use of limited finite personnel resources [5]. A novel system was developed which combines SARs with non-immersive VR to address the personnel limitations and lack of engagement with pure VR systems with the goal of engaging cognitive, social, and physical skills to improve their quality of life [16]. Additionally, to make the system more naturalistic, it needs to be sensitive to the affective states [17] experienced by the older adults during the activities, specifically stress [18–21]. Supervised Learning algorithms can be used along with physiological data to create a model that can approximate affective states to allow an HCI system to be dynamic and responsive to the users. Creating a fully labeled dataset is labor intensive and prone to errors even by experts. So, we developed a data annotation tool that allows for easy annotation in online and offline settings with the goal of streamlining the steps from data collection and data annotation to creating an affective computing agent.

The data annotation tool consists of a four-page flow where the first page allows for experts to modify the tool in real time for their use case, the second and third page allow the expert to annotate in an online and offline setting respectively, and the final page provides a summary. As the expert uses the tool, a JSON object is build that keeps track of the timestamped labels. Once the labels have been created, a synchronization step is followed where the data from all sensors is fused together along with the labels to create a fully labeled dataset.

While this tool was initially built for the SAR and VR system, it can be used universally for any online and offline data acquisition needs due to its run-time modifiability.

References

1. Alzheimer's Association: 2021 Alzheimer's disease facts and figures. Alzheimer's Dementia **17**, 327–406 (2021). https://doi.org/10.1002/alz.12328
2. USD of Health, Services H, et al.: Long-term services and supports: nursing workforce demand projections 2015–2030 (2018)
3. Volicer, L.: Behavioral problems and dementia. Clin. Geriatric Med. **34** (2018). https://doi.org/10.1016/j.cger.2018.06.009
4. Lanctôt, K.L., AgüeraOrtiz, L., Brodaty, H., et al.: Apathy associated with neurocognitive disorders: Recent progress and future directions. Alzheimer's Dementia **13**, 84–100 (2017). https://doi.org/10.1016/j.jalz.2016.05.008
5. Brodaty, H., Burns, K.: Nonpharmacological management of apathy in dementia: a systematic review. Am. J. Geriatr. Psychiatry **20**, 549–564 (2012). https://doi.org/10.1097/JGP.0b013e31822be242
6. Yu, R., Hui, E., Lee, J., et al.: Use of a therapeutic, socially assistive pet robot (PARO) in improving mood and stimulating social interaction and communication for people with dementia: study protocol for a randomized controlled trial. JMIR Res Prot. **4**, e4189 (2015)
7. Šabanović, S., Bennett, C.C., Chang, W.-L., Huber, L.: PARO robot affects diverse interaction modalities in group sensory therapy for older adults with dementia. In: 2013 IEEE 13th International Conference on Rehabilitation Robotics (ICORR), pp 1–6 (2013)
8. Görer, B., Salah, A., Akin, H.: A robotic fitness coach for the elderly. In: Augusto, J.C., Wichert, R., Collier, R., Keyson, D., Salah, A.A., Tan, A.H. (eds.) AmI. LNCS, vol. 8309, pp. 124–139. Springer, Cham (2013). https://doi.org/10.1007/978-3-319-03647-2_9
9. Fasola, J., Matarić, M.J.: A socially assistive robot exercise coach for the elderly. J. Hum.-Robot Interact. **2**, 3–32 (2013)
10. Matsusaka, Y., Fujii, H., Okano, T., Hara, I.: Health exercise demonstration robot TAIZO and effects of using voice command in robot-human collaborative demonstration. In: RO-MAN 2009-The 18th IEEE International Symposium on Robot and Human Interactive Communication, pp 472–477 (2009)
11. McColl, D., Louie, W.-Y.G., Nejat, G.: Brian 2.1: a socially assistive robot for the elderly and cognitively impaired. IEEE Robot. Autom. Mag. **20**, 74–83 (2013)
12. Wu, Y.-H., Wrobel, J., Cornuet, M., et al.: Acceptance of an assistive robot in older adults: a mixed-method study of human–robot interaction over a 1-month period in the Living Lab setting. Clin. Interv. Aging **9**, 801 (2014)

13. Eisapour, M., Cao, S., Domenicucci, L., Boger, J.: Virtual reality exergames for people living with dementia based on exercise therapy best practices. In: Proceedings of the Human Factors and Ergonomics Society Annual Meeting, pp 528–532 (2018)

14. Mann, J.A., MacDonald, B.A., Kuo, I.-H., et al.: People respond better to robots than computer tablets delivering healthcare instructions. Comput. Hum. Behav. **43**, 112–117 (2015)

15. Bainbridge, W.A., Hart, J.W., Kim, E.S., Scassellati, B.: The benefits of interactions with physically present robots over video-displayed agents. Int. J. Soc. Robot. **3**, 41–52 (2011)

16. Migovich, M., Ghosh, R., Khan, N., Tate, J., Mion, L., Sarkar, N.: System architecture and user interface design for a human-machine interaction system for dementia intervention. In: Gao, Q., Zhou, J. (eds.) HCII 2021. LNCS, vol. 12787, pp. 277–292. Springer, Cham (2021). https://doi.org/10.1007/978-3-030-78111-8_19

17. Hogg, M.A., Abrams, D.: Social cognition and attitudes. In: Martin, G.N., Carlson, N.R., Buskist, W. (eds.) Psychology, 3rd edn., pp 684–721. Pearson Education Limited (2007)

18. Kerous, B., Bartecek, R., Roman, R., Sojka, P., Becev, O., Liarokapis, F.: Examination of electrodermal and cardio-vascular reactivity in virtual reality through a combined stress induction protocol. J. Ambient. Intell. Humaniz. Comput. **11**(12), 6033–6042 (2020). https://doi.org/10.1007/s12652-020-01858-7

19. Ahmed, N., Rony, R.J.: Understanding self-reported stress among drivers and designing stress monitor using heart rate variability. Qual. User Exp. **6**(1), 1–21 (2021). https://doi.org/10.1007/s41233-020-00043-0

20. Mohammed, S., Karim, A.: A survey on emotion recognition for human robot interaction. J. Comput. Inf. Technol. **28**, 125–146 (2020). https://doi.org/10.20532/cit.2020.1004841

21. Hazer-Rau, D., Meudt, S., Daucher, A., et al.: The uulmMAC database—a multimodal affective corpus for affective computing in human-computer interaction. Sensors **20** (2020). https://doi.org/10.3390/s20082308

22. Richter, M., Wright, R.A.: Sympathetic nervous system (SNS). In: Encyclopedia of Behavioral Medicine, pp. 1943–1944 (2013)

23. Glick, G., Braunwald, E., Lewis, R.M.: Relative roles of the sympathetic and parasympathetic nervous systems in the reflex control of heart rate. Circ. Res. **16**, 363–375 (1965)

24. Mohri, M., Rostamizadeh, A., Talwalkar, A.: Foundations of Machine Learning. MIT Press, Cambridge (2018)

25. Sharma, S., Singh, G., Sharma, M.: A comprehensive review and analysis of supervised-learning and soft computing techniques for stress diagnosis in humans. Comput. Biol. Med. **134**, 104450 (2021). https://doi.org/10.1016/j.compbiomed.2021.104450

26. Education BIBMC: What is supervised learning? IBM (2020)

27. Zheng, Z., Staubitz, J., Weitlauf, A., et al.: A predictive multimodal framework to alert caregivers of problem behaviors for children with ASD (PreMAC) a predictive multimodal framework to alert caregivers of problem. Sensors **21** (2021). https://doi.org/10.3390/s21020370

28. Schmidt, P., Reiss, A., Duerichen, R., et al.: Introducing WESAD, a multimodal dataset for wearable stress and affect detection. In: Proceedings of the 20th ACM International Conference on Multimodal Interaction, New York, NY, USA, pp 400–408. Association for Computing Machinery (2018)

29. Bevilacqua, F., Engström, H., Backlund, P.: Game-calibrated and user-tailored remote detection of stress and boredom in games. Sensors **19** (2019). https://doi.org/10.3390/s19132877

Why It is Easier to Slay a Dragon Than to Kill a Myth About Older People's Smartphone Use

Eugène Loos[1]([✉]), Mireia Fernández-Ardèvol[2,3], Andrea Rosales[2,3], and Alexander Peine[4]

[1] Utrecht University School of Governance, Utrecht University, Utrecht, The Netherlands
e.f.loos@uu.nl

[2] Internet Interdisciplinary Institute (IN3), Universitat Oberta de Catalunya/ Open University of Catalonia, Barcelona, Catalonia, Spain
{mfernandezar,arosalescl}@uoc.edu

[3] Faculty of Information and Communication Sciences, Universitat Oberta de Catalunya/Open University of Catalonia, Barcelona, Catalonia, Spain

[4] Copernicus Institute of Sustainable Development, Utrecht University, Utrecht, The Netherlands
a.peine@uu.nl

Abstract. Our study focuses on myths about older people's smartphone use. Self-reported data, from Eurostat for example, report access rather than actual usage and are of limited use. What respondents report does not necessarily correspond with their actual smartphone usage behaviour in everyday life. We therefore conducted a tracking study to gain insight into smartphone usage among older adults. Smartphone activity logs were collected from individuals aged 60–79 (N = 303) throughout a period of 28 days between February and May 2019 in Canada, the Netherlands, Spain and Sweden. The data thus obtained on actual smartphone use were critically examined in the light of seven myths related to the smart phone usage of older people in everyday life. We also analysed the data in the context of empirical studies in the field of older people's digital behaviour. Finally, after drawing our conclusions, we present limitations and sketch implications for future research.

Keywords: Older adults · Smartphone use · Everyday life · Tracking · Digital practices · Myths

1 Introduction

It is easier to slay a dragon than to kill a myth [1]. This also applies to older people's use of digital devices. In 2012, Wandke et al. [2, p. 564] discussed and debunked the following myths related to ICT use by older people: (1) Just wait and see. Future generations of older people will use computers without problems; (2) Older people are not interested in using computers; (3) Older people consider computers to be useless and unnecessary; (4) Older people lack the physical capabilities to use ICT; (5) Older people simply cannot understand interactive computing technology; and (6) You can't teach an old dog new

Q. Gao and J. Zhou (Eds.): HCII 2022, LNCS 13330, pp. 212–223, 2022.
https://doi.org/10.1007/978-3-031-05581-2_16

tricks. In 2013, Durick et al. [3, p. 470] dispelled a number of prevailing myths about ageing in connection with technology design, stating: "Within the context of designing technology, we explore and present alternative approaches to the myths that all old people are the same; socially isolated and lonely; a burden on society; chronically ill; incapable of learning new, mainstream, technologies, and unable to use technology." In 2018, Quan-Haase et al. [4, p. 1207] deconstructed myths about the online activities, skills, and attitudes of older adults and developed a "typology that moves beyond seeing older adults as Non-Users to include Reluctants, Apprehensives, Basic Users, Go-Getters, and Savvy Users."

Our study focuses on myths related to older people's smartphone use. We first consulted statistics from Eurostat to gain insight into real life smartphone use by older people. The Eurostat data (2019) [5] showed that 73% of the EU-27 population between the ages of 16 and 74 accessed the internet on their mobile phones in 2019, a percentage that dropped to 45% when focussing on the group in the upper end of the age range, i.e., those aged between 55 and 74 years old. However, these self-reported data refer to access rather than actual usage and have limited use: the information provided by respondents in such a survey does not necessarily correspond with the reality of their actual smartphone usage behaviour in everyday life. We therefore conducted a tracking study to gain insight into the smartphone usage of older adults. To that end, we collected the smartphone activity logs from individuals aged 60–79 years old (N = 303) throughout a 28-day period between February and May 2019 in Canada, the Netherlands, Spain and Sweden, enabling us to critically examine the following myths related to older people's actual smart phone usage in everyday life:

Myth #1: Digital technologies are alien to older people
Myth #2: Older people are not able to interact with technology
Myth #3: The older the individual, the less the smartphone is used
Myth #4: Older people are a homogeneous population
Myth #5: Older people are defined by their medical conditions, creating specific digital needs
Myth #6: Older people don't use the smartphone to play, they don't need fun
Myth #7: Older people don't use their smartphone for self-representation

Our results will be presented within the context of empirical studies on smartphone usage by older people.

2   Method

The data we analyse here come from the More Year Better Lives (MYBL) research project BCONNECT@HOME [6]. A more detailed clarification of the data collection process and research design is given elsewhere [7, 8]. Here, we provide the relevant information to contextualize the obtained results. We used data that was collected by tracking the smartphone usage of a sample of older adults. The total sample was comprised of individuals aged 55 to 79 (N = 430), although in the present paper, the focus was on the older individuals between the ages of 60 to 79 (N = 303) within this group, who provided almost 900,000 logs (or valid observations) corresponding to more than 3.000

different apps. We collected the smartphone activity logs in a period of four consecutive weeks (28 days) between February and May 2019 in Canada, the Netherlands, Spain and Sweden. The geographical scope provided ample diversity in terms of internet and smartphone use in later life (see also [7]). The length of data collection allowed us to gain an in-depth picture of the everyday digital practices of the participants and to study the actual use of digital technology in daily life. This is important as it is impossible to be certain that the information provided by respondents in surveys and interviews corresponds with their actual digital behaviour. We aim to shed light on the digital practices of this group, although the selected sub-sample does not seek representativeness at the population level. The analysis we propose here relies exclusively on what can be considered a classical 'big data' analysis. Except for age, a critical dimension of our analysis, we study the smartphone logs without any other socio-demographic, contextual information. We conducted a relatively simple descriptive analysis of smartphone usage to build a robust narrative.

Usage indicators commonly rely on device screen activity. These are by-product indicators that, while less than perfect, are generally used in the field (see [7] for a discussion on the data analysed here). For instance, usage is generally measured as screen time, which is calculated by the time the screen remains active. However, use of such a proxy is not without its problems. On the one hand, the screen can turn on and remain active afterwards without an actual interaction, as when a notification pops up. On the other hand, some applications do not need screen time to run. Audio applications, such as Spotify, can run for hours but is counted as screen time only when the user turns on the application and at other scattered moments, such as when the user selects songs, channels or other sources of music.

First of all, we decided, following usual standards, to measure access as the number of times the screen turned on. Accessing apps is interpreted as evidence of usage: the higher the number of accesses, the higher the usage. Second, following a similar approach, we measured the usage time, or activity length, as the number of seconds the screen remained on once an app pops up. Both variables (number of accesses and access length) were assigned a minimum value of zero (indicating no usage) and no upper threshold (the higher the values, the higher the intensity of use). We examined the average daily usage and how this was distributed over the 24 h of the day. We also analysed the kind of apps used by the participants. We first looked into the most popular apps (either in general or within the sample) to provide analytically relevant examples. We then organised them into the following categories for a more systematic perspective on smartphone appropriation:

1. Image, Audio & Video. These are apps to create, edit or publish images, audio & video content.
2. News, Media & Publications. Refers to digital content consumption.
3. Email, Messaging & Phone. Includes instant messaging, email and calls –either regular or over IP.
4. Social Network Sites. Includes general purpose sites as well as dating sites.
5. Games. Refers to games, lotteries and gambling apps.
6. Health & Fitness. Includes trackers of physical activity and diet (calory counters), activity bracelet controllers and other health-related apps.

7. Travel, Transportation & Navigation. Refers to apps that support users during trips and commuting.
8. Productivity & Education. Consists of personal/office productivity and educational tools.
9. Weather. Refers to weather forecast apps.
10. Finance. Comprises banking, stocks management, micro-payment and PayPal-like apps.
11. Shopping. Refers to online shopping, price comparisons and loyalty apps.
12. Tools. Any tool not related to the previous categories.
13. System. Includes launchers and other apps with a transparent interface for the user (not explicit, not noticeable when in operation). The analysis will exclude this category.

3   Results

Myth #1: Digital technologies are alien to older people

Are digital technologies really alien to older people? If this were the case, why would they use the smartphone the whole day, as Fig. 1 clearly shows? The participants used their mobile phones more than 100 times per day on average. This usage is distributed over the day, curving upward from 5 AM on and remaining high until starting to decrease in the evening from 6 PM on. Usage is minimal at night (between 1 and 5 AM). We agree with Durick et al. (2013, p. 472) [3] that "(…) a lack of perceived benefit appeared to generate negative opinions of new technology. (…) older users expect a clear vision of how technology will allow them to retain their independence and achieve practical benefits that will help them maintain their everyday wellbeing. However, one could argue that this is an important to all ages."

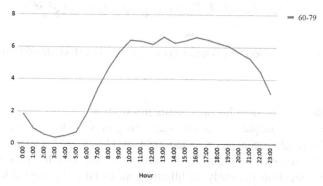

Fig. 1. Average number of accesses to smartphone apps/webs per hour (aged 60–79)

Myth #2: Older people are not able to interact with technology

Figure 1 also clearly shows that it is not true that older people are unable to master internet skills: they apparently have the internet skills to know how to access smartphone apps/webs, as they are attached to their smartphone all day. They use their mobile phones (=screen turns on) more than 100 times per day on average. The distribution of this usage over the day shows that smartphone use is shaped by social uses of time (sleeping time, etc.). Usage rises from 5 AM in the morning and remains high until 6 PM in the evening, when it once again starts to decrease. At night (between 1 and 5 AM), usage is minimal but even then it does not totally disappear. Our findings are consistent with insights from studies such as [2–4, 9].

Myth #3: The older the individual, the less the smartphone is used
Age is generally considered to negatively affect digital engagement. Depending on factors such as attitudes, motivations and skills older people can be digitally engaged [see e.g., 4, 9]. The data in Fig. 2 and 3, split by age group (60–69 and 70–79), challenges the myth that the older old use their smartphone less than the younger old. We found no difference in usage throughout the day, nor in the duration of the smartphone session. We observed similar patterns in both cohorts: the differences are small and the curves for both age groups follow each other closely.

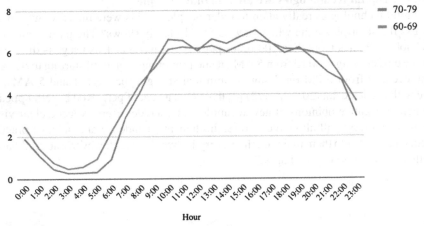

Fig. 2. Average number of accesses to smartphone apps/ webs per hour (60–69, 70–79 years old)

Myth #4: Older people are a homogeneous population
It is a myth that older people form a homogeneous group. On the contrary, older adults represent a highly heterogeneous population [4, 9–11]: the older people become, the more diverse they become as a group, a phenomenon called 'aged heterogeneity' [9–11]. Table 1 presents data from our study, highlighting the fact that different older individuals rely on different apps in daily life and use these with different intensity. The overview of selected apps clearly shows the diversity of usages and differences in popularity, which illustrates the heterogeneity in activities and communication interests mediated by the smartphone.

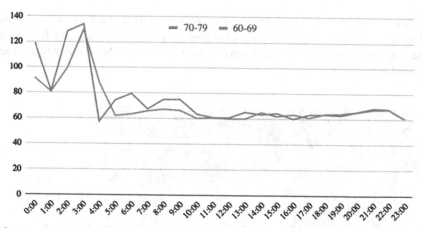

Fig. 3. Average duration of accesses to smartphone apps/webs per hour – units: seconds (60–69 years old, 70–79 years old)

Though differences in digital proficiency between users can play a role to a certain extent [12–14], it is also important to be aware of the fact that studies reporting internet use, often report average behavior, with the diversity of internet users among older adults remaining unacknowledged (see [4, 9] for a more critical approach).

Table 1. Use on average per app (60–79 years old)

Ages: 60–79	Users		Usage (on average)	
	N	%	Accesses per user in the 28-day period	Duration of accesses (seconds)
Google Maps	227	75%	15	133
WhatsApp Messenger	191	63%	300	83
Spotify Music	48	16%	14	–
Google Fit	11	4%	144	–
Pokémon GO	9	3%	351	334
Candy Crush Friends Saga	5	2%	28	655

Note: Duration of access is measured in terms of time screen. Apps as Spotify or Google Fit mostly run on the background and do not count as time screen usage

Myth #5: Older people are defined by their medical conditions, creating specific digital needs

The myth that older people are defined by their medical conditions and their digital needs (an assumption that is part of a patronizing attitude towards older adults [15]) does not hold up. We present data in Fig. 4, showing the different categories of apps used by the participants use (number of accesses during the observed period). These very clearly show that the typology of apps used by the participants does not appear to be shaped by medical conditions alone, but also by personal interests, such as calls & messaging, using social networks, games & gambling (see also Myth #6), news & media and travel & transportation.

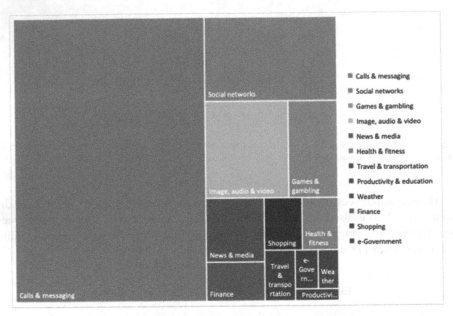

Fig. 4. Different categories of apps' use (aged 60–79)

Myth #6: Older people don't use the smartphone to play, they don't need fun

Our data clearly show that older people have fun and do play games (see for example Candy Crush and Pokémon Go in Table 1). Moreover, Fig. 4 clearly shows that "Games and Gambling" is the fourth – out of 12 – most relevant category of apps. This category is more relevant than news & media, and health & fitness apps. Though most gaming reports do not include much data on age (or any at all, see Statista [16] for Spain), there are a few examples that do provide some information about age. According to the ESA gaming report, 30% of men in the USA in the age group 55–64 play on a game console, while 31% of the women play on a tablet or a wireless device [17]. And Statista (2020), which presents the data for Sweden, shows that in Sweden, 21% of the 45–64 years old and 15% of the 65–79 years old [18] engaged in playing video games on a daily basis in 2018. In the first half of 2016, some 8% of internet users gaming online on mobile devices were aged 55 and up in the Netherlands, rising to 12% in the second half of 2016, 14% in the first half of 2017 before dropping to 11% in the 2nd half of 2017 [19].

Myth #7: Older people don't use their smartphone for self-representation

If it were true that older people do not use their smartphone for self-representation, why do they use Instagram, Facebook or even dating apps, such as Tinder? There are studies reporting that older people are not interested in social network sites [20]. But our data in Table 2 clearly show that that older people most certainly do use social network sites. Self-representation could be one of the reasons.

Table 2. Overview of app use (60–79 years old)

Ages: 60- 79	Users		Usage (on average)	
	N	%	Accesses per user in the 28-day period	Duration of accesses (seconds)
Facebook	178	58,7	114	201
Instagram	111	36,6	67	144
Twitter	40	13,2	87	125
LinkedIn	35	11,6	18	69
Snapchat	5	1,7	58	78
Pinterest	4	1,3	23	95
Tinder	1	0,3	6	9
Nextdoor	1	0,3	1	262

4 Conclusion

We collected the smartphone activity logs from individuals aged 60–79 (N = 303) over a period of 28 days between February and May 2019 in Canada, the Netherlands, Spain and Sweden to critically examine seven myths related to older people's actual smart phone usage in everyday life. The obtained data were assessed in the light of empirical studies in the field of older people's smartphone usage. This led to the following results:

Myth #1: Digital technologies are alien to older people
Figure 1 clearly shows that on average, participants use their mobile phones more than 100 times per day. This usage is distributed throughout the day, curving upward from 5 AM in the morning and remaining high until 6 PM, when this starts to decrease. In line with the findings of Durick et al. (2013) [3], usage is minimal at night (between 1 and 5 AM). If older people are using their smartphone the whole day long, digital technologies are anything but alien to them.

Myth #2: Older people are not able to interact with technology
Figure 1 also clearly shows that older people are able to master internet skills: They apparently know how to accesses smartphone apps/webs as they are attached to their smartphone throughout the day: they use their mobile phones (=screen turns on) on average more than 100 times per day. Our findings are consistent with insights from studies such as [2–4, 9].

Myth #3: The older the individual, the less the smartphone is used
The data in Fig. 2 and 3, split by age group (60–69 and 70–79), challenges the myth

that the older old use their smartphone less. We found no differences either in usage throughout the day or in duration of the smartphone sessions during the day. We observed similar patterns in both age groups: only minor differences were seen between the groups, with neither one exceeding the other. Depending on factors such as attitudes, motivations and skills, older people can be said to be digitally engaged [see e.g., 4, 9].

Myth #4: Older people are a homogeneous population
Our findings clearly show that older people form a heterogeneous group (in line with [4, 9–11]). Table 1 presents data from our study showing that different older individuals rely on different apps in their everyday life and use these with different intensity. The overview of selected apps clearly demonstrates the diversity of usages and differences in popularity, which illustrates the heterogeneity in activities and communication interests mediated by the smartphone.

Myth #5: Older people are defined by their medical conditions, creating specific digital needs
Older people are not defined by their medical conditions and their digital needs (an assumption that is part of a patronizing attitude towards older adults [15]). Our data in Fig. 4, presenting different categories of apps used by the participants (number of accesses during the observed period), clearly show that the typology of apps would not appear to be shaped only by medical condition, but also by personal interests, such as calls & messaging, using social networks, games & gambling (see also Myth #6), news & media and travel & transportation.

Myth #6: Older people don't use the smartphone to play, they don't need fun
Most gaming reports do not include much age-related data [16, 18, 19], but our data clearly show that older people have fun and do play games (see for example Candy Crush and Pokémon Go in Table 1). Moreover, Fig. 4 clearly shows that "Games and Gambling" is the fourth – out of 12 – most relevant category of apps. It has more relevance than news & media, and health & fitness apps.

Myth #7: Older people don't use their smartphone for self-representation
There are studies reporting that older people are not interested in social network sites [20], but our data in Table 2 clearly show that they are also users of Instagram, Facebook or even dating apps such as Tinder. Self-representation could be one of the reasons.

5   Limitations and Implications for Future Research

The explorative quantitative data that we present and discuss in this paper is embed-ded in a conceptual framework that is now widely referred to as the co-constitution of ageing and technology [21, 22]. This line of research breaks away from the usual tendency to conceptualize technologies as interventions to the problems of ageing and later life, and instead studies "how the contemporary experience of aging is alreadyco-constituted by gerontechnology design, the socio-material practices it enacts, and policy discourses around innovation and aging". [23, p. 19] So far, however, most of the studies in this emerging tradition have been qualitative, focusing in depth on particular, situated forms of ageing-technology relations in practice.

The study presented in this paper, therefore, is unique in the presentation of quantitative data to explore the co-constitution of ageing and technology. The tracking approach that we pursued allowed us to map out real world encounters of older people with technology in their everyday lives in a comparative perspective and with a large sample size. Its data thus goes beyond existing quantitative overviews that use self-reported data about the possession and use of digital technology among older people, and of smartphones in particular. This particular perspective has allowed us to provide additional understanding of the diversity and extent of digital uses based on a large sample from across four countries.

While our approach is explorative, it has allowed us to complement and thus corroborate existing qualitative studies that had already shown how digital device use by older people is more diverse than existing policy discourses around gerontechnology innovations would indicate. [24–30].

We consider this an important step towards complementing existing narrative evidence and the establishing of a broader database that we can use to inform policy making in the field. To be more precise, we argue that this study demonstrates the value of more mixed methods research in socio-gerontechnology, whereby quantitative data about digital technology use can further underpin the relevance of richer and broader narratives about ageing technology relations. For instance, where Beneito-Montegut et al. [24] show in depth the role social media play in the everyday life and caring relations of older people, our data in relation to myth #5 (e.g., calls & messaging in Fig. 4) demonstrates that such co-constitutive relations between older people, caring and social media are indeed widespread and thus relevant. Together, then, we find an equally deep and broad evidence base to inform more creative and productive encounters of socio-gerontechnology with innovation policy or technology design.

There are of course also limitations to our approach, in particular regarding the representativeness of our sample. Our study sampled study subjects that owned a smartphone and who had previously indicated that they regularly used it. In future research, this approach can be adopted for studies in other countries than just the four in our research project and may be combined with population data to assess how widespread the passion for smartphones is in the studied population. Moreover, future research may also try to understand more specifically the relationship between digital technology use and place, so as to be able to contextualize better where and why certain apps are being used. Finally, existing qualitative studies in ageing and technology may be more systematically used to devise hypotheses about specific relations in the data, and thus move beyond the (mostly) descriptive analysis of "big data" on ageing and digital technology use.

Acknowledgements. The research project BConnect@Home – Making use of digital devices in later life (https://jp-demographic.eu/projects/beconnected-at-home/) is funded by the JTP 2017 - JPI More Years, Better Lives (Grant Agreement n. 643850). Canada: Canadian Institutes of Health Research (201704MYB-386097); the Netherlands: ZONMW (Project 9003037411); Spain: MINECO (ref. PCI-2017–080), Sweden: TBC and. It also received partial funding from the Ageing + Communication + Technology project http://actproject.ca/ (ref. 895–2013-1018, Social

Sciences and Humanities Research Council of Canada), and the Spanish Ministry of Science, Innovation, and Universities (ref: FJCI-2015–24120).

References

1. Gabriel, Y.: On organisational stories and myths: why it is easier to slay a dragon than to kill a myth. Int. Sociol. **6**(4), 427–442 (1991)
2. Wandke, H., Sengpiel, M., Sönksen, M.: Myths about older people's use of information and communication technology. Gerontology **58**(6), 564–570 (2012)
3. Durick, J., Robertson, T., Brereton, M., Vetere, F., Nansen, B.: Dispelling ageing myths in technology design. In: Proceedings of the Australian Computer-Human Interaction Conference (OzCHI'13), pp. 467– 476 (2013) https://doi.org/10.1145/2541016.2541040
4. Quan-Haase, A., Williams, C., Kicevski, M., Elueze, I., Wellman, B.: Dividing the grey divide: deconstructing myths about older adults' online activities, skills, and attitudes. Am. Behav. Sci. **62**(9), 1207–1228 (2018)
5. Eurostat 2021: Individuals used a mobile phone (or smart phone) to access the internet. Dataset: Individuals - mobile internet access [ISOC_CI_IM_I__custom_1985172]. Accessed 27 Jan 2022 (2019) https://ec.europa.eu/eurostat/databrowser/view/ISOC_CI_IM_I__custom_1985172/default/table
6. BCONNECT@HOME: Being Connected at Home – Making use of digital devices in later life (2017) https://www.jp-demographic.eu/wp-content/uploads/2017/01/BCONNECT_2017_conf2018_brochure.pdf
7. Fernández-Ardèvol, M., et al.: Methodological strategies to understand smartphone practices for social connectedness in later life. In: Zhou, J., Salvendy, G. (eds.) HCII 2019. LNCS, vol. 11593, pp. 46–64. Springer, Cham (2019). https://doi.org/10.1007/978-3-030-22015-0_4
8. Fernández-Ardèvol, M., Rosales, A., Morey, F.: Methods matter: assessment of the characteristics of a sample to analyze digital practices and social connectedness in later life. In: Gao, Q., Zhou, J. (eds.) HCII 2020. LNCS, vol. 12209, pp. 58–68. Springer, Cham (2020). https://doi.org/10.1007/978-3-030-50232-4_5
9. Loos, E.F.: Designing for dynamic diversity: Representing various senior citizens in digital information sources. Observatorio (OBS*) **7**(1), 21-45 (2013)
10. Nelson, E.A., Dannefer, D.: Aged heterogeneity: fact or fiction? the fate of diversity in gerontological research. Gerontologist **32**(1), 17–23 (1992)
11. Stone, M.E., Lin, J., Dannefer, D., Kelley-Moore, J.A.: The continued eclipse of heterogeneity in gerontological research. J. Gerontology Series B **72**(1), 162–167 (2017)
12. van Deursen, A.J.A.M., van Dijk, J.A.G.M.: The first-level digital divide shifts from inequalities in physical access to inequalities in material access. New Media Soc. **21**(2), 354–375 (2019). https://doi.org/10.1177/1461444818797082
13. Robinson, L., et al.: Digital inequalities and why they matter. Inf. Commun. Soc. **18**(5), 569–582 (2015). https://doi.org/10.1080/1369118X.2015.1012532
14. Robinson, L., Schulz, J., Blank, G., Ragnedda, M., Ono, H., Hogan, B., Mesch, G., Cotten, S.R., Kretchmer, S.B., Hale, T.M., Drabowicz, T., Yan, P., Khilnani, A.: Digital Inequalities 2.0 Legacy inequalities in the information age. pp. 1–29 (2020)
15. Ryan, E.B., Boich, L.H., Hummert, M.L.: Communication predicaments of aging: patronizing behavior toward older adults. J. Lang. Soc. Psychol. **14**, 144–166 (1995). https://doi.org/10.1177/0261927X95141008
16. Statista: Video game industry in Spain. (2020) https://www.statista.com/topics/6035/video-game-industry-in-spain/

17. ESA: Esential Facts About the Video Game Industry (2021) https://www.theesa.com/wp-content/uploads/2021/08/2021-Essential-Facts-About-the-Video-Game-Industry-1.pdf
18. Statista: Video games in Sweden. (2018) https://www.statista.com/outlook/dmo/digital-media/video-games/sweden
19. Statista: Gaming Market in the Netherlands. (2020) https://www.statista.com/study/59212/gaming-market-in-the-netherlands/
20. Rosales, A., Fernández-Ardèvol, M.: Beyond whatsapp: older people and smartphones. Romanian J. Commun. Public Relat. **18**(1), 27–47 (2016)
21. Peine, A., Marshall, B.L., Martin, W., Neven, L. (eds.): Socio-Gerontechnology — Interdisciplinary Critical Studies of Ageing and Technology. Routledge, London (2021)
22. Peine, A., Neven, L.: The co-constitution of ageing and technology – a model and agenda. Ageing Soc. **41**(12), 2845–2866 (2021)
23. Peine, A., Neven, L.: From intervention to co-constitution: new directions in theorizing about aging and technology. Gerontologist **59**(1), 15–21 (2019)
24. Beneito-Montagut, R., Begueria, A.: "Send me a whatsapp when you arrive home": mediated practices of caring about. In: Peine, A., Marshall, B., Martin, W., Neven, L. (eds.): Socio-Gerontechnology - Interdisciplinary Critical Studies of Ageing and Technology, pp. 119–132. Routledge, London (2021)
25. Katz, S., Marshall, B.L.: Tracked and fit: fitbits, brain games, and the quantified aging body. J. Aging Stud. **45**, 63–68 (2018)
26. López Gómez, D.: Little arrangements that matter. rethinking autonomy-enabling innovations for later life. Technol. Forecast. Soc. Change **93**, 91-101 (2015)
27. Carlo, S., Bonifacio, F.: Elderly, ICTs and qualitative research: some methodological reflections. In: Gao, Q., Zhou, J. (eds.) HCII 2021. LNCS, vol. 12786, pp. 3–20. Springer, Cham (2021). https://doi.org/10.1007/978-3-030-78108-8_1
28. Loos, E., Haddon, L., Mante-Meijer, E. (eds.): Generational Use of New Media. Ashgate, Adlershot (2012)
29. Loos, E.F.: De oudere: een digitale immigrant in eigen land? Een terreinverkenning naar toegankelijke informatievoorziening. (oratie) [Older people: Digital Immigrants in their own country? Exploring accessible information delivery (inaugural lecture)]. Boom/Lemma, The Hague (2010)
30. Loos, E.F.: Senior citizens: digital immigrants in their own country? Observatorio (OBS*) **6**(1), 1-23 (2012)

3D QR Cube for Elderly Information System Design

Ameersing Luximon[1] , Ravindra S. Goonetilleke[2] , and Yan Luximon[3]($\boxtimes$)

[1] EMEDS Ltd., Kowloon, Hong Kong SAR
[2] Department of Industrial and Systems Engineering, Khalifa University, Abu Dhabi, UAE
ravindra.goonetilleke@ku.ac.ae
[3] School of Design, The Hong Kong Polytechnic University, Hung Hom, Hong Kong SAR
yan.luximon@polyu.edu.hk

Abstract. The worldwide population is aging, even though more and more elderly people are living independently and alone. Moreover, pandemics such as COVID-19 are putting enormous pressure in health care systems all around the world. To deal with the growing elderly population and health care challenges, there is an emerging focus on technology and IT products. Technology such as mobile devices with their ever-increasing computational power, and differing sensors show immense usefulness for elderly as well as people with disability. This study proposes the development of 3D QR codes for improved safety, security, and customization of user interfaces. This study proposes multiple QR codes aligned together to create a QR cube (or QR cuboid) to store an increasing amount of information about the user. Individual QR codes will be compatible with existing systems. On the other hand, nearly, all individual information is stored with the user, enabling better privacy. Even with the development of future technologies, QR cubes can be used to access digital information.

Keywords: QR code · QR cube · Privacy and security · Personalization and customization · Digital and information systems

1 The Aging Population

1.1 Population Trends

Elderly populations are concentrated in specific geographic distribution creating specific social and economic challenges and having serious implications for government and private spending on pensions, health care, education and, more generally, for economic growth and welfare [1]. Based on 2020 data there are 16 countries (Japan, Italy, Finland, Greece, Portugal, Germany, Bulgaria, Croatia, Latvia, France, Slovenia, Estonia, Hungary, Sweden, Czech Republic, Denmark) with an elderly population of more than 20%. Japan has the highest percentage of elderly population at 28.79% [1]. Apart from the 16 countries [1], more places including Hong Kong (latest elderly population 17.8% [2]) and Singapore (latest elderly population 15% [1]) will also have more than 20% elderly population by 2050 [3]. The elderly population is expected to increase to

© The Author(s), under exclusive license to Springer Nature Switzerland AG 2022
Q. Gao and J. Zhou (Eds.): HCII 2022, LNCS 13330, pp. 224–236, 2022.
https://doi.org/10.1007/978-3-031-05581-2_17

16% of the world population by 2050 [3, 4]. On the other hand, the UAE population is relatively young with a 1.3% elderly population [5]. Despite a low percentage of the elderly population, even in the UAE there are concerns as the population is aging and this will create financial, social, and medical pressures for families and the UAE government [5].

In most countries, elderly do not work and depend on the working population. Hence, the elderly dependency rate is an important economic indicator and is calculated as the ratio between the elderly population (>65 years) and the working age (15–64 years) population [4]. While the population is greying, the total labor supply (people aged 20 to 64) is projected to fall (in the EU by 9.6% over 2016–70) [6]. With increasing cost of aging and decreasing labor supply, most government consider aging a major concern and many governments have developed policies to promote active and healthy aging.

Elderly experience one or many medical conditions such as hearing loss, eye problems such as cataracts and refractive errors, back and neck pain and osteoarthritis, chronic pulmonary disease, diabetes, depression, and dementia [3]. Most of the health conditions are influenced by people's physical and social environments rather than genetics. Also, there are large variations among people. For example, some 80-year-olds have physical and mental capacities like many 30-year-olds [3]. Hence, it is important to consider individual and environmental factors to enable healthy aging. In addition, globalization, technological developments, urbanization, migration and changing gender norms also need to be considered. Recently, during the COVID-19 pandemic, conventional health-care systems have performed poorly while providing health care to the public [7]. The COVID-19 pandemic has shown the importance of a seamless interaction between healthcare, society, and technology. Human rights-based access to lifesaving and life-enhancing knowledge, services, and supports based on and implemented through technology are the future of healthcare systems to support the elderly population. In addition to healthcare, elderly need to adapt with the ever-changing technology. Therefore, for elderly to have healthy and active aging, the focus is beyond healthcare with a complete ecosystem for happy aging.

1.2 Elderly Technology and Information System

Due to the ever-increasing elderly population and decreasing percentage of working people, elderly healthcare must be transformed by the adoption of technology. For Japan, with a high percentage of elderly, it is not surprising that the government has developed several strategies regarding healthcare information technology (HIT). The first government HIT strategy was the "E-Japan Strategy" in 2001 [8]. There were several other strategies that have been developed and the general trend has been to move from e-Japan (use Information and communication technology (ICT) widely) in 2001 to u-Japan (U stands for Ubiquitous, Universal, User-oriented, and Unique). On July 17, 2020, the Japanese government approved a new IT strategy aimed at being the World's Most Advanced IT Nation [9]. This will affect how people, especially elderly in Japan live and interact with technology and information systems. Other countries, such as China, which expects to have 26% elderly by 2050 with 5% elderly above 80 years old, will have a growing demand for elderly care and health services [10]. A survey on the use of internet by old people (>60 years old) found that 38.6% used the Internet and their favorite online activity was online dating (74.2%), health information (63.1%) and exercise (47.1%). The participants somewhat demanded smart bracelets, emergency callers, telemedicine, and online health consultation [10].

Devices and systems have been developed to support aging by improving seniors' quality of life and reducing caregivers' burdens. It is often referred as Assistive Ambient Living (AAL). Several health care system and projects such as My-Heart, an EU FP6 project, HeartCycle project, Continua Health Alliance project has been initiated [11]. The CoSHE [12], a cloud-based smart home system, uses ubiquitous health monitoring by collecting daily physiological signals through non-invasive wearable sensors and record location in the home. The sensor data is processed in real time and provided for remote care givers [12]. There are many other systems based on sensors and wearable technology for health care monitoring, health care data processing and communication. Among them smart phone seems to be a good gateway to connect the user environment to the cloud system [11].

In addition to technology and information systems related to health, such as online shopping, especially in China, have grown rapidly. Chinese customers prefer online shopping systems such as Taobao more than physical stores because of price, convenience, customer service quality, searching and browsing process, easy access to information about products, and less pressure about status [13]. Some people find that the sales in the physical stores are aggressive, discriminate minorities and care about social status. Online shopping systems are extremely useful to the elderly as they can shop online at their own pace and get goods delivered to their home. In addition, Chiang et al. [14] discussed an augmented reality (AR) application that supported the elderly in searching books and videos in a large library (SearchAR). When using SearchAR, sixty percent of the elderly felt they save time searching library materials, felt easier to associate 3D images to library materials rather than reading complicated online catalogs.

Although the use of technology is important, several studies have shown difficulties in elderly to adapt to new technologies. In the USA, 40% of all medical expenditure is on elderly and with increasing elderly (20% by 2030) population, the medical expenditures for seniors will continue to grow. Although more than 80% of USA adult users have searched the Internet for health information [15], elderly participants from the USA seemed to adhere to a physician-centered model of care [16]. Given the tendency towards physician-centered model of care in USA, the health care system will be overburdened if new strategies based on technology and information are not widely implemented. In Sweden, elderly patients reported uncertainty towards e-health and raised concerns about costs, mistrust in the system, accessibility to e-health systems and impaired abilities to cope with technology [17]. Elderly e-health system needs to consider cost, usefulness, user-friendliness, security, confidentiality, and accessibility. Also given huge variations among elderly, the system needs to be designed such that it can be personalized or customized based on different individual needs.

In addition to adaptation to new technology, several studies have indicated ethical and privacy concerns when elderly and elderly with disability use technology and information systems. Elderly with Parkinson's Disease perceived the internet as mysterious and confusing. This contributes to fears about online information privacy and concern for information privacy breaches [18]. AAL technologies, devoted to support aging population, opens the ethical issues related to human personal space [19]. Since more elderly will live independently at home, Panico et al. [19] encouraged a person-oriented approach when designing healthcare facilities for future generations of personalized AAL devices [19]. When elderly are not at home, people with dementia can have tracking devices using Global Positioning Systems (GPS). This raises ethical concerns and there need to be clearer policies and practical guidelines [20]. Similarly, Intelligent assistive technology (IAT), making use of artificial intelligence (AI), robotics and wearable computing promises to reduce global burden of population aging and improving the quality of life of elderly, raises important ethical challenges as it involves machine intelligence, collect sensitive data, and operate near human body [21]. Furthermore, an overview of the literature by Niemeijer et al. [22] shows that application and use of surveillance technologies in residential care, especially for elderly and people with intellectual disability, generates considerable ethical debates, especially when there is conflict of interests between institution and resident. Resident concerns include freedom and consent, privacy, and dignity/stigma. Fortunately, over the past decades several changes have taken place in the development of ethical support in elderly care [23]. Developers of Intelligent digital healthcare systems are concerned about security, privacy and ethics and they pay particular attention to data security and consider the user's best interest [24].

2 Quick Response Code (QR Code)

Quick Response code (QR code) is a two-dimensional or matrix code invented in 1994 by Masahiro Hara from the Japanese automotive company Denso Wave [25]. The initial purpose was to track vehicles during manufacturing and a QR code allowed high-speed component scanning. QR Codes were developed as a quick way to access information. The amount of data that can be stored in a QR code depends on the data type (Numeric, alphanumeric, binary, Kanji/Kana), QR code version (1 to 40) and error correction level (Low (L), Medium (M), Quartile (Q) and High(H)). For L, M, Q, and H 7%, 15%, 25% and 30% of data bytes can be restored. The number of dots is equal to (4 × version number + 17 dots on each side). For example, version 40 has 117 × 117 dots and the maximum storage capacities occur for version 40 and error correction level L (low) and it can store either 7089 numeric only characters or 4296 alphanumeric characters. Estimated number of numeric data (N) equals to $3.7085*v^2 + 28.501v$ or estimated number of alphanumeric data (A) is equal to $2.276v^2 + 17.272v$, where v is the version number when using Low data correction level. Businesses quickly saw the value of QR Codes and QR codes are now widely used in industrial and commercial applications. Many web-based generators are available.

QR codes based on URL link, plain text, contact information, phone, SMS, 'App QR code' that can open android app can be created (www.the-qrcode-generator.com/). Figure 1 shows 3 types of QR codes as an example. The plain text QR code was created using the abstract of this paper. Other website (supercode.com, www.denso-wave.com) provides a Q-platform to manage QR codes and provide different QR code types such as URL, E-mail, vCard, social media, SMS, Feedback, plain text, Bulk codes, WhatsApp QR code, Images and PDF file. For example, the QR code created using an image or PDF provide a link to the image (or PDF) rather than the image being encoded in a static QR code. The website can also provide view scan analytics as the created QR code provide a link to the stored data. The QR code can be dynamic, static and can be customized based on color scheme, logo, and branding guidelines. QR codes based on web platforms (Q-platform) are extremely useful. However, there may be concerns about privacy and security.

(a) URL code   (b) vCard   (c) Plain text

Fig. 1. Different types of QR codes

2.1 QR Security

A QR Code is space-saving and has relatively large capacity. The use of smartphones with sensors and QR code readers and encoders have increased the use of QR code applications [26] such as shopping [27], banking [28], sensor and internet of Thing (IoT) [29, 30] and medical applications [31–38]. There are many uses of QR codes in elderly and medical applications including COVID19 pandemic control using leave home safe apps [31] and health QR code [32]; medication safety support system [33]; safer use of medication [34]; medication adherence [35]; medical surgery related applications [36]. However, since any device can read the same information, including private and classified information, the traditional QR code is not secure.

New QR codes (SQRC) are being developed by Denso Wave [25], that are secure. A single QR code carries two types of data: public and private. The private data can be read only with a dedicated reader having the cryptographic key, which provides data protection. Since SQRC looks the same as the regular QR Code, it can prevent forgery and tampering. In addition to Denso Wave, many researchers are working on security and privacy when using QR codes many of which can be used in smart phones rather than using dedicated readers. After a comprehensive security and privacy analysis, Wahsheh and Luccio [39] found that some apps provide security services such as checking URLs and using cryptographic solutions, while other apps claim to guarantee user privacy. The apps that claim to guarantee user privacy may deceive the users by providing security and privacy protections that are weaker than what is claimed. Security and privacy system should have built in cryptographic solutions with preferable private keys rather than relying on claimed security by websites. Yu et al. [40] has developed a high-capacity

QR code with three-layers of information to protect the sensitive information using characteristics of the Hamming code. Zhou et al. [41] have proposed dynamic QR code system for banking and payment using several cryptographic algorithms. QR codes can be used for communication like handshaking protocol, known as Screen-camera communication [42], for security and privacy checks before transferring data. Data such as text, picture and audio files can be transferred without error using Screen-Camera Communication System based on Dynamic QR Code [42]. Alphanumeric private keys are common, but visual cryptography [43–47] including steganography can be very secure and have been used for mobile payments [43] and transfer of medical images and data [45, 47]. The 3D QR cube proposes a multi-platform QR code system that uses visual cryptography techniques for secure data transfer, and Screen-Camera Communication System for privacy and ethical checks.

3 3D QR Cube (QR3D Code)

3.1 System Structure

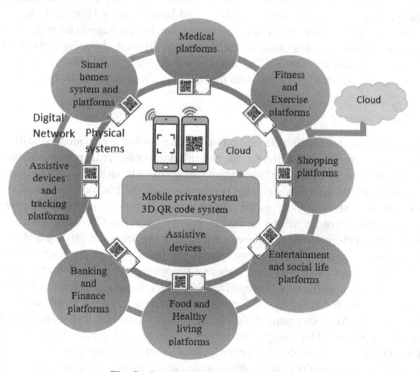

Fig. 2. System structure of 3D QR code

The heart of the 3D QR cube system is the smart phone technology and different types of application platforms (Fig. 2). The mobile phone is connected to assistive and measurement devices such as heart rate monitor, blood pressure monitoring system, wheelchair, exoskeleton and robotic system for rehabilitation and mobility support, and electronic walking stick, through wireless technology. In addition, current mobile phones have many sensors that can be used directly without any extra expense for elderly assistance. For example, a built-in smart phone GPS system and/or Wi-Fi positioning system (WPS) can be used for tracking; while voice, video and images can be used for taking data to evaluate posture, physical, mental, and emotional state; and accelerometers can be used for gait, fall and fitness evaluation. With the current trend in technology, the smart phone of the future will have more sensors to aid in elderly care such as infrared cameras, and heart rate monitor. The smart phone will store private keys that can be alphanumeric and image based. In some cases, biometric data such as fingerprint or face scan can be used as private keys. Some mobile data is stored in the cloud in private folders, while others are stored in hard disks or other storage devices as 'cold storage' for better security and privacy. The mobile phone will communicate with the different application platforms via camera, screen, and wireless technology. There can be many application platforms that can be accessed via the smart phone for the benefit of the elderly.

These platforms can be related to health and medical applications, fitness and exercise, smart homes and IoT devices, assistive devices especially for mobility, and platforms for shopping, entertainment, banking, and healthy living (Fig. 2). Other future platforms and applications can be added to the system. For each application there can be more than one platform. For example, there are many different shopping platforms such as Amazon, Alibaba and Taobao. The aim is to use the open patent QR code technology while using the different platforms with the access to data controlled by the user.

3.2 User-Centered

The user controls the data and the amount of information that is provided to the different systems. For example, today different shopping platforms have a user profile and based on the user profile the shopping platform suggests new products, target marketing campaign and promotions. When a new shopping platform is used, the platform does not have the user information and shopping profile. The user needs to register and after shopping for some time, a user profile will be created in the new platform. Currently, the company who own the platforms controls the user data and many times the privacy and opinion of the users are ignored. With a user-centered QR based system, the user profile data is stored by the user. When the user goes to a shopping platform, a dynamic QR code which has the user profile is presented. This shopping QR code does not include private user information. The shopping platform is configured based on the profile information in the QR code. After shopping, the shopping platform provides a shopping history in the existing platform. This shopping history can either be used to modify the user profile and stored in the private mobile system or ignored based on the user privacy and security settings of the shopping QR code. In any shopping platform, the user-controlled shopping profile can be used, hence creating a secure shopping experience with customization and personalization attributes. A similar method is used for different platforms, as the users have control over their personal data. Using this method, services can be customized and personalized based on user data and still the user information can be privately stored. For payments, a dynamic payment QR code is activated (Fig. 3).

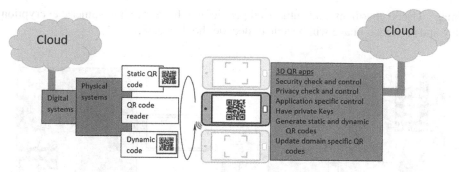

Fig. 3. Screen-Camera communication via QR codes

When interacting with physical and digital QR code systems, a screen-camera communication protocol can be used. Here, we can use a hospital as an example. Assume a hospital of the future where there are less health care personnel, but more assistive systems such as Health Bots, autonomous wheelchair, and automated storage and retrieval pharmacy system. In a simple situation, the user scans the QR code at the entrance of the hospital. The user smart phone system uses the QR code information and checks whether there are any appointments and other visits. A dynamic QR code is created in the phone to indicate any appointments, current health status, medical history, and other important information for better triage. Based on the user presented QR code, a decision will be made using the hospital information system and a QR code presented to the user. The user can get this QR code and access the hospital. The initial dynamic QR code can have information on the different facilities to use, access to any autonomous systems (such as wheelchair), and the different sections of the hospital. The GPS system or the Wi-Fi positioning system (WPS) in the phone tracks the user and makes sure the user does not go in any unrestricted area. After meeting the medical professional, the dynamic QR code will be modified, and the user can collect the drugs at the pharmacy. The QR code will be used during drug dispensing to reduce errors. Also, all the drugs will have a QR code including information about dosage and the frequency the medicines should be taken. The user QR code is updated and stored in a mobile private system. Depending on the required security, safety and ethical concerns different levels of cryptographic algorithms are used.

3.3 Security

For secure data sharing in a public network, cryptographic algorithms such as digital steganography can be used. Figure 4. shows a method for transferring medical images and data over public platforms such as Q-platform or commercial websites. In this case, images and data are first encrypted using an alphanumeric key. After the first encryption, the images look more like noisy data. The encrypted data is then embedded inside a reference image to create a new image which looks like the reference image but has encrypted data. The data is then uploaded on a Q-platform. The Q-platform generates a URL QR code and sends it to the user. Any third party will not be able to decode the image without a private alphanumeric encryption key and the reference image. Users, guardians, and authorized people who have the alphanumeric encryption key and reference image will be able to decode the data correctly.

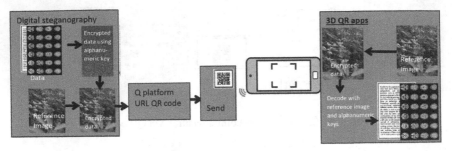

Fig. 4. Secure data transfer using digital steganography and private key on public network

3.4 Scalable

Given that many QR codes are used (see a montage of QR images in Fig. 5), it is important to have a system and database to access these codes efficiently. In this study we propose to stack the QR codes together to create a 3D QR cube (Fig. 6). Many QR codes can also be included into a movie type of format. In a dynamic QR code, when data are added, the version might change given that different version support different amount of data. When the version changes, the size of the QR code also changes. As 3D cube size is standardized, any changes in version will not change the 3D cube structure. By proper design, the sides of the QR cube can be used for error checking and validation. The QR cube system, although complex to develop, is simple for the elderly. The elderly do not need to know many aps or different languages. The screen to camera communication or the security coding are done inside the mobile system. In general, the 3D QR cube is scalable as more layers of QR codes can be added.

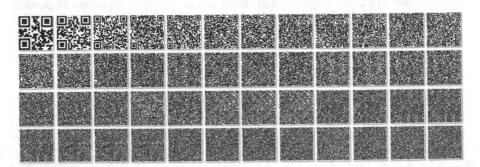

Fig. 5. Montage of QR codes

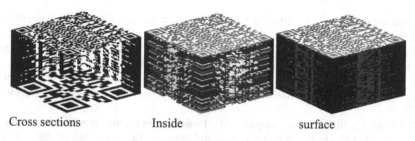

Cross sections   Inside   surface

Fig. 6. 3D QR cube

4   Conclusions

The world population is aging rapidly. Elderly people have many diseases associated with aging and a traditional physician-centered health care will not be able to handle the cost and burden of the greying population. Social services and systems must be designed and developed so that the elderly can have a healthy and active lifestyle for a longer period. Technology, especially mobile technology, seem to be a crucial element for active aging as it can easily link offline systems with online systems. However, elderly often find it difficult to use technology and they are also concerned about security and privacy. Among elderly, there are large variations in the perception and use of technology and elderly from different generation will have different knowledge of technology. In this paper, we proposed a multi-application framework with different platforms that rely on smart technology, Screen-Camera communication via QR codes, and alphanumeric and visual encryptions. A QR code is based on open patent and has seen wide acceptance in many applications. In the proposed system many QR codes are arranged and stored together creating an indexed 3D QR cube for better access using a database system. The system is scalable and also takes account of different level of security issues which can improve elderly's technology acceptance and usage. Although the system is proposed for the elderly, it could be applicable to younger adults too. Based on this theoretical proposal, more research could be conducted in this area to further develop and test the system in the future.

Acknowledgement. The work described in this paper was supported by grants from The Hong Kong Polytechnic University (School of Design Collaborative Research Funding Project No. P0035058) and Laboratory for Artificial Intelligence in Design (Project Code: RP1–3), Innovation and Technology Fund, Hong Kong Special Administrative Region.

References

1. OECD: Elderly population https://data.oecd.org/pop/elderly-population.htm, Accessed 7 Feb 2022
2. Wong, K., Yeung, M.: Population aging trend of Hong Kong. Population (Mn) 18, 64 (2019)
3. WHO: Global Health and Aging, World Health Organization (2018)
4. United Nations: World Population Aging 2019 (ST/ESA/SER.A/444), (2020)

5. Almarabta, S., Ridge, N.: What the UAE population thinks of aging and aged care (Strategic Report No. 5). Sheikh Saud bin Saqr Al Qasimi Foundation for Policy Research. (2021)
6. European Union: The 2018 Aging Report: Economic and Budgetary Projections for the EU Member States (2016–2070), (Institutional Paper 079), (2018)
7. Khasnabis, C., Holloway, C., MacLachlan, M.: The digital and assistive technologies for aging initiative: learning from the GATE initiative. Lancet Healthy Longevity 1(3), e94–e95 (2020)
8. Abraham, C., Nishihara, E., Akiyama, M.: Transforming healthcare with information technology in Japan: a review of policy, people, and progress. Int. J. Med. Inform. 80(3), 157–170 (2011)
9. JETRO: ICT government initiatives, https://www.jetro.go.jp/en/invest/attractive_sectors/ict/government_initiatives.html Accessed 11 Feb 2022
10. Sun, X., et al.: Internet use and need for digital health technology among the elderly: a cross-sectional survey in China. BMC Public Health 20(1), 1–8 (2020)
11. Pham, M., Mengistu, Y., Do, H.M., Sheng, W.: Cloud-Based Smart Home Environment (CoSHE) for home healthcare. In: 2016 IEEE international conference on automation science and engineering, (CASE). IEEE, pp. 483–488 (2016)
12. Al-khafajiy, M., et al.: Remote health monitoring of elderly through wearable sensors. Multimedia Tools Appl. 78(17), 24681–24706 (2019)
13. Tian, X.: Escaping the interpersonal power game: online shopping in China. Qual. Sociol. 41(4), 545–568 (2018)
14. Chiang, C.W., Liu, Y.H., Wang, C.P.: An elderly assistive device substitutes for traditional online library catalogs. The Electron. Libr. 38(2) 223-237 (2020)
15. Fox, S., Fallows, D.: Health Internet Resources. Washington, DC: Pew Internet & American Life Project (2003, Jul 16)
16. Campbell, R.J., Nolfi, D.A.: Teaching elderly adults to use the Internet to access health care information: before-after study. J. Med. Internet Res. 7(2), e128 (2005)
17. Nymberg, V.M., Bolmsjö, B.B., Wolff, M., Calling, S., Gerward, S., Sandberg, M.: Having to learn this so late in our lives 'Swedish elderly patients' beliefs, experiences, attitudes and expectations of e-health in primary health care. Scand. J. Prim. Health Care 37(1), 41–52 (2019)
18. Donelle, L.: Perceptions of online information privacy among older Canadians with Parkinson's disease. In: Medicine 2.0 Conference. JMIR Publications Inc., Toronto, Canada (2012)
19. Panico, F., Cordasco, G., Vogel, C., Trojano, L., Esposito, A.: Ethical issues in assistive ambient living technologies for aging well. Multimedia Tools Appl. 79(47), 36077–36089 (2020)
20. Landau, R., Werner, S.: Ethical aspects of using GPS for tracking people with dementia: recommendations for practice. Int. Psychogeriatr. 24(3), 358–366 (2012)
21. Wangmo, T., Lipps, M., Kressig, R.W., Ienca, M.: Ethical concerns with the use of intelligent assistive technology: findings from a qualitative study with professional stakeholders. BMC Med. Ethics 20(1), 1–11 (2019)
22. Niemeijer, A.R., Frederiks, B.J., Riphagen, I.I., Legemaate, J., Eefsting, J.A., Hertogh, C.M.: Ethical and practical concerns of surveillance technologies in residential care for people with dementia or intellectual disabilities: an overview of the literature. Int. Psychogeriatr. 22(7), 1129–1142 (2010)
23. van der Dam, S., Molewijk, B., Widdershoven, G.A., Abma, T.A.: Ethics support in institutional elderly care: a review of the literature. J. Med. Ethics 40(9), 625–631 (2014)
24. Garner, T.A., Powell, W.A., Carr, V.: Virtual carers for the elderly: a case study review of ethical responsibilities. Digital health 2, 2055207616681173 (2016)

25. Denso-Wave: Information capacity and versions of QR Code. www.qrcode.com, Accessed 7 Feb 2022
26. Iancu, I., Iancu, B.: Designing mobile technology for elderly. a theoretical overview. Technol. Forecast. Soc. Chang. **155**, 119977 (2020)
27. Yan, L.Y., Tan, G.W.H., Loh, X.M., Hew, J.J., Ooi, K.B.: QR code and mobile payment: the disruptive forces in retail. J. Retail. Consum. Serv. **58**, 102300 (2021)
28. Liu, R., Wu, J., Yu-Buck, G.F.: The influence of mobile QR code payment on payment pleasure: evidence from China. Int. J. Bank Mark. **39**(2), 337–356 (2021)
29. Madsen, S.S., Santos, A.Q., Jørgensen, B.N.: A QR code-based framework for auto-configuration of IoT sensor networks in buildings. Energy Inf. **4**(2), 1–19 (2021)
30. Gligoric, N., Krco, S., Hakola, L., Vehmas, K., De, S., Moessner, K., Van Kranenburg, R.: Smarttags: IoT product passport for circular economy based on printed sensors and unique item-level identifiers. Sensors **19**(3), 586 (2019)
31. LeaveHomeSafe: Technical specifications for LeaveHomeSafe mobile app (version1.5), The government of the Hong Kong Special Administrative Region of the People's Republic of China, https://www.leavehomesafe.gov.hk/en/ Accessed 11 Feb 2022
32. Tai, Z., Yu, X., He, B.: Locked down through virtual disconnect: navigating life by staying on/off the health QR code during COVID-19 in China. Convergence **27**(6), 1648–1662 (2021)
33. Tseng, M.H., Wu, H.C.: A cloud medication safety support system using QR code and Web services for elderly outpatients. Technol. Health Care **22**(1), 99–113 (2014)
34. Mira, J.J., et al.: Use of QR and EAN-13 codes by older patients taking multiple medications for a safer use of medication. Int. J. Med. Inf. **84**(6), 406–412 (2015)
35. Capranzano, P., et al.: Suitability for elderly with heart disease of a QR code-based feedback of drug intake: overcoming limitations of current medication adherence telemonitoring systems. Int. J. Cardiol. **327**, 209–216 (2021)
36. Cho, J., et al.: The usefulness of the QR code in orthotic applications after orthopedic surgery. In: Healthcare (Vol. 9, No. 3, p. 298). Multidisciplinary Digital Publishing Institute, (2021)
37. Jayant, C.: Non-Visual Mainstream Smartphone Camera Interactions for Blind and Low-Vision People. University of Washington, Seattle, USA (2011)
38. Su, S., Yang, X., Su, Q., Zhao, Y.: Prevalence and knowledge of heavy menstrual bleeding among gynecology outpatients by scanning a WeChat QR Code. PLoS ONE **15**(4), e0229123 (2020)
39. Wahsheh, H.A., Luccio, F.L.: Security and privacy of QR code applications: a comprehensive study, general guidelines and solutions. Information **11**(4), 217 (2020)
40. Yu, B., Fu, Z., Liu, S.: A Novel Three-Layer QR code based on secret sharing scheme and liner code. Security Commun. Networks 2019, Article ID 7937816 (2019)
41. Zhou, Y., Hu, B., Zhang, Y., Cai, W.: Implementation of cryptographic algorithm in dynamic QR code payment system and its performance. IEEE Access **9**, 122362–122372 (2021)
42. Liu, W., Wang, B., Li, Y., Wu, M.: Screen-camera communication system based on dynamic QR code. In: IOP Conference Series: Materials Science and Engineering (Vol. 790, No. 1) p. 012012, IOP Publishing (2020)
43. Lu, J., Yang, Z., Li, L., Yuan, W., Li, L., Chang, C.C.: Multiple schemes for mobile payment authentication using QR code and visual cryptography. Mobile Inf. Syst. 2017, Article ID 4356038 (2017)
44. Wei, Y., Yan, A., Dong, J., Hu, Z., Zhang, J.: Optical image encryption using QR code and multilevel fingerprints in gyrator transform domains. Optics Commun. **403**, 62–67 (2017)

45. Seenivasagam, V., Velumani, R.: A QR code based zero-watermarking scheme for authentication of medical images in teleradiology cloud. Comput. Math. Methods Med. 2013, Article ID 516465 (2013)
46. Chen, S.K., Ti, Y.W.: A design of multi-purpose image-based QR code. Symmetry **13**(12), 2446 (2021)
47. Mathivanan, P., Jero, S.E., Ramu, P., Ganesh, A.B.: QR code-based patient data protection in ECG steganography. Australas. Phys. Eng. Sci. Med. **41**(4), 1057–1068 (2018)

Willingness to Participate in Smartphone-Based Mobile Data Collection Studies

Alexander Seifert$^{(\boxtimes)}$ (iD)

University of Applied Sciences and Arts Northwestern Switzerland (FHNW), 4600 Olten,
Switzerland
`alexander.seifert@fhnw.ch`

Abstract. Today, digital and mobile forms of data collection are increasingly
being used to capture information on the real lives of older adults. One method used
is smartphone-based mobile data collection, which uses a standard smartphone to
collect information related to people's daily lives. Even though smartphones are
useful in measuring the daily variance of behaviors and the situational context in
which these behaviors take place, little is known about openness to participate in
mobile data collection studies among the general population. By utilizing representative data from Switzerland, this paper presents data on adults' openness to
participate in those studies and their willingness to share self-recorded smartphone
data with researchers. Analyses were based on a cross-sectional survey involving
1,394 participants aged 18 years and older (age range: 18–93 years; mean age:
48 years). The survey was conducted at the end of 2020. Both univariate and multivariate analyses were conducted. The results indicate that 24.8% are very open
to participate, while 31.1% are willing to share their self-recorded smartphone
data with researchers in mobile data collection studies. Nevertheless, the bivariate
analyses show that those in the younger age group (18–64 years) are more open
to participate than those in the older age group (aged 65 years and older). Multivariate analyses indicate that aside from age, interest in science is a predictor of
openness to participate. While the results reveal that only 25% are open to participate, this initial evaluation of openness to participate in mobile data collection
studies among younger and older adults should nevertheless enrich discussions on
the acceptance of wearables as data collection tools in future research.

Keywords: Smartphones · Data collection · Seniors · Research · Ambulatory
assessment

1 Introduction

At present, smartphones are increasingly being used for research purposes within gerontology studies [1]. In particular, researchers have used smartphones to collect data on the
daily lives of older adults [2]. Mobile data collection, which is part of the methodological family of ambulatory assessment, is an approach to assessing and tracking people's
ongoing thoughts, feelings, behaviors, or environments in the context of seniors' daily
lives [3]. The primary goal of this method is to directly collect in-the-moment, actively

© The Author(s), under exclusive license to Springer Nature Switzerland AG 2022
Q. Gao and J. Zhou (Eds.): HCII 2022, LNCS 13330, pp. 237–247, 2022.
https://doi.org/10.1007/978-3-031-05581-2_18

logged (i.e., self-reported survey responses) and/or passively sensed data (e.g., data collected from mobile sensors or phone logs) from people's smartphones within their natural environments [4]. Current studies have demonstrated the benefits of mobile data collection using smartphones by showing the daily variations and contexts of older adults' behaviors, feelings, and social and physical activities [5–7].

At present, mobile data collection is possible because smartphones are now widely available and come with the computational power and embedded sensors needed to obtain real-world information. A main advantage of this approach is that it permits ecologically valid research designs, given that data are collected during people's day-to-day lives outside of the research laboratory [8]. Thus, by using smartphones to collect data, researchers can capture self-reports by setting random, continuous, or event-based notifications prompting participants to respond to questions as they go about their day. These in-the-moment reports are less prone to memory bias than retrospective assessments and provide important information, for example, about the dynamic patterns of real-life feelings and thoughts [9]. Moreover, intensive repeated measurements of one participant can capture information at the within-person level (i.e., the extent to which a person shows variations in themselves over time). Within-person research allows for the study of the mechanisms that underlie behavior, which can be contrary to findings based on information at the between-person (i.e., comparison of two participants or groups) level [10].

Mobile data are also rich in contextual information, because they allow for the combination of subjective self-reports and more objective assessments, such as daily activities or social interactions, using the sensors that are built into smartphones. The use of sensors allows researchers to extract not only information about the current feelings of one participant, but also the distinct situational contexts in which they emerge (e.g., that he/she is currently in a place that is unpleasant for him/her) [11]. Finally, many older adults (aged 65 years and older) own smartphones, so they are already familiar with the use of apps and hardware [12, 13].

From a research perspective, mobile data collection with smartphones is becoming increasingly relevant for gerontological research, as it offers unique and innovative opportunities for studying older people's behaviors and daily processes in real-life contexts. This is highlighted by the theoretical model of "healthy aging" proposed by the World Health Organization [14], which conceptualizes healthy aging as an ongoing interaction between the characteristics of individuals (including their real-life activities) and the environment. This definition takes into account the fact that individuals' real-life activities and context data are important contributors to health; therefore, we have to conduct studies that measure such data. However, measuring and understanding healthy aging requires access to real-life data collected by older adults on their own devices (e.g., smartphones, tablets). Thus, when considering the future of healthy aging research, the question arises as to whether older users of smartphones are open to participate in mobile data collection studies and are willing to share their recorded data with researchers.

2   Research Questions

Given the current research background and the fact that research on the openness of older adults to participate in mobile data collection studies remains scarce [4], the present study investigated participants' openness to participate and willingness to provide self-tracked smartphone data for research purposes by using a representative sample from Switzerland.

Thus far, only a few studies have focused on the issue of the general population's willingness to share self-collected smartphone data [13, 15–17]. For example, Bietz et al. [15] and Chen et al. [16] found high (77%–78%) levels of willingness among younger and middle-aged participants to share smartphone-based self-recorded personal health data with researchers. A major drawback of these studies, however, is that the analyses are based either on a younger sample or deal with small, non-representative sample sizes. To the best of our knowledge, no study has investigated, in a nationally representative sample, openness to participate in mobile data collection studies and willingness to share data among individuals aged 65 years and older compared to younger adults.

Therefore, the aim of this study is to examine the extent to which older adults aged 65 years and above (compared to younger adults) are (1) open to participate in mobile data collection studies and (2) willing to share the data from these devices and apps with researchers. Furthermore, the study evaluates the factors that explain the differences in the levels of openness and willingness among the participants. Based on previous studies [13, 15–17], this study hypothesizes that sociodemographic factors (age, education, income) and interest in science, in general, influence openness to participate in those studies and willingness to share self-recorded data with researchers.

3 Methods

3.1 Sample

The study took place between October 12, 2020 and December 12, 2020. A total of 1,394 adults aged 18 years and older from all language regions of Switzerland (German, French, Italian) were interviewed using a computer-assisted web interview (CAWI) format (n = 1336), in addition to a paper-and-pencil-based survey for households without internet access (n = 58). The response rate of the survey was 19%. All participants consented to participate in the study. A standardized questionnaire was administered with questions about personal details (age, sex, education, sports, subjective health, and subjective quality of life), openness to participate in mobile data collection studies, willingness to share data, and open attitude toward sciences. A random sample of the permanent-resident population of Switzerland aged 18 years and older was selected from the AZ-Direct database (based on a public phonebook). The sample was post-weighted according to age group, language region, gender, and education. The ages of the respondents in the sample ranged from 18–93 years, with a mean age of 48.4 years; 52% were female.

For our analyses, we only included participants who reported that they owned a smartphone or used it with others. Therefore, we excluded 97 participants who did not use a smartphone or did not provide an answer to this question, resulting in a sample of 1297 participants for the subsequent analyses. Table 1 provides a description of the study sample.

3.2 Measures of Study Variables

The first dependent variable, "openness to participate in mobile data collection studies," was measured with the statement, "I could well imagine taking part in a project in which I fill out a questionnaire on my smartphone every day about how I'm feeling at the moment," and was rated on a Likert scale from 1 ("do not agree at all") to 5 ("agree completely") (M: 2.37; SD: 1.274). Two dummy variables were calculated from this information to subdivide the evaluation: people who were rather or very open to participate (values 4 and 5) vs. all other people (values 1–3).

The second dependent variable, "willingness to share self-collected smartphone data," was measured with the statement, "I would agree to make my smartphone-recorded data available for scientific purposes if the objectives are explained to me," and was rated on a Likert scale from 1 ("do not agree at all") to 5 ("agree completely") (M: 2.55; SD: 1.359). Two dummy variables were calculated from this information to subdivide the evaluation: people who were rather or very willing to share (values 4 and 5) vs. all other people (values 1–3).

To examine whether standard demographic variables were significant predictors of openness and willingness, a set of variables was included in the univariate and multivariate models: age (in years), gender (female/male), education (primary/secondary/tertiary), and household income (gross household income in Swiss francs [CHF], from low (1, "under 2,001") to high (8 "over 10,000")). Table 1 presents specific details of the scales used in the survey. Apart from those basic variables, information on life situations was also used, including perceived quality of life (M: 4.25; SD: 0.817) and subjective health (M: 4.14; SD: 0.827), both of which were measured with a five-point Likert scale, from 1 ("very bad") to 5 ("very good").

People's openness to participate in mobile data collection studies and, therefore, in research in general, is often influenced by their "interest in science" [18, 19]. Thus, the analyses included information about people's attitudes toward science or, more precisely, their interest in science and research. This was based on the statement, "I am very interested in science and research," which was rated on a Likert scale from 1 ("does not apply at all") to 5 ("applies fully") (M: 3.54; SD: 1.115).

3.3 Analytic Strategies

SPSS (version 28) was used for the statistical analyses. Univariate analyses were conducted to describe the differences in the characteristics of the supporters of mobile data collection studies (openness to participate and willingness to share data) and non-supporter groups by applying Student's t-test and chi-square testing. In addition, two binary logistic regressions based on the openness and willingness variables were calculated to analyze the statistical predictors of those evaluations.

4 Results

4.1 Descriptive Data on Openness to Participate and Willingness to Share Data

Among the sample used for analyses (n = 1297), including only the participants who used smartphones, 89.0% reported using them daily. Regarding the first statement on their openness to participate in mobile data collection studies, 24.8% of the respondents agreed or strongly agreed with this statement, while the others answered "do not agree at all" (34.0%), "do rather not agree" (24.8%), "partly, partly" (16.4%), "rather agree" (19.5%), and "strongly agree" (5.3%), resulting in a mean of 2.37 (SD: 1.274). Comparing those in the 18–64 and 65 + age groups, we can see that the younger participants (M: 2.53) are statistically significantly [t-test: t (1199) = 7.51, $p = < .001$] more open than the older ones (M: 1.84). If a distinction is made between high (values 4 and 5) and rather low openness (values 1–3), it becomes clear that 24.8% of the sample are within the high openness group, whereas 75.2% are not.

In terms of standard demographics, the bivariate analyses (see Table 1) reveal that, aside from age, education, income, subjective health, and interest in science significantly distinguish between participants with high and low/non-openness. Thus, in general, people who are open to participate in mobile data collection studies are more often younger, have a high education background, have higher incomes, are in good health, and are interested in science and research.

In relation to the second statement regarding willingness to share self-recorded data in mobile data collection studies, 31.1% of the respondents agreed or strongly agreed (values 4 and 5) with this statement, while 68.9% do not. The participants answered "do not agree at all" (32.3%), "do rather not agree" (20.0%), "partly, partly" (16.6%), "rather agree" (22.8%), and "strongly agree" (8.3%), resulting in a mean of 2.55 (SD: 1.359). Comparing those in the 18–64 and 65 + age groups, we can see that the younger participants (M: 2.66) are statistically significantly [t-test: t(1199) = 4.30, $p = < .001$] more open than the older ones (M: 2.22). Furthermore, the first and the second statements are intercorrelated (r = .685; $p < .001$), indicating that those who are open to participate in mobile data collection studies are also willing to share their data with the researchers in such studies.

Regarding the standard demographics, the bivariate analyses (see Table 1) reveal that, aside from age, education, income, subjective health, and interest in science also significantly distinguish between participants with high and low/non-willingness to share data. Similarly, people who are willing to share their smartphone data in mobile data collection studies are more often younger, have a high education background, have higher incomes, are in good health, and are interested in science and research.

Table 1. Sample and group descriptions

Parameter	Range	M or %	High openness to participate (n = 304)	Low or non-openness to participate (n = 922)	High willingness to share data (n = 378)	Low or non-willingness to share data (n = 838)
Gender						
Female		50.8%	52.6%	50.3%	50.5%	50.6%
Male		49.2%	47.4%	49.7%	49.5%	49.4%

(*continued*)

Table 1. (*continued*)

Parameter	Range	M or %	High openness to participate (n = 304)	Low or non-openness to participate (n = 922)	High willingness to share data (n = 378)	Low or non-willingness to share data (n = 838)
Age						
Age mean	18–93	48.44	41.30***	50.93***	46.23**	49.46**
Age group: 18–25		12.4%	21.5%***	9.4%***	14.9%*	11.2%*
Age group: 26–44		28.5%	39.3%***	24.2%***	31.1%*	26.5%*
Age group: 45–64		39.4%	29.0%***	43.9%***	37.5%*	41.4%*
Age group: 65–93		19.7%	10.2%***	22.5%***	16.5%*	20.8%*
Education						
Primary		15.1%	8.9%***	16.2%***	12.6%***	16.3%***
Secondary		61.1%	58.3%***	62.1%***	52.9%***	64.4%***
Tertiary		23.7%	32.8%***	21.7%***	34.5%***	19.3%***
Household income[1]	1–8	5.90	6.13*	5.85*	6.15*	5.81*
Quality of life[2]	1–5	4.25	4.17	4.27	4.25	4.25
Subjective health[3]	1–5	4.14	4.26*	4.11*	4.20*	4.10*
Interest in science[4]	1–5	3.54	3.78***	3.46***	3.88***	3.40***

Notes: n = 1297. [1] *Household income* (in Swiss francs [CHF]), from 1 (< 2,001) to 8 (> 10,000). [2] *Perceived quality of life*: scale from 1 ("very bad") to 5 ("very good"). [3] *Subjective health*: scale from 1 ("very bad") to 5 ("very good"). [4] *Interest in science* ("I am very interested in science and research"): scale from 1 ("does not apply at all") to 5 ("applies fully"). T-test T (p) or chi-square-test (p): *$p < 0.05$, **$p < 0.01$, ***$p < 0.001$

4.2 Multivariate Test of Group Differences

Additional analyses were conducted to check the bivariate results using a multivariate approach. Table 2 shows the results of two binary logistic regressions to address openness to participate in mobile data collection studies and willingness to share data. In both models, the openness/willingness groups [1 = high values (4 and 5), 0 = all other values (1–3)] were considered the dependent variable, while age, gender, education, household income, quality of life, subjective health, and interest in science were included as the independent variables. The tests of both full models showed statistical significance (see

Table 2 notes), indicating that the predictors, as a set, reliably distinguished between the two groups.

Table 2. Multivariate binary logistic regression analysis for the predictors of openness and willingness

Parameter	Openness A			Willingness B		
	OR	p value	95% CI	OR	p value	95% CI
Female (ref. male)	**1.412**	**.027**	1.039; 1.918	1.298	.072	.977; 1.726
Age	**.959**	**< .001**	.959; .979	.995	.241	.986; 1.004
Tertiary education (ref primary and secondary)	1.200	.306	.846; 1.702	**1.689**	**.002**	1.218; 2.342
Household income[1]	1.048	.296	.960; 1.143	1.058	.169	.976; 1.147
Quality of life[2]	.858	.139	.701; 1.051	.956	.649	.789; 1.159
Subjective health[3]	1.906	.426	.875; 1.372	1.023	.825	.837; 1.251
Interest in science[4]	**1.238**	**.004**	1.069; 1.434	**1.355**	**< .001**	1.181; 1.555

Notes: [1] *Household income* (in Swiss francs [CHF]), from 1 (< 2,001) to 8 (> 10,000). [2] *Perceived quality of life*: scale from 1 ("very bad") to 5 ("very good"). [3] *Subjective health*: scale from 1 ("very bad") to 5 ("very good"). [4] *Interest in science* ("I am very interested in science and research"): scale from 1 ("does not apply at all") to 5 ("applies fully"). A: Openness to participate in mobile data collection studies: model fit ($\chi^2 = 70.215$ [7], $p = < .001$, Nagelkerke's $R^2 = .103$, n = 969). B: Willingness to share data within mobile data collection studies: model fit ($\chi^2 = 49.981$ [7], $p = < .001$, Nagelkerke's $R^2 = .071$, n = 958). Bold = significant values ($p < .05$)

Model A (openness) shows that gender, age, and interest in science are significant prediction factors, whereas education, income, quality of life, and subjective health are not predictors based on the multivariate analyses. Thus, females, younger people, and those with a high interest in science are generally more open to participate in mobile data collection studies than males, older adults, and those with a low interest in science.

Model B (willingness) shows that education and interest in science are significant predictors, whereas gender, age, income, quality of life, and health are not predictors based on the multivariate analyses. Thus, the participants who have a higher education level and those who are interested in science are generally more willing to share their smartphone-collected data within mobile data collection studies than those with less interest in science and have a lower education level.

5 Discussion

Using data drawn from Switzerland, this paper presents the potential interest of particular segments of the population regarding participation in mobile data collection studies among younger and older Swiss adults. Following the first research question regarding openness to participate in mobile data collection studies, the analysis revealed that 24.8% were rather or very open to this idea of participatory research. This seems to be a moderate number of people who are interested in participating in such studies. Nevertheless, the majority of the people are more cautious and skeptical about this form of research.

Those who are more open to participate are mostly younger people and those with a high interest in science and research in general. This could be why gerontological researchers face difficulties convincing older adults (aged 65 years and above) to join their smartphone-based studies. Therefore, researchers should address, above all, older adults who have an interest in research.

This paper's second research question addresses potential study participants' willingness to share smartphone-based, self-collected data with researchers in mobile data collection studies. The univariate analyses show that age, education, income, subjective health, and interest in science are significant distinguishing factors between those who are more willing and those who are less/not willing at all to share data, whereas gender and quality of life are not significant predictors of group differences. The multivariate analyses partly confirm the results of the univariate analyses by showing that education and interest in science predict willingness to share data. Thus, people with a high education level and a high interest in science in general are more willing to share their self-collected smartphone data. The role of education as a predictor has also been established in other studies [13, 17], which have reported that proximity to higher education favors individuals' attitudes toward research. However, the studies themselves also showed that interest in technology positively influences willingness, which could probably be related to their participants' positive evaluations of digital transformation in general.

The findings also show that, regardless of age, people who are more interested in topics, such as science and research, are more open to join mobile data collection studies, thus indicating that personal interests are especially important in evaluating the necessity of those specific research methods. Chen et al. [16] reported that participants are more willing to share their health-tracking records with researchers in the following situations: (a) when they already shared their health-tracking records with someone, (b) when they have an interest in the topic of scientific study, (c) when they already registered in a scientific database, and (d) when they are interested in self-measurement. Therefore, interest in research and trust in science are important factors motivating participants to join mobile data collection studies.

To be able to use participants' self-recorded data, discussions must be held around issues of practical data and sharing management, as well as legal, ethical, social, and technical framework conditions [20, 21]. These discussions should also consider other issues, such as informed consent, data privacy, data security, and data ownership. These concerns may require new models of participant involvement, with the goal of creating a trustworthy relationship between data providers and research institutions working with data.

In the future, the use of smartphones could be an interesting field within gerontological research because of the opportunities they provide as tools to collect data on older adults' daily lives [22]. Nevertheless, mobile data collection also brings challenges that provide interesting avenues for future developments (for an overview, see [4]). First, it is important to keep in mind that mobile data collection studies require research questions that reflect the dynamics of daily life (e.g., day-to-day variations in activities). Second, to avoid usability problems, the training of participants is recommended as part of the informed consent process. For example, it can be helpful to anticipate older adult participants' potential lack of smartphone skills by adapting tutorials and providing them with information on how to use smartphones. Third, working with different data types (e.g., self-reported and sensor data) that can be considered forms of "big data" requires technical expertise. Furthermore, after data collection, skills in advanced statistical analyses (e.g., multilevel modeling) are also required. The final challenge has to do with the ethical considerations surrounding data security and respecting participants' privacy. This is because the collection of traceable real-life data requires securing ethical and legal approvals, safeguarding participants' privacy, and establishing data privacy practices [23]. The abovementioned aspects should thus be considered when planning a mobile data collection study.

5.1 Limitations

Several limitations must be noted. First, the present study has a specific regional focus (Switzerland), so the findings have limited generalizability. Second, the data provided only a cross-sectional view of the various interplays examined in the study. Thus, future studies should investigate the dynamics of these interplays, especially the evaluation of openness pre- and post-participation in mobile data collection studies. Third, because the population survey was conducted online and by mail, we were unable to reach all older persons (e.g., those living in long-term care facilities). Nevertheless, our study had a good response rate (19%) for those population surveys. Fourth, because of the limited width of the study variables that could be used, other important background factors, such as personality, technical skills, and attitudes toward smartphones in general, were not controlled for. Therefore, further studies using longitudinal designs and a wider range of variables may be required to examine this topic in more detail.

5.2 Conclusion and Implications for Future Research

This study has presented representative data from Switzerland regarding the openness to participate in mobile data collection studies and willingness to share self-recorded smartphone data with researchers in the general population aged 18 years and older. The results indicate that around 25% are open to participate in such studies, and 31% are willing to share their self-recorded smartphone data with researchers. Nevertheless, the bivariate analyses show that younger adults (18–64 years) are more open to participate than older adults (65 years and older). Multivariate analyses also indicate that interest in science is a specific predictor of openness to participate and willingness to share self-recorded data.

   The findings reveal that, at present, older adults with a marked interest in science and younger people are the ones who are interested in mobile data collection studies. The current study also provides evidence of the potential of mobile data collection studies for scientific research, in general, and for gerontological studies, in particular. Although few older adults are very open to participate in mobile data collection studies today, they make for interesting study subjects because researchers can examine their daily lives through smartphone-based research [22].

Future mobile data collection studies should not only focus on research-affine older people, but also on those with a certain distance to research and no experience in the use of smartphones in their daily lives.

References

1. Seifert, A., Harari, G.M.: Mobile data collection with smartphones. In: Gu, D., Dupre, M.E. (eds.) Encyclopedia of Gerontology and Population Aging, Springer, Cham, CH (2019)
2. Brose, A., Ebner-Priemer, U.W.: Ambulatory assessment in the research on aging: contemporary and future applications. Gerontology **61**, 372–380 (2015). https://doi.org/10.1159/000 371707
3. Harari, G.M., Müller, S.R., Aung, M.S., Rentfrow, P.J.: Smartphone sensing methods for studying behavior in everyday life. Curr. Opin. Behav. Sci. **18**, 83–90 (2017). https://doi.org/ 10.1016/j.cobeha.2017.07.018
4. Seifert, A., Hofer, M., Allemand, M.: Mobile data collection: smart, but not (yet) smart enough. Front. Neurosci. **12**, 971 (2018). https://doi.org/10.3389/fnins.2018.00971
5. Gruenenfelder-Steiger, A.E., et al.: Physical activity and depressive mood in the daily life of older adults. GeroPsych. **30**, 119–129 (2017). https://doi.org/10.1024/1662-9647/a000172
6. Reichert, M., et al.: Ambulatory assessment for physical activity research: state of the science, best practices and future directions. Psychol. Sport Exerc. **50**, 101742 (2020). https://doi.org/ 10.1016/j.psychsport.2020.101742
7. Wolf, F., Naumann, J., Oswald, F.: Digital social interactions in later life: effects of instant messaging on situational mood of older smartphone users. In: Gao, Q., Zhou, J. (eds.) HCII 2021. LNCS, vol. 12786, pp. 443–458. Springer, Cham (2021). https://doi.org/10.1007/978-3-030-78108-8_33
8. Wrzus, C., Mehl, M.R.: Lab and/or field? measuring personality processes and their social consequences: lab and/or field? Eur. J. Personal. **29**, 250–271 (2015). https://doi.org/10.1002/ per.1986
9. Hektner, J.M., Schmidt, J.A., Csikszentmihalyi, M.: Experience Sampling Method: Measuring the Quality of Everyday Life. Sage Publications, Thousand Oaks, California (2007)
10. Hamaker, E.L.: Why researchers should think "within-person": A paradigmatic rationale. In: Mehl, M.R., Conner, T.S. (eds.) Handbook of Research Methods for Studying Daily Life, pp. 43–61, Guilford, New York, NY (2012)
11. Wolf, F., Seifert, A., Martin, M., Oswald, F.: Considering situational variety in contextualized aging research - opinion about methodological perspectives. Front. Psychol. **12**, 570900 (2021). https://doi.org/10.3389/fpsyg.2021.570900
12. Pew Research Center: Mobile Fact Sheet, https://www.pewresearch.org/internet/fact-sheet/ mobile/, Accessed 26 Apr 2021
13. Seifert, A., Vandelanotte, C.: The use of wearables and health apps and the willingness to share self-collected data among older adults. Aging Health Res. **1**, 100032 (2021). https:// doi.org/10.1016/j.ahr.2021.100032
14. WHO: Decade of healthy ageing: Baseline report. (2021)
15. Bietz, M.J., et al.: Opportunities and challenges in the use of personal health data for health research. J. Am. Med. Inform. Assoc. **23**, e42–e48 (2016). https://doi.org/10.1093/jamia/ ocv118
16. Chen, J., Bauman, A., Allman-Farinelli, M.: A study to determine the most popular lifestyle smartphone applications and willingness of the public to share their personal data for health research. Telemed. E-Health. **22**, 655–665 (2016). https://doi.org/10.1089/tmj.2015.0159

17. Seifert, A., Christen, M., Martin, M.: Willingness of older adults to share mobile health data with researchers. GeroPsych. **31**, 41–49 (2018). https://doi.org/10.1024/1662-9647/a000181
18. Schäfer, M.S., Füchslin, T., Metag, J., Kristiansen, S., Rauchfleisch, A.: The different audiences of science communication: a segmentation analysis of the Swiss population's perceptions of science and their information and media use patterns. Public Underst. Sci. **27**, 836–856 (2018). https://doi.org/10.1177/0963662517752886
19. Füchslin, T., Schäfer, M.S., Metag, J.: Who wants to be a citizen scientist? identifying the potential of citizen science and target segments in Switzerland. Public Underst. Sci. **28**, 652–668 (2019). https://doi.org/10.1177/0963662519852020
20. Christen, M., Domingo-Ferrer, J., Herrmann, D., van den Hoven, J.: Beyond informed consent—investigating ethical justifications for disclosing, donating or sharing personal data in research. In: Powers, T.M. (ed.) Philosophy and Computing. PSS, vol. 128, pp. 193–207. Springer, Cham (2017). https://doi.org/10.1007/978-3-319-61043-6_10
21. Sula, C.A.: Research ethics in an age of big data. Bull. Assoc. Inf. Sci. Technol. **42**, 17–21 (2016). https://doi.org/10.1002/bul2.2016.1720420207
22. Fernández-Ardèvol, M., et al.: Methodological strategies to understand smartphone practices for social connectedness in later life. In: Zhou, J., Salvendy, G. (eds.) HCII 2019. LNCS, vol. 11593, pp. 46–64. Springer, Cham (2019). https://doi.org/10.1007/978-3-030-22015-0_4
23. Beierle, F., et al.: Context data categories and privacy model for mobile data collection apps. Procedia Comput. Sci. **134**, 18–25 (2018). https://doi.org/10.1016/j.procs.2018.07.139

Research on the Age-Appropriate Design of Mobile Phone APPs Based on the Experience of Using Smartphones for Chinese Young-Old

Yuxuan Xiao[1] (ID), Yanghao Ye[2]([⊠]) (ID), and Yi Liu[3] (ID)

[1] Hunan University (Changsha University of Science and Technology), Changsha, China
[2] Changsha University of Science and Technology, Changsha, China
yeyanghao@csust.edu.cn
[3] Hunan University, Changsha, China

Abstract. With the development of "intelligent" society, smart terminals have been used in many occasions of daily life. Smart phones have become an extension of people, which is an indispensable medium that people connect with each other and the society. Currently, among the 274 million elderly mobile phone users in China, 134 million are elderly smartphone users. Nearly 140 million seniors are connected to the Internet through smartphones. Through an online questionnaire survey on smartphone use experience for young-old, this paper attempts to investigate the actual needs and difficulties of young-old in the use of smartphones, and the preference of this group for the age-appropriate design of mobile phones. Based on the 500 valid samples of the survey, we found that the young-old tend to actively learn the use of mobile phones, but the current smartphone APPs does not take into account the special need of the young-old, and the adaptability of the touch-screen experience. We suggest that it's necessary to consider the need of the old users in terms of functions, interfaces, menu settings, so as to improve the willingness of the old to use mobile APPS and improve the effect of human-computer interaction.

Keywords: Aged-appropriate design · Smartphone APPs · Young-old

1 Introduction

Smartphones integrate clothing, diet, housing, transportation, entertainment, education, medicine, health care, and wealth on one screen. However, the convenience and rapidity of digital intelligence iteration cannot cover the problems of the use of smart phones by young-old people, such as difficulties in logical understanding, degradation of functional memory, and decline in audio-visual resolution. With the accelerated aging of China's population, the adaptation of the elderly to the use of smartphones is affected by economic conditions, education levels, work experience, social status, family pension environment and other factors, as well as psychological and physiological changes after retirement at home, the digital gap between the elderly and the smart age is growing. In order to enable the old to adapt to complete social, economic and cultural activities in the smart

Q. Gao and J. Zhou (Eds.): HCII 2022, LNCS 13330, pp. 248–262, 2022.
https://doi.org/10.1007/978-3-031-05581-2_19

age and improve their quality of life, it's imperative to design smartphone APPs for the old.

The current research is based on the experience of using smartphones of Chinese young-old people, the respondents are the people between the age of 50–70 years old. They are the accurate objects for the current smartphone APPs aging-appropriate design. The results of the study are aimed to provide the basis for the decision-making of better Apps design the old. The data from the questionnaires shows that the number of people who filled in is relatively evenly distributed among the three age groups: 50–55 years old, 55–60 years old, and 60–65 years old, with a proportion of about 30%, and the least number of people filling in from the 65–70 years old stage. Among the young-old people who participated in the questionnaire, the ratio of male to female is about 4:6, and most of them have junior high school education, half of them live together with elderly couples, 77.4% of young-old people filled out this questionnaire by themselves, 22.6% of young-old people fill out this questionnaire with the assistance from their families.

Age-appropriate design is a human-centered design concept. In order to make products and services meet the needs of the old, special emphasis is placed on the physical and psychological characteristics of the elderly, as well as behavioral characteristics, habits, and preferences in the design process. In recent years, research on age-appropriate design has mostly focused on product development in home furnishing, architecture, landscape, and auxiliary elderly care. In November 2020, the State Council of China issued the "Implementation Plan on Effectively Solving the Difficulties of the Elderly in Using Intelligent Technology". In the same year, the Ministry of Industry and Information Technology of China also organized a one-year special campaign for the aging and barrier-free transformation of Internet applications across the country. In the first stage, 115 websites in 8 categories and 43 APPs in 6 categories were ordered to carry out aging and barrier-free renovation. Larger fonts, simplified icons, removal of complicated functions, removal of advertisements, "elders mode", "care mode" and other methods are enabled. However, there are other problems such as "water injection" in the aging transformation of smartphone APPs. Some APPs designers simply believe that larger fonts and optimizing the homepage icons is what the elderly need, ignoring the fact that the elderly group is not only difficult to read the text, but also has a common problem of complex menu interfaces. Larger icons and font sizes can only improve the look and feel of the smartphone APPs for the elderly to a certain extent, but it cannot guide the elderly to understand the logic of smartphone software and learn to use the software more easily. There are endless APPs, and the versions are updated quickly, the elderly are constantly facing the learning of new interfaces and the search for old functions, the entrances of suitable functions such as "Elders Edition" and "Senior Zone" are not placed in the visual center, but hidden behind the complex multi-level menus. The cross-generational design ignores the differences in the use logic between groups, the aging-appropriate function is difficult to achieve. Therefore, it is of great practical significance to take the young-old as the research object, according the use demands of smartphones as the core issue, and the age-appropriate design of smartphone APPs as the research content.

The survey data shows: Young-old people generally have the willingness to integrate into the digital life, but their learning ability and need for using smartphones have been underestimated for a long time. The aging-appropriate upgrade of smartphone APPs is conducive to help young-old people improve their digital literacy and bridge the digital gap.

(1) Among the young-old who participated in the questionnaire, more than 60% use smartphones for their daily needs. Although they are influenced by the people around them, they want to pursue new things and have more fun by mastering smartphones skills.
(2) Young-old people generally have the willingness to actively learn the use of mobile phones. They do not only learn from children and grandchildren, friends, neighbors, and senior colleges, but also learn by reading books and self-study as high as 41.2%, and even click on the built-in play function of mobile phones to learn to use them.
(3) The use of smartphones by young-old people is relatively rich, and there is no obvious preference. While using mobile phones to communicate and connection, they also have a high degree of participation in Internet entertainment, shopping, and information consultation. They achieved their usage goals and experienced convenience and relaxation.
(4) Nearly half of the younger seniors have more than 10 applications on their mobile phones, and nearly 90% of the young-old know how to obtain the Apps they want through various ways.
(5) The current mobile phones and software have varying degrees of difficulty in the use of young-old people in terms of color graphic design, ease of operation, and running speed. Young-old also have worries about their own health, knowledge screening, misunderstanding of expenses, network security and other aspects in the application of smart phones, and they have a certain "touch screen phobia" about smart devices.
(6) The young-old generally have a demand for the aging-appropriate transformation of mobile APPs, and the functions and designs they pursue are closer to "traditional elderly devices".

2   Literature Review

The extant research on the age-appropriate design of smartphone APPs based on the experience of using smartphones of young-old in China are mainly carried out in the following aspects:

(1) Mobile APPs interaction design based on Kano model. Xu Yuwen et al. (2017) used the Kano model for smartphone APPs user interface design to improve the satisfaction of elderly users. Similarly, He Weishan (2020) designed the online learning APPs interactive interface based on the Kano model.
(2) Explore the interface design of mobile APPs based on the cognitive needs of elderly users. For example, Wang Yue (2018) constructs typical character models and scenes from the cognitive characteristics of vision, memory, and emotion of elderly users, and explore the age-appropriate interface interaction design method in line with the cognitive characteristics of the elderly from three aspects: the information architecture layer, the interaction layer and the presentation layer of the smart phone, and

verify its rationality through practice. Liu Xiaolu et al. (2017) conducted research on the age-appropriate design of information APPs interface based on the cognitive needs of the elderly.

(3) Research on the utility of each element of the mobile phone interactive interface. For example, Huang he et al. (2017) decomposed and reconstructed smartphone elements through the joint analysis method, and analyzed the user's tendency to choose 18 virtual new schemes to obtain the best design element combination scheme.

(4) Research on the evaluation of APPs usage experience of elderly users. For example, Li Yongfeng et al. (2018) constructed an elderly user experience evaluation system based on the grey analytic hierarchy process, and took mobile medical APPs as a case to collect samples to provide a basis for application optimization design decisions.

(5) Appeals and reflections on the age-Appropriate design of an "intelligent" rational society. For example, Li Yiyu et al. (2021) believe that the development of intelligent services exacerbates the intergenerational cultural gap, which decreases the sense of identity and acquisition of the elderly. Therefore, it is necessary to bridge the gaps in resources, institutions and cultures through social "intelligence" and "appropriate aging". Also, Fan Yuji et al. (2021) described the subjective and objective dilemma of the elderly using smartphones, and proposed that multiple entities should cooperate to ensure the use of smartphones by the elderly in terms of industry development, policy subsidies, and usage data.

3   Method

This paper adopt the questionnaire survey on the experience of smartphone use among the young-old groups, and conducts research on smartphone usage behavior, age-appropriate needs and applicability of mobile phone software. Specifically, the research involves the preferences, experiences, difficulties and situational design of young-old in the process of using smartphones. We also provide suggestions on the aging-appropriate design of smartphone APPs, clarifying the smartphone APPs aging-appropriate design ideas. After reviewing the returned questionnare, 500 valid samples were finally obtained in this experiment. The questionnaires used are shown in the appendix.

4   Experiment

The research is mainly carried out from three dimensions: the use behavior of smartphones of the young-old, the needs of suitable aging and the applicability of the current APPs, and the design situation of suitable aging. Based on the questionnaire data, the results are shown in the following sections:

4.1 Smartphone Use Behavior of Young-Old

• **Smartphone usage.**
The questionnaire lists several possible situations of smartphones using, and conducts a survey on "How is your smartphone usage?". The statistical results are as follows (Fig. 1):

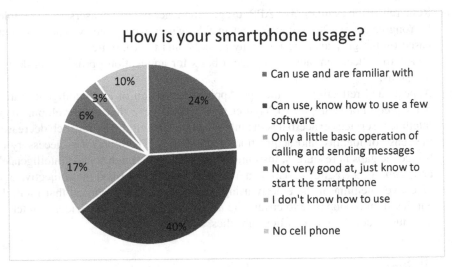

Fig. 1. Smartphone usage classification chart. (Self-Designed Form)

Statistics show that 64% of young-old people think they can use smartphones, but 40% of them only use a few Apps, and not many elderly people are very familiar with using mobile phones. 17% of the elderly only have some basic operations such as making calls and sending short messages. smartphones provide no more digital life experience for them.

• **How and why of learning smartphones.**
In response to the question "How do you learn about smartphones?", the young-old are mainly taught by others, supplemented by self-learning. Teaching from sons and daughters is the most important source of their skills acquisition. 41.2% of young-old are familiar with the use of smartphones by taking classes in senior colleges and self-learning by reading books, which is almost close to the proportion of friends and neighbors' teaching. It is worth noting that 28.6% of the young-old will use the smartphone's own tutorial to learn (Table 1).

Table 1. Statistics of the way to learn smartphones. (Self-Designed Form)

The way to learn smartphones	Percentage
Sons and daughters' teaching	48.4%
Grandchildren's teaching	34.8%
Friends and neighbors' teaching	43.6%
Self-taught through senior college and reading	41.2%
Self-learning through the smartphone's own teaching skills	28.6%

Statistical results also show that the overall level of engagement with learning smartphones is relatively high, which reveals that they have a sense of initiative. This tendency to actively learn new things has been revealed in the question about "Why do you want to learn smart phones?" in the questionnaire. Most of the young-old people who fill out the questionnaire are learning to use smart phones based on their own reasons, or based on life needs, or hope to add fun to their boring old age with cell phone, avoiding drifting to an island in the internet wave.

• **Smartphone usage and experience.**
Among the six major functions listed in the questionnaire, there is no significant preference for the young-old, and the maximum value comes from "listening to music, watching news and reading short videos", and 57.8% of the young-old chose this item. The popularity of short videos has not diminished that young-old people are immersed in short videos to learn how to cook, dance, and maintain health. they have long been loyal digital workers on short video platforms. Among them, 48.2% of the young-old will use smartphones to "take photos or short videos" to contribute UGC content belonging to them, showing the potential of old bloggers and old uploaders to attract fans. Secondly, 54.2% of the young-old have strong social needs, so WeChat maintains and reconstructs their social circle. In terms of online shopping needs, 43.2% of the young-old will order their favorite products through online shopping platform, whether it is half-day delivery of food or supermarket delivery the next day. The younger age group is slowly following the development of Internet plus e-commerce in the use of smartphone software. Finally, using the Internet to get information and playing games are also a need that young-old people cannot ignore (Table 2).

Table 2. Statistics of the way to learn smartphones. (Self-Designed Form)

Purpose of using a smartphone	Percentage
Contact others	54.2%
Take photos or short videos	48.2%
Listen to music, watch news, watch short videos	57.8%

(continued)

Table 2. (*continued*)

Purpose of using a smartphone	Percentage
Internet consultation	37.2%
Online shopping	43.2%
Play games to relax (Such as Happy Match)	28.2%

The young-old also achieved the goal of using smartphones, and gained experiences such as "getting information", "social communication", "convenient contact", "leisure and relaxation", and "catching up with fashion". Although the most commonly used APPs for young-old people are to listen to music, watch news and short videos, the basic value such as "Convenient Contact" was not affected by the user experience. It shows that the emergence of smartphones has reduced the loneliness of young-old people to a large extent. Only 8.6% of the young-old believe that their experience of using mobile phones is to follow the fashion. It shows that the young-old people do not blindly follow the digital trend, and they have a more rational use and experience.

4.2 Aging Needs and Current APPs Applicability

Smartphones attract people to approach with the advantages of mobile and deep access to the Internet. At the same time, they also make young-old people experience psychological fear of touching the screen and the physical difficulties of using them. We can understand the aging-appropriate transformation logic by understanding the attitudes and needs of young-old people about the current smartphone usability.

• **Software quantity and download method.**
According to the statistical results, 21.8% of the young-old people have more than 15 Apps on their smartphones, and 26.4% of the young-old people have 10–15 Apps. That is to say, among the interviewees, nearly half of the young-old people have more than 10 Apps on their smartphones. If the number of Apps is evenly allocated to functions such as social networking, health preservation, audio and video, short video, browser, information, shopping, games, then 10 software is not too many. In response to the question "What is the main way for you to obtain mobile phone software?", 12.6% of the elderly still said that they did not know. The conventional method such as download through the software store that comes with the system, followed by the application store or Baidu search, which will still be a problem for this part of the elderly.
• **Current APPs applicability.**
The results also show that in the process of using smartphones, young-old people generally encounter difficulties in using Apps result from complicated Apps design or smartphone operating failures. "Complicated software operation" is the biggest problem for the elderly when using mobile APPs. 49.4% of the young-old also feel frustrated by "too many Apps". 41% of the young-old have experienced "phone freezes and doesn't respond", and the visual experience of "uncomfortable color graphics and text" also affects their sense of use (Table 3).

Table 3. Difficulty classification table based on the mobile phone itself. (Self-Designed Form)

What difficulties or problems have you encountered while using your smartphone ?	Percentage
Uncomfortable color graphics and text	33.4%
Complicated software operation	57.6%
Too many software	49.4%
Phone freezes and doesn't respond	41%
Others	14%

- **Difficulty in use based on the characteristics of the young-old(Table 4).**

Table 4. Difficulty classification table based on the use of smartphones by the young-old themselves. (Self-Designed Form)

The biggest problem you face while using your smartphone?	Percentage
Health problems, such as blurred vision, decreased limb flexibility, etc	48.8%
Knowledge problems, such as inability to discern the content of a pop-up prompt box, etc	42.6%
Cost issues, smartphones and their associated costs	39.8%
Environmental issues, less information specific to the elderly	46.4%
Security issues, unfamiliar with software functions, worry about property safety, etc	36%

The questionnaire data shows that the "health problems, such as blurred vision, decreased limb flexibility, etc." of the young-old are major obstacles to use smartphones. For example, 48.8% of them chose this option. In terms of physiological characteristics, the physical movement, hearing, and visual abilities of young-old will have varying degrees of loss and decline. For example, the visual ability to distinguish colors is weakened, and it is more sensitive to high-contrast color blocks; the movement of the body gradually becomes slower, so it is difficult for their fingers and eyes to lock the target area synchronously, and the finger touch area tends to become larger, and the operation speed gradually decrease. Sorted by numerical percentage, "environmental issues, such as less information specific to the elderly", "knowledge issues, such as inability to discern the content of a pop-up prompt box, etc.", "cost issues, smartphones and their associated costs," "security issues, unfamiliar with software functions, worried about property safety, etc.", there are four categories of use dilemmas involve the physical changes of the young-old, such as the degradation of memory function, the delay in receiving and converting information, the psychological fear of touching the screen, and questions about intelligent technology. The volume of mobile APPs is increasing day by day, and the function of one-stop service is pursued, but it has not taken into account the changes in the physiology and psychology of young-old. In the face of complex intelligent logic and high sensitivity to unfamiliar information, the elderly have slowed down the pace of embracing technology and reduced their willingness to use it.

4.3 Aging Design Scenarios

The data also shows that young-old have demands for the aging-appropriate design of smartphone APPs. The design logic of the "Elderly Phone" is more in line with the habit of the young-old, which reveal that they have low awareness and dissatisfaction with the use of smartphones for human-computer interaction. This doesn't affect their use of smartphones to participate in social life and self-entertainment, and it stimulated their expectations for intelligent technology.

• **Preferences for new features in the software (Fig. 2).**

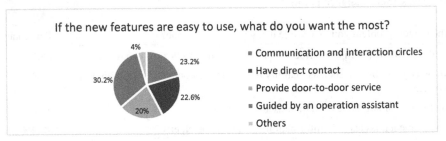

Fig. 2. Classification of preferences for new smartphone functions among young people. (Self-Designed Form)

First of all, 30.2% of the elderly hope that the smartphone software is "guided by an operating assistant", which is related to the question of "living style of young-old" in the questionnaire. More than 70% of the elderly surveyed don't live with their children, so remote teaching aids increase the difficulty of intergenerational communication, and it's difficult to take care of usage needs in a timely manner. Secondly, 23.2% of the survey respondents hope that "communication and interaction circles" in the software account for the interactive experience on the cloud allows them to share life and happiness independently. Furthermore, 22.6% of the young-old expect the software to "have direct contacts", and 20% of the young-old prefer that the software can "provide door-to-door services". For young-old, the most convenient way to know is still to make phone calls or face-to-face manual answers.

• **Smartphone aging-friendly design trends.**
In the question of "Which design is more likely to be a smartphone?", the maximum value comes from the design of "simple interface", followed by the requirement of "handwriting input", as shown in the following figure (Fig. 3):

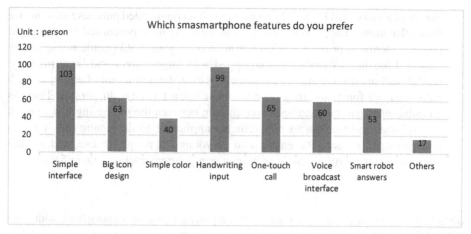

Fig. 3. A classification chart of the aging-Appropriate design trend of smart phones for the young and elderly. (Self-Designed Form)

Research shows that the vital design needs of smart phones by the elderly includes "simple interface", "big icon design", "simple color", "handwriting input", "one-touch call", "voice broadcast interface", "smart robot answer" and so on. It is easy to find that these demands are closer to the "old man's mobile phone" which is very convenient in terms of making calls, calling announcements, menu reading, automatic time reporting, and keyboard input. This type of mobile phone has a small screen and does not have the Internet access function, but the manually set pages and function lists are displayed in the form of large icons and plain text, and the use logic is simpler and the target functions are accessible. Most of young-old people have difficulties in getting used to the design of APPs in current smartphones. They prefer "elderly phones" with large screens. However, there are still 10.6% of young-old people who hope to have "smart robot answer". They are curious and eager for human-computer interaction dialogue and willing to try AI scientific and technological achievements.

5   Conclusion

Based on the data and analysis, this study concluded that:

(1) Younger elderly people generally tend to learn and use smartphones, and generally can achieve their own goals. However, in terms of the degree of "use", only a few young-old people can be very familiar with smartphones, most of the young-old people still have a lot of space for learning.

(2) In terms of aging needs and the applicability of current smartphones, smartphones produced by mobile phone brands are constantly being updated or upgraded, and each with its own selling points. However, it has not changed the difficult situation that young-old people face, either based on the design of the smartphone itself, or based on their own physiological and psychological characteristics. This article selects the latest four smartphones with prices around 1,000 yuan from the two major

brands of Huawei and Honor. By combining its recommended purchase reasons, we found that these smartphones, which are more likely to be purchased by young-old people in terms of price, are neither promoted for young-old people nor specially designed for them. Whether it is equipped with large battery and large memory, or high-definition pixel high-brush screen, or even the promotion of equipped with chips and 5G functions, they do not aim to attract young-old people. There is an unbalanced and mismatched contradiction between the increasing functions of smartphones and the logical requirements applicable to the young-old. This, to a large extent, reduces the enthusiasm of young-old people to use, and are not conducive to the virtuous circle of human-computer interaction (Table 5).

Table 5. List of promotional selling points on the purchase page of a smartphone with price around 1,000 yuan.

The price around 1,000 yuan smartphones' purchase page promotes selling points				
Brand	HUAWEI		Honor	
Series	Low-range: Changxiang Series	Entry model: Changwan Series	Low-range: Play series	Mid-range: X series
Model	Changxiang 20e	Changwan 30plus	Play 5T Vitality Edition	X30i
Price	999–1399 yuan	1099–1499 yuan	1599 yuan	1399–1899 yuan
Big battery	√	√	√	
Large/Narrow screen	√			√
Loud volume	√			
Large storage		√	√	
Thin and light				√
Camera pixel	√		√	√
Smart system	√			
Fast charge		√	√	√
High brush eye protection screen		√	√	
Storage expansion		√	√	
5G		√		√
Chip				√

(3) In the context of age-appropriate design, the process of human-computer interaction produces a nostalgic context that is not easily perceived. This is because, first, the young-old tend to have simple designs such as large icons and one-button type; simple operations such as handwriting input and voice broadcast; tend to retain the "elderly machine" function of smartphones. Second, the young-old expect to have a direct contact to answer questions or provide door-to-door teaching services during the installation and use of smartphone software. The third is that young-old have expectations for intelligent AI situations in human-computer interaction. they believe that intelligent robot solutions are helpful to reduce operational errors, and improve communication willingness, and forming better human-computer interaction. Overall, although the current smart phones have limited cognition and mastery of young-old, they are still active in frequency of use and enthusiasm for learning. The young-old people are nostalgic for functional design expectations, but they are also full of expectations for technological iterative updates.

Based on these results, the aging-appropriate design of smartphone APPs should be improved in the following aspects. First, we suggest to reduce the complexity of human-computer interaction, reduce the difficulty of self-learning for young people to use smartphone APPs, and rationally plan the settings of teaching skills that come with smartphones. It is not limited to the basic functions of the smartphone APPs, but also how to learn common software, demonstrate design logic, and create integrated videos of practical operations, so as to establish a human-machine trust relationship and help optimize the use of the APPs. Secondly, as far as the consumer psychology of the young-old is concerned, warm words that cares for the elderly can be used in the advertising and APPs interface of smartphones, such as "being your assistant in life" and "a smartphone that makes your life more convenient", so as to alleviate old people's resistance to new things, and to achieve a unified design for physical aging and psychological aging. In addition, the physiological characteristics of young-old require that the age-appropriate design of smartphone APPs should use a simple and easy-to-read interface, easy-to-recognize colors, increase the finger touch area during using, and lock the contacts after exiting, and reduce the cumbersome steps, avoid using time limits etc. Finally, the age-appropriate design should enhance the sense of human-computer interaction between the young-old and the smartphone, developing a tailor-made age-appropriate situation for the young-old. The big data algorithm should calculate the applicable characteristics of people of different ages, so as to avoid the perceived barriers due to differences in the use of logic, and to miss the data that really helps to improve the use effect of the young-old group.

Because this study has not conducted in-depth interviews with the young-old who participated in the questionnaire, other improvements in the age-appropriate design of the smartphone APPs may not have been fully considered. It may be more able to verify the findings of this paper if future research presents the data of the effect evaluation of the one-year APPS aging modification that has not been carried out in the current study.

Acknowledgments. The research is supported by the 2022 Hunan social science achievement evaluation committee Research Program (Project No.: XSP22YBZ016).

Appendix

A Survey on Smartphone Usage Experience of Young-Old

Hello, thank you very much for filling out this questionnaire! We are the research team of the School of Design and Art of Changsha University of Science and Technology. Please rest assured that the anonymous information obtained in this questionnaire is for research and statistical purposes only. There is no standard answer to the following questions, please fill in the truth, thank you for your support and cooperation!

1. This questionnaire is filled out by () ?(radio)
A. Myself
B. Fill in on behalf of my family

2. What is your gender?(radio)
A. Male
B. Female

3. What is your age?(radio)
A. 50–55 years old
B. 55–60 years old
C. 60–65 years old
D. 65–70 years old

4. What is your education level?(radio)
A. Illiterate
B. Elementary school and below
C. Junior high school
D. Secondary school high school
E. College
F. Bachelor degree and above

5. What is your current residence status?(radio)
A. Living alone
B. Elderly couple living together
C. Living with children
D. Other

6. How is your smartphone usage?(radio)
A. Can use, and be familiar with
B. Can use, know how to use a few software
C. Only a little basic operation of calling and sending messages
D. Not very good at, just know how to start the smartphone
E. I don't know how to use
F. No cell phone

7. Why do you want to learn about smartphones? (Optional)
A. I like to accept new things
B. Influenced by the people around me
C. Life needs

D.   Life is too boring, want to find some fun

8.   How did you learn about smartphones?(Optional)
A.   Sons and daughters' teaching
B.   Grandchildren's teaching
C.   Friends and neighbors' teaching
D.   Self-taught through senior college and reading
E.   Self-learning through the smartphone's own teaching skills

9.   What is your smartphone generally used for?(Optional)
A.   Contact others
B.   Take photos or short videos
C.   Listen to music, watch news and short videos
D.   Internet consultation
E.   Online shopping
F.   Play games to relax (such as matchmaking)

10.   The main way you get mobile software is()(radio)
A.   System's own application store
B.   Third-party application store
C.   Search through Baidu, etc.
D.   Not clear

11.   How much software do you have in your smartphone now?(radio)
A.   5 or less
B.   5–10
C.   10–15
D.   15 or more

12.   For you, what has been your experience with your smartphone? (radio)
A.   Get information
B.   Communication platform
C.   Easy to contact
D.   Leisure and relaxation
E.   Successfully catch up with fashion

13.   During the process of using your smartphone, have you encountered () difficulties or problems with your smartphone. (Optional)
A.   Uncomfortable color graphics and text
B.   Complicated software operation
C.   Too many software
D.   Phone freezes and no respond
E.   Others

14.   The biggest problem you face while using your smartphone is?(Optional)
A.   Health problems, such as blurred vision, decreased limb flexibility, etc.
B.   Knowledge problems, such as inability to discern the content of a pop-up prompt box, etc.
C.   Cost issues, smartphones and their associated costs.
D.   Environmental issues, less information specific to the elderly.

E. Security issues, unfamiliar with software functions, worry about property safety, etc.

15. If the new function is easy to use, what you want most is the () function.(radio)
A. Have a communication and interaction circle.
B. Have direct contact
C. Provide door-to-door service
D. Guided by an operating assistant
E. Others

16. Which smartphone features do you prefer?(radio)
A. Simple interface
B. Big icon design
C. Simple color
D. Handwriting input
E. One-touch call
F. Voice broadcast interface
G. Smart robot answer
H. Others

References

Xu, Y., Li, Y., Zhu, L.: Research on the user interface design of smartphone APP for the elderly based on Kano model. Packaging Eng. **38**(16), 163–167 (2017)

He, W.: Research on aging-adaptive design of online learning app interactive interface based on Kano model. (2020) https://doi.org/10.12783/dteees/peee2016/3853

Yue, W.: Research on interface interaction design based on cognitive characteristics of the elderly. (2018)

Liu, X., Ding, H., Wei, X.: Research on the interface design of information APP based on the cognitive needs model of the elderly. Design (01), 26–27 (2018)

Huang, H., Yang, M.: Research on the interactive interface design of smart phone for the elderly based on conjoint analysis method. Packaging Eng. **38**(04), 133–137 (2017)

Li, Y., Shi, W., Zhu, L.: Research on the evaluation of APP user experience for the elderly based on gray analytic hierarchy process. J. Graphics **39**(01), 68–74 (2018)

Li, Y., Yang, X., Meng, F.: From "falling distance" to "integration": why is the social "intelligence" theory "appropriate for aging"?. Academic Exploration (08), 96–103 (2021)

Fan, Y., Li, Z.: From empowerment to empowerment: a study of smartphone use among older adults. Future Commun. **28**(05), 29–37 (2021)

Aging, Social Media and Digital Literacy

Challenges of the Intergenerational Feminist Movement(s): Some Reflections

Carla Cerqueira[(⊠)] and Célia Taborda Silva

Lusófona University/CICANT, Rua Augusto Rosa n°24, 4000-098 Porto, Portugal
{carla.cerqueira,celia.taborda}@ulp.pt

Abstract. This paper focuses on the feminist movement(s) today and the controversies that tend to permeate the notions of "waves" and "(inter)generations". It falls within the scope of feminist media studies, in a line of approach that seeks to traverse feminist activisms and their communication strategies, including mainstream and alternative media and the digital and offline spaces of interaction.

Throughout history, feminist movements have conducted several protests worldwide. Feminism has been asserting itself since the 19th century and its struggles have evolved, with current studies pointing to the existence of three "waves" of the feminist movement, each corresponding to different demands and conquests of rights for women. Some research, however, foretells the emergence of a fourth "wave" of the feminist movement, marked by the digital world, transnational demands, intersectionality, an intergenerational approach and the inclusion of new agendas and performance repertoires.

In this paper, we will question the "wave" narrative to explain the inception and evolution process of the feminist movement and the challenges of intergenerational feminist movement(s) nowadays. This is a critical reflection, anchored in international scientific literature, that intersects feminist activism and the sphere of (online and offline) communication and the media. We will also include examples of feminist movements/initiatives/protests/projects how demonstrate nowadays it is crucial to talk and understand what the idea of "intergenerational feminisms" can mean, and what are its impacts in strategies of mobilization in diverse spaces and platforms.

Keywords: Feminist movement(s) · Waves · Intergenerational relations

1 Introduction

The contemporary feminist movement is the result of a historical movement marked in time and space, which attempts to converge globally what is its essential matrix, women's rights, and gender equality. As Nancy Cott states, "feminism allows a range of possible relations between belief and action, a range of possible denotations of ideology or movement" [1]. From this relationship between belief and action, a group consciousness was born that has been built up over time, and the concept of "wave" was used to explain it. The conception of "waves" for thinking about the feminist movement has been much criticised and has generated controversy. It is often pointed to as creating splits between different generations of feminists. Simultaneously, it is often seen as presenting a linear and reductionist line, implying divisions and reifying oppositions. There are, however, approaches that look at "waves" as metaphors that allow us to understand what has been done, what the current agendas are and how the movement positions itself vis-à-vis the future. Chamberlain points out that "the wave can be a means by which to approach feminist temporality, considering how the past and future inform the affective immediacy of the present moment" [2]. We see waves as a process of the feminist movement, conditioned to the historical contexts of the countries that embraced it, occurring at different times within Europe and between Europe and the rest of the world [3].

Thus, in this paper we will enter the problematisation of the wave narrative to explain the process of the feminist movement's formation and evolution, and the challenges of intergenerational feminist movement(s) nowadays. This is a critical reflection, using a hermeneutic methodology, anchored in international scientific literature that crosses feminist activism and the sphere of communication and the media. This reflection will also include examples of feminist movements/initiatives/protests/projects that demonstrate how nowadays it is crucial to talk about and understand intergenerational feminisms.

2 Feminist Movement Waves

The feminist movement is historically marked by several periods corresponding to cycles of demands of several generations of women. These phases have been termed "waves" to show continuity and change in the politics of feminist contestation [4]. As a social movement, it resulted from a confrontation between opponents throughout history. Della Porta and Diani point out that social movements are "involved in conflicting relations with clearly identified opponents; they are linked by dense informal networks; they share a distinct collective identity" [5]. It is consensual that there are three "waves" within the feminist movement [6], with some authors considering that we are already in a fourth "wave" of the movement, as will be discussed later.

To understand where we are today, it is necessary to do a brief historical trajectory since the emergence of the feminist movement. The first wave of women's collective action in the public space occurred in England at the end of the 19th century, when several British women took to the streets in demonstrations, marches or strikes to have their right to vote recognized, in open confrontation with the State. Women's activism gave rise to several organizations such as the Women's Freedom League, the Actresses' Franchise League, and the most important, the National Union of Women's Suffrage Societies (NUWSS), led by Millicent Fawcett [7]. In 1903, Emmeline Pankhurst and her daughters Christabel and Sylvia, breaking with the NUWSS, founded the Women's Social and Political Union (WSPU), and were nicknamed the suffragettes. Their action was much more programmed and radical than that of the other organizations. All their public action – demonstrations or marches – was staged for newspaper coverage, and they even had their own newspaper. Arrests, hunger strikes, and force-feeding were widely publicized in order to impact society and political power. Between 1911 and 1914, the WSPU supported violent actions by the suffragettes. Bombing the homes and mailboxes of parliamentarians opposed to women's suffrage, cutting telegraph cables, and setting fires in churches, castles, and abandoned buildings were some of the violent acts the movement engaged in [7, 8]. The result was internal division within the organization and hostility in the public opinion, which rejected this type of performance. The height of the suffragette extremism came in 1913 when Emily Davison stormed the track in the Epsom Derby horse race, and threw herself in front of the king's horse. She succumbed to her injuries days later, and the funeral, although widely reported by the newspapers, did not garner popular support for the cause. In fact, the international suffragists distanced themselves from the radical methods of the suffragettes and the WSPU. With the outbreak of war in 1914, the founders of the WSPU became patriots, forgot the demand for the right to vote and abandoned the suffragist cause. This, however, did not fall by the wayside, the suffragettes continued negotiations in Parliament, winning the partial right to vote in 1918, and the vote for all women in 1928. This demand for human and citizenship rights, that is, for the recognition of women as subjects, was also expressed in the USA. In other countries these citizenship rights, such as voting, were only achieved much later, as is the case of Portugal.

The two world wars had a great impact on this first wave of the feminist movement and on the social position of women, who entered the public space and the labor market in a way never seen before [9]. Obviously, this period coincided with the rise of many dictatorial regimes that contributed to the retreat and silencing of feminisms.

It is in this context that the 2nd wave of feminism emerges, dating back to the post-war period, between the years 1960 and 1980. With the end of World War II came peace and economic and social development. The golden years of capitalism allowed an expansion of the labor and consumer market and a change in mentalities. The population increased, gained purchasing power, and education was democratized [10], leading to the emergence of an educated, qualified middle class, very connected to public functions [11] and whose protests no longer resulted from industrialization but from post-industrialization, in which conflicts no longer revolved around capital-labor and centered on cultural and informational issues.

These post-war political and social changes gave rise to a set of social movements (student, pacifist, ethnic) and a new wave of the feminist movement, all of them endowed with an identity and cultural character, which academics referred to as the New Social Movements (N.M.S). Some of the theorists of the New Social Movements [12, 13] see them as the reflection of a new middle class [11, 14], less concerned with materialistic or elementary social issues and more focused on universal issues such as peace, the environment or gender inequalities.

The sixties were years of social contestation, against the Vietnam war, against racial injustice, against bourgeois conservatism, against gender inequalities. In the sixties, women founded liberation movements inspired by feminists. For example, in America they founded the National Organization for Women (NOW) inspired by the feminist Betty Fridan, who intervened socially in search of greater freedom and equality for women, emphasizing that their function was not exhausted in reproduction. Medicine lent a hand with the emergence of the birth control pill, which revolutionized customs and gave women a, previously nonexistent, sexual boldness.

France saw the occurrence of "May of 68". In Paris, students occupied the Sorbonne, calling into question the centuries-old established academic order, in search of new cultural forms. Young women also participated in the occupation of universities and in street demonstrations [15], although men were most visible. In 1967 the Féminin, Masculin, Avenir (FMA) movement had emerged, born within the Mouvement démocratique féminin, and this mixed-constitution movement played an important role in the Sorbonne assemblies on the role of women. In the United States, having won the right to vote in 1919, the second wave emerged after the 1960s, around the Women's Liberation Movement (WLM), whose activists protested against discrimination, all forms of sexism of which they were victims, and claimed equal rights to men. Scott mentions that the concept of gender emerged when American feminists rejected "sexual distinctions" [16]. That decade ended with women in the streets protesting all over the world. In late 1968, a gathering of women, about 400 activists from the Women's liberation movement tried to stop the Miss America pageant in Atlantic City [17]. They intended to hold a bonfire to burn bras and other women's paraphernalia. Although they were prevented from protesting by the authorities, the episode that became known as the "bra burning" spread to Europe, where bonfires actually took place. In 1970, they held a strike in New York that brought 50,000 people into the streets. The early 1970s saw the appearance of new women's movements. In France, the Mouvement de Libération des Femmes appeared as heir to previous movements (French League for Women's Rights, Women's Democratic Movement, Féminin, Masculin, Avenir), but as an all-women movement, not mixed [18]. This movement promoted various collective actions, from manifestos, such as the "Manifesto 343," for the right to contraception and abortion, to demonstrations. On November 20, 1971, in Paris, they organized an international demonstration in favor of free contraception and abortion. Women swarmed the streets in joyful agitation, using colorful banners and balloons, dances and songs composed of familiar melodies [19]. In 1972 they demonstrated, after the Bobigny case (a young woman who was raped and had an abortion), for the decriminalization of the voluntary interruption of pregnancy. These demonstrations were joined by other feminist movements, whose force of protest was echoed by Simone Veil, health minister in Jacques Chirac's government, resulting in the proposed law for decriminalizing the voluntary interruption of pregnancy, which came into force in January 1975. The women of the Mouvement de Libération des Femmes profoundly transformed French values and society when it came to contraception, abortion, and parental equality.

These manifestations of feminists, sharing common experiences, and reflecting on the condition of women and their role in society forged a collective identity [20] and from there their recognition as social actors. In fact, the feminist social movement drove the Feminisms of the 20th century. In the midst of the activist effervescence of the sixties, according to Offen, there is an "eruption of feminisms" [21], although with different cadences in European countries. And, according to Young, the various currents of feminism affirmed Feminism as the "most far-reaching cultural policy movement" in the twentieth century [22].

By the end of the century, in Europe and the United States, the feminist movement managed to get some of women's demands heard and met by sectors of political and civil society. Discussions around issues such as sexuality, contraception, and abortion subsided as they became legal conquests.

The third wave began around the 1990s (between 1990–2000) and emerged almost as a reaction to the criticism that, from the 1980s onwards, had been leveled at the second wave and at feminism. While conceptually and ideologically Feminism was trying to find itself, the concept of post-feminism emerged, which mirrored the plurality of feminisms. There was also an emergence of anti-feminist movements (feminist backlash). As a social movement, feminism was moving towards transnational action, owing to women having managed to assert their female identity and win certain rights. From then on, they sought internationalization and recognition of the movement on a global scale. It was in this context that the World March of Women (WMW) movement emerged, which began on March 8, 2000, International Women's Day. The Women's World March was not a one-off mobilization, it became a platform for action of a more permanent nature, promoting major marches and demonstrations every five years and participating often in world social forums. Defined as a worldwide feminist network, the Women's World March is part of movements on a global scale. It acquired a large dimension, bringing together several international movements, and intended to project the movement and draw attention to its cause through dissemination in the media. Like other movements, its purpose was "to produce visibility through the media and symbolic effects for the protesters themselves (in the political-pedagogical sense) and for society in general, as a form of political pressure of the most expressive in contemporary public space" [23]. The inspiration for the creation of the World March of Women came from a demonstration held in 1995 in Canada, when 850 women marched 200 km between Quebec and Montreal, symbolically asking for "Bread and Roses". At the end of this action, several conquests were achieved, such as an increase in the minimum wage, more rights for immigrant women and support for the solidarity economy.

The motto of the 2000 march was the fight against violence and poverty. Actions were organized in more than 150 countries, involving more than 6000 women's groups [24]. At the end of the march, these participating groups drafted a document with seventeen points of demands to be delivered to the UN. The collective actions ended on October 17th with a demonstration in New York City.

The feminist movement, by acting transnationally, aims for the empowerment of all women in the world, because the achievements of European women are not yet a global reality and only global collective action can endow the movement with the intersectionality, plurality of repertoires, and performative actions that this third wave aims for.

3 Fourth Wave? or a Feminist Tsunami?

"The wave can be a means by which to approach feminist temporality, considering how the past and future inform the affective immediacy of the present moment" [2]. It is within this context that this author mentions the importance of speaking of a fourth wave of the movement, which emerges from 2013. According to Chamberlain [2], this new wave of feminism is characterized by a series of protests and resistance movements, which intersect various social movements and allow for the expansion to human rights issues, with concerns that intersect gender with issues of class, sexuality, ethnicity, race, generation, functional diversity and environment, among others. Gender intersects with other identity, belonging, and social problems, and should not be discussed outside of this approach, which accentuates the focus on "sidestreaming", that is, on the multiple oppressions that occur beyond gender. It should be noted that at a stage when the movement is characterized by social and political mobilizations occurring within an increasingly transnational frame, driven by the proliferation of information and communication technologies, it is crucial to analyze the culture in which women are embedded [25], and how the interaction between activists is established. This may not be a new issue, the need to address local specificities, to aim for situated knowledge [26], but the interconnection between the global and the local, as well as the relevance of the digital sphere in this equation is assumed to be very pressing.

Matos, Chamberlain, Perez & Ricoldi also refer to new forms of relationship with the state, seeking the depatriarchalization of state institutions, whilst being characterized by new relations between the state and civil society (polycentric: state and anti-state, at the same time depatriarchalizing and decolonizing). Also noteworthy is the existence of a renewed theory, with "a profound theoretical reformulation with a strong concentration on decolonial contemporary feminist theoretical-critical traditions and aiming at a new framework for a cosmopolitan feminism" [27]. Finally, according to the same authors, what marks this new phase is action in digital media; digital activism or cyberactivism that uses blogs, social networks such as Youtube, Facebook, and Instagram to create and disseminate feminist causes, enabling the multiplication of non-hegemonic ideas and other voices in public space. The attention to the "place of speech" [28] is very relevant for this new phase of feminism, with many voices and causes within feminisms, which historically have been silenced, gaining expression.

Naming a new periodization of the historical moment as the fourth wave is a way to empower its enunciators and enhance their political agenda [29]. It is a way of seeking visibility for the resumption of women's claims that often address old, and little achieved agendas. This is where movements like Slutwalk, #Metoo, LaManada, 8M Feminist Strike, etc. arise, which are internationally recognized, and involve dynamics in the digital space, but also in the streets. One can then ask: How different are these new feminist movements from previous forms, and what differences and continuities divide and unite the generations, the diverse women/people who make up these movements, what are the voices that gain expression and the struggles that gain visibility and public recognition?

Maybe we are not talking about a feminist wave, but the designation "feminist tsunami" [30] seems to us the most adequate to explain the dynamics of the feminist movement today. It is an expanding movement, designed for the 99%, intergenerational, defined by technology, feminism 4.0. It politicizes new generations without losing ties with the old ones and bonds together the various types of political, social and cultural struggles that cross the world today.

4   Intergenerationally Between "waves"

"Feminism is a historically constituted, local and global, social and political movement with an emancipatory purpose and a normative content. It posits a subject (women), identifies a problem (…), and expresses various aims (…) in the name of specific principles (e.g., equality, rights, liberty, autonomy, dignity, self-realization, recognition, respect, justice, freedom)" [31].

As Dietz points out, Feminism is a historical movement, and as such, several generations of women have played a part in it over the three waves. The question of intergenerationality in an enduring movement like Feminism is as controversial as the metaphor of waves, but it refers to the inheritance, the legacy from one generation to the next. As with other social movements, Feminism accrued a set of repertoires of action from previous generations and innovated in each new one. The suffragettes started a whole collective action in the public space with marches, demonstrations, representations, strikes and journalistic mobilization that was followed by the generations of women of the subsequent "waves", who innovated, albeit within their temporal and spatial context. Between the first and second waves, the world changed a lot in political, economic and social terms, so if the context changes, the social actors also change. As Nancy Cott [1] says, it is in the beginning of the 20th century that the term "Feminism" appears to designate a binding ideology among women, which did not happen in the 19th century when women united and fought for a notion of a feminine sphere. The Wars contributed to women thinking about the world and themselves differently. Writers such as Simone de Beauvoir, Betty Fridan, and Carol Hanish bring into the public sphere themes previously belonging exclusively to women's private sphere, which were not discussed at all or, when touched upon, done so from a patriarchal perspective. In 1963, Betty Fridan launched the book "Feminine Mystique", in which she described what middle-class American women thought, deconstructing the male discourse of the happy mother and housewife. Fridan showed that women felt a dissatisfaction, an anxiety, and this "nameless problem" came from the fact that they wanted something more than merely their husbands, children, and home [32].

Feminism also progressed into the academies, and studies on women or Women's Studies began to appear. These revealed that the category "woman" was insufficient as a field of research and study and the concept of gender emerged in research [16]. However, many black and lesbian women considered the concept of gender to be metanarrative, continuing interests of the hegemonic identity of heterosexual and white women.

In the West, in the 1960s, Feminism emerges as a women's liberation movement. However, as Caughie states, "the first phase of the women's movement in non-Western contexts is roughly coterminous with the Western understanding of the first wave and often connected to women's participation in the anti-colonial nationalist movement from the late nineteenth century to the 1930s" [33], which demonstrates that approaching an intergenerationality between distinct historical contexts is more difficult. Between the first and second waves, there is a western intergenerational identification, because the memory of the struggles and conquests for the rights of equal citizenship is kept alive, even by the fact that women did not secure the right to vote at the same time in all European countries. In France, women only won the vote in 1945, with remnants of suffragism remaining in the second French feminist wave.

There is also an intergenerational approach in social terms, given that second wave feminists are white, educated, heterosexual, middle-class women, just as they were in the first wave (at least in the beginning). In the 1980s, the movement was very focused on gender differences, excluding other 'axes of difference', including race, sexuality, class, and ethnicity [34]. In the 20th century, the movement became more socially heterogeneous, which gave rise to several currents of feminism (e.g. liberal, socialist, radical), not all of which claim this bourgeois heritage. In fact, more recently we see that this typification of currents does not reflect the diversity of voices and claims existing within the feminist movement at all.

Although the generations are closer together temporally, it is evident what separates the second and third waves. According to Fraser, it was the abandonment of the "exclusive focus on gender difference" that made the third wave emerge [34], a wave marked by multiculturalism. For Fraser, multiculturalism 'has become the rallying cry for a potential alliance of new social movements', and promotes a cultural pluralism that recognizes all identities as equally valuable in their particularity [34]. Thus, blacks, lesbians, and transsexuals are no longer the "other" within feminism. The identity of feminisms evolves [35], points to the intersectional bias and assumes the new "places of speech" [28] historically marginalized.

It was Rebecca Walker that brought the term "third wave" into public conscious-ness, when she founded the Third Wave Foundation in 1992. Springer considers that the term signals "a new generation of feminists" that "credits previous generations for women-centered social and political advances" [36], but also thinks that it "deprioritizes generational differences in the interest of historical, activist continuity" [36]. For this author the non-inclusion of race in earlier movements created a generational rift and "the wave model perpetuates the exclusion of women of color from women's movement his-tory and feminist theorizing" [36]. Furthermore, the issue of intergenerationality among Black feminists, their conflicts and distinctions, is little talked about [36].

Intergenerationality between waves is still present, as no current of feminism has reneged on the historical past of the movement, but it does not encompass all realities, as waves do. Just as "waves do not efface feminist history. When a new wave is declared, or emerges, it does not eradicate previous efforts of previous waves" [2], also the knowledge and forms of collective action acquired by one generation of women did not disappear in the following generations. Now, it is a fact that the progress of each era pushes for innovation [2], but there remains an "affective temporality" that unites all women generationally, that was forged in the struggles and that gave birth to a group-conscious identity, a unity within the diversity that characterizes women.

5 Final Reflections

The feminist movement has always been eclectic, marked by a plurality of ideas and forms of action. It is important to reflect on the challenges faced today, because trying to classify what involves feminist activism in contemporary times is a difficult task.

Of course, thinking about feminist activism today implies thinking about the plural-ity of organizations, collectives, movements, actions, mobilization platforms, agendas and performative repertoires of action. It implies looking at an action that takes place in the digital networks, but also in the streets and in the interconnection between the two. For feminism, the digital world has enabled the expansion and almost unlimited access to its discourse, empowering even more women, allowing a new place of speech. The internet enables the large-scale dissemination of feminist ideas and facilitates the mobilization and organization of protests. Of course, many of them move to the streets, as is the case of Slutwalk, 8M Feminist Strike, #MeToo and others of more localized expression. These are transnational feminist movements, marked by the intersectionality and intergenerationality of struggles, and which allow feminist causes to re-energize themselves in public space. They need to be further studied in order to better frame an understanding of transnational communication strategies, but also local specificities.

The metaphor of waves seems valid to us in the sense of showing these interconnections that permeate the feminist struggles, which are passed down from generation to generation, renewing themselves. As matter of fact, feminist activism has historically had moments of growth, retraction, and retreat, and these are obviously related to the historical, social, economic, and political contextualization. The term wave is seen here from Chamberlain's [2] perspective, in an attempt to overcome the difficulties of generations, identities, and divisions. The author asserts that feminism must develop its own methods for time-keeping, in which past activism and future aspirations touch the present moment. Through this unique temporality, she continues, feminism can create space for affective bonds to create intense moments of activism, in which passion catalyzes and sustains action. Social movements are tied to emotional convergences, in which feelings transfer between wider groups, encouraging them to action. This is central to initiating and then sustaining feminist activism, drawing in a range of subjects through shared investment within a specific historical moment. This idea obviously leads us to the discussion about intergenerationality and its dynamics, the projects now emerging and that bring together people of different generations, who interact in multiple ways, both digitally and in person. One of the challenges that can be raised in this field emerges precisely from the pandemic we are experiencing, and it leads us to question how these forms of activism will be reconfigured, how affection is lived through the digital.

Perhaps here we should also take up Nuria Varela's [30] concept of a feminist tsunami to characterize what is currently happening in this field of social mobilization, marked by an intense dynamic, by voices that multiply, by intersecting agendas, and by the somewhat overwhelming way in which certain movements, such as #MeToo, have marked the public, political and media agenda. In fact, if we turn to Sara Ahmed [37], the author states that "what is the hardest for some does not even exist for others. It is necessary to understand that intersectional identities recognize situations of privilege and oppression and how feminist activism makes visible the voices that have been most oppressed and allows this intergenerational dialogue". This is the challenge that will occupy us in the near future in terms of empirical research in a study that we are developing regarding the Portuguese context, in which we intend to understand the dynamics of the glocalized contemporary feminist movement ("FEMglocal - Glocal feminist movements: interactions and contradictions - PTDC/COM-CSS/4049/2021).

Acknowledgements. This chapter resulted from several discussions started in the SMART-EU Social Media Resilience Tookit project (LC-01563446), so we are grateful for all the support for academic reflection and economic support for participation in scientific activities. Moreover, this chapter is part of the ongoing research being developed by the project team ("FEMglocal - Glocal feminist movements: interactions and contradictions - PTDC/COM-CSS/4049/2021), supported by national funds through FCT — Foundation for Science and Technology, I.P.

References

1. Cott, N.: The Grounding of Modern Feminism. Yale University Press, New Haven and London (1987)
2. Chamberlain, P.: The Feminist Fourth Wave: Affective Temporality. Palgrave Macmillan, London (2017)
3. Dean, J., Aune, K.: Feminism resurgent? Mapping contemporary feminist activisms in Europe. Soc. Mov. Stud. **14**(4), 375–395 (2015). https://doi.org/10.1080/14742837.2015.1077112
4. Cullen, P.: Conceptualising generational dynamics in feminist movements: Political generations, waves and affective economies. Sociol. Compass **8**, 282–293 (2014). https://doi.org/10.1111/soc4.12131
5. Della Porta, D., Diani, M.: Social Movements: An Introduction, 2nd edn. Blackwell Publishing, Malden, USA (2006)
6. Kaplan, G.: Contemporary Western European Feminism. University Press, New York (1992)
7. Walters, M.: Feminism: A Very Short Introduction. Oxford University Press, Oxford (2005)
8. Bearman, C.J.: An examination of suffragette violence. Engl. Hist. Rev. **120**(486), 365–397 (2005). https://doi.org/10.1093/ehr/cei119
9. Thébaud, F.: Introdução. In: Duby, G., Perrot M. (eds.) História das Mulheres, Afrontamento, Porto (1991)
10. Hobsbawm, E.: A Era dos Extremos. Presença, Lisbon (1996)
11. Offe, C.: New social movements: challenging the boundaries of institutional Politics. Soc. Res. **52**(4), 817–868 (1985)
12. Touraine, A.: Pourrons-Nous Vivre Ensemble? Editions Fayard, Paris (1998)
13. Melucci, A.: Challenging Codes. Collective Action in the Information Age. Cambridge University Press, Cambridge (1996)
14. Habermas, J.: The Theory of Communicative Action. The Critique of Functionalist Reason, vol. 2. Polity Press, Boston (1986)
15. Chaperon, S.: Les années Beauvoir (1945–1970). Fayard, Paris (2000)
16. Scott, J.W.: Gender: a useful category of historical analysis. Am. Hist. Rev. **91**(5), 1053–1075 (1986)
17. Buchanan, P.D.: Radical Feminists: A Guide to an American Subculture. Geenwood (2011)
18. Chaperon, S.: La radicalisation des mouvements féminins Français de 1960 à 1970. Vingtième Siècle: Revue d'Histore **48**(1), 61–74 (1995)
19. Fournel, M.Z.: Notre corps, nous-mêmes. In: Gubin, E. et al. (dir.), Le siècle des feminisms, pp. 209–222. Les Editions de L'Atelier, Paris (2004)
20. Melucci, A.: A invenção do presente: movimentos sociais nas sociedades complexas. Vozes, Petrópolis (2001)
21. Offen, K.: Erupções e fluxos: reflexões sobre a escrita de uma história comparada dos feminismos europeus, 1750–1950. In: Cova, A. (dir.), História Comparada das Mulheres, pp. 29–45. Livros Horizonte, Lisboa (2008)
22. Young, I.M.: La Justicia y la Politica de la diferencia. Ediciones Cátedra, Madrid (2000)
23. Scherer-Werren, I.: Das mobilizações às redes de movimentos sociais. Sociedade e Estado **21**(1), 109–130 (2006). https://doi.org/10.1590/S0102-69922006000100007
24. Tavares, M., Bento, A., Magalhães, M.J.: Feminismos e Movimentos Sociais em tempos de Globalização: o caso da MMM. In: VIII Congresso Luso-Afro-Brasileiro de Ciências Sociais, pp. 1–17. CES, Coimbra (2004)
25. Cochrane, K.: All the Rebel Women. The Rise of the Fourth Wave Feminist. Guardian Books, London (2013)
26. Haraway, D.: Situated knowledges: the science question in feminism and the privilege of partial perspective. In: Haraway, D. (org.) Symians, Cyborgs and Women: The Reinvention of Nature, pp. 183–202. Routledge (1988/1991)

27. Matos, M.: A Quarta onda feminista e o Campo crítico-emancipatório das diferenças no Brasil: entre a destradicionalização social e o neoconservadorismo político. Anais 38o Encontro Anual da ANPOCS, pp. 1–28, ANPOCS, Caxambu (2014)
28. Ribeiro, D.: O que é: Lugar de fala? Editora Letramento, Belo Horizonte (2017)
29. Gomes, C., Sorj, B.: Corpo, geração e identidade: a Marcha das vadias no Brasil. Sociedade e Estado **29**(2), 433–447 (2014). https://doi.org/10.1590/S0102-69922014000200007
30. Varela, N.: Feminismo 4.0. La cuarta ola. Ediciones B, Barcelona (2019)
31. Dietz, M.G.: Current controversies in feminist theory. Annu. Rev. Polit. Sci. **6**, 399–431 (2003). https://doi.org/10.1146/annurev.polisci.6.121901.085635
32. Fridan, B.: Mística Feminina. Vozes, Petrópolis (1971)
33. Caughie, P.L: Introduction: theorizing the first wave globally. Fem. Rev. **95**, 5–9 (2010). https://doi.org/10.1057/fr.2009.63
34. Fraser, N.: Justice Interruptus: Critical Reflections on the 'Postsocialist' Condition. Routledge, New York (1997)
35. Maluf, S.W.: Políticas e teorias do sujeito no feminismo contemporâneo [Resumo]. In: Anais do VII Encontro Internacional Fazendo Gênero. UFSC, Florianópolis (2006)
36. Springer, K.: Third wave black feminism? Signs **27**(4), 1059–1082 (2002). https://doi.org/10.1086/339636
37. Ahmed, S.: Living a Feminist Life. Duke University Press Books, Durham and London (2017)

Why the Elderly Indulges in Live Shopping: Optimization of Interaction Mechanism Under the Live E-commerce Scenario?

Xinyi Ding, Cong Cao$^{(\boxtimes)}$ (iD), and Dan Li

Zhejiang University of Technology, Hangzhou, China
congcao@zjut.edu.cn

Abstract. In recent years, the addition of the elderly to live e-commerce broadcasting has become a phenomenon. In order to clarify the formation of consumption intention of the elderly in live e-commerce, this paper proposes a model based on digital affordance theory. It uses partial least squares structural equation model (PLS-SEM) to analyze 198 questionnaire data to evaluate the model. The results show that the ease of interaction, the anchor's charm, and the attraction of live content significantly impact the elderly's consumption intention formation. This study fills the gap in the consumption intention of the elderly in live e-commerce. It provides a reference for living e-commerce enterprises to understand elderly consumers better.

Keywords: Live e-commerce · Elderly · Digital affordance · Interaction

1 Introduction

The participation of the elderly in live shopping is becoming a new trend. With the popularity of the mobile Internet and the continuous progress of information technology, more and more older people have learned how to use mobile phones to surf the Internet. In the post epidemic era, the control of offline activities limits the entertainment channels of the elderly to further spend time online for entertainment. According to China's seventh national census data, China's population aged 60 and overreached 260 million, accounting for 18.7% of the country's total population. The scale of the elderly population is still growing rapidly. Meanwhile, according to the 45th Statistical Report on Internet Development in China, from 2010 to 2020, the number of Internet users aged 60 and over increased from 8.67 million to 60.54 million, and the proportion of elderly Internet users in the elderly population increased from 4.9% to 23.8% [1]. The process of population aging is accompanied by the rapid development of digitization and informatization. To actively deal with population aging, we cannot ignore the role of digital products and services.

The webcast provides new tools for the contemporary elderly to acquire knowledge, social entertainment and show themselves, strengthens the social connection of the elderly, and improves the social adaptation and social participation of the elderly

Q. Gao and J. Zhou (Eds.): HCII 2022, LNCS 13330, pp. 276–290, 2022.
https://doi.org/10.1007/978-3-031-05581-2_21

after they withdraw from the labour market. Nevertheless, at the same time, widespread pseudoscience and rumours [2–5], violations of personal privacy[6–8]; False publicity [9], fraud and other issues also bring significant risks for the elderly to participate in a live interaction. The information gap between generations makes the ability of the elderly to screen and distinguish information on the Internet weaker than the younger generation who are old Internet residents or aborigines [10, 11]. At the same time, due to the lack of spiritual sustenance and material entertainment, in reality, the elderly are eager to find the so-called "confidants" on the Internet. Their emotional investment in the anchor is much higher than young people. Once this emotional connection breaks down, it will have a tremendous negative impact on the psychology of the elderly and is not conducive to social stability and harmony.

Just as the Internet and live broadcasting are new to the elderly, the elderly group is also strange to enterprises. Is the behaviour pattern of the elderly in live shopping different from that in traditional scenes? How does the consumption intention of the elderly come into being? How should enterprises improve their products and services to serve the elderly better? What measures should be taken to avoid all kinds of risks?

The theory of digital affordance provides a reference for solving the above problems. Digital affordance theory depicts the "Relationship Attribute" between subject and technology. On the one hand, it reveals the opportunities brought by digital technology as the subject of the environment [12]. On the other hand, it emphasizes that the grasp of opportunities is affected by the joint action of subject cognition and situation. Gibson [13] expressed digital influences as digital technologies and infrastructures. This concept was later extended by Nambisan, Autio and other scholars, which can better explain that the possibilities brought by the progress of digital technology are grasped and utilized by different subjects in different degrees [14–16]. In the scene of middle-aged and older people participating in live e-commerce, the progress of digital technology as an environment has brought opportunities for the elderly and e-commerce enterprises. For the elderly, technology makes live broadcasting available and easy to use. They can obtain new knowledge, leisure and entertainment, social interaction, life sharing, purchase products and other needs through live broadcasting. For enterprises in the live e-commerce track with an increasingly saturated market and increasingly fierce competition, the participation of the elderly undoubtedly brings a new growth point.

Based on the theory of digital affordance, this paper constructs a model of purchase intention of elderly consumers in the live e-commerce environment. It analyzes 198 sample data using the partial least squares structural equation model (PLS-SEM) to test the model and hypothesis. The research results show that the ease of use of the interactive function of the live broadcast room and the attraction of the anchor's personal and live content will significantly affect the digital availability to promote the shopping intention of elderly consumers. At the same time, the transformation of perceived digital availability into actual availability to promote the consumption intention needs the subjective grasp of elderly consumers and e-commerce enterprises. These studies will provide a reference for enterprises to make targeted adjustments and improvements for the new live broadcast object of elderly consumers, guide enterprises to better seize this development opportunity, and also provide some reference materials for the social phenomenon of the elderly addicted to living shopping, which is generally concerned by the society, and can provide support for all kinds of relevant decisions. Also, based on the perspective of live broadcasting for the middle-aged and elderly, this paper explores the behaviour mode of elderly consumers in the context of live broadcasting e-commerce, which provides a particular theoretical reference for future related research.

This paper's research ideas and contents are arranged as follows: firstly, this paper combs and summarizes the relevant research and results of live shopping and consumption intention of the middle-aged and the elderly. Secondly, based on the theory of digital availability and the consumption intention model of relevant literature, this paper puts forward the framework of this study and constructs the corresponding research hypotheses. Then the questionnaire is designed according to the scale of the existing literature. Relevant data were collected from the middle-aged and elderly through an online questionnaire, and the research model and hypothesis were evaluated and tested by PLS-SEM. Finally, the corresponding research conclusions and theoretical and practical significance are discussed. In addition, this paper also explains the limitations of this study and the direction of future research.

2   Theoretical Background and Hypotheses

The middle-aged and the elderly are becoming a new driving force for e-commerce consumption. Scholars believe that the simplicity and ease of use of online shopping can improve the participation of elderly consumers' participation and optimize the consumption interface, links, and processes [17–21]. With the progress of technology, the improvement of usability and the development of overall social cognition, the attitude of the elderly towards online shopping has changed from scepticism to resistance [19, 22–25], which has also extensively promoted the online consumption of the middle-aged and elderly.

Social media attracts older people to indulge in it. The existing literature found that social networks have gradually become the primary way for the elderly to participate in society [26]. The study of Jin et al. pointed out that there was a positive correlation between the likes of the elderly and their concerns [12]. Other studies have discussed the time for the elderly to watch the live broadcast [27], the factors affecting the elderly to watch the live broadcast [28], and some new live broadcast application scenarios [29].

By searching and combing the relevant literature, the online participation of middle-aged and elderly groups is receiving extensive attention in the academic circles, and their live participation has also been studied to a certain extent. However, there is little literature to focus on the live shopping behaviour of middle-aged and older people. The preferences of middle-aged and older people in live e-commerce are different from their traditional shopping preferences and preferences when watching live, and it is not a simple sum of the two. However, there is no article to distinguish and discuss this. In addition, the decision-making mode and the generation of consumption intention of the middle-aged and elderly in live e-commerce also lack sufficient consideration.

The participation of middle-aged and older people in live e-commerce benefits from the development of digital technology. In the live e-commerce scenario, enterprises and consumers are the main interaction body. Therefore, digital affordance provides excellent theoretical support for this study. Digital availability research focuses on people's grasp of the possibilities provided by digital technology and the process of opportunity discovery and pursuit based on this [14]. Digital affordance has fundamental and practical characteristics. The actual availability reflects that the digital technology in the environment is "objectively" presented to the subject. It is necessary to analyze the relevant parties and gather the opportunities according to the possibility presented in front of them. Perceived availability reflects the deepening of the relevant parties' understanding of digital technology. It then analyzes how they use opportunities to create value for themselves with the help of perceived availability. This paper studies the discovery and pursuit of the possibility of live broadcasting technology from the perspective of two participants: Live Broadcasting e-commerce enterprises and middle-aged and elderly consumers (Fig. 1).

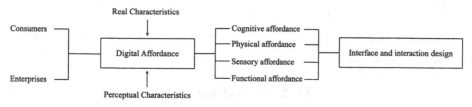

Fig. 1. Affordance mechanism.

In the interaction design and evaluation, Hartson defines affordance as four complementary types: cognitive affordance, physical affordance, sensory affordance and functional affordance [30] (Table 1, Fig. 2).

Table 1. Affordance types.

Affordance type	Description	Example
Cognitive affordance	Design feature that helps users in knowing something	Online live broadcasting room
Physical affordance	Design feature that helps users in doing a physical action in the interface	Applicability of interaction, convenience of transaction
Sensory affordance	Design feature that helps users sense something (especially cognitive affordances and physical affordances)	Provide rich sound, visual and tactile stimuli during live broadcasting
Functional affordance	Design feature that helps users accomplish work (i.e., the usefulness of a system function)	Provide product related knowledge and product origin information during live broadcasting

Note. Reproduced from Susan (2019)

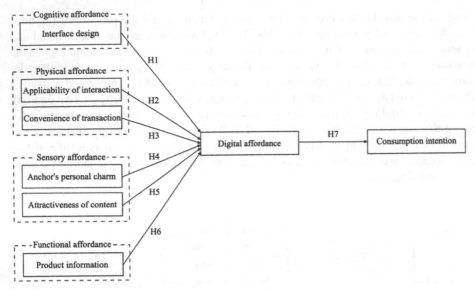

Fig. 2. Research framework.

Cognitive affordance refers to a design feature that helps users recognize, understand and think [30]. In the context of live broadcasting, the most significant cognitive affordance is the clarity and accuracy of each function key in the interface design. Only when customers face an interface, clearly know what they can do, and quickly find the corresponding functions when they need them can they have more motivation to stay in the live studio [31, 32]. This is also the basis of all affordance. Everything else will be empty talk once the live broadcasting room cannot retain consumers due to inconvenient operation. For the elderly, their vision and responsiveness have decreased, and they are more attracted to good aging friendly interface design than young people [33, 34]. Based on this, this paper puts forward the following assumption:

H1: Simple and clear interface design positively impacts digital affordance.

Physical affordance refers to the design module that helps users realize a specific action [30]. In the context of live e-commerce, physical affordance is mainly reflected in the ease of interaction between the anchor and consumers and the convenience of consumers' consumption. The attraction of live shopping primarily comes from the unique sense of presence, and the sense of presence comes from the excellent interaction and atmosphere between the anchor and consumers [35–37]. Interaction with strong usability can significantly improve consumers' sense of presence to improve consumers' shopping experience and immersion because it is easier to generate a willingness to consume [38]. Moreover, as consumers in live e-commerce tend to consume impulsively, the blocked and unsmooth payment experience will significantly reduce the trading volume. Based on this, this paper puts forward the following assumptions:

H2: Applicability of interaction has a positive impact on digital affordance.
H3: Convenience of transaction has a positive impact on digital affordance.

Sensory affordance refers to the design module that helps users perceive (see, hear, feel) [30]. In the live e-commerce context, the anchor is the subject of user perception, followed by the content conveyed by the anchor. Many studies have shown that the anchor's charm significantly impacts consumers in the live broadcasting room [39–41]. The content itself is one of the most critical factors of the media [42], but in the context of live e-commerce, its carrier has become the anchor. Based on this, this paper puts forward the following assumptions:

H4: Anchor's personal charm has a positive impact on digital affordance.
H5: Attractiveness of content has a positive impact on digital affordance.

Functional affordance refers to the design of modules to help users achieve specific purposes [30]. In the anchor e-commerce environment, the ultimate goal of consumers is to conduct consumer behaviour. In order to realize this behaviour, the decision-making process needs the support of all kinds of information, and the most important one is the product information. Providing product information is one of the most basic functions of live e-commerce [43–46]. Based on this, this paper puts forward the following assumptions:

H6: Product information has a positive impact on digital affordance.

A user performs cognitive, physical, and sensory actions during interaction and requires affordances to help with each [30]. Digital affordance uses information technology to provide many possibilities for elderly consumers to contact and use live e-commerce and consume in it. Based on this, this paper puts forward the following assumption:

H7: Digital affordance has a positive impact on consumption intention.

3 Research Methodology

There are two main methods to solve the structural equation model: one is the covariance structure analysis method based on maximum likelihood estimation (ML); The other is the analysis method based on partial least squares (PLS). The latter has advantages in data distribution requirements, sample size and model identification conditions and is more applicable to causal prediction structural equations. Therefore, this paper uses the PLS-SEM model to study the formation of shopping intention of the elderly in the live studio.

The scale design of the questionnaire in this paper refers to the mature scale in the relevant literature. It has been appropriately modified and adjusted according to the characteristics of live shopping. In the initial scale, except for the basic information of the respondents, other questions were measured with the 5-point Likert scale. Specifically, these questions are expressed in 1–5, one strongly disagree, and five strongly agree. After completing the initial questionnaire design, a small-scale pre-test was conducted within the target sample range. A total of 35 questionnaires were collected to check whether the semantic and grammatical expressions of the options in the questionnaire are easy to understand and whether the reliability and validity meet the requirements. Also, according to the respondents' feedback, some expressions of the questionnaire were modified, and finally, a formal questionnaire was formed.

Aiming at the research problem of "the generation of consumption intention of the elderly in live e-commerce", this paper limits the survey participants to two levels. First, the age of the participants in the questionnaire should be 50 years old and above. Secondly, based on the phenomenon of "addiction", we excluded some mild live e-commerce users. We required the questionnaire participants to have at least 5 h of short video browsing time per week.

This paper adopts the online questionnaire distribution. After screening the collected questionnaires, 198 valid questionnaires were obtained. According to the standard ten times principle of PLS-SEM, the sample size of this study is at least 70. The effective questionnaire collected in this study has far exceeded this minimum limit, which can improve accuracy.

The demographic characteristics of 198 samples are shown in Table 2. Regarding gender ratio, female respondents are slightly more than men, but the gap is small, and the distribution is relatively uniform. In terms of the age distribution of the sample, it is relatively difficult to obtain the elderly over 60 years-old data. Therefore, nearly 70% of the samples are mainly concentrated in 50–60 years old. In terms of education level, due to the objective factors of social development, the education level of the elderly is lower than the average level of the current society. However, nearly 40% of the participants still have a bachelor's degree or above.

Table 2. Demographic profile of respondents, N = 198.

Measure	Category	N	Percent
Gender	Male	86	43%
	Female	112	57%
Age	50–60	137	69%
	Over 60	61	31%
Education	College or below	122	62%
	Undergraduate	48	24%
	Postgraduate	28	14%

4   Results

4.1   Measurement Model

Reliability test includes internal consistency reliability and combination reliability. Internal consistency reliability is used to measure the consistency of multiple measurement indicators of the same concept. Its measurement indicator is the Cronbach coefficient.

If $\alpha > 0.7$, indicating that it is suitable for further research. Combination reliability reflects the consistency of internal indicators of latent variables. Its measurement index is CR (composite reliability), which is generally required to be CR > 0.7. This study α Value and CR value meet the conditions (as shown in Table 3), indicating that the data is acceptable.

The structural validity of this study is mainly evaluated by content validity, convergence validity and discriminant validity. Because the scale of this study is adjusted according to the existing literature, it has content validity. Discriminant validity is used to judge the degree of difference between latent variables. Its measurement index is the square root of the mean extracted variance (AVE) and the correlation coefficient between other latent variables. If the square root of AVE is greater than the correlation coefficient between other latent variables, it indicates that discriminant validity exists; that is, there are significant differences between variables. It can be seen from Table 4 and Table 5 that the square root of AVE in this study is greater than the correlation coefficient between this variable and other latent variables, which proves that there is good discriminant validity between variables. The AVE value measures introverted validity, generally considered AVE > 0.5. It can be seen from Table 2 that the AVE values of this study meet the conditions, and the introverted validity exists.

Table 3. Descriptive statistics for the constructs.

	Cronbach's Alpha	CR	AVE
Anchor's personal charm (APC)	0.956	0.972	0.920
Applicability of interaction (AI)	0.921	0.950	0.864
Convenience of transaction (CT)	0.919	0.948	0.860
Product information (PI)	0.925	0.952	0.870
Attractiveness of content (AC)	0.846	0.907	0.765
Digital affordance (DA)	0.919	0.961	0.925
Consumption intention (CI)	0.920	0.962	0.926
Interface design (ID)	0.974	0.983	0.950

Table 4. Correlations among constructs and the square root of the AVE.

	APC	AI	CT	PI	AC	DA	CI	ID
APC	**0.959**							
AI	−0.051	**0.930**						
CT	0.156	0.658	**0.927**					
PI	−0.383	−0.372	−0.395	**0.933**				
AC	0.297	0.784	0.569	−0.467	**0.875**			

(continued)

Table 4. (*continued*)

	APC	AI	CT	PI	AC	DA	CI	ID
DA	0.454	0.698	0.581	−0.408	0.821	**0.962**		
CI	0.470	0.696	0.549	−0.342	0.822	0.920	**0.962**	
ID	0.436	0.195	0.311	−0.643	0.452	0.439	0.394	**0.975**

Note: Bold number represent the square roots of the AVEs

Table 5. Factor loadings and cross loadings.

	API	AI	CT	PI	AC	DA	CI	ID
API.1	**0.962**	−0.062	0.151	−0.341	0.295	0.447	0.455	0.411
API.2	**0.958**	−0.036	0.160	−0.379	0.277	0.430	0.445	0.406
API.3	**0.957**	−0.049	0.136	−0.382	0.282	0.427	0.451	0.438
AI.1	−0.028	**0.931**	0.620	−0.363	0.737	0.679	0.689	0.220
AI.2	−0.063	**0.924**	0.597	−0.298	0.722	0.653	0.632	0.164
AI.3	−0.052	**0.933**	0.617	−0.377	0.727	0.610	0.617	0.156
CT.1	0.164	0.632	**0.939**	−0.402	0.564	0.551	0.540	0.329
CT.2	0.125	0.612	**0.933**	−0.326	0.537	0.582	0.533	0.294
CT.3	0.146	0.584	**0.909**	−0.376	0.477	0.473	0.445	0.234
PI.1	−0.338	−0.340	−0.360	**0.920**	−0.406	−0.329	−0.290	−0.542
PI.2	−0.401	−0.333	−0.379	**0.950**	−0.435	−0.426	−0.345	−0.649
PI.3	−0.324	−0.370	−0.366	**0.927**	−0.465	−0.375	−0.315	−0.597
AC.1	0.263	0.672	0.520	−0.386	**0.869**	0.729	0.736	0.411
AC.2	0.298	0.699	0.486	−0.435	**0.895**	0.743	0.737	0.419
AC.3	0.215	0.687	0.488	−0.406	**0.859**	0.680	0.682	0.354
DA.1	0.460	0.674	0.586	−0.414	0.810	**0.963**	0.898	0.447
DA.2	0.412	0.668	0.531	−0.369	0.768	**0.960**	0.870	0.397
CI.1	0.440	0.687	0.529	−0.305	0.807	0.903	**0.964**	0.361
CI.2	0.465	0.652	0.528	−0.353	0.775	0.867	**0.961**	0.399
ID.1	0.428	0.168	0.301	−0.624	0.419	0.424	0.370	**0.977**
ID.2	0.417	0.244	0.326	−0.649	0.476	0.461	0.418	**0.976**
ID.3	0.431	0.151	0.278	−0.605	0.423	0.395	0.360	**0.970**

Note: Bold number indicate outer loading on the assigned constructs

4.2 Structural Model

In this paper, the scaling determination coefficient obtained by the bootstrap algorithm of SmartPLS 3.3.4 software is used to test the explanatory ability of the model and reflect the explanatory degree of latent variables to endogenous variables to reflect the explanatory ability of the model. The T-test is used to verify the research hypothesis proposed in this paper, reaching the significance level $p < 0.05$. Figure 3 shows the standardized path coefficients and T values. Five of the seven hypotheses proposed in this paper passed the statistical significance test. The results show that interactive ease of use, personal anchor charm, content attraction, and product information significantly impact digital availability, and digital availability significantly impacts consumers' purchase intention. In addition, among the influencing factors of digital availability, interactive ease of use, personal anchor charm, and content attraction have the most prominent influence. In contrast, the influence of product information is slightly weaker.

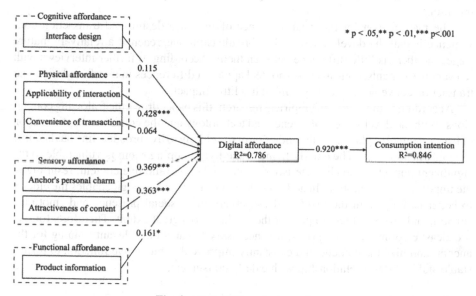

Fig. 3. PLS-SEM analysis results.

The coefficient of certainty (R^2) is the most commonly used coefficient to evaluate the structural model, which is used to evaluate the model's prediction ability. R^2 is between 1 and 0, and the higher the value, the stronger the prediction ability. Generally speaking, when R^2 is between 0.5–0.75, the interpretation ability is medium. If R^2 is higher than 0.75, it has significant explanatory power. In this study, the R^2 of digital availability reached 0.786, and the R^2 of consumption intention reached 0.846, indicating that the model proposed has excellent explanatory ability.

5   Discussion and Implication

5.1   Summary of Results

Based on the theory of digital affordance and combing the existing literature, this paper first expounds on the phenomenon and origin of the elderly participating in or even indulging in live e-commerce and points out the great possibility that the development of science and technology brings to the elderly and enterprises. Then, from the perspective of elderly consumers, combined with the affordance theory, and comprehensively considering the factors such as interface design, interactive ease of use, transaction convenience, anchor personal charm, content attraction and product information, this paper constructs the generation model of consumption intention of elderly consumers in the live broadcast situation. Through the questionnaire survey of 198 samples, the model is evaluated by PLS-SEM. The results show that the consumption intention of elderly consumers in live shopping is mainly affected by interactive ease of use, content attraction, personal anchor charm and product information. At the same time, the convenience of interface design and transaction has no significant effect on promoting their consumption intention.

The main reason for the weak influence of interface design and transaction convenience is that the development of live broadcasting has reached a relatively mature stage, and there is little difference between them. According to further interviews with relevant participants, consumers do not feel apparent differences in interface design and transaction convenience, so they think it has little impact.

According to the results of empirical research, this paper draws the following conclusions. With the development of science and technology and the continuous optimization of live e-commerce platforms, the addiction of the elderly to live broadcasting has become a social phenomenon. The elderly living in the live shopping room is vulnerable to the significant impact of the characteristics of the anchor and the live content, resulting in the impulse of consumption. In addition, the good interactive design enables the elderly to better participate in the live broadcast, obtain more social presence and emotional support, and promote them to pay for the products to a great extent. Therefore, for live broadcast e-commerce enterprises, it is necessary to carry out relevant training for the anchor, optimize the content, and constantly improve the interactive function to form a stable and long-term relationship with elderly consumers.

5.2 Implication for Theory

Aging is becoming a global trend, and the new phenomena and problems brought about by aging have attracted more and more attention. With the continuous development of technology and the continuous improvement of the overall ideology and literacy of the elderly, coupled with the limited offline life of the elderly in the post epidemic era, forcing the elderly to "touch the Internet", more and more elderly people begin to be active in the Internet world. The elderly are often more likely to indulge in the virtual world and webcast because of poor discrimination and lack of real emotional connection. Based on the theory of digital affordance and the existing literature, this paper discusses the generation mechanism of consumption intention of the elderly in live shopping through empirical research. Relevant research results have laid a foundation for understanding the behaviour of elderly consumers in live e-commerce and promoting the development of relevant theories.

The existing literature has thoroughly discussed the relevant factors affecting consumers' purchase intention and consumers' behaviour patterns in live e-commerce. There are also relevant studies on the shopping behaviour of the elderly. However, as a new phenomenon, the elderly are addicted to living e-commerce, but there is little literature attention. The research results aim to provide a new perspective for understanding the consumption behaviour of the elderly in the live e-commerce environment. In addition, this study thoroughly discusses the specific impact of various factors on the consumption behaviour of the elderly and distinguishes the differences. This will help scholars further understand the internal mechanism of the consumption intention of the elderly in the live e-commerce situation.

5.3 Implication for Practice

Live e-commerce has become a mainstream marketing method, but many problems also accompany its rapid development. In recent years, more and more social events caused by live e-commerce have attracted more and more attention. The elderly indulge in live broadcasting, blindly purchasing health care products to exhaust all their property. Place their emotions too much on a single anchor, resulting in psychological problems, indulge in live broadcasting day and night and affect their everyday life. These problems will negatively affect individuals, families and society to varying degrees. If live broadcast e-commerce enterprises want to achieve peaceful and long-term development, they are bound to participate in solving these problems. On the one hand, the research results of this paper can help enterprises better understand consumers and make corresponding improvements. On the other hand, it provides a reference for enterprises to standardize live broadcasting further and guide the elderly to use live shopping correctly.

5.4 Limitations and Future Research

This paper thoroughly discusses the generation mechanism of purchase intention of elderly consumers in live e-commerce, but there are still some limitations. Firstly, the number of samples in this paper is 198, which is higher than the minimum requirement of the structural equation model, but further expanding the sample size can improve the accuracy of evaluation. Secondly, this study is aimed at users of the platform. Tiktok can investigate the elderly consumers in different platforms in the future to discuss the impact of the differences of interface design on the generation of shopping intention of the elderly consumers. Therefore, it is necessary to conduct more in-depth research in the future.

6 Conclusion

The entry of the elderly into the e-commerce live broadcasting room not only provides new growth points for enterprises, but also brings many new problems and challenges. Enterprises should consider not only how to better serve the elderly to fully transform their potential consumption power, but also how to standardize themselves, guide the elderly to correctly participate in e-commerce live broadcasting and truly enjoy the convenience brought by the Internet. Only by training and restricting the employees and anchors in the enterprise, continuously optimizing and improving the live broadcast interface, aging design, participating in the co creation of live broadcast content and giving sufficient supervision can the enterprise truly embrace elderly consumers. Besides enterprises, the problems of the elderly also need wider social participation, so that the elderly can enjoy the convenience brought by technology without worry, which is also a necessary move for our common future.

Acknowledgments. This study is supported by grants from the Zhejiang University of Technology Humanities and Social Sciences Pre-Research Fund Project (GZ21731320013), the Zhejiang University of Technology Subject Reform Project (GZ21511320030), and China's National Undergraduate Innovation and Entrepreneurship Training Program (File No. 202110337048).

References

1. C. A. o. China (CNNIC): The 45th statistical report on the development of China's Internet. http://www.cac.gov.cn/2020-04/28/c_1589619527364495.htm. Accessed
2. Jones, N.L.: Should Social Media Censor Pseudoscience? (2018)
3. Gsenger, R.: Digital literacy and pseudoscience in crisis response. The Case of COVID-19 in Austria. In: MEi: CogSci Conference, p. 67 (2020)
4. Aupers, S., De Wildt, L.: Down the rabbit hole: heterodox science on the internet. In: Houtman, D., Aupers, S., Laermans, R. (eds.) Science under Siege. Cultural Sociology, pp. 65–87. Palgrave Macmillan, Cham (2021). https://doi.org/10.1007/978-3-030-69649-8_3
5. Chutian, W.: Analysis of the communication mode of internet rumors: taking top ten online rumors about COVID-19 epidemic in China in April as examples. In: 7th International Conference on Humanities and Social Science Research (ICHSSR 2021), pp. 784–788. Atlantis Press (2021)
6. Hameed, K., Rahman, N.: Today's social network sites: an analysis of emerging security risks and their counter measures. In: 2017 International Conference on Communication Technologies (ComTech), pp. 143–148. IEEE (2017)
7. Alben, A.: Privacy, freedom, and technology-or how did we get into this mess. Seattle UL Rev. **42**, 1043 (2018)
8. Xia, L., Lin, H., Huang, N., Li, J.: Risk analysis of college students' e-commerce live broadcast based on data in survey. J. Phys. Conf. Ser. **1774**(1), 012010. IOP Publishing (2021)
9. Wang, Z.: Analysis of the problems existing in network live broadcast. In: E3S Web of Conferences, 2020, vol. 218. EDP Sciences (2020)
10. Zadražilová, I.: Information literacy of elderly people: bridging the digital gap. In: Kurbanoğlu, S., Boustany, J., Špiranec, S., Grassian, E., Mizrachi, D., Roy, L. (eds.) ECIL 2017. CCIS, vol. 810, pp. 545–554. Springer, Cham (2018). https://doi.org/10.1007/978-3-319-74334-9_56
11. Vidal, E.: Digital literacy program: reducing the digital gap of the elderly: experiences and lessons learned. In: 2019 International Conference on Inclusive Technologies and Education (CONTIE), pp. 117–1173. IEEE (2019)
12. Jin, L.: Digital affordances on WeChat: learning Chinese as a second language. Comput. Assist. Lang. Learn. **31**(1–2), 27–52 (2018)
13. Gibson, J.J.: The theory of affordances. Hilldale USA **1**(2), 67–82 (1977)
14. Autio, E., Nambisan, S., Thomas, L.D., Wright, M.: Digital affordances, spatial affordances, and the genesis of entrepreneurial ecosystems. Strateg. Entrep. J. **12**(1), 72–95 (2018)
15. Nambisan, S.: Digital entrepreneurship: toward a digital technology perspective of entrepreneurship. Entrep. Theory Pract. **41**(6), 1029–1055 (2017)

16. Nambisan, S., Lyytinen, K., Majchrzak, A., Song, M.: Digital innovation management: reinventing innovation management research in a digital world. MIS Q. **41**(1), 223–238 (2017)
17. McCloskey, D.W.: The importance of ease of use, usefulness, and trust to online consumers: an examination of the technology acceptance model with older customers. J. Organ. End User Comput. (JOEUC) **18**(3), 47–65 (2006)
18. Chen, Y.: Usability analysis on online social networks for the elderly. Helsinki University of Thechnology (2009)
19. Sukson, C.: Factors motivating elderly to go shopping online (2018)
20. Li, S.: LAMPO. Online shopping products based on analysis of usability factors for the elderly users (2020)
21. Zhou, J., Zhou, M.: Human computer interaction design of online shopping platform for the elderly based on flow theory. In: Ahram, T., Taiar, R., Groff, F. (eds.) IHIET-AI 2021. AISC, vol. 1378, pp. 280–284. Springer, Cham (2021). https://doi.org/10.1007/978-3-030-74009-2_35
22. Eastman, J.K., Iyer, R.: The elderly's uses and attitudes towards the Internet. J. Consum. Mark. **21**(3), 208–220 (2004)
23. Iyer, R., Eastman, J.K.: The elderly and their attitudes toward the internet: the impact on internet use, purchase, and comparison shopping. J. Mark. Theory Pract. **14**(1), 57–67 (2006)
24. Kuo, H.-M., Fu, H.-H., Hsu, C.-H.: Exploring the difficulties of Internet shopping behavior between the elderly and young consumers. J. Inf. Optim. Sci. **30**(3), 447–462 (2009)
25. Aldousari, A.A., Delafrooz, N., Ab Yajid, M.S., Ahmed, Z.U.: Determinants of consumers' attitudes toward online shopping. J. Transnatl. Manag. **21**(4), 183–199 (2016)
26. He, T., Huang, C., Li, M., Zhou, Y., Li, S.: Social participation of the elderly in China: the roles of conventional media, digital access and social media engagement. Telematics Inform. **48**, 101347 (2020)
27. Sun, J., Liu, Z.: Analysis of Public Satisfaction on the Webcast in Taiyuan City, Shanxi Province (2019)
28. Sun, Y.: Research on the influence of celebrity live streaming on Chinese consumers' purchase intention. In: 2021 International Conference on Social Development and Media Communication (SDMC 2021), pp. 933–937. Atlantis Press (2022)
29. Lu, J., Xu, Z.: Can virtual tourism aid in the recovery of tourism industry in the COVID-19 pandemic? (2021)
30. Hartson, R.: Cognitive, physical, sensory, and functional affordances in interaction design. Behav. Inf. Technol. **22**(5), 315–338 (2003)
31. Najjar, L.J.: Advances in e-commerce user interface design. In: Salvendy, G., Smith, M.J. (eds.) Human Interface and the Management of Information. Interacting with Information. Human Interface 2011. LNCS, vol. 6772, pp. 292–300. Springer, Berlin, Heidelberg (2011). https://doi.org/10.1007/978-3-642-21669-5_35
32. Hunsinger, J.: Interface and Infrastructure in Social Media. In: The Social Media Handbook: Routledge, pp. 13–25 (2013)
33. Chang, J.J., Binti Zahari, N.S.H., Chew, Y.H.: The design of social media mobile application interface for the elderly. In: 2018 IEEE Conference on Open Systems (ICOS), pp. 104–108. IEEE (2018)
34. Nugraha, K.A., Sebastian, D.: Mobile social media interface design for elderly in Indonesia. In: Stephanidis, C., Antona, M., Ntoa, S. (eds.) HCI International 2020 – Late Breaking Posters. HCII 2020. CCIS, vol. 1294, pp. 79–85. Springer, Cham (2020). https://doi.org/10.1007/978-3-030-60703-6_10
35. Nou, A.A., Sjolinder, M.: Live broadcasting--the feeling of presence and social interaction. In: 2011 IEEE Third International Conference on Privacy, Security, Risk and Trust and 2011 IEEE Third International Conference on Social Computing, 2011, pp. 678–683 (IEEE)

36. Wohn, D.Y., Freeman, G., McLaughlin, C.: Explaining viewers' emotional, instrumental, and financial support provision for live streamers. In: Proceedings of the 2018 CHI Conference on Human Factors in Computing Systems, pp. 1–13 (2018)
37. Su, Q., Zhou, F., Wu, Y.J.: Using virtual gifts on live streaming platforms as a sustainable strategy to stimulate consumers' green purchase intention. Sustainability 12(9), 3783 (2020)
38. Deng, F., Wang, Y., Liang, X.: Research on the impact of Taobao live broadcasting on college students' online consumption behavior based on TAM model. In: Xu, J., Duca, G., Ahmed, S.E., García Márquez, F.P., Hajiyev, A. (eds.) ICMSEM 2020. AISC, vol. 1190, pp. 771–782. Springer, Cham (2020). https://doi.org/10.1007/978-3-030-49829-0_57
39. Al-Emadi, F.A., Ben Yahia, I.: Ordinary celebrities related criteria to harvest fame and influence on social media. J. Res. Interact. Mark. 14(2), 195–213 (2020)
40. Chen, T.Y., Yeh, T.L., Lee, F.Y.: The impact of Internet celebrity characteristics on followers' impulse purchase behavior: the mediation of attachment and parasocial interaction. J. Res. Interact. Mark. 15(3), 483–501 (2021)
41. Gerrath, M.H., Usrey, B.: The impact of influencer motives and commonness perceptions on follower reactions toward incentivized reviews. Int. J. Res. Mark. 38(3), 531–548 (2021)
42. Geng, R., Wang, S., Chen, X., Song, D., Yu, J.: Content marketing in e-commerce platforms in the internet celebrity economy. Ind. Manag. Data Syst. (2020)
43. Ho, R.C., Rajadurai, K.G.: Live streaming meets online shopping in the connected world: interactive social video in online marketplace. In: Strategies and Tools for Managing Connected Consumers: IGI Global, pp. 130–142 (2020)
44. Pang, Q., Meng, H., Fang, M., Xing, J., Yao, J.: Social distancing, health concerns, and digitally empowered consumption behavior under COVID-19: a study on Livestream shopping technology. Front. Public Health 9, 748048 (2021)
45. Li, Y.: Livestream sales: a breakthrough in the retail industry. In: ECSM 2021 8th European Conference on Social Media, Academic Conferences Inter, p. 299 (2021)
46. Wu, Q., Sang, Y., Wang, D., Lu, Z.: Malicious Selling Strategies in Livestream Shopping: A Cast Study of Alibaba's Taobao and ByteDance's Douyin, arXiv preprint arXiv:2111.10491 (2021)

A Generational Approach to Fight Fake News: In Search of Effective Media Literacy Training and Interventions

Elena-Alexandra Dumitru[1]([⊠]), Loredana Ivan[1], and Eugène Loos[2]

[1] Communication Department, National University of Political Studies and Public Administration, 012244 Bucharest, Romania
{alexandra.dumitru,loredana.ivan}@comunicare.ro
[2] Utrecht University School of Governance, 3511 ZC Utrecht, The Netherlands
e.f.loos@uu.nl

Abstract. The rise of Internet and the pervasiveness of communication and information technologies have allowed many societies to successfully reduce inequalities in access to information. However, the spread of fake news endangers the value and trustworthiness of the information being accessed. Although the dominant approach to reduce the spread of fake news includes legal measures and technological innovations (e.g., automatic fact-checking applications), Media Literacy Training and Interventions are also ways to empower people to fight fake news. The present scoping literature review examines the Media Literacy Training and Intervention options available, offering an overview of the extent to which they include an explicit fake news component, whether they are evidence based and the social groups (including different generations) for which they were tailored. We found that students and educators were the main target groups, almost wholly to the exclusion of other groups; that they took place mainly in educational settings; and that, at least in the case of the training sessions, they were not evidence based, which meant that neither the long-term nor short-term efficacy could be tested. Such findings shed light on the relatively poor reliability of the available training and interventions, and on their limited effectiveness in the target groups.

Keywords: Fake news · Media literacy training · Media literacy interventions · Generational approach · Evidence-based instruments

1 Introduction

To achieve equal opportunities in our society, access to credible information [1, 2] is of crucial importance. Fake news endangers the accessibility of information for all citizens, younger and older [3]. In this context, two compelling questions arise – how can we fight fake news and how can we do so in a more generationally inclusive manner?

One approach to fighting fake news is through legal measures that push tech platforms such as Google, Facebook and Twitter to institute self-regulatory controls. In June 2020, the EU requested these platforms to provide monthly reports

Q. Gao and J. Zhou (Eds.): HCII 2022, LNCS 13330, pp. 291–310, 2022.
https://doi.org/10.1007/978-3-031-05581-2_22

on their fight against disinformation (https://reut.rs/3o19Kg8). As part of these self-regulatory measures, Facebook and Google committed to a more stringent policing of the content that is tolerated on their platforms (https://about.fb.com/news/2020/04/covid-19-misinfo-update/, https://blog.google/outreach-initiatives/google-news-initiative/news-brief-april-2021-updates-google-news-initiative/). And Twitter stated: "As the global community faces the COVID-19 pandemic together, Twitter is helping people find reliable information, connect with others, and follow what's happening in real time (…)" (https://blog.twitter.com/en_us/topics/company/2020/covid-19#protecting). See also [4, 5].

Another initiative launched by the EU was the introduction of a code of principles: "This code of principles is for organizations that regularly publish nonpartisan reports on the accuracy of statements by public figures, major institutions, and other widely circulated claims of interest to society. It is the result of consultations among fact-checkers from around the world and offers conscientious practitioners' principles to aspire to in their everyday work" (https://ifcncodeofprinciples.poynter.org/know-more). In 2019, evaluation of this code of principles showed, on the one hand, that it had indeed triggered various positive changes in platform policies (https://ec.europa.eu/digital-single-market/en/news/study-assessment-implementation-code-practice-disinformation) (p. 3), but, on the other hand, that criticism remained: "The main criticism of the Code relates to its self-regulatory nature, lack of uniformity of implementation – evidenced by the unevenness of progress made under the specific Pillar – monitoring, and lack of clarity around its scope and some of the key concepts" (https://ec.europa.eu/digital-single-market/en/news/study-assessment-implementation-code-practice-disinformation) (p. 4). In short, the extent to which a legal approach using self-regulation and a code of principles really works to fight fake news remains unclear. See also Duke's Reporters LAB (https://reporterslab.org/fact-checking/) and the International Fact-Checking network fact-checkers' code of principles: "The International Fact-Checking Network has seven counselors who represent the geographical diversity of the network. They are pioneers in the development and implementation of fact-checking in their countries and regions. All board members are unpaid. The pool of assessors is a group of journalism and media experts who know the fact-checking context in their countries, and they act as the first filter for each application received" (https://www.poynter.org/ifcn-fact-checkers-code-of-principles). Meanwhile, Google has already started using labels to fact-check articles in Google News (https://blog.google/outreach-initiatives/google-news-initiative/labeling-fact-check-articles-google-news/), while Facebook recently introduced an oversight board (an international committee of judges, journalists and academics) that will help steer the company's policy on freedom of expression (https://www.oversightboard.com/).

Another approach is technological and uses automatic fake news detection [e.g., 6, 7]. Innovative technological detection might help to fight fake news to some extent, but it can never provide a full solution. Apart from technical feasibility - fake news will become more and more sophisticated and harder (if not impossible) to detect - there is an even more fundamental issue. Who is going to decide on the criteria for determining the trustworthiness of online information: the state, the platform companies, or the press? Giving sophisticated tools to withhold certain news from citizens could in the end threaten their information access, which eventually erodes democracy. Access to (digital) information about services and products is of prime importance [8]. Van den Hoven [9], referring to Rawls [10], goes so far as to refer to accessible information as a "primary good", as all citizens have an equal right to access to information. Research on digital inequalities shows that individuals from socially disadvantaged backgrounds are less skilled in the use of digital means which could considerably improve their lives [11]. Bovens [12] and Bovens & Loos [13] even advocate granting citizens information rights, next to the classic (freedom) rights. Fake news [14] endangers the access to information by younger and older citizens [3]. The question is how we can fight fake news, so that all generations continue to have access to credible information.

We argue that a more durable solution is to empower citizens so that they themselves are able to establish the trustworthiness of news. An educational approach using media literacy [15, 16] is an intervention that can be used in schools and in other institutions and community centers as well. Media literacy should not only focus on people's ability to use certain devices and technologies, but also on promoting a deep understanding of modern forms of media, how these work and how they produce and use news items, all of which may be attained through systematic media education programs [17]. It is not only important to investigate the feasibility of interventions at an early age to empower young citizens such that they are able to establish the trustworthiness of news. It is also essential to involve other generations as due to the paucity of studies in this field, it would be naive to assume that they are not vulnerable to fake news.

In our paper, we therefore explore the Media Literacy Training and Intervention landscape, to gain insight into how evidence based such training activities are and the extent to which they include a fake news component. We pay especial attention to the design of such training activities and to the target groups for which they have been developed. We examine whether different age groups are considered and how evidence-based the instruments are. When determining whether or not the studies were evidence-based, we examined whether scientific data was used to structure the activities and tasks. We focused on effectiveness, which we assessed based on the criterion of whether or not the studies tested for long term and short-term effects on the target groups.

First, we underline the importance of empowering citizens of different social categories to fight fake news, through the use of educational means. We then analyze the characteristics of the current Media Literacy Training and Intervention landscape, based on a systematic literature review previously conducted by Eisemann and Pimmer and complement this with a review of the types of training and interventions found in large-scale European projects and small-scale interventions.

A literature review is the starting point of our inquiry. We first present an overview of group differences relative to the vulnerability to fake news. We use Brites et al. [18] to gain insight into generational perspectives on EU Documents tackling disinformation, as well as Loos & Nijenhuis [3]. In addition, we will refer to the systematic literature review on educational approaches to address fake news conducted by Eisemann & Pimmer [19]. Furthermore, we will present evidence of fake news interventions, based on a scoping literature review of studies selected in an exploratory manner using Google Scholar, on Media Literacy Interventions designed to reduce individuals' vulnerability to fake news. Also, we will add a case study on interventions in studies referenced in the US-based Center for Media Literacy's online Reading Room and Media & Values Archive (https://www.medialit.org/how-teach-media-literacy). The results from the case study will be compared with those of the systematic literature review by Eisemann & Pimmer [19] and with the overview of the media literacy projects conducted in the EU 28 countries – The European Council report: "Mapping of media literacy practices and actions in EU-28" [20]. Finally, conclusions will be drawn about the extent to which training and interventions can be used as evidence-based methods to fight fake news in an effective and inclusive way.

2   Literature Review

The term fake news is commonly used today as a collective term to refer to any kind of inaccurate information, from journalistic errors to automated amplification techniques. Disinformation alludes, more specifically, to misleading information that is shared with the intention of causing harm or for profit, while misinformation is simply false information that is disseminated without malicious intent [21]. In this paper, we use the term fake news to refer to any kind of misleading information that could mistakenly be considered accurate, regardless of the mechanisms that led to its propagation.

2.1   A More Inclusive Perspective on Fighting Fake News

Brites et al. [18] analyzed the following five EU key documents to gain insight into the extent to which the EU addresses disinformation from a generational-driven perspective:

- European Commission. A multi-dimensional approach to disinformation: Report of the independent High Level Group on fake news and online disinformation (2018) [21]
- European Commission. Commission Recommendation of 14.2.2018 on enhancing the European nature and efficient conduct of the 2019 elections to the European Parliament. European Commission: Brussels (2018) [22]
- European Commission. EU Code of Practice on Disinformation. European Commission: Brussels (2018) (https://bit.ly/3EQRZGo)
- European Commission. Tackling online disinformation: a European Approach. European Commission, Brussels (2018) (https://bit.ly/3u8k5rD)
- European Commission. Fake News and Disinformation Online. Flash Eurobarometer 464. European Commission, Brussels (2018) (https://bit.ly/39AQtJW)

The documents all date from 2018. That was the year the EU tackled disinformation, as "for political reasons, 2018 was a strategic year to engage citizens in the democratic process anticipating EU parliament elections" [18] (p. 353).

The researchers concluded that two recurring weak generational imageries – on the one hand, adults, and on the other hand, children and young people – are created through an unspecific identification of citizens and that no significant efforts were made to identify different generational groups and their needs. The authors show that the intergenerational perspective is only mentioned in relation to lifelong learning. They explain that viewing "adulthood" as a homogeneous group, instead of recognizing the heterogeneity of the different generational groups precludes any understanding of the different generations' specific needs and their learning opportunities arising from community public policies that consider European citizens attending at the macro level and the various micro-levels [18]. Generalizing adult individuals into a generic age group without taking into consideration the specificity of their needs in their different life stages reinforces the nescience regarding fake news and the need for media literacy.

The conclusions drawn by Brites et al. [18] are in line with the findings from a study by Loos & Nijenhuis [3], who show that generational differences relating to the consumption of fake news have been virtually ignored in the edited volume Detecting fake news on social media [23], as well as in The Handbook of Research on Deception, Fake News, and Misinformation Online [24], and in the Reuters Institute digital news report 2017 [25]. They note the dearth of research in this area: "a Google Scholar search (01.02.2020) using the key words 'social media' AND 'fake news' AND 'generation' OR 'Age' OR 'young' OR 'old' also failed to return any hits for scientific papers on this topic" [3]. Closing the gap in the study of fake news and how different age groups consume fake news, the ways they experience its effects, and their media literacy needs would bring relevant insights into discussion, potentially offering a new perspective on the ways fake news could be tackled.

Media Literacy Training and Interventions, the focus of this chapter, should therefore not be limited to young people only; these activities should also be targeted at other age groups, including older adults. Moreover, they should also take into consideration the vulnerability of different ethnic and socio-cultural groups to fake news, as media content is often accessed in the native languages of these different groups – an aspect that is overlooked in the current EU initiatives to fight fake news.

2.2   Characteristics of Current Media Literacy Training and Interventions

In order to have a structured overview of the media literacy initiatives and to better understand the types and the effectiveness of the training and interventions currently being deployed, we turned to the systematic literature review recently produced by Eisemann and Pimmer [19]. These two authors screened 995 articles spanning a period of twenty years (2000–2020), obtained through a database search (ERIC, OVID Medline, APA PsycInfo and PsycARTICLES) for media literacy training and interventions. After reviewing the corpus, fourteen articles were found that met the criteria of including training or interventions that contained an explicit fake news component; were evidence based; boasted a solid methodology; and reported outcomes (the effectiveness of the intervention was checked). The authors added five more articles found on Google Scholar, ending with a final corpus of nineteen articles, three of which fell into more than one training category. Three types of training were distinguished: (1) reactive training targeted at a fact-based correction of misinformation (nine articles); (2) proactive training in a specific fake news detection method (eleven articles); and (3) training to develop a critical understanding of the media system (four articles).

In nine of the articles resulting from the systematic analysis of Eisemann and Pimmer [19], the interventions examined were of the first type, i.e. aimed at correcting existing misconceptions about what is right and what is wrong in a fact-based manner. A typical example would be the current vaccination debate and the selective views towards the media information provided about this issue. In these studies, various strategies for addressing such situations were tested, ranging from the provision of information about the lack of scientific evidence to the recital of dramatic narratives – going from strategies following the central route to strategies following the peripheral route of information processing (see [26] for describing the ELM – a two-way mode of information processing). Although some strategies were more effective than others, generally speaking their efficacy was limited and tended to fade over time. Their efficacy is, moreover, difficult to generalize beyond the specificity of the tasks and the groups in which they were used.

The second type of training and interventions distinguished by Eisemann and Pimmer [19], consisting of a proactive approach aimed at improving people's abilities to detect fake news, was found in eleven articles. We refer to this approach as explicit fake news training. It involved equipping the participants with a set of tools, ranging from guidelines and regulations to technical tools such as fact-checkers, cross-checking and inverse image search, that can serve to improve their ability to detect fake news. It also included observational guidelines, such as looking at the author's style or performing a reactive search to check the truthfulness of some content (asking questions of the author). The effectiveness of such training proved to be higher and more constant over time in comparison with the first intervention category. Nonetheless, the success of this approach should not be taken for granted. Additional factors may also play a role in reducing its efficacy, such as (1) the educational context – such training proved to be less effective in higher educational contexts; and (2) the prior attitudes of the participants: it was found that a type of confirmation bias (see [27] for an analysis of the concept) might occur, with such training being more effective if this is consistent with people's attitudes and beliefs.

The third approach identified by Eisemann and Pimmer [19], found in four articles, was directed at the development of a critical understanding of the media system, helping people to critically reflect on media content and the way such content is created and re-created. Although this category has been dominant in the scientific literature for the past 20 years (as Eisemann and Pimmer showed), it has produced limited evidence of effectiveness, features a rather inconsistent methodology and a poor research design.

Inspired by the work of Eisemann and Pimmer [19], we used Google Scholar to investigate, in an exploratory way, articles spanning the period from 2010 to 2020 on research studies that included interventions aiming to reduce people's vulnerability to fake news. The selection of articles on fake news interventions was initially triggered by the project "Fighting Fake News: A New Literacies Approach for Young People", coordinated by Eugène Loos at Utrecht University. In our project, we aimed to use a game as a form of intervention to understand how school pupils could be trained to decode fake news about climate change. We first used the search term "fake news interventions" to identify potential articles that could serve as a starting point, using Google Scholar (2010–2020). This yielded 20,000 hits, from which we then selected the review articles only (1400 hits). We focused on the contributions in which a game was used and in which the interventions targeted issues of climate change. In the next step, we selected articles which had a research component designed explicitly to improve the ability to fight fake news and included a clear description of the results. Our aim was to evaluate the value of such interventions in helping people to better detect/recognize fake news. We discarded all articles that did not report the outcome of the intervention as well as those that did not present a research methodology. Also, we selected studies with a unique methodology; of the studies employing similar methodologies on similar groups of participants (e.g., students), only one was selected. Many of the interventions were Media Literacy Interventions that did not focus on improving people's ability to avoid or detect fake news. We selected only articles in which the object of the intervention was to help people learn to detect/recognize fake news. Table 1 presents an overview of the nine articles we identified and coded using the following coding scheme: (1) country where the intervention was conducted; (2) type of intervention (large-scale or small-scale) and the intended results; (3) the target group(s); (4) methodology and (5) the effects, if any, of the intervention on the target group.

The interventions analyzed in Table 1 proposed either a gamified method [28–32], a news evaluation approach [16, 34, 35], or a combination of the two [33]. Most of the technical innovations used in the studies mentioned in Table 1 were designed for online use but could also be adapted for in-person settings at various locations specific to different social groups, from classrooms to workshop spaces. A noteworthy aspect that could have important implications for the results of this analysis is the rather less diverse localization of the studies, as the majority were conducted in the US, the UK or The Netherlands.

Roozenbeek & van der Linden [28, 29, 31] extensively researched the efficacy of specific gamified approaches to fighting fake news through online games like The Bad News Game or Harmony Square. The Bad News Game, an online game the authors created in collaboration with the Dutch media platform DROG (https://politi.co/2Y6aGFq) was the instrument on which several studies, including the only intervention identified in our online search process that studied the mid-term and long-term effectiveness of active inoculation on identifying and resisting fake news [30], were based. The results of this research showed that inoculation interventions using The Bad News Game or similar instruments helped against misinformation over time, with regular assessment having a positive impact on the longevity of the effect. Other inoculation interventions used gamified methods [31, 32] and had results that suggested that this type of educational activity could be feasible in equipping people with cognitive assets for withstanding fake news.

The news evaluation approaches summarized in Table 1 were effective in proving the urgent need for instruments to support individuals in distinguishing between real news and disinformation and were, with one exception, evidence based. However, the studies did not test the effectiveness of the interventions in consolidating fake news resistance. The studies exclusively included younger participants, from school children to college undergraduates and were mainly focused on the importance of media literacy in students at different educational stages.

Another study [33] proposed a method that combined the two approaches. Factitious is an online game that requires participants to assess various types of news and indicate which of the items they consider to be unreliable. Similar in structure to Tinder, a popular dating app, Factitious presents news evaluation in an interactive manner. The study was

Table 1. Overview of research studies which included interventions to empower people to fight fake news

Authors	Country	Type of intervention/intended results	Target Group(s)	Methodology	Effects on the target group
Roozenbeek & van der Linden (2019a) [28]	UK	Large-scale evaluation of *The Bad News Game*	N = 15.000 Age groups: under 18, 19–29, 30–49, 50+	Evaluation of the game in a pre-post game design. Players learn about six fake news techniques: impersonation, emotional language, polarization, conspiracy theories, discrediting opponents, trolling	The results offer positive initial evidence about people's ability to identify fake news regardless of education, age, political ideology, or cognitive style
Roozenbeek & van der Linden (2019b) [29]	The Netherlands	Pilot intervention seeking to test the effectiveness of *The Bad News Game* in improving students' ability to recognize and resist fake news	N = 95 16- to 19-year-olds	Players were placed in groups and were asked to produce a news article impersonating one of four characters – the denier, the alarmist, the clickbait monger, or the conspiracy theorist. The group choosing the most correct answers won	The results suggest that the inoculation used in the study reduced the perceived reliability of fake news articles
Maertens, Roozenbeek, Basol & van der Linden (2020) [30]	UK	Intervention testing the long-term effectiveness of active inoculation in building resistance to disinformation	N = 515 19–66	Participants played either Bad News (inoculation group) or Tetris (gamified control group) and rated the reliability of news headlines that did or did not use a disinformation technique. The experiment took place again after four weeks and after eight weeks	The results suggested that regular exposure to weakened doses of fake news could reinstate the inoculation effect, and that the inoculation effect decays over the course of two months

(*continued*)

Table 1. (*continued*)

Authors	Country	Type of intervention/intended results	Target Group(s)	Methodology	Effects on the target group
Roozenbeek & van der Linden (2020) [31]	US & International	Intervention using the *Harmony Square* with the purpose of probing the game's effects on students' media literacy skills	N = 681 41,4% 18- to 24- year-olds	2 (treatment vs. control) × 2 (pre vs. post) mixed design measuring perceived reliability of disinformation social media posts before and after the intervention. The treatment group played Harmony Square, while the control group played Tetris for 10 min	The results show that people playing the *Harmony Square* game find fake news less reliable and are more confident in their fake news assessment skills
Chang et al. (2020) [32]	US	Evaluation of the *Lamboozled!* -card game's efficiency in enhancing students' news literacy skills	N = 76 middle school and high school students and N = 11 teachers	Players took part in *Lamboozled!*, where they tried to acquire the best hand of cards, each of which contained clues about the veracity of a specific story. After the game, the students created their own cards about a fake and a true story and offered feedback about the game. The authors interviewed 11 teachers after they implemented the game in the classroom	The authors found the game to be effective in practicing media literacy skills and transfer media literacy strategies to real life contexts. The efficiency was shown to depend on the teachers' level of preparation

(*continued*)

Table 1. (*continued*)

Authors	Country	Type of intervention/intended results	Target Group(s)	Methodology	Effects on the target group
Grace & Hone (2019) [33]	N/A	Study investigating the utility of the *Factitious* game in measuring news literacy skills	N = 45.000 All ages	Large-scale online study. Participants played *Factitious*, an online game where they evaluated several news stories, then swiped to the right if they thought the story was real or to the left if they perceived the story as fake. Answers were scored depending on correctness	Findings indicate that older participants generally outperformed younger participants. Younger participants tended to make their decision faster, people with higher education levels (PhD) completed the game in less time
Bråten & Strømsø (2010) [34]	Norway	Intervention examining students' understanding of texts in different task conditions	N = 184 Mean age: 22.6 years old	Participants read seven texts about climate change in three task conditions: argument, summary, and global understanding. Tests and measures used in the study were: word decoding test, prior knowledge measure, personal epistemology measure, and measure of multiple-text understanding	Intervention findings suggest that students' prior beliefs and the task instructions matter in their text understanding abilities
Loos, Ivan & Leu (2018) [16]	The Netherlands	Intervention examining schoolchildren's ability to identify a hoax website as being fake	N = 27 11–12 years old	The participants accessed a hoax website and completed a questionnaire. Those willing to sign a petition to save the animal presented by the site were considered to trust the source. A new media literacies training and a debriefing followed	Only 2 of the 27 (4%) schoolchildren recognized the source as being a hoax and explained why

(*continued*)

Table 1. (*continued*)

Authors	Country	Type of intervention/intended results	Target Group(s)	Methodology	Effects on the target group
McGrew, Ortega, Breakstone & Wineburg (2017) [35]	US	Intervention testing students' ability to distinguish between reliable sources and disinformation sources	N = 7.804 Middle and high school students	The authors administered 56 tasks to students, measuring participants' ability to (1) identify the real source of the information presented (2) evaluate the evidence presented, and (3) investigate other sources on the subject	Close to 70% of the high school students failed to identify the unreliable news pieces. They proved to be attracted by interesting visuals when assessing the material

not evidence based; the authors sought to identify a news literacy improvement tool and did not test the effectiveness of the game. Nevertheless, we consider the intervention to be relevant, as it could be a useful method to fight fake news, mainly because of its simple play instructions that could be easily understood by individuals of all ages.

Only a few of the studies that touched on the efficacy of interventions in building fake news recognition [28, 30, 33] also included different age groups in their research (19–66; under 18 to 50+; 0–9 to 70–79 and over 79). However, these were large-scale studies that concentrated on presenting extensive results, and not necessarily on approaching the subject from a generational perspective.

In line with the findings of similar studies, the effectiveness of gamified inoculation interventions appears encouraging [19, 36]. These interventions offer the potential to become valuable instruments in fighting fake news, and the majority are evidence-based. Moreover, some of the game-based studies discussed included multiple age groups in their research [28, 30, 33], with one study even suggesting that older adults were better than younger participants at identifying fake news [33]. Such a gamification approach could form the starting point for future studies to identify or formulate tools to help build resistance to fake news.

3 Large-Scale Projects and Small-Scale Interventions

The European Council Report "Mapping of media literacy practices and actions in EU-28" [20] offers an overview of some of the most significant media literacy projects undertaken at the national or regional level between 2010 and 2016 in all 28 member states of the EU. The report is part of the European Audiovisual Observatory (EAO). Data were collected retrospectively, in April 2016, using a questionnaire which was addressed to experts in each of the 28 EU member states. The experts were asked to list 20 media literacy projects in their countries and to provide an overview of the five most significant of these projects. The responses were then double-checked with the

EU Media Literacy Expert Group (MLEG) to increase the validity of the data. In this particular report, the following details of each project were recorded: (1) the stakeholders; (2) type of engagement of each stakeholder (i.e., academia, public institutions, media regulatory authorities); (3) type of project; (4) type of media literacy aimed for; (5) the magnitude of the project and its duration; (6) the significance of each project. The latter - the significance of each project - is particularly relevant for the present article. Significance was described as: the size of the target group; the total budget; success in terms of outcomes; the level of public awareness of the project, and the level of engagement of the targeted groups. Note that the report did not check whether the Media Literacy Interventions were evidence based, nor did it verify the effectiveness of these interventions (in terms of measured effect on the target groups).

The above-mentioned European Council Report [20] gathered data on 547 projects, spanning a period of six years, on media literacy at the EU level. The majority of these projects (409) were national projects; 95 were regional and 43 projects targeted all the countries in the EU zone.

None of the projects in the report included a specific, clearly-stated component designed to reduce people's vulnerability to fake news. Also, most of the projects fell into the categories of "Resources" and "End-user engagement", which meant they were intended to equip people with the media skills and competencies they need in daily life and to teach them how to engage more with different media. None of the projects described as "Policy Development" featured a component on defusing fake news or enabling people to recognize and avoid fake media content. Instead, the "Policy Development" projects aimed more to increase cooperation between different stakeholders or countries.

Some of these projects were labeled as research projects by the experts involved (78) – meaning that they were qualitative or quantitative research projects that explored on an aspect of media literacy that had previously been investigated in the scientific literature. Among the 78 projects, 20 were considered significant enough to be extensively analyzed in the report. Only one Swedish project (https://www.niemanlab.org/2014/12/in-sweden-traditional-tabloid-rivals-are-taking-their-battle-to-viral-sites/) had an explicit fake news component. The Viral Eye project (Viralgranskaren), which won an award in 2014 in Sweden for its contribution to journalism, aimed to help Swedish journalists to detect fake news and to raise their awareness of what can happen when distributing different types of content through social media (for example, sharing a link). Although targeted at journalists - the project examined how some unreliable stories go viral and how important it is for journalists to be critical of their information sources - it eventually percolated through to a larger audience than media professionals alone. The project itself was an initiative of a newspaper (Metro publisher) and to our knowledge it was never replicated in other countries. This is in line with the conclusion of the European Council Report, which noted that many of the media literacy projects undertaken at the EU level were relatively small-scale (mainly national or regional), one-off initiatives with little impact and no long-term vision.

Many of the projects that ran at the EU level aimed to develop the critical thinking skills of the target groups to improve media literacy, while others sought to promote the capability to master different media, including the ability to develop creative media content. Little attention was paid to the risks and vulnerabilities confronting people on being exposed to content in various media formats.

In terms of the target groups, the EU projects on media literacy were mainly directed at teenagers and students (81 projects) and professionals (76 projects). Other targeted audiences were parents (41 projects) and children (51 projects). Some 34 projects were addressed at the general public, while seven of the 409 projects analyzed in the report focused on older adults, all in the 5 European countries of Belgium, Estonia, Greece, Luxembourg, and Spain. Older people appear indeed to have been a neglected category in media literacy projects (at least in the period 2010–2016), and were perceived to be the less media savvy and less skilled group in critically analyzing media content.

What is probably even more important when analyzing the magnitude of these projects at the EU level is their relatively small scale. The total budget for the majority of the initiatives presented in the report was between €10,000 and €20,000, implying these were relatively limited in scope and activities.

Taking this report as our starting point, we then investigated the articles on small-scale training courses and interventions available in the US-based Center for Media Literacy's online Reading Room and Media & Values Archive (https://www.medialit.org/how-teach-media-literacy). We located a total of 54 articles and reports at the Center for Media Literacy. These were subsequently analyzed and the items with an educational training design aimed at improving media literacy, were selected. Unavailable online pages and articles approaching media literacy from a theoretical point of view, as well as articles explaining the design of the intervention without applying this or with an unclear design were excluded, resulting in six relevant educational items that are further analyzed in the present paper.

Table 2. Overview of Media Literacy Training and Interventions from the Center for Media Literacy (https://www.medialit.org/how-teach-media-literacy)

Authors	Topic/Country	Type of training/intended results	Target groups	Methodology	Evidence based
Anderson (2005) [37]	Food advertisements/US	Three-week pilot media literacy/nutrition program/improve media literacy	N = 19 Middle-schoolers	Learning experience was tested using role play (experimental/vs control group)	Yes
Tripp (2017) [38]	Education/US & Canada	Practical ideas for the classroom/ **improve media literacy**	Teachers, graduates/specialists	Video presentations, discussions, and role-playing (theory driven)	No
Tripp (2000) [39]	Education/US& Japan	Practical ideas to be used in the teaching activities/ **improve media literacy**	N = 15 Teachers (all grades)	Presentations, lively discussions, role-playing activities and brainstorming sessions)	No

(*continued*)

Table 2. (*continued*)

Authors	Topic/Country	Type of training/intended results	Target groups	Methodology	Evidence based
Tripp (n.a) [40]	Education/ US & Japan	Experience how media literacy supports learning skills in class/**improve media literacy**	Teachers (primary and secondary school)	Analysing movie ads – discussing how women appearing as less defined, highly sexualized and subordinate to men	No
Hobbs (1996) [41]	Education/US	Teachers using small-scale interventions in class/ **raise the awareness of the ways ads and media use emotions to reach a certain audience**	Teachers (primary and secondary school)	Examples and discussion/ experiential learning	No
Phillips (2012) [42]	Media, ads, politics/US	Four classroom activities that could help students become savvy media consumers/**critical views on media content**	Students	Experiential learning & debates	No

When analyzing types of training and interventions on media literacy (ML), using those referenced by the Center for Media Literacy (https://www.medialit.org/how-teach-media-literacy) as typical examples, we identified a number of aspects of these training courses that called for further discussion. First, as Table 2 shows, all of these interventions are in English, with no thought for the possible needs of different ethnic groups. Indeed, the Center for Media Literacy is located in the US, mainly targeting the audience in the US. Nonetheless, many cultural groups (also those living in the US) are exposed to media information in their native language and consequently susceptible to fake news.

Second, although some of these training courses and interventions touched on the risks of exposure to media messages, they did not explicitly address the actual problem of fake news, i.e., the inability to recognize misinformation and non-reliable sources of information. The goal of these initiatives was not to teach people to check the trustworthiness of media information or to doubt the accuracy of the messages distributed by various types of media. Nor was the term "fake news" used as such, either in the presentation of the trainings or in the description of the sessions or the results.

Third, the training courses we analyzed were not evidence based. Except for one course, scientific data on media literacy and media literacy components [e.g., 43, 44] played no part in these initiatives. Instead, these tended to be more experiential in nature, with participants learning by doing while reflecting on the experience itself. Most of the training courses and interventions consisted of interactive tasks, such as role-playing, projective activities (in which people have to imagine certain situations), brainstorming sessions and debates. Others were more mixed, combining classic presentations and examples (including video materials) with more interactive tasks when critically analyzing media content.

Fourth, the main targets were usually students at different levels of education, and teachers. Not only did these training courses and interventions not tackle the issue of fake news, but they tended to remain a rather isolated learning experience, associated with the process of learning in schools. But the fake news phenomenon does not affect only people enrolled in the formal education; it affects people from different generations and socio-economic backgrounds. It is true that such initiatives start from the assumption that by improving our media literacy, we will be more critical of the media content we are exposed to and, consequently we will be better equipped to fight fake news. However, this is hard to do if the sessions are not targeted at a large audience or the general public and are not evidence based.

Last but not the least, the training initiatives and interventions in the articles we analyzed did not follow a particular methodology, nor were the results evaluated. In only one case [37] (see Table 1) was the starting point scientific evidence and had the effectiveness of the training been tested using an experimental design. This was done by comparing individuals who had taken part in the training session (the experimental group) with a control group who had not participated in the training session. We strongly endorse the practice of testing the efficiency of Media Literacy Training in general and of sessions dedicated to fake news, in particular. However, it is a practice that remains rarely encountered.

The analysis conducted by Eisemann and Pimmer [19] indicated that proactive training and interventions aimed at improving the ability to detect fake news have the greatest effect. They are also the most prevalent type of interventions found in the scientific literature to fight fake news. Still, in practice, as our examples from the Center for Media Literacy show, many of these courses did not fall into this category; they were neither based on scientific evidence nor was their effectiveness checked by assessing the results. Also, one thing that needs to be considered is the fact that the analysis of Eisemann and Pimmer [19] turned up only a relatively small number of articles from the past twenty years (19 out of 955 screened articles), all based on evidence produced in educational settings, using students as participants. We found similar results in our literature review search (10 articles on interventions to empower people to fight fake news, over the past 10 years – using Google Scholar as a searching platform). We took note of the fact that Eisemann and Pimmer [19] showed that a higher educational context could be a variable that impacts the efficiency of such interventions. Also, a serious limitation of this type of training and interventions might well be the fact that their audience tends to be a homogeneous one (often school children and students). The possibility of more diverse groups of people should be considered, as the effectiveness of these interventions may differ among different social groups.

4   Conclusions

When we embarked on this study, we sought to answer two questions: how to fight fake news and how to do this in a more generationally inclusive manner?

In the fight against fake news, the strategies employed to strengthen resistance to such news commonly include technical innovations such as fact-checking apps. However, more consideration should be given to educational approaches using training courses and interventions that empower people to distinguish between what is reliable media content and what is not. Such an approach might be more generally accessible to a larger audience and could be tailored for groups with various levels of media skills.

Yet many of the training programs and interventions described in the research conducted over the past ten years still favor the technical approach. Studies incorporating a clear fake news intervention are scarce. Instead, the majority of studies that included interventions to increase the ability to fight fake news were far more focused on enhancing the critical thinking skills of individuals exposed to various types of media content.

When searching for initiatives that fight fake news in a more generationally inclusive manner, we found that the majority of the research studies, but also small-scale and large-scale initiatives in the media literacy (training and interventions) targeted younger participants, mainly students at different educational stages. Some targeted professionals, such as educators and journalists. It is important for researchers and practitioners to consider a more inclusive audience for training and interventions of this kind consisting of different socio and cultural groups: people from different generations, with different socio-economic and cultural background. In many cases, access to media content is facilitated by other languages than the official language of a country, an aspect that has hitherto been wholly disregarded in the current initiatives.

Moreover, the majority of the studies in which news evaluation interventions or training were included took place in a formal environment – usually a classroom. This setting excludes individuals who are not part of the formal education system but could also potentially bias the participants through the authority of the space and/or the teachers present [45, 46], thus influencing the results of studies scrutinizing individuals' reactions to certain fake news related tasks or situations.

Most of the interventions, regardless of their specificity, only measured the short-term effectiveness of the instrument they proposed, but they generally report positive results. However, the training courses analyzed in this study for the most part failed to evaluate the results. Furthermore, with little exception, the trainings were not evidence based. An interesting, evidence-based approach was seen in several of the gamified intervention studies. This could arguably be a more inclusive, pressure free, but relevant method for supporting individuals in fighting fake news.

Probably the most important finding is the lack of continuity of most of the training courses and interventions discussed in this manuscript: many were too small to influence the target group in a significant way and the level of replication or cross-cultural collaboration is low. Interventions and training to empower people to fight fake news that have only small budgets and are organized more like one-off events lack long-term efficacy. Even interventions aiming to develop critical thinking skills in individuals exposed to media content lack long-time perspective and continuity. This was evident, not only in the small-scale initiatives in the articles at the Media Literacy Center (here considered as a typical case), but also in the European projects on Media Literacy conducted in the EU-28 countries [20].

5   Limitations

When referring to the current study, several limitations should be kept in mind. First, it is not claimed to be an exhaustive analysis, but an exploration of existing Media Literacy Interventions and Training initiatives, with a focus on interventions featuring a gamification component. Also, as we looked particularly at interventions in which climate change issues were taken as the starting point, our conclusions may not simply be generalized to other types of training. Still, we have no reason to believe that the patterns we have identified in the current manuscript are necessarily different from the types of training used to address other issues. In fact, the systematic literature review by Eisemann and Pimmer, discussed extensively here, appears to indicate as much. Hence, there could be more than a few studies that fall within the scope of this paper, but were not included, even though their findings could be relevant. Also, as we focused mainly on interventions with a gamification component, this limited our conclusions on other types of interventions (e.g., fact-checking interventions). Using Google Scholar to search for articles that discuss interventions and training in the field of fake news might have introduced some limitations regarding the articles we found, as the output of a Google Scholar search process is dependent on the search history of a particular device. However, the current research is exploratory in nature. It provides an overview of the way interventions and training incorporating an explicit fake news component are approached in the literature. For such purposes, Google Scholar is useful as it aggregates the data from different scientific databases. Second, most of the studies we discussed were conducted in the US, the UK and The Netherlands, thus the rather limited localization of the papers could possibly affect the results of the analysis. Third, the studies suggested as potentially efficient educational instruments for fighting fake news have their own limitations that should be considered when trying to replicate them, or when integrating the instruments they propose into education curriculums.

6   Implications for Future Research

Future studies could take note of the instruments analyzed in this paper and test their effectiveness in various educational environments, while also including different age groups in their research (e.g., https://www.stopcoronafakenews.com/toolkit/, http://smart-toolkit.eu/). An interesting perspective in fighting fake news could be gamification, as shown by some of the discussed studies. Gamification might offer a useful option for instruments used in interventions with participants of various ages, especially since the relaxed, less formal format of the method could possibly help in potential polemic contexts, for example when addressing political subjects. Future studies might also undertake to compare the effectiveness of the different types of available training [37–42] and interventions [28–35]. Finally, we recommend that future studies focus on an evidence-based approach, and that they adopt a longitudinal approach to measure whether the training and interventions deployed retain their effectiveness after a certain period of time.

References

1. Flanagin, A.J., Metzger, M.J.: The role of site features, user attributes, and information verification behaviors on the perceived credibility of web-based information. New Media Soc. **9**(2), 319–342 (2007). https://doi.org/10.1177/1461444807075015
2. Metzger, M.J., Flanagin, A.J., Medders, R.B.: Social and heuristic approaches to credibility evaluation online. J. Commun. **60**(3), 413–439 (2010). https://doi.org/10.1111/j.1460-2466.2010.01488.x
3. Loos, E., Nijenhuis, J.: Consuming fake news: a matter of age? The perception of political fake news stories in Facebook ads. In: Gao, Q., Zhou, J. (eds.) HCII 2020. LNCS, vol. 12209, pp. 69–88. Springer, Cham (2020). https://doi.org/10.1007/978-3-030-50232-4_6
4. Singh, L., et al.: A first look at COVID-19 information and misinformation sharing on Twitter. Arxiv (2020). https://arxiv.org/pdf/2003.13907.pdf
5. Rodríguez, C.P., Carballido, B.V., Redondo-Sama, G., Guo, M., Ramis, M., Flecha, R.: False news around COVID-19 circulated less on Sina Weibo than on Twitter. How to overcome false information? RIMCIS **9**(2), 107–128 (2020). https://doi.org/10.17583/rimcis.2020.5386
6. Conroy, N.K., Rubin, V.L., Chen, Y.: Automatic deception detection: methods for finding fake news. Proc. Assoc. Inf. Sci. Technol. **52**(1), 1–4 (2015). https://doi.org/10.1002/pra2.2015.145052010082
7. Zhou, X., Zafarani, R., Shu, K., Liu, H.: Fake news: fundamental theories, detection strategies and challenges. In: Proceedings of the twelfth ACM international conference on web search and data mining, Melbourne, Australia, 11–15 February 2019, Association for Computing Machinery: New York, United States, pp. 836–837 (2019). https://doi.org/10.1145/3289600.3291382
8. De Jong, J., Rizvi, G.: The State of Access: Success and Failure of Democracies to Create Equal Opportunities. Brookings Institution Press, Washington, D.C. (2008)
9. Van den Hoven, M.J.: Towards Ethical Principles for Designing Politico-Administrative Information Systems. In: Weckert, J. (eds.) Computer Ethics, 1st ed. Routledge, London, England, pp. 193–213 (2017). https://doi.org/10.4324/9781315259697
10. Rawls, J.: A Theory of Justice. Belknap Press and Harvard University Press, Cambridge, United States (1971)
11. Hargittai, E., Dobransky, K.: Old dogs, new clicks: digital inequality in skills and uses among older adults. Can. J. Commun. **42**(2), 195–212 (2017)
12. Bovens, M.A.P.: Information rights. Citizenship in the information society. J. Polit. Philos. **10**(3), 317–341 (2002). https://doi.org/10.1111/1467-9760.00155
13. Bovens, M.A.P., Loos, E.F.: The digital constitutional state: democracy and law in the information society. Inf. Polity **7**(4), 185–197 (2002). https://doi.org/10.3233/IP-2002-0017
14. Tandoc, E.C., Jr., Ling, R., Westlund, O., Duffy, A., Goh, D., Zheng Wei, L.: Audiences' acts of authentication in the age of fake news: a conceptual framework. New Media Soc. **20**(8), 2745–2763 (2018). https://doi.org/10.1177/1461444817731756
15. Leu. D.J., Kinzer, C.K., Coiro, J., Cammack, D.: Towards a theory of new literacies emerging from the Internet and other ICT. In: Ruddell, R.B., Unrau, N. (eds.) Theoretical Models and Processes of Reading, pp. 1570–1613, 5th ed. International Reading Association, Newark, USA (2004)
16. Loos, E., Ivan, L., Leu, D.: Save the pacific northwest tree octopus: a hoax revisited. Or: how vulnerable are school children to fake news? Inf. Learn. Sci. **119**(9–10), 514–528 (2018). https://doi.org/10.1108/ILS-04-2018-0031
17. Buckingham, D.: The Media Education Manifesto. Polity Press, Cambridge, UK (2019)
18. Brites, M.J., Amaral, I., Simões, R.B., Santos, S.J.: Generational perspectives on EU documents tackling disinformation. In: Gao, Q., Zhou, J. (eds.) HCII 2021. LNCS, vol. 12786, pp. 349–360. Springer, Cham (2021). https://doi.org/10.1007/978-3-030-78108-8_26

19. Eisemann, C., Pimmer, C.: Educational approaches to address fake news–preliminary insights from a systematic review. In: Proceedings of the CELDA 2020: 17th International Conference on Cognition and Exploratory Learning in Digital Age. Lisbon, Portugal, 18–20 November 2020

20. Insights, M., Chapman, M.: Mapping of media literacy practices and actions in EU-28, European Audiovisual Observatory and Council of Europe (2016). https://ketlib.lib.unipi.gr/xmlui/handle/ket/1185

21. De Cock Buning, M.: A multi-dimensional approach to disinformation: Report of the independent High level Group on fake news and online disinformation, Publications Office of the European Union, Luxembourg (2018).https://doi.org/10.2759/739290

22. European Commission: Fake News and Disinformation Online. Flash Eurobarometer 464, European Commission, Brussels, Belgium (2018). https://doi.org/10.2759/559993

23. Shu, K., Liu, H.: Detecting fake news on social media. Morgan & Claypool, Williston United States (2019).https://doi.org/10.2200/S00926ED1V01Y201906DMK018

24. Chiluwa, I.E., Samoilenko, S.A.: Handbook of Research on Deception, Fake News, and Misinformation Online. IGI Global (2019). https://psycnet.apa.org/doi/10.4018/978-1-5225-8535-0

25. Newman, N., Fletcher, R., Kalogeropoulos, A., Levy, D., Nielsen, R.K.: Reuters Institute digital news report (2017). https://ssrn.com/abstract=3026082

26. Cacioppo, J.T., Petty, R.E.: The elaboration likelihood model of persuasion. NA–Adv. Consum. Res. **19**(11), 673–675 (1984)

27. Nickerson, R.S.: Confirmation bias: a ubiquitous phenomenon in many guises. Rev. Gen. Psychol. **2**(2), 175–220 (1998). https://doi.org/10.1037/1089-2680.2.2.175

28. Roozenbeek, J., van der Linden, S.: Fake news game confers psychological resistance against online misinformation. Palgrave Commun. **5**(1), 1–10 (2019). https://doi.org/10.1057/s41599-019-0279-9

29. Roozenbeek, J., van Der Linden, S.: The fake news game: actively inoculating against the risk of misinformation. J. Risk Res. **22**(5), 570–580 (2019). https://doi.org/10.1080/13669877.2018.1443491

30. Maertens, R., Roozenbeek, J., Basol, M., van der Linden, S.: Long-term effectiveness of inoculation against misinformation: three longitudinal experiments. J. Exp. Psychol. Appl. **27**(1), 1–16 (2020). https://doi.org/10.1037/xap0000315

31. Roozenbeek, J., Van der Linden, S.: Breaking harmony square: a game that inoculates against political misinformation. HKS Misinf. Rev. **1**(8) (2020). https://doi.org/10.37016/mr-2020-47

32. Chang, Y.K., et al.: News literacy education in a polarized political climate: how games can teach youth to spot misinformation. HKS Misinf. Rev. (2020). https://doi.org/10.37016/mr-2020-020

33. Grace, L., Hone, B.: Factitious: large scale computer game to fight fake news and improve news literacy. In: Extended Abstracts of the 2019 CHI Conference on Human Factors in Computing Systems, Glasgow, United Kingdom, 4–9 May 2019, pp. 1–8. Association for Computing Machinery, New York, United States (2019). https://doi.org/10.1145/3290607.3299046

34. Bråten, I., Strømsø, H.I.: Effects of task instruction and personal epistemology on the understanding of multiple texts about climate change. Discourse Process. **47**(1), 1–31 (2010). https://doi.org/10.1080/01638530902959646

35. McGrew, S., Ortega, T., Breakstone, J., Wineburg, S.: The challenge that's bigger than fake news: civic reasoning in a social media environment. Am. Educ. **41**(3), 4–9 (2017). https://files.eric.ed.gov/fulltext/EJ1156387.pdf. Accessed 14 Apr 2021

36. van Helvoort, J., Hermans, M.: Effectiveness of educational approaches to elementary school pupils (11 Or 12 Years Old) to combat fake news. Media Lit. Acad. Res. **3**(2), 38–47 (2020). https://bit.ly/3m2Eo6m. Accessed 18 May 2021

37. Anderson, K.: CML Pilots Media Literacy Unit for Obesity, Nutrition Education. Center for Media Literacy (2005). https://bit.ly/2ZvTQQI. Accessed 14 Sep 2021
38. Tripp, A.: Workshop report: How to do Assessment and Evaluation in Media Literacy. Center for Media Literacy (2017). https://bit.ly/3COTQd3. Accessed 14 Sep 2021
39. Tripp, A.: Workshop report: Integrating Media Literacy across the curriculum. Center for Media Literacy (2000). https://bit.ly/3m0MkFb. Accessed 14 Sep 2021
40. Tripp, A.: Summer seminars take on hot topics in media literacy. Center for Media Literacy (n.a). https://bit.ly/3i6ZMpH. Accessed 14 Sep 2021
41. Hobbs, R.: Teaching media literacy. In: Dennis, E., Pease, E. (eds.) Children and the media, pp. 103–111. Transaction Press, New Brunswick, United States (1996). https://bit.ly/3i1ltr1. Accessed 14 Sep 2021
42. Phillips, M.: It's Not a Pipe: Teaching Kids to Read the Media. Edutopia (2012). https://edut.to/3zySFwc. Accessed 14 Sep 2021
43. Meyrowitz, J.: Multiple media literacies. J. Commun. **48**(1), 96–108 (1998). https://doi.org/10.1111/j.1460-2466.1998.tb02740.x
44. Potter, W.J.: Media Literacy, 9th edn. Sage Publications, London, England (2018)
45. Ivan, L., Frunzaru, V.: The use of ICT in students' learning activities. J. Media Res. **7**(1/2), 3–15 (2014)
46. Dumitru, E.A.: Testing children and adolescents' ability to identify fake news: a combined design of quasi-experiment and group discussions. Societies **10**(3), 71 (2020). https://doi.org/10.3390/soc10030071

Missing Voices and Gendered Ageism –Patterns of Invisibility in Global News Media

Maria Edström(✉) (iD)

Department of Journalism, Media and Communication,
University of Gothenburg, Gothenburg, Sweden
`maria.edstrom@gu.se`

Abstract. News media has an agenda-setting function in society and has an important role for democracy. Earlier research has indicated that there is a male bias in the news. This paper suggest that there is also a global pattern of age bias in the news. Using data from the sixth Global Media Monitoring Project (GMMP) from 2020 that covers news from 116 countries, patterns on gendered invisibility and ageism is revealed, creating a symbolic annihilation of voices and perspectives.

The data collected from newspapers over the world indicate a clear imbalance in terms of visibility. Men dominate all adult age groups in the news. Children are rarely seen in the news, with girls are slightly more visible than boys. Teenagers are slightly more visible and have a gendered balance. Men in the ages 50–64 years are most likely to be in the news. Men keep the media attention even after retirement ages, but when passing 80 years, men and women are more or less invisible, but still with a male dominance. The global trend over time in newspapers is that women above 50 years has become more invisible. This indicates that news media contributes to gendered ageism.

Keywords: Gendered ageism · Global news · Journalism. Global Media Monitoring project (GMMP)

1 News, Gender and Age

1.1 The Agenda-Setting Function of the News Media

News media has an agenda-setting function in society and they contribute to shape our ideas and opinions on different topics (Weaver 2007). Through the media, we understand the world. Journalists in news media scrutinize power, spotlight events, inform the citizen and give voice to individuals as well as different group interests, which means that news media plays important role for democracy.

If you are *not* part of the media narratives, you become more or less invisible in society. Therefore, the symbolic power of the media is a key concern for many researchers. Media scholar Nick Couldry claims that we have a growing crisis of voice across political, economic and cultural domains (Couldry 2010, 2019). This is not just an issue for the individual. Social representation is considered to be an important part of democracy,

Q. Gao and J. Zhou (Eds.): HCII 2022, LNCS 13330, pp. 311–320, 2022.
https://doi.org/10.1007/978-3-031-05581-2_23

especially in the political sphere. The representation and presence of various age groups in the news media can therefore be seen as a proxy for their communication rights and political rights (Bergström and Edström 2022). In the late 1970-ies the sociologist Gaye Tuchman talked about a symbolic annihilation of women in the news (Tuchman 1978). This paper will argue that there is an ongoing symbolic annihilation of women's voices and perspectives in all age groups.

1.2 Ageing and Ageism

When talking about age, it is important to remember that age can mean many things, depending on the situation and conversation. This paper focus on years lived, the chronological age, understanding that social, biological or other age concepts are equally important. However, the chronological age is what most quantitative data is based on, and that is the pre-conditions for the studies mentioned here. The broad patterns of age representation in the news will be discussed, with a focus on the older age groups.

Globally, the population aged 65 and above is growing faster than all other age groups in society. The improved longevity is experienced in all regions and the concern for the growing aging populations is captured by the United Nations slogan 'leave no one behind' as a guiding light for Sustainable development goals (United Nations 2015). According to World Health Organization, WHO, there are more than 1 billion people aged 60 years or older, with most living in low- and middle-income countries (WHO 2021). Older people now have better lives both in terms of biological health (lung capacity, balance, etc.) and in terms of life satisfaction (Skoog et al. 2022). But while many people live longer and heathier lives, the attitudes towards older persons is problematic. Ageism is a relatively new concept, closely related to more commonly known phenomena such as racism, and sexism. In fact, when ageism was first mentioned in scientific press in 1969 by gerontologist Robert Butler, he used the concepts of racism and sexism to underline and explain the similar patterns regarding ageism, how stereotyping and prejudice based on race, gender or age, may lead to discrimination (Butler 1969). Since then ageism has been in central focus for many research discussions (Schonfield 1982; Gullette 2017; Krekula et al. 2018; Loos and Ivan 2018). The United Nations has a long engagement in age issues and recently launched the UN Decade of Healthy Ageing 2021–2030, where countering ageism is one of the priorities. Ageism is considered to affect people throughout their lives and it permeates institutions and many parts of society. The World Health Organization (WHO), regards tackling ageism as critical to human well-being and human rights, it is considered a threat to all ages in one way or another. In 2021 the organization launched a global campaign to combat ageism where some key aims is to foster intergenerational solidarity and change the narratives around age and ageing (WHO 2021).

1.3 Ageism in the Media

It is reasonable to believe that ageism might be fueled by the media. Media representations may all have gendered or/and ageist components regarding presence, roles and topics. Data from Global Media Monitoring Project indicate that the very young and the very old rarely makes the news agenda. While young people are at the center for new media and technology development, their presence in the news is almost non-existent. This might be explained by that young people don't fit into the news valuecriterias such as belonging to the power elite, being a celebrity, or being able to deliver a story of magnitude (For a list of news values see for example Harcup and O'Neill 2017). That said, there are of course example of young people that makes the news, like educational activist and Nobel laureate Malala Yousafzai and climate activist Greta Thunberg. A literature review of scientific articles about children, young people and the news indicate that it is a small research field, with no large comparative news content analysis. Reception and representation studies are major research interest, but when it comes to research on representation, the focus is often about one specific person, media or topics, usually empirically based in one or two countries (Fillol and Pereira 2020).

Earlier research indicate that older persons seldom are present in the media, but when they are, they are often stereotyped into polarized categories like the active silverback or the voiceless, frail person. The advertising industry want to reach the resourceful healthy older people, often called 'golden agers' (Bai 2014) and the media interest for older age groups often derives from a consumer perspective, with a focus on agelessness and successful ageing (Kenalemang 2021). The news media on the other hand tend to focus on representations of older persons as frail and having problems of declining health (Lundgren and Ljuslinder 2011; Nilsson and Jönsson 2009; Wien 2003). However, compared to young people, there is no lack of older persons who might fit many of the news value criterias, in terms of being an expert, elite or celebrity person.

Some of them also makes the news, such as Queen Elizabeth of England, actor Anthony Hopkins who won his first Oscar in 2020 at the age of 83, and the US president Joe Biden, born 1942.

As mentioned earlier, ageism is based on stereotypes and negative stereotypes on ageing seem to have existed for a long time. A study that used computational linguistics to the Corpus of Historical American English found a clear shift from positive to negative age stereotypes already in 1880, possibly due to the growing aging population, a development that has continued since then (Ng et al. 2015). Negative stereotypes of ageing seem to be very resilient (Levy et al. 2015), and news media may reinforce negative beliefs about older persons (Kroon et al. 2019).

1.4 The Gender Bias of the News

In 1995, The UN Beijing Declaration and Platform for Action pointed out media as one of twelve areas where actions need to be taken if we are to achieve gender equality in the world. At that time, only 17% of the news subjects were women, a share that since then has increased to 25%, indicating a slow progress towards a gender balance in the news (Macharia 2021). The male dominate in the news when it comes to presence, and topics and roles are gendered with a clear dominance of men as spokespersons and experts, and women are more likely to talk from personal experience (Macharia 2015, 2021; Ross and Padovani 2017). The gendered newsroom culture is considered to be a part of the problem (Byerly 2013). When comparing the global news content with indexes on the factual gender equality in society, such as the Global Gender Gap Index, there is a persistent global pattern where news media seem to be less gender equal than the 'real' world (Djerf-Pierre and Edström 2020).

1.5   Gender Ageism in the News

Media research combing gender and age are often based on a one-country study, or studies of one media title or genre. A literature review of ageing and media studies also indicates that the reflective side regarding concepts of age and media is often missing (Mosberg and Wilinska 2019).

Using Sweden as an example, the author of this paper has been involved in two studies regarding gender and age in the media. Both studies indicate similar patterns, the most visible persons in the media are adults related to the labour market years, belonging to the age category 20–65 years. Younger women are more visible than older women. After passing the retirement years, (you may retire when you are 61–67 years), both men and women are underrepresented, compared to their share of the population in Sweden (Edström 2006; 2018). As a methodology test, a third study was conducted in order to find gender and age patterns in a large material of news. (39 online news sites and 4, 7 million news). Similar patterns appeared, with gendered over- and underrepresentation in the news where the very young and the 60+ were underrepresented (Kokkinakis et al. 2018). A question for this study is if these national patterns from Sweden are reflected in the global patterns of the news.

On a minor note, since early 2020, the news media has been dominated by Covid-19. The GMMP 2020 report (Macharia 2021) indicate that women voices are absent in the conversation about covid, as well as the 80+ population. This is also confirmed by studies undertaken by the Bill and Melinda Gates Foundation that commissioned a mapping of the underrepresentation of women and gender perspectives in the news in six countries (Kassova 2020). Gerontologists and geriatrics have also expressed concerns that the pandemic is magnifying prejudices based on age, and that ageism that was displayed in social media during Covid-19, is causing intergenerational tensions (Ayalon 2020).

2   Methodology and Material

This paper provide an analysis of collected data from the 6th, Global Media Monitoring Project (GMMP), provided both from the published report in 2021 [Macharia 2021] and from in-depth analysis of non-published data from GMMP. The GMMP is the largest and longest longitudinal study on gender in the world's news media, conducted every fifth year since 1995. The monitoring of news by the GMMP is conducted during one day around the world, catching a snapshot of the news. The monitoring in every country is overseen by national coordinators that submits the data to the project management who process all the data for a global report. The national reports are produced by the local teams. When coding the age of people in the news, GMMP use the criteria how 'the person appears', meaning what age the person appears to be on an image and/or age information is appearing within the news story. (It is quite common to mention the age of a person in the news). There is room for misjudgment when coding, but there should not be any systematic errors in the age estimation. For the full methodology the GMMP, see the project website [whomakesthenews.org].

The empirical data consist of content analysis of news media and television news, collected within sixth study from Global Media Monitoring Project (GMMP) and predicted population statistics from the United Nations for 2020. In the GMMP 2020, a total of 30172 news stories were monitored from 2215 news outlets in 116 countries. The analysis presented here is primarily based on news subjects where age can be identified (Newspapers N = 4636, Television news N = 11958). The 2020 study was the first time an 80+ category was included in the age variable. An intention for this paper was to break down the data regarding the most marginalized groups, children and older persons 80+. Unfortunately, due to the age group 80+ is almost invisible in the news, the analysis is limited.

3 Results

3.1 The Age Gaps Between the World Population and People in the News

There is a substantial discrepancy between the age patterns in the world compared with the age representation in the news. Figure 1 compare the share of different age groups within the world population compared with the age representation in newspapers.

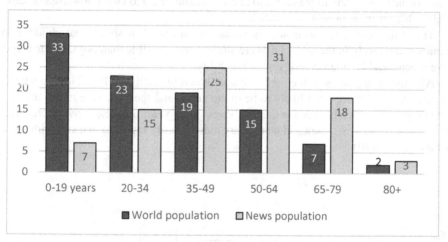

Fig. 1. Share of population in different age groups, in the world and in newspapers 2020 (percent). The news population is based on news subjects where age of the person was appearing N = 4636. Please note that the age categories from the UN data is 0–19 years and for the GMMP it is 0–18 years. Source: United Nations Populations Data 2020 and GMMP2020, www.whomakesthen ews.org

The GMMP 2020 indicate that the youngest and the oldest people are the least likely to appear in news media around the world. The share of the 80+ population is globally still quite small, two percent, and the representation in the news is quite similar. For the young population it is another matter. Globally, 33% of world's population is below the age of 19 years, making it the largest population group. This is in stark contrast with the GMMP study where only 7% of the people in the news are below 18 years, see Fig. 1.

The underrepresentation of young people in the news continues in the age group of young adults, 20–34 years. People 35–49 years are more often in the news, and if you pass 50 years the visible in the news increase even more, in fact, 50–64 year olds represent the largest age group in the news 31% belong to that category, more than double the share of 50–64 year olds in the world's population. This can partly be explained by the news logic that values people in power, experts and spokespersons, usually it takes some years to achieve those positions and they are older. On the other hand, societal development and decisions made at the top, concerns people everywhere and news could easily cover a broader age selection by shifting perspectives.

From a Swedish perspective, it is interesting to note the large overrepresentation in the news of people between 65–79 years in the global news, 18% vs 7% in the global population, since content studies of Swedish news media indicate that the age group 65–79 years is clearly underrepresented in the Swedish news, compared to the population. 80+ is also underrepresented in Swedish news media.

3.2 Gendered Age Representation in Newspapers

As mentioned earlier, men still dominate the news. Overall there is a 75% male dominance of news subjects in press, radio and television in 2020 (with newspapers have a slightly higher male dominance, 76%).

The patterns of age and gender is visualised in Fig. 2. It shows that children and teenagers are rarely in the news. Girls are slightly more visible than boys, and teenagers have a gendered balance in terms of (in)visibility.

All other age groups in the news are dominated by men (see Fig. 2). Men who are 50 years and older are most likely to be in the news, and they keep the media attention until they are 79. Men between in the 65–79 age group years are clearly overrepresented. When passing 80 years, men and women are more equally invisible, but still with a male dominance (60/40).

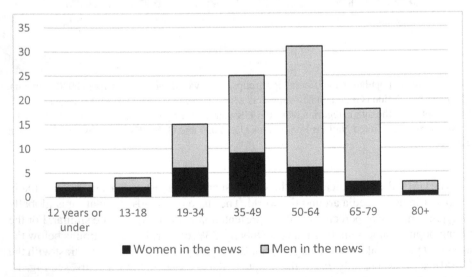

Fig. 2. Gender and age representation in newspapers 2020 (percent). Based on cases where age of the news subjects was appearing. N = 4636. Source: GMMP2020, www.whomakesthenews.org

Women are less visible in the news in all the adult age groups, the chances for women to make the news are highest *below* 50 years of age, the largest age group for women in the news is 35–49 years. This means that women have their peak of visibility earlier than men. After 50 women move into invisibility, again, see Fig. 2.

Worth mentioning is that the trend over time in the GMMP studies are that women above 50 years has become more and more invisible.

3.3   Topics

The largest topics in the news are also permeated by age patterns. Children and youth are most likely to be present when crime & violence is the topic, of if the news are about social& legal issues. Celebrity, art, media and sports is the third area of where children and youth appear. The 80+ people are also likely to be in the news when the topic is about celebrity, art, media and sports, but the largest topic for the oldest age category is to be present when the news are about politics and governance.

3.4   Roles and Functions in the News

Many news stories often contains typical casting; experts and spokesperson who contributes to the understanding of the topics, often complemented with individual 'cases' that may be represented by a personal experience, an eye witness or popular opinion. The role of experts and spokespersons are almost exclusively casted by people between the age of 19–64 years; 91% of the experts belong to that age group and 89% of the spokespersons. This confirms that news media have a clear focus on people in the labour market and don't consider 65+ that might have expertise as newsworthy.

3.5   Covid and the Lack of the Oldest People in the News

The 2020 GMMP-study made it possible to specifically investigate the representation in the news of the age group 80 years and older. On a global scale, more people are getting older and healthier, 2020 was also the first year into to the global Covid-19-pandemic, where old age was considered a common denominator for being at risk. Both these scenarios, a growing older population and a pandemic with age as a risk factor could indeed have been considered to be seen as newsworthy. However, this is not appearing in the news covered by GMMP 2020-study. Very few persons in the global news study are 80+. In fact, it was the smallest age group of all in the study, and women 80+ were even more invisible than the men in that age group. On the other hand, even though life expectance increase all over the world, the factual representation of 80+ in the world corresponded with the representation in the global news.

4   Conclusions/Discussion

Mediated representations of different age groups and ageing has an effect on all of us, they might open up our imagination, confirm or limit ideas of ageing. The paper has focused on global patterns of representation in the news media, indicating large discrepancies between age groups in real life and in the global news, especially regarding children and teenagers, and women are underrepresented in all adult age groups, especially the older age groups. As mentioned earlier, representation and presence of various age groups in the news media can be seen as a proxy for communication rights and political rights. When some age groups are not present in the news, it means a devaluation of those voices and negative attitudes based on age might occur.

Of course, news can't be expected to exactly mirror all age groups in society, but when large age groups are not present in the news, it is easy to understand that it might create tensions. A democratic society needs informed citizens, when large groups are invisible in the news, more stereotypical ideas might be nourished that leads to prejudice and discrimination.

The patterns of visibility in the news may be interpreted as an ongoing symbolic annihilation of voices and perspectives, especially regarding people from the youngest age groups. The analysis of the GMMP 2020 also confirms that the news contributes to a gendered ageism, where women below 50 years of age are seen as more news-worthy and older women are almost invisible. Older men on the other hand, keep their newsworthiness way beyond the retirement age.

During the Covid-19 pandemic, geriatrics feared that the isolation experienced by older people increased the risk of mental health problems among previously healthy older people (Skoog 2020). This feeling of isolation could have been mitigated by the news media by spotlighting the lives of the oldest people during Covid-19. But instead, that seems to not have been the case.

The news media have a clear focus on people in the labour market, this is in line with the commercialisation of the news during the digital era. But it also highlights the question about the role of news for democracy. If some age groups are considered to be more newsworthy than others, what narratives of society are the news contributing to?

A way forward could be to encourage the newsrooms to become more age-competent and learn more about ageing, and by that becoming more aware of the skewed images of aging and age groups that news media tend to produce. Regardless of commercial arguments, editors and journalist in newsrooms should be able to argue for a more varied and nuanced reporting that includes a broader segment of population. At least, it is time for them to consider the importance if media accountability and their responsible for that everyone is heard in the public sphere of the news media.

People from age groups affected by the symbolic annihilation in the news could also benefit from increasing their media literacy in order to understand the news media logic, why certain age groups are not present, and possibly also learn how to contribute to more diverse media images themselves.

Needless to say, more studies are required on age representation in news media, both in order to reveal more in depth studies of global patterns, and to learn more about news content and age patterns in specific countries.

Acknowledgements. The author thank Sarah Macharia, Principal Investigator for the Global Media Monitoring Project for making the data accessible.

Disclosure Statement. The author is the national coordinator for Sweden in the Global Media Monitoring Project.

Additional information. Funding: This work was supported by AgeCap, Centre for Ageing and Health, at the University of Gothenburg.

References

Ayalon, L.: There is nothing new under the sun: Ageism and intergenerational tension in the age of the COVID-19 outbreak. Int. Psychogeriatr. 1–4 (2020)

Bai, X.: Images of ageing in society: a literature review. J. Popul. Ageing **7**(3), 231–253 (2014)

Bergström, A., Edström, M.: Invisible or powerful? Ageing in a mediatised society. In: Falk Erhag, H., Lagerlöf Nilsson, U., Rydberg Sterner, T., Skoog, I. (eds.) A Multidisciplinary Approach to Capability in Age and Ageing. IPA, vol. 31, pp. 191–205. Springer, Cham (2022). https://doi.org/10.1007/978-3-030-78063-0_14

Butler, R.N.: Age-ism: another form of bigotry. Gerontologist **9**(4), 243–246 (1969)

Byerly, C.M. (ed.): The Palgrave International Handbook of Women and Journalism. Palgrave Macmillan, Basinstoke (2013)

Couldry, N.: Why Voice Matters. Culture, Politics and neo Liberalism. Sage, London (2010)

Couldry, N.: Capabilities for what? Developing Sen's moral theory for communication research. J. Inf. Policy **9**, 43–55 (2019)

Djerf-Pierre, M., Edström, M.: Introduction: comparing gender and media equality across the globe: understanding the qualities, causes, and consequences. In: Djerf-Pierre, M., Edström, M. (eds.) Comparing Gender and Media Equality Across the Globe: A Cross-national Study of the Qualities, Causes, and Consequences of Gender Equality in and through the News Media. Nordicom, Göteborg (2020)

Edström, M.: Tv-rummets eliter. Föreställningar om makt och kön i fakta och fiktion. [The television elites. Imgaes of gender and poert in fact and fiction. Diss. Department of journalism, media and communication, University of Gothenburg (2006)

Edström, M.: Visibility patterns of gendered ageism in the media buzz: a study of the representation of gender and age over three decades. Fem. Media Stud. **18**(1), 77–93 (2018)

Fillol, J., Pereira, S: Children, young people and the news: a systematic literature review based on communication abstracts. Comunicação e sociedade (37), 147–168 (2020)

Gullette, M.: Ending Ageism: Or How Not to Shoot Old People. Rutger University Press, New Brunswick (2017)

Harcup, T., O'Neill, D.: What is news? News values revisited (again). Journal. Stud. **18**(12), 1470–1488 (2017)

Levy, B., Slade, M.D., Chung, P.H., Gill, T.M.: Resiliency over time of elders' age stereotypes after encountering stressful events. J. Gerontol. B Psychol. Sci. Soc. Sci. **70**(6), 886–890 (2015)

Lundgren, A.S., Ljuslinder, K.: Problematic demography: representations of population ageing in the Swedish daily press. Popul. Ageing, **4**, 165–183 (2011). https://doi.org/10.1007/s12062-011-9048-2

Loos, E., Ivan, L.: Visual ageism in the media. In: Ayalon, L., Tesch-Römer, C. (eds.) Contemporary Perspectives on Ageism. International Perspectives on Aging, vol. 19, pp. 163–176. Springer, Cham (2018). https://doi.org/10.1007/978-3-319-73820-8_11

Kassova, L.: The Missing Perspectives of Women in Covid-19 News. The Bill and Melinda Gates Foundation, London (2020)

Kenalemang, L.: Visual ageism and the subtle sexualisation of older celebrities in L'Oréal's advert campaigns: a multimodal critical discourse analysis. Ageing Soc. 1–18. (2021)

Kokkinakis, D., Edström, M., Berggren, M.: Ageism and Swedish news media. In: 24th Nordic Congress of Gerontoloy (NKG), 2–4 May 2018. Oslo, Norway (2018)

Krekula, C., Nikander, P., Wilińska, M.: Multiple marginalizations based on age: gendered ageism and beyond. In: Ayalon, L., Tesch-Römer, C. (eds.) Contemporary Perspectives on Ageism. International Perspectives on Aging, vol. 19, pp. 33–50. Springer, Cham (2018). https://doi.org/10.1007/978-3-319-73820-8_3

Kroon, A.C., Trilling, D., Van Selm, M., Vliegenthart, R.: Biased media? How news content influences age discrimination claims. Eur. J. Ageing **16**(1), 109–119 (2019)

Macharia, S. (ed.): Who makes the news? Global media monitoring project 2015. WACC (2015). https://whomakesthenews.org/gmmp-2015-reports/. Accessed 01 Feb 2022

Macharia, S. (ed.): Who makes the news? In: 6th Global Media Monitoring project. WACC, Toronto (2021). https://whomakesthenews.org/gmmp-2020-final-reports/. Accessed 01 Feb 2022

Mosberg Iversen, S., Wilinska, M.: Ageing, old age and media: critical appraisal of knowledge practices in academic research. Int. J. Ageing Later Life IJAL **14**(1), 1–29 (2019)

Ng, R., Allore, H., Trentalange, M., Monin, J., Levy, B: Increasing negativity of age stereotypes across 200 years: evidence from a database of 400 million words. PloS One **10**(2), e0117086 (2015). https://doi.org/10.1371/journal.pone.0117086

Nilsson, M., Jönson, H.: Äldre i massmedierna – osynliga eller förknippade med problem. l In H. Jönsson (Ed.), Åldrande, åldersordning, ålderism. Linköpings universitet (2009)

Ross, K., Padovani, C.: Gender Equality and THE Media: A Challenge for Europe (Routledge studies in European communication research and education; 11). Routledge, Abingdon-on-Thames (2017)

Schonfield, D.: Who is stereotyping whom and why? Gerontologist **22**(3), 267–272 (1982)

Skoog, I., Falk Erhag, H., Kern, S., Rydberg Sterner, T., Samuelsson, J., Zettergren, A.: The capability approach in epidemiological studies. In: Falk Erhag, H., Lagerlöf Nilsson, U., Rydberg Sterner, T., Skoog, I. (eds.) A Multidisciplinary Approach to Capability in Age and Ageing. IPA, vol. 31, pp. 29–50. Springer, Cham (2022). https://doi.org/10.1007/978-3-030-78063-0_4

Skoog, I.: COVID-19 and mental health among older people in Sweden. Int. Psychogeriatr. **32**(10), 1173–1175 (2020)

Tuchman, G.: Introduction. The symbolic annihilation of women in the mass media. In: Tuchman, G., Daniels, K., Arlene, M., Benet, J. (eds.) Hearth and Home: Images of Women in the Mass Media. New York, NY, Oxford U.P. (1978)

UN Decade of Healthy Ageing 2021–2030. https://www.who.int/initiatives/decade-of-healthy-ageing. Accessed 01 Feb 2022

United Nations.: The Beijing Declaration and the Platform for Action: Fourth World Conference on Women. New York: Dept. of Public Information, United Nations (1995)

United Nations General Assembly: Transforming our world : the 2030 Agenda for Sustainable Development (2015)

United Nations Populations Data: World Population Prospects (2019). POP/DB/WPP/Rev.2019/POP/F15-1, https://population.un.org/wpp/Download/Standard/Population/. Accessed 01 Feb 2022

United Nations: Global Issues Ageing. https://www.un.org/en/global-issues/ageing. Accessed 01 Feb 2022

Weaver, D.H.: Thoughts on agenda setting, framing, and priming. J. Commun. **57**(1), 142–147 (2007)

Wien, C.: Aeldrebilledet i medierna gennem 50 år. [Images of older people in the media during 50 years] Syddanskt universitetsforlag, Odense (2003)

Who makes the news: https://whomakesthenews.org. Accessed 01 Feb 2022

World Health Organization: Global report on ageism. (electronic version) (2021). ISBN 978-92-4-001686-6, https://www.who.int/publications/i/item/9789240016866. Accessed Feburary 2022

An Interface Design of Chat Application for the Elderly Based on Color Cognition and User Demand

Linlin Feng and Jing Luo[✉]

School of Arts and Design, Shenzhen University, Shenzhen, Guangdong, China
luojng@szu.edu.cn

Abstract. Population aging is a defining demographic reality of our era. Meanwhile, the global information technology industry has rapidly developed. People usually use online chat applications to communicate with each other. In this case, the interface design should not overlook the needs of the elderly. Nevertheless, the surveys show that the current Easy Mode for the elderly of chat applications does not adequately address the issue. In order to study these issues, firstly, this project constructs a flow chart through questionnaires and interviews based on Grounded theory, flow chart showing the usage process of chat applications by the elderly, and it could help us to find the most critical factors affecting the usage of the elderly. Secondly, improving the UI design of Easy Mode based on color cognition and user demand to solve the identified problems. Finally, we chose quantitative experiments to verify this method's feasibility, and then users need to make subjective evaluations to assist in proving the conclusions.

Keywords: The elderly · Interface design · Color cognition · User demand · Chat application · Grounded method · Mann-Whitney test

1 Introduction

As we are all aware, the 21st Century is an era of information, especially digital information. While most middle-young people enjoy the conveniences of mobile applications, the requirements of the elderly are ignored [1]. As the global aging is more severe in recent years, The United Nations has predicted that the global aging population will continue to grow at an average rate of 2.5% per year, while the figure for China is 3.3% for the same period, which combined with the large base of the Chinese population, it means that the aging problem in China will be even more severe [2]. We should emphasize the elderly's needs and obstacles regarding mobile phone applications [3]. At the same time, the United Nations pointed out that the number of the elderly living independently and with their spouses has increased. The report means that these senior citizens will have more requirements of communicating with the outside world and studying to communicate with their children by mobile phones [2]. As per the surveys, among the elderly who have a mobile phone, more than half of them carry smartphones. They mainly use smartphones to keep in touch with their family and friends [4]. Since the elderly have trouble accepting new things, recognizing graphics and text, or learning operations [5], they are unwilling to use online chat applications. For example, in a population-based survey of the elderly (a sample of 349 senior citizens) in Shijiazhuang, China, it was pointed out that 71.94% of the elderly think that mobile application operations are complicated [6]. In response to this problem, it is necessary to provide an effective Easy Mode for the elderly.

According to this research, we found some design insights. Firstly, the functions of the chat applications are usually more than those needed for the elderly [7]. The elderly mainly use chat-related functions, the functions of leisure and entertainment popular among young people are rarely used by them [6]. The interface design also has simplified and integrated colors and is mainly distinguished through graphics. Nevertheless, the elderly will have reduced cognition in the graphics and texts. Through the investigation, we found that many senior citizens believed that color could promote orientation both as a code and a cue and were agreeable to the idea of using color as memory support [8]. Therefore, we can optimize the interface design of the Easy Mode for the elderly by using colors properly.

2 Methods

This project used a combination of qualitative and quantitative experiments. The experiment method was employed in the present study to investigate the main factors influencing the study and use of chat applications in the elderly and understand their demand. The interface design of the chat application was improved based on color cognition and functional requirements, then based on quantitative experiments to verify whether it is effective and using subjective evaluation to measure user acceptance. The study was carried out mainly based on WeChat (the most commonly used chat application in China).

2.1 Questionnaire

Participants. A total of 63 people were surveyed. The participants with an average age of 74.68 years old (SD = 5.62; age range: 61–83). In order to more accurately understand the use of online communication software for the elderly, the survey respondents were randomly recruited in Taoyuan Street, and they all lived in first-tier cities.

Research Approach. The primary purpose of the questionnaire survey was to obtain information on the use of online chat applications for the elderly user needs and to identify suitable candidates for follow-up interviews. Considering that the elderly may not be able to read the text or choose the wrong options, this questionnaire was conducted in the form of questions, it ensured the authenticity and accuracy of the data. The questionnaire mainly consists of two parts. We first listed five fundamental questions and grouped them into two main themes: (a) personal information. (b) usage of WeChat. After filling out the basic information, we asked participants a multiple-choice question about WeChat usage, subsequent questions depending on how they answered the second question: (a) If they are using WeChat. Firstly, they needed to choose the most frequently used functions.

Secondly, they should choose or answer whether they have difficulties in the learning process of WeChat, and finally, choose or answer the questions encountered during the use process. (b) If they have used it before. Firstly, they need to choose or answer why not to continue. Secondly, choose or answer any inconveniences when learning or using WeChat. (c) If they have never used WeChat before, they were asked to answer their reasons for not using it.

2.2 In-Depth Interview

Participants. Among the participants who participated in the questionnaire, we recruited ten senior citizens in the interviews, they are still using WeChat but had difficulties using it or had used it before but gave up due to some difficulties. And Family members who taught them to use WeChat were interviewed too. A total of 20 people (ten senior citizens and ten of their families) were interviewed. The elder participants with an average age of 73.5 years old (SD = 6.08; age range: 64–83).

Research Approach. To understand their usage, and find problems for improving the UI design, we investigated and constructed the process of learning and using online chat applications for the elderly. The grounded theory approach was adopted in data collection and analysis (Charmaz, 2006; Glaser & Strauss, 2009). What's more, the 'mosaic method' was used to reconstruct the process of learning, memory, and use. This process has not been systematically studied, therefore we need to collect and encode meaningful references and group them into coding categories.

For the accuracy and completeness of the overall process construction, during this process, we adopted two criteria for selecting research targets: (a) First of all, the elderly participating in the survey must be using WeChat or having used WeChat for some time to prevent narrative bias caused by subjective factors. (b) Data collection in the form of interviews is conducted on both the elderly who use the application and the family members who teach them to use WeChat to ensure the integrity of the data. In this way, we could get the actual situation of users from learning to using this application. Then, the collected information was classified and summarized according to the research groups, and through interviews with their family members, the process and difficulties of teaching the use of WeChat to the elderly were mainly obtained. Through the interviews of the elderly, we mainly got the process and inconvenience of their operation memory and usage. Finally, we aggregate and integrate the classified information.

In order to construct the process from learning to using WeChat of the elderly, the interview data should be transcribed and organized systematically. Firstly, 'process elements' were identified. Secondly, we draw out partial processes through each person's teaching or use process narrative. Next, we combined all partial processes in each group into the overall processes using the 'mosaic method'. After constructing overall processes, we simplified them with 'process chunks' to identify each process. Finally, we visualized them as a learning-memory-operation model. Figure 1 shows the research procedure.

Interview Data	Partial Using Process/Teaching Process	Combined Process (combine)	Overall Process

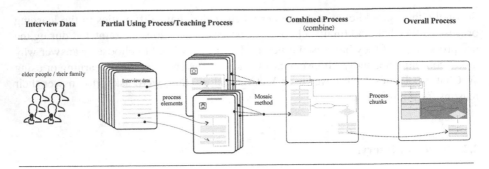

Fig. 1. Research procedure.

Interview Procedure. In-depth interviews were used to investigate the operation process from learning to using WeChat. Firstly, we let the elderly participating and their families restore the process of using or teaching on the spot. Secondly, we asked which part has been the most repeated one of the overall process. Finally, ask them which is the most challenging part of the overall process and why?

Identifying Using and Teaching Processes. Although all transcribed data contained information related to design processes, they did not describe it in the most straightforward language, and the data was intermingled with other information, such as the description of the button and the personal feelings, Etc. Firstly, we distinguished each step from their utterances and demonstration actions, then reduced them to process elements. Lastly, using the conjunctions they said in the narrative process as structural lines to connect the process elements.

The next stage was to combine each participant's processes into overall processes via a 'mosaic method'. In this process, we added process elements or merged process elements according to the narratives of different participants. Through this stage, we could better define these operating processes, and at the same time, it is easy to make up for some problems caused by personal expressions and make the logic of the constructed process system more compact.

Simplifying the Processes. In this process, on the one hand, we classified and summarized related processes and classified them with different chunks; on the other hand, we divided the overall process into three stages—learning phase, memory phase, and operation phase. This simplified and systematic classification will make it easier for us to find and define problems in the overall process. Figure 2 is the overall process from learning to using WeChat for the elderly. Furthermore, Fig. 3 is the simplified one.

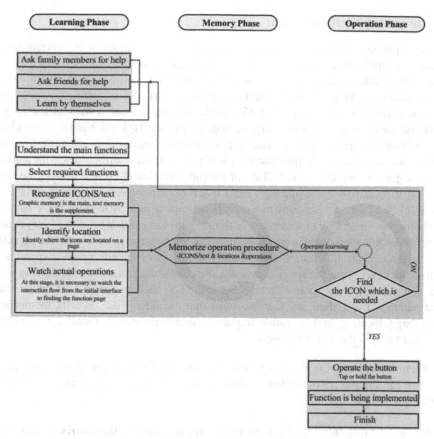

Fig. 2. The process of learning and using WeChat for the elderly.

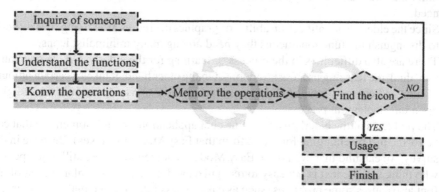

Fig. 3. The simplified process.

2.3   Improved Interface Design

Result Analysis. Through the questionnaire analysis, we can know the current use of online chat applications by the elderly and find out the problems subjectively found by users. The questionnaire analysis shows the following three points: (a) there are 33% of people still using WeChat and found it inconvenient; (b) 22% of them gave up using it and found it challenging to use; (c) 35% of them could not use it without teaching or think the learning process is too complicated; (d) the rest 10% can handle it quickly).

Although the Easy Mode of chat application has been widely used, through this survey, we can also clearly find that the elderly have specific difficulties with learning and using it. Among them, (a) 77.78% of people think that the functions they need are not easy to find; (b) 44.44% of people think that the operation is complicated and hard to learn; (c) 56.67% of people think that it is challenging to recognize icons and characters (including not being able to see clearly or thinking the recognition process is very tiring).

In order to understand the problem more comprehensively, we found five objective factors through the flow chart: First, family members or friends need to spend a lot of time and energy on the specific process, especially the process of identifying icons and confirming the location of icons. Second, they need to repeat and demonstrate continuously. Third, there are few functions that the elderly use. Fourth, memorizing icon shape, location, and operation requires constant repetition. Finally, it takes time and effort to find the icon they need.

Problem Definition. Combined with questionnaire data analysis and process chart analysis, we can summarize the following four questions for the elderly in the process from learning to using:

- We can find that only few functions are commonly used by the elderly. Before using it, they identify first the very few functions they want to learn. At the same time, they think that there are too many functions and even affect the use of the functions they need.
- Since the elderly's identification ability of graphics decreases after aging, it is difficult to distinguish the functional icons they need among many minimalist icons.
- There are also difficulties in the process of learning for the elderly. On the one hand, they think the learning process is arduous. On the other hand, it takes a certain amount of time and energy of their family to teach them how to use it, and it is easy to give up in this unpleasant process.
- The problems of the elderly using online chat applications are not something that can be solved just by enlarging fonts (the form that Easy Mode now takes). Because in the survey, we can find that even if the Easy Mode is adopted, there are still many people who think that the text is not easy to recognize, and the excessive enlargement of the font also causes some problems (such as easy to miss information, make the interface unsightly, Etc.).

Design Philosophy. After discovering these problems, We hope to find an easier identification and memory method for the elderly and minimize the impact of superfluous functions on their primary functions. We found that color could promote orientation as a cue during the research process, and the elderly think using color as memory support is practical [8]. In this case, many reports show that non-pathological aging will cause visual problems. We found that the elderly have a better memory of orange in general [9]. Therefore, we adopted orange as the main colour which is easy to remember and identify in the interface design. At the same time, we found that color can represent some emotional meaning [10], orange can give people a sense of vitality, and the elderly prefer bright colors.

Interface Redesign. In the process of interface design, to ensure the accuracy of the experimental results, it is necessary to control variables, so we should make as few changes as possible. Therefore, in prototyping, we kept the original layout format and changed the following three points:

- Change the color of the primary button.
- Change the color lightness to distinguish the importance of buttons.
- Simplify the interaction of the primary function.

On the one hand, by observing the data, the functions most frequently used by the elderly are voice message (77.78%), voice call (77.78%), and video call (66.67%). We can clearly find in the improved prototype Fig. 4 that the particular buttons are marked with different brightness of orange to indicate the importance of icons. Compared with the original UI design, which only deepens the color in the dialog box, the improved color indication design hopes to make the learning process and use process of the elderly simpler and faster. On the other hand, in the interaction process of the prototype with the

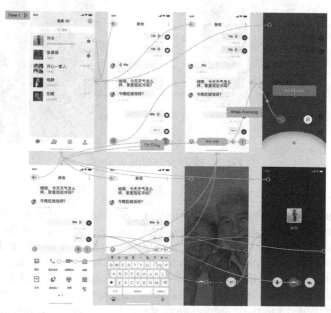

Fig. 4. Hi-Fi prototype with color indication & simplified operation

original UI design Fig. 5, the voice call and video call instructions are placed together under a video icon so that the interaction is complicated, and it takes two clicks to select the function they need. Therefore, in the modified prototype Fig. 4, they are placed respectively under the icons representing phone and video.

2.4 Experiment

Participants. A total of 20 participants were involved in this study. They all use WeChat occasionally. All of the elder participants were recruited from the townships in Henan. All the participants were in good physical and cognitive condition and had the ability to read Chinese characters and operate the mobile phone. The participants were divided into two groups: Group A with an average age of 64.7 years old (SD = 4.11; age range:59–73); and Group B with an average age of 60.7 years old (SD = 4.14; age range:58–70).

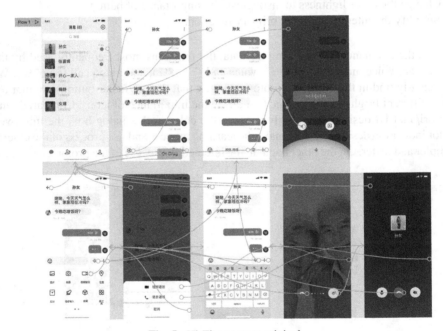

Fig. 5. Hi-Fi prototype original

Experimental Design. The UI design was changed based on color cognition and user demand to investigate whether it will positively impact the usage of the application. The experiment is carried out under the condition that the UI interface design of the two prototypes is only different in color and few buttons to control the variables. We used Figma to make the Hi-Fi prototypes used in the experiment, and the participants operated with an iPhone 11 adjusted to the same brightness during the experiment.

Firstly, recorded the basic information about the subjects. Secondly, 20 subjects were equally divided into two groups, ten people in each group. Group A used the Hi-Fi prototype original to complete the experiment, and Group B used the Hi-Fi prototype with color indication & a simplified function to complete the experiment. Then, five minutes of teaching and answering questions were conducted on the operation steps of the three functions most frequently used by users.

After that, the participants were asked to operate the prototype immediately to complete the three commands in turn. According to the Ebbinghaus forgetting curve, it can be known that memory declines most rapidly within twenty minutes. After 15 min, repeated the operation of the three commonly used commands. The time used for the above operation is timed during the operation, and the number of clicks is recorded. Then, the experimental data were analyzed to determine whether the improved chat application UI design based on color cognition and user demand is effective for the elderly.

In the final phase of the experiment, the other prototype's usage was introduced to each group. So they could better understand their different UI design. And then, subjective evaluation was measured by the 5-point Likert scales based on five aspects: ease-of-use, ease-of-study, the effort needed, helpfulness, and satisfaction. The entire experimental process will be controlled within 30 min.

Procedure. We tried our best to control the external interference during the experiment. The experiment was conducted in well-lit and relatively quiet external places, with one participant and two experimenters there at one time.

Before the experiment, each participant had learned how to use the basic three-function operations through the teaching of the experimenters, and they were allowed to freely explore the usage of the prototype and ask questions for 5 min. Following that, participants completed three tasks, and the experimenter recorded the time and the number of clicks they took from receiving the instruction to finishing the operation.

After the experiment, the experimenter gave a brief introduction to the operation of another prototype, and the participants were asked to fill out a subjective evaluation questionnaire.

3   Results

The experiment compared the performance in two groups and subjective evaluation of the participants. The possible effects of color cognition and user demand were also investigated.

3.1   Data Analysis

We can find that the data was not normally distributed through the normality test. The non-parametric testing was then utilized to analyze the results in SPSS. Specifically, the Mann-Whitney test was employed to compare the differences in operational performance between two groups.

Comparison Between Two Groups (Immediately). Mann-Whitney test analysis was used to compare the difference of operating performance between two groups using different prototypes. This analysis mainly studies the operation performance of starting the

Table 1. Statistics of app operation time (*immediately*).

Task	Group	Operation time	Z	p
Task 1	1	15.695 (12.863−16.910)	−3.780	0.000
	2	8.160 (7.340−9.130)		
Task 2	1	15.525 (12.205−23.010)	−3.780	0.000
	2	7.585 (6.863−8.978)		
Task 3	1	15.410 (10.100−21.705)	−3.630	0.000
	2	6.895 (5.665−8.428)		

Table 2. Statistics of app operation time (*after 15 min*).

Task	Group	Operation time	Z	p
Task 1	1	8.655 (6.825−10.363)	−1.209	0.274
	2	5.975 (4.8875−10.313)		
Task 2	1	10.440 (9.003−11.678)	−3.780	0.000
	2	4.645 (3.558−5.980)		
Task 3	1	10.390 (9.490−11.340)	−3.780	0.000
	2	4.185 (3.185−5.513)		

Table 3. Statistics of the number of clicks (*immediately*).

Task	Group	Number of clicks	Z	p
Task 1	1	4.00(3.00−5.00)	−0.698	0.529
	2	3.50(3.00−4.25)		
Task 2	1	5.50(4.00−7.00)	−2.131	0.035
	2	4.00(3.00−5.00)		
Task 3	1	5.50(4.75−6.00)	−3.191	0.001
	2	3.00(3.00−4.25)		

Table 4. Statistics of the number of clicks (*after 15 min*).

Task	Group	Number of clicks	Z	p
Task 1	1	3.00(3.00−4.25)	−3.107	0.002
	2	6.00(4.00−7.00)		
Task 2	1	8.00(7.00−9.00)	−3.628	0.000
	2	4.00(3.00−5.00)		
Task 3	1	8.00(6.75−9.00)	−3.506	0.000
	2	4.00(3.00−5.25)		

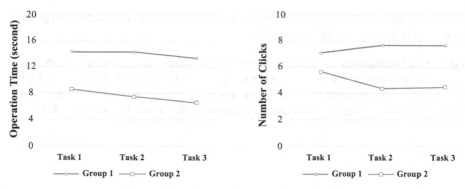

Fig. 6. Operation performance (*immediately*).

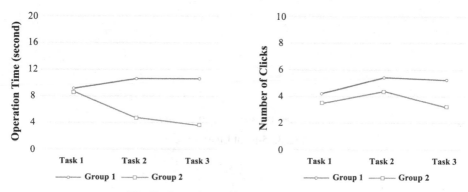

Fig. 7. Operation performance (*after 15 min*).

operation immediately among two groups. Firstly, Fig. 6 clearly shows us the difference in the operation time and the number of clicks using a visualization of the weighted median change. Secondly, through the analysis of the completion of task 1 (send a voice message). In terms of the data, the results in Table 1 and Table 3 revealed that the operation of two groups with different prototypes did not show much difference in time (Z = −1.209, p = 0.274), and the number of clicks (Z = −0.698, p = 0.529), which also proved that there was no significant difference in the instantaneous memory between the participants from two groups. Third, the improved UI design simplified the operation. On the one hand, the data of manipulation time in task 2 (Z = −3.780, p = 0.000) and task three (Z = −3.780, p = 0.000) showed that the time required for the experimental operation of Group 2 was shorter than Group 1. On the other hand, the data in task two (Z = −2.131, p = 0.035) and task three (Z = −3.191, p = 0.001) showed no significant difference in the number of clicks.

Comparison Between Two Groups (After 15 min). This analysis mainly studies the operation performance after 15 min among two groups. Firstly, Fig. 7 clearly shows us the difference in the operation time and the number of clicks using a visualization of the weighted median change. Secondly, From the data analysis in Table 2, it shows that the participants from Group 2 need shorter operation time in three tests (p < 0.05) than

Group 1. Finally, the analysis from Table 4 indicates that the participants from group 2 need a fewer number of clicks in three tests.

Subjective Evaluation. A comparison of 5-point Likert scale evaluations in Fig. 8 shows the participants of two prototype designs. They evaluated significantly higher in the prototype with optimized UI design among C1: ease-of-use, C2: ease-of-study, C3: helpfulness, C4: satisfaction, and they also think that it needs less effort (C5).

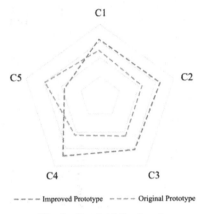

Fig. 8. 5-point Likert scale

4   Discussion

First of all, when online chat application has become an indispensable part of communication today, this project considers the needs of the elderly and finds out the problems of the usage from learning to using. Secondly, this project takes WeChat (the most widely used chat software in China) as the reference. For the first time, we studied the elderly's operation process from learning to use of chat applications systematically. The problems existing in the use process were found from an objective point of view through the flow chart. Combined with the subjective issue collected by the questionnaire, the usage problems were summarized. We found that it is a good penetration point to improve the UI design based on color cognition and user demand based on the research. In that case, an optimized UI design is made based on WeChat.

After that, data were analyzed using Mann-Whitney test analysis. The data shows that: the improved prototype requires fewer operations time and fewer clicks. Therefore, it can be seen that the guidance of colors and the simplification of commonly used functions are beneficial to learning and memory. At the same time, we also found the main effect of this improvement by analyzing the data: the optimized UI design mainly shortens the time it takes for users to find the button. Even if we changed the brightness of the icon, this design only has a modest positive impact on users' misclicks, so it is vital to discuss the number and color change of the colored icons.

What's more, even with objective data comparison, we believe that the user experience is essential. Therefore, at the end of the experiment, the participants subjectively rated the operation of the improved prototype and the original prototype, and the results showed that users received the optimized UI design well. The interface design of chat application for the elderly based on color cognition and user demand are effective.

Finally, the elderly are major users of mobile applications that cannot be ignored. This experiment provides a new approach to interface design in Easy Mode that uses specific colors as cues and memory aids. Many excellent experiments have proved that the elderly have minor deviations in specific color memory. However, this research result has not been used in the design of the aging-friendly interface. Therefore, in the case of elderly cognitive function and visual function degradation, the application of color-assisted memory in the UI design process can be further explored. Indeed, changing the color scheme is very easy to implement in UI design.

5 Conclusion and Future Work

According to the data analysis, the interface design of chat applications for the elderly based on color cognition and user demand is helpful. During this period, the optimized UI design based on color cognition positively impacts the user's use, but appropriate use of color becomes a new problem. At the same time, due to some limitations, the number of participants in the experiment is small.

At the same time, we can also know that some senior citizens are not only satisfied with the convenience brought by social software, many of them also use many entertainment applications that young people commonly use, and it also brings many problems for the elderly. The problem of the aging population is getting worse; the elderly will be a significant user group of mobile applications that cannot be ignored. Encoding the usage process of users into a systematic process instead of just making a questionnaire may contribute to the UI design of particular users because the user can not articulate the real problem sometimes.

Therefore, we hope that this project can provide a new idea for the Easy Mode design on the mobile application. Use color wisely, and consider the real needs and physiological conditions of users in the design of the age-friendly interface.

References

1. Law, K.A., Bhaumik, A., Yin, H., et al.: Study on Urban elder mobile phone users in China: in the perspective of aging issue. Int. J. Control Autom. 12(5), 99–106 (2019)
2. Palen, L., Salzman, M.: Welcome to the wireless world: problems using and understanding mobile telephony. In: Springer Computer Supported Cooperated Work Series, pp. 135–153. Springer, New York (2001). https://doi.org/10.1007/978-1-4471-0665-4_10
3. Navabi, N., Ghaffari, F., Gannat, A.Z.: Older adults' attitudes and barriers toward the use of mobile phones. Clin. Interv. Aging 11, 1371–1378 (2016)
4. Briede-Westermeyer, J.C., Pacheco-Blanco, B., Luzardo-Briceño, M., Pérez-Villalobos, C.: Mobile phone use by the elderly: relationship between usability, social activity, and the environment. Sustainability 12(7), 2690 (2020)

5. Van Biljon, J.A.: A model for representing the motivational and cultural factors that influence mobile phone usage variety. Ph.D. Thesis, School of Computing, University of South Africa, Pretoria (2007)
6. Zhang, J.: Analysis on current situation and influencing factors of smart phone use among the urban elderly. In: Hebei University of Economics and Business (2021)
7. Kim, H., et al.: Contextual research on elderly users' needs for developing universal design mobile phone. In: International Conference on Universal Access in Human-Computer Interaction. Springer, Berlin, Heidelberg (2007). https://doi.org/10.1007/978-3-540-73279-2_106
8. Wijk, H., Berg, S., Sivik, L., Steen, B.: Color discrimination, color naming and color preferences in 80-year olds. Aging Clin. Exp. Res. **11**(3), 176–185 (1999). https://doi.org/10.1007/BF03399660
9. Pérez-Carpinell, J., Camps, V.J., Trottini, M., Pérez-Baylach, C.M.: Color memory in elderly adults. Color Res. Appl. **31**, 458–467 (2006)
10. Won, S., Westland, S.: Colour meaning and context. Color Res. Appl. **42**, 450–459 (2017)

Digital Literacy of Older People and the Role of Intergenerational Approach in Supporting Their Competencies in Times of COVID-19 Pandemic

Igor Kanižaj[1]([⊠])(iD) and Maria José Brites[2](iD)

[1] Faculty of Political Science, University of Zagreb, Zagreb, Croatia
ikanizaj@fpzg.hr
[2] Lusófona University, CICANT, Lisbon, Portugal
mariajosebrites@ulp.pt

Abstract. This paper presents the preliminary results of two research projects conducted in Croatia and Europe that tackle the issues of digital literacy and the digital divide among older citizens. This methodology combines both quantitative and qualitative research methods, including a public opinion poll and a case study with intergenerational workshops on digital and media literacy. Both studies were conducted during the pandemic, after the second half of 2020 and in 2021, thus providing information about unexpected and imposition uses of digital technologies among older people and both revealed low levels of participation in the digital environment associated with the lack of digital skills and weak infrastructure. The innovative concept of the research was also highlighted through the involvement of journalism students, which contributed to the promotion an intergenerational guidance and support to older people. This support was provided mainly in terms of promoting online digital literacy.

Keywords: Digital divide · Digital literacy · Participatory workshops · Older people · COVID-19 · Croatia

1 Introduction

In an ageing European society, the intergenerational approaches towards improving media use in the context of everyday life constitute a safer path. Therefore, through the Green Paper on Ageing, the European Commission has recently promoted actions and attitudes of solidarity and responsibility between generations, which includes using technologies in learning-based contexts, as well as with regard to the issues such as health and work. [1]. Nevertheless, age is still one of the essential variables in Internet use. In the meantime, research has shifted from the classical concept of "digital divide" to the concept of "digital inequality" defined by Büchi and Hargittai [2] as "the systematic differences between individuals of different socioeconomic backgrounds concerning their access to, skills in, uses of and outcomes derived from engagement with digital media".

Q. Gao and J. Zhou (Eds.): HCII 2022, LNCS 13330, pp. 335–345, 2022.
https://doi.org/10.1007/978-3-031-05581-2_25

Research has mainly focused on the participation of individuals in society concerning media literacy activities [3]. However, researchers have also established that older people, for the most part, were not addressed as citizens with active roles at local, regional and international levels. Moreover, the age usage gap has become even more dominant in the pandemic due to an increased media and social networks usage during lockdowns.

In the last two years, we have also learned that the global pandemic has emphasised the relation between digital literacy, media literacy and health literacy, especially concerning older people [1, 4]. Research has also shown a positive correlation between media literacy and health literacy; the higher health literacy, the higher media literacy [5]. Moreover, social isolation has become a growing problem in hyper-connected societies, especially among older citizens [6]. Surprisingly, in an unexpected situation of the pandemic, news can positively influence making a connection between older people and society, thus contributing to their well-being [7]. This particular aspect is relevant to the research presented in this paper, since some of the subjects addressed by our survey conducted with older people were related to disinformation contexts. The European project SMaRT-EU – Social Media Resilience Toolkit (European Commission, LC-01563446) evidenced these aspects, not only in terms of the digital divide but also in terms of the foundational relationship that older citizens establish with news and through this relationship with their social and health needs as well, in an interdisciplinary form [8].

SMaRT-EU has developed participatory workshops in Croatia, Estonia, Belgium, Portugal and Wales. This article will focus on specific experiences of older adults in retirement homes in Croatia, their media usage, and digital competencies. In the time of lockdown, they could not meet members of their families and relatives in person. Even after the 2020 lockdown, the measures proclaimed by the governments made it more difficult for them, as users of retirement home services, to communicate in person, face to face with their families.

Nevertheless, this challenge has been tackled with ICT, communication platforms, and different applications without previous knowledge and experience. This has led to significant exposure to disinformation and misinformation on the Internet and social networks. However, even before the pandemic, certain challenges of digital literacy of seniors were identified [9, 10]. It was established that "they initially approach new technologies by applying the media practices they picked up during adolescence, including the logic inherent in these practices, and then repeatedly find themselves confronted with – and above all amazed by – all the other possibilities these technologies have to offer" [9]. As they advance their skills necessary for using social network platforms to establish communication, they become aware of many risks and opportunities of the digital world. However, mainly due to a lack of any previous experience in digital literacy education, there is still no evidence-based usage strategy concerning the challenges mentioned above.

2   Theoretical Framework

Despite the increase in the use of new technologies among older people, the percentage of senior citizens using them is still lower than in other age groups [11], particularly among those living in care homes, who are most likely to be digitally excluded or restricted [11].

In this line of thought, the research with older people has to reinforce the need to consider the context, including the individual needs and the risk of exclusion in many variables. Neves and Mead [11] call attention to the need to avoid implementing measures that try to fit the same recipe in diverse contexts:

"A comprehensive digital inclusion policy must account for diverse social contexts and avoid the 'one-size-fits-all'. For example, digital literacy programmes targeting older people should consider both individuals' needs and aspirations personalisation) and their social contexts, such as living settings or family interaction contextualisation)".

Supported by data from a longitudinal mixed-methods study of a co-designed app for older people, the research team also established that "learning to use new technology in later life rests on various socio-technical factors; these factors challenge assumptions of homogeneity or passivity of frail older people and highlight the need for a relational understanding of people and technology" [11].

Internet use among older people is very diverse and fluctuant; "[it] is an all-or-nothing issue: seniors tend to be either intense Internet users or non-users with only few in between" [12]. The research showed a significant difference between the media consumption of youth and older people in our society [8]. However, the digital divide is yet primarily identified with older people [12], with income and education to be indicated as relevant predictors, without neglecting the social context (friends and family) [13].

"(…) the access divide is only the first gap, and many more gaps need to be closed before we can assume an inclusion of seniors within today's new media society. However, the finding that only about a third of all seniors older than 65 are online indicates that the first and very basic digital divide is still the one that needs to be overcome first" [12].

Improving digital literacy skills among the so-called digital immigrants is demanding. The challenge increases if we consider older citizens and especially among those that are in care homes and retirement homes. A systematic literature review on the empirical studies promoting media literacy among senior citizens [8] indicated that creative processes were rarely used in the research, opening the door to participatory and innovative proposals. The same happened with blended and online pedagogical interventions. The online recommendations were related mainly to the need to improve basic technological skills or to use health devices. At the same time, the role of tutors, educators, volunteers and young people were considered as decisive in the success of the intervention processes [6, 8], which indicates the relevance of the intergenerational approaches.

As emphasised at the beginning of this text, all these challenges were raised as the pandemic broke out in 2020. As Skałacka and Pajestka [14] point out, physical distancing helped to avoid COVID-19 spread. On the other hand, however, it reinforced social distancing, notably in contexts of older people's lives, and online communication was and still is a form of surpassing the isolation. Some studies, however, show that this online life has had negative implications on mental health [13, 14]. The research we present in the next sections will precisely address the issue of how older citizens faced and interacted with technology during the COVID-19 pandemic.

3 Methodology

Our research design consists of one quantitative and one qualitative research methods: a public opinion poll and a case study, namely intergenerational workshops on digital and media literacy.

3.1 Public Opinion Poll, General Audience – National Level

In 12/2020 Croatia was one of the first countries in Europe that implemented the public opinion poll on the attitudes of the public towards the media and the pandemic. The new research insights were made possible through the scientific research project JOURLAB – Journalism Research Lab: Credibility of Media through Culture of Experiments and innovation in the newsrooms financed by the Croatian Science Foundation. This research was organised by a research team at the University of Zagreb, Faculty of Political Science and was conducted by IPSOS PULS in November and December 2020 on a N = 1009 (18 +) representative national sample. A 50-min questionnaire in households has been implemented in combination with an Internet panel. Our overall goal was to gain new insights into trends of trust in media and professions, news avoidance and the role of media in the COVID-19 crisis.

3.2 Intergenerational Workshops on Digital and Media Literacy

As our second method, we used a case study of participative activities with local inter-generational communities in five European countries on seven different topics and six languages, implemented and organised in 2021 within the EC-funded project SMaRT-EU – Social Media Resilience Toolkit, an intergenerational project. In 2021, a total of 50 workshops were implemented for 400 participants with the support from project partners but also with assistance from eight institutional partners at the local level. Thanks to the support from the institutions providing services to older adults such as the Retirement Home Sveta Ana (Dom za starije osobe Sveta Ana Zagreb) or the Foundation Joint Path (Zaklada Zajednički put), in Zagreb, the capital city of Croatia, we had the opportunity to test the new innovative face-to-face (F2F) intergenerational approach to digital media education as a possible solution to overcoming the digital literacy gap between younger generations and older people. Other studies had previously identified the lack of an intergenerational approach [8]. In the centre of our model are older people empowered, guided, and supported in navigation through digital challenges by young journalism and communication science students.

4 Key Findings from the Public Opinion Poll

In the second half of 2020, the research on public opinion towards media credibility and the role of media and social networks in providing information about COVID-19 at the European ground was scarce. To the best of our knowledge, this research is the first of its kind in virtue of being the first European national representative research study in peer-reviewed journals with public opinion research at the national representative sample focusing on media and COVID-19 in 2020 as keywords.

The Croatian research within the JOURLAB scientific project, as explained in the introduction, offered new insights into the role of media in times of pandemic and identified significant differences between different age groups. The data gathered in Croatia suggest that there is an evident digital divide that increased even further during the pandemic. There were significant differences in consumption of social media and Internet portals among different age groups during the pandemic.

With regard to our research we asked the respondents the following question: *How do you get informed about societal and political events (Internet portals)?* The great majority (83%) of those 70 + have never used an Internet portal to be informed about societal and political events, in comparison to only 5,6% in the 18–29 age group. Yet, this age group is not the one with the highest percentage in the overall daily consumption (62,2%). Actually, 64,5% of those in the 40–49 age group claim to use Internet portals on a daily basis (Fig. 1).

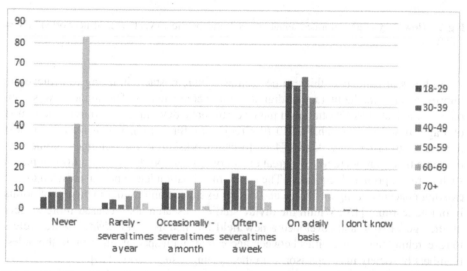

Fig. 1. How do you get informed about societal and political events (Internet portals)? (N = 1009)

Nevertheless, this digital divide turns out to be even more prominent when respondents are asked about the usage of social networks when trying to be informed about societal and political events (Graph 2). 92% of those above 70 have never used it for this purpose and only 4% are using it on a daily basis. At the same time, 56,1 of those aged 18–29 are using it on a daily basis. The difference in usage of social networks is thus further emphasised, which confirms that the age variable is significant (Fig. 2).

If 92% of senior citizens in a specific country such as Croatia never use social networks and 83% never use Internet portals for information about societal and political events, it can be noticed that the fundamental precondition for digital literacy and media literacy – the possibility and capability to use media and these channels – has not been fulfilled.

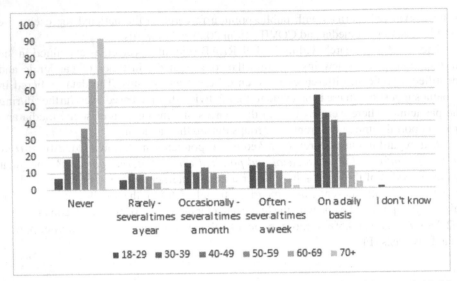

Fig. 2. How do you get informed about societal and political events (social networks)? (N = 1009)

In times of pandemic, this can be seen as a huge obstacle in trying to achieve the improvement in media literacy or digital literacy competences. The situation was even more complicated as Croatia faced major earthquake devastation in March (the region of Zagreb) and in December 2020 (the region of Banovina), which made it almost impossible to provide any kind of face-to-face workshop in the retirement homes. At the same time, seniors relied to a great extent on content produced by traditional media such as radio, print and television. The pandemic situation led to new discussion on the existing concepts of digital choice and digital exclusion and digital inclusion of adults in online learning [15]. Within the divide studies, research also focused more closely on the age variable and developed a new field labelled as *"grey divide"* which refers to researching the "inequalities between age groups with special attention to the oldest members of society in comparison with their younger successors" [16].

Yet, if we focus on the general role of media in better understanding of crises we see that, on the whole, the media helped in better understanding of crises, especially in the age group 70 + where 66% mostly or totally agree with the above statement. A significant reliance on the media by seniors was increased during the pandemic. In general, we can see that the older the audience, the reliance on the media content will have a more significant role. This is especially important in times of pandemic and lockdown, and primarily for those vulnerable members of society that are not in a position to discuss and share their thoughts and opinions with others (Fig. 3).

Finally, we asked the respondents to share their opinion on the role of different actors and stakeholders in "fight against disinformation and fake news". In previous graphs we provided evidence of overall usage of social networks and Internet portals contextualised in the COVID-19 pandemic. Within all target groups, media were identified as the most responsible stakeholder for fighting against disinformation and fake news. In

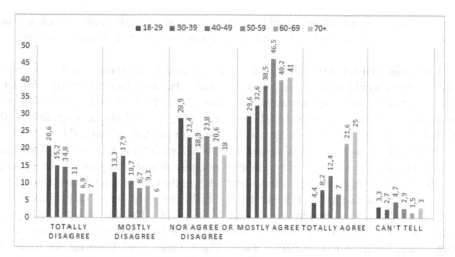

Fig. 3. The media has helped me in better understanding of crisis (N = 1009)

the youngest and oldest target groups, almost the same opinion on the role of media can be identified (Fig. 4).

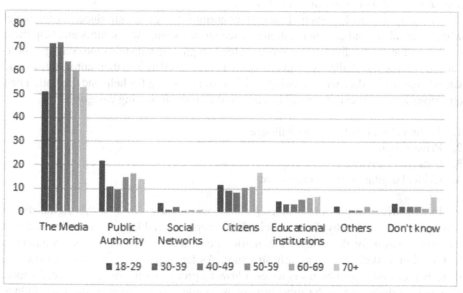

Fig. 4. In your opinion, who should fight against disinformation and fake news? (N = 1009)

5   Intergenerational Workshops on Digital and Media Literacy

In the previous section, we presented the results of the public opinion poll in Croatia that identified an urgent need to overcome the evident divide and exclusion of seniors from the digital environment. Based upon the presented research results, we know that the digital divide is omnipresent in all countries in the region, to a greater or smaller extent.

Our main goal was to create, prepare and implement intergenerational workshops where seniors would meet young people and students, share their knowledge, reflect, analyse and evaluate media messages and learn about the risks and opportunities of social networks and Internet portals. In this case study, we will give an overview of 50 workshops implemented in six languages in five countries throughout 2021.

As one of the cornerstones of our local activities, we introduced a new pedagogical model in times of pandemic – face-to-face individual consultations primarily in Zagreb, Croatia, with the support from local partners such as the City of Zagreb and the Retirement Home Sveta Ana and the Foundation Zajednički put. Even during the pandemic, we were able to provide support to seniors. One of the users in Croatia made the following statement: *"I would like to personally thank you. I'm 90 years old and although I've been using the Internet since 2010. I would like to thank you"*. However, for some of the users this was the first time they had used a tablet and even the first time they had used a search engine. As we were introducing the different topics such as disinformation and fake news, as well as topics such as social media and clickbait, the reactions of the seniors were surprising: *"This was a totally new topic for me. What a great surprise"*. At the same workshop, another 70 + user said: *"I would like to thank you for thinking also about seniors in this pandemic time"*.

Beside F2F consultations in three partner countries, we also introduced a new model where journalism and communication science students empower seniors and help them overcome the digital divide. This model helped us gain new insights into seniors' motivation, but also the challenges and fears they face, as well as into their competences and knowledge, while they were opening to the students asking for help and support. Their questions and interventions could be classified into the following categories:

1. Technical – infrastructural challenges
2. Privacy issues
3. E-citizen activities
4. Critical digital literacy perspective

In line with the previous studies - where we already saw that the digital divide concept is determined by diverse socio-demographic variables - we have learned that the main reason for the evident low participation level in the digital environment is lack of digital skills and weak infrastructure. As far as privacy issues are considered, there is a growing need by users to learn how to protect their privacy in virtual space. This was perhaps one of the most prominent challenges in our workshop spotlighted by our users: *"Can you please teach me how to make my own FB profile, but without being visible to others? Can you help me with cookies?"* Even from the perspective of journalism students, these types of questions were not expected as none of the workshop curators could predict these upper intermediate interventions. Thirdly, we also recognised a possible opportunity to promote e-citizenship as an increasing number of seniors in Croatia showed interest to improve their usage, knowledge, and participation in the e-citizenship platform. In individual consultations, journalism students were enthusiastic to empower users and try to find answers to their questions such as: *"I would like to open my e-citizen profile. How hard is it?"* Lastly, at the final stage of our workshops - Critical digital literacy perspective - we promoted critical digital literacy discussions on disinformation and clickbaits. In general, this activity opened a new perspective on understanding our users' needs as they were able to reflect and recognise the side-effects of media content they were exposed to. Table 1 is original evidence of the huge interest in disinformation and fake news as topics with the greatest number of implemented workshops. Finally, among users that participated in the workshops in Croatia, 97,5% (47 respondents) would recommend these workshops to their colleagues and friends. Even after the official end of the project, this cooperation has been continued in 2022 based on the need analysis.

Although SMaRT-EU had already been implemented by different types of institutions (universities, NGOs, and private companies), we established cooperation with eight local supporting institutions as well. Among those already mentioned from Croatia, intergenerational programmes will be promoted on a long-term scale thanks to the support from S-Plus vzw (Belgium), the second biggest membership organisation for

Table 1. SMaRT-EU workshops participants.

Institution	Topic of the workshop	Online/Offline	End users	Participants	Workshops
DKMK (HR)	Disinformation and Fake News	Offline	Seniors, Journalism Students	55	4
	Social Media and Good Manners	Offline	Seniors	20	2
	Privacy and Digital Footprint	Offline	Seniors	20	2
	The Role and Influence of Influencers	Offline	Seniors	20	2
	Clickbaits in Social Media	Online-webinar	Seniors	92	1
	Individual Consultations	Offline	Seniors	12	12
COFAC (PT)	Disinformation and Fake News	Online	Journalism Students, Youth, Adults	7	3
	Social Media and Good Manners	Online	Journalism Students, Youth, Adults	16	1
	Privacy and Digital Footprint	Online	Journalism Students, Youth, Adults	17	1
	The Role and Influence of Influencers	Online	Journalism Students, Youth, Adults	13	1
	Civic Engagement	Online	Journalism Students, Youth, Adults	8	1
	Clickbaits in Social Media	Online	Adults	5	2
PONTYDYSGU SL (UK)	Disinformation and fake news	Online/Offline	International group/youth and seniors	9	2
	Privacy and Digital Footprint	Online/Offline	International group/youth and seniors	9	2
	Civic Engagement	Offline	International group/youth and seniors	11	2
	Clickbaits in Social Media	Online/Offline	International group/youth and seniors	10	2
IMEC/MEDIAWIJS (BE)	Disinformation and Fake News	Online	Seniors	32	4
	Social Media and Good Manners	Online	Seniors	9	2
	Clickbaits in Social Media	Online	Seniors	3	1
	General Introduction	Online	Youth	3	1
TARTU UNI (EST)	Disinformation and Fake News	Online	Journalism Students, Youth, Teachers	56	2
	The Role and Influence of Influencers	Online	Journalism Students	19	1

seniors in Flanders-Belgium; COFAC – Civitas Braga, Escolhe Vilar and Daycare senior institution (Portugal); TARTU - Energia avastuskeskus (Estonia).

6   Conclusion

Our research has confirmed that the *"digital divide"*, *"digital inequality"*, the *"grey divide"* and *"digital exclusion"* are present within the European context as showcased by Croatia. These challenges were boosted by pandemic context and further reinforced within the population of seniors in retirement and care homes, especially in times of lockdown throughout the world. Their participation in society is far more than just an everyday usage of diverse applications for communication with friends and relatives. Hence, pandemic has also led to a new understanding of the advantages of digital inclusion, especially in relation to health literacy. Seniors, as the oldest members of our society indeed have a need to be informed and to participate in our digital societies. However, they also differ through so many variables: their experience, previous knowledge, media usage habits, expectations from media, etc. Yet, there is an evident need that they want to learn more and to find new ways of communication and participation with digital media usage. This was proved by our intergenerational workshops and individual consultations as a new model of curation and educational space where youth and students together with seniors gain new knowledge and understanding of the challenges in the digital society. The digital divide gap between youth and seniors is asking for a new policy approach and for large-scale cooperation between all stakeholders in our societies with the goal to empower seniors and create better conditions for them to participate in the virtual space. Their digital literacy and media literacy competences are the main precondition for inclusion and participation as e-citizens in their respective societies, especially in times of pandemic and dramatic changes where seniors are still one of the most vulnerable members of our societies.

References

1. European Commission.: Green Paper on Ageing - Fostering solidarity and responsibility between generations (2021). https://op.europa.eu/en/publication-detail/-/publication/d91 8b520-63a9-11eb-aeb5-01aa75ed71a1/language-en. Accessed 02 Jan 2022
2. Büchi, M., Hargittai, E.: A Need for Considering Digital Inequality When Studying Social Media Use and Well Being, Social Media + Society January-March, 1–7 (2022). https://doi.org/10.1177/20563051211069125
3. Livingstone, S., Papaioannaou, T., del Mar Grandío Pérez, M., Wijnen, C.: Editors' note: critical insights in European media literacy research and policy. Media Stud. 3(6). 2–12 (2012)
4. Ruseva, G., All Digital.: O3 Policy Recommendations for stakeholders and policy makers (2021). https://ict4theelderly.com/wp-content/uploads/2022/01/O3.Policy-Recommendations_FINAL.pdf. Accessed 02 Jan 2022
5. Afshar, P.P., et al.: International Quarterly of Community Health Education 0(0), 1–7 (2020). Doi: https://doi.org/10.1177/0272684X20972642, Sage
6. Lee, O.E.-K., Kim, D.-H.: Bridging the digital divide for older adults via intergenerational mentor-up. Res. Soc. Work. Pract. 29(7), 786–795 (2019)

7. Fisher, C., Park, S., Lee, J.Y., Holland, K., John, E.: Older people's news dependency and social connectedness. Media Int. Australia **181**(1), 183–196 (2021)
8. Rasi, P.i., Vuojärvi, H., Rivinen, S.: Promoting media literacy among older people: a systematic review. Adult Educ. Quart. **7**(1), 37–54 (2021)
9. Schäffer, B.: The digital literacy of seniors. Res. Comp. Int. Educ. **2**(1), 29–42 (2007)
10. Treumann, K., Baacke, D., Haacke, K., Hugger, K.-U.: Vollbrecht, R: Medienkompetenz im digitalen Zeitalter: wie die neuen Medien das Leben und Lernen Erwachsener verändern. Leske & Budrich, Opladen (2002)
11. Neves, B.B., Mead, G.: Digital technology and older people: towards a sociological approach to technology adoption in later life. Sociology **55**(5), 888–905 (2021)
12. Friemel, T.N.: The digital divide has grown old: Determinants of a digital divide among seniors. New Media Soc. **18**(2), 313–331 (2016)
13. Neves, B.B., Waycott, J., Maddox, A.: When technologies are not enough: the challenges of digital interventions to address loneliness in later life. Sociological Research Online, pp. 1–21 (2021)
14. Skałacka, K., Pajestka, G.: Digital or in-person: the relationship between mode of interpersonal communication during the COVID-19 pandemic and mental health in older adults from 27 countries. J. Fam. Nurs. **27**(4), 275–284 (2021)
15. Eynon, R., Helsper, E.: Adults learning online: digital choice and/or digital exclusion? New Media Soc. **13**(4) 534–551 (2010). https://doi.org/10.1177/1461444810374789
16. Morris, A., Brading, H.: E-literacy and the grey digital divide: a review with recommendations. J. Inf. Literacy **1**(3), 13–28 (2007)

A Social-Media Study of the Older Adults Coping with the COVID-19 Stress by Information and Communication Technologies

Najmeh Khalili-Mahani[1,2,3](✉) ⓘ, Kim Sawchuk[3,4], Sasha Elbaz[3],
Shannon Hebblethwaite[3,5], and Janis Timm-Bottos[3]

[1] Department of Design and Computation Arts, Concordia University, Montreal, QC, Canada
najmeh.khalili-mahani@concordia.ca
[2] Division of Social and Transcultural Psychiatry, McGill University, Montreal, QC, Canada
[3] engAGE Centre for Research on Aging, Concordia University, Montreal, QC, Canada
[4] Department of Communication Studies, Concordia University, Montreal, QC, Canada
[5] Department of Applied Human Sciences, Concordia University, Montreal, QC, Canada

Abstract. In this paper, we convey the results of our digital fieldwork within the current mediascape (English) by examining online reactions to an important source of cultural influence: the news media's depiction of older adult's stress, the proposals offered to older adults to assist them in coping with the stress of living in the COVID-19 pandemic, and finally, the responses of online commentators to these proposals. A quasi-automated social network analysis of 3390 valid comments in seven major international news outlets (Jan-June 2020), revealed how older adults were generally resourceful and able to cope with COVID-19 stress. For many in this technology-using sample, information and communication technologies (ICTs) were important for staying informed, busy, and connected, but they were not the primary resources for coping. Although teleconferencing tools were praised for facilitating new forms of intergenerational connection during the lockdowns, they were considered temporary and inadequate substitutes for connection to family. Importantly, older adults objected to uncritical and patronizing assumptions about their ability to deal with stress, and to the promotion of ICTs as *the* most important coping strategy. Our findings underline the necessity of a critical and media-ecological approach to studying the affordances of new ICTs for older adults, which considers changing needs and contextual preferences of aging populations in adoption of de-stressing technologies.

Keywords: Older adults · Social media · COVID-19 · Social isolation · Stress · Coping · ICT · Communication · News media · Ageism

1 Introduction

1.1 Background

Being the first to experience the hazards of COVID-19 (Corona Virus Disease, 2019) in terms of contagion vulnerability and social isolation, older adults became the subject

Q. Gao and J. Zhou (Eds.): HCII 2022, LNCS 13330, pp. 346–364, 2022.
https://doi.org/10.1007/978-3-031-05581-2_26

of many inquiries into how to reduce their stress by increasing their access to the safest tool for staying connected: information and communication technologies (ICTs).

Often, technological innovations are promoted to reduce the stresses of living in an unpredictable natural world by increasing the ability of humans to control this world and by extending the capacity for prediction, prevention, and intervention against harm. However, in doing so, all new technologies impact the lives of those who must negotiate their use. This negotiation is not only related to how physical aspects of life are affected by ICTs, but also to their psychological and cultural effects [1].

A host of discourses and debates on the conflicting social impacts of ICTs have been raised in the academic literature: they have been promoted as a means for providing tele-health or social connectedness, but there is fear of ICTs becoming used for surveillance [2], reducing the complexity of human experience to machine learned data [3], propagating mis-information [4] and promoting stigma [5, 6].

Even when technologies are not perceived negatively, they are not necessarily effective. A pre-pandemic feasibility study by Apple et al. (2019) illustrated that introducing VR (360 videos of nature) to 66 individuals in their 80s was successful and feasible; yet after trying the VR systems, participants felt less rested, less curious, and significantly more lonely [7]. While on the one hand, social media seem to provide a relief from the stresses related to COVID-19, they may become emotionally overwhelming, stressful and a source of false information and negative messaging [8].

An important factor in the mediation of cultural and psychological stresses of new technologies is that the media-created stereotype of age-related deficits. For example, by paying significant attention to age-related limitations in cognitive and physical abilities of older adults, perceptual limitations or corrective benefits of ICTs, there is often an implicit equation of aging with quantifiable and deterministic forms of disability. However, research indicates that age alone is not a predictive factor in determining usage or non-usage of ICTs [9–11]. It has also been shown that older adults deviate and tailor ICTs to their own needs, irrespective of the purpose for which they are promoted [12].

The trend towards mediatization of aging, in which media plays an important role in creating social, political and institutional cultures that are created from the omnipresence of media (or ICTs) in today's world, could become detrimental when age becomes equated with deficit and exclusion [13]. In their examination of discourses within a Canadian newspaper (The Globe and Mail) Fraser et al. (2016) found that the majority of articles created negative stereotypes of aging that reduced the willingness of older adults to seek help when needed [14]. In the context of COVID-19, Morgan et al. [15] conducted a similar study, examining 91 articles that referred to older adults and COVID-19. They found that the news coverage typically referred to older adults as a nameless, homogeneous 'other' group who were overwhelmingly framed as being at risk and passive, thus stigmatising older adults as inherently vulnerable, rather than as situationally at risk. A study of the Chinese news media yielded similar results, finding that an overemphasis on age framed as a biomedical disability and as risk factor, led to less attention being paid to the socioeconomic circumstances that would alter the quality of older people's lives at any age [16]. Messaging about the vulnerability of older adults during COVID-19 led to strict measures to reduce risk, but that subsequently increased their isolation [17].

Media creates messages not only by its content, but also by creating public reactions to itself which deserve attention. A qualitative analysis of 18,000 tweets containing the keywords "elderly," "older," and/or "boomer" plus the hashtags "#COVID19" and/or "#coronavirus" in March 2020, demonstrated that almost a quarter of tweets downplayed the importance of COVID-19 because it was 'only' deadlier among older individuals, and that 14% contained offensive content or jokes disparaging older adults [18]. Expanding the same search to more than 82,000 tweets using automated methods, another group found more concerning results: almost 73% of jokes ridiculed older adults, half of which were death jokes [19]. Interestingly, performing a thematic analysis of the Weibo (the Chinese equivalent of twitter), revealed a different pattern of representation: "older adults contributing to community" [20].

As such, the aim of this study is to examine the mediated discourses on being old (or senior), COVID-related stress, and ICTs (published in news media articles), against the on-line responses of the older readers of those articles, expressed in comments on the websites, Facebook and Reddit feeds of those articles.

1.2 Research Objective and Approach

This study deploys a novel methodological framework at the intersection of Lazarus' Transactional Theory of Stress [21] and McLuhan's ecological Media Theory [22]. We have provided examples of this interdisciplinary mixed-methodological approach elsewhere [8, 23, 24]. Briefly, media ecology argues that while technological innovations aim to extend our body's capacity for surviving more easily and comfortably, they affect both physical and cultural (thus psychological) aspects of our lives [1, 22]. In Richard Lazarus' Transactional Theory of Appraisal and Coping, stress is understood as an adaptive mechanism that is tied to a host of perceptual and behavioral variables that vary with an individual's appraisal of the significance of the stressor, and its potential impact on one's life [21]. As early as in 1960s, it has been shown that different perceptions of the same media-experience would induce different bodily stress responses [25].

The unique context of the COVID pandemic allowed for an examination of the interactions between a stressful event, the diffusion of ICTs among those who are presumed to be vulnerable to physical and mental harm, and the potential beneficiaries of ICTs that mitigate these harms: older adults.

Our methodological approach is informed by an early study of the affordances of mobile phones by 'seniors' (those over the age of 65), where Sawchuk and Crow [26] asserted that to engage in an open discussion about use and non-use of technology outside the standard frameworks for quantitative research (e.g., surveys. or usage monitoring) or qualitative inquiries (e.g., structured interviews or focus groups) might better reveal the complexities created by the specificity of context, thus painting a nuanced picture of why and how older adults adopt or resist these technologies.

To understand the appraisal of COVID-related stress and ICTs use among older adults, we explored the following questions:

1. What stressors and resources are identified and become dominant in the discussions of the stress of COVID-19 from the perspective of age?

2. How are ICTs implicated in the discussions of older adults coping with stress during COVID-19?
3. What themes emerge from older adults' discussions of the topic of COVID-related stress, ICTs and coping?

2 Materials and Methods

To conduct our research, we used a mixed-methods recursive data-mining approach that included a quantitative analysis of frequent topics, followed by a qualitative textual analysis of emerging themes [27], followed by a quantitative network analysis of overlapping themes [28] and a final reflective analysis. This recursive approach allowed us to map dominant patterns of discursive correlation between the themes (stress, resources, ICTs and age) that were co-present in online discussions.

2.1 Data Sources

Between March 2020 and September 2020, we searched 20 major Anglo-American news media outlets with a global readership (*The Guardian, The Wall Street Journal, New York Times, The Washington Post, CNN*, and *Fox News*), as well as Canadian (*The Toronto Star* and *CBC*), and Montreal (local) newspapers (*Le Devoir, Le Soleil*, and *The Montreal Gazette*); using the following keywords: "Senior" OR "Older Adults" OR "Elderly" AND "Technology" AND "Coping" AND "Covid19" AND" <the name of the media outlet> ". Articles that did not have any social media engagement were excluded. In the remaining 7 articles, we used a web-scraping technique to gather data from three sources of public engagement with the articles including: a) the comments left on the Facebook pages of each media outlet examined (using FacePager https://github.com/str ohne/Facepager), b) the comments on the articles on Reddit were extracted by Simple Scraper (https://simplescraper.io), and c) the comments on the permanent websites of the news organizations where the articles initially appeared were copy-pasted manually. Two members of the team, SE and MKM, examined all comments and cleaned the data to exclude irrelevant content, such as single response words, advertisements, or emoticons. We then performed a thematic analysis on the remaining valid 3390 comments cases, following a procedure detailed below.

2.2 Content Analysis and Visualization

Using NVivo for Mac (2020, QSR Inc.) we conducted a semi-structured thematic analysis of the content using the following procedures:

Step1: Exploratory Word-Frequency Analysis. All articles (referred to as Source) and comments (referred to as Response) were aggregated. Using NVivo, we computed a word cloud for each to identify the most prevalent words. This practice allowed us to gain a visual perspective on the prevalence and frequency of specific words, related to coping, aging and technology, in Source and in Responses. Counting the word frequency in all Sources and all Responses showed that the words "Older" and "Help" were the most frequently used terms in the Source articles, while the words "Living" and "Reading" were the most frequently used words in Responses. Neither the word "Stress", nor "Media" or "Technology" were dominant in the Responses (Fig. 1).

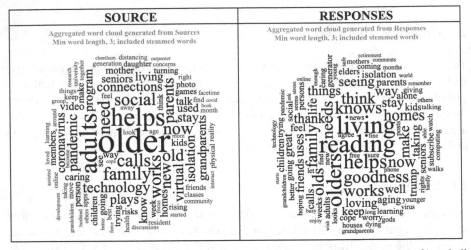

Fig. 1. Word clouds created from aggregated text from all news articles (Source, Left) and all comments (Response, Right)

Step 2: Coding Comments Under Primary Categories. We then coded each comment under four general thematic categories:

Age: Any Responses that explicitly referred to age (e.g., by stating the responder's age, age of parents, or identification of oneself or others with phrases including old, older, senior, grandparent, age, aging). When the commentors referred to themselves as a target of the article as a 'senior', they were coded under *Older*; and if they referred to examples of a senior person in their life or in their care, they werecoded under *Younger*.

Resources: Any Responses that referred to one or other forms of coping strategies. These included practical strategies including specific activities, such as reading, or support networks, as well as conceptual mechanisms such as experience.

Stressors: Any Responses that expressed an anxious or worrying opinion about the ramifications of the COVID-19 pandemic, such as not seeing friends or family, were coded under this theme.

Technology: Any Responses that explicitly referred to usage of ICTs, such as the Internet, phone, or the computer were coded as technology.

Step 3: Identifying Sub-themes. Table 1 provides the actual titles of the articles and the differences in distribution of the categories (% of coverage) that emerged from the comments. As can be seen, the highest number of comments were about available resources.

To obtain a more granular picture of different topics within each primary theme, we coded each comment inductively. For example, a comment like "*We're vulnerable seniors [Age: Older], and we've been socially isolated [*Stress: *Social Isolation] for more than two months. Our groceries are delivered, and we don't go out except to exercise and wave and smile at neighbors [*Resource: *People]. We both Text and email quite a bit and are on Facebook a lot. I'm also on twitter and the comments sections of various web sites. [*Resource: *Communication; Technology: email, Facebook, SMS, Internet, Positive View of Technology]. We don't have kids or pets, but we're used to being together and are adapting to the new situation.*" [Resource: *Coping strategy, People, Family.]* This hierarchical re-coding of the primary thematic categories revealed a total of 71 specific but nested sub-themes.

Table 1. Primary Thematic code, and the percentages of coverage per Source

Code	Age		Resources		Stressors		Technology	
Title	Count	%	Count	%	Count	%	Count	%
Ways Older Adults Can Cope With the Stress of Coronavirus								
	514	22.5	872	26.3	783	29.1	239	12.0
For isolated older people, pandemic is 'a cruel event at this time in our lives'								
	152	40.2	213	34.9	280	54.0	35	7.5
Ok Zoomer: how seniors are learning to lead more digital lives								
	138	45.4	217	47.4	109	40.1	185	53.4
The Grandparents Who Dropped Everything to Help Out During COVID								
	120	50.2	260	66.0	114	45.5	9	5.21
It's Grandparents to the Rescue for Stressed Working-From-Home Parents								
	24	12.6	40	14.7	9	6.3	6	2.4
Just What Older People Didn't Need: More Isolation								
	44	40.7	144	65.1	131	61.6	31	13.1
These seniors are turning to cutting edge technology to stay connected during the pandemic								
	7	3.7	20	7.4	31	20.0	4	2.2
Total	999		1766		1457		509	

Step 4: Network Analysis. Using the matrix coding query function in NVivo, we created a matrix whose cells indicated the number of times that any two sub-themes (codes) were expressed in the same comment. This matrix can be understood as a correlation matrix, which can be represented as a network, with the weight of an edge corresponding to the number of co-occurrences of any two codes. We then used the software Gephi 0.9.2 to compute the components that were more likely to form a community, or network, of interconnected sub-themes (network modularity), using edge weights and a 0.8 resolution, resulting in 6 networked communities [29, 30]. The sub-themes that were

most connected across different thematic communities were determined using a computational function known as eigenvector centrality, which indicates the network hubs that have the largest number of connections to other important hubs in the network. Network communities were organized by colour, and filtered by edge weight, to illustrate any edges that weighed more than 50. The thickness of the edges relates to the weight of connections between subthemes.

Step 5: Reflective Analysis and Validation. Having identified the network hubs and major edges, we then re-examined each comment to guide our interpretation and the ensuing discussion of our findings.

3 Results

3.1 Mapping the Pattern of Co-occurring Discussions

Figure 2 provides a visual representation of the centrality of themes and correlation between sub-themes. Consistent with initial coding, we found 4 large clusters (identified by colour and named reflectively) and a small additional cluster related to political skepticism (Yellow).

The size of letters in each cluster indicates high eigenvector centrality, meaning that the theme was important in the collective discourse emerging from the data. The highest centrality values were found in nodes *Older* and *Coping Strategy* (EC = 1, both in the same green cluster), followed by *People and Socialization* Strategy (EC = .993; both in the magenta cluster), *Covid-Specific stress* and *Social Stress* (EC = 1, and 0.98, respectively; both in the orange cluster) and *Media, Information and Entertainment* (EC = 0.953 and 0.950, respectively, in the blue cluster). This indicates that although important, the ICTs are not the central theme of the discussions about age and COVID-related stress.

The main hub of interest to our study *Older*, belonged to a network community that also included *Coping Strategies, Activities, Generation, Perspective* and *Experience* (coded under Resources) and *Ageism (coded under Stressors)*. We refer to this cluster as *Older Adults' Coping Strategies* (green).

The second significant hub, *Covid-Stress* was linked to *Older*, but belonged to a different cluster that included *Social Stress, Health Worries, Isolation, Economy, boredom, Lost time, Worries about the young*, as well as *Independent Elder*. We refer to this cluster as *Age-Related Covid Stressors* (orange).

Interestingly, we found a split in sub-themes that were coded under primary codes *Resources* and *Technology*. Specifically, the central hub *People* and *Socialization Strategy*, which was coded under Resources, were in a cluster that also included *Younger* (initially coded under Age), Communication and ICTs that were used for such connections (*Zoom, Phone, Facebook, Chat, SMS, email*). This indicates that these communication technologies pertained to facilitating connections for the younger respondents on the social media. We call this cluster *Intergenerational Connections* (magenta).

On the other hand, the cluster (blue) that included central hubs such as *Media* and *Information and Entertainment* technologies (including *Computer, Watching TV, Games*) which were initially coded as Resources, also included subthemes that reflected individual appraisal of ICTs (such as *Positive view of tech, Tech stress, Luddite, Indifferent to tech, Cost*) which were initially coded under *Technology*, and technological self efficacy such as *Nerdy Elder* (initially coded under Age). We call this cluster *Older Adults ICT Appraisal* (blue).

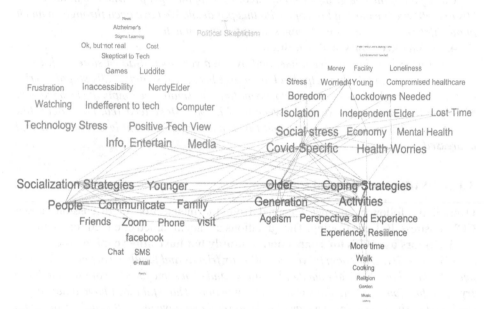

Fig. 2. Network clusters (identified by different colours) emerging from network analysis of co-occurrence matrix of 71 subthemes in comments. The letter size indicates the centrality of the theme in the cluster.

3.2 Age, COVID-Stress and Resources

A substantial portion of the public discussions on the topic of seniors' stress during COVID-19 focused on cultural assumptions about the relationship between ageing and vulnerability and stated resistance to the implied ageism explicitly. Overall, the following themes emerged from studying the intersection of discussions about Coping, COVID-stress, and Age. (**The** *quotations* **are not modified or edited for language.**)

1. Senior isolation is not new.

C1:... America has treated senior citizens, in general, as a nuisance and a frequent topic of geriatric jokes for as long as I can remember. [...]. Millions of them are living just as they did before the Coronavirus...isolated and alone. I am hopeful that this tragic time and articles like this, will give more of us a sense of responsibility to reach out, in some way, to acknowledge that they are out there.

2. The young are presumptive about senior's stress.

C2: This journalist must be young! Thanks for thinking of us but we are handling today's situation quite well. The senior community can cope with this historic Pandemic but we pray for our nation's young adults who are being tested with this social, medical and financial crisis. The writer does not realize our wealth of knowledge from years of life experiences, going back to the world situation of 1930's to this year, 2020 as well as our deep faith and trust in a higher being than ourselves.

3. Seniors are resilient and can help.

C3: Of all of the age groups who are dealing with this- people who are in their 70s, 80s and 90s are the most apt to cope with this pandemic We have been through so much in our lifetimes, seen so many changes, adapted to so much.

4. Seniors keep busy with routines.

C4: I am 86, widowed, live alone, and live in a very locked-down state […]. I will describe something I do that helps but I apologize because it sounds really stupid. I write a list of every single thing I intend to do, no matter how small, like Empty the Dishwasher, Make the Bed, Manicure my Nails, Sweep the Balcony, Make Iced Tea, Pay Cable Bill, etc. etc. […] This imposes structure and I feel more organized and less rudderless and depressed.

3.3 COVID-Stress, ICT and Coping

Overall, the following themes emerged from the intersection of discussions about COVID-stress, ICT and Coping. The quotations are not modified or edited for language.

5. Seniors use ICTs for connection to family but have other coping resources.

C5: FaceTime and Zoom let you see all your friends and family easily enough- I just keep thinking how thankful I am that I'm not stranded in some foreign country like India trying to find food on long lines with so many people. Thankful that I have a house and backyard to sit in each day- so many books to read and have my crafts and music and a stockpile of food to eat. I'm just grateful for all I do have.

6. Seniors take advantage of ICTs to taking care of the young.

C6: My parents have played virtual hide and seek with my five- and three-year olds. They take turns trying to find the person that hides. So my mom will hide in her house and my Dad will try to find her while my kids suggest hiding spots to him. It's good for at least a half hour of fun!

7. Seniors have discovered and enjoy new forms of intergenerational connections.

C7: To me this is the upside of the pandemic which is spending time with grandkids who I just saw on holidays and select weekends. Now I have learned Zoom and brushed off my multiplication tables, and experienced the joy of reading books out loud. I turned the guest bedroom into their sanctuary and my lower level into a learning/ arts and crafts room. I am no longer just a grandmother who brings gifts.

8. Seniors have enjoyed learning new skills for staying connected.

C8: My own father never went to high school, but when made redundant in his 50s, became interested in computers and actually became pretty confident (with some occasional nudging from me). But when he passed away recently in his early 70s, it left my mum quite disconnected, as she was previously not interested in computers/tech. She is the kind of person who struggled with the remote control, and would cry with frustration when she couldn't get the wifi to work at home. […], I installed whatsapp for

her, and now we have family chats, and she sees get grandkids by video chat everyday-
[…]. I think it has been a primary part of her mental health not deteriorating.

9. Seniors use different ICTs to fill the time with different activities.

C9: As a comfortable retiree, I was thinking what about if this had happened circa
1975 when I was just starting out and living in a small efficiency (i.e. one room) apart-
ment. No internet, no cable, TV only NBC/CBS/ABC/PBS and independent channels
5 and 20 (anyone else remember "Channel 20--The Great Entertainer"?), an AM/FM
radio. It there's a time in my life to be constrained as I am this is it. Hundreds of
cable channels, all of the knowledge of humanity accessible via the internet, ebooks I
can buy or borrow from the library, Kindle/Nook, Apple Music with almost every song
ever recorded and Apple News with hundreds of magazines, streaming services (Netflix,
Disney +, Apple TV, all the HBO/Showtime/Starz premium channels)--the choices are
limitless. Throw in Facetime and Zoom.

3.4 Age, COVID-Stress and ICT

To specifically investigate the topic of age and ICT in relation to COVIS-stress, we
examined the links between the *Older* hub, ICTs and what stresses can be linked to
them. This analysis revealed the following common themes.

10. ICT does not fully address the stress of separation from loved ones.

C10: The biggest issue is we can't see our two grandchildren. We now interact with
them using FaceTime but it's not the same.

C11: I was introduced to Zoom by my grandson and have converted to online tuition
via this app. I prefer face to face tuition but will tutor online until an antibody test or
vaccine is found.

11. Physical Inaccessibility of technology causes stress.

C12: I'm 84 and macular degeneration and arthritis. I'm willing to help myself any
way I can but crawling on the floor to check modems and black cords plugged into black
tech items with teensy white numbers and names on black surfaces while talking with
a clutched phone at my ear while some young person "talks me through it" at a mile a
minute drives me crazy. Every time I manage to climb up to my chair again and see a
working TV screen I cheer.

12. Constantly changing User Interfaces cause stress.

C13: Perhaps it should have been at greater pains to say that both types of older
people exist - those who embrace technology well and those who struggle - with a massive
sliding scale in between.\n\nMy mother, in her 70s struggles, but we have got her using
Facebook video Messenger and Zoom. I feel a lot of it is about keeping up with these
things as the years progress as the 'grammar' of using them changes quite a bit. […].

13. Costs of technology cause stress.

C14: The real issue for older people is not the inability to use technology but the
fact that when you give up regular work you may no longer have access to either the
funds to buy and keep up to date the hardware you need or the informal access to help
and support which comes with working in many office/educational etc. environments.
[…]Digital exclusion and the issues this poses for all ages is a far more pertinent issue
in the current lockdown than whether someone in their 80s who can afford to buy a
laptop or tablet can use zoom for an online reading group or class.

12. Some seniors do not trust the surveillance features in new ICTs.

C15: Perhaps after a certain age a person becomes less concerned with having their private data mined, placing themselves under home surveillance, whilst being manipulated by clandestine third party interests.

C16: I can't believe the amount of people suckered in to using Alexa etc. having your actions monitored and paying for the privilege.

13. Pushing technology on older adults while neglecting their choices causes stress.

C17: As an older person, I do find this article and comments a bit patronising. Technology is straightforward and easy for most people, older people who do not use it, chose not to.\nA friend of mine has parents, who will not even consider using a tablet or computer, saying they are too old to learn and for the majority of older people that is a choice not a fact.\nWhen my mother was in her mid eighties (she has been dead for 15 years), she insisted on having a go and mastered the tech available then with no issue. In fact she said that using a keyboard was helping to keep her arthritic hands mobile.\nAnother friend has lost speech and mobility due to a stroke and now has taught herself to communicate using a ipad, we talk to her daily.\nIf anyone of any age has mental capacity they can use IT if they want to, it's a choice.

14. The implied ageism in technology adoption discourses cause stress.

C18: Oh dear. Yet another simplistic lumping of\"seniors\" into one class of computer-illiterati. I'm 74. I wrote my first computer program in 1968 had an Apple II in 1982 was using modems over telephone lines to communicate like iMessage back in 1984. Maybe I'm atypical but it illustrates the oversimplification. Like saying \"all journalists are stupid\". May be true for some obviously not for all. "

15. Stigmatization of older adults' digital literacy stifles learning.

C19: But it is simply a reality that the majority of seniors still are not comfortable enough with technology to be independent with it. Denying that there is a problem only creates a stigma about getting help.

4   Discussion

The aim of this study was to investigate the older adults' reaction to mainstream media's depiction of older adult's COVID-19 stress, and their appraisal of ICTs as a coping strategy. Mapping the discourse emerging in the context of the public discussions about the stress of COVID-19 for older adults, we found that the themes of age and coping resources (green cluster in Fig. 2) and COVID stressors (orange cluster) were linked, but not co-occuring enough to form a common network community. We also found a thematic split in how ICTs were used to cope with COVID stress: ICTs that were related to dealing with boredom, or staying active and entertained (blue cluster) were independent of the COVID-stress (orange cluster)--although linked to older adults coping strategies (green cluster). However, ICTs that were specific to connecting with family and friends (such as Zoom, Facebook and telephone) were related to social resources for coping and were linked to COVID-specific stress of social isolation. Reflective analysis of the links between these clusters indicated that the negative appraisals of ICTs, were related to a host of well-known concerns that predate the pandemic (e.g., physical and financial accessibility; disinterest or lack of trust; and technology shaming). The positive appraisals were related to new-found opportunities for intergenerational connection, albeit with emphasis on the temporary necessity of ICTs and the fact that they would not replace real and in-person experiences. We highlight the following important conclusions:

4.1 Older Adults Are Resilient and Concerned About the Young

Our observations corroborate other studies that have taken place in North America, suggesting that older adults have found ways to be resilient and proactive in coping with COVID-related stress [31–33]. In a literature review study published in 2020, Fleth and Heisel, argued that to feel valued and respected for their ability to contribute and offer experience matters most to older adults who need to cope with the biological hazards of this pandemic [34]. This is in fact what this data reveals as well, both because age-related experience was often referred to as a source of resilience, and also because older adults expressed concern for the young, and took pleasure from finding new ways (e.g. learning to babysit via Zoom) to help their children in the workforce.

For those who identified themselves as older adults (*Older*), besides social isolation, worrying about the effects of the pandemic on younger generations were a source of concern. Similarly, in a quantitative survey of >400 60 + adults, Nimrod demonstrated that although the respondents reported moderate to high levels of stress due to COVID, the greatest contributor to the score was their concern about others and not the immediate threat to themselves [35]. This finding was replicated in a qualitative study of 826 older adults of the same age group [36].

4.2 ICTs for Staying Active and ICTs for Connection Address Different and Independent Needs

We found that the benefits of ICTs in the COVID-19 context were in: 1) allowing one to stay safely connected to others while practicing social distancing; 2) helping working children by tutoring or playing with grandchildren, either via Zoom or via other online activities; and 3) learning new things because of the need to connect to others, including younger generations, *via* such technologies. These findings are consistent with Freeman *et al.*'s TILL study, which identified intergenerational connections as one of the main motivational factors for older adults to adopt technologies that are introduced to them by the younger generations [37]. However, it is also important to underscore that beyond serving as a social strategy, various other activities such as reading, gardening, cooking, or sitting on a porch were equally important to coping with COVID-19 related boredom and isolation. In general, too little attention is being paid to the desire for leisure activities, for meaning and for general social equity are rarely the primary concerns for technological innovation [38, 39]. Misunderstanding the needs and desires of older adults might, in turn, may stifle technology adoption [37].

The use of ICTs for leisure entertainment and information have previously been linked to coping with stress--independent of age [8, 24, 37, 40], however studies in older adults to date do not indicate that ICTs act as the primary coping strategy for older adults throughout the COVID-19 pandemic [36, 40–42]. We found that although new technologies like Zoom were appreciated for creating possibilities for connecting with family and friends--especially creating new ways of connecting with grandchildren--they were not fully replacing face-to-faced contact. While many researchers are exploring whether older adults will accept and adopt smart ICTs [43, 44], choice, accessibility and agency continue to remain critical factors [11, 45, 46].

4.3 Media's Role in Ageist Messaging Is Remarkable

Exaggerated attention to age-related limitations in cognitive and physical abilities of older adults contributes to a messaging environment in which ageist narratives that simplistically equate aging with decline propagate.

Our study corroborates other studies that argue that ageism is a pervasive theme in COVID-19 discourses [47]. Media have been known to perpetuate ageist stereotypes, [14, 16, 48], and our data shows that older adults object to it. In a cultural milieu, where ageism is manifest in the uncritical valorization of ideals of 'successful', 'healthy' or 'positive' aging, it is critical to understand how the zealous promotion of these alternative images may unwittingly reinforce their very opposite intended effect, including age-related shaming and blaming [49].

Examining comments on news articles that promoted new technologies such as VR, show a certain level of skepticism emerging from being pushed into rapid adoption of technology due to COVID-19. As many older commenters stated, this is not because all older adults are luddites, but because technology may threaten a way of living in which they have already flourished. Our findings confirm that, the 'pandemic precarity', i.e., the risk of further marginalizing older adults in the presumptive development of homogenizing stress-relief solutions must be considered [38]. As numerous comments in our study corroborated, in the context of the pandemic, ignoring situational vulnerability prevents attending to the diversity of socio-economic circumstances and intersecting identities, including ethnicity and gender [15].

4.4 Implied Ageism in Discussions of Older Adult's Relation to ICT Is a Potential Obstacle to Their Adoption

Ageism, an unintended consequence of focusing on older age, has at least three facets: the stereotyping of older adults based on their age and abilities; discrimination based on age; and institutional and policy practices that perpetuate those stereotypes [50]. Positive stereotypes of old age may have detrimental consequences too; for example, positive images of ageing may make those who do not live up to these norms feel like they have failed and often contain new normative values that promote successful aging as individual achievement, rather than as a shared social responsibility [48].

In examining the link between technology and ageism, Ivan and Cutler have argued that there is a circular relationship between ageism and technology, in that being designed by the younger innovators, technologies are not always meaningful or accessible to many older adults, and thus internalized stereotypes (even by older adults themselves) perpetuate this disconnect further [51]. This is when messaging around the issue of age-stress and destressing-ICT can become a source of stress in and of itself.

In our research, three issues associated with ICTs and aging were identified as frustrating, ageist and contributing to their stress: 1) discourses on older adults as ICT illiterate (citing examples of the fact that many septuagenarians (like Bill Gates) are the pioneers of computing technology; 2) the assumption (presumably) by young writers of the articles that older adults were disinterested in technologies and 3) the lack of acknowledgement of structural and systemic issues including the insufficiency of financial and human resources that would facilitate the adoption of ICTS by octogenarians.

Indeed, several of those who raised objections to 'ageist' attitude of the mainstream media, pointed out that many new ICTs did not serve any purpose in their lives, and that it was their choice, not inability to learn, that made them refuse adoption of new technologies. These observations corroborate previous research that age alone is not a predictive factor in determining usage or non-usage of ICTs [9–11], suggesting that choice, agency and systemic conditions are also critical factors [11, 45, 46].

Our findings corroborate results from a pre-COVID qualitative study of older adults in various communities in the UK and Canada. Marsten et al. identified the two sources of resistance to technology: apprehension about how to use it because of feeling ashamed for not knowing about it or not being able to learn it; lack of interest stemming from concerns about technology replacing actual human connections [10]. Here we observed that many older adults saw this pandemic as an 'opportunity' for learning ICTs (e.g., as a new tool to babysit grandchildren) for new purposes. These findings corroborate Sawchuk's observation in the RECCA study, where a community of older adults who pushed back against mainstream depictions of ageing as a hindrance, adopted technology as an activist strategy to advance their agenda [11]. In other words, as difficult and 'stressful' as technology might be, if there is a good reason for using it, age is not an impediment in adoption--although physical and cognitive abilities remain challenging.

5 Conclusion

5.1 Addressing Research Questions

Our first research question was: "What stressors and resources dominated the discussions of the stress of COVID-19 from the perspective of age?" We found that proportionately, there were more references to *Resources* than to *Stressors* and that to be *Older*, in and of itself, was identified as a major asset for coping with the stress of pandemic--primarily due to the experience of having lived a long and eventful life. However, *People* and *Activities* were important resources, especially to cope with the social limitations created by lockdowns.

Our second question was about how ICTs were implicated in the discussions of older adults coping with stress during COVID. We found that in general, ICTs were not the primary resource for coping, except to alleviate the stress of being cut-off from the family members. In addition to serving their usual purpose of providing information and entertainment, they were also referred to as important for creating new intergenerational experiences. To have to learn new skills to foster such relations was welcomed by all who mentioned such benefits.

Finally, we wanted to explore what themes emerged from older adults' discussions of the topic of COVID-related stress and coping through ICTs. We found that even when the social affordances of ICTs were acknowledged, they were not seen as a replacement for actual physical human contact and interaction. Moreover, the prevalence of ageist discourses on older adults' experience of stress during COVID, and presumptions about aging with technology, were frustrating to many older adults within our sampling range.

Our findings suggest that the physical and financial accessibility of ICTs, especially for the oldest of this cohort was important, but to consider older adult's agency, and decision-making, irrespective of their experience with technology was important to all age groups.

5.2 Limitations

A major constraint of our study is in that we only focused on Anglo-American and Canadian news media websites, mainly targeting an educated readership.

Conclusions of this study are based on the comments of a group of older adults who already have access to ICTs and who possess enough digital proficiency to interact with news media via social networks. The majority of those who commented often reflected on their own privilege in possessing the financial and technological means to take advantage of ICTs. Therefore, these results do not address the reality of digital divide, that is still pervasive even in countries like Canada.

5.3 Implications for Future Research

Despite limitation of not being inclusive-enough, and given the fact that access was not an issue for the commenters that informed this study, it is noteworthy that ageism emerged as a significant theme, both in protest to presumptions about older adults coping with COVID-19, and in protest to presumptions about their ability or needs to take advantage of ICTs. This observation highlights the fact that the mediatization of ageing creates cultural and psychological tensions that need to be carefully considered while new technologies for alleviating stress are pushed into the lives of older adults.

The interdisciplinary methodological approach of this study, applied to data gathered from social media of major news media outlets where the answers were framed by the topic of the articles, but unsolicited point of views of participants were expressed on Social Media) provides an opportunity for a critical approach to studying aging within our current media ecology, which all too often neglects or misrepresents older-users' appraisals of the proposed tech-based solutions that industry and academic scholars may design for them.

Acknowledgements. This paper is part of research projects **Meet me At the Mall: engAGE Living Lab,** funded by the Fond de Recherche du Québec (JTB, PI; NKM & SH, co-investigator); and **Aging in Data,** funded by Social Sciences and Humanities Research Council of Canada (KS, PI; NKM, co-investigator).

References

1. Mumford, L.: The drama of the machines. Scribner's Mag. **88**, 150–161 (1930)
2. Jung, G., et al.: Too much information: assessing privacy risks of contact trace data disclosure on people with COVID-19 in South Korea. Front. Public Health **8** (2020). https://doi.org/10.3389/fpubh.2020.00305
3. Bachtiger, P., Peters, N.S., Walsh, S.L.F.: Machine learning for COVID-19—asking the right questions. Lancet Digital Health. **2**(8), e391–e392 (2020). https://doi.org/10.1016/s2589-7500(20)30162-x
4. Eysenbach, G.: How to fight an infodemic: the four pillars of infodemic management. J. Med. Internet Res. **22**(6), e21820 (2020). https://doi.org/10.2196/21820
5. Anwar, A., et al.: Role of mass media and public health communications in the COVID-19 pandemic. Cureus (2020). https://doi.org/10.7759/cureus.10453
6. Atehortua, N.A., Patino, S.: COVID-19, a tale of two pandemics: novel coronavirus and fake news messaging. Health Promot. Int. **36**(2), 524–534 (2021). https://doi.org/10.1093/heapro/daaa140
7. Appel, L., et al.: Older adults with cognitive and/or physical impairments can benefit from immersive virtual reality experiences: a feasibility study. Front Med. (Lausanne) **6** 329 (2019). https://doi.org/10.3389/fmed.2019.00329
8. Pahayahay, A., Khalili-Mahani, N.: What media helps, what media hurts: a mixed methods survey study of coping with COVID-19 using the media repertoire framework and the appraisal theory of stress. J. Med. Internet Res. **22**(8) e20186 (2020). doi:https://doi.org/10.2196/20186
9. Fernández-Ardèvol, M., Sawchuk, K., Grenier, L.: Maintaining connections. Nordicom. Review **38**(s1), 39–51 (2017). https://doi.org/10.1515/nor-2017-0396
10. Marston, H.R., et al.: Older adults' perceptions of ICT: main findings from the technology in Later Life (TILL) study. Healthcare (Basel) **7**(3) (2019). doi:https://doi.org/10.3390/healthcare7030086
11. Sawchuk, K.: Tactical mediatization and activist ageing: pressures, push-backs, and the story of RECAA. MediaKultur. **54**, 47–64 (2013)
12. Loos, E., Peine, A., Fernandéz-Ardèvol, M.: Older people as early adopters and their unexpected and innovative use of new technologies: deviating from technology companies' scripts. In: Gao, Q., Zhou, J. (eds.) HCII 2021. LNCS, vol. 12786, pp. 156–167. Springer, Cham (2021). https://doi.org/10.1007/978-3-030-78108-8_12
13. Christensen, C.L.: and L. Nybro Petersen. Introduction. Nordicom Rev. **38**(s1), 3–7 (2017). https://doi.org/10.1515/nor-2017-0399
14. Fraser, S.A., et al.: Stereotypes associated with age-related conditions and assistive device use in canadian media: table 1. Gerontologist **56**(6), 1023–1032 (2016). https://doi.org/10.1093/geront/gnv094
15. Morgan, T., et al.: COVID-19 and the portrayal of older people in New Zealand news media. J. R. Soc. N. Z. **51**(sup1), S127–S142 (2021). https://doi.org/10.1080/03036758.2021.1884098
16. Zhang, J., Liu, X.: Media representation of older people's vulnerability during the COVID-19 pandemic in China. Eur. J. Ageing **18**(2), 149–158 (2021). https://doi.org/10.1007/s10433-021-00613-x

17. Monahan, C., et al.: COVID-19 and ageism: How positive and negative responses impact older adults and society. Am. Psychol. **75**(7), 887–896 (2020). https://doi.org/10.1037/amp 0000699
18. Jimenez-Sotomayor, M.R., Gomez-Moreno, C., Soto-Perez-de-Celis, E.: Coronavirus, Ageism, and Twitter: an evaluation of tweets about older adults and COVID-19. J. Am. Geriatrics Soc. **68**(8) 1661–1665 (2020). doi:https://doi.org/10.1111/jgs.16508
19. Xiang, X., et al.: Modern senicide in the face of a pandemic: an examination of public discourse and sentiment about older adults and COVID-19 using machine learning. J. Gerontol. Ser. B. **76**(4), e190–e200 (2021). https://doi.org/10.1093/geronb/gbaa128
20. Xi, W., et al.: A thematic analysis of weibo topics (Chinese Twitter Hashtags) regarding older adults during the COVID-19 outbreak. J. Gerontol. Ser. B. **76**(7), e306–e312 (2021). https://doi.org/10.1093/geronb/gbaa148
21. Lazarus, R.S., Folkman, S.: Stress, Appraisal, and Coping. Springer Pub. Co., New York xiii, 445 p. (1984)
22. McLuhan, M., Ralph Ellison Collection (Library of Congress).Understanding media; the extensions of man. 1st ed., vii, 359 p. McGraw-Hill, New York (1964)
23. Khalili-Mahani, N., De Schutter, B.: Affective game planning for health applications: quantitative extension of gerontoludic design based on the appraisal theory of stress and coping. JMIR Serious Games. **7**(2), e13303 (2019). https://doi.org/10.2196/13303
24. Khalili-Mahani, N., Smyrnova, A., Kakinami, L.: To each stress its own screen: a cross-sectional survey of the patterns of stress and various screen uses in relation to self-admitted screen addiction. J Med Internet Res. **21**(4), e11485 (2019). https://doi.org/10.2196/11485
25. Lazarus, R.S.: A laboratory study of psychological stress produced by a motion picture film. Psychological monographs: general and applied, 35 p. American Psychological Association, Washington (1962)
26. Sawchuk, K., Crow, B.: Into the 'Grey Zone': Milieus that Matter. Wi: Journal of Mobile Media. **5**(Special Issue: Observing the Mobile User Experience) (2011)
27. Leech, N.L., Onwuegbuzie, A.J.: Beyond constant comparison qualitative data analysis: using NVivo. Sch. Psychol. Q. **26**(1), 70–84 (2011). https://doi.org/10.1037/a0022711
28. Papadopoulos, S., et al.: Community detection in social media. Data Min. Knowl. Disc. **24**(3), 515–554 (2011). https://doi.org/10.1007/s10618-011-0224-z
29. Blondel, V.D., et al.: Fast unfolding of communities in large networks. J. Stat. Mech. Theory Exp. **2008**(10) (2008). https://doi.org/10.1088/1742-5468/2008/10/p10008
30. Lambiotte, R., Delvenne, J.-C., Barahona, M.: Random walks, Markov processes and the multiscale modular organization of complex networks. IEEE Trans. Network Sci. Eng. **1**(2), 76–90 (2014). https://doi.org/10.1109/tnse.2015.2391998
31. Klaiber, P., et al.: The Ups and downs of daily life during COVID-19: age differences in affect, stress, and positive events. J. Gerontol. Ser. B. **76**(2), e30–e37 (2021). https://doi.org/10.1093/geronb/gbaa096
32. Pearman, A., et al.: Age differences in risk and resilience factors in COVID-19-related stress. J. Gerontol. Ser. B. **76**(2), e38–e44 (2021). https://doi.org/10.1093/geronb/gbaa120
33. Vahia, I.V., Jeste, D.V., Reynolds, C.F.: Older Adults and the Mental Health Effects of COVID-19. Jama. **324**(22) (2020). https://doi.org/10.1001/jama.2020.21753
34. Flett, G.L., Heisel, M.J.: Aging and feeling valued versus expendable during the COVID-19 pandemic and beyond: a review and commentary of why mattering is fundamental to the health and well-being of older adults. Int. J. Ment. Heal. Addict. **19**(6), 2443–2469 (2020). https://doi.org/10.1007/s11469-020-00339-4
35. Nimrod, G.: Changes in internet use when coping with stress: older adults during the COVID-19 pandemic. Am. J. Geriatr. Psychiatry **28**(10), 1020–1024 (2020). https://doi.org/10.1016/j.jagp.2020.07.010

36. Whitehead, B.R., Torossian, E., Meeks, S.: Older adults' experience of the COVID-19 pandemic: a mixed-methods analysis of stresses and joys. Gerontologist **61**(1), 36–47 (2021). https://doi.org/10.1093/geront/gnaa126

37. Freeman, S., et al.: Intergenerational effects on the impacts of technology use in later life: insights from an international, multi-site study. Int. J. Environ. Res. Public Health **17**(16) (2020). https://doi.org/10.3390/ijerph17165711

38. Hebblethwaite, S., Young, L., Martin Rubio, T.: Pandemic precarity: aging and social engagement. Leisure Sci. **43**(1–2) 170–176 (2020). https://doi.org/10.1080/01490400.2020.1773998

39. De Schutter, B., Vanden Abeele, V.: Towards a gerontoludic manifesto. Anthropol. Aging. **36**(2) 112–120 (2015). https://doi.org/10.5195/aa.2015.104

40. Khalili-Mahani, N., Elbaz, S., Pahayahay, A., Timm-Bottos, J.: Role of social media in coping with COVID-19 stress: searching for intergenerational perspectives. In: Meiselwitz, G. (ed.) HCII 2021. LNCS, vol. 12775, pp. 373–392. Springer, Cham (2021). https://doi.org/10.1007/978-3-030-77685-5_28

41. Pahayahay, A., Khalili-Mahani, N.: What media helps, what media hurts: a mixed methods survey study of coping with COVID-19 using the media repertoire framework and the appraisal theory of stress. J. Med. Internet Res. **22**(8) (2020). https://doi.org/10.2196/20186

42. Fuller, H.R., Huseth-Zosel, A., Bowers, B.J.: Lessons in resilience: initial coping among older adults during the COVID-19 pandemic. Gerontologist **61**(1), 114–125 (2021). https://doi.org/10.1093/geront/gnaa170

43. Wang, S., et al.: Technology to Support Aging in Place: Older Adults' Perspectives. Healthcare **7**(2) (2019). https://doi.org/10.3390/healthcare7020060

44. Carnemolla, P.: Ageing in place and the internet of things – how smart home technologies, the built environment and caregiving intersect. Visualization Eng. **6**(1), 1–16 (2018). https://doi.org/10.1186/s40327-018-0066-5

45. Christensen, C.L., Nybro Petersen, L.: Being old in the age of mediatization. Nordicom Rev. **38**(s1), 3–7 (2017). https://doi.org/10.1515/nor-2017-0399

46. Hebblethwaite, S.: The (in)visibility of older adults in digital leisure cultures. In Digital leisure cultures : critical perspectives. In: Carnicelli, S., McGillivray, D., McPherson, G. (eds.) 94–106. Routledge, Taylor & Francis Group, London ; New York (2017). doi:

47. Fraser, S., et al.: Ageism and COVID-19: what does our society's response say about us? Age Ageing **49**(5), 692–695 (2020). https://doi.org/10.1093/ageing/afaa097

48. Loos, E., Ivan, L.: Visual ageism in the media. In: Ayalon, L., Tesch-Römer, C. (eds.) Contemporary Perspectives on Ageism. IPA, vol. 19, pp. 163–176. Springer, Cham (2018). https://doi.org/10.1007/978-3-319-73820-8_11

49. Brunton, R.J., Scott, G.: Do we fear ageing? a multidimensional approach to ageing anxiety. Educ. Gerontol. **41**(11), 786–799 (2015). https://doi.org/10.1080/03601277.2015.1050870

50. Butler, R.N.: Age-Ism: another form of bigotry. The Gerontologist **9**(4 Part 1), 243–246 (1969). https://doi.org/10.1093/geront/9.4_Part_1.243

51. Ivan, L., Cutler, S.J.: Ageism and technology: the role of internalized stereotypes. Univ. Tor. Q. **90**(2), 127–139 (2021). https://doi.org/10.3138/utq.90.2.05

Older Adults and Communication Technologies During the Lockdown in Romania

Luminița-Anda Mandache[1](✉) [ID] and Loredana Ivan[2] [ID]

[1] School of Anthropology, University of Arizona, Tucson, AZ 85721, USA
lmandache@email.arizona.edu
[2] Communication Department, National University of Political Studies and Public Administration, 012244 Bucharest, Romania
loredana.ivan@comunicare.ro

Abstract. Current available data suggest that already vulnerable populations are being disproportionately affected by the COVID 19 epidemic. The same is valid for older adults, who have been labeled at the beginning of the pandemic as a high-risk population and advised to be precautious in meeting others and take part in large gatherings. In the current study, we use data from 12 semi-structured interviews conducted between 15th and 30th of May 2020, in Romania, with old adults aged 65 and above, from urban and rural areas. The interviews approached topics such as use of technology during the pandemic, ways of obtaining information about the COVID-19 pandemic and overall challenges experienced during the pandemic. The findings reveal that digital technologies have been used more during the pandemic than before, especially in the urban areas. Family communication via digital technologies revolved around pandemic related topics, everyday life, and safety measures. Contrary to popular believes, Romanian seniors consumed information about the COVID-19 pandemic with caution, triangulating sources of information from several TV channels and social media. Lastly, seniors' greatest challenge was the lack of physical contact with family members and physical movement, particularly related to their daily routines. They have used social media to cope with the loneliness of being apart from their children and grandchildren, and some even reconnected with older friends or distant family members.

Keywords: ICT · COVID-19 · Older adults and ICT · Older adults and communication technologies

1 Introduction

The Covid-19 pandemic has been challenging to everyone and a devastating period especially during the initial months when measures of social isolation and social distancing become the norm worldwide [1]. Moreover, the Covid-19 pandemic proved to be particularly harmful for older adults [2], due to their preexisting risk of loneliness and on average lower level of technology skills [3, 4]. To maintain contact with family and friends and to provide social interactions needed for critical situations (as for example interaction with doctors and carriers), older adults had to appeal to Internet

Q. Gao and J. Zhou (Eds.): HCII 2022, LNCS 13330, pp. 365–380, 2022.
https://doi.org/10.1007/978-3-031-05581-2_27

based tools and use them effectively. Once online, they faced additional challenges in finding the relevant information and avoid scamming and disinformation [5]. Some were helped by families and acquaintances and others were probably pushed to learn using new applications or use new digital devices compared with their usual digital repertoires [6]. Given this context, digital inequalities have been exacerbating representing a major risk of vulnerability not only to the virus but also to social isolation [7]. In fact, Covid-19 increased pressure on "vulnerable" groups to improve their digital skills [8].

Information and communication technologies (ICTs) have been presented as a way of reducing the effects of social isolation, provide remote health care at a distance, carry on working and training activities, but also maintain basic services (as shopping and appointments). Older adults who were not using the new technologies (e.g., smartphone, tablets) or did not have access to Internet were particularly excluded from the so-called "digital participation" [9] which eventually meant that they were deprived of online services and content (as for example content regarding health information), digital social networking, online shopping and entertaining. This resulted in increasing feelings of loneliness [1] and isolation [10]. For older adults who were already online, Covid-19 has been a challenging period as there was a bi-directional relation between the Covid-19 crisis and digital inequalities: Covid-19 deepened the digital divide phenomena and digital inequalities accentuated people's vulnerabilities to Covid-19 [7].

There is a general understanding that older adults are the most affected by the digital divide phenomenon [9]. For example, "digital immigrants", the term coined by Prensky [11] —, described the presumed digital gap between older and younger people, the latter being described as "digital natives" (the group that was born and raised when the new technologies were largely available). Consequently, the lockdown and the subsequent measures of social isolation presumably affected older adults to a larger extent, as they lagged in using Internet-based tools. While the digital gap between old and younger citizens has reduced during past years, especially in developed countries, at the beginning of the Covid-19 pandemic there was a significant number of older adults with low digital skills [12, 13]. Indeed, the Internet adoption rate increased almost exponentially during the past two decades both in European Union (EU) and in the United States (US), and the general attitude toward digital technologies has become more positive across people of different ages and socio-economic backgrounds. However, costs and affordability continue to be a barrier for some of social groups (for example the oldest-old, living in rural areas or in the nursing homes) in many developing countries [14, 15].

Nevertheless, in the past years, the problem of access to digital technologies became rather peripheral, as the groups who were considered being at risk of social exclusion due to the lack of access and Internet use (women, seniors, persons with lower levels of education, and people who have lower incomes) have recorded the highest increase of Internet use from 2004 to 2019 [15]. For example, the percentage of adults aged 65 and above who use the Internet tripled during 2004–2019 in the EU and the US, from 20% to more than 60% [12, 13], the largest increase compared with other age groups. Current literature focuses more on the gap between different social groups (as for example the gap between older and younger users) in terms of digital skills and type of usage [16, 17] – as such gaps are translated in differences and opportunities (digital participation) and knowledge (e.g., select and use the relevant information). Consequently, studies have been focused on the third level of digital divide [17, 18], describing a gap between the groups who hold digital skills at a level that would allow then to convert those skills in solving different issues of daily live (from finding your way in a city to finding the relevant information for a health problem) and those who are not able to "benefit". The divide shows that it is those with higher levels of education, who already have good jobs, and the young, who benefit more from the use of the Internet than those who have lower levels of education, those who belong to the lower classes, and older adults. Thus, the lack of digital skills reinforces an already existing structure of social stratification [18]. The third level of digital divide is a relevant concept for better understanding the Covid-19 pandemic. Particularly, it can explain differences in the way people found credible information and avoided unreliable online sources, how different people coped with the health issues by making use of the online services and how they used the online shopping and online leisure activities to overcome social isolation and loneliness during lockdown.

The current study investigates how Romanian older adults from urban and rural areas used digital technology during the lockdown period. The study reveals what applications they have start using during the pandemic and who assisted them, how they found the relevant information regarding Covid-19 and what challenges they have experienced during the first months of the pandemic. By focusing on people aged 65 and above we investigate challenges faced by the oldest-old, who in the literature are described as being the most marginalized in the digital divide. Romania is a typical case of the Eastern European countries strongly affected by migration for work, and where older adults, especially from the rural localities, were at high risk of social isolation already prior to the Covid -19pandemic. Many rural localities face demographic decline, and an increased number in the oldest-old population who neither have the resources to purchase digital technologies nor the skills to benefit from Internet opportunities [19, 20]. For such groups of adults, the Covid-19 pandemic would have probably increased their isolation or brought no changes at all.

2   Literature Review

In April 2019, 89 countries and more than a third of the global population had experienced lockdowns due to the outbreak of an unpreceded situation [4]. Most of the countries in Europe, but not only, have enforced lockdown measures in the first few months, and measures of quarantine, self-isolation, closure of some shops and public services, accompanied by social distancing rules, raised concerns in terms about how older adults will cope with such changes and the impact for their well-being. Systematic studies showed the negative impact of loneliness and social isolation on older adults, on their health status and their general well-being [21, 22]. In general, social isolation and loneliness have been linked to poor physical and mental health [4]. Although the lockdown measures have been useful in decreasing the spread of Covid-19 in the initial months of the pandemic, there are studies showing that in the case of older adults, such measures might have been accompanied by "increased blood pressure, heart disease, obesity, diminished immune system functioning, depression, anxiety, poorer cognitive functioning, increased risk of Alzheimer's disease, and mortality" [4, p. 5].

Also, the risk of loneliness and isolation was not only present among older adults, who previously reported being lonely and isolated, but also among those who were socially active. The risk of loneliness was triggered by the removal of older adults social contacts in their communities including interactions when doing shopping, attending community centers gatherings and places of worship and other such activities that were part of the daily pre-pandemic routine [23]. Also, older adults who were far away from their family members or did not have families, experienced higher vulnerability, when some of the community services or public services were disrupted.

The use of information and communication digital technologies was regarded as an alternative to the face to face economic and social activities, at least during the initial months of the pandemic [24]. Digital technologies have been described as ways of responding to the challenges of loneliness and isolation faced by older adults [25]. Communication tools (as WhatsApp, Zoom, Social Network Sites and other platform) were discussed as having the potential of preventing loneliness and isolation, by keeping people physically distant but still connected. Again, such an understanding of the role of technology in preventing the negative impact of loneliness and social isolation at older adults is based on previous studies: "Systematic reviews have revealed that Internet- and mobile-based apps, companion robots, video games (Wii and TV gaming systems), video calls, and general computer usage are effective tools to reduce social isolation and loneliness for older adults in the short term" [25, p. 983].

During the first months of the Covid-19 pandemic, the role of digital technologies was acknowledged even by the most critical voices. There was a general understanding of the role or ICTs in developing a sense of connection between people, in offering them the support they would need in carrying on daily activities and interests. Particularly in the case of older adults, digital technologies were associated with the assistive role of caregivers and health care workers and service providers [25, 26]. Moreover, the role of digital skills and people's experience in using digital technologies prior to Covid pandemic was considered important for understanding why some older adults managed to use digital communication in a more efficient way than others [27]. For example, an online survey conducted on older adults in 2016 and 2020 showed that participants were more experienced, and their Internet use was more diverse and intense in 2020. Some important predictors help explaining the role of Internet use as a coping mechanism during the pandemic: older adults' health status (with those in frail conditions being less efficient in converting the Internet use in well-being), number of years of using digital devices and number of hours of use on a regular week, and the diversity of Internet functions (showing that those having limited experience and less diverse digital repertoires have had actually fewer resources to benefit from the use of Internet tools in terms of well-being and reduced loneliness).

There are many studies that emphasize the role of digital technologies for older adults' strategies to cope with social isolation and restrictive measures of the Covid pandemic. For example, a study conducted on older adults with pre-frailty and frailty condition has shown that most participants limited their contact with families and friends and experienced social disconnectedness and symptoms of depression and anxiety in the initial months. Such feelings were less present in the case of those who were active in online discussion forums or used the online content to stay in contact with family and friends [28]. Another study [29] tested older adults' ability to harness the Internet for coping with pandemic-induced stress, showing that leisure use was associated with the reduced stressed and enhanced well-being. The study concluded that although the use of Internet-based technology per se does not automatically count as an efficient coping strategy for the pandemic-induced stress, using digital tools for leisure and entertainment was an important predictor in reducing such stress. Also, the study showed that participants reported using more Internet based functions compared to prior to the pandemic and the largest increase was in platforms allowing video-calls and chatting as Zoom, Skype and WhatsApp, but also online shopping, financial management and medical appointments, social network services and online newspapers, navigating websites related to their hobbies and interests. Overall, only the online activities associated with hobbies and interests, but also downloading content (as films or music), playing digital games, or writing blogs – all labeled as online leisure activities, were connected with subjective wellbeing and reduced stress. The study also shows evidence of the digital divide phenomenon, with older persons from the higher socio-economic background and living in urban settings being more able to convert online activities in coping strategies to reduce pandemic-induced stress, as compared with people from lower socio-economic background or living in rural areas. Other studies [30] have shown the same disparities between older residents from the urban and rural areas. For example, veterans living in rural settings in the US were less willing and less able to participate in video connections for clinical care, compared to those from the urban areas, again during the Covid pandemic. Instead, older adults from the rural areas preferred phone call clinical visits [30]. Again, education and socio-economic background was a moderator factor, proving that the traditional social inequalities would have to be considered when discussing the way older adults used Internet-based technologies during the Covid-19 pandemic.

When discussing the role of Internet based tools in helping older adults cope with the pandemic-induced stress, one important aspect to be considered is the type of sources they used where they received Covid-19-related information and the perceived reliability and trustworthiness of those sources. On this topic the current literature is scarce and the few studies addressing Covid-19 information seeking at older adults point in the direction of differences between young and older Internet users. For example, a recent study [5] comparing younger and older adults revealed that older Internet users received information from a diversity of sources, more frequently from traditional media (as for example TV) and from interpersonal sources (information shared by family and friends), compared to younger Internet users. The study underlined the fact that older adults relied more on information received through personal connections (spouses, family members, friends) about Covid pandemic issues (including information regarding health) and found more relevant the traditional media (e.g., radio, printed newspapers and TV). This study indicated that older adults might be more selective in information they search and consider credible, but they also rely on fewer information sources and especially the information provided from people they know.

3   Covid-19 in Romania and Research Questions

The World Health Organization declared Covid-19 a pandemic in March 2020 [31]. In the following months, governments have applied different restrictive measures to prevent the outbreak. Health authorities warned older adults that they are at higher risk of death associated with Covid-19 [23]. Consequently, the recommendations for older adults were to a stay at home and avoid social contacts, at least in the initial months of the pandemic. Moreover, in some countries, older adults faced more restrictions than the general population. For example, in Romania during the Covid 19 lockdown (March-May 2020), the government invoked the 15th Amendment of the European Convention of Human Rights for emergency situations and issued an *Emergency State Presidential Decree* (first put into effect on March 16 and extended until May 15, 2020). This amendment allowed for exemptions from broad categories of human rights (e.g., the right to privacy and intimacy). Older people became the main target of the Romanian government's plans for isolation. First, elders were not allowed to leave their houses; then, they were allowed to go out exclusively to shop for food and medicine, but only for two hours per day; finally, there was an extension of the time period they could shop for basic goods.

The research questions that drove the present study were inspired by both prior research in the field of aging and technology but also by our needs, as researchers, to connect with older acquaintances that fall in the age bracket of what we call in this study "older people." By older people we mean seniors of 60 years and above. Therefore, the questions we aimed to answer were:

1. How can access to technology during the Covid-19 pandemic be described?

    a. What technologies and applications have older adults used before and during the lockdown?
    b. Did older adults learn to use new technologies and applications and if so, how and why?

2. Who assisted older adults in using technology during the pandemic?
3. How did older adults use technology to find news/ information about Covid-19?
4. What are some of the material and emotional challenges older adults experienced during the pandemic and how did they use technology to cope with these challenges?

4   Methodology

We are now seeing the first publications on how the Covid-19 pandemic shapes social research as we knew it. For example, some anthropologists propose a "A Manifesto for Patchwork Ethnography" that questions binary assumptions between "home" and "field" and neoliberal university labor conditions [32] as tenants of "traditional" anthropological method. Questioning these binaries seems timelier now than ever; for example, this study was planned and carried out entirely at "home." Anthropologists propose "research efforts that maintain the long-term commitments, language proficiency, contextual knowledge, and slow thinking that characterizes so-called traditional fieldwork"

[32]. Even though the present study is not anthropological study, we think that such commitments could apply to the field of social sciences more broadly. Additionally, as this research underscores, new epistemological reflections in the social sciences should also consider the importance of cross-disciplinary, collaborative approaches among women social scientists, this study being one of them.

In conducting the research and selecting the sample of participants we took an ethnographic approach. Particularly, we recruited as participants older adults (N = 12) with whom we had a certain familiarity. They included neighbors, former research participants or acquaintances. This choice was motivated by the need to situate these experiences into the larger context of the life histories of these participants. Additionally, this approach allowed us to probe into aspects of our participants' life from prior the pandemic. Lastly, since we had a relationship of trust with these participants, we were able to also capture a genuine description of their experiences. Interviewing these participants often led to moments of emotional overlap, or the mutual share of vulnerabilities, around the unprecedented experience of the Covid-19 pandemic [33]. Such moments included sometimes long pauses, nostalgia for the pre-pandemic life or the mutual understanding that overall "things have changed, but they will get better." Another characteristic of the research sample was our strategic choice for seniors from both rural and urban areas, considering (1) rural – rural economic and social discrepancies in Romania and (2) the fact that most studies on seniors in Romania tend to focus on the urban population, who tends to be, in general, better served by social services and infrastructure.

As Table 1 shows, participants' ages ranged between 63 and 80, they varied in education levels; 80% of participants used social media applications while all had access to a smart phone and some to a laptop as well.

With the entire research project being planned and conducted at home, we scheduled interviews by phone and conducted them both over the phone and WhatsApp and Facebook Messenger. Interviews lasted about 40 min and started with an introductory discussion on participants' access to technology prior and during the Covid-19 pandemic. Then we discussed ways in which seniors acquired information about the pandemic and the reasons that made them trust these sources of information. The last and more extensive part of the interview covered participants' challenges during the pandemic and how technology helped or not overcome these challenges. We transcribed all interviews and analyzed them thematically. For the purpose of the analysis, we clustered these themes as follows, in the Results section: i) support for and use of technology prior and during the pandemic; ii) acquiring information about the Covid-19 pandemic, and iii) older adults' challenges during the pandemic.

Table 1. Participants' socio-demographic information and access to technology

Participant	Gender	Age	Education level	Income	Access to technology	Social media usage	Rural/urban
P01	F	65	High school	Bellow the mean	Phone Laptop	Facebook WhatsApp	Urban
P02	F	65	High school	Bellow the mean	Phone Laptop	Facebook WhatsApp	Rural
P03	F	63	High school	Bellow the mean	Phone	Facebook WhatsApp	Rural
P04	F	68	High school	Above the mean	Phone	Facebook WhatsApp	Rural
P05	M	70	College degree	Bellow the mean	Phone Laptop	Facebook WhatsApp	Rural
P06	F	71	Professional school	Bellow the mean	Phone	Facebook WhatsApp	Rural
P07	M	71	Professional school	Above the mean	Phone	None	Rural
P08	F	70	High school	Above the mean	Phone Laptop	Facebook WhatsApp	Urban
P09	M	67	High school	Bellow the mean	Phone Laptop	Facebook WhatsApp	Urban
P10	F	66	College degree	Bellow the mean	Phone Laptop	Facebook WhatsApp	Urban
P11	M	80	Graduate degree	Above the mean	Phone Laptop	Facebook WhatsApp	Urban
P12	M	73	Professional school	Bellow the mean	Phone	None	Rural

5 Results

5.1 Use of Technology Among Old Adults Prior and During the Covid-19 Pandemic

Most participants we interviewed had access to and were constantly using a smartphone, with two exceptions including male seniors who didn't own smartphones connected to the internet. One participant used a laptop for work and another one used a tablet, from time to time. The apps used by all participants but two were Facebook (including Facebook Messenger) and WhatsApp. Only two participants out of the total of twelve learned new apps (one Facebook and the other one WhatsApp) because their children had either given them phones with these apps installed or installed the application themselves to keep in touch with distant relatives. During the pandemic they used these apps and the phones in the same way as before the pandemic: to keep in touch with close and distant family members or friends. Some used the phones to play games or watch videos on the Facebook app. One participant started shopping online, drawn by a Facebook ad, shortly after opening a Facebook account. Another participant mentioned that she used to shop online before the pandemic, but she was reluctant to do so now because of fear that products might be contaminated with the Covid-19 virus.

In terms of frequency, most participants used technology more during the pandemic than before the pandemic. Yet, older adults from the rural areas conformed less to this pattern since the beginning of the pandemic coincided to the moment of the year (the spring) when most took care of their gardens. Many older adults in rural Romania use subsistence agriculture to complement their household needs. Canning food and sharing it with their children is a common practice, rooted in the socialist era. P4 below discusses how she kept in touch with her neighbors and friends:

"We didn't have time to meet, but we [kept in touch] via WhatsApp or Messenger. We sent each other a post or ask each other about life but now everybody here in the countryside is busy with the gardens, planting, you know? .... But in general, the only way to stay in touch with each other is the Internet." (P4).

For these participants social media usage decreased overall but not also the frequency of communication with children or grandchildren, which intensified just like for the other participants. Communication with children and grandchildren revolved around the everyday life and Covid-related safety measures. Besides family and friends, some older adults also reconnected with school friends and distant relatives.

None of interviewees mentioned needing help using technology or learning to use social media apps. One interviewee, P3, discussed how she learned by herself to find the block button on the Facebook app:

"One day Tatiana (her friend) came by, and I was showing her that I received a suspicious friend request. One guy, with tattoos, thought that I was a girl of his age, and I must have "accepted" him as a friend. One day, early in the morning 'good morning', at night 'good night' and he was just starting off, but I blocked him. Tatiana asked me how I did, but I searched until I figured out, right? Speaking of who wants to learn...." (P3).

By "speaking of who wants to learn" P3 alludes to her husband who only uses his phone to give phone calls and refuses to use learn how to use the internet and look for things such as the weather forecast or stay in touch with his children through WhatsApp. Overall, participants we interviewed used technology during the beginning of the pandemic just like pre-pandemic times; those living in urban areas used it even more frequently while those in the countryside not because they kept themselves busy with subsistence agriculture practices.

5.2   TV and Social Media as Covid-19 Information Sources

All older adults interviewed said that the TV was the main source of information regarding the Covid-19 pandemic. All participants had at least one TV at home, some even up to three, one for each member of the household. As P1 mentioned below:

"The TV is the only direct means of information. It's becoming so that you cannot live without it. In our house the TV is on." (P1).

When watching TV and learning about the pandemic they were interested in following the progress of the pandemic around the world including the number of deaths, learn about the impact the virus might have on people of their age, how to avoid contagion, but also learn about the evolution of the pandemic in countries where some had children or other family members. As P6 mentions:

"I was interested in seeing how the pandemic evolved in Germany and Italy because Dani (her daughter) is in Germany and her husband was in Italy and the pandemic caught them separated." (P6).

Contrary to popular believes in Romania, framed by the current economic, social and generational divides, old adults we interviewed consumed news with skepticism and precaution. The popular media narratives present seniors as easy to persuade by different TV stations. What we learned is that most of interviewees consumed news from at least three different TV channels and triangulated the findings in order to decide what is truly "credible." They noticed discrepancies between different political discourses, political framings of the same events or differences between the voices of experts and non-experts.

"I start with Romania 1, Digi 25, Antena 3, Observator, Romania TV, Realitatea TV and I make a summary; which one would be credible? In any case, there is a lot of misinformation; it's not reality 100%." (P7).

"On TV I compare the news. I have 2–3 sources, or even more. There are many contradictions, so it depends on the TV channels you see. Digi TV, for me, is more operative and unexpectedly impartial comparing to Antena TV and Romania TV. These last 2 seem to be paid. They are subjective and they should mind their own business." (P5).

Two out of the 12 participants compared between the news they watch on TV and the information they read on Facebook or legal decisions they received by WhatsApp:

"On Facebook I have many friends, including from America, Canada for example. I have 7–8 friends who surprise me by the absolute fairness with which they send information from there; they select and filter information from there. (…) It looks like intelligent people from diaspora represent an important filter." (P9).

"I have a friend who sends me any new legal decision. I don't even have the time to look for it because he sends it to me by WhatsApp." (P5).

Even though at the beginning of the pandemic older adults were consuming news heavily, with the time they started watching TV less because they became frustrated and fatigued by (1) the contradictory information, which created confusion, and the (2) reporting on the increased number of deaths because it created panic.

"I stopped watching even doctors [on TV] because, I told you, each with their own opinion. Some say one way, other the other way, some say that it's useless wearing masks and gloves, others say we shouldn't leave the house without them. It's contradictory so..." (P10).

"At the beginning of I was curious to see how many people are infected, what happened but then I got scared and I stopped watching, seeing how many cases there were I became afraid. I was still watching news, but I wasn't as interested anymore because of the fear. They kept announcing that so many more got infected, I don't know what else happened, they checked the airports...It was a period...I never thought I would live something like that." (P4).

A few seniors we interviewed were skeptical of getting their information from social media also because they read news that didn't seem credible or confused them. For example:

"I read an article that my sister sent me saying that it [the virus] was created in a lab and the Chinese let it go, that there there the interests of this guy from Google. So, I don't know how to say it, but I believe both virus variants, but I think there are indeed people ill intended. The TV news, I don't take that literally, I pass them through a personal filter." (P2).

"There is much fake news, but you can easily figure out what's going on. (...) Yesterday I received news saying that we should be very cautious because there is a group of young people who say they come from med schools and want to test people. I received this [news] from acquaintances. We inject you; we get a little bit of blood...In reality they say they are part of an ISIS group. What would ISIS do here? It doesn't seem credible, and I ignore that. They were warning us not to be injected, not to accept that." (P6).

Overall, older adults we interviewed learned about the Covid-19 mainly from TV. They were interested in information about the evolution of the pandemic in Romania and in the world, but especially in the countries where they had relatives. In watching TV, they triangulated information from around three TV channels and focused on experts' voices to decide what was trustworthy. Over time, old adults became scared by the constant alarming news and fatigued by contradictory advice. Social media was a secondary source of information; some used it to compare the information received on social media apps with what they saw on TV, but often information from these channels was confusing because it presented the events under an unusual framework and therefore was deemed less trustworthy.

5.3 Challenges and Coping Strategies for Romanian Older Adults During the COVID-19 Pandemic

The most prevalent challenge that older adults encountered during the period of imposed isolation was the restriction imposed to their physical movement, including the very narrow window when they could do all their chores. In the two hours per day most seniors had to do groceries, pay bills, and sometimes visits doctors. Those living in rural areas also had to find ways to get to the city. For example, P6 lives in a village and to her:

"We, seniors of over 65 had [to leave the house] since 11 am until 1 pm. What can you do between 11 am and 1 pm because this wasn't enough even for groceries? Not to mention leaving the village and going to the city. I haven't been to the city because buses circulate every two hours. This must be done with the declaration. The declaration must be written by hand; there is no place where you can get some [printed]. (....) Then they changed our schedule, it wasn't from 11 am until 1 pm anymore because people were unhappy. In some places it started to become warm outside. They changed it from 7 am until 11 am. Which seniors would wake up at 7 am to go on the streets and where can you go when shops open at 9 am? In our village we only have small grocery stores. Then we had from 7 pm until 10 pm. Do old people hang out on the streets at night? So, they made us a schedule only for the sake of having one. "(P6).

For older adults living in the city, this limitation meant a disruption to their daily routines, which often included going in parks, seeing friends, or taking their grandchildren for walks. Even though all seniors we interviewed had the support of their children or other family members, so accessing food wasn't a challenge, they did insist that the having their movement limited and punished harshly was painful. Some mentioned that drastic application of the law, which punished older adults for not respecting these rules with harsh fines that were disproportionate to their monthly incomes. Part of the freedom to move, many older adults emphasized the need to socialize with friends and be in touch with others:

"This freedom to circulate, to see each other, to enjoy each other's presence, to go on walks, it was a joy. I don't know what more I can say. At our age this is what we have left." (P3).

Secondly, and equally important, many older adults felt the pain of being separated from their children and grandchildren. Even though a few of those interviewed lived away from their children and grandchildren, most participants interviewed were involved in the childrearing of their grandchildren and prior to the pandemic were in close contact with them. For these people:

"It was a sad time. The fact that we couldn't see each other, we feel a hole in the soul because we miss them [the children and grandchildren]. Our son, firstly, we cannot enjoy his presence. He was filling our soul. They are freshly married so it's good for them but for we, as parents, missed them a lot. [We miss] seeing each other in person, not through WhatsApp. We receive pictures but to see each other, to hug each other, to feel each other's soul, that's what hurts the most." (P1).

Thirdly and lastly, few participants felt the need to be in public, to see the "spectacle of the street, to watch people" (P11) or be in nature. These challenges were experienced differently by people in rural areas who, as mentioned earlier, were able to be outside or take care of their gardens, and even see family or neighbors across the fences.

In the face of these challenges, older adults employed two coping strategies. First, it was the more intense use of technology. Technology partially covered old adults' need to socialize, care for others and be taken care of:

"I see Tatiana (friend) ten times per day on the phone. I had a friend who used to visit me, but she didn't come during that period. They [children] called us all the time." (P3).

"I can't say it was very difficult. We spoke all the time with the children on WhatsApp, and they are well in their own ways so I can't say it was something very difficult." (P8).

Secondly, older adults turned their energy inwards, towards their homes. Those living in in rural areas planted seeds for spring fruits and vegetables or took care of the flowers. One person painted the entire house, checked the sanitary and electrical installation, and cleaned the storage spaces. Even urban older adults had the same drive:

"I am active person, and I don't like to stay in the house even if you kill me. It was hard for me at the beginning. But I was lucky because before Easter I started cleaning the house. In turned the house upside down; there wasn't an untouched corned in the house. I didn't rush; I took it easy so I can have work to do. (...) I was working all day until I was working until I could not stand on my feet. (...) You will laugh but my mom copied me. She would ask me: what are you doing now? I will start as well. So, since there was no one there to help her, she started doing like me." (P8).

In conclusion, older adults' challenges during the period of imposed isolation included a time window too narrow for their chores and the inability to continue their pre-pandemic routines, the need to socialize with friends and family and the overall need to be in public places. Their coping strategies included using technology to respond to the need to care of and be taken care of and doing chores around their houses to use their energy.

6 Conclusion

The present study investigated how Romanian older adults from urban and rural areas used digital technology during the lockdown period to cope with the challenges of the Covid-19 pandemic. The findings revealed that digital technologies were used more at the beginning of the pandemic than before it, especially in the urban areas. While in rural areas the beginning of the pandemic period coincided to the spring gardening activities, older Internet users from the rural setting have used those activities to cope with the pandemic-induced stress. Family communication using digital technologies revolved around pandemic related topics, everyday life and safety measures. Some of the older adults interviewed reduced their social contacts and restraint more to family communication, whereas others found new friends online, for example from old school mates and friends, with whom they had not talked for years or from distant relatives. The pandemic time proved to be not only a time of social isolation, but also a proper moment to re-connect and regain a sense of community. Additionally, contrary to popular believes, Romanian older adults consumed information about the Covid-19 pandemic with caution, triangulating sources of information, relying on the voices of experts and mainly TV for information and treated with suspicion and distrust information they received on social media. Lastly, their greatest challenge was the lack of physical contact with family members and physical movement, particularly their daily routines. Therefore, they used social media to cope with the loneliness of being apart from their children and grandchildren, and some even reconnected with older friends or distant family members.

7 Limitations

The research has some limitations regarding the structure of the sample. Participants had a medium or high-level education, and many of them were young old aging between 65 and 70. Even so, the structure of our sample is still rather close to the profile of typical older Internet user in Romania [34, 35]. In addition, we did not manage to capture the opinions of very old adults, living in remote rural settings, who might have faced the most challenges caused by the social isolation and potentiated by the Covid-19 pandemic. Also, our interviews did not capture the challenges faced by older adults with transnational families. This deserves to be approached in a separate study.

8 Implications for Further Research

The present study revealed the importance to have a better understanding of the role of the information sources older people use in time of crisis and how such sources are selected, invested with trust and credibility, and used to shape behaviors. The role of traditional media (e.g., TV, radio and printed newspapers) in the process of finding relevant information at this age group is insufficiently explored in the literature. Particularly in the case of Covid-19, the role of traditional media in combination with the new media in generating (dis)information becomes relevant there are lower levels of vaccination rates among old adults in Eastern European countries compared with the Western countries. Issues of fake news and misinformation were advanced in the public discourse to explain older adults' reluctance to vaccination. By studying older adults' ways of selecting and treating information in time of crisis, we bring an important and understudied topic into discussion: the vulnerability of older adults to fake news and disinformation. Nevertheless, the strategies older people used to cope with an unpreceded situation are related to the cultural context in which we have conducted the investigation, for example lifestyle and routines people from different countries might have once they get to the retirement age. We managed to partially capture such contextual factors in explaining the findings of the current study. However different social contexts might trigger other coping strategies, as well as different roles of the digital technologies or ICTs.

Acknowledgments. The work of the second author is supported by a Horizon 2020 European grant COFUND-ENUTC, project City & Co, Code: COFUN-ENUTC-City&Co.

References

1. Heid, A.R., Cartwright, F., Wilson-Genderson, M., Pruchno, R.: Challenges experienced by older people during the initial months of the COVID-19 pandemic. Gerontologist **61**(1), 48–58 (2021)
2. Moore, R.C., Hancock, J.T: Older adults, social technologies, and the coronavirus pandemic: challenges, strengths, and strategies for support. Soc. Media+Society **6**(3) (2020)
3. Stuart, A., Katz, D., Stevenson, C., Gooch, D., Harkin, L., Bennasar, M., Nuseibeh, B: Loneliness in older people and COVID-19: Applying the social identity approach to digital intervention design (2021, in press)

4. Wu, B.: Social isolation and loneliness among older adults in the context of COVID-19: a global challenge. Global Health Res. Policy **5**(1), 1–3 (2020)
5. Chu, L., Fung, H.H., Tse, D.C., Tsang, V.H., Zhang, H., Mai, C: Obtaining information from different sources matters during the COVID-19 pan-demic. Gerontologist **61**(2), 187–195 (2021)
6. Hänninen, R., Pajula, L., Korpela, V., Taipale, S: Individual and shared digital repertoires–older adults managing digital ser-vices. Inf. Commun. Soc., 1–16 (2021)
7. Beaunoyer, E., Dupéré, S., Guitton, M.J.: COVID-19 and digital inequalities: Reciprocal impacts and mitigation strategies. Computers in human behavior, 111 (202)
8. Voinea, C., Wangmo, T., Vică, C.: Respecting Older Adults: Lessons from the COVID-19 Pandemic. J. Bioethical Inquiry, 1–11 (2022)
9. Seifert, A.: The digital exclusion of older adults during the COVID-19 pandemic. J. Gerontol. Soc. Work **63**(6–7), 674–676 (2020)
10. Smith, M.L., Steinman, L.E., Casey, E.A.: Combatting social isolation among older adults in a time of physical distancing: the COVID-19 social connectivity paradox. Front. Public Health **8**(403) (2020)
11. Prensky, M.: Digital natives, digital immigrants. Part 2: Do they really think differently? On the Horizon **9**(5),1–6 (2021)
12. Eurostat. Digital economy and society statistics - households and individuals. ec.europa.eu/eurostat/statisticsexplained/index.php?title=Digital_economy_and_society_statistics. Accessed 2 Sept 2022
13. Pew Research Center. Digital Divide. www.pewresearch.org/fact-tank/2019/05/07/. Accessed 2 Sept 2022
14. Barrantes, R., Matos, P.: Who benefits from open models? In Making Open Development Inclusive, International Development Research Center, MIT Press, The role of ICT access (2019)
15. Ivan, L., Cutler, S.J.: Older adults and the digital divide in Romania: implications for the Covid-19 pandemic. J. Elder Policy **1**(3), 131–154 (2021)
16. Hargittai, E: Second-level digital divide: Differences in people's online skills. First Monday **7**(4) (2002). https://doi.org/10.5210/fm.v7i4.942. Accessed 2 Sept 2022
17. Van Deursen, A.V., Van Dijk, J.A.: The digital divide shifts to differences in usage. New Media Soc. **16**(3), 507–526 (2014)
18. Van Dijk, J.A.: The Digital Divide. Polity Press, Cambridge (2020)
19. Ducu, V.: Displaying grand parenting within Romanian transnational families. Global Netw. **20**(2), 380–395 (2020)
20. Ivan, L., Fernández-Ardèvol, M.: Older people and the use of ICTs to communicate with children and grandchildren. Trans. Soc. Rev. **7**(1), 41–55 (2017)
21. Cacioppo, J.T., Hawkley, L.C.: Perceived social isolation and cognition. Trends Cogn. Sci. **13**(10), 447–454 (2009)
22. Luo, Y., Hawkley, L.C., Waite, L.J., Cacioppo, J.T.: Loneliness, health, and mortality in old age: a national longitudinal study. Soc. Sci. Med. **74**(6), 907–914 (2022)
23. Brooke, J., Jackson, D.: Older people and COVID-19 isolation, risk and ageism. J. Clin. Nursing **29**, 2044–2046 (2020)
24. Marston, H.R., et al.: COVID-19: technology, social connections, loneliness, and leisure activities: an international study protocol. Front. Sociol. **89**, 1–15 (2020)
25. Chen, K.: Use of gerontechnology to assist older adults to cope with the COVID-19 pandemic. J. Am. Med. Dir. Assoc. **21**(7), 983–984 (2020)
26. Ehni, H.J., Wahl, H.W.: Six propositions against ageism in the COVID-19 pandemic. J. Aging Soc. Policy **32**(4–5), 515–525 (2020)
27. Nimrod, G.: Technostress in a hostile world: older internet users before and during the COVID-19 pandemic. Aging Mental Health **18**, 1–8 (2020)

28. Chen, A.T., et al.: Reactions to COVID-19, information and technology use, and social connectedness among older adults with pre-frailty and frailty. Geriatr. Nurs. **42**(1), 188–195 (2021)
29. Nimrod, G.: Changes in internet use when coping with stress: older adults during the COVID-pandemic. Am. J. Geriatr. Psychiatry **28**(10), 1020–1024 (2020)
30. Padala, K.P., Wilson, K.B., Gauss, C.H., Stovall, J.D., Padala, P.R.: VA video connect or clinical care in older adults in a rural state during the COVID-19 pandemic: cross-sectional study. J. Med. Internet Res. **22**(9), e21561 (2020)
31. WHO. (2020). Advice for the public on COVID-19 – World Health Organization. https://www.who.int/emergencies/diseases/novel-coronavirus-2020/advice-for-public
32. Gunel, G., Saiba, V., Watanabe, C.: A Manifesto for Patchwork Ethnography. Society for Cultural Anthropology. https://culanth.org/fieldsights/a-manifesto-for-patchwork-ethnography. Accessed 2 Sept 2022
33. Feldman, L, Mandache, L.A.: Emotional overlap and the analytic potential of emotions in anthropology. Ethnography **227–244**, 1–18 (2018)
34. Ivan, L., Schiau, I.: Older audiences and digital media: focus on Romania. Manage. Dyn. Knowl. Econ. **6**(3), 423–447 (2018)
35. Ştefăniţă, O., Ivan, L.: Characteristics of the digital divide in Romania and differences in internet use in comparison with internet use in Europe. J. Media Res. **11**(2), 5–21 (2018)

Digital Campaigning: Challenges for Older Bulgarian Electorate

Lilia Raycheva(✉) ⓘ, Andreana Eftimova ⓘ, Neli Velinova ⓘ, and Lora Metanova

Faculty of Journalism and Mass Communication, The St. Kliment Ochridski Sofia University, 49, Moskovska str., 1000 Sofia, Bulgaria

`lraycheva@yahoo.com, a.eftimova@uni-sofia.bg, nelikdkd@gmail.com, loranikolova76@gmail.com`

Abstract. 2021 was an election year for the Bulgarians - they had to go to the polls for three national parliamentary votes (one regular and two early) and once again - for president. The pre-election campaigns for all these votes were held in the conditions of COVID-19 epidemic, hard political confrontation and some concomitant factors such as the European Football Championship, the summer vacations and the strong inflationary trends. Internet platforms and especially social networks became increasingly popular channels for politicians to communicate with voters. That is why the aim of the study focuses on the digital pre-election campaigns. The object is the dynamics of the internet connection between the voters (especially the older adults) and the MP candidates. The subject refers to the election messages of the leaders of the political forces, presented in their Facebook profiles. The methodology is comparative analysis and empirical study, conducted by academic research team from the Faculty of Journalism and Mass Communication at The St. Kliment Ohridski Sofia University. The scope of the study includes those political forces that have passed the 4% electoral threshold. The results are indicative for those interested in digital political communication during social pandemic isolation.

Keywords: Digital communication · Older adults · Social networks · Pre-election campaign

1 Introduction

During the period of democratization - since 1989, the election campaigns in Bulgaria have developed in parallel with demonopolization, liberalization and transformation of the media system. Nevertheless, the deregulation of the radio and television broadcasting sector was protracted, giving way to the rise of two interrelated processes - politicization of media and mediatization of politics [1]. Since the beginning of the new century, these processes have accelerated with the widespread use of digital technologies in everyday communication.

The high-speed spread of the online platforms enhanced the burst of social movements, instigated by the growing economic inequality. Bulgaria quickly joined the global protest movements, which shared a common autonomous digital network basis, supported by the Internet and wireless communication. Manuel Castells called these movements "evolution of liberty and dignity" [2]. The protesters in Bulgaria followed this digital pattern – they gathered horizontally through decentralized social networks and acted in a direct, participatory democracy of equals. Thus, spontaneously organized (thanks to the social networks) the mass protests have managed to redefine the communication processes. Internet enabled activists to plan, plot and co-ordinate the protests at low costs, anonymity and speed. Traditional mainstream media, especially radio and TV, were lagging dramatically behind in the high-speed race for consumers' attention [3].

Thus, nourishing ground for rigorous development of populism as a political concept and rhetorical style has been created. Nowadays the political environment in Bulgaria is characterized by almost permanent merge of political entities, which gradually escalates the usage of populist approaches, styles and rhetoric by all political parties in the country, whether left or right-oriented. Political leaders and parties with pronounced populist behavior have mixed, often changing characteristics. In the last decade, some of the newly formed populist parties have gradually won considerable numbers of seats in the national Parliament and were represented in the European Parliament as well. The strong critical attitude of populists towards the status quo, and towards what they regard as the chimera of democracy, is generally intertwined with the function of the media as a corrective factor with regard to government authorities. The growing impact of social networks on the process of communication between society and political leaders points out the reasonable assumption that this model of interaction will rigorously develop, especially in times of social isolation, such as the COVID-19 pandemic has caused. Dealing with the pandemic not only in medical and economic, but also in social and communication terms posed significant challenges to the institutions and the population in the country during the state of national emergency.

That is why it is of particular importance to outline the trends and the peculiarities of the developments of these online relationships in the context of the dynamics of the pre-election online communication between politicians and the public (especially the older people). Bulgaria is a country with high rate of population ageing and people 65+ sustain 29% of all voters [4] and there exists a telling risk of digital generation divide, i.e. of vulnerability and of social exclusion of older people from the modern information and communication environment and from certain civic rights such as informed choice for voting.

2   Aim and Research Methods

The aim of this study focuses on the dynamics of online Parliamentary'2021 pre-election communication between politicians and society in the context of the COVID-19 restrictions in Bulgaria, so that the structured and analyzed information be utilized into patterns for policy support for decision makers, academia, media, telecommunications, general publics, and private sector. The object is the specifics of the internet connection between the digital audiences and the MP candidates during the one-month pre-election campaigns. The subject of the research refers to the digital election messages of the political party leaders, presented in their Facebook profiles. The scope of the study includes those political forces, which passed the 4% threshold.

The study examines the verbal and non-verbal communication of the MP candidates, the quality of their messages in terms of positivism, negativism or neutrality, as well as their commitment to social, health, economic, technological and other important topics related to the welfare of the population in the country as an EU member-state. The frequency of the usage of Facebook by the political leaders, the issues that dominate their messages, and the digital activity of the audiences (especially the older adults) are also tracked.

The study raises three main research questions:

1. Do politicians actively use online communication with people?
2. Is there a connection between the activity in the social network and the number of interactions with the result of the elections?
3. Do older people have equal opportunities to participate in the online election campaign and exercise their informed choice when voting?

The study is interdisciplinary and it uses mixed research methods, among them:

– Comparative analysis of the derived data from academic sources, sociological surveys, regulatory frameworks and media and telecommunications practices;
– Qualitative research study, conducted via written semi-structured interviews with older adults 65+.

In addition, cross-combining technique for data collection and analysis was applied in order to compensate some of the inherent limitations.

Some of the findings have been disseminated to decision makers, media and academia [5, 6].

3   Results

3.1   Bulgarian Parliamentary Elections of 2021

Regular Parliamentary Election (04. 04. 2021). The regular election for national Parliament'2021 was held on 04.04. in a situation of global insecurity in spheres such as healthcare, economy, social life, etc. Besides, in the summer of 2020 street protests broke out in the country with a variety of demands, such as: convening a Grand National Assembly for reforming of the Bulgarian Constitution; lustration of former communists in power; modernization of the administration; sustaining greater freedom of speech, etc. The accumulated negative public energy targeted mainly the fight against corruption and the need for judicial reform. The protesters called for immediate resignation of the running Government and the Prosecutor general and for summoning of early elections. The President of the country supported the unrest. Despite the challenges of the COVID-19 infection, the protesters started to block on daily basis key intersections in the capital and some other cities in the country, thus hindering the normal functioning of the urban environment. They kept throwing tomatoes, eggs and fish against government buildings. The Diaspora also supported national demonstrations. The protests were mostly rhisomatic, although they were coordinated by the so-called "Poisonous trio" (consisted of a journalist, sculptor and lawyer) and backed by an oligarch with a number of legal allegations, who has fled from the country. In attempt to brush-up their image, some non-parliamentary represented politicians rubbed shoulders with the demonstrators. The protesters, no matter that some of their demands were reasonable, could not formulate clear constructive goals and could not nominate a charismatic and competent person as a leader to unite the nation. On the contrary, the motivation of the non-protesters to state their disagreement with the public discontent was related to their skepticism about the ability of any alternative to the ruling political party to change the status quo in the system. The protests lasted until October 2020 and led to the resignation of five ministers. Despite the political insecurity, the Government accomplished its term.

Among the main reasons for the public dissatisfaction with the government was the accumulated fatigue from the ruling of the three cabinets with the leading participation of the center-right *Citizens for European Development of Bulgaria (CEDB)* political party (2009–2013, 2014–2017, and 2017–2021), as well as with the loss of trust in the state institutions. Indeed, its last coalition government has achieved certain success in: handling of the corona virus crisis; sustaining good macroeconomic indicators and infrastructure modernization; managing the migrant crisis; increasing the country's international outlook, etc. However, the Parliamentary opposition and the protesters' allegations that this political party did not resolutely fight corruption and did not put much effort to defend the rule of law, have helped to form a prevailing critical attitude towards it.

The tense relationships between the prime minister and the president further polarized the political environment. Under pressure from protesters, the Electoral Code has been amended to provide parallel use of voting machines in polling stations with a minimum of 300 registered voters. Shortly before the elections some new parties and coalitions were established, mainly by former high-ranking public officials and by participants in the street protests. Candidates from 67 political formations, organized in 19 political parties and 11 coalitions run for the 240 seats in the National Parliament. MPs from 2 political parties and 4 coalitions, representing 20 political entities were elected. From the former political forces only the *Movement for Rights and Freedoms (MRF)* political party improved its results by gaining 4 seats. *Citizens for European Development of Bulgaria-Union of Democratic Forces (CEDB-UDF)* lost 20 seats and *Bulgarian Socialist Party for Bulgaria (BSP for Bulgaria)* Coalition – 37. The nationalist coalitions, such as the *United Patriots* and *Will* suffered from splits and lost their representation in the new Parliament. Some of the new participants in the political race such as *Democratic Bulgaria (DB)* coalition, *There Is Such a People (TISP)* political party and *Stand up! Goons Out! (SUGO)* coalition passed over the 4% electoral threshold.

Voter turnout in the country was 50. 61% - 3,334,283 out of 6,588,372 eligible voters went to the polls. The election apathy somehow displaced the initial political euphoria in society – a definitely protest vote of the Bulgarians against the political class. Bulgarian voters refused to yield to any mass media, political and sociological propaganda, especially when dished out along negative lines [7].

According to the Preliminary Standpoint of the Organization for Security and Co-operation in Europe (OSCE) fundamental freedoms were respected in the election [8].

Early Parliamentary Election (11.07.2021). Although *CEDB-UDF* became the first political force in the 45th Parliament and offered a structured cabinet, the attitudes of the other five political formations put this coalition in isolation. The first actions of a number of the newly elected MPs were not encouraging in terms of expertise and political culture, demonstrating aggression and disregard for parliamentary rules. The second-ranked political force *There Is Such a People,* despite the huge support from other MPs of its program, returned the mandate wrapped in silence. Its leader is unique in the Bulgarian parliamentary life in that he is the only MP who did not appear at any sitting of the National assembly. The *BSP Coalition for Bulgaria* also did not propose a government. The lack of a clear majority and the inadequacy of many of the new MPs turned unproductive in legislative activity. The only legislative result was the hastily revised Electoral Code, voted on the eve of Good Friday in violation of the Rules of Procedure, but with the intention to ensure greater fairness of the vote. A new Central Election Commission has been appointed, compulsory machine voting has been introduced for sections with more than 300 voters, and the restriction of 35 sections in non-EU countries has been removed.

Negativism against the winner *CEDB-UDF* seemed to be a more unifying factor for the other five parliamentary represented political forces, instead of the consensus discussion on important issues for the country. The caretaker government, appointed by the President, and the narrow perimeter of its actions would hardly help for their solution. Thus, it became quite possible to add a political crisis to the health, economic, social and institutional ones – a telling trend to the erosion of democracy.

Although this was considered the most expensive election in the country's history, turnout in July was unusually low - 42.19% or 8.42% less than the vote in April [7]. The activity of the early vote seemed to refute the effectiveness of the machine voting. Thus, only 38% of those obliged to vote with machines in sections with 300 and more voters went to the polls, while significantly more - 55%, were those who voted with paper ballots. Resistance to machines refused many (especially the older people) to go to the polls. Preventive police actions of law enforcement agencies and police forces in places where there were suspicions of control votes, although loudly announced, were not fair and effective enough.

The Bulgarian people gave a second chance to those political forces elected in April, without again having the upper hand of any political formation.

If for the regular elections in April the participating political entities could be divided into two: parliamentary (Coalition *Citizens for European Development of Bulgaria–CEDB/Union of Democratic Forces–UDF;* Coalition *Bulgarian Socialist Party-BSP for Bulgaria,* and political party *Movement for Rights and Freedoms-MRF* and non-parliamentary (political party *There Is Such a People - TISP*, Coalition *Democratic Bulgaria-DB* and Coalition *Stand up! Goons out! - SUGO*), in the July déjà vu all six ranked equalized as parliamentary represented, regardless of the time of their stay in the National Assembly or the effectiveness of their activities in it for the formation of policies and legislation ensuring sustainable development of the country.

All participants in the election campaign, both in the regular and in the early vote, and not only those who crossed the 4% barrier, have bet extremely seriously on their presence on the social network Facebook during both one-month campaigns. The candidates who ran for the 240 seats in the National Assembly for the early vote in July did not differ significantly from the ones for the regular vote in April: 64 (vs.71) were the political formations organized in 15 (vs. 18) political parties, 8 (vs. 12) coalitions and 1 independent candidate. In the remake, the winners were again the same - two parties and four coalitions, representing 33 political entities, formed the 46th Parliament. However, the change in the rules led to a shift in the ranking. And not only that: the massive negative rhetoric against the former ruling *CEDB-UDF* coalition by all ranked political formations, by the President and by some ministers of the caretaker government and during the campaign period contributed to this.

During the early parliamentary elections, 3,973,856 registered voters (57.81%) were not represented in the 46th National Assembly, which is a challenge to its legitimacy [7]. All these people were not asked about the program and composition of the government, nor how to outline the priorities for governing the country, which is counterproductive for democracy.

Early Parliamentary Election (14.11.2021) and Presidential Election (14-21.11. 2021). The early Parliamentary election of July 11, 2021 resulted in a narrow victory for the newly established political party *There Is Such a People (TISP)* over the then ruling *CEDB-UDF* coalition, however, *TISP* won only 65 out of 240 seats in the National Assembly. *TISP* opted to form a minority government with potential partners (the coalitions *Democratic Bulgaria - DB, Stand Up! We Are Coming! – SUWAC (the* renamed *Stand Up! Goons Out! – SUGO*, and *Bulgarian Socialist Party for Bulgaria – BSP for Bulgaria*). These attempts proved unsuccessful. After the other two political forces in the row (*CEDB-UDF* and *BSP for Bulgaria*) refused to propose a government, the Parliament was dissolved and new early Parliamentary election was scheduled together with the regular vote for President.

On 14 November 2021 were held the first round of regular election for President (the second round was on 21 November 2021 as no candidate was able to receive a majority of the vote in the first round) and early election for Parliament. Nationwide the turnout in the Parliamentary election and in the first presidential round fell below 41% - Bulgaria's lowest participation rate in 30 years for both presidential and legislative elections. Nationwide turnout in the second presidential round experienced another drop, featuring only 34.84% (2,310,903 of the registered 6,632,375 voters). In the runoff it was won by incumbent president Gen. Rumen Radev with 66.72% (1,541,834 ballots) against the rector of the largest and most renowned University in the country Prof. Anastas Gerdzhikov [7].

The 47th Parliament consists of thirty three political formations (three political parties and four coalitions, representing thirty political forces). Although with no majority (25.67%), the newly formed electoral alliance *We Continue the Change (WCC),* unregistered political formation, led by Kiril Petkov and Asen Vasilev, the former caretaker ministers of Economy and Finance, respectively, appointed by President Radev, and US backed, won the most seats (67). Kiril Petkov has been appointed on May 12 by President

Radev a minister of economy in the caretaker cabinet, in violation of the Constitution, according to which ministers must only be Bulgarian citizens. Being previously a citizen of Canada, Petkov stated that he had renounced his citizenship on April 2021, but Canadian government documents showed that the procedure was not officially completed until August 2021. The leaders of the electoral alliance *We Continue the Change (WCC)*, the coalition *Bulgarian Socialist Party for Bulgaria (BSP for Bulgaria)*, the political party *There Is Such a People (TISP)*, and the coalition *Democratic Bulgaria (DB)* announced that they had agreed to form a coalition to put an end to the months-long political crisis. On 13 December 2021 the National Assembly approved the incoming government of Kiril Petkov. The other three political forces – the coalition *CEDB-UDF*, the political party *MRF* and the new nationalist political party *Revival* stayed in opposition. This whole long process of power switch, which went through three parliamentary votes, was carefully engineered and closely guided by President Radev, who is also seeking to amend the Constitution for a new polity - a presidential republic. Coincidentally or not, the President scheduled both votes on days that do not stimulate the turnout - 04. 04. coincided with the Catholic Easter, and 11. 07. - with the finals of the European Football Championship. The coincidence of the last parliamentary elections with the first round of the presidential election could be linked to his intention for the parliamentary vote to provide the necessary turn out of over 50% of the voters in order to avoid the second round.

During the early parliamentary election, 3,966,045 registered voters (55.77%) were not represented in the 47th National Assembly, which is again a challenge to its legitimacy and stability. Among the main reasons for the low turnout (especially for older people) was the lack of meaningful debate on the social, economic and civil priorities in the public agenda; the frustration from the ongoing COVID epidemic; and the challenges of the machine voting.

Obviously, most Bulgarians refused to comply with media, political and sociological propaganda, especially when they did not meet their needs. It seems that their idea of a democracy in which causes, values and principles are upheld was undermined by the wave of populism, defending interests and unenforceable promises, skillfully playing with people's fears, hopes, and expectations. Fairly criticizing previous managerial shortcomings, the populists had no vision of proposing a meaningful program for their correction and energy to implement it. And any social change is a long, consensual process, not a momentary "erasure" of the political legacy (both good and bad). The remake of the neglect of the dialogue, of the belittled prioritization of the public order, leads to the replacement of the people's discontent by a fake democracy.

3.2 Challenges of Media Literacy to Debates on Civic Rights

Media are among the main factors of the deliberative democracy, which should ensure fair and reasonable debate among citizens (especially in pre-election times).

Defining media literacy in contemporary communication process faces multicomplex approach. Within five decades only the concept of the transition from an economy based on material goods to one based on knowledge [9] was transformed to knowledge divide - the gap between those who can find, create, manage, process, and disseminate information and those who are impaired in this process [10]. While in post modernity [11] diffusion between information and technology has been prerequisite for blurring the lines between the physical, digital, and biological spheres, nowadays transmedia storytelling and participatory culture already represents a process where integral elements of a fiction get dispersed systematically across multiple delivery channels for the purpose of creating a unified and coordinated entertainment experience [12]. In today's flat globalized world 'never before in the history of the planet have so many people – on their own – had the ability to find so much information about so many things and about so many other people' [13].

Information literacy forms the basis for lifelong learning, enabling individuals of different educational background to find, critically and competently evaluate, accurately and creatively use, and responsibly communicate information in all its various formats efficiently and effectively, in regard with acquisition of knowledge, as well as in situations requiring decision making or problem solving.

Unifying information literacy and media literacy as a composite concept considering the right to freedom of expression and access to information through ICTs has been tackled by UNESCO in the first of a kind significant publication on the matter. *Media and Information Literacy. Policy & Strategy Guidelines* offers a multifaceted harmonized approach to developing national policies, legal framework, and regulatory mechanisms for better media and information environment [14]. Also, A UNESCO handbook *Journalism, "Fake News" & Disinformation* provides an internationally-relevant open model curriculum, responding to the emerging global problem of disinformation that confronts societies in general, and journalism in particular [15].

Digitalization has led to significant proliferation of information spread across the Internet. Nowadays the possibilities of people all over the world to connect via mobile devices with unprecedented speed, scope, processing power, storage capacity, and access to knowledge, are practically unlimited. It was in 1997, when the citizens of the Net representing the new globalized way of communication were named netizens [16]. Later, other terms were introduced for the internet users, such as digital natives, digital immigrants, smart mobs [17, 18], etc. However, many users lack awareness of the mechanisms that frame their digital engagement with information online and offline. Further on, content personalization and private moderation may have various positive or negative effects as well as may cause serious threats for access to information and freedom of expression [19]. In addition, age-based inequalities and socio-economic disparities may deepen the digital divide, thus hampering the citizens' informed participation in democratic processes. That is why the ability of digital literacy to find, organize, evaluate, create, and disseminate information in various platforms using digital technology supplements the managerial particularities of information literacy and the communication specifics of media literacy, thus contributing to knowledge developments.

Taking into account the radically transforming media economy due to mobility, user generated communication, Internet and booming availability of digital products, in 2007 the Commission launched the Communication *A European Approach to Media Literacy in the Digital Environment.* It defines media literacy as "the ability to access media, to understand and to critically evaluate different aspects of the media and media contents and to create communications in a variety of contexts" [20].

Recital 59 of the revised Audiovisual Media Services Directive provides that: in order to enable citizens to access information and to use, critically assess and create media content responsibly and safely, citizens need to possess advanced media literacy skills. Media literacy should not be limited to learning about tools and technologies, but should aim to equip citizens with critical thinking skills required to exercise judgment, analyse complex realities and recognise differences between opinion and fact. It is therefore necessary that both media service providers and video-sharing platforms providers, in cooperation with all relevant stakeholders, promote the development of media literacy in all sections of society, for citizens of all ages [21].

Of particular importance in this digital communication is the effective participation of different generations in it and the approach to overcome the digital generation divide. The majority of studies have focused on older people's *access* and *use* of digital technologies and media, while the *creation* of media content has been researched less within the traditional dimensions of media literacy. The studies have concluded that while older people exhibit a variety of digital media practices, they typically use digital technologies and media less and somewhat differently than younger age groups [22].

Many studies focus on the need to prevent possible exclusion of digitalization on older people by providing them with media education. There is diversity among older people's online activities, their range is narrower than that of younger age groups, and there are more Internet non-users among older people. Researches indicate that the so-called warm experts, often family members and friends, play a important role in older people's use of digital devices and media. It is especially important to analyze the use of social networks, and in particular Facebook, by the elderly, in order to protect them from the impacts of fake news and Internet trolls [23, 24]. Nowadays, for example, the election campaign are increasingly shifting from traditional media to social networks, and efforts to enhance media literacy would help vulnerable people to make informed choice while exercising their vote.

The Facebook Facade of the Bulgarian Parliamentary Campaigns'2021. All participants in the election campaign, both in the regular and in the two early votes have bet extremely seriously on their presence online, especially on the social network Facebook, during the three one-month pre-election campaigns.

Following the aim of this study, focused on the dynamics of pre-election online communication in the three parliamentary votes in 2021, the messages of the leaders of political parties presented in their Facebook profiles during the one-month campaigns for the regular elections (04.03.-04.04.2021) and for the early voting (11.06.-11.07.2021 and 14.10.-14.11.2021) were examined and compared. Due to the limited size of this text, the results will be presented only for those political forces that have crossed the 4% barrier.

Overall, the campaigning of Boyko Borisov - the leader of the coalition *CEDB-UDF* and former Prime Minister's via Facebook were rational and pragmatic. He was trying to play the role of a unifier of the nation. In the three campaigns, among the posts published on his Facebook page, were listed those of some European leaders who declared their support for him, such as the one by Manfred Weber, the chairman of the Group of the European People's Party in the European Parliament.

The Facebook populist campaign of the leader of *There Is Such a People* Slavi Trifonov is perhaps best characterized in Katherine Calvait's comment in Süddeutsche Zeitung: "A model for success? More mockery. Trifonov, musician, presenter, TV star, neo-politician, no program. During the election campaign, he hardly showed up, his ideas were deliberately formulated in a vague way. Now that he can form a coalition with other reformist forces and will have to present a government program, he comes up with conditions that cannot be met, so the question arises: Is the man a visionary or a charlatan?" [25]. The party is named after one of his musical albums - *There Is Such a People*. He himself has an inscription tattooed on his back with the famous Wyatt Earp's (performed by Kurt Russel) phrase from the 1993 US western *Tombstone*: "I'm Coming and the Hell's Coming with Me". His success actually continues a trend in both Europe and the United States: TV and show business stars are entering politics, such as US Donald Trump, Italian Beppe Grillo, Ukrainian Volodymyr Zelensky, Slovenian Marian Sharec, etc. The general conclusion is that Slavi Trifonov's emotional campaign focuses on the position of "anti-status quo", against fear, the importance of people's opinions, and patriotism.

The *Bulgarian Socialist Party* suffered from contradictions within the party between its leader Korneliya Ninova and various fractions. The coalition gradually has departed from its clear-cut social democratic left profile, combining up to nineteen political formations, ranging from communism and nationalism to environmentalism. The Facebook profile of the leader of the coalition *BSP for Bulgaria* Kornelia Ninova in the three campaigns was moderate in intensity. The key words of her messages were predictability and stability.

The coalition *Democratic Bulgaria* has two chairpersons. While campaigning in his official Facebook page one of them - Hristo Ivanov, relied on expert speech, not so much on emotional personal posts. The main message was the need for change and the statement that the *DB* coalition knows how to make this change. In general, the style and approach of the online campaign on Facebook of the other co-chairman of the *DB* coalition Atanas Atanasov also did not differ much from the campaign for all the parliamentary elections. He also relied on a rational rather than emotional approach. Most of his posts were linked to interviews and media publications.

The centrist liberal *Movement for Rights and Freedoms* political party, perceived as a "Turkish party", has been one of the consolidated Parliamentary entities since its foundation in 1990. Although the law does not permit parties on racial or religious basis, a number of ethnic Turkish and Roma candidates run in minority-populated areas. The Facebook profile of the leader of the political party *MRF* Mustafa Karadayi in all pre-election campaigns of 2021 was characterized by an unobtrusive and casual election strategy. Karadayi's Facebook profile published addresses of international leaders, such as: Hans van Baalen (former Chair of ALDE); Dr. Hakima el Haite (Chair of the Liberal International); Graham Watson (former Chair of ALDE); Dacian Ciolos (Chair of the Renew Europe EP Group); Roman Jakic (Chair of the Liberal South East European Network); Dita Charanzova (Vice President of the EP), etc. Verbal communication was almost non-existent in the three pre-election campaigns. The agitation was reduced to modest photos and videos. There is no tension from the upcoming race, but rather confidence. It seems that the *MRF* leader does not rely only on the election campaign on the social network, but rather on a hard electorate.

The most eclectic coalition *Stand Up! Goons Out!* united several political formations of quite different profiles – social democratic, environmental, populist, liberal, agrarian, etc. The two leaders - Maya Manolova, a former member of the socialist party and a former national ombudsman and Nikolay Hadgigenov, lawyer and one of the three members of the "Poisonous Trio"- the coordinators of the 2020 protests, did not provide consolidated platform for the regular election of 04.04 and for the early one on 11.07. For the early election of 14.11, although the political formation changed its name to *Stand Up! We are coming! (SUWAC)* and only one leader was left - Maya Manolova, the coalition did not pass the 4% threshold. The Facebook page of the leader of the coalition *SUGO/SUWAC* Maya Manolova was very active but in her strategy dominated populist promises.

Teamwork was the leitmotif of the campaign of the newcomer *We Continue the Change* - the winner of the 14.11. early Parliamentary election. One of the two co-chairpersons - Kiril Petkov, is a relatively new face to the Bulgarian political system. The impression was that people are talking about him, not he about himself. This approach was different from that of most other politicians, who presented themselves in their profiles and the publications on their behalf were at the heart of their campaign. A key publication was the one of October 27, accompanied by a photo on which he holds a poster with the inscription "I am Kiril Petkov and I am not afraid." He said that he accepts the negative decision of the Constitutional Court on his false declaration for Bulgarian citizenship when appointed Minister of Economy in the caretaker cabinet, but he does not agree with it and his head was held high because he denunciated his Canadian citizenship and handed over his Canadian passport before that, claiming that he had fulfilled his obligation to the Constitution. This is Petkov's most liked post, as well as the post with the most interactions - 29 thousand likes, 36 comments, over 6 thousand shares. The other co-chairman of *We Continue the Change* Asen Vassilev did not run a campaign on his own Facebook profile.

The 4% threshold at the 14.11. early election was crossed also by another newcomer - the nationalist political party *Revival*, founded in 2914. Its leader Kostadin Kostadinov was extremely active on his page occupying the current far-right political space. He held 320 posts during the election campaign, 213 of which contain video. Kostadinov's populist style was revealed in direct speech, attacks on political opponents, expressive language.

The comparative study of the three election campaigns (for the regular vote in April and for the early ones in July and in November) analyzed the verbal and non-verbal communication of the leaders of the political forces, overcoming the 4% barrier. The quality of their messages on Facebook in terms of positivism, negativism or neutrality, as well as their commitment to social, health, economic, technological and other important issues related to the welfare of the population in the country as a Member State of the European Union were also studied. Moreover, the digital activity of the audience was also monitored.

Digital Challenges to Older Adults During the 2021 Pre-election Campaigns.
Although the introduction of compulsory machine voting in polling stations with more

than 300 voters was adopted with the intention of clearing the electoral process off from the practices of buying votes, it was definitely not in favour for older adults 65+. Besides, data from the National Statistical Institute show that in 2021 83.5% of the households in the country have internet access. 73.9% of persons aged between 16 and 74 years used the Internet every day or at least once a week at work, at home or elsewhere, and 61.4% used the resources of the global network several times a day. The most active users of the Internet were people with higher education (92.7%) and young people aged between 16 and 24 - 92.9%. Only 30.8% of people over the age of 65 used this access every day, and 18.5% - several times daily, with 50.6% stating that they have never used the internet [26].

Despite the rapid development of ICT and online services, television continues to be the most preferred source of information and entertainment for most Bulgarian households. In addition to traditional media and online-only news sites, using of other social media platforms, as well as networking and microblogging services such as Facebook, Google Plus, Instagram, Twitter, TikTok, and hashtags, is becoming more and more popular. The use of online social networks every day or almost every day is 56% (in EU it ranges from 46% in Germany and France, to 77% in Lithuania) [27].

The creative potentials of the new information and communication environment appear to be a key factor in the development of Bulgarian media reality. More than 76% of all Bulgarians use Facebook for any purpose and 64% for news; 70% use YouTube for any purpose and 64% for news; 54% use Facebook Messenger for any purpose and 17% for news; 61% use Viber for any purpose and 16% for news; 36% use Instagram for any purpose and 12% for news; and 13% use Twitter for any purpose and only 8% for news. Thirty-eight per cent share news via social media, messaging or e-mail (Reuters, 2021) [28]. After the massive civil protests of 2013 that were fomented by the widespread involvement of social networks, the influencing effects of various communication channels were acknowledged by the Bulgarian citizens. However, the majority of the older population remained non-inclusive in this communication.

When assessing the vulnerability of elderly people in Bulgaria in the contemporary media environment, it should be borne in mind that they are not a homogeneous group of people. Apart from the traditional division of people at pre-retirement and retirement age, there is another intermediate generation, whose characteristics are sharply different from the traditional perception of older adults in Bulgaria. The "technological" generation (today's Bulgarians at the age of 55–74), which ensured the boom of the high-tech industry in Bulgaria in two socio-economic systems, has a high social status, a good financial position and opportunities for coping in the modern technological and information environment. Media, marketing, and political PR specialists should view them as a group with significant, underestimated potential, rather than as people with disruptive functions in society. However, the oldest, poorly educated, mostly living in the countryside users of media content can be considered as truly vulnerable participants in the contemporary media ecosystem.

Along with the increase in the activity of the middle aged people on social networks, the older people's aspirations to learn about online skills are growing. Enhancing the communication and media literacy of the elderly should be encouraged by the governmental and the non-governmental sector as it satisfies several needs simultaneously:

communicating with relatives who have emigrated abroad, overcoming social exclusion by establishing contacts with people with similar interests, diversifying the channels for obtaining a variety of information, providing an opportunity to check its credibility, etc. A survey, conducted by research team of the St. Kliment Ohridski Sofia University in 2017, showed that this is the group that has no other means of protection against unreliable and manipulative information, apart from the credibility and professionalism of journalists and of its own long life experience. Elderly people can withstand media impact when it is contrary to their established beliefs, knowledge and patterns of behavior. However they can not counteract the personified, reliant on their feelings and highest values, influence (as seen, for example, by the success of phone fraudsters who take huge sums of money from old people, on the pretext that they are treating their heavily injured loved ones). Against the backdrop of the popularity of traditional media, journalists in the radio, the television and the press should try to justify and preserve their trust, otherwise they risk losing some of their most faithful admirers - the older audiences. This can be done by providing reliable information on topics that are eager for the elderly: internal politics, security and public order, economy and finance.

In compliance with the EU provisions for the ICTs and the ageing population to stay socially active and creative, through networking and access to public and commercial services, thus reducing the social isolation of older people, particularly in rural areas [29], the research team from the Faculty of Journalism and Mass Communication at the St. Kliment Ohridski studied qualitatively the attitudes of the older adults 65+ (N = 22) to the 2021 election process. A non-representative survey as part of a broader research on media usage patterns was conducted with MA and BA students as interviewers. The respondents were approached with three questions, related to their attitude to: the machine voting, the election campaign, and their trust in the media – all under the umbrella topic of the possibility for informed choice in the vote. Almost all respondents pointed out television in the first place in terms of trust (public BNT and commercial, nationally distributed, bTV and Nova), followed by the public radio (BNR). Depending on their educational background, those with a minimum of upper secondary or higher education indicated that they had no problem with the machine voting, while those with lower educational status and residents of smaller settlements responded that they were embarrassed by the lack of choice for voting with paper ballots. Some admitted that they did not go to the polling stations due to this frustration. It turns out that the COVID epidemic was not such a deterrent for the voting process. The reactions to the qualities of the election campaign were most diverse. Many answers tied up around the notion that the participants in the political race have failed to understandably present their management programs. Some claimed that the media have failed to offer meaningful debates on important topics for society, such as healthcare, economics, and social issues. Few have paid attention to the messages on social networks and Facebook, describing them as propaganda and full of unproductive confrontation. In cases of suspicion of misinformation and fake news, a large number of the respondents either did not trust the message or sought other communication channels to verify the information. None of the respondents answered that the election campaign influenced his or her choice. They relied mainly on their previous many years of experience, their political preferences and their sense of public duty.

The results of the analysis show that during the 2021 election campaigns Bulgarians preferred to be informed first by television, and then - by social networks - mostly - by Facebook. Online communication replaced live political contacts with the public, and the numerous likes, comments and shares expanded the boundaries of the audiences. However, the number of publications, the frequency of use of the social network, as well as the invested funds did not turn out to be directly proportional to the achieved success. Judging by the quality of the content of the posts, relying on populism in its various dimensions was the most profitable strategy. For some of the new political formations, aggressive rhetoric was also effective. In a few of the Facebook profiles surveyed, political leaders clearly set out their intentions so that voters had the opportunity to make informed choices [30].

4   Conclusion

No matter how positive the impact of digitalization and ICT applications and media developments on progress in all areas of life might be, it is no less true that they pose challenges to the social stratification of society. The different speed, extent, and level of utilizing the digital competence by the different layers of the population determine the need to update the mechanisms for accessing, using and perceiving information disseminated online. Therefore, media and information literacy programs acquire additional importance in today's communication environment.

The 2021 elections (one regular – 04.04. and two early – 11.07. and 14.11) for National Assembly in Bulgaria were organized in a tense political confrontation and epidemiological restrictions of COVID-19. The pre-election campaigns have developed alongside two mutually bound processes – politicization of media and mediatization of politics.

When answering the first research question related to the extent to which the social network is used by politicians in their communication, the results of the research show that all the politicians who took part in the elections have accounts and are relatively active in their Facebook campaigns. Some of them share their TV interviews, thus duplicating all their media appearances on Facebook.

Regarding the second research question related to the effectiveness of online campaigns the analysis shows that there is no direct correlation between the Facebook presence and the results of the elections. The findings of the study showed that funding invested in political advertising, scope of media activity, populism, hate speech, and Facebook interactions were not sufficient for electoral prevalence. It also became evident that the risks of communication competencies of political and media entities in the country are related to the insufficient level of media literacy of media users (especially the older adults), who, lost in a bulk of contradictory information, could not impartially exercise their informed election vote. Deficits in purposeful political messages and in clear party programs were the more serious challenges to the developments of deliberative democracy.

As for the third research question whether the older people can equally participate in the election campaign and exercise their informed choice when voting, it turned out that there is a risk for this age group (over half of elderly have never used the internet) to cope with the political messages in Facebook. The Internetization of the campaign created to some extent the effect of excluding older people from the pre-election process.

The limitations of the study are mainly related to the more detailed outline of the effects of the attraction of older people to the political election campaign, developed on social networks. Future empirical studies should address such issues as tracking of interactions and evaluating of political messages by older audiences against the backdrop of the popularity of traditional media,

The results of the study are indicative to those interested in digital political communication during social isolation of pandemic.

Acknowledgements. The paper has been developed within the framework of the academic research projects and MEDIADELCOM project of H2020 of the EC. KP-06-M35/4-18.12.2019 of the National Scientific Fund of Bulgaria.

References

1. Raycheva, L.: Mediatization of politics VS politicization of the media in the situation of the election campaign. In: Krumov, K., Kamenova, M., Radovic-Markovic, M. (eds.) Personality and Society: the Challenges of Change. Sofia: Bulgarian Academy of Sciences and Arts, Serbian Royal Academy of Sciences and Arts, European Center of Business, Education and Science, 2014, pp. 75–98 (2014)
2. Castells, M.: Networks of Outrage and Hope: Social Movements in the Internet Age. Polity, pp. 328 (2015)
3. Raycheva, L., Velinova, N., Tomov, M.: The 2013 social protests in Bulgaria: iconic photographs and image events. In: Stephen, C., Barbara, L.-T., Paul, W. (eds.) Conflict, Mediated Message, and Group Dynamics, pp. 53–66. Intersections of Communications. Lanham, USA (2017)
4. National Statistical Institute. Population by Statistical Regions, Age, Place of Residence and Sex (2021). https://nsi.bg/en/content/2977/population-statistical-regions-age-place-res idence-and-sex
5. Velinova, N., Tomov, M., Raycheva, L., Metanova, L.: Digitization of pre-election messages during the 2021 parliamentary campaign in Bulgaria. Paper presented at the International Conference on Human Systems Engineering and Design: Future Trends and Applications (2021). Dubrovnik, Croatia. http://www.ihsed.org/program.html
6. Raycheva, L., Velinova, N., Tomov, M., Metanova, The Great Downfall: the Facebook Election Campaign' 07.2021: Remake, D´êjà Vu or False Democracy. Bulgarian Academy of Arts and Sciences (2021). https://www.basa.bg/images/%D0%93%D0%BE%D0%BB% D0%B5%D0%BC%D0%B8%D1%8F%D1%82_%D1%81%D1%80%D0%B8%D0%B2_ Facebook_%D0%BF%D1%80%D0%B5%D0%B4%D0%B8%D0%B7%D0%B1%D0% BE%D1%80%D0%BD%D0%B0_%D0%BA%D0%B0%D0%BC%D0%BF%D0%B0% D0%BD%D0%B8%D1%8F_07.2021_remake_deja_vu_%D0%B8%D0%BB%D0%B8_% D1%84%D0%B0%D0%BB%D1%88%D0%B8%D0%B2%D0%B0_%D0%B4%D0% B5%D0%BC%D0%BE%D0%BA%D1%80%D0%B0%D1%86%D0%B8%D1%8F.pdf
7. Central Election Commission of the Republic of Bulgaria. Parliamentary elections (2021). https://www.cik.bg
8. OSCE International Election Observation Mission Bulgaria – Parliamentary Elections. Statement of Preliminary Findings and Conclusions (2021). https://www.osce.org/files/f/docume nts/8/2/482801_0.pdf

9. Drucker, P.: The Age of Discontinuity. Heinemann, London (1969)
10. Rheingold, H.: Net Smart: How to Thrive Online. MIT Press, Cambridge (2012)
11. Lyotard, J.: The Postmodern Condition. Manchester University Press, Manchester (1984)
12. Jenkins, H.: Convergence Culture. New York University Press, New York (2006)
13. Friedman, T.: The World Is Flat: a Brief History of the Twenty-First Century. Farrar, Straus and Giroux, New York (2006)
14. UNESCO. Media and Information Literacy. Policy & Strategy Guidelines (2013). http://une sdoc.unesco.org/images/0022/002256/225606e.pdf
15. Ireton, C., Posetti, J.: Journalism, "Fake News"& Disinformation. UNESCO (2018). https:// digitallibrary.un.org/record/1641987?ln=en
16. Hauben, M.: The Netizens and Community Networks. Computer-Mediated Communication Magazine 4(2) (1997). http://www.december.com/cmc/mag/1997/feb/hauben.html
17. Prensky, M. : Digital Natives, Digital Immigrants. Part 1 & 2. On the Horizon. 9(5), 1–6 & 9(6), 1–6 (2001)
18. Rheingold, H.: Smart Mobs: The Next Social Revolution. Basic Books, New York (2002)
19. Spitzer, M.: Digitale demenz. Droemer, München (2012)
20. European Commission. A European Approach to Media Literacy in the Digital Environment. Communication from the Commission to the European Parliament, the Council, the European Economic and Social Committee and the Committee of the Regions (2007). http://eur-lex.eur opa.eu/legal-content/EN/TXT/?uri=celex%3A52007DC0833
21. European Parliament. Directive (EU) 2018/1808 of the European Parliament and of the Council of November 14, 2018 amending Directive 2010/13/EU on the coordination of certain provisions laid down by law, regulation or administrative action in Member States, relating to the provision of audiovisual media services (Audiovisual Media Services Directive) (2018). https://eur-lex.europa.eu/eli/dir/2018/1808/oj
22. Brites, M.J., Amaral, I., Simões, R.B., Santos, S.J.: Generational perspectives on EU documents tackling disinformation. In: International Conference on Human-Computer Interaction, pp. 349–360 Springer International Publishing (2021)
23. Dumitru, E.-A., Ivan, L., Loos, E.F.: Generational approach to fight fake news: search of effective media literacy trainings and interventions. In: Zhou, J., Gao, Q. (eds.) Human Aspects of IT for the Aged Population, Technology and Society, 7th International Conference, ITAP 2022, Held as Part of the 23nd HCI International Conference, HCII 2022, Gothenburg, June 26–1 July 2022
24. Loos, E., Nijenhuis, J.: Consuming fake news: a matter of age? the perception of political fake news stories in Facebook ads. In: Zhou, J., Gao, Q. (eds.) Human Aspects of IT for the Aged Population, Technology and Society, 6th International Conference, ITAP 2020, Held as Part of the 22nd HCI International Conference, HCII 2020, Copenhagen, July, 19–24. Proceedings, Part III, pp. 69–88. Springer International Publishing (2020)
25. Kahlweit, C.: Hauptsache, alles anders (2021). https://www.sueddeutsche.de/meinung/bulgar ien-slawi-trifonow-parlamentswahl-1.5351874
26. National Statistical Institute. Households with Internet Access (2021). https://www.nsi.bg/ en/content/2808/households-internet-access-home
27. European Commission. Standard Eurobarometer: Report 92: Media Use in the European Union (2021). https://op.europa.eu/en/publication-detail/-/publication/d2dbcf78-11e0-11ec-b4fe-01aa75ed71a1/language-en/format-PDF
28. Reuters Institute Digital News Report 2021 10th Edition (2021). https://reutersinstitute.pol itics.ox.ac.uk/sites/default/files/2021-06/Digital_News_Report_2021_FINAL.pdf

29. European Commission. Europe 2020: A European Strategy for Smart, Sustainable, and Inclusive Growth (2010). http://eur-lex.europa.eu/LexUriServ/LexUriServ.do?uri=COM:2010:2020:FIN:EN:PDF

30. Raycheva, L., Miteva, N., Peicheva, D.: Overcoming the Vulnerability of Older Adults in Contemporary Media Ecosystem (International Policies and Bulgarian Survey). J. Zhou and G. Salvendy (Eds.) Human Aspects of IT for the Aged Population. Acceptance, Communication and Participation. © Springer International Publishing AG, part of Springer Nature 2018. ITAP 2018. LNCS, vol. 10926, pp. 118–133 (2010). https://doi.org/10.1007/978-3-319-92034-4_10

"Online Gameable Communities": Social Digital Games in the Infocommunication Ageing Society

Francisco Regalado(✉) and Ana Isabel Veloso

DigiMedia, Department of Communication and Art, University of Aveiro, Aveiro, Portugal
{fsfregalado,aiv}@ua.pt

Abstract. Technological ubiquity has brought countless paradigmatic changes – *e.g.* the rise of the network society; new forms of entertainment, socializing, and learning; and a digital divide that is still limiting the access and use for a large part of the population. Concurrently, an increasing ageing of the population has been witnessed, bringing additional challenges when developing digital platforms suitable for this audience. Considerable research has studied the impact that digital platforms, such as online communities and digital games, may have on promoting an active and healthy ageing. However, little is known regarding the combined interaction of these two media within the ageing citizen context. This research, in light of the paradigms of complexity and informationalism, epistemologically and antagonistically analyzes the relationship between the older adults, online communities, and digital games. As a result of this disruptive thinking, a new transdisciplinary term emerges – *online gameable communities*. In conclusion, it is believed that this new medium will allow a greater involvement of older adults with technology, while fostering socialization, technological learning, well-being, and an active and healthy ageing.

Keywords: Social digital games · Online communities · Active and healthy ageing · Infocommunication society

1 Introduction

The growing ageing population [1], alongside the increasing use of digital platforms by older adults [2], has been overlooked by developers and marketers. Therefore, despite the numerous advantages that digital platforms can present for an active and healthy ageing – *e.g.* fostering physical activity [3]; promoting socialization [4]; and increasing self-confidence [5] and cognitive functions [6] – there is still a big usage barrier.

As described by Castells [7], with the ever-increasing technological ubiquity, new social contexts emerge. In this vein, and as part of digital platforms, (social) digital games arise as amplifiers of social connections [8], while benefiting from all the advantages that digital games have – *i.e.* provide playful and fun contexts that promote knowledge learning [9], increase quality of life; improve well-being and health, by alleviating depression [10]; and stimulate older adults' cognitive abilities [11]. Moreover, online communities – *i.e.* spaces where people or organizations can discuss various issues together [12] – are also part of this digital evolution.

© The Author(s), under exclusive license to Springer Nature Switzerland AG 2022
Q. Gao and J. Zhou (Eds.): HCII 2022, LNCS 13330, pp. 398–410, 2022.
https://doi.org/10.1007/978-3-031-05581-2_29

When analyzing from a complex point of view – *i.e.* understand the epistemological problematic based on the paradox of unity and multiplicity of physical, biological, and anthropological systems, while exploring uncertainty within richly organized systems [13] – it is possible to deconstruct the problematic and reach new visions and conclusions. Therefore, in this paper it is possible to perceive the transdisciplinary and complex combination of the various areas addressed – *i.e.* gerontology, online communities, and digital games – that when combined create new opportunities for learning, socializing, participating, and promoting an active and healthy ageing.

This paper is divided into three sections, including the Introduction and Final Considerations. The first section – 1. *The Infocommunication Ageing Society* – is devoted to describing the worldwide ageing of the population in the context of a growing use of digital platforms. Then, the second section – 2. *Social Digital Games* – introduces digital games as part of the digital world. Moreover, the advantages of using games to incite an active and healthy ageing are presented, and the addition of the social aspect is described. Lasly, the third section – 3. "Online Gameable Communities" – is dedicated to the introduction of this new term as a transdisciplinary combination of *online communities* and *social digital games*. It is believed that this new concept could be one of the answers to mitigate the effects of the ageing population, while promoting socialization and technological learning. Throughout all sections, an intersection is made between the theme addressed and the two macro-paradigms of complexity and informationalism.

2 The Infocommunication Ageing Society

2.1 Active and Healthy Ageing Society

The World is witnessing an accelerated ageing of the population, highly motivated by the historically low fertility levels, and increasing longevity due to the medical advances [1]. In fact, it is predicted that by 2050 people aged 65 or over will outnumber teenagers and youngsters between the ages of 15 and 24 [1]. Despite the massive disruption caused by the COVID-19 outbreak on the economies and societies [14], and the various levels of mortality impact reported around the World [15], Wilson and colleagues [14] suggest that the previously mentioned ageing trend will prevail in the upcoming years.

Alongside with ageing, older adults may experience some psychological [16], physiological [17], and social declines [18], greatly conditioning the way they perceive, experience and relate to the world.

According to the World Health Organization's perspective, the concept of *active ageing* has been replaced and updated to *healthy ageing*. Active ageing refers to the process where opportunities are optimized for an healthy, participative and secure ageing life, mainly focusing on the continuous participation in the "social, economic, cultural, spiritual and civic affairs" (WHO - World Health Organization, 2002, p. 12). However, the term *healthy ageing* has been introduced in 2015, and goes beyond the definition of absence of disease or infirmity, since this is not a requirement for an healthy ageing [20, 21]. In fact, "healthy ageing is about creating the environments and opportunities that enable people to be and do what they value throughout their lives" [20], para. 2], which can be accomplished even if one experiences some health condition, as is common among older adults [20].

Within the context of this paper, the term *active and healthy ageing* will be used, representing the union between the two aforementioned concepts – since they are not antagonistic or incompatible. Despite no official definition of this new term, it is an attempt to deeply and more completely characterize what a successful and optimal ageing should be.

2.2 The Infocommunication Ubiquity

Before analyzing the ubiquity of the infocommunication ageing society, and characterize its impacts on people's lives, it is important to clarify the *information, communication* and *digital platform* terms that will be used throughout this paper.

Firstly, information can be defined as the encoded mental product that derives from cognitive processes inherent to knowledge – *i.e.* the processes associated with cognition [22]. Moreover, it is crucial to distinguish information from communication. As mentioned by Daniel Bougnoux [23], in their book *Introduction aux sciences de la communication*, the *homo communicans*[1] uses a set of signs to act on another *hommo communicans*, *i.e.* communication can be seen as the perpetual transmissions of signs between entities who are simultaneously receivers and transmitters.

This infocommunicational process which has its origin in an analog format, can be digitalized [24]. In fact, and according to Manuel Castells [25], we live in a world that has become digital – where the current technological development augments exponentially the ability to create digital artifacts that allow the creation, storage, recovery processing, and transmission of information.

In this vein, there is the emergence of *digital platforms*, which can be defined as "the extensible codebase of a software-based system that provides core functionality shared by the modules that interoperate with it and the interfaces through which they interoperate" [26]. An example of a module is the applications (commonly called *apps*), *i.e.* a piece of software that connects to the *digital platform* and adds functionalities to it [26]. According to Ghazawneh and Henfridsson [27] applications are "executable pieces of software that are offered as applications, services or systems to end-users of the platform". Therefore, digital platforms and its applications can have a vast array of possible uses, materializing in the most diverse devices that are part of our daily life, and fulfilling the transmission of information between social actors, thus allowing communication – as a medium for the Information and Communication Technologies (ICT).

The disruption of ICT started in the 70s, as it began to unevenly spread around the world [28]. Since then, the society has been shaping the needs, values, and interests of technology, determining what technology is [28]. In fact, Internet-connected devices have been growing in number and complexity of use and features [29]. Alongside these

---

[1] *Homo communicans* can be defined as a being without interiority and without a body, who exists by capturing and exchanging information, while being completely turned towards the social aspect [55].

technological advances, Castells [7] also emphasizes the exponential emergence of inter-twined nodes – *i.e.* networks, social and information transmission spaces *par excellence*. Therefore, in the 90s, it starts to surface in the literature the study of a *network society* [29], *i.e.* a ubiquity of networks within networks, with impacts on industry, education, leisure, entertainment, and home life, leading us – *hommo communicans* – to where we stand today: individuals immersed in digital platforms [29], part of a society that navigates towards hyper-connectedness [12].

Although it is registered a great adherence to the Internet and its products – *i.e.* digital platforms –, there is still a large digital divide – a social and global problem that shapes and conditions the access to the opportunities enabled by technology [30]. In fact, the rapid growth of knowledge regarding technology, increases inequality between those who have it and those who do not, thereby extending the problem to a planetary scale [31].

Since the year 2000, the digital divide measured according to access has been dimin-ishing [25]. However, according to Dijk [30] the term 'access' is no longer used in preference to the term 'use'. Thus, instead of just considering the access to devices, which *per se* doesn't guarantee any digital literacy, the emphasis has shifted to the abil-ity to use and perceive digital platforms and the technological paradigm of which they are part of [25]. Manuel Castells [25] emphasizes three characteristics of the aforementioned paradigm, also known as informationalism: (i) technology plays an active role on infor-mation; (ii) the effects of technology are constant and pervasive, impacting the society's individual and collective processes, and (iii) the new information technologies allow the emergence of increasingly complex interaction network logics with unpredictable patterns.

Over the years, technological ubiquity has forced a narrowing of the digital divide. As it is possible to observe on Fig. 1, the data reported by PORDATA [2] – a data bank of certified statistics on Portugal – shows that Internet usage is clearly growing, with special emphasis on the age groups over 55. It is worth noting that in 2020 there was an increase of nearly 6 percentage points over the prior year in the oldest age group – the largest increase yet when comparing consecutive years. In the same year, the values regarding computer use also had a similar increase [2]. This was the year that the first case of the COVID-19 outbreak appeared in Portugal, having a huge impact on the way society perceives and practices togetherness and connectivity [32]. In fact, and as proven, during this era of social distancing, a Canadian study suggested a possible increase in technology use by older adults [33].

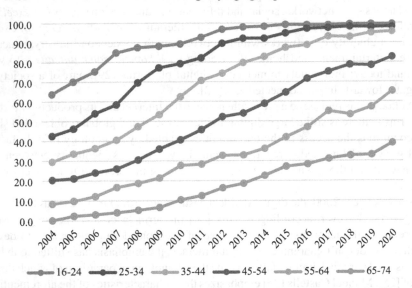

Fig. 1. Internet usage by age group (% per year). Adapted from PORDATA [2].

Forsman and their colleague [34] found a correlation between the Internet use and the well-being experience of older adults. In fact, the increasingly used digital platforms [2], play a crucial role in active and healthy ageing by (i) fostering physical activity [3]; (ii) promoting socialization – at a time of great disconnection, as is the case of COVID-19 pandemic, digital platforms can strengthen relationships with service providers [4]; and (iii) increasing self-confidence [5] and cognitive functions [6].

Older adults are a very heterogeneous group [35]. Therefore, it is essential to analyze them in a complex, paradoxical, and systemic way, perceiving the individual and collective needs. When considering their increasing use of digital platforms, one should not overlook the barriers imposed by a technology that is not made for them [36], which emphasizes the use by youngsters.

By analyzing Fig. 2, it is possible to understand the correlation of the constituent axes of a complex transdisciplinary system – *i.e.* the union of gerontology with technology, forming gerontechnology. According to Edgar Morin [13], transdisciplinarity allows understanding simultaneously the unity of science and the differentiation of the sciences, while systemically analyzing the problem of a *whole* that is not reduced to the *sum* of physical, cognitive, and social system's parts. Transdisciplinarity doesn't strive to master the various intervening areas, but rather to understand what crosses and goes beyond them [31]. The migration of concepts between the various areas, creating phenomena of disintegration and decay, allow an epistemological and complex vision, which will ultimately result in the construction of new thoughts. To this process of creating "new insights, new visions, new discoveries, and new reflections" (p. 77), Morin [13] gave the name of *complexity paradigm*.

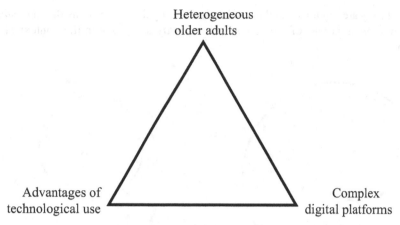

Fig. 2. Systematization of the relationship between the elements that constitute the infocommunicational complexity for older adults (Authors' copyright).

In fact, isolating older adults from technologies, and not equating the advantages these may have, but also the barriers they present, could lead to an extremely reductionist thinking that is unable to assess reality and build appropriate technological solutions.

3 Social Digital Games

Considering the older adults' free time and their growing acceptance of technologies' use [37], there is an important adherence in the particular case of digital games – 15% of US game players are over 55 years old [38]. Therefore, it is crucial to develop video games with this target audience in mind [37].

As an integral part of digital platforms on an infocommunication ecosystem, games, and in particular digital games, play an important role in multiple fields and disciplines, such as education, business, and healthcare [39]. According to Avedon and Sutton-Smith [40], a game can be defined as a voluntary exercise of system control, enclosed by rules, in which through a competition between powers there is a production of an unbalanced result. Moreover, the key elements to this definition are [41]: (i) physical or intellectual activity are requirements in games; (ii) games are completely voluntary; (iii) a conflict between players is built-in; (iv) games are limited by rules; and (v) the game's output is the final goal, being always different from the initial state.

Although the game play's focus is entertainment, challenge is a constant variable allowing game structures to be adapted for use in other contexts, where values of "self-motivation, learning, skill practice, and meeting challenges" (p. 1) are also promoted [42]. Due to entertaining, motivating and fun activities, games are known for their high levels of engagement [39]. In fact, games are designed to stimulate high levels of motivation and engagement, allowing results that educational materials are not capable of [42].

Salen and Zimmerman [41] emphasize the importance of distinguishing the terms *game* and *play* – something that languages other than English usually do not allow (*e.g.* the phrase "play a game", in Portuguese, uses different versions of the same word – "jogar um jogo"). As can be observed in Fig. 3, a twofold approach is allowed: (a) some forms of *play* are organized and formalized, allowing them to be considered *games*; and (b) *play* a *game* is part of the games, placing *play* and *game* in the context of game design.

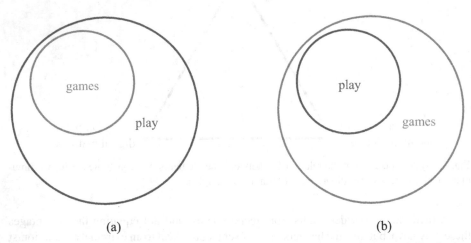

Fig. 3. – Relationship between *games* and *play*. (a) games are a subset of play; and (b) *play* is a component of *game*. [41] Adapted from *Rules of Play: Game Design Fundamentals*, p. 73].

The growing ubiquity of technology, as part of the informationalism described by Manuel Castells [25], led to the combination of the term *digital* with the *games*. According to Nicola Whitton [43], the combination of this two terms refers to the use of information electronic devices of some kind, which can be an integral part or just a peripheral one of the game – *e.g.* "computers, game consoles, handheld devices, mobile phones, digital audio players," (p. 20), and mobile game consoles. Moreover, the digital part of the game can be integral and fundamental, or it can be merely peripheral and be part of specific actions of the game [43].

Similarly to the reality of digital platforms, the focus of game marketers is on younger audiences – thus sacrificing the development of games that keep seniors' needs in mind [44], and limiting feelings of accomplishment and satisfaction that make games enjoyable [45], leading to a potential state of frustration [35].

Nevertheless, digital games can be used by seniors to provide a playful and fun context that promotes social interactions [11] – suppressing feelings of loneliness [10] – and new knowledge learning [9]. Thus, they can also increase quality of life; improve well-being and health – by alleviating depression [10]; and stimulate older adults' cognitive abilities [11], thus promoting an active and healthy ageing. Moreover, Motti and their colleagues [46] emphasize the importance that digital games may have in preventing the technological exclusion – thus helping to narrow the digital divide.

The inherent complexity of digital games when applied to the context of older adults becomes clear when, similarly to digital platforms – which games are part of –, there is a barrier of usage imposed by the age-related changes that affects usability issues [47], preventing one from benefiting from the ultimate gaming experience. Moreover,

IJsselsteijn and colleagues [47] emphasize the importance of targeting older adults' motivations, and highlights the potential benefits to engage them with new technology.

As previously stated, digital games play an important role in promoting social interactions, which can be highly amplified by *social digital games* – *i.e.* games that feature a shared understanding of the intentionality of players' goals, prioritizing social interactions and making actions in the game socially meaningful [8]. Once again, the complex epistemological problematic unveils itself, revealing the enormous challenge of combining the various units of a complex and heterogeneous (eco)system – older adults, games, digital games, and social digital games. Despite the enormous advantages already presented, there is still a usage barrier, thus making it complex thinking about social digital games that can simultaneously be the problem and the solution.

In the next section, it will be examined how the addition of social digital games to online communities can amplify engagement and the social component, thus promoting social connection and learning of digital platforms usage. Moreover, the concept of "online gameable communities" will be introduced, combining the definition of *online* communities and *gameable*, while amplifying the possibility of social connections, motivation and engagement.

4   "Online Gameable Communities": Bursting Social Connections

As previously mentioned in the first section – *cf.* 1. *The Infocommunication Ageing Society*, online communities are an integral part of digital platforms and a world that is leaning towards hyper-connectivity [12]. In a transdisciplinary way – as a systemic virtue, like described by Morin [13], when combining *online communities* with *social digital games*, the gaming and socializing potential in an online community increases exponentially. Thus, in the context of this paper, a new term will be introduced later: *online gameable communities*. As can be observed in Fig. 4, the term *Online Communities* comprises two characteristics of the term *Social Digital Games*, *i.e. Online* for *Digital* and *Communities* for *Social*; leaving the term *Game(able)* to join *Online Communities*.

Fig. 4. Representative scheme of the construction of the term "Online Gameable Communities" (Authors' copyright).

4.1   Defining Online Communities

Online communities can be divided in its two terms: *online* and *communities*, where the former adds a new dimension to the latter. The term community can be used to describe the relations established interpersonally, within a geographic area, and with a shared bond [48]. When appending the term *online*, the concept of community acquires new dimensions, contexts, and meanings. According to Plant [12], the term *online community* can be defined as a "collective group of entities, individuals or organizations that come together either temporarily or permanently through an electronic medium to interact in a common problem or interest space". Furthermore, Preece [49] adds to this definition that an online community is also (i) a place where people can satisfy their own needs by interacting with each other; (ii) rules that guide people's conduct in these online spaces; and (iii) computer systems that facilitate and amplify social interaction between users. This new social phenomenon was motivated by the ubiquity of technological break-throughs, and to meet Human's basic needs for connection, knowledge, and information (Plant, 2004).

Online communities, as part of ICT and a world that tends towards hyper-connectedness [12], play a key role in maintaining and expanding interpersonal relation-ships [50]. Having the potential to incorporate digital social games, online communities exponentially amplify the social interactions promoted by games, and it is noteworthy the tightening of intergenerational relationships and a bridging of geographic distance [37], having a positive outcome, even if for seniors it means having to learn to handle technology and deal with the frustrations of systems not designed for them [51].

4.2 Defining Gameable

Gameable is a blend of the word *game* and the suffix -*able*. Just like the word *able*, the term -*able* is an adjectival suffix that has its etymological origin in the Latin expression -*ābilis*, meaning "capable or worthy of being acted upon" [52]. Therefore, when added to the word *game*, a new dimension is added. According to the WordSense dictionary [53], *gameable* is an adjective that can be defined as "capable of being gamed" (para. 1), *i.e.* something that is capable of becoming a game or having a game integrated in a seamless way.

4.3 Defining "Online Gameable Communities"

Having already defined the terms *Online Communities* and *Gameable,* and clarified the concept of *(social) digital games*, the term "Online Gameable Communities" is introduced in this paper to refer to:

- *A technologically mediated space where people can share common interests and infor-mation, while having the potential to incorporate social digital games, thus amplifying social interactions promoted by games.*
  Additionally, it can be added:
- *It is the ideation of a community where social digital games promote digital liter-acy, the tightening of intergenerational relationships and a bridging of geographic distance. It is added to online communities the engaging, motivating, and social capabilities of social digital games.*

Owing to the high potential of games to engage and motivate its players [39] – by promoting a potential flow state [54], it is believe that Online Gameable Communities will not only mitigate some of the effects of ageing – such as social decline [18] by unleashing the social potential of online communities; but also assist in the integration and education for the use of digital platforms [9] in an increasingly digital world [25].

5   Final Considerations

The growing technological ubiquity, as posited by Manuel Castells [25], makes the older adults' use of digital platforms a central topic in contemporary debates. In fact, technology has been pervading the world, shaping everyday life, letting itself be shaped by people and information, and allowing new social contexts to emerge. A giant set of new realities are surfacing in this new digital world – which is not yet fully ready to welcome older adults. Furthermore, digital platforms play a key role in integrating senior citizens within a digital society, preventing their exclusion or marginalization, while mitigating the effects of ageing and promoting an active and healthy one.

Despite the vast array of benefits presented by digital platforms to older adults – *e.g.* promotion of physical activity, boost of self-esteem, better socialization, and improvement of cognitive processes – they still lack attention to the needs, impairments, and motivations of the heterogeneous older adult. In light of this diversity, Castells [25] advises the use of complexity thinking for its epistemological value, while allowing the creation of order out of chaos, through interactivity between the elements at the origin of the problem.

Therefore, considering respectively the three principles of the complexity paradigm – *i.e.* dialogic, organizational recourse, and hologrammatic [13] –, it is possible to make the following analysis regarding this research:

1. There is a clear confrontation between older adults and digital platforms. But at the same time, and antagonistically, they manage to organize and collaborate;
2. By using digital platforms to promote active and healthy ageing, it is being allowed the problem-making product to act as a solution;
3. The older adult as an individuality belongs to the whole, but this whole is made of heterogeneous individualities. Therefore, researchers are responsible to develop solutions in an interactive and inter-retroactive way with this audience, countering simplifying thinking – opposed to *unitat multiplex.*

This paper has shed a light on the potential that online communities, social digital games, and their combination – *i.e.* online gameable communities – can pose for an active and healthy ageing. That said, this paper introduces a transdisciplinary concept of online gameable communities – a digital space where games play a key role in engaging and motivating the older adults, promoting their intergenerational socialization, helping them to learn to use digital platforms – which is crucial in this modern and digital World, while mitigating psychological and physical declines.

Aside the evident complexity of the topics discussed throughout this paper, it is believed that digital platforms, in particular online gameable communities, may cease to be the problem and become part of the solution to the problem itself.

Acknowledgments. This work was supported by FCT – Foundation for Science and Technology (Fundação para a Ciência e Tecnologia), I.P. nr. 2021.06465.BD, DigiMedia Research Center, under the project UIDB/05460/2020, and the project SEDUCE 2.0 - Use of Communication and Information in the miOne online community by senior citizens, funded by FCT – Fundação para a Ciência e a Tecnologia, I.P., COMPETE 2020, Portugal 2020 and European Union, under the European Regional Development Fund, POCI-01-0145-FEDER-031696 SEDUCE 2.0.

References

1. The United Nations: World Population Prospects 2019 Highlights (2019)
2. PORDATA: Indivíduos com 16 e mais anos que utilizam computador e Internet em % do total de indivíduos: por grupo etário. https://www.pordata.pt/Portugal/Indivíduos+com+16+e+mais+anos+que+utilizam+computador+e+Internet+em+percentagem+do+total+de+individuos+por+grupo+etário-1139. Accessed 23 Oct 2021
3. Vollenbroek-Hutten, M., et al.: Rest Rust ! Physical active for active and healthy ageing. Translational medicine @ UniSa. **13**, 19–28 (2015). https://doi.org/10.14273/unisa-2005
4. Sixsmith, A.: COVID-19 and AgeTech. Quality Ageing Older Adults. **21**, 247–252 (2020). https://doi.org/10.1108/QAOA-07-2020-0029
5. Park, C., Lee, J.H.: Factors influencing the accessibility of online social game. In: 2012 IEEE Symposium on E-Learning, E-Management and E-Services, IS3e 2012, pp. 83–86 (2012). https://doi.org/10.1109/IS3e.2012.6414950
6. Pappas, M.A., Demertzi, E., Papagerasimou, Y., Koukianakis, L., Voukelatos, N., Drigas, A.: Cognitive-based E-learning design for older adults. Soc. Sci. **8** (2019). https://doi.org/10.3390/socsci8010006
7. Castells, M.: A Galáxia Internet: reflexões sobre a Internet, negócios e a sociedade. Bolsas, Fundação Calouste Gulbenkian. Serviço de Educação e Bolsas, Lisboa (2004)
8. Juul, J.: A Casual Revolution: Reinventing Video Games and Their Players. The MIT Press, London, England (2010)
9. Kaufman, D., Sauve, L.: Digital gaming by older adults: can it enhance social connectedness? In: Zhou, J., Salvendy, G. (eds.) HCII 2019. LNCS, vol. 11593, pp. 167–176. Springer, Cham (2019). https://doi.org/10.1007/978-3-030-22015-0_13
10. Wollersheim, D., Merkes, M., Shields, N., Liamputtong, P.: Physical and psychosocial effects of Wii video game use among older women. Int. J. Emerg. Technol. Soc. **8**, 85–98 (2016)
11. Hausknecht, S., Schell, R., Zhang, F., Kaufman, D.: Building seniors' social connections and reducing loneliness through a digital game. In: Proceedings of the 1st International Conference on Information and Communication Technologies for Ageing Well and e-Health, pp. 276–284. SCITEPRESS - Science and and Technology Publications (2015). https://doi.org/10.5220/0005526802760284
12. Plant, R.: Online communities. Technol. Soc. **26**, 51–65 (2004). https://doi.org/10.1016/j.techsoc.2003.10.005
13. Morin, E.: Introdução ao Pensamento Complexo. Editora Meridional, Ltda. Porto Alegere (2005)
14. Wilson, T., Temple, J., Charles-Edwards, E.: Will the COVID-19 pandemic affect population ageing in Australia? J. Popul. Res. **2021**, 1–15 (2021). Doi:https://doi.org/10.1007/S12546-021-09255-3
15. Johns Hopkins University: Coronavirus Resource Center - COVID-19 Dashboard. https://coronavirus.jhu.edu/map.html. Accessed 19 Oct 2021

16. Forsell, Y., Jorm, A.F., Winblad, B.: Suicidal thoughts and associated factors in an elderly population. Acta Psychiatr. Scand. **95**, 108–111 (1997). https://doi.org/10.1111/j.1600-0447.1997.tb00382.x

17. Pak, R., McLaughlin, A.: Designing Displays for Older Adults. CRC Press, Boca Raton (2011)

18. Eng, P.M., Rimm, E.B., Fitzmaurice, G., Kawachi, I.: Social ties and change in social ties in relation to subsequent total and cause-specific mortality and coronary heart disease incidence in men. Am. J. Epidemiol. **155**, 700–709 (2002). https://doi.org/10.1093/aje/155.8.700

19. WHO - World Health Organization: Active Ageing: A Policy Framework. A Contribution of World Health Organization to the Second United Nations World Assembly of Ageing. , Madrid (2002). https://doi.org/10.1080/713604647

20. WHO: Ageing: Healthy ageing and functional ability. https://www.who.int/westernpacific/news/q-a-detail/ageing-healthy-ageing-and-functional-ability. Accessed 19 Oct 2021

21. WHO: World report on ageing and health. World Health Organization (2015)

22. Passarelli, B., Malheiro, A., Ramos, F.: e-Infocomunicação : estratégias e aplicações. , Rio de Janeiro (2014)

23. Bougnoux, D.: Introduction aux sciences de la communication. La Découverte, Paris (2001)

24. Floridi, L.: Information: A Very Short Introduction. Oxford University Press (2010). https://doi.org/10.1093/actrade/9780199551378.001.0001

25. Castells, M.: The Rise of the Network Society: With a New Preface, Volume I: Second Edition With a New Preface. The Rise of the Network Society: With a New Preface, Volume I: Second Edition With a New Preface (2010). https://doi.org/10.1002/9781444319514

26. Tiwana, A., Konsynski, B., Bush, A.A.: Research commentary—platform evolution: coevolution of platform architecture. Govern. Environ. Dyn. **21**, 675–687 (2010). https://doi.org/10.1287/ISRE.1100.0323

27. Ghazawneh, A., Henfridsson, O.: Balancing platform control and external contribution in third-party development: the boundary resources model. Inf. Syst. J. **23**, 173–192 (2013). https://doi.org/10.1111/J.1365-2575.2012.00406.X

28. Castells, M., Cardoso, G.: The Network Society: From Knowledge to Policy. Center for Transatlantic Relations, Jhu-Sais (2006)

29. Hassan, R.: Media. Politics and the Network Society. Open University Press, New York (2004)

30. Dijk, J.: The Digital Divide. Polity Press, Cambridge (2020)

31. Freitas, L., Morin, E., Nicolescu, B.: Carta de Transdisciplinaridade. Primeiro Congresso Mundial da Transdisciplinaridade (1994)

32. Lopez, K.J., Tong, C., Whate, A., Boger, J.: "It's a whole new way of doing things": the digital divide and leisure as resistance in a time of physical distance. **63**, 281–300 (2021). https://doi.org/10.1080/16078055.2021.1973553

33. AGE-WELL: COVID-19 has significantly increased the use of many technologies among older Canadians: poll. https://agewell-nce.ca/archives/10884. Accessed 24 Oct 2021

34. Forsman, A.K., Nordmyr, J.: Psychosocial Links Between Internet Use and Mental Health in Later Life: A Systematic Review of Quantitative and Qualitative Evidence **36**, 1471–1518 (2015). https://doi.org/10.1177/0733464815595509

35. Fisk, A.D., Rogers, W.A., Charness, N., Czaja, S.J., Sharit, J.: Designing for Older Adults: Principles and Creative Human Factors Approaches, Second Edition. CRC Press, Boca Raton, Florida (2009). https://doi.org/10.1201/9781420080681

36. McMurtrey, M.E., Zeltmann, S.M., Downey, J.P., McGaughey, R.E.: Seniors and technology: results from a field study. J. Comput. Inf. Syst. **51**, 22–30 (2011). https://doi.org/10.1080/08874417.2011.11645498

37. Villani, D., Serino, S., Triberti, S., Riva, G.: Ageing positively with digital games. In: Giokas, K., Bokor, L., Hopfgartner, F. (eds.) eHealth 360°. LNICSSITE, vol. 181, pp. 148–155. Springer, Cham (2017). https://doi.org/10.1007/978-3-319-49655-9_20

38. ESA: 2020 Essential Facts About the Video Game Industry. , Washington, DC (2020)
39. Pyae, A., Luimula, M., Smed, J.: Investigating the usability of interactive physical activity games for elderly: a pilot study. In: 6th IEEE Conference on Cognitive Infocommunications, CogInfoCom 2015 – Proceedings, pp. 185–193 (2016). https://doi.org/10.1109/COG INFOCOM.2015.7390588
40. Avedon, E., Sutton-Smith, B.: The Study of Games. Wiley, New York (1971)
41. Salen, K., Zimmerman, E.: Rules of play: game design fundamentals. Int. J. Artif. Intell. Tools 9 (2004)
42. Watters, C., et al.: Extending the use of games in health care. In: Proceedings of the Annual Hawaii International Conference on System Sciences, vol. 5, (2006). https://doi.org/10.1109/HICSS.2006.179
43. Whitton, N.: Learning with Digital Games. Routledge, New York (2010)
44. Nimrod, G.: The fun culture in seniors' online communities. Gerontologist **51**, 226–237 (2011). https://doi.org/10.1093/geront/gnq084
45. Schell, R., Hausknecht, S., Kaufman, D.: Barriers and adaptations of a digital game for older adults. In: Proceedings of the 1st International Conference on Information and Communication Technologies for Ageing Well and e-Health, pp. 269–275. SCITEPRESS - Science and and Technology Publications (2015). https://doi.org/10.5220/0005524002690275
46. Genaro Motti, L., Vigouroux, N., Gorce, P.: Design of a social game for older users using touchscreen devices and observations from an exploratory study. In: Stephanidis, C., Antona, M. (eds.) UAHCI 2014. LNCS, vol. 8515, pp. 69–78. Springer, Cham (2014). https://doi.org/10.1007/978-3-319-07446-7_7
47. IJsselsteijn, W., Herman Nap, H., Poels, K., de Kort, Y.: Digital game design for elderly users. In: Proceedings of the 2007 Conference on Future Play - Future Play '07 (2007). https://doi.org/10.1145/1328202
48. Willie, C.: The evolution of community education: content and mission. Harvard Educ. Rev. **70**, 191–210 (2000). https://doi.org/10.17763/haer.70.2.838w67647mq44168
49. Preece, J.: Online communities: designing usability, supporting sociability. Ind. Manag. Data Syst. **100**, 459–460 (2000). https://doi.org/10.1108/imds.2000.100.9.459.3
50. Leist, A.K.: Social media use of older adults: a mini-review. Gerontology **59**, 378–384 (2013). https://doi.org/10.1159/000346818
51. Osmanovic, S., Pecchioni, L.: Beyond Entertainment: motivations and outcomes of video game playing by older adults and their younger family members. Games Culture. **11**, 130–149 (2016). https://doi.org/10.1177/1555412015602819
52. WordSense Dictionary: -able: meaning, origin, translation. https://www.wordsense.eu/-able/# English. Accessed 24 Oct 2021
53. WordSense Dictionary: gameable: meaning, origin, definition
54. Zichermann, G., Cunningham, C.: Gamification by Design: Implementing Game Mechanics in Web and Mobile Apps. O'Reilly Media Inc, Sebastopol (2011)
55. Breton, P.: L'Utopie de la communication - Le mythe du "village palnétaire." 182 (1992)

Tech Mentors, Warm Experts and Digital Care Work: Pandemic Lessons from a Remote Digital Literacy Training Program for Older Adults

Kim Sawchuk[(✉)] and Constance Lafontaine

Communication Studies, Concordia University, Montreal, QC H2S 3J1, Canada
kim.sawchuk@concordia.ca

Abstract. This paper discusses a Canadian tablet distribution and digital training program that involved two non-profit organizations. The program targeted older adults during the fall and winter of 2020/2021, an especially dire period of the pandemic in Canada. Drawing on data collected from surveys, interviews and observations, we report on our evaluation of the impact of the program on the older adults and the organizations, highlighting the key role and potential played by *paid* "tech mentors" who we consider as "warm experts" in the program's success. As this study suggests, the term warm expert can be expanded beyond the circle of the family. The digital care work needed within society, provided by warm experts, needs recognition and consideration by policy makers.

Keywords: Aging · Older adults · ICTS · Warm expert · Digital literacy · COVID-19 · Canada · Remote learning · Digital care work

1 Introduction

Across the globe and within Canada, the COVID-19 pandemic has had a disproportionate impact on older adults from heightened infection rates in senior residences, to higher chances of fatal illness, to regulations on movement, to limitations on social contact [1]. In this context, a lack of access to digital technologies within this population has provoked public awareness of the dire consequences of age-related digital divides [2–5].

The disparity in age-related digital access has generated a plethora of projects to put digital technologies into the hands of older adults, in the midst of a major crisis in public health [6, 7]. In this pandemic context, aging, digital technologies and age-related digital divides have become a hot topic of conversation in the media [8, 9] and academia. For those living on fixed incomes after retirement in Canada, maintaining digital access either through cellular services or WiFi connections remains a challenge. This is for a multiplicity of reasons: from the lack of connectivity in rural and remote regions, to the costs of broadband and cellular services, to the affordances of the technology and software, to lack of experience with their use [10, 11].

In this paper, we discuss a Canadian tablet distribution and digital training program led by two non-profit organizations that targeted older adults during the fall and winter

Q. Gao and J. Zhou (Eds.): HCII 2022, LNCS 13330, pp. 411–431, 2022.
https://doi.org/10.1007/978-3-031-05581-2_30

of 2020/2021, an especially dire period of the pandemic in Canada. Drawing on data collected from surveys, interviews and observations, we report on our evaluation of the impact of the program on the older adults and the organizations, highlighting the key role and potential played by paid "tech mentors" in the program's success. We ask and attempt to answer the following questions: what did the older adults find valuable about the program? What did they identify as the main challenges to remote learning? As a corollary, we ask what skills were identified as essential for effective tech mentoring by the older participants, the community organizers and the tech mentors themselves?

Paying attention to the benefits and the challenges of instigating a remote digital training program in this context, we draw upon and critically expand the concept of the "warm expert" [12], a term that has gained traction within Internet studies since its introduction by Bakardjieva in 2005. We challenge the de facto association of the warm expert to the domains of the familial and the unpaid, and argue for an expanded definition of the "warm expert" that accounts for the myriad of skills that are required to support older adults in a transition to on-line, digitally mediated communications.

2   Literature Review

Strategies for increasing the digital literacy skills of older adults have been identified as a means to counter social isolation [13] and misinformation [14], two salient phenomena that occurred during the pandemic. The pandemic created conditions that have necessitated older adults go online, accelerated the need to address existing digital divides [3], and have increased older adults' interest in learning digital technologies [15]. However, the pandemic also has impacted older adults' ability to partake in face-to-face activities that promote connectedness and the development of skills [16], including digital literacy workshops or classes [12].

The outsized importance and heightened need for digital skills of older adults in Canada during the pandemic and the difficulty delivering programming at this time has created a conundrum. Researchers have identified the need for effective strategies to implement digital training virtually for older populations who have no or low digital skills [12, 17] and who thus may find themselves socially and digitally isolated. Garcia et al. describe this dilemma well: "Teaching older adults with low or no skills how to use computers and smartphones by using these same technologies as tools to enable general teaching is an extraordinary challenge". It is in this context that we turn to the literature on the "warm expert", a term originating with Maria Bakardjieva's 2005 influential discussion of the integration of the Internet into everyday life activities.[1] The warm expert has long been referenced as an important tenet in approaches to digital literacy for older adults. In Bakardjieva's words: "The warm expert is an Internet/computer technology expert in the professional sense or simply in a relative sense compared with the less knowledgeable other. [...] The warm expert mediates between the technological universal and the concrete situation, needs and background of the novice user with whom

---

[1] This approach builds upon the domestication of technology theory discussed by Roger Silverstone and Leslie Haddon [18]. The domestication of technology, which describes the conditions under which new technologies become 'tamed' and integrated in household routines has been taken up in recent work for example by Stephen Neville [19].

he is in a close personal relationship." [12]. Three terms are critical here: in the original articulation of a warm expert, this expertise is relational, and relative to the learner; warm experts play a mediating role and warm experts have a close personal relationship to the potential user.

While the term warm expert is often cited in passing, there have been more extensive explorations of the concept of the warm expert in the literature on ICTs and aging. Within studies of the adoption of technologies by older users, the warm expert has been used to examine the reason for the non-adoption of mobile phone service by "have-nots" in Sweden, including "elderly users" [20], the adoption of telehealth [21] and "unboxers" on YouTube videos [19]. In all of this literature, including the study of aging and ICTs, most often foregrounds the role of family members as warm experts. For example, in their study of ICT adoption of older adults in Sweden, Olsson, Samuelson and Viscovi describe warm experts as non-professional persons who are typically a "closely-related person, often a child or grandchild" [22]. In his excellent 2019 book Intergenerational Connections and Digital Families, Sakari Taipale provides one of the most expansive discussions of the warm expert in the context of aging, devoting an entire chapter to a discussion of the key role of "Warm Experts 2.0" [23]. Taipale outlines four different types of warm experts that have emerged in the context of the family, changes in media and Internet access, drawing upon extensive ethnographic research in three European countries. Research on warm experts and aging has generated new and important empirical work on the "heterogeneity of ICT use" among older adults [24], and discussions of the role of warm experts in assisting older adults to access online services [24]. Ironically, Bakardjieva does not explicitly make an argument for the warm expert as a family member in her 2005 book, nor does she investigate in any depth issues of aging or inter-generationality. Yet, as we can see, the evolving literature on warm experts tends to underscore and emphasize the import of familial relationships in the development of digital literacy for older adults.

3 Methodology

The data for this paper was initially collected as part of a joint effort with two collaborating Canadian non-profit organizations who wanted to evaluate the impacts of their digital tablet distribution and training program so that they could build upon this iteration for future initiatives. Participants for the project were selected by one of the non-profit organizations through their networks after a formal submission process. Recruitment for this study was done *via* this organization, who contacted all of the participants on our behalf and informed them of our research project. Participation in the study was voluntary. Our participation in the data collection is commensurate with our position, as a team concerned with data justice [25], towards creating community-driven data that draws upon traditions of participatory action research [26] and is greatly influenced by researchers such as Virginia Eubanks, and her writing on collaborative action research [27].[2] Each instance of creating data sets with community organizations is a negotiation

---

[2] Several research assistants were involved in the data collection and data analysis: Marie-Ève Durocher, Nicole Fornelli, Margaret Johnston, Xiaxue Li, Maggie McCutcheon, Valerie Thomas and Andrea Tremblay.

of objectives and resources, on both sides. In this case, this entailed co-creating projects that assist community and non-profit organizations to meet their objectives, furnishing concrete information independently, and providing information that can be used for further project and funding development.

Surveys. We undertook surveys with 27 older adults who participated in the program. These surveys comprised 35 close-ended questions and one open-ended question, structured along five themes. The surveys were all undertaken by phone with participants in March of 2021. Each conversation lasted between 21 and 60 min, with the average interview lasting 46 min. The surveys were translated into three languages to accommodate the needs of the respondents (English, French and Mandarin). A team of five ACT research assistants and a translator administered the survey. The surveys were not audio recorded, but quantitative results and additional qualitative comments were documented on a spreadsheet. The results of the survey were tabulated to provide an overall picture of how participants responded to the program, and we thematically coded the responses to the open-ended questions.

Semi-directed Interviews. We undertook a series of semi-directed interviews with various actors involved in the planning and delivery of the program, from multiple angles. This included staff members from the non-profit organizations involved in developing the program (four). These interviews, in particular, helped to guide the development of the survey and all other interview grids. We then interviewed tech mentors who were hired to train older adults (four) and the coordinator of the tech mentors (one). Finally, we conducted interviews with community leaders or community organization personnel who are knowledgeable of their local contexts and responsible for connecting older adults to the program (four). The interviews were transcribed and a code frame was developed to analyze the data.

Participant Observation. The last element of our data collection entailed participant observation, undertaken locally in Montreal. A local organization, with which we have a long history of collaboration, received seven iPads through the program, which it distributed to local older adults. In this case, two members of the organization and one member of our research team followed training by the program leads and took on the role of tech mentors, working remotely with local older adults. By working with a local organization and older participants, we learned first-hand of the benefits and challenges associated with delivering the training program remotely in a pandemic. The three team members involved in the participant observation recorded field notes throughout the process.

Analysis: The survey data was collected and tabulated using a spreadsheet. Two researchers double checked the data to verify it for accuracy. After transcription, a thematic analysis of the comments on the open-ended portion of the survey and the interview material was undertaken by two readers A longer report covering a wider range of themes and more details on the responses of interviewees was submitted to the non-profit organization. For the purposes of this paper, we have foregrounded the themes that emerged most frequently in the transcripts. We did not intend to study warm experts. In the tradition of "grounded theory" the theoretical concept that guides this paper emerged from our reflections on our conversations with participants and reading of the transcripts [28].

4 Background

4.1 Program Overview

The digital literacy program we analyze was developed over 2020, immediately following the onset of the pandemic by two partnered Canadian non-profit organizations that wanted to address two simultaneous crises. On the one hand, older adults who found themselves on the wrong side of the digital divide and isolated with no access to the conveniences offered by services that rapidly moved online. On the other hand, mostly young service industry workers, like restaurant servers or other members of the 'hospitality industry', who were left unemployed due to closures and in a precarious financial situation. This digital learning program sought to a) assist older adults without digital access and b) offer training and employment to service and hospitality industry workers who had been laid off so they could work as "tech mentors". These tech mentors, most of whom were based in an urban centre in Eastern Canada, would provide remote training to older adults from across the country to help them in the development of their digital skills.

Seventy-five tablet computers (iPads) were purchased, along with four-month data plans for each tablet. A call was made to community organizations across the country to identify socially-isolated and economically-disadvantaged local seniors who might be keen to learn to use digital devices. Tablets were distributed in five Canadian provinces in one of two ways. First, the tablets could be distributed directly to older adults identified by a local community organization. These seniors would then follow the weekly training given remotely, mostly by telephone, by the tech mentors over three months. Second, and alternatively, the tablets could be given to the community organizations who would have control over the tablets, virtually. In this case, the community organizations would deliver the bulk of the training to local older adults, and lent the tablets to them as they saw fit. This was done according to their organizational programming and capacity. It also depended greatly on the housing situation of the older adults vis-à-vis the participating organization: in some cases, older adults were in a long-term care facility, where staff were on hand to assist the learners with the devices, directly. In other cases, the older adults were members of an organization, but lived alone. There were some overlaps between these two branches of the program (e.g., some organizations received training from tech mentors, some older adults received training from tech mentors and community organizations).

As one might imagine, this flexibility in the program was appreciated by participating organizations. But this flexibility also meant that there existed a wide range of program applications and appropriations locally, which were contingent on organizational priorities and local realities. In this paper, we primarily focus on the first program delivery model, which gave individual older adults tablets and remote support on a weekly basis from a bank of paid tech mentors. If needed, to create a point of comparison, we also refer to data on culled from older participants in the other program, which mainly focused on delivering tablets to community organizations. Without getting bogged down by the complexities of the program delivery, the unifying thread among the data considered for this study is that the digital literacy training undertaken *via* remote tech mentors and directed to autonomous older adults. We do not examine, in detail, the specifics of the program itself.

There are at least three ways we consider this particular digital literacy program, and the uniqueness of our case study. First, it was delivered almost entirely remotely, primarily over the phone, over the course of a pandemic and entailed teaching basic digital literacy from a distance. Second, it relied on *paying* the tech mentors, who were trained and hired exclusively to provide digital skills to older adults. The employment of tech mentors is in contrast to digital literacy programs that are centred on volunteers [13] or individuals already employed by organizations with a diverse set of functions, who are then deployed to do the work of digital training. Third, the program included some skills training, a five-gigabyte data plan, and the device. After the three months, the tablets were given to the older adults or to the organizations who wanted to keep them. The data plan was extended for roughly a month beyond the three-month training period. After this, the older adults and organizations had to procure their own Internet through either purchasing a SIM card for their device, or by purchasing a Internet plan to access a WiFi network, if they wanted to remain online.

4.2 Demographic Portrait of Participants

Recent research on later life often stresses the heterogeneity of the older adult population as critical to factor into any analysis of aging [29]. The term older adults can cover a wide range of life course experiences, as well as key differences in the use of media technologies related to other mitigating factors, such as gender, education and social class [30].

In this study, our participants were indeed heterogenous. Of the 27 older adults surveyed out of 75 participants, the majority were between the ages of 75 and 85, a group sometimes referred to as "the old old", a population who is often understudied in ICT work [31]. Most of our participants–68%–identified as female while 27% identified as male. The majority (77%) of the participants lived in urban areas. About 55% of the participants disclosed earning an income that is under the national annual average for older adults (estimated as $28,190 CAD by Statistics Canada). The group was largely well-educated, with 68% of the respondents reporting having a college or university education. English was the first language of 68% of our respondents, followed by 9% French and 13% a language other than French or English. A diversity of communities were included in the program: one cohort were Mandarin-speakers living in a senior's apartment complex; another came from a long-term residence that catered to Eastern European-Canadians; another were Francophone with histories of addiction, dwelling in their own homes; another were a group of Indigenous Elders living in British Columbia. As we see from this quick overview, the living situation of older adults also varied significantly amongst the participants in this program. Some of them lived autonomously in houses or apartments, others lived in private or publicly subsidized independent-living facilities for older people, while others lived in low-income housing for older adults.

5 Findings

In the sections that follow, we first provide an overview of the challenges of providing remote digital learning, during a pandemic, primarily from the point of view of the older participants. We then describe what the older participants learned and the reported impacts that their participation in the program had on their daily lives during the pandemic, as well as on the community organizations who played a critical mediating role in recruiting individual participants into the program. Next, we present our findings from interviews with tech mentors, focusing on the specific qualities and skills they identify as essential in the delivery of remote digital learning to older adults. Following this, we discuss our amendment to and expansion of the definition of the term "warm expert" as it is currently used in the literature on aging and ICTs. We argue, first, that the category of warm expert should not be narrowly confined to pre-existing social relations that are mostly restricted to the family. Second, we question the assumption that this expertise should be *unpaid* work. The warm expertise needed to assist others in their digital learning needs acknowledgement as a skill, whether paid or unpaid.

5.1 Challenges of Remote Digital Learning: Older Participants' Feedback

A key theme that emerged from the data collection centred on the difficulties of learning a new skill remotely in a pandemic. For many of the participants in the program, learning to use a tablet was a new experience: only 32% of the respondents had prior experience using a smartphone or a tablet, and only 5% stated they were experienced users of digital technologies before starting the program.

In the case of our respondents, the one-on-one training took place almost exclusively by phone. A team of paid tech mentors, most of whom were based in the Eastern Canada, were matched with older adults from across the country. While the phone was the primary method for delivering remote training and providing follow-up assistance, the tablets given to the older participants were loaded with an application that enabled tech mentors to visualize and manipulate the learner's device remotely to carry out the training. While circumstances dictated the use of the telephone, respondents–including community leaders, older adults and tech mentors–remarked on the difficulty of remote teaching and learning by phone. When we asked the participants about their learning experience, the respondents were split on whether or not they found it easy to learn remotely (45% agreed and 45% disagreed). In the following subsections we present the primary challenges encountered, from the point of view of the older participants.

Language Barriers Exacerbated by Remote Training. In the context of digital learning and training, words matter. Long-time users of digital technologies have accrued a complex lexicon of technical terms that can be overwhelming for a learner. Technical language can be used by people with power and knowledge of this language to disempower those who have not acquired it [32].

The challenge of finding a common language and the right terms and vocabulary to use to engage older participants in digital learning was exacerbated by the remote nature of this training. For example, if and when verbal language fails, in a face-to-face situation, the trainer or mentor can point to a feature on the screen or on the device. The learner also can develop their skills by observing how a trainer manipulates their device. In this program and in this COVID-19 context, the learner and mentor relied primarily on verbal instructions rather than visual cues in a situation of proximity.

Frustration with the absence of physical proximity was experienced both by the learner and the teacher: tech mentors stated that they wished they could point to the actual device when the older adult was having difficulty knowing what to do. Controlling the screen was rarely discussed as an option. Further, despite their best efforts to find a common language, for 41% of our older participants, the terms used by the tech mentors were ultimately an impediment to the training. The tech mentors likewise noted the difficulty of finding the appropriate terminology to communicate with the older adults as something they had to work on and finesse for the duration of their involvement in the program.

The participant observation undertaken in Montreal sheds light on this challenge. For the older adults who had never manipulated a tablet or used a computer, learning to use the distributed tablets remotely was extremely difficult. Knowing that the tech mentors assigned to them, in this particular case, were in the same city was a cruel reminder to the older participants, that spending time face-to-face was needed to problem-solve. One telephone session between a tech mentor and an older adult took three hours, and left the older adult frustrated with her inability to use the tablet within this time-frame. For this reason, when the COVID-19 restrictions temporarily allowed for a face-to-face interaction, the Montreal tech mentors seized the moment and delivered one in-person session in person with the participants. This one-time face-to-face contact enable the older adults to get started and to continue their remote learning in later sessions.

Barriers due to the use of specific lexicon were made even more apparent when teaching those whose first language was neither French or English. The Mandarin-speakers were able to cope with this by relying heavily on the acquired expertise of one of the group members who ended up playing a critical mediating role, furnishing trouble-shooting assistance, but also finding activities and information culturally relevant to the interests of this particular population, from music to YouTube videos depicting Chinese holidays.

A Need for Print Materials. The need for more printed materials was identified in the open-ended section of our survey: in fact, 32% of our participants expressed this need, without prompting. All five of the Mandarin-speakers interviewed requested more written materials so that they could "do homework" and double check their understanding of the content. Five participants mentioned that they had slight memory problems that hindered their learning and suggested that notes and written instructions would have been useful. To this point, several organizations observed that some of their older clients had experienced memory loss: "when you are working with older people, you have to be mindful that they can forget things". These organizers, who have a wealth of experience working with older adults, told us that many adults do not like to ask for special treatment, nor do they want to be stigmatized by having to admit, in a session, that they needed assistance with learning. Providing materials in advance meant that individuals did not feel pressured to reveal their health status to others.

The community organizations who connected individuals to the tech mentors, largely had positive impressions of the remote training, yet they too highlighted the need for better and more visual and textual aids. This, they thought, was especially needed in the remote learning setting, to compensate for the lack of face-to-face interactions. They emphasized that written materials could promote autonomous use outside of the training session, especially important for new users who wanted to practice and who did not know how to access online tutorials on social media, such as YouTube. Some tech mentors created print materials on an *ad hoc* basis. One organization developed their own manual. This practice was haphazard and usually done at the request of an older adult.

We also encountered the need for printed complementary materials in our participant observation in the Montreal organization. Explaining to older adults over the phone where the home button was located on an iPad, one of the first lessons, proved a daunting task for some. In a non-remote learning scenario, this hurdle would have been easily overcome but it could simply not be solved by phone. This organization produced drawings of the iPads that identified their most important features clearly in both French and English, for their clientele.

5.2 Impacts from the Point of View of the Older Adults, Community Organizations and Tech Mentors

Over the course of the program, the majority of the respondents (55%) used the tablet every day. When we asked older participants to explain what other activities they did with the tablet: 55% used their tablets to access social media, 55% used their tablets to speak with a family member on video, 50% used the tablets for email and 45% used the tablets to watch videos. Other activities that were less popular with participants but that are still notable, included accessing books or podcasts (23%), sending text messages (23%), playing a game (18%), attending a religious or spiritual event (18%), partaking in cultural activities (9%) and accessing content from the library (9%). None of our respondents said that they used the tablet for shopping or online banking. In the open-ended section of the survey, several older adults reported using the tablets to obtain health information and information related to the pandemic. This was contingent on location and access to service: those living in residences had no need for health information, while those living autonomously, particularly those speaking languages other than French or English wanted to know where to search for reliable, scientific information on COVID-19 and other health matters.

A sizable proportion of the older participants disclosed having acquired important basic skills like checking the news or the weather (64% stated they could) or sending an email (50% stated they could). These numbers reveal that significant portions of the participants, from this highly motivated group, were concerned about manipulating their tablets autonomously for basic tasks, indicating varying degrees of proficiency as a result of the program. This points to the need for ongoing access to assistance beyond the three-month period provided.

When asked if they felt they had acquired a sufficient amount of training to become proficient with their devices, and if they could use them in the future, the responses had a mostly positive outlook, with a majority of respondents (56%) stating that they had learned a lot from the program. Encouragingly, 86% of respondents agreed or were in strong agreement that they would be able to use the devices after the program was over with their current skill set. Only 14% did not think they would be able to use the devices in the future. At the same time, significant hurdles could be envisaged by this group. For example, only 27% of participants said they were able to establish a WiFi Internet connection without assistance, and only 9% were able to update or install an application. Beyond this data, older participants and community organizations discussed the impact that the program had on the quality of life of the participants, which we detail in the sections below.

Maintaining Social Connections During Social Distancing. We asked the respondents a number of questions about how the program changed the quality of their lives. The majority of participants (68%) stated that their quality of life had improved as a result of the program. Further, 73% stated that they were more informed about what was going on in the world after following the digital learning program. Approximately 77% of the respondents felt more connected to other people because of the program.

In the open-ended discussions with older participants, the most frequent response addressed the ability to connect with family members through Zoom. Prior to this program, most of the older participants had never used Zoom, and while the tech mentors established learning goals with the older adults after an initial basic training session, Zoom often became a key focus. Older adults recounted their joy at being able to "see" the faces of family members or friends for the first time in the pandemic. Another community organizer, described the importance of seeing an unmasked face on the iPad screen for residents in confinement. That said, another care worker recounted that for another resident, seeing the faces of people through a screen who could not visit them face-to-face was too disturbing.

Especially salient, and described with frequency, was the ability to partake virtually in family events. For an older adult in Montreal, the tablet and training gave him virtual access to his family's Christmas celebration. The organizations reported that many of the older adults who benefited from the program had family in other provinces or countries and many "suffered" from the cancellation of plans that prevented them from seeing their loved ones. For some who had immigrated and had few visits at any time, the tablet was a thrill that boosted their wellbeing. As a community organizer reported:

...he's 101 years old, and he's in Canada alone. His family lives [in another country]. And he doesn't have anyone here. [...] He doesn't have anyone to talk with. Especially, you know, it's important to receive support from his family. Once he received an iPad, the first thing he wanted to learn was to get in touch with his family through FaceTime.

This particular older adult, who had a background in engineering, was also able to use the iPad, within the three-month period, to search for music, videos and other programming in their own language without assistance. As other studies have noted, older adults come to the training program with a range of skills and experiences that allow them to be comfortable with new technologies more readily than others [33].

The importance of facilitating social connection was shared by the tech mentors, who had a unique insight into the progression of older adults based on week-to-week interactions, including the perceived psychological benefits. As one mentor gushed:

It's just amazing and you know, just mentoring her is just such a treat, just seeing this person go from zero to starting [her] own blog soon, so things like that, I mean that's empowerment. She feels like a million bucks and just the difference in her, like her depression is just vanishing, her family says. And I'm not saying, you know, clinically that this is the solution to it, but [she] is definitely showing traits of not feeling so isolated and scared and lonely.

In other words, one key benefit of the program from the perspective of older adults, the community organizers and tech mentors is that the program gave them the ability to connect to friends and family. This is especially significant in a country like Canada where distances can make visiting on a regular basis difficult at any time.

Connecting to Local Networks of Support. In the context of the pandemic, many older adults also were deprived of contact with activities and services, from grocery outings to casual socializing in the corridors over coffee that are a critical part of daily routines and rituals. During the pandemic many organizations wanted to support their older community members who suddenly found themselves socially, culturally and digitally disconnected. As they reported, this became a strong impetus for organizations to become involved in this digital literacy program.

While this created challenges for organizations, an unforeseen benefit, from the point of view of the community organizers and the older adults is that sometimes made the older adults aware of the existence of other services available to them to improve their quality of life. For example, in trying to participate in the digital literacy program, one person revealed that they were dealing with low general literacy, which made digital learning all the more difficult. Although this person did not continue with the digital learning program at this time, the organization enrolled them in a local literacy program. Several care workers we spoke to disclosed that having to find out what people wanted to do digitally, so they could assist them, gave them profound insight into the specific interests of individual residents.

5.3 The Tech Mentors Experience

Patience, Empathy, Understanding. Anticipating the challenge of undertaking remote teaching to older adults in a pandemic, in addition to providing a simple template on how to provide older adults with skills in a particular order, the non-profit organizations who initiated this project put much effort and reflection into hiring tech mentors who they thought would succeed in meeting this challenge.

According to the coordinator for the tech mentors, it was essential to be "really good at selecting people and recognizing [the tech mentors'] skills, and then assigning them to the best positions to fit their skills so that everyone can best benefit: this increases chances for people to feel successful in what they do." The tech mentors received significant training as part of their position. This included regular check-ins and follow-ups. They also had access to a training manual that had been devised by one of the participating non-profit organizations, to support them in their work.

We asked the tech mentors to describe the key skills that they thought were critical to teaching older users how to acquire the digital skills they needed. The mentors were emphatic that their work did not require a particularly high degree of digital proficiency beyond what they had acquired in their day-to-day life. Several mentors mentioned that their prior experience in the restaurant industry, including dealing with a variety of customers, as assisting them in their new role as a virtual tech mentor.

The mentors repeatedly articulated the qualities and attributes of patience, empathy, understanding and flexibility as essential to assisting older learners to acquire the confidence needed to feel empowered. As one mentor put it:

> You need patience, you need empathy, you need to be understanding, someone who just understands who these people are, how they're feeling with technology and what you can do to improve that. [...] giving them a sense of [...] empowerment is so important.

Key to creating confidence, or feelings of "empowerment" was demonstrating a willingness to engage for long periods at a time. Both tech mentors and older adults recounted calls that lasted for hours, an investment in time that demonstrated "care".

Flexibility. The tech mentors often used the term "flexibility" as a key attribute in remote learning. In analyzing the transcripts, flexibility was used in three different ways: in terms of the digital content; in terms of scheduling; and in terms of the conversation.

Recognizing the diversity of their clients, the tech mentors first described flexibility as an ability to tailor skills training to the particular interests of an older adult, a process that began right at the beginning of the program, and led to a search for appropriate apps to meet those needs. While each tech mentor would work with several older adults, they also would fine tune their approach to teaching over time, as they came to know each individual learner better. In this way, the activities selected for learning by the older adults were not merely the end goal, but became part of the means for delivering effective training.

Secondly, flexibility was discussed in terms of scheduling. As one respondent recounted, the mentors were amenable to sudden changes in the availability of older adults, which could happen from time to time, as during the pandemic older adults faced health emergencies and medical appointments: "I know sometimes residents would have emergency appointments and they were flexible with us, they would reschedule". They appreciated the flexibility of the tech mentors in adapting to the needs, and schedules, of the older adults.

Thirdly, flexibility was discussed in terms of the goals of sociability, including the importance of the tech mentors being able to make participants feel "relaxed" and "not rushed". A representative of a community organization witnessed how the relationships evolved between the tech mentors and the older adults beyond discussing access to digital content, or solving more technical problems: "sometimes they would have very nice talks, they would share the experiences, they would talk about their towns. You know, it's not only about learning technology, but it's also, you know, talking about different topics and sharing their life stories".

Reliability, Professionalism and Ritual. Tech mentors were asked to be flexible, however, at the same time, interviewees stressed the importance of reliability. While the tech mentors were praised for their patience, calmness, and flexibility these were not seen as oppositional to the qualities of reliability and professionalism. As one organizer stated: "I liked that the program had them taking the lead and had them being the ones to talk to the elders. They took on the effort, connected with the elders, did everything and followed up".

Reliability was critical, as well, because of a context in which so many other rituals and routines were in abeyance and disrupted. The digital program offered a weekly social connection to the older adults during periods of isolation and disruption. Community organizers and tech mentors both expressed that this weekly contact was appreciated by the older adults as a moment of connection and interaction that broke from the monotony and loneliness of confinement. In the words of one tech-mentor this "is really cool, because a lot of it makes them not feel alone, and they feel like, 'Oh, here's my social hour, you know, I get to socialize, feel like I'm a human being now'". Likewise, many older adults and mentors liked working with the same person from week to week, as this consistency also helped to build trust, confidence and enhanced the learning experience because one knew the whole person.

These comments underscore the empathic nature of communications. The importance of ritual and routine to creating bonds, tying community to communication, reverberates with the theoretical work of media and cultural theorists, such as James Carey. In *Communication as Culture*, Carey underscores two dominant modes of communications: the transmission model of communications, which stresses the efficient diffusion of information across space; communication understood as a ritual event and symbolic activity of shared meaning-making occurring in time [34]. In the case of remote learning, both modes of communication were in evidence. Transmitting information clearly and efficiently was important, but even more valued but were the affective bonds created between mentor and learner. Comments from the tech mentors convey the reciprocal nature of this modality of ritual communications. In interview they enthusiastically shared their genuine and vested interest in their assigned older participants, and the thrill they experience in seeing older adults learn new skills and becoming "empowered":

When that light bulb goes on in their head they, you know, you can just know [...] that they're feeling differently than they felt before with technology and the number one feeling they all have beforehand is intimidation, it's so rewarding to turn that intimidation into empowerment. There's nothing like that.

As researchers, we were asked to evaluate the impact of the program on the quality of lives of older adults. The comments of the tech mentors and organizers make it clear that the encounter between the tech mentors and the older participants was not simply impactful, but could be meaningful, was oft-times reciprocal, and potentially empowering for both the older adults and the tech mentor. Skills were transmitted to older participants, who gained access to email, games, social media, video calls, and information on a search engine. The experience, when it worked, also transformed the tech mentors positively.

Several mentors mentioned how the mentoring experience transformed their understanding of aging and the potential rewards of life-long learning opportunities: "hearing them and experiencing that they actually learned something at 90 years old, or whatever the case happens to be, and they didn't find it scary" was identified as "rewarding". Another mentor reflected that the encounter with older clients had affected her perceptions of her own aging process, hinting at the transformative power of their encounters: "Just knowing that when you're older you can still learn things is a wonderful thing for younger people to appreciate because we all get older. We're all going to be on that opposite side of the phone call someday you know, potentially."

5.4 Structural and Systemic Challenges

The program had many successes, particularly those due to the ability of the tech mentors. Our research highlighted areas for improvement, but our interviews also revealed challenges that would be difficult to rectify. While 73% of respondents thought that the digital learning program made them feel more comfortable learning new technologies in the future and a significant majority of the older adults we surveyed (82%) wanted to keep using their devices after the end of the program, other systemic and structural contingencies were revealed as stressful. In several interviews, stress over the data use and future data costs was mentioned. As one organizer commented: "Just from a really practical standpoint, we were always very nervous about going over that five gigabytes of data. And they did assure me that if we were to go over it, it would just sort of slow down our it's a worse thing to go over." While the program allowed older adults to keep their tablets, it could provide only short-term access to data. So, while a small majority of respondents (55%) stated that they would be likely to acquire a data plan or WiFi so that they could keep using their tablets to connect to the Internet, continuing data access was not so clear. Some organizations took it upon themselves to investigate other service providers with whom they could broker advantageous deals on behalf of their older clients. Other organizations, specifically those where older adults congregated in a common space like residences for older adults or community centres, explored the idea of installing a WiFi connection that could be used on-site by several older adults. The reality remains, in these cases, that Internet plans are costly in Canada and continue to serve as a barrier to digital access for older adults [10].

6   Discussion

As mentioned previously, the majority of the research in ICT studies focuses on the role of family members as warm experts in providing support to older users learning new ICT skills. Indeed, Bakardjieva's theory of the warm expert [12] suggests that warm experts already have a relationship to the learner, and an *a priori* familiarity with their needs, habits, and learning styles. "he or she possesses knowledge and skills gained in the System world of technology and can operate in this world but, at the same time, is immediately accessible in the user's lifeworld as a fellow man/woman' [12]. This affective relationship of comfort and caring has been demonstrated, empirically, to facilitate learning in numerous studies [20, 23, 24, 35, 36]. However, our discussions with older participants, community organizers and tech mentors themselves suggest another possibility for meeting the needs of digital learners to have access to "warm experts". These warm experts do not necessarily need to be family members and the attributes associated with warmness and kindness can be genuine even when it is paid work, Vanwynsberghe and Boudry describe in their study of librarians [37]. Others may play this pivotal role, of warm expert given the right skills in combination with training, temperament and experience [17]. It is possible, in other words, to establish new relationships and to become a *paid* warm expert. Acting as a warm expert is a skill, whether it is paid or unpaid. In this discussion, we further discuss some of the socio-political implications that may result from the assumption that the best type of digital training is family-driven and free.

A Narrow Approach to Warm Experts Reifies a Heteronormative/ Chrononormative Approach to Later Life. The warm expert is often figured as a family member of the older learner, and thus an integral actor in the development of digital skills. In the original definition of the warm expert, and subsequent uses of the term, the approach disproportionately values the pre-existence of "close relationships". It foregrounds the family as the source of digital training, potentially taking for granted a particular trajectory through the life course structured through temporal milestones centred on heteronormative expectations, akin to what Freeman has termed chrononormativity [38]. It also disproportionately positions the existence of the family, whether nuclear or extended or intergenerational as a precursor to digital integration. Those who are socially isolated– who share many of the socio-economic factors of social disconnection–may be among the least likely to have access to this sort of familial support.

Assuming warm experts are unpaid suggests that digital training does not require professionally-valuable skills. Our interviews with tech mentors indicated that digital knowledge is not the primary skill-requirement when it comes to working with older adults and ICTs. While the mentors had basic digital knowledge and some training in program delivery, they possessed high levels of communication skills acquired through years of hard work in the service industry. This gave the mentors experience in engaging with a diversity of publics, often under high pressure, stressful conditions.

The tech mentors were valued for their ability to communicate with the older adults, for their patience, respect and ability to adapt the training to engage with their clients' needs and interests in a manner that was respectful. In the words of one community worker: "Our mentors, were able to talk to them in a professional way and in a courteous way, and treated them like people- not anything different [...] they understood that that's what we were trying to do was just to help them guide them not belittle them." This made the engagement of both client and mentor meaningful. This ability to adapt to expressions of hesitancy or fear is akin to "articulation work" or the "often unacknowledged management of awkward intersections among the social worlds of people, technology and organizations," that is often developed through jobs that require interaction with the public [39].

Positioning digital training as a natural part of family relations and care duties may assume that the skills most helpful for digital training are inherent features of family relationships. This tacitly may devalue what is termed 'soft skills' in the context of remunerated work and promote the assumption that patience and empathy are innate and cannot be developed [40]. From a feminist perspective, this idea of natural caregiving in the family may also reify a classist and sexist devaluation of the skills that are crucial for success in traditionally gendered sectors like care work, education, hospitality or in the service industry–and indeed digital literacy training. The idea of "warmth" in the act of communication is underpinned by a converging set of characteristics that actually are valued by customers, for example, in professional settings, as the term captures traits "that are related to perceived intent, including friendliness, helpfulness, sincerity, trustworthiness and morality" [41]. While we agree the value of warmth, as years of feminist research into the persistence of gendered divisions of labour in the workplace have revealed, work associated with these characteristics are not remunerated equally, particularly in the context of care work [1, 42, 43].

Warm Expert 3.0? In his discussion of warm experts in intergenerational family settings, Taipale reconceptualizes and updates the term warm expert in light of different conditions locally, and historically in terms of the development and rapid diffusion of ICTs [23]. Building on this insight, in the wake of an epidemic that became a pandemic in 2020, the relationship with and reliance on digital media and online communications has evolved since 2005. So, too, should our understanding of warm expertise shift in light of these historical events, as well as changes in media. The relationship to technology and the rapid domestication of the Internet has been in constant transformation since the concept of the warm expert was introduced in 2005. Over the past decades, there has been a steady, persistent digitization of nearly all spheres of life often associated with the term mediatization [44].

We remain critical of the idea that digital technologies, and new developments such as artificial intelligence, provide a panacea for all that ails, along with other critics of the "digital sublime" [45]. However, the pandemic should cement once and for all our understanding that digital access is now a fundamental aspect of life in Canadian society. The Internet itself–at all times but especially in times of crises–mediates access to other necessities of life like information, food, health care and other people. The digital literacy gap within the older population is a sufficiently consequential and urgent issue that requires the mobilization of skilled interventions. In this regard, tech mentors, motivating older adults to learn, providing them with access to tools, and skills are only one part of the solution. As the data anxieties of community organizers and older participants alike indicates, in the Canadian context, ensuring inexpensive, reliable access to the Internet to older adults, no matter where they reside, is essential.

7 Conclusions, Limitations and Implications for Future Research

In this paper, we attempted to answer the following questions: what did the older adults find valuable about the program? What did they identify as the main challenges to remote learning? As a corollary, we ask what skills were identified as essential for effective tech mentoring by the older participants, the community organizers and the tech mentors themselves? For the older adults participating in this remote learning program receiving a tablet, a paid connection and "tech mentoring" furnished them with the ability to connect with family and friends throughout this period, during an extremely difficult moment in the pandemic in the Fall and Winter of 2020–2021.

The main challenge to remote learning, for this highly motivated group of older learners, was that instructions were largely given by telephone, while they were asked to find buttons on the tablets, enter information, and access specific applications. Support materials, including written instructions, and exercises were requested, and in many cases developed on the fly, by intermediaries at the participating organizations. Once basic skills were acquired, participants were able to personalize their digital experience by adding applications to their tablets that reflected their specific interests and needs.

In addition to acquiring a device and skills, they described the pleasure of learning because of the patience, care and flexibility of the tech mentors. These encounters were described with enthusiasm and the caring attitude and attributes of the mentors, were emphasized by the interviewees as the most essential element that assisted them in their learning, and helped them to acquire not only skills but confidence, often expressed as "empowerment". In the words of one community organizer: "The digital empowerment, it just hit us in the face, right. I think that's the silver lining, the other silver lining to all of this is that our partners, everybody is coming out of their silos and they're working together."

7.1 Limitations and Implications

Limitations. Our research, which included surveys, interviews and observations make clear, the pandemic has forced a recognition of the need for greater attention to the digital knowledge and practices of their older adults. The program we discussed largely succeeded in empowering the 75 older adults who participated, helped the community organizations who became involved accelerate their digital agenda, and furnished the tech mentors with meaningful paid employment. This is, to be sure but one case study and the research was collected during or just soon after the program took place.

What would be helpful would be a follow-up study to analyze and understand the longer-term effects of the program on individuals and on the organizations. Are they still using the tablets? Are they using them in the same way or differently? How did they manage a data connection after the program stopped furnishing it? Did the organizations transform their programming? And finally, who updates and maintains those tablets and provides assistance troubleshooting when things don't work as they should? Who acts as a "warm expert" now that the tech mentors are gone? There are questions for the future.

Despite its limited scope, this remote digital learning program filled a gap at an important moment, allowing organizations to consider how their usual face-to-face services could be reconfigured for the online world. Organizations could test out, on a small scale, how the virtual could be incorporated in their day-to-day operations and potentially be carried over in a post-pandemic context. It made individuals and organizations envision other future scenarios where digital access would be necessary, such as snowstorms or other climate emergencies. In the Canadian context, the pandemic also accelerated funding for digital training programs locally through government support to the non-profit sector, including through umbrella organizations, such as the United Way. What remains uncertain for these organizations is the longer-term implication of the need to create access to the digital world, and the enduring knowledge gap of some older adults. What is largely absent, and needs policy attention, is a sustained strategy that provides necessary resources to bridge the digital gap, including the human resources needed to accompany older adults in a digital transition. Much needed are governmental and multi-sectoral investments and strategies for a digital future that is inclusive of older adults.

Another limitation, theoretically, is to examine in detail the relationship of this work to communications policies, age-friendly city strategies, and ways to these structural issues and systemic issues, including the links between this research and feminist political economy. We agree that the concept of the warm expert, in discussions of aging in a digital world that is replete with a multiplicity of digital divides, can be generative and an acknowledgement of the work that goes on within families. Indeed, as Taipale's research discusses the challenges faced by "Warm Experts 2.0" in the family context, such as the amount of time this work takes, the burden of responsibility and duty it entails in the wake of other commitments, or the fear of burdening a family member with calls and questions [23]. It requires an expertise in the art of communication. Certainly, no amount of digital training alone can overcome the entangled social issues that continue to exclude older adults from digital society, but the valuing of these skills, and the recognition of their importance to our society, should be part of the solution. As researchers in media and communication studies there is the need to consider the need to recognize the value of this work of digital maintenance, or "digital housekeeping" [23] as an emergent form of care work, digital care work, in the delivery of remote learning and in the push to get older adults online. This is particularly critical for those older adults who may not have a circle of family or friends to provide them with this assistance.

Implications: Digital Care Work. The implications of this research into the possibility of paid warm experts to play a role in the digital education of older adults is theoretical and political, as we have detailed. The development of strategies to empower older adults, and not simply force them to become digital, "forced mediatization" [46], entails valuing the expertise, at a social and political level, of those who become digital trainers, or digital care workers. These skills are not merely technical. They may come from experience outside of the tech realm. They may become a part of an education in the social sciences and humanities that raises awareness of the power of social discourses that too often stigmatize older adults as inept, incompetent or irrelevant. Becoming a warm expert is no only about patience and caring: it requires an expertise that accounts for the heterogeneity of older adults, and that is aware of the intersectional dynamics of power at play.

As we discuss, these findings indicate the ongoing significance of Bakardjieva's term, the "warm expert", which has been used in key works examining aging and digital literacy, with caveats. While most of these studies focus on the key role of family members who do unpaid digital care work, our study suggests that this work can also be effectively carried out by *paid* workers. The tech mentors themselves highlighted how the most important asset that they brought to the remote learning experience was their background in the service industry (mostly restaurants), confirming the importance of the same qualities identified by the participants as essential [41].

To be clear, our intention is in no way to disparage or minimize the impact of the many who take on the work of digital literacy within their families and social circles–some of us play this role in our own families–or those who volunteer to bridge the age-related digital divide [47, 48]. However, in the same way that informal or natural caregivers have been positioned as indispensable in the face of underfunded healthcare systems, we suggest that in this new environment, family members have taken on the added responsibility to lessen age-related digital divides in addition to other responsibilities, a hallmark of neo-liberal political agendas [47–49, 50].

While the consequences of digital disconnection may be felt at a highly personal and intimate level, overcoming these divides cannot simply be the responsibility of individuals or of families. In positioning families and close-knit social circles as the *de facto* providers of digital training and warm expertise, we ask this: are we missing an opportunity to advocate for skilled digital training and digital access for older adults as a matter of social justice? If we are all being forced to become digital, then should not this access be afforded to all and not just to those fortunate enough to have the social capital to benefit from the free labour of family or friends?

References

1. Béland, D., Marier, P.: Covid-19 and long-term care policy for older people in Canada. J. Aging Soc. Policy **32**(4–5), 358–364 (2020)
2. Garcia, K.R., et al.: Improving the digital skills of older adults in a COVID-19 pandemic environment. Educ. Gerontol. **47**(5), 196–206 (2021)
3. Nash, S.: The Pandemic has Accelerated the Need to Close the Digital Divide for Older Adults. Stanford Center on Longevity (2021). https://longevity.stanford.edu/the-pandemic-has-accelerated-the-need-to-close-the-digital-divide-for-older-adults/. Accessed 3 Feb 2022
4. Seifert, A.: The digital exclusion of older adults during the COVID-19 Pandemic. J. Gerontol. Soc. Work **63**(6–7), 674–676 (2020)
5. Seifert, A., Cotten, S.R., Xie, B.: A double burden of exclusion? Digital and social exclusion of older adults in times of COVID-19. J. Gerontol. Ser. B **76**(3), 99–103 (2021)
6. Hanes, A.: Montrealers deliver phones and tablets to isolated seniors, Montreal Gazette, 17 April 2020. https://montrealgazette.com/news/local-news/hanes-montrealers-gather-and-deliver-phones-tablets-to-isolated-patients-in-care-homes. Accessed 3 Feb 2022
7. TELUS Communications: TELUS delivering over 10,000 free mobile devices to help isolated seniors, hospitalized patients and vulnerable Canadians stay connected during the COVID-19 pandemic. GlobeNewswire News Room, 20 April 2020. http://www.globenewswire.com/news-release/2020/04/20/2018511/0/en/TELUS-delivering-over-10-000-free-mobile-devices-to-help-isolated-seniors-hospitalized-patients-and-vulnerable-Canadians-stay-connected-during-the-COVID-19-pandemic.html. Accessed 3 Feb 2022
8. Conger, K., Griffith, E.: As Life Moves Online, an Older Generation Faces a Digital Divide, New York Times, 28 March 2020. https://www.nytimes.com/2020/03/27/technology/virus-older-generation-digital-divide.html. Accessed 3 Feb 2022
9. Patille, R., Mahmood A., Chyrva, P.: How to Empower Older Adults to Become Digital Citizens in our Tech-dependent World, The Conversation, 23 September 2021. https://theconversation.com/how-to-empower-older-adults-to-become-digital-citizens-in-our-tech-dependent-world-167010. Accessed 3 Feb 2022
10. Middleton, C., Sawchuk, K., Lafontaine, C., DeJong, S., Henderson, J.: Meeting the needs of all Canadians: older adults, affordability and mobile, wireless services, Intervention (CRTC-2019-57) Review of mobile wireless services (2019)
11. Lafontaine, C., Sawchuk, K.: Accessing InterACTion: ageing with technologies and the place of access. In: Zhou, J., Salvendy, G. (eds.) Human Aspects of IT for the Aged Population. Design for Aging. ITAP 2015. LNCS, vol. 9193, pp. 210–220. Springer, Cham (2015). https://doi.org/10.1007/978-3-319-20892-3_21

12. Bakardjieva, M.: Internet Society: The Internet in Everyday Life. SAGE Publications Ltd., London (2005)
13. McGinty, J.M.: Developing a training program for digital literacy coaches for older adults: lessons learned from the train-the-trainer program. J. Educ. Train. Stud. **8**(11), 62–69 (2020)
14. Xie, B., Charness, N., Fingerman, K., Kaye, J., Kim, M.T., Khurshid, A.: When going digital becomes a necessity: ensuring older adults' needs for information, services, and social inclusion during COVID-19. J. Aging Soc. Policy **32**(4–5), 460–470 (2020)
15. Sin, F., Berger, S., Kim, I.J., Yoon, D.: Digital social interaction in older adults during the COVID-19 pandemic. Proc. ACM Hum.-Comput. Interact. **5**(CSCW2), 1–20 (2021)
16. Son, J.S., Nimrod, N., West, S.T., Janke, M.C., Liechty, T., Naar, J.J.: Promoting older adults' physical activity and social well-being during COVID-19. Leis. Sci. **43**(1–2), 287–294 (2021)
17. Weil, J., Kamber, T., Glazebrook, A., Giorgi, M., Ziegler, K.: Digital inclusion of older adults during COVID-19: lessons from a case study of older adults' technology services (OATS). J. Gerontol. Soc. Work **64**(6), 643–655 (2021)
18. Silverstone, R., Haddon, L.: Design and the domestication of Information and communication technologies. In: Silverstone, R., Mansell, R. (eds.) Communication by Design: the Politics of Information and Communication Technologies. Oxford University Press, Oxford (1996)
19. Neville, S.J.: The domestication of privacy-invasive technology on YouTube: unboxing the Amazon Echo with the online warm expert. Convergence Int. J. Res. New Media Technol. **27**(5), 1288–1307 (2021)
20. Annafari, M., Axelsson, S., Bolin, E.: A socio-economic exploration of mobile phone service have-nots in Sweden. New Media Soc. **16**(3), 415–433 (2014)
21. Wyatt, S., Henwood, F., Hart, A., Smith, J.: The digital divide, health information and everyday life. New Media Soc. **7**(2), 199–218 (2005)
22. Olsson, T., Samuelson, U., Viscovi, D.: At risk of exclusion? Degrees of ICT access and literacy among senior citizens. Inf. Commun. Soc. **22**(1), 55–72 (2019)
23. Taipale, S.: Intergenerational Connections in Digital Families. Springer, Cham (2019). https://doi.org/10.1007/978-3-030-11947-8
24. Hänninen, R., Taipale, S., Luostari, R.: Exploring heterogeneous ICT use among older adults: the warm experts' perspective. New Media Soc. **23**(6), 1584–1601 (2021)
25. Redden, J.: The Harm that Data Do: Paying Attention to how algorithmic systems impact marginalized people worldwide is key to a just and equitable future, Scientific American, 1 November 2018
26. Reason, P., Bradbury, H. (eds.): The SAGE Handbook of Action Research, 2nd edn. SAGE Publications Ltd., London (2020)
27. Eubanks, V.: Digital Dead End: Fighting for Social Justice in the Information Age. MIT Press, Cambridge (2012)
28. Leavy, P.: Research Design: Quantitative, Qualitative, Mixed Methods, Arts-Based, and Community-Based Participatory Research Approaches. Guilford, New York (2017)
29. Stone, M.E., Lin, J., Dannefer, D.: The continued eclipse of heterogeneity in gerontological research. J. Gerontol. B Psychol. Sci. Soc. Sci. **72**(1), 162–167 (2017)
30. Sawchuk, K., Crow, B.: Into the grey zone: seniors, cell phones and milieus that matter. Observing the mobile user experience. In: Poppinga, B., Magnusson, C. (eds.) Proceedings of the 1st International Workshop held in Conjunction with NordiCHI, pp. 17–21 (2010)
31. Fernández-Ardèvol, M., Sawchuk, K., Grenier, L.: Maintaining connection: octogenerians and nonagenarians speak. In: Christensen, C.L., Peterson, L.N. (eds.) Becoming Old in the Age of Mediatization Nordicom Review, vol. 38, no. 1 (2017)
32. Hargittai, E., Dobransky, K.: Old dogs, new clicks: digital in equality in skills and uses among older adults. Can. J. Commun. **42**(2), 195–212 (2017)
33. Carey, J. W.: Communication as Culture: Essays on Media and Society. SAGE Publications Ltd., London (1992)

34. Selwyn, N.: Digital division or digital decision? A study of non-users and low-users of computers. Poetics **34**(40), 273–292 (2006)
35. Madsen, C., Kræmmergaard, P.: Warm experts in the age of mandatory e-government: interaction among danish single parents regarding online application for public benefits. Electron. J. E-Govern. **14**, 87–98 (2016)
36. Olsson, T., Viscovi, D.: Warm experts for elderly users: who are they and what do they do? Hum. Technol. **14**(3), 324–342 (2018)
37. Vanwynsberghe, H., Boudry, E.: Experts as facilitators for the implementation of social media in the library? A social network approach. Libr. Hi Tech **32**(3), 529–545 (2014)
38. Freeman, E.: Time Binds: Queer Temporalities, Queer Histories. Duke University Press, Durham (2010)
39. Hampson, I., Junor, A.: Invisible work, invisible skills: interactive customer service as articulation work. N. Technol. Work. Employ. **20**(2), 166–181 (2005)
40. Garavan, T.N.: Interpersonal skills training for quality service interactions. Ind. Commer. Train. **29**(3), 70–77 (1997)
41. Burns, P.M.: Hard-skills, soft-skills: undervaluing hospitality's 'service with a smile.' Prog. Tour. Hosp. Res. **3**(3), 239–248 (1997)
42. Grist, H., Jennings, R.: Carers, Care Homes and the British Media: Time to Care. Palgrave Macmillan, London (2010)
43. Marier, P., Van Pevenage, I.: The Invisible women: gender and caregiving in francophone newspapers. Rom. J. Commun. Public Relat. **18**(1), 77–88 (2016)
44. Sawchuk, K., Lafontaine, C.: Precarious ageing: questioning access, creating interACTion. In: da Silva, P.D., Alves, A. (eds.) TEM 2015: Proceedings of the Technology & Emerging Media Track – Annual Conference of the Canadian Communication Association (2015)
45. Mosco, V.: The Digital Sublime: Myth Power and Cyberspace. MIT Press, Cambridge (2004)
46. Sawchuk, K.: Tactical mediatization: pressures, push-back and learning from RECAA. MedieKultur J. Media Commun. Res. **29**(54) (2013)
47. Friemel, T.N.: The digital divide has grown old; determinants of a digital divide among seniors. New Media Soc. **18**(2), 313–331 (2016)
48. Schreurs, K., Quan-Haase, A., Martin, K.: Problematizing the digital literacy paradox in the context of older adults' ICT use: aging, media discourse and self-determination. Can. J. Commun. **42**(2), 359–377 (2017)
49. Martinez-Alcala, et al.: The effects of Covid-19 on the digital literacy of the elderly: norms for digital inclusion. Front. Educ. **6**(19) (2021)
50. Moore, R.C., Hancock, J.T.: Older adults, social technologies, and the coronavirus pandemic: challenges, strengths, and strategies for support. Soc. Media Soc. **6**(3) (2020)

Understanding Older Adults' Stickiness Intention of Health Information on Social Media: A Time and Gratification Perspective

Xindi Wang[(⊠)] and Yuxiang Chris Zhao

School of Economics and Management,
Nanjing University of Science and Technology, Nanjing 210094, China
wxdkust@163.com

Abstract. With increasing concern about aging and its associated problems, China is taking measures to cope with its aging population. Improving geriatric health conditions is part of China's effort to provide better lives for the elderly. The broad impact of social media can play a vital role in the control or reduction of the onset of potential diseases. The future time perspective (FTP) is a cardinal tenet of the socioemotional selectivity theory (SST) that could explain older adults' health information behavior. This study aims to identify the effects of FTP and the gratifications that contribute to older adults' health-oriented stickiness on social media. Online survey data from 303 elderly Chinese users (above 55 years) were collected and analyzed using the structural equation modeling. This study indicates that both the open-ended time perspective and the limited time perspective have significant positive effects on hedonic, informational, emotional, and social gratification, and the open-ended time perspective has a more significant influence on gratification than the limited time perspective. The time perspectives affect different perceived gratifications, which in turn affect the health-oriented stickiness intention on social media. The results also prove the importance of informational, emotional, social gratification, and the irrelevance of hedonic gratification in examining older adults' health-related stickiness intention.

Keywords: Social media · Health information · Older adults · Stickiness · Socioemotional selectivity theory · Gratification · Future time perspective

1 Introduction

An aging populace will become more technology-dependent due to the progression of technology and its invasive nature [1–3]. The 45th China Statistical Report on Internet Development reported that 6.7% of their Internet users are over 60 years old [4]. While people are living longer, societies are getting older; thus, to cope with the problems associated with an aging population, China is taking measures to help senior citizens bridge the digital divide and provide them with smart facilities and life services. Due to the support of national policies, some social media applications (apps) added an easy model to be friendlier to aged people. Recently, there are 43 apps and 115 websites

Q. Gao and J. Zhou (Eds.): HCII 2022, LNCS 13330, pp. 432–447, 2022.
https://doi.org/10.1007/978-3-031-05581-2_31

that focus on designing elderly-friendly versions to assist with geriatric transportation, health, living environments, and even work activities [5]. A case in point is WeChat, a typical social and instant messaging app, which added functional guidance and dialect recognition. This indicates that social media may gradually change into a wide resource for obtaining hedonic, informational, social, and emotional support, and will set up efforts to bridge the digital gap faced by seniors.

With geriatric health being considered as the most concerning issue, it is necessary to encourage older adults to engage in formal-health related activities on the ubiquitous mass media. Social media greatly encourage the public to engage with health information [6], and successively attract the elderly for health-oriented usage [7]. However, older adults' decreased biological, physiological, and cognitive capacity could block their long-term using intention. To address the fundamental needs of senior citizens and control or mitigate the onset of potentially risky diseases, it is meaningful to make social media more hospitable for older adults. This will increase their involvement in health-related activities and active behavior responses.

Although older adults are more likely to be resistant to new forms of information and communication technologies, this does not mean that they are technophobic or dislike technology [1]. In discussing the current state of social media usage among the elderly, previous studies on the elderly and their health-related information behavior have focused on psychological factors and other influencing factors as well as obstacles or constraints [8, 9]. However, the effect of time perception on older adults' health information behavior has not been extensively discussed. Previous researchers explained the relationship between time perception and gratification [10, 11]. Future time perspective (FTP) is one of the cardinal tenets of the socioemotional selectivity theory (SST). When people perceive an open-ended temporal horizon, they tend to prioritize goals that prepare them for a long and nebulous future [12]; otherwise, they prefer instant gratification. Based on the perspectives of time and gratification, this study aims to identify the factors that contribute to older adults' stickiness intention on social media for health-related activities.

Consequently, adopting the SST to investigate elderly users' health-oriented propensity to stick with social media from the time perspective could answer the following questions:

RQ1. How could the perspective of time influence users' gratification?
RQ2. What kinds of psychological gratification can predict users' stickiness intention with health information on social media?

Overall, our results revealed the inherent influencing mechanism of FTP on elderly stickiness of health information and confirmed the compatibility of the time perspective and the gratification theory. In terms of information technology and managerial implications, the current findings could contribute to informing the user experience design of elderly-oriented social apps and bringing more social inclusion for successful aging.

2 Theoretical Background

2.1 Future Time Perspective

The SST suggests that individuals' social goals are influenced by their perceptions of future time [13]. The FTP is related to social motivations following the perception of the temporal horizon, instead of chronological age [14, 15]. There are two kinds of social goals divided by function: knowledge-related goals and emotional goals [16]. According to the SST, people prioritize knowledge-related goals about gaining instrumental information for their future when time is perceived as open-ended [16]. Conversely, when the perception of the future is limited, people relatively tend to gratify their present needs about emotion and hedonism because such goals often pertain to the acquisition of short-term benefits [12].

The pioneers of SST focused on time perspectives, namely, FTPs, which were divided into limited time and open-ended time [13], and the respective effects of these ramifications of time perspective on individuals' social network and well-being [17]. In view of this, Wright (2010) suggests that individuals' age and health conditions influence their online social preference [18]. If people had a limited time horizon perspective, they would prefer strong-tie social support over weak-tie networks. Whereas, people with an open-ended temporal horizon would prefer to stick with social communication technologies for weak-tie interaction to expand their social network and gain more social benefit. The benefits of strong-tie relationships that contract with age enhance geriatric technology adopters' well-being more than weak ties do [19]. The SST also underscores that the change of individuals' perception of future time also changes their adaptive behavioral responses [20]. Indeed, Settanni (2018) argues that the time perspective can also work on the addictive stickiness of social media among elderly users [21].

The role of psychological demands within the geriatric populace should be considered principally. As chronological age relates to issues that affect how people perceive time remaining in life, older adults are more likely motivated toward gratifying emotional and meaningful goals with enjoyment and pleasure [16, 22]. According to the relationship between individuals' gratification and their time perspective [12], social media should not only satisfy older adult's psychological need for social contact or emotional support but also enable users to benefit from the information and hedonic elements, and further contribute to life satisfaction and well-being [3, 23]. This paper uses FTP to explore older adults' behavioral responses on social media for their health-related purpose based on two motivations.

First, psychological factors are a prominent topic in the study of the information behavior of the elderly [24]. According to the SST, FTP has been a key indicator for older adults' psychological needs. This kind of awareness of the temporal horizons could be viewed as an open-ended or limited dichotomy. Older adults' gratifying perceptions of enjoyment, knowledge, social benefits, and emotional rewards would promote their engagement with social media to achieve personal goals under the influence of FTP [3]. Second, social media began to incorporate more age-appropriate design elements to meet the fundamental health needs of the senior population [25]. FTP provides a time-structural manner to understand the effects of different time perspectives on the gratification of older adults, and in turn, their intention to stick to social media for health-related purposes.

2.2 Time Perspective and Hedonic Gratification

Hedonism is a type of benefit identified by the gratification framework [26]. Hedonic gratification refers to the need for escape and diversion from problems and routines [27]. In this study, hedonic gratification reflects the nature of individuals' expectations of enjoyment and pleasure in the context of social media. According to Jochemczyk (2017), a present-hedonistic time perspective can positively influence people's behavioral responses [28]. He explained how different time orientations play imperative roles in the desire for hedonic benefits. According to the SST, older adults reported higher levels of positive emotions than younger adults [12, 29]. Those older adults who have an open-ended time perspective would prefer to engage with emerging technologies, and their higher levels of well-being would make them gratify hedonic expectations easier than younger adults. Thus, the following hypothesis is proposed:

H1a: Open-ended time perspective will positively influence the elderly users' hedonic gratification.

Individuals with limited time perspective would be aware of constraints on time and therefore tend to be selective with affective events that afford them immediate pleasure [30]. If older adults perceived a limited time perspective, their preferential goals would change to acquire present hedonic gratification [28]. Hence, elderly users are more likely to use social media for instant entertainment gratification [20]. Furthermore, based on their limited FTP, older adults' higher levels of positive effects would also have a positive effect on hedonic gratification. Thus, we propose the hypothesis as:

H1b: Limited time perspective will positively influence elderly users' hedonic gratification.

2.3 Time Perspective and Information Gratification

The gratification of informational needs predominantly motivates older adults' engagement with health information on social media [31]. According to the SST, there is an age-related reduction in information seeking, which may lead to negative outcomes for older adults' health interventions [30]. To promote information seeking in late life, Löckenhoff (2004) suggested that health information about protection from threats of illness is more palatable than those health threats for older adults [30]. Furthermore, social media affords elderly users access to health-related information through multiple ways such as seeking health-related information, encountering health news, communicating with family or friends, following certified health-oriented celebrities in the online community. When time is perceived as open-ended, individuals prioritize the acquisition of knowledge [12, 16]. With the expeditious development of social media technology, a myriad of health information has been accessible on the Internet. Thus, it is assumed that elderly users with open-ended time perspectives would like to perceive the benefits and gratification of health information through the health-oriented utilization of social media [31, 32]. Therefore, the following is hypothesized:

H2a: Open-ended time perspective will positively influence elderly users' information gratification.

Limited time-oriented individuals' positive affect generally remains highly stable [12]. Older adults with limited-time perspectives desire to maintain high levels of well-being and tend to process information with positive affect. Social media can afford users to receive health information and contribute to life satisfaction [23]. Because of the limited time perspective, elderly users with positive attitudes were more likely to satisfactorily receive useful and meaningful health information than younger adults [32]. Therefore, the following was hypothesized:

H2b: Limited time perspective will positively influence elderly users' information gratification.

2.4 Time Perspective and Emotional Gratification

Emotional gratification refers to a user's emotional fulfillment, pleasant feelings from social contact, and aesthetic experience of the utilization of an IT artifact [27]. To achieve emotional fulfillment, open-ended time-oriented users tend to get acquainted with new friends and expand their social networks. Studies have shown that people who perceived time as a distant future report greater emotional well-being if they had extensive social networks [12, 23]. Social media enables people to get emotional support from others when communicating health-related issues with friends, family, and even strangers [33]. Therefore, elderly users with open-ended time perspectives would like to achieve emotional gratification through engagement with health information on social media. Hence:

H3a: An open-ended time perspective will positively influence the elderly users' emotional gratification.

On the contrary, as people age and time horizons are constrained, they tend to view the closeness of relationships as a more pertinent issue instead of the social network size. Social media offers limited time-oriented individuals a virtual space to express their emotions of fearfulness, happiness, and panic with other users to get comfort. The elderly user could talk about health conditions to get instant emotional gratification through health-related interactions with intimate partners on social media [31, 32]. Hence:

H3b: Limited time perspective will positively influence the elderly users' emotional gratification.

2.5 Time Perspective and Social Gratification

In this study, social gratification refers to the benefits of social media that satisfy user desires [32]. According to the SST, when the future is perceived as relatively open-ended and filled with positive rewards, people are expected to widen their exposure to make new friends [13]. The elderly user with an open-ended time perspective tends to seek social gratification which is associated with more positive social experiences through expanding social networks. Hence:

H4a: An open-ended time perspective will positively influence the elderly users' social gratification.

While limited time-oriented individuals consider the future time perspective as restrictive, they prefer to keep company with intimate partners. Narrowing the social scale is likely to result in greater social satisfaction for people who feel the future time is limited [13]. Zhang (2021) asserted that keeping in touch with familiar partners is one of the most important factors for older adults' active engagement with health information on social media [31]. Hence:

H4b: Limited time perspective will positively influence elderly users' social gratification.

2.6 Gratification Perspective and Stickiness Intention

Both individuals with open-ended time and limited time-oriented perspectives would have the rudimentary demands of health issues while social media gratifies health-related goals in several ways. A case in point is Baldensperger's (2018) set hypotheses derived from the SST which suggested that FTP may play a crucial role in future disease management programs [34]. Several studies suggest that perceived gratification enhances users' stickiness on social media [35, 36]. According to previous studies, hedonic gratification, informational gratification, emotional gratification, and social gratification are the most prominent factors to adopt social media for health-related purposes [33], instead of professional healthcare platforms [37, 38]. Kim (2001) suggested that users' information gratification, social support, and entertainment are the predominant motivations for engagement with social media [39]. Furthermore, studies have shown that the elements of hedonism, the emotional fulfillment from self-expression, and the social benefits from communication with acquaintances positively influence users to adopt social media services [6, 40, 41]. Hence:

H5: Hedonic gratification will positively influence the elderly health-oriented stickiness intention on social media.

H6: Information gratification will positively influence the elderly health-oriented stickiness intention on social media.

H7: Emotional gratification will positively influence the elderly health-oriented stickiness intention on social media.

H8: Social gratification will positively influence the elderly health-oriented stickiness intention on social media.

In the end, the conceptual model was built as shown in Fig. 1 (see Fig. 1).

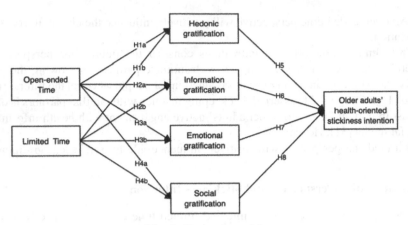

Fig. 1. Research model.

3 Methodology

3.1 Measures

All construct items in this study were adapted from existing studies. Each item was measured according to a seven-point Likert scale ranging from 1 (strongly disagree) to 7 (strongly agree). There were two stages of questionnaire formation. Initially, we invited 22 senior citizens with health-oriented experience of social media use to participate in the initial questionnaire. Based on their feedback, we revised the questionnaire and obtained the final version. The construct items and references are detailed in Table 1.

Table 1. Research items and references.

Constructs	Items	Source
Open-ended time	OT1: Many things await me to do in the future OT2: It seems to me that my future plans are pretty well laid out OT3: I get the work done on schedule and on time OT4: I'll be proactive about what happens in the future	[13, 22]
Limited time	LT1: I have the sense that time is fleeting LT2: I begin to experience that time is limited LT3: I try to live in the moment LT4: I worry about my health in the future	[13, 16]

(continued)

Table 1. (*continued*)

Constructs	Items	Source
Hedonic gratification	HG1: I feel relaxed about engagement with health-related activities through social media HG2: I find it interesting to get health-oriented information through social media HG3: I use social media for health-related purposes with pleasure HG4: The dissemination of health information on social media is entertainment for me	[42, 43]
Information gratification	IG1: Health information from social media help me to prevent illness IG2: I can get useful health-related information on social media IG3: Through social media, I can get good advice on health issues IG4: Searching for health information on social media could solve my problem	[31, 43]
Emotional gratification	EG1: By talking with others about my health situation on social media, I feel the emotional concern and encouragement EG2: Sharing health-related experiences and knowledge on social media make me comfortable EG3: Health information on social media has eased my worries about health risks EG4: Talking with others about my health situation on social media has eased my loneliness	[13]
Social gratification	SG1: Social media has enhanced my opportunities to communicate with family and friends about health issues SG2: When I share health-related information on social media, I can get support from others' likes and comments SG3: Exchanging health-related information on social media can make me get closer to my family or friends	[42, 44]
Health-related stickiness intention	HSI1: I will continue to use social media for health-related information HSI2: I hope to continue to talk with others about health-related issues on social media HSI3: I will continue to engage in health-related activities through social media	[35, 45]

3.2 Data Collection and Sample

Although the definition of "older adults" varies in the literature [46, 47], people over 55 years of age were selected as potential respondents in the current study as this population segment is usually considered in studies related to health-related usage of social media among older adults. Moreover, this age group is associated with a greater potential need and concern for health information [7]. To examine the proposed research model, we conducted an online survey focused on older adult users over 55 years of age in China and adopted the snowball sampling approach for data collection. Finally, a total of 303 questionnaires were collected. Table 2 summarizes the demographic information of the 303 participants. The age of the participants mostly ranged from 55 to 65. 53.1% were male and 46.9% were female. About 79.6% thought they were completely healthy. Five participants reported their health status as very poor due to poor immunity, high blood pressure, glaucoma, heart disease, and so on. We set up a multiple-choice question and found that children were selected most frequently as the main contact person in their social networks, which is also consistent with the prior findings [48].

Table 2. Demographic information of participants (N = 303).

Measure	Items	Frequency	Percentage (%)
Gender	Male	161	53.1
	Female	142	46.9
Age	55–60	119	39.3
	60–65	106	35.0
	65–70	44	14.5
	70–75	20	6.6
	75–80	5	1.7
	80–85	5	1.7
	Over 85	4	1.3
Health status	Very well	96	31.7
	Good	145	47.9
	Poor	57	18.8
	Very poor	5	1.6
Main contact on social media (multiple choices)	Spouse	166	54.8
	Children	257	84.8
	Parents	88	29.0
	Relatives	178	58.8
	Friends	176	58.1
	Colleagues	78	25.7

4   Results and the Analysis

In this study, we utilized partial least squares (PLS) to test the proposed model and employed SmartPLS to test both the measurement and structural models. The statistical significance levels of the structural model path coefficients were verified using the bootstrapping technique.

4.1   The Measurement Model

The reliability and validity of the research model were evaluated through multiple data analyses. Reliability is a test of the consistency or stability of survey data. The value of Cronbach's alpha (α) and the composite reliability (CR) were used to examine the internal consistency of the conceptual model constructs. Cronbach's alpha values exceeded the recommended level of 0.6, indicating acceptable reliability [49]. CR values exceeded the recommended level of 0.7, indicating good reliability. Furthermore, the average variance extracted (AVE) was used to measure the convergent and discriminant validity of the research model. First, the AVE values of all constructs exceed the 0.5 thresholds, suggesting qualified convergence validity and proving that items can effectively show the corresponding constructs [7]. The reliability and convergence validity results are detailed in Table 3. Moreover, the diagonal of Table 4 is the square root of AVE, and its values were all higher than the correlation of inner constructs, confirming that the measurement model has good discriminant validity.

Table 3. Reliability and convergence validity

Construct	Composite reliability	AVE	Cronbach's alpha
EG	0.855	0.596	0.773
HG	0.803	0.505	0.672
IG	0.847	0.581	0.759
LT	0.832	0.556	0.736
OT	0.842	0.572	0.750
SG	0.835	0.628	0.705
HSI	0.851	0.656	0.738

Table 4. Discriminant validity

Construct	EG	HG	IG	LT	OT	SG	HSI
EG	**0.772**						
HG	0.677	**0.711**					
IG	0.571	0.640	**0.762**				

(*continued*)

Table 4. (*continued*)

Construct	EG	HG	IG	LT	OT	SG	HSI
LT	0.296	0.264	0.263	**0.746**			
OT	0.491	0.518	0.445	0.037	**0.756**		
SG	0.683	0.709	0.647	0.280	0.462	**0.793**	
HSI	0.642	0.626	0.696	0.309	0.405	0.709	**0.810**

4.2 The Structural Model

The test of the structural model included the examination of path coefficients and the corresponding significance levels. Figure 2 presents the results of the PLS analysis (see Fig. 2). The hypothesis testing results are listed in Table 5. We also adopted the bootstrapping technique that can directly test the influence of the independent variable on the dependent variable. The results show that the positive effects of open-ended time perspective and limited time perspective on each gratification are significant, supporting H1a, H1b, H2a, H2b, H3a, H3b, H4a, and H4b. Regarding gratification perspectives, information, emotional, and social gratification significantly influence stickiness intention, indicating H6, H7, and H8 are supported. Results indicate that the influences of the hedonic gratification on HSI are not statistically significant. Hence, H5 is not supported.

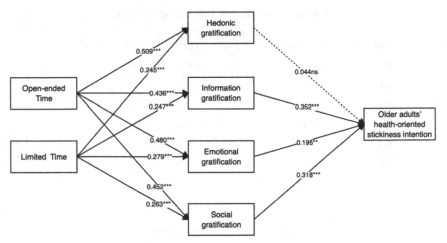

Fig. 2. Structural equation model with standardized coefficients. Note: *p < .05, **p < .01, ***p < .001, ns = nonsignificant, Nonsignificant paths are presented by a dashed line.

In total, eleven of twelve hypotheses were supported. In sum, these significant links indicate that older adults' FTP and health-related social media usage have the relationships specified in the model.

Table 5. Results of hypothesis testing

Hypothesis	Paths	Path coefficients	t-value	p-value	Hypothesis validation
H1a	OP → HG	0.509	7.829	0	Supported
H1b	LP → HG	0.245	3.606	0	Supported
H2a	OP → IG	0.436	6.810	0	Supported
H2b	LP → IG	0.247	3.876	0	Supported
H3a	OP → EG	0.480	7.949	0	Supported
H3b	LP → EG	0.279	4.347	0	Supported
H4a	OP → SG	0.452	7.901	0	Supported
H4b	LP → SG	0.263	4.485	0	Supported
H5	HG → HSI	0.044	0.644	0.520	Not supported
H6	IG → HSI	0.352	5.025	0	Supported
H7	EG → HSI	0.195	2.874	0.004	Supported
H8	SG → HSI	0.318	4.535	0	Supported

5 Discussion

This study aimed to investigate the influence factors of elderly health-oriented stickiness intention on social media and the perspective of time on old adult users' gratification. Our research developed a model based on an integrity model of FTP and gratification perspective to examine the influence factors that affect users' stickiness intention of health information behavior on social media platforms. We conducted an online survey for 303 users of social media such as WeChat, Weibo, and other mainstream social media platforms in China. The findings were as follows.

5.1 Gratification Perspective

First, consistent with the framework of the gratification perspective, we found that elderly health-oriented stickiness intention on social media is significantly affected by IG, EG, and SG. Specifically, the results of this study indicate that information gratification was the most salient factor. The results showed there was a significant strong effect of social gratification toward older adults' stickiness intention. This result has been confirmed in most previous studies [31, 42]. A previous study on WeChat found that activities with social ties were more likely to attract people to stick with social media applications [42]. In this study, according to the gratification theory, social gratification which is driven by health-oriented social interaction satisfies older adults' demands for getting support or maintaining social contacts. We also found that emotional gratification is another indispensable influence factor that has significant positive effects on older adult users' health-oriented stickiness intention. Numerous studies revealed that adopting social media technology can alleviate emotional difficulties and enhance the level of well-being [19, 23]. Therefore, the elderly-oriented design of social media platforms should give full consideration to the emotional demands of elderly users toward different relationships. Considering the critical role of health information for older adults, social media platforms should also design a relatively simple user interface where health information can be obtained and particularly highlight the health information from close friends to gratify elderly users' emotional rewards. Besides, service providers should focus on the real meaning of healthcare and aim at the importance of the popularization related knowledge of the public health emergencies of control and prevention disease on social media for elderly users to promote both their information and social gratification.

Second, examining the effect of hedonic gratification toward stickiness showed that there was no significance. This finding reflects that the purpose of users' health-oriented stickiness on social media is not for pure entertainment. Although according to previous studies [33, 42], hedonism is an important element of social media. However, the stickiness of health information may not gratify users' hedonic needs. This shows that the recreational health information of social media, such as health-related videos, photos, and so on, increases users' pleasure, but does not bring functional affordances for health-oriented purposes. It can also be explained that the particularity of health information makes users pay more attention to their benefits from information, social and emotional rewards when forming their stickiness about health information. Therefore, for elderly users, social media should focus more on the quality and effectiveness of health information instead of entertainment properties, meanwhile, maintain the social network with close partners especially.

5.2 Future Time Perspective

From the FTP, we found that elderly health-oriented hedonism, information, emotion, and social gratification on social media are significantly affected by open-ended time perspectives and limited time perspectives. First, this study shows that future time perception positively affects health-oriented stickiness on social media among older adults through perceived gratification. According to the SST, elderly users with an open-ended time perspective would prefer knowledge acquisition, while the emotional rewards of social interaction are more attractive to the elderly with a perception of limited time. However, the current elderly-oriented design genres in social media pay more attention to the simplification of social affordances and ignore the elderly's motivation to seek health information. Therefore, social media's elderly-oriented future design should focus more on the demands of knowledge acquisition to meet older adults' usage gratifications.

Second, our results suggested that the effects of an open-ended time perspective on gratification were more significant than a limited time perspective. According to the SST, older people are more likely to evoke emotion for positive information. The open-ended time perspective increases older adults' desire for health information with rich content and high quality, while a limited time perspective makes them prefer emotional benefits. However, it is difficult to use current social media technology to widely measure and classify older adults' FTPs. Moreover, this study shows that hedonic gratification has no significant impact on the stickiness intention of the elderly. Therefore, health information disseminated on social media should contain more positive effects and usefulness while retaining entertainment elements that are not distracting to cater to all older adults' positive preferences for information processing.

6 Conclusion

This study makes theoretical and practical contributions. First, it confirms the compatibility between the SST and the gratification theory. Although the SST is the main theory used in exploring the technology adoption of elderly users [1], there are few studies on health-related stickiness intention on social media guided by SST. In this study, the FTP is considered an important factor and is combined with perceived gratifications to explore the influencing mechanism of health-oriented stickiness. This study not only echoes the previous research on stickiness intention described by the gratification theory but also expands the application of SST on social media. Our results also provided a new perspective for elderly-oriented technology research and filled the knowledge gap regarding FTP in the context of health information practice. Second, this study establishes the connection between elderly users and their health-oriented behavior responses on social media. Our findings are useful for informing the development of optimal designs for elderly-oriented social media applications to bridge the digital gap between older adults' endorsements and new forms of social media.

References

1. Czaja, S.J., et al.: Designing for Older Adults: Principles and Creative Human Factors Approaches, 3rd edn. CRC Press, New York (2020)
2. Chou, W.H., Lai, Y.-I., Liu, K.-H.: User requirements of social media for the elderly: a case study in Taiwan. Behav. Inf. Technol. 32(9), 920–937 (2013)
3. Hämmerle, V., Pauli, C., Braunwalder, R., Misoch, S.: WhatsApp's influence on social relationships of older adults. In: ICT4AWE, pp. 93–98 (2020)
4. China Internet Network Information Center (CNNIC): The 45th China Statistical Report on Internet Development. http://www.cnnic.cn/gywm/xwzx/rdxw/20172017_7057/202004/t20 200427_70973.htm. Accessed 4 Jan 2022
5. iiMedia Report, Research Report on Internet Access Behavior of Chinese Middle-aged and Elderly People in 2021. https://baijiahao.baidu.com/s?id=1704784780357614149&wfr=spi der&for=pc. Accessed 4 Jan 2022
6. Song, S., Zhao, Y.C., Yao, X., Ba, Z., Zhu, Q.: Short video apps as a health information source: an investigation of affordances, user experience and users' intention to continue the use of TikTok. Internet Res. 31(6), 2120–2142 (2021)
7. Shang, L., Zhou, J., Zuo, M.: Understanding older adults' intention to share health information on social media: the role of health belief and information processing. Internet Res. 31(1), 100–122 (2020)
8. Chen, K., Chan, A.H.S.: Gerontechnology acceptance by elderly Hong Kong Chinese: a senior technology acceptance model (STAM). Ergonomics 57(5), 635–652 (2014)
9. Kruse, C., Fohn, J., Wilson, N., Patlan, E.N., Zipp, S., Mileski, M.: Utilization barriers and medical outcomes commensurate with the use of telehealth among older adults: systematic review. JMIR Med. Inform. 8(8), e20359 (2020)
10. Chatman, E.A.: Life in a small world: applicability of gratification theory to information-seeking behavior. J. Am. Soc. Inf. Sci. 42(6), 438–449 (1991)
11. Twenge, J.M., Catanese, K.R., Baumeister, R.F.: Social exclusion and the deconstructed state: time perception, meaninglessness, lethargy, lack of emotion, and self-awareness. J. Pers. Soc. Psychol. 85(3), 409 (2003)

12. Charles, S.T., Carstensen, L.L.: Social and emotional aging. Annu. Rev. Psychol. **61**, 383–409 (2010)
13. Lang, F.R., Carstensen, L.L.: Time counts: future time perspective, goals, and social relationships. Psychol. Aging **17**(1), 125 (2002)
14. Kuppelwieser, V.G.: Towards the use of chronological age in research-a cautionary comment. J. Retail. Consum. Serv. **33**, 17–22 (2016)
15. Zacher, H., Frese, M.: Remaining time and opportunities at work: relationships between age, work characteristics, and occupational future time perspective. Psychol. Aging **24**(2), 487 (2009)
16. Carstensen, L.L., Isaacowitz, D.M., Charles, S.T.: Taking time seriously: a theory of socioemotional selectivity. Am. Psychol. **54**(3), 165 (1999)
17. Kozik, P., Hoppmann, C.A., Gerstorf, D.: Future time perspective: opportunities and limitations are differentially associated with subjective well-being and hair cortisol concentration. Gerontology **61**(2), 166–174 (2015)
18. Wright, K.B., Rains, S., Banas, J.: Weak-tie support network preference and perceived life stress among participants in health-related, computer-mediated support groups. J. Comput.-Mediated Commun. **15**(4), 606–624 (2010)
19. Chan, M.: Multimodal connectedness and quality of life: examining the influences of technology adoption and interpersonal communication on well-being across the life span. J. Comput.-Mediated Commun. **20**(1), 3–18 (2015)
20. Lai, K.P., Chong, S.C.: Influences of time perspectives and perceived values on continuance intention to engage in social media amongst older adults for healthcare-related purposes. Univ. Access Inf. Soc. **167**, 1–15 (2021). https://doi.org/10.1007/s10209-021-00845-9
21. Settanni, M., et al.: The interplay between ADHD symptoms and time perspective in addictive social media use: a study on adolescent Facebook users. Child. Youth Serv. Rev. **89**, 165–170 (2018)
22. Chang, P.F., et al.: Age differences in online social networking: extending socioemotional selectivity theory to social network sites. J. Broadcast. Electron. Media **59**(2), 221–239 (2015)
23. Leist, A.K.: Social media use of older adults: a mini-review. Gerontology **59**(4), 378–384 (2013)
24. Fisk, D., Charness, N., Czaja, S.J., Rogers, W.A., Sharit, J.: Designing for Older Adults. CRC Press, Boca Raton (2004)
25. Sciarretta, E., Ingrosso, A., Volpi, V., Opromolla, A., Grimaldi, R.: Elderly and tablets: considerations and suggestions about the design of proper applications. In: Zhou, J., Salvendy, G. (eds.) ITAP 2015. LNCS, vol. 9193, pp. 509–518. Springer, Cham (2015). https://doi.org/10.1007/978-3-319-20892-3_49
26. Nambisan, S., Baron, R.A.: Interactions in virtual customer environments: implications for product support and customer relationship management. J. Interact. Mark. **21**(2), 42–62 (2007)
27. Saad, N.M., Alias, R.A., Ismail, Z.: Initial framework on identifying factors influencing individuals' usage of telehealth. In: 2013 International Conference on Research and Innovation in Information Systems (ICRIIS), pp. 174–179. IEEE (2013)
28. Jochemczyk, Ł., et al.: You only live once: present-hedonistic time perspective predicts risk propensity. Pers. Individ. Differ. **115**, 148–153 (2017)
29. Kellough, J.L., Knight, B.G.: Positivity effects in older adults' perception of facial emotion: the role of future time perspective. J. Gerontol. Ser. B Psychol. Sci. Soc. Sci. **67**(2), 150–158 (2012)
30. Löckenhoff, C.E., Carstensen, L.L.: Socioemotional selectivity theory, aging, and health: the increasingly delicate balance between regulating emotions and making tough choices. J. Pers. **72**(6). 1395–1424 (2004)
31. Zhang, X., Xu, X., Cheng, J.: WeChatting for health: what motivates older adult engagement with health information. Healthcare **9**(6), 751 (2021)

32. Parida, V., Mostaghel, R., Oghazi, P.: Factors for elderly use of social media for health-related activities. Psychol. Mark. **33**(12), 1134–1141 (2016)
33. Song, S., Zhao, Y.C., Yao, X., Ba, Z., Zhu, Q.: Serious information in hedonic social applications: affordances, self-determination and health information adoption in TikTok. J. Documentation (2021)
34. Baldensperger, L., et al.: Social network, autonomy, and adherence correlates of future time perspective in patients with head and neck cancer. Psycho-Oncol. **27**(6), 1545–1552 (2018)
35. Hsieh, P.S., Ou, J., Xu, J.: Users' emotional attachments to internet celebrities: based on the perspective of extended-self. IN: Proceedings of the 52nd Hawaii International Conference on System Sciences (2019)
36. Chavez, L., et al.: The role of travel motivations and social media use in consumer interactive behaviour: a uses and gratifications perspective. Sustainability **12**(21), 8789 (2020)
37. Fornace, K.M., Surendra, H., Abidin, T.R., et al.: Use of mobile technology-based participatory mapping approaches to geolocate health facility attendees for disease surveillance in low resource settings. Int. J. Health Geogr. **17**(1), 1–10 (2018)
38. Utama, D.Q., et al.: Mobile health application for drug supply chain management: case study national population and family planning board. In: 2017 5th International Conference on Instrumentation, Communications, Information Technology, and Biomedical Engineering (ICICI-BME). IEEE (2017)
39. Kim, Y., Sohn, D., Choi, S.M.: Cultural difference in motivations for using social network sites: a comparative study of American and Korean college students. Comput. Hum. Behav. **27**(1), 365–372 (2011)
40. Putri, M.F., Harahap, N.C., Pramudiawardani, S., Sensuse, D.I., Sutoyo, M.A.H.: Usage intention model for mobile health application: uses and gratification perspective. In: 2019 International Conference on Electrical Engineering and Informatics (ICEEI), pp. 500–505. IEEE, July 2019
41. Jung, T., Youn, H., McClung, S.: Motivations and self-presentation strategies on Korean-based "Cyworld" weblog format personal homepages. CyberPsychol. Behav. **10**(1), 24–31 (2007)
42. Wu, X., Kuang, W.: Exploring influence factors of wechat users' health information sharing behavior: based on an integrated model of TPB, UGT and SCT. Int. J. Hum.-Comput. Interact. **37**(13), 1243–1255 (2021)
43. Park, N., Kee, K.F., Valenzuela, S.: Being immersed in social networking environment: Facebook groups, uses and gratifications, and social outcomes. Cyberpsychol. Behav. **12**(6), 729–733 (2009)
44. Lin, C.P.: Assessing the mediating role of online social capital between social support and instant messaging usage. Electron. Commer. Res. Appl. **10**(1), 105–114 (2011)
45. Li, D., Browne, G.J., Wetherbe, J.C.: Why do internet users stick with a specific web site? A relationship perspective. Int. J. Electron. Commer. **10**(4), 105–141 (2006)
46. Asla, T., Williamson, K., Mills, J.: The role of information in successful aging: the case for a research focus on the oldest old. Libr. Inf. Sci. Res. **28**(1), 49–63 (2006)
47. Zhao, Y.C., Zhao, M., Song, S.: Online health information seeking behaviors among older adults: systematic scoping review. J. Med. Internet Res. **24**(2), e34790 (2022)
48. Song, X., Song, S., Chen, S., Zhao, Y.(C.), Zhu, Q.: Factors influencing proxy internet health information seeking among the elderly in rural China: a grounded theory study. In: Zhou, J., Salvendy, G. (eds.) HCII 2019. LNCS, vol. 11592, pp. 332–343. Springer, Cham (2019). https://doi.org/10.1007/978-3-030-22012-9_24
49. Jen, W., Hu, K.-C.: Application of perceived value model to identify factors affecting passengers' repurchase intentions on city bus: a case of the Taipei metropolitan area. Transportation **30**(3), 307–327 (2003)

Technology Acceptance and Adoption: Barriers and Facilitators for Older Adults

Work, Digital Devices and Later Life:
A Quanti-qualitative Research

Simone Carlo[1]([✉]) [iD] and Giulia Buscicchio[2]

[1] Università Cattolica del Sacro Cuore, 20131 Milan, Italy
simone.carlo@unicatt.it
[2] Luxembourg Institute of Socio-Economic Research, LISER and University of Luxembourg,
4365 Esch-sur-Alzette, Luxemburg

Abstract. This article presents the results of a qualitative-quantitative research on the relationship between work background and digital media use among the elderly. The aim of the study is to investigate the relationship between gender, employment status and professional level, and the technological endowments, skills, use and appropriation processes of ICT by the elderly. A sample of 900 Italians between 65 and 74 years old was used for quantitative analysis, together with 20 in-depth interviews. The research was conducted between December 2013 and April 2014. From the results it emerges that gender, working condition and professional level differently influence technological endowment, frequency of use of Internet and PC and Social Networks, while gender, income and educational qualification determine IT competence. This evidence was further corroborated and enriched by the ethnographic investigation.

Keywords: Elderly · Ageing · Gender · ICT · Job · Active ageing · Digital media

1 Introduction

The ageing of population is a global trend that challenges society in its entirety, by producing massive transformations that involve almost every sector of society in every part of the world [1].

Italy, in particular, is one of the countries with the higher average age among citizens [2]. Ageing arguably and dramatically affects welfare costs, nonetheless the elderly can also age actively and healthily [3–5]. Older people, when healthy, are also dynamic beings in terms of work as well as social and cultural capital. Within this theme, ICT (Information and Communication Technologies) are often considered as a viable way to guarantee active ageing thanks to their potential for inclusion [6]. The empowerment of the elderly through the use of ICT is in turn influenced by their learning process in both a formal (e.g. work environment) and informal (e.g. social and family life) capacity [7].

There are however still very few studies, especially when it comes to Italy, on the role played by ICT in active ageing taking into account key elements such as work and social conditions.

© The Author(s), under exclusive license to Springer Nature Switzerland AG 2022
Q. Gao and J. Zhou (Eds.): HCII 2022, LNCS 13330, pp. 451–465, 2022.
https://doi.org/10.1007/978-3-031-05581-2_32

This research, by using a mixed methodology (quantitative and ethnographic), thus aims to fill that existing gap and to examine the work status of the elderly in its ability to affect ICT access, use and acquisition.

2 State of the Art

The topic of the relation between use of ICT and users age generates from the premise of massmediological researches on digital divide [8] and revolves around the study of the connection between digital alphabetization and social inclusion of the elderly [9]. More recently, an increasing number of empirical studies focused on the implementation of ICT among the elderly with the purpose of promoting active ageing and wellbeing [10]. For example from a psychological point of view it would seem that the implementation of ICT betters their elderly users' quality of life by impacting variables such as personal affirmation, autonomy and stress [11]. In addition, it also appears as if the use of ICT helps the elderly in maintaining and growing their social networking, especially in high-mobility or migration contexts [12]. Heo et al. [13] stressed how patterns of frequency in Internet use by older people can attest positively to their social support net, life fulfillment and wellness, and negatively to their loneliness.

As was the case for the studies on digital divide, the research on active ageing has been criticized for the excessive (neoliberal) emphasis put on the elderly individual traits and responsibilities [14], as well as for neglecting the social dimension of aging processes and their context of development [15]. On this matter there is an urgency of an understanding that goes beyond the study of the "present" and the individuality of older people but rather examines their "past" and the life instances that led them to be more or less prone to the use of ICT today.

Nowadays various researches correlate the elderly use of ICT to socio-demographic variables (such as income, age, education [16]), but very few of them explore the elderly work experience and Internet use. It however appears clear that retirement represents a pivotal element in each individual's biography, and that their previous work condition heavily affects the processes of digital technologies implementation [17]. The digital skill set (e.g. e-mail, processing of texts and calc sheet, video calls, etc.) acquired in the workplace can directly influence the ways seniors utilize ICT in private [18]. Besides, retirement has a tendency to reduce IT alphabetization and the frequency of Internet use in both men and women (ibidem). Also, the negative effect of retirement on PC use is greater on former workers who used to be employed in positions requiring a more advanced and intense application of digital skills than on those who learned and used ICT outside the workplace. Additional studies [19] stress how senior employees who use the PC at work, feeling useful and motivated longer, postpone retirement.

3 Context, Research Questions, Sample, Methodology

This paper's intention is that to investigate the link between work background and use of ICT among the elderly with the aim to provide new evidence on a still underdeveloped topic. According to Colombo et al.[9], only 21,3% of Italians aged 65–74 owns a PC, and 49,8% of senior digital users declare to have learned their skills in the workplace. Among the latter, more than half (57,8%) are men, while women are fewer (37,6%). Based on these data, it appears important to conduct a further examination on the existing connection between ICT implement and work position and condition of the elderly, with a focus on gender: older women seem to have been less exposed than men to the digitalisation process, probably due to their different work placement [20].

Therefore the following research questions have been formulated:

1. Does gender determine a difference in technological equipment (*1a*), Internet (*1b*) and social networks (*1c*) use?
2. Does employment status determine a difference in technological equipment (*2a*), Internet (*2b*) and social networks (*2c*) use?
3. Does professional rank determine a difference in technological equipment (*3a*), Internet (*3b*) and social networks (*3c*) use?
4. Do seniors former work placement (*4a*), level of education (*4b*), income (*4c*), gender (*4d*) and age (*4e*) favourably or unfavourably predict the acquired IT knowledge and skills?
5. Do seniors former work placement (*5a*), level of education (*5b*), income (*5c*), gender (*5d*) and age (*5e*) favourably or unfavourably predict the frequency of use of IT technologies?

In order to answer these questions between December 2013 and January 2014 a sample of 900 Italian seniors aged 65–74 were each asked to compile a face-to-face questionnaire. The sample is representative of the Italian population between 65 and 74 years: the participants were selected with a random, proportional sampling, stratified by region and size of the Municipality of residence. 1600 names were extracted from the electoral lists of 90 municipalities, using a systematic method, carried out in two stages with a 56% response rate and 900 respondents (Error sample: 3%. Confidence error: 0.05%). 776 individuals responded in full.

The remaining sample averages an age of 69.34 ($DS = 3.01$) and is equally divided between women (365) and men (411). The age bracket taken into consideration within the research exhibits a high percentage of non-workers (homemakers, retirees): 80,2% among men and 92,9% among women, and only 10,5% of men and 2,2% of women work full-time.

In addition, 20 non-structured and in-depth home interviews took place among younger seniors aged 65–74, all residents of Lombardy and users of ICT. The finding of the subjects to be interviewed took place through the recruitment of a professional agency.

As regards the qualitative portion of the research, its specific objective was the deepening of certain aspects surfaced during the quantitative analysis. In particular, that of pinpointing the biographic trajectories that influenced choices in the use of digital technologies, digital skills and typology of services used, as well as the composition of the domestic contexts of learning and the processes of implementation of ICT within the households [21].

4 Results

4.1 A Subsection Sample

All analyses were processed through the statistic software SPSS v. 24. The variables used in the analyses are displayed in the notes. In order to answer research questions 1–3, we ran a χ^2 test on independent samples and examined the relation among gender (1), employment status (2), professional level (3), technological equipment and use of Internet and social networks in the elderly. It was possible to detect significant connections between gender and Technological Equipment Index (χ^2 (2) = 25.47, p < .001) (1a), PC and Internet Use Index (χ^2 (2) = 33.51, p < .001) (1b) and Social Networks Use Index (χ^2 (2) = 11.97, p = .003) (1c). The statistical significance for each of our investigated relationships was quite strong, below the 5% threshold level. As regards technological equipment, women own an inferior number of devices compared to men, as well as it is almost inexistent their PC use. Lastly, the presence of both men and women on social networks is extremely scarce, although slightly more common – albeit still limited – when it comes to the former. Moreover, there is an statistically significant strong link between employment status and technological equipment (χ^2 (8) = 48.93,p < .001) (2a), showing that the latter's Index is quite low when referred to retirees, as opposed to seniors who are still employed in any capacity (see Table 4), reaching its peak values with those who are working on a full-time basis. Also strongly statistically significant are the relations between employment status and PC and Internet Use Index (χ^2 (8) = 54.61, p < .001) (2b), and Social Networks Use Index (χ^2 (8) = 17.04, p = .03) (2c). The data in Table 1 show how PC and Internet Use disappear with retirement but are still present among active workers, even more so in full-time jobs, while limited in part-time or occasional occupations. Social networks are instead sporadically used only by those who are currently employed. Professional level is also linked to technological equipment at high statistically significant level (χ^2 (6) = 169.01, p < .001) (3a) as well as PC and Internet Use Index (χ^2 (6) = 170.29, p < .001) (3b) and Social Networks Use Index (χ^2 (6) = 85.61, p < .001) (3c). Surprisingly, the level of technological equipment is lower for individuals occupying medium/high positions (i.e. intellectuals, businessmen) than for manual workers, who indeed hold the highest numbers; exactly the same happens regarding the use of social networks, which is paltry within the first group and more frequent within the second. Results show a complete opposite trend in relation to PC and Internet use, which are a common practice among higher-level professionals and scarce among the others.

In order to answer research questions 4 and 5, a correlation analysis was run between all continuous variables of interest. As shown in Table 2, the variables put in correlation were: Internet use frequency, IT proficiency, professional level, education, gender and age. It appears clear that all independent variables are in fact correlated to dependent variables IT proficiency and Internet use frequency.

In order to answer research question 4 (from 4a to 4e), a multiple linear regression was run. The regression model is statistically significant, F (7, 434) = 33.94, p < .001 with a correct R2 of .35. As shown in Table 3, the participant's professional level ($\beta = -.001$; p = .95) (4a) is not a significant predictor of IT proficiency, with a p-value way above the statistically significant threshold of 5%. Meanwhile, education is a statistically strong

Table 1. χ^2 Technological equipment index, pc and internet use index, social networks use index by gender and employment status

Factors	Total sample	Gender		Employment status					Professional level			
		Male	Female	Retired	Not working - disabled	Full-time worker	Part-time worker	Occasional worker	Intellectual	Executive	Manager	Manual worker
Technological equipment index												
n	775	417	483	651	17	52	27	30	221	228	47	67
% Low	.685	.638	.789*	.711*a	.904*a	.400	.431	.671	.393*f	.405*f	.083	.119
% Medium	.185	.201	.128*	.179	.121	.184	.334	.208	.153	.403*g	.104	.340*g
% High	.132	.154	.083*	.110	.000	.409*b	.223	.119	.096	.183	.077	.644*g
PC and internet use index												
n	776	270	388	472	15	20	11	21	226	232	47	68
% Nil	.695	.647	.804*	.904*a	.384*a	.400	.715	.695*c	.082	.110	.401*h	.387*h
% Limited	.088	.082	.074	.056	.077	.256	.156*d	.088	.176	.382*g	.162	.279
% High	.217	.271	.122*	.065	.533	.332*e	.127	.217	.561*f	.275*f	.076	.086

(*continued*)

Table 1. (*continued*)

Factors	Total sample	Gender		Employment status					Professional level			
		Male	Female	Retired	Not working - disabled	Full-time worker	Part-time worker	Occasional worker	Intellectual	Executive	Manager	Manual worker
Social networks use index												
n	776	337	429	548	17	34	22	24	238	269	58	115
% Nil	.832	.807	.889*	1,025	.647	.809	.812	.832	.350*f	.396*f	.085	.169
% Limited	.124	.144	.076*	.000	.275	.150*d	.161	.124	.116	.263	.116	.505*g
% High	.045	.049	.034	.000	.071	.028	.025	.045	.111	.278	.056	.556*g

Note. The comparative analysis was based on the χ^2 test; men and women were compared according to the Technological Equipment Index (χ^2 (2) = 25.47, p < .001), the PC and Internet Use Index (χ^2 (2) = 33.51, p < .001) and the Social Networks Use Index (χ^2 (2) = 11.97, p = .003). Different professional statuses were compared according to the Technological Equipment Index (χ^2 (8) = 48.93, p < .001), the PC and Internet Use Index (χ^2 (8) = 54.61, p < .001) and the Social Networks Use Index (χ^2 (8) = 17.04, p = .03). Lastly, the Professional level (considered as a category rather than a metric variable) was again compared to the Technological Equipment Index (χ^2 (6) = 169.01, p < .001), the PC and Internet Use Index (χ^2 (6) = 170.29, p < .001), and the Social Networks Use Index (χ^2 (6) = 85.61, p < .001). The asterisks, when added, signal significant differences in categories on the same line. [a] A significant difference was recorded in relation to "Full-time worker" and "Part-time worker". [b] A significant difference was recorded in relation to "Retired" and "Occasional worker". [c] A significant difference was recorded in relation to "Full-time worker". [d] A significant difference was recorded in relation to "Retired", "Not working-Disabled" and "Occasional worker". [e] A significant difference was recorded in relation to "Retired". [e] A significant difference was recorded in relation to "Retired", "Not working-Disabled" and "Occasional worker". [f] A significant difference was recorded in relation to "Manager" and "Manual worker". [g] A significant difference was recorded in relation to "Intellectual" and "Executive". [h] A significant difference was recorded in relation to "Intellectual" and "Manager"

Table 2. Correlation table

Variable	N	M	SD	1	2	3	4	5	6
1.Internet use frequency	231	3.59	0.73	-					
2.IT Proficiency	775	1.23	0.72	.380[**]	–				
3.Professional level	810	2.77	1.12	−.275[**]	−.351[**]	-			
4.Education	896	2.29	1.64	.277[**]	.525[**]	−.553[**]	–		
5.Income	795	2.81	1.26	.241[**]	.399[**]	−.430[**]	.540[**]	-	
6.Gender	900	1.54	0.50	−.111	−.200[**]	−.039	−.152[**]	−.183[**]	–
7.Age	900	69.34	3.01	−.189[**]	−.153[**]	.063	−.119[**]	−.110[**]	.015

Note. [**]p < .01

and positively predictor of IT proficiency ($\beta = .19$; p = .001) (4b) as well as income ($\beta = .12$; p = .001) (4c). Self-assessed IT proficiency seems to higher for males than females ($\beta = −.26$; p = .001) (4d), and to decrease with aging ($\beta = −.03$; p = .01) (4e).

Table 3. Regression coefficients of professional level, education, income, gender and age predictors

Variable	B	SE	95% CI		p
			LL	UL	
Constant	3.092	.773	1.574	4.611	.000
3. Professional level	−.001	.008	−.016	.015	.947
5. Education	.187	.030	.128	.246	.000
7. Income	.118	.031	.056	.180	.000
8. Gender	−.257	.065	-.383	−.130	.000
9. Age	−.029	.011	−.050	-.008	.007

Note. Gender is codified with 1 for male and 2 for female

In order to answer research question 5 (from 5a to 5e) the same multiple regression as before was run, by substituting Internet use frequency to IT proficiency as an independent variable. The regression model is statistically significant, F (7, 434) = 3.86, p < .001 with a correct R2 of .11. As shown in Table 4 none of the independent variables listed is a valid predictor of Internet use frequency among the elderly, thus implying the following answer: in this case neither professional level, education, gender nor income have a real impact in determining Internet use frequency (all the p-value were highly above the maximum statistical significance threshold of 5%, Table 4).

Table 4. Regression coefficients of professional level, education, income, gender and age predictors on Internet Use

Variable	B	SE	95% CI		p
			LL	UL	
Constant	5.753	1.353	3.076	8.422	.000
3. Professional level	−.007	.012	−.032	.017	.558
5. Education	.003	.040	−.077	.082	.947
7. Income	.091	.062	−.030	.213	.139
8. Gender	−.160	.119	−.395	.074	.179
9. Age	−.031	.019	−.069	.006	.097

Note. Gender is codified with 1 for male and 2 for female

In summary, the survey shows how users' former professional level does not really affect IT knowledge and proficiency (p-values equal to .947 and .558 respectively, above to 5% threshold). It however assumes a more central role when paired with work conditions in determining the number of devices owned and PC, Internet and social networks use frequency. It is specifically evident that being still employed, either on a full-time or part-time basis, entails an increase in numbers pertaining the matter.

As regards proficiency, technological equipment and frequency in the use of devices, the results highlight two staple points. The first concerns the impact caused by the professional level: the higher it is, the lower is the number of devices owned and of hours spent utilizing social networks, while more time is dedicated to PC and Internet use. The second concerns gender difference: the number of older women who are familiar with and utilize IT technologies is significantly inferior to that of men, so gender is a definite predictor of perceived IT proficiency as a factor inversely proportional to being a female. Plus, technological equipment as well as Internet and social networks use are characterize women way less than men.

It is also worth of notice to mention how although professional level doesn't affect self-assessed IT proficiency, education and income, when higher, do entail a better IT proficiency and efficiency. Data as such confirm what already established in previous studies [22]: seniors with upper income, education and social standing are more suitable to own and use ICT.

4.2   Ethnography

After the survey, which marked a starting point, in 2014 the research continued through an ethnographic study. In the following pages some of the latter's results will be explained, paying particular attention to the link between the elderly work experience and their processes of acquisition of ICT. The transcripts of the interviews were analyzed through a grounded and inductive approach. The comparative method was used [23] for the qualitative analysis of the interviews and the processing of data and recurring themes emerging from the reading of the transcripts.

Based on the analysis of the interviews, it is possible to outline three separate profiles of senior ICT users, each entailing a different way of implementing technologies connected to the elderly work conditions.

1. Senior "White Collar" Retirees, i.e. Teachers and Office Workers in the 1990's

It is the more representative group in terms of number among the owners of ICT interviewed, corresponding to the professional categories of intellectuals and managers.

It includes those seniors who started to use digital and communication technologies at work. They were part of the late 80's-early 90's digitalization process involving administration and office procedures that saw the replacement of typewriters with PCs. These people learned at work how to use the Microsoft Office package, various accounting programs and the computerised management of orders. Almost all of them decided later on to purchase their own home PC and Internet connection quite in advance compared to their peers [24].

Already having to use it at work I quickly realised its usefulness, so I was one of the firsts among my friends to have an Internet connection at home in 1998 (M, 69, Retiree/Former office worker)

Technological literacy in the workplace embodied the driving force behind the accelerated entrance of certain groups of people into the IT and digital universe: workers from the 1990's (nowadays seniors) did rapidly understand the advantages provided by the implementation of ICT [24]. For them, digital technologies are a well-acquired skill set that they were able to pass onto other family members (especially their children) by teaching them how to use a PC.

I started to teach (how to use) the PC to my children: how to start it, to move the mouse, they needed to do researches for school and I reckoned it was useful to have one and show them how it worked (F, 69, Retiree/Former teacher)

For these aforementioned seniors the use of PC at home derives from the application background learned at work and, at least at first, leaves no room for leisure and entertainment. After retiring though, thanks to all the free time available their approach undergoes a transformation switching from a task-related utilitarian application to a recreational activity. Nonetheless, their primary use of ICT remains focused on utility rather than leisure, as demonstrated by their implementation in online e-Commerce, e-Banking, e-Government and e-Health related practices.

Thus it is not by chance that the desktop PC (often equipped with printer, keyboard, mouse, USB chargers etc.) is presently recognised as the main IT device for digital use, while smart phones, tablets and even laptops are considered with a certain scepticism as fun "toys".

2. Still-Working Seniors

A more limited, although consistent, number of seniors are still employed. Their working status has a great impact on their chosen way to spend their free time and therefore on their ICT use. They are mainly men with a reduced personal time who are active beings and live primarily outside the family environment and in the workplace.

This group can first be divided into those whose jobs are ICT use-oriented and those whose jobs don't require their use. The formers are office workers (insurance agents, consultants, vendors) who need PCs in order to manage all the suppliers/clients communication but also softwares specific to their work. The latter are artisans, small businessmen, restaurateurs and more generally employees in low-digitalised sectors, who resort to digital technologies in their free time and for personal purposes.

Regarding the first category, their professional activity represented a means to keep up with the times and stay on par with younger colleagues [19]:

I decided to continue working as an insurance agent, but in order to do so I have to be able to use the PC like my younger colleagues as well as the programs for opening new policies or Whatsapp to contact my clients (M, 67, Insurance agent)

Such work-related technological proficiency only marginally applies to their private life:

To me the PC is just a work tool, my wife has way more free time than me and she's the one keeping in touch with the grandchildren on Facebook, but when the time comes for the tax return I get the mouse (M, 66, Consultant)

These seniors are apt ICT users at work but less capable in private:

If I need to enter a new policy in the database I do it and I do it quickly, if I have to upload a photo on Facebook I'm always afraid to make mistakes, but maybe is more important to do one's job properly, I don't really care about those other silly things... (M, 67, Insurance agent)

As concerns the second category instead, the opposite stands: they are barely proficient in ICT use at a professional level but more open to employ them to manage personal matters. Therefore at times ICT are seen as proof of their shortcomings from a work point of view.

Everybody tells me to get Facebook for example for the restaurant, the bookings, but I say no, I'm not good at managing it. I leave it to the new restaurants downtown, we are something different... I'm going to work for a couple of years more and then I'll stop, so this is not the time to get into this tangle (F, 65, Restaurateur)

This type of reduced implementation of ICT in the workplace translates into a similarly restricted use in the private sphere, also due to the limited free time available that doesn't facilitate an explorative approach to technologies:

My friends spend plenty of time on the PC and became very good, I don't have time and am lousy at it: I can send an e-mail or search for a supplier on the Internet, but it takes a lot of effort (F, 65, Restaurateur)

3. Senior "Blue Collar" Retirees, i.e. Workmen and Homemakers in the 1990's
Together with the first group, are the more numerous among the interviewed. These workers in the 90's were employed in positions that didn't require any form of PC use (factory workers, artisans) or were simply unemployed (a large number of homemakers). They never learned how to use such technologies at work and are only now starting to approach digital media.

I've always been a homemaker and I haven't needed the PC for it up until now... perhaps now with all the recipies online things are going to change...[laughing] (F, 71, Retiree/Homemaker).

These people are somewhat conscious of their digital delay compared to their contemporaries who throughout their lives had more opportunities to employ IT technologies. Their former work conditions are thus considered at fault for their lack of proficiency:

I see my relatives who used to work at a desk job and ten, twenty years ago already had a PC at home: I only started to use one two years ago and it was the first time that I actually sit down typing (M, 71, Retiree/Former artisan)

They are senior who only recently bought (or were gifted) a PC, when all their children were already living elsewhere. The input for the purchase is a general curiosity toward the new digital world as well as a vague need to keep up with the times. They are still at the explorative phase and their digital skills are basic. They are very interested in some of the services provided on the Internet (homebanking, newsfeed) and in the opportunities that it offers.

I wasn't so passionate about it, but people used to tell me it was useful...then I bought it, saw some interesting stuff, and thought "it's like with the dishwasher, I can save a lot of time" (M, 71, Retiree/Former artisan)

They are mostly self-taught: only few of them attend IT literacy courses, interestingly with an approach similar to that of a professional training at a new job, and encounter significant difficulty in applying the various tools.

I was worried I couldn't use it. So I sign up for a course [...] I finished it at Easter time and now I can use it. It's like with a new job, before starting you need to study and learn how to do it (F, 72, Retiree/Homemaker).

A professional background non-related to an office job of some sort often entails for the elderly an initial hurdle in handling keyboard and mouse. That is why they are the ones who prefer to choose the more intuitive and simple "touch" devices, such as tablets and smartphones.

A PC with a keyboard is something completely new to me, back when I was young I never even used a typewriter. So in the end I decided to buy the tablet where you only need to press with your finger and it's the same, no, it's better (M, 71, Retiree/Former artisan)

This attitude reflects in the different types of services used, which show a limited fruition of writing and data management programs (e.g. Office Word and Office Excel) and activities that are almost exclusively connected to the Internet and certain apps (Facebook, Whatsapp, YouTube, public utility apps, games). While for the seniors belonging to the previous two categories ICT are mainly connected to utilitarian functions like work, news and service management applications, those comprised in this last group employ the Internet and everything digital as a source of entertainment.

5 Conclusions, Limitations and Implications for Future Research

We here summarize the evidence that emerged from our results.

Q1. Does gender determine a difference in technological equipment (1a), Internet (1b) and social networks (1c) use?
The results of our study showed that not only do women have a lower number of devices than men (technological equipment), but they use the Internet and social networks much less than men. This finding is not only in line with all the other studies [e.g., 20, 22, 29, 30] that attest to the presence of gender differences in the use of ICT, but also with what emerged from the qualitative interviews. Indeed, from the interviews with the few women present in the qualitative sample it emerges that the use of the PC is almost none and if used only out of necessity but not for recreational purposes is due to an actual lack of skill (e.g., "Everybody tells me to get Facebook for example for the restaurant, the bookings, but I say no, I'm not good at managing") and time (" I don't have time and am lousy at it: I can send an e-mail or search for a supplier on the Internet, but it takes a lot of effort ").

Q2. Does employment status determine a difference in technological equipment (2a), Internet (2b) and social networks (2c) use? and Q3. Does professional rank determine a difference in technological equipment (3a), Internet (3b) and social networks (3c) use?
The empirical results showed that although both occupational status and the level of the position previously held were significantly correlated with technological equipment, Internet and social network use, the relationships diverged between the two. In fact, if for employment status, that is, whether or not the respondents were still working, it seems that those who were still working owned more devices, who made a higher use of the Internet than those who were retired or inactive, for employment status this trend changed slightly. That is, those in intellectual positions had fewer technology devices than manual workers. The same trend, however, was seen for frequency of internet use greater for both employed and intellectual occupations, and for low use of social. Again, these trends seem to have partially emerged in the ethnographic interviews as well: respondents belonging to the intellectual professions show greater use of ICT than those in manual professions (e.g., "I started to teach (how to use) the PC to my children" - F, 69, Retiree/Former teacher- "I wasn't so passionate about it, but people used to tell me it was useful" -Retiree/Former artisan-), as well as those who still work compared to those who no longer work ("I decided to continue working as an insurance agent, but in order to do so I have to be able to use the PC like my younger colleagues" -Insurance agent- "A PC with a keyboard is something completely new to me" -Retiree/Former artisan-).

Q4. Do seniors former work placement (4a), level of education (4b), income (4c), gender (4d) and age (4e) favourably or unfavourably predict the acquired IT knowledge and skills? and Q5. Do seniors former work placement (5a), level of education (5b), income (5c), gender (5d) and age (5e) favourably or unfavourably predict the frequency of use of IT technologies?

It is interesting to note that the level of education, gender and age were significantly related to the acquired IT knowledge, the higher the level of education and income the greater the acquired IT knowledge, on the contrary the higher the age the lower the acquired IT knowledge, as well as once again confirming the gender pattern, whereby men have a greater acquired IT knowledge than women. These latter findings support our hypotheses as we expected and are in line with other studies on ICT and the elderly.

The starting point in our research was the overcoming of the biological and individualistic approach to the discussion on the relations between seniors and technologies [24] and overall to the processes of active ageing [25]. Neither age nor an alleged natural difficulty in the use of ICT by the elderly affect the paths of technological acquisitions [26], but are rather social contexts and life choices that determine the significance of ICT in older people's everyday life. In particular, our study shows quite the important role played by work conditions in the practices of ICT implementation, role that is confirmed both at a quantitative and a qualitative level. Indeed, while one's former professional status does not seem to influence IT knowledge and proficiency, work conditions do. A senior still employed in any capacity is closer to IT technologies than an unemployed or retired one. Being professionally active, especially in "intellectual" or office jobs, entails a stronger awareness in the use of devices for practical purposes and a look at IT sciences as a place of useful tools and services that revolve around the use of a PC. On the contrary, retired seniors with plenty of free time available tend to a less technical ICT use favoring leisure and entertainment contents accessed via tablets and smartphones. The same can be said regarding professional status: the lower the former position covered the greater the time spent in the recreational use of ICT, interacting on social networks through a wide range of devices such as PCs, tablets and smartphones. Those who used to work in intellectual, executive or management roles are more oriented toward the exclusive use of PCs and utilitarian digital services (eCommerce, eBanking, eGovernment, eHealth). When the past work life was characterized by an active implementation of ICT, during the retirement years is more probable that the skill set formerly acquired will continue to provide a significant awareness in the use of technologies, even when trying a more recreational approach. When the past work life was instead set in a digital-free environment, a present use of technologies verges almost exclusively toward the entertainment and an explorative rather than intense approach to digital media, tablet and smartphones in primis.

All of the above allows for a reflection on the processes of digitalization involving the elderly. Although ICT are undoubtedly and rapidly spreading among mature citizens, our research shows that not all of them get digital in the same way, at the same speed and with the same opportunities to make ICT use significant in terms of inclusion and digital citizenship. In particular those who are poorer, less educated, retired and inactive risk to approach the digital world only as a place for low-cost entertainment and not as an instrument for developing new skills. In a classic dynamic of radicalization of digital-operated inequities [27], the outbreak of ICT in the elderly life may expand the social divide between biographically "rich" (in income, culture, relations, work) and poorer (of resources able to transform ICT into multipliers of chances for active ageing) seniors. ICT are not an element of active ageing in themselves, but they can paradoxically embody an obstacle to healthy ageing [28].

A second instance surfaced from both the quantitative and the ethnographic analysis and is related to gender. Women not only appear to be less IT-proficient than men but also, as a consequence, have reduced technological equipment and ICT use frequency. This further confirms that, whilst the digital gender gap is progressively disappearing among the youth, older women are still behind their male counterparts as regards the ICT implementation [22]. In adults this discrepancy can be explained according with a "life course" perspective [20]. Throughout the years men and women have been exposed to different expectations and occasions, especially concerning education, family duties and job opportunities [29] and such diversities came to affect also ICT acquisition practices and overall active ageing. A lesser education, less free time and less qualified work placements all contributed to the present-day minor digitalization of females as opposed to males among the elderly, carrying until the end the effects of lifelong disparities. This last observation reminds us how active ageing opportunities are strongly influenced by individual traits such as the elderly digital and social resources as well as gender. Therefore, it becomes urgent a redesigning of the current digital inclusion and active ageing policies in order to stop them from being "blind to gender" [30], and instead part of the understanding of the differences at play within ageing (and ICT use) processes between men and women.

References

1. UNDESA: World Population Ageing 2019. World Population Ageing 2019, vol. 64 (2019)
2. ISTAT: IndicatoriDemografici—Year 2020, vol. 12 (2020)
3. Rossi, G., Boccacin, L., Bramanti, D., Meda, S.G.: Active ageing: intergenerational relationships and social generativity. Stud. Health Technol. Inform. **203**, 57–68 (2014)
4. Rosina, A.: Il futuro non invecchia. Vita e Pensiero (2018)
5. Bordone, V., Arpino, B., Rosina, A.: Forever young? An analysis of the factors influencing perceptions of ageing. Ageing Soc. **40**(8), 1669–1693 (2020). https://doi.org/10.1017/S01446 86X19000084
6. Carlo, S., Sourbati, M.: Age and technology in digital inclusion policy: a study of italy and the UK. ESSACHESS – J. Commun. Stud, **13**(2(26)), 107–127 (2020)
7. Hänninen, R., Taipale, S., Luostari, R.: Exploring heterogeneous ICT use among older adults: the warm experts' perspective. New Media Soc. **23**(6), 1584–1601 (2021)
8. Ragnedda, M.: Conceptualizing digital capital. Telemat. Inform. **35**(8), 2366–2375 (2018)
9. Colombo, F., Aroldi, P., Carlo, S.: Nuevosmayores, viejas brechas: TIC, desigualdad y bienestaren la tercera edad en Italia. Comunicar: Revista Científica de Comunicación y Educación **23**(45), 47–55 (2015)
10. Walker, A., Maltby, T.: Active ageing: a strategic policy solution to demographic ageing in the European Union'. Int. J. Soc. Welf. **21**(S1), 117–130 (2012)
11. Sims, T., Reed, A.E., Carr, D.C.: Information and communication technology use is related to higher well-being among the oldest-old. J. Gerontol. Ser. B Psychol. Sci. Soc. Sci. **72**(5), 761–770 (2017)

12. Khvorostianov, N.: "Thanks to the internet, we remain a family": ICT domestication by elderly immigrants and their families in Israel. J. Fam. Commun. **16**(4), 355–368 (2016)
13. Heo, J., Chun, S., Lee, S., Lee, K.H., Kim, J.: Internet use and well-being in older adults. Cyberpsychol. Behav. Soc. Netw. **18**(5), 268–272 (2015)
14. Tadic, D.: Virpi T: Beyond Successful and Active Ageing: A Theory of Model Ageing, 119 p. Policy Press, Bristol (2018). ISBN 978-1-4473-3017-2 (hardback). Int. J. Ageing Later Life **11**(2), 87–88 (2016)
15. Carney, G., Macnicol, J.: Neoliberalising Old Age, 242 p. Cambridge University Press, Cambridge (2015). pbk £25.83, ISBN 13-978-1-107-53554-1. Ageing Soc. **37**(4), 874–875 (2017)
16. Pirone, F., Pratschke, J., Rebeggiani, E.: Un'indagine sull'uso delle Ict tra gli over 50: Considerazioni su nuovi fattori di disuguaglianza sociale e territoriale. SOCIOLOGIA DEL LAVORO (2008)
17. Arief, M., Rissanen, S., Saranto, K.: Influence of previous work experience and education on Internet use of people in their 60s and 70s. BMJ Health Care Inform. **25**(3) (2018)
18. Cavapozzi, D., Dal Bianco, C.: Does retirement decrease the familiarity with ICT of older individuals? In: Working Paper 2020:01, Department of Economics, University of Venice «Ca' Foscari» (2020)
19. Biagi, F., Cavapozzi, D., Miniaci, R.: Employment transitions and computer use of older workers [Post-Print]. HAL (2011)
20. Kim, J., Lee, H.Y., Christensen, M.C., Merighi, J.R.: Technology access and use, and their associations with social engagement among older adults: do women and men differ? J. Gerontol. Ser. B **72**(5), 836–845 (2017)
21. Silverstone, R., Hirsch, E.: Consuming Technologies: Media and Information in Domestic Spaces. Routledge; CRC Press, Abingdon (1993)
22. Sala, E., Gaia, A.: Older People’s use of «information and communication technology» in Europe. The Italian Case. Autonomielocali e servizi sociali, February 2019 (2019)
23. Glaser, B., Strauss, A.: The Discovery of Grounded Theory. Weidenfeld and Nicholson, London (1967)
24. Loos, E.F.: Senior citizens: digital immigrants in their own country? Observatorio (OBS*) J. **6**(1), 1–23 (2012)
25. Peacock, S.E., Künemund, H.: Senior citizens and internet technology. Eur. J. Ageing **4**(4), 191–200 (2007)
26. Loos, E.F.: Generational use of new media and the (ir)relevance of age. In: Colombo, F., Fortunati, L. (eds.) Broadband Society and Generational Changes, pp. 259–273. Peter Lang, Berlin (2011)
27. van Dijk, J.A.G.M.: The evolution of the digital divide—the digital divide turns to inequality of skills and usage. Digit. Enlightenment Yearb. **2012**, 57–78 (2012)
28. Carlo, S., Vergani, M.: Benefici e rischi percepiti negli usi delle ICT tra gli anziani italiani. Stud. Sociol. **54**(2), 169–186 (2016)
29. Setftersten, R.A., Lovegreen, L.D.: Educational experiences throughout adult life: new hopes or no hope for life-course flexibility? Res. Aging **20**(4), 506–538 (1998)
30. Paz, A., Doron, I., Tur-Sinai, A.: Gender, aging, and the economics of "active aging": setting a new research agenda. J. Women Aging **30**(3), 184–203 (2018)

Barriers and Facilitators to Technology Among Older Adults During COVID-19 Pandemic: A Systematic Review Using Thematic Analysis

Susann Keohane[1,2(✉)], Caroline Swarbrick[1], and Sumi Helal[1,3]

[1] Centre for Health Research, Lancaster University, Lancaster, UK
skeohane@us.ibm.com
[2] Digital Health, IBM Corporation, Armonk, USA
[3] Computer Information Science and Engineering, University of Florida, Gainesville, USA

Abstract. World Health Organization and local governments recommended that older adults self-isolate due to the elevated risk for adverse health outcomes faced when contracting COVD-19. Technology offers better access to virtual communications for social connections and healthcare. Yet, the barriers and facilitators of older adults' use of technology during this world-changing event are, for the most part, unknown. The purpose of this paper is to synthesize using inductive thematic analysis the literature on broader health and social impacts on older adults from lockdown-related measures caused by the pandemic. The findings consisted of three dichotomous themes regarding older adults' barriers and facilitators to technology. The first theme centers on personal belief and perception of oneself. The second theme explores the digital literacy continuum. The third theme focuses on older adults' barriers and facilitators when adopting technology. The practical significance of these findings is to better inform the design and delivery of accessible technology to older adults.

Keywords: Older adults · Technology · Pandemic

1 Introduction

As many countries forced a self-isolation policy during the COVID-19 pandemic, better access to virtual communications for social connections and healthcare became imperative to improve the well-being of older adults. World Health Organization and local governments recommended that people aged 65 and older self-isolate because contracting COVD-19 brought elevated risk for adverse health outcomes in the aging population [1]. Because older adults are disproportionally affected by the COVID-19 pandemic, it is critical to understand the barriers and facilitators to technology adoption during this world-changing event.

This paper synthesizes the literature on broader health and social impacts on older adults from lockdown-related measures caused by the pandemic. The themes in the literature were identified and assessed using a thematic synthesis method with inductive coding. The purpose of this review is to learn from the lived experiences of older adults.

Q. Gao and J. Zhou (Eds.): HCII 2022, LNCS 13330, pp. 466–484, 2022.
https://doi.org/10.1007/978-3-031-05581-2_33

The practical significance is understanding the key themes to better inform the design and delivery of accessible technology to older adults.

2 Method

In preparation for the systematic literature review, a pilot search was conducted to inform and improve the search strategy. The goal of the pilot search was to identify a set of gold standard articles that are relevant to the topic and will be used to test the accuracy of the final search results. Key terms were refined and re-evaluated using an iterative approach to identify and capture the gold standard articles. A Lancaster University librarian supported the search strategy in online consultations.

The pilot search yielded six gold standard articles to validate the final search results. Given the anticipation of a high number of studies in this area, proximity operators were used, including words like acceptance, barriers, and attitudes, to yield more precise and inclusive search results. The final search strategy (Table 1) was run against titles and abstracts of peer-reviewed studies for six databases (i.e., Cumulative Index to Nursing and Allied Health Literature (CINAHL), MEDLINE, Academic Search Ultimate, PsycINFO, Web of Science, and Scopus), resulting in 8498 articles. After importing

Table 1. Search strategy

Concept	Synonym		Similar	
COVID	covid* or coronavirus* or "corona* virus*" or coronovirus* or "corono* virus*" or coronavirinae* or "corona* virinae*" or Cov or "2019-nCoV*" or 2019nCoV* or "19-nCoV*" or 19nCoV* or nCoV2019* or "nCoV2019*" or nCoV19* or "nCoV-19*" or "HCoV-19*" or HCoV19* or "HCoV-2019*" or HCoV2019* or "2019 novel*" or Ncov* or "n-cov" or "COVID-19" or COVID-19 or "Coronovirus Disease 2019" or pandemic	OR	"SARS-CoV-2*" or "SARSCoV-2*" or "SARSCoV2*" or "SARS-CoV2*" or SARSCov19* or "SARS-Cov19*" or "SARSCov-19*" or "SARS-Cov-19*" or SARSCov2019* or "SARS-Cov2019*" or "SARSCov-2019*" or "SARSCov-2019*" or SARS2* or "SARS-2*" or SARScoronavirus2* or "SARS-coronavirus-2*" or "SARScoronavirus 2*" or "SARS coronavirus2*" or SARScoronovirus2* or "SARScoronovirus-2*" or "SARScoronovirus 2*" or "SARS coronovirus2*" or "severe acute respiratory syndrome*"	AND

(*continued*)

Table 1. (*continued*)

Concept	Synonym		Similar	
Technology	technolog* or "smart tech*" or "digital technology" or digital or videoconferenc* or "video conferenc*" or zoom or skype or "virtual reality" or telehealth or tele-health or "tele health" or "digital health" or "mobile health" or "tele-medicine" or "tele medicine" or "telemedicine" or eHealth or "virtual care" or virtual or internet or digital or email or e-mail or alexa or "app" or "instant messaging" or "search engines" or "social networking" or "online shopping" or "telecare" or "smart homes" or robots or gerontechnology or "home health technology" or WhatsApp or "smart watch" or Fitbit or ICT or "internet-based communications" or "social media" or "online social contact" or "social network" or mHealth or "internet communication" or Facetime or "video chatting"	N/10	accept* or barrier* or understand* or useful* or reject* or confiden* or frail* or ability or literac* or access or attitude or utilizati* or activ* or facilitators, attitudes or beliefs or behaviors or behaviours	
Older adults	elder* or geriatric* or grandmother* or grandfather or grand-father* or grand-mother* or grand-parent* or grandparent* or older or aged or senior or old or senior or aging or ageing	N/5	citizen* or person* or population* or parent* or man or woman or men or women or male or female or segment, participants or people or adults or patients	

these studies into EndNote 20 software for de-duplication and removal of non-English articles, 4955 articles advanced to the screening step.

The inclusion criteria included articles published in English, in a peer-reviewed journal, targeted at adults aged 60 years or above, and presented results from the analysis of primary outcomes. Included studies focused on the phenomenon of interest using a qualitative method to capture the lived experience and views of independent older adults on using technology during the pandemic. The exclusion criteria were studies focused on older adults with cognitive impairment (e.g., dementia, Alzheimer's) who lived in a long-term nursing facility (e.g., nursing home, institution, or hospital) and did not personally interact with technology. The titles and abstracts screening resulted in thirty-nine articles retrieved for full-text eligibility screening. The full-text screening led to the removal of fifteen articles due to not meeting the inclusion criteria.

The Preferred Reporting Items for Systematic Reviews and Meta-Analyses (PRISMA) guideline (Fig. 1) presents the search strategy that resulted in twenty-four articles identified for analysis. The quality of each study was assessed using the Critical Appraisal Skills Programme (CASP) Qualitative Checklist [2] tool, resulting in half of the articles rated as high quality, third of the articles rated as medium quality, and the rest as low quality.

The information was extracted and analyzed from the studies following the thematic synthesis method guidance developed by Thomas and Harden [3]. The literature was imported into the software package NVivo 12 for data organization, management, and

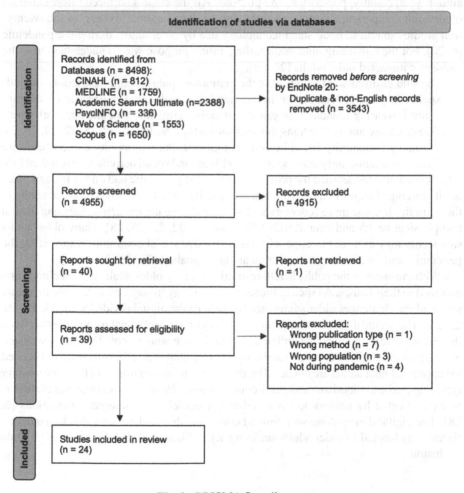

Fig. 1. PRISMA flow diagram

coding. Following a thematic analysis as defined by Braun and Clarke [4], an iterative inductive coding process was implemented. The codebook was tested and refined with each reading of the literature focusing on the critical aspects related to the research questions.

3 Literature Summary

In March 2020, the World Health Organization declared the COVID-19 outbreak a global pandemic [5]. Across the globe, government-imposed restrictions went into effect to reduce the viral spread amongst citizens. The twenty-four articles in the literature review span thirteen countries across six continents and have 2317 older adults who participated in open-ended surveys and semi-structured interviews during the pandemic. The literature summary shown in Table 2 provides a synopsis of each article, including author, year, country, population, and purpose. All the studies surfaced information on older adults' experience with technology during the pandemic. Fifteen of the twenty-four studies sought to understand technology use by older adults during the pandemic [6–20]. For the remaining nine studies, the guiding purpose was to understand how the pandemic impacted older adults [21–29].

The studies discussed the impact of the mandatory public health restrictions, including shelter-in-place orders, stay-at-home mandates, lockdowns, curfew laws, quarantines, mask wearing mandates, physical distancing guidelines, public space closures, travel restrictions, and public transport shutdowns [6, 7, 9, 13–15, 17, 18, 22–24, 26, 28, 29]. At many community-living housing complexes, the community centers, exercise facilities, restaurants, and game rooms were closed, and social activities were halted [18, 22]. Several articles detailed the profound impact the pandemic had on the lives of older adults forcing changes in their daily routines [9, 16, 17, 21, 23, 26]. The older adults in these studies became more sedentary and isolated during the pandemic, harming mental and physical health and overall well-being [14, 17, 22, 23, 25, 28]. Many older adults saw technology as a tool to cope with the restrictive social conditions imposed by the pandemic, and its use was to support meaningful goals [6, 7, 13, 19, 21–29].

With the onset of the public health restrictions, many older adults were secluded and confined to their homes. As society turned to technology to stay connected, the literature surfaced the challenges older adults face because of the digital divide [6, 13, 14, 16, 20, 22, 24]. The digital divide is "the economic, educational, and social inequalities between those who have computers and online access and those who do not" (Merriam-Webster, n.d.). The main challenges are cost and access to technology and the infrastructure needed to support it. Older adults are impacted by the digital divide regardless of their community type (e.g., urban, suburban, and rural communities). However, the rural population is heavily affected by limited access to reliable electricity and internet connections [6, 28]. The digital divide along with limited contact with social network due to pandemic restrictions has led to older adults suffering what Ekoh et al. [6] describes as "double exclusion".

Table 2. Literature summary

First author	Year	Country	Participants	Purpose
Bakshi [6]	2021	India	N = 30	Explore the experience older adults, living in urban India, had with technology during COVID
Bardach [7]	2021	USA	N = 30	Understand how to support older adults with technology to inform the development of training interventions
Carenzio [8]	2021	Italy	N = 24	Explore older adults' digital competencies, internet use, and desired support and training
Chen [21]	2020	USA	N = 10	Gather the perspective of older adults during the onset of the pandemic through a group discussion forum
Daly [22]	2021	USA	N = 21	Assess the impact the pandemic has on the mental and physical health of older adults
Ekoh [9]	2021	Nigeria	N = 11	Explore how older adults in Nigeria are dealing with double exclusion from the digital divide and pandemic

(continued)

Table 2. (*continued*)

First author	Year	Country	Participants	Purpose
Greenwood-Hickman [23]	2021	USA	N = 25	Understand directly from older adult narratives how the pandemic affected their mental, social, and physical health and to characterize the ways they were coping with these challenges
Javanparast [10]	2021	Australia	N = 30	Explore the telehealth experience of patients at high risk of poor health outcomes during the pandemic to discern the value of continuing with telehealth visits post-pandemic
Jiwani [11]	2021	USA	N = 20	Explore modified behavioral lifestyle intervention using mHealth and the impact of "real world" stressors due to the pandemic
Johnson [12]	2021	USA	N = 33	Identify the barriers and facilitators of older adults' adoption of teledermatology during the pandemic
Kotwal [24]	2021	USA	N = 115	Understand experiences of social isolation and loneliness among older adults during the COVID-19 pandemic and health needs stemming from changes in social interaction is needed

(*continued*)

Table 2. (*continued*)

First author	Year	Country	Participants	Purpose
Lee [25]	2021	USA	N = 18	Understand how COVID-19 affected older adults' mobility and daily lives
Liu [26]	2021	China	N = 248	Explain the underlying causes of old adults' persistence of mobility
Llorente-Barroso [13]	2021	Spain	N = 27	Explore the impact of the use of ICT on the emotional well-being of elderly people during their confinement
Lopez [14]	2021	Canada	N = 20	Explore the impact of pandemic on older adults' social connection and digital connectivity
McCabe [15]	2021	Scotland	N = 10	Explore the design and delivery of technological interventions to create solutions to reduce the impingement of older adults' human rights to fully participate in society
O'Connell [16]	2021	Canada	N = 25	Explore older adults' perceptions, barriers, and facilitators when using of videoconferencing platform for social interaction

(*continued*)

Table 2. (*continued*)

First author	Year	Country	Participants	Purpose
Pisula [27]	2021	Argentina	N = 39	Explore the emerging needs related to the mental health of isolated older adults in this period and to identify their main support networks they have and the emerging coping strategies in the face of the situation
Rao [17]	2020	India	N = 15	Understand older adults needs, preferences, and problems associated with using technology for managing their routine health and fitness
Saldanha [18]	2020	Canada	N = 1	Provides the perspectives and experiences of an active senior in an independent living facility who transitioned to online groups during the pandemic
Tomaz [28]	2021	Scotland	N = 1198	Explores the impact of social distancing during the COVID-19 pandemic on loneliness, wellbeing, and social activity, including social support, in Scottish older adults
vonHumboldt [19]	2020	Italy, Mexico, Portugal, and Spain	N = 351	Understand smart technology's impact on the meaning of life for older adults during COVID
Wagner [29]	2021	Austria	N = 8	Explores how older adults' lives have changed because of the pandemic

(*continued*)

Table 2. (*continued*)

First author	Year	Country	Participants	Purpose
Wang [20]	2021	China	N = 8	Explores how the COVID-19 pandemic high-lighted the age-based mobile digital divide in China, and what are the implications for gerontological internet-based social work

4 Findings

4.1 Dichotomous Themes

Three dichotomous themes regarding older adults' barriers and facilitators to technology were identified in the literature analysis.

Theme 1 - Personal belief and perceptions of oneself	
Keep up with the times	Diminished future time
Overcome fear	Internalized agism
Strong independence, empowerment	Lack of confidence

Theme 2 - Digital literacy continuum			
Prior experience with technology	Digital literacy is tied to purpose and social connection	Real-time learning	New normal

Theme 3 – Barriers and facilitators	
Physical abilities and native language	Technology support from Family
Cost and infrastructure	Supporting peer

The first theme centers on personal belief and perception of oneself. On one end of the spectrum, findings indicated that older adults cited strong perseverance to keep up with the times, overcome fear, and strive for independence. On the other end of the spectrum, the findings noted that older adults who had internalized ageism perceived a diminished future lifespan, viewed technology as only for the youth, and had an overall lack of confidence in adopting technology into their lives.

The second theme explores the digital literacy continuum. The American Library Association defines digital literacy as "the ability to use information and communication technologies to find, evaluate, create, and communicate information, requiring both cognitive and technical skills" [30]. The digital literacy continuum plots the progression of someone with no digital skills to someone who has mastered competency with technology. Whereas some older adults began the pandemic as digital literates, others started the pandemic digital illiterate. Irrelevant to where they started, the primary factor driving the decision to improve their technology skills depended on the purpose of use.

Some adults came into the pandemic with competencies due to prior workplace exposure to technology. Purpose-driven need motivated the move along the digital continuum to reach a certain level of digital competency. Older adults require specific and straightforward training to help with the transition to become digitally literate and independent technology users. There was a greater emphasis on real-time learning to acquire knowledge to meet an immediate need.

The third theme focuses on the barriers and facilitators older adults faced when adopting technology. Barriers to technology included physical limitations, limited infrastructure, and financial costs. Older adults were often in digital poverty, measured by one's ability to afford and access technology. Family, friends, and peers were the most significant facilitators to technology use in older adults.

4.2   Theme 1 - Personal Belief and Perceptions of Oneself

Keep Up with the Times. Resilience and perseverance enable older adults to adapt to adversity caused by the pandemic and, no matter the difficulties or opposition, to continue trying to achieve their desired outcome. Some older adults revealed a positive personal view of technology with comments like: "I love technology!" and "I'm an old fella, but I love modern technology" [6, p.3]. One older adult overcame the negative typecasting of older adults with strong perseverance: "I'm still living in this world, and things are changing, I mean things are changing so fast that you have to keep up! Or you're left behind" [14, p. 291]. For these older adults, it was vital to keep up with the times: "Technology wasn't in our time, but it is in our time now… when I retired I realised I was going to be left behind, I had stayed up with everything during my working life but realised that I would be left behind, so I went out and bought all the gear" [15, p. 10]. These older adults believed their age did not impact their ability to learn: "I might be old, but I still am teachable. It's just a whole new, way of doing things and learning. I guess I want to know, some seniors I think maybe don't want to know. But I want to know. And so, and I'd like to know, I don't like to be left" [14, p. 290]. Nothing was going to stop these older adults from learning new technology: "I would be willing to learn how to use the app… They're (apps) important, they really do help in times like this…like Zoom" [12, p. 1586].

Overcome Fear. Along the continuum, the literature reveals that some older adults expressed fear, anxiety, and isolation when adopting technology: "I really wish I could use the computer… It's time I learn a little technology. I'll be stuck at home; the world will pass me by. All my friends are on the Internet" [24, p. 25]. For one participant, the fear corresponded with the initial use. Still, then she became more comfortable: "once I found out not to be afraid of technology, I was a lot more comfortable…I learned that I cannot break it if I make a mistake" [7, p. 4]. During the pandemic, older adults slowly increased their adoption: "It does feel a bit isolated but I have replaced some direct contact with online communications" [21, p. 192]. One participant showed pride in overcoming his fear of technology: "at first, I was afraid of losing things with technology. Now I love all this stuff and ability to do things. No fear anymore" [7, p. 4]. Some boldly repudiated the ageist stereotype, like one participant who stated: "I'm fine with it [technology], I'm not one of those little old ladies that is scared of it" [7, p. 5].

Strong Independence, Empowerment. As older adults gained competency with digital technology, it brought a strong sense of independence and empowerment. One participant shared their view of learning technologies as "very important to develop myself emotionally, physically and economically. I feel more empowered, I feel I grew up another step" [19, p. 718]. Many older adults were interested in developing their digital competencies to be "more autonomous" and not having to "depend on others" [8, p. 13]. One participant shared their journey to independence leading to a high self-efficacy: "before I depended a lot on my children, now I learned a lot on my own; maybe with their help, but I had to learn myself" [27, p. 6].

Diminished Future Time. Finally, on the opposite end, personal beliefs and perceptions of oneself were based on a perceived age limitation. Some older adults perceived how much time they had left to live in this world as a limitation to learning and using technology. This sentiment aligns with Socioemotional Selectivity Theory (SST), which states that as we age, we become more selective with our activities as our future time perspective diminishes; our motivation shifts from knowledge acquisition to emotionally rewarding goals [31]. SST explains the older adults who felt too old to bother with technology. One participant's response toward learning new technology was that she is "not interested at all. I'm 87 and won't be around much longer" [7, p. 4]. Another participant explained: "I don't find it necessary at my age"; "not anymore, you know?! My mind is too tired" [8, p. 11]. Some participants felt they reached the age where it was unnecessary: "no, I don't want to use technology more. If I were 5 years younger it would be entirely different" [7, p. 4]. Another participant expanded on the idea of being too old for technology, stating there is more benefit to technology if he was younger: "I think it would depend on my age! I mean if I'm 92 I'm not going to worry about it. In my 80s, early 80s I would probably go ahead and do it" [12, p. 1591].

Internalized Agism. Social messaging has ingrained an idea that technology is primarily for the youth. The media often depict older people struggling to use or manage technology, such as the Saturday Night Live [32] sketch about an Amazon Echo Silver for Seniors. While the intent is to be humorous, it works like most stereotypes to undermine views of older adults as technology users. Many participants perceived that modern technology solutions are for young people and do not benefit older adults. Some older adults kindly reject technology with a fondness for traditions or ideas from the past: "I don't get on with the computer, I'm a bit old-fashioned" [10, p. 4]. Other older adults expressed an outright renunciation, characterizing the use of technology as frivolous and lacking any worthwhile purpose. As stated by one participant's lack of interest in technology: "no I can't feel bad about that I'm not a child" [9, p. 636].

The negative stereotyping of older adults' use of technology feeds into a harmful narrative, which may become a self-fulfilling prophecy that can impact technology use. The stereotype depicts older adults as incompetent learners who are incapable of using technology. Older adults internalize the agism and believe they could not learn or use technology solely because of their age. As one participant reflected on technology: "I am too old to start learning such things" [9, p. 637]. For those older adults who struggle with internalized ageism, a problematic experience using technology can further reinforce their negative perception as incompetent learners.

Lack of Confidence. A challenge accompanying internalized ageism is low perceived self-efficacy and many older adults who lack confidence in their ability resign themselves as perceptual novices. One participant described how society's rapid adoption of technology made him feel inferior: "my only concern would be my personal incapability of using iPhones like everybody else uses them… it's not a comfort zone for me" [12, p. 1586]. The lack of comfort lends itself to self-blame and despair, as shared by a participant: "I am limited by not being comfortable on my iPhone for anything other than as a telephone, e-mail, texts, and banking. It is my own fault so I get down on myself for that" [24, p. 25]. The dependency on others for help seems inevitable, as expressed by a participant: "when your PC crashes and you don't have the basic notions to work on it and you always have to ask for external help" [8, p. 11]. Ultimately, internalized ageism manifests as a lack of confidence that impacts older adults from reaching a proficiency level to achieve the desired outcome: "taking online classes and preparing ppt is a new thing for senior teachers like us. So I'm struggling, learning and relearning to get used to the new normal" [6, p. 199].

4.3   Theme 2 - Digital Literacy Continuum (Directional Dichotomy)

At the onset of the pandemic, older adults could land on various points along the digital literacy continuum, with some starting with a higher degree of computer literacy and others having none. Those with a higher degree of digital literacy often had prior exposure to technology in the workplace. The personal computer entered the market in the mid-1980s and changed the workplace [33]. Younger older adults, individuals in their 60s, more than likely had an opportunity to use computers in the workplace compared to someone in their 80s [33]. Older adults of today are not the older adults of tomorrow. So, the younger older adults may have more exposure to technology, but technology continues to evolve. Tablets, smartphones, mobile applications, and the sharing economy entered the market in the 2010s. The evolution of new technology causes an ever-expanding digital literacy continuum. The literature analysis shows that emotionally meaningful goals were the greatest motivator for older adults to gain the necessary knowledge to move along the continuum.

Prior Experience with Technology. Some participants acknowledge that they had developed functional competencies with technology before the pandemic [6, 8, 13, 14]. One participant described her level of comfort with computers: "we had a computer when computers-personal computers were really new. And we've always had them since then" [14, p. 292]. Participants with more digital literacy had higher educational levels and previous work experience exposure to technology. Older adults who had higher levels of self-efficacy had computer training at her workplace and were required to use technology as part of their careers: "I started with the PC when there was no Windows, eh… because of my job, I had to take all possible and imaginable courses and, in particular, get a PC… immediately" [8, p. 11]. These participants believe their use of technology when they were younger positively impacted their current use during the pandemic. Their use of technology earlier in life provided them the confidence to adopt new technology: "I did not use the internet a lot before COVID-19. Now, I do use it more to shop than going into the stores, even for household items … I started with computers and worked in a business in 80's … I'm not afraid of computers. I was able to load Zoom on my phone, on my iPad, and on my laptop without any problems. That was surprising to me" [26, p. 4].

Digital Literacy is Tied to Purpose and Social Connection. Technology was purpose-driven for older adults who lacked digital literacy. Acquiring new competency was typically associated with a specific upcoming need rather than a general desire to increase competence. The perceived benefit of the technology eclipsed even low perceptions of personal competency and compelled them to put forth the effort and time needed to learn new technology. During the pandemic, an example of the purpose-driven use of technology was to stay connected to friends and family: "Connecting with my grandchildren over the video call. That was the driving force…empowering me to move forward" [13, p. 12]. Other participants learned new technologies to stay connected: "We've tried to learn the new technology as much as possible so we can at least try to stay connected through different types of social media and using Zoom and stuff, to visit that way, and that's been really helpful" [23, p. 7]. Most older adults preferred human interaction: "There's nothing like being able to sit down and look into a person's eyes and verbally express what's in a person's heart" [7, p. 4]. Even though physical contact is preferred, older adults use technology to stay connected: "It was hard not having close contact with family but we FaceTimed daily" [28, p. 15]. Some older adults are resigned to technology use because it's necessary during the pandemic: "I do not like using technology but do because it is the means to communicate" [24, p. 25]. Another example of a specific need driving older adults' technology use was to acquire groceries safely: "I'm trying to figure out how to order my groceries online" [7, p. 5]. Once older adults gain the technological competency to meet specific needs, they become fulfilled with their new knowledge: "I don't know of anything I would want to do that I can't already do" [7, p. 4].

The importance of technology to help them emotionally cope with the confinement and safety issues brought forth by the pandemic led even those with a lower level of digital literacy to step outside their comfort and learn how to use technology to meet their goals. Equipping older adults with an understanding of the benefits and addressing their training needs empowers their use of technology: "I like the idea of more Zoom activities for meetings and things like that. The one thing that is needed, though, is a concerted effort to educate people and help them set their computers up [22, p. 5).

Real-Time Learning. The literature revealed how the training was a vital part of enabling older adults to move along the continuum to reach a level of digital literacy. The training empowered older adults to use technology and helped them move along the continuum to reach a level of digital literacy. Findings revealed that easy-to-follow learning material facilitated independence, but complicated material was a barrier. One participant shared her struggle with complex training: "after, certain point of time, it becomes difficult to follow or remember the steps. So, the more the instructions are simple and 'nontechnical' the easier it is. Luckily in my case whenever I have asked for help in such matters, I didn't get any undignified responses from my children" [6, p. 199]. Many adults expressed a need for additional or refresher training to avoid dependency on others: "I know the basis of online payments, but I wish I learnt all about it previously so that I did not have to call up my son or ask my neighbour to guide me through the steps" [6, p. 197]. The fear of relearning causes older adults to be locked into outdated technology. As an example, for older adults, upgrading from a mobile flip phone to a smartphone and learning and using mobile apps was often difficult and even frustrating because "there are always new functions or updates I don't know how to deal with" [20, p. 55]. It seems to indicate the need for real-time learning and knowledge acquisition based on immediate needs: "training needs to be right then, because if I do it way ahead, I will forget" [7, p. 5].

New Normal. Contrary to the stereotype that technology is for the youth, the pandemic has proven older adults can and want to adopt technology into their lives. As one participant said: "sometimes new situations are good to break up myth" [19, p. 716]. Older adults use technology to accomplish rewarding activities and express appreciation for technology during lockdowns: "the virtual thing is a blessing" [18, p. 5). The primary use of technology focused on staying connected with family and friends: "You can be isolated in home during the lockdown and not feel isolated at all because you can instantly connect with anyone at any part of the world. I make video calls to my grandchildren because I don't want to miss seeing them grow inch by inch during this period" [6, p. 197]. Some participants found video conferencing software improved their pre-pandemic connections: "I am communicating more than ever, I have a new friend…I guess I want to say I am better with technology" [24, p. 25].

Because of social distancing, technology has replaced in-person activities: "I did not use the internet a lot before COVID-19. Now, I do use it more to shop rather than going into the stores, even for household items" [25, p. 4]. Older adults' religious engagement has moved online: "I continue to attend masses, but now on the internet" [19, p. 717]. Cultural institutions have adjusted to serving older adults during the pandemic better: "Church has a livestream. I'm doing Zoom now as far as we have Bible study" [25, p. 4]. The use of the specific application has been beneficial for social distancing requirements: "Zoom opportunities have substituted for some religious and exercise programs that I previously would attend in person" [24, p. 25]. Older adults have adapted to using technology for one specific purpose and expanded to use it for other purposes: "I do some Zoom stuff like Zoom exercise and book club" [24, p. 25]. Older adults seek out other technology to serve their interest: "I have explored the topics that interest me on YouTube, I listen to podcasts, I have time to explore important apps. Technology has served my interests" [19, p. 718]. Older adults have transitioned from purpose-driven use of technology to using it for entertainment: "the last year and a half I really came into YouTube and I'm enjoying it. Love some information and learning" [25, p. 5]. For older adults, digital literacy in the pandemic ushered in a new normal of daily technology use: "Today, I used the computer to check my emails and order some useful products for the family from Amazon, [and I used] the smartphone to check the bank account and the tablet to read the news of the local newspapers" [8, p. 10].

4.4 Theme 3 - Barriers vs facilitators

Physical Abilities and Native Language. Physical abilities and native language barriers are impediments to digital literacy. Older adults grow into physical challenges that make technology use difficult, including but not limited to lack of dexterity, hearing loss, and poor vision. To overcome dexterity issues, one user chose to use voice-activated control; however, new challenges emerged: "only thing is that I don't have the dexterity of…people… I don't like…texting. I don't have the feeling.., That's why I will often dictate…for texts. And I get frustrated 'cause…Siri doesn't…understand me" [12, p. 1587]. Unfortunately, older adults with physical impairments might not realize how to modify their devices to accommodate their impairment. One participant said she is "always looking for my eyeglasses" when options exist to enlarge the text on the screen [20, p. 55]. Some older adults experience from mild cognitive impairment can make memory recall difficult. One participant kept written notes to refer to when making a WhatsApp video. The training notes were necessary to remind her of the steps as she would "forget if not used frequently" [17, p. 39]. Others found using the on-screen keyboard to be discomforting: "the (smartphone) screen is too small" and "I hate typing on the mobile phone" regretting not having purchased a "mobile phone with a big screen" [20, p. 55]. For non-English language users: "not having a good hold of English" seems the main obstacle to technology use [17, p. 39]. The default language setting on many devices is English. This default setting will present the on-screen keyboard in English, and users do not know they can install an on-screen keyboard in their native language. The physical abilities and native language barriers are not addressed because, as one participant shares: "the people designing the technology are not sitting in our world" [15, p. 9].

Cost and Infrastructure. Financial costs and physical infrastructure may exacerbate access to technology. For those with access to technology, the cost of internet service was potentially prohibitive: "the hospital was where I could just go in because they had different activities for the seniors. They still have a program online, but I don't have access to that [the internet]" [25, p. 5]. Technology was around them but not available to them: "I don't have it (smartphone) oh, but some people do show me things that happens in there" [9, p. 635]. Some older adults understand the benefits of technology and stated that they would like to own a smart phone to connect to their children and relatives. Still, the cost was a prohibitor: "I heard that I can even be seeing my children on the phone if I have that kind of phone, but I cannot afford to buy that kind of phone. If my children can buy it for me, it will be good oh. At least I will be seeing them whenever I want" [9, p. 636]. The lack of access made it problematic for older adults to participate in social events online: "I try to use Zoom every Sunday, but everybody else is on the internet so it's hard to get it in the mornings because I don't have the best internet service. But yes, I do. I try to watch something as far as I can go, as long as my internet is working" [25, p. 5]. Older adults who reside in rural regions are impacted by limited electricity, lack of internet service, and the cost of digital devices. One rural participant recommended a focus on improving the infrastructure: "in this village, we don't always have light [electricity]. How will I charge the phone if I have a phone? I can't start going to look for where to charge the phone like all these children. They should start giving us constant electricity first before you talk about us using phones" [9, p. 363].

Technology Support from Family. When needing support with technology, older adults expressed relying on children, grandchildren, and other family members. The supportive tasks include acquiring and setting up devices, suggesting software or social media applications, downloading software onto devices, and training participants to navigate the devices and software. One participant shared that she "went to buy a "ludo" board, but the shops were closed. So my granddaughter has downloaded it on my phone" [6, p. 197]. Another participant expressed having to "ask my granddaughter again and again" because "the (interface of) those apps are so complicated" [20, p. 55]. Many older adults needed guidance from family to set up social media applications like Zoom: "The majority of my activities and Drs. visits can be done by Zoom. I have help from granddaughter or others if I have a technology issue. I am trying to update my skills" [24, p. 25]. Grandchildren appear to be a great source of supportive help: "I use that [Facetime] whenever my grandkids call. Nobody had been able to teach me how to use it. They walked me through it. You call that number and then their face pops up. My granddaughter told me that. That's all you gotta do Grandma, it's not that hard" [25, p. 5].

Supporting Peers. As older adults become comfortable with technology, they can gain the skills independently: "In this time I learned a lot about technology and that and the positive side of it." [27, p. 6]. The newly gained confidence enabled them to encourage others, as one participant stated: "Well I will try to encourage my friends to use Zoom more. Not just so I can talk to them but, also, I think it would be a benefit to them" [16, p. 5]. As older adults become more independent and competent with technology, they expressed the desire to help others their age: "I have learned more … [about] technology … I had opportunity to help other people through technology" [24, p. 25]. Another participant shared how her new skills enabled her to support her peers: "It reassures me that I can connect. I've used Zoom for different types of meetings like [community group],… and a new member orientation meeting where I had to give a presentation. And I was able to provide support and advice to the new members just like others do to me. So, Zoom lets me be social" [16, p. 5].

5 Conclusion

Older adults may be disproportionately affected by lockdown-related efforts to contain the COVID-19 pandemic because they tend to have more significant health problems. Pre-pandemic inequities due to the digital divide impacted older adults on multiple levels: access, skills and usage, and the tangible outcomes from the use of technology. Due to the pandemic, the government-imposed lockdown, travel restrictions, and ongoing social distancing limited older adults' physical and social contact. The lockdown and the digital divide inequities amplified older adults' isolation, causing a double exclusion.

The findings re-emphasize older adults are not a homogenous population that can be easily segmented solely by the length of time a person has lived. The literature review surfaced interesting dichotomous themes regarding older adults' acceptance and adoption of technology. Older adults' resilience affects how technology can impact their aging experience in a positive and empowering way. The rewards can be life-changing for those who persevere with technology during a pandemic: staying connected with family and friends during self-isolation, utilizing digital services to complete tasks like acquiring groceries, and increasing independence.

References

1. World Health Organization Older people & COVID-19 website. https://www.who.int/teams/social-determinants-of-health/demographic-change-and-healthy-ageing/covid-19. Accessed 01 Feb 2022
2. Critical Appraisal Skills Programme (CASP) Qualitative Checklist. https://casp-uk.b-cdn.net/wp-content/uploads/2018/03/CASP-Qualitative-Checklist-2018_fillable_form.pdf. Accessed 01 Feb 2022
3. Thomas, J., Harden, A.: Methods for the thematic synthesis of qualitative research in systematic reviews. BMC Med. Res. Methodol. **8**, 1–10 (2008)
4. Braun, V., Clarke, V.: Qualitative research in psychology using thematic analysis in psychology using thematic analysis in psychology. Qual. Res. Psychol. **3**(2), 77–101 (2006)
5. World Health Organization Director-General's opening remarks at the media briefing on COVID-19 website. https://www.who.int/director-general/speeches/detail/who-director-general-s-opening-remarks-at-the-media-briefing-on-covid-19---11-march-2020. Accessed 01 Feb 2022
6. Bakshi, T., Bhattacharyya, A.: Socially distanced or socially connected? Well-being through ICT usage among the Indian elderly during COVID-19. Millennial Asia **12**(2), 190–208 (2021)
7. Bardach, S.H., Rhodus, E.K., Parsons, K., Gibson, A.K.: Older adults' adaptations to the call for social distancing and use of technology: insights from socioemotional selectivity theory and lived experiences. J. Appl. Gerontol. **40**(8), 814–817 (2021)
8. Carenzio, A., Ferrari, S., Rasi, P.: Older people's media repertoires, digital competences and media literacies: a case study from Italy. Educ. Sci. **11**(10) (2021)
9. Ekoh, P.C., George, E.O., Ezulike, C.D.: Digital and physical social exclusion of older people in rural Nigeria in the time of COVID-19. J. Gerontol. Soc. Work **64**(6), 629–642 (2021)
10. Javanparast, S., Roeger, L., Kwok, Y., Reed, R.L.: The experience of Australian general practice patients at high risk of poor health outcomes with telehealth during the COVID-19 pandemic: a qualitative study. BMC Fam. Pract. **22**(1), 1–6 (2021)
11. Jiwani, R., et al.: Assessing acceptability and patient experience of a behavioral lifestyle intervention using fitbit technology in older adults to manage type 2 diabetes amid COVID-19 pandemic: a focus group study. Geriatr. Nurs. **42**(1), 57–64 (2021)
12. Johnson, A., et al.: Barriers and facilitators to mobile health and active surveillance use among older adults with skin disease. Health Expect. **24**, 1582–1592 (2021)
13. Llorente-Barroso, C., Kolotouchkina, O., Mañas-Viniegra, L.: The enabling role of ICT to mitigate the negative effects of emotional and social loneliness of the elderly during covid-19 pandemic. Int. J. Environ. Res. Publ. Health **18**(8) (2021)
14. Lopez, K.J., Tong, C., Whate, A., Boger, J.: "It's a whole new way of doing things": the digital divide and leisure as resistance in a time of physical distance. World Leisure J. **63**(3), 281–300 (2021)

15. McCabe, L., Dawson, A., Douglas, E., Barry, N.: Using technology the right way to support social connectedness for older people in the era of covid-19. Int. J. Environ. Res. Publ. Health **18**(16) (2021)

16. O'Connell, M.E., Haase, K.R., Grewal, K.S., Panyavin, I., Kortzman, A., Flath, M.E., Peacock, S.: Overcoming barriers for older adults to maintain virtual community and social connections during the COVID-19 pandemic. Clin. Gerontol. (2021)

17. Rao, P., Joshi, A.: Design opportunities for supporting elderly in India in managing their health and fitness post-covid-19. In: IndiaHCI 2020: 11th Indian Conference on Human-Computer Interaction, pp. 34–41 (2020)

18. Saldanha, K.: A view from the other side: a senior's view of participating in online groups during the pandemic. Soc. Work Groups (2020)

19. von Humboldt, S., et al.: Smart technology and the meaning in life of older adults during the Covid-19 public health emergency period: a cross-cultural qualitative study. Int. Rev. Psychiatry **32**(7–8), 713–722 (2020)

20. Wang, J., Katz, I., Li, J., Wu, Q., Dai, C.: Mobile digital divide and older people's access to 'Internet plus social work': implications from the COVID-19 help-seeking cases. Asia Pac. J. Soc. Work Dev. **31**(1–2), 52–58 (2021)

21. Chen, A.T., et al.: Reactions to COVID-19, information and technology use, and social connectedness among older adults with pre-frailty and frailty. Geriatr. Nurs. (42), 188–191 (2020)

22. Daly, J.R., et al.: Health impacts of the stay-at-home order on community-dwelling older adults and how technologies may help: focus group study. JMIR Aging **4**(1) (2021)

23. Greenwood-Hickman, M.A., et al.: "They're going to zoom it": a qualitative investigation of impacts and coping strategies during the COVID-19 pandemic among older adults. Front. Publ. Health **9**, 1–10 (2021)

24. Kotwal, A.A., et al.: Social isolation and loneliness among san francisco bay area older adults during the COVID-19 shelter-in-place orders. J. Am. Geriatr. Soc. **69**(1), 20–29 (2021)

25. Lee, K., et al.: Exploring factors enhancing resilience among marginalized older adults during the COVID-19 pandemic. J. Appl. Gerontol. 1–9 (2021)

26. Liu, Q., Liu, Y., Zhang, C., An, Z., Zhao, P.: Elderly mobility during the COVID-19 pandemic: a qualitative exploration in Kunming, China. J. Transp. Geogr. **96** (2021)

27. Pisula, P., et al.: Qualitative study on the elderly and mental health during the COVID-19 lock-down in Buenos Aires, Argentina - Part 1. Medwave **21**(4) (2021)

28. Tomaz, S.A., et al.: Loneliness, wellbeing, and social activity in Scottish older adults resulting from social distancing during the COVID-19 pandemic. Int. J. Environ. Res. Publ. Health **18**(9) (2021)

29. Wagner, P., Winkler, A., Paraschivoiu, I., Meschtscherjakov, A., Gärtner, M., Tscheligi, M.: Tracing COVID-19 - older adults' attitudes toward digital contact tracing and how to increase their participation. In: ACM International Conference Proceeding Series, pp. 349–353 (2021)

30. American Library Association: Digital Literacy (n.d.)

31. Carstensen, L.L., Isaacowitz, D.M., Charles, S.T.: Taking time seriously. Am. Psychol. **54**(3), 165–181 (1999)

32. Saturday Night Live Amazon Echo Silver. https://www.youtube.com/watch?v=YvT_gqs 5ETk. Accessed 01 Feb 2022

33. BBC How the computer changed the office forever. https://www.bbc.com/news/magazine-23509153. Accessed 01 Feb 2022

Virtual Cardiac Rehabilitation in a Pandemic Scenario: A Review of HCI Design Features, User Acceptance and Barriers

Irina Kondratova[1] (✉) ⓘ and Helene Fournier[2] ⓘ

[1] Human-Computer Interaction, Digital Technologies Research Centre, National Research Council Canada, Fredericton, New Brunswick, Canada
Irina.Kondratova@nrc-cnrc.gc.ca
[2] Human-Computer Interaction, Digital Technologies Research Centre, National Research Council Canada, Moncton, New Brunswick, Canada
Helene.Fournier@nrc-cnrc.gc.ca

Abstract. We report on the literature review of best practices in virtual cardiac rehabilitation (VCR), with a focus on technology usability, acceptance, and adoption barriers. We reviewed recent papers published in scientific conferences and journals on the topics of virtual cardiac rehabilitation and remote cardiac monitoring, with a publication dates from 2019 to 2021. Cardiovascular disease is a leading cause of mortality in elderly populations worldwide, and older adults are at an increased risk of COVID-19. Before the pandemic, the uptake of VCR technologies was slow due to concerns about technology effectiveness and cost. Since early 2020, better acceptance and adoption of VCR into routine care have been observed in many countries, including Canada. Some VCR components, like patient education or consultations are digitized relatively easy with online education sessions and resource repositories available for patients. Other elements such as supervised exercise and safe physical activity are more difficult to implement and require use of home cardiac monitoring technology. A proper HCI design of VCR services can contribute to better technology adoption by both service provider s and patients, and lead to improved patient outcomes. Design recommendations to increase adoption and improve user engagement with VCR by older adults include using multimodal interfaces, providing structured training and support, tailoring content and mode of delivery to the user, enabling automatic data transfer and easy integration across various systems and devices, improving accuracy of home cardiac monitoring devices, and conducting systematic technology validation studies, including remote usability evaluations for VCR technologies as part of the technology adoption life cycle.

Keywords: Virtual cardiac rehabilitation · Usability · Technology acceptance

1 Background

1.1 Virtual Cardiac Rehabilitation

This paper reports on the literature review of best practices in implementing virtual cardiac rehabilitation (VCR), with a focus on technology usability, acceptance, and adoption barriers. Cardiovascular disease (CVD) is a leading cause of mortality in elderly

Q. Gao and J. Zhou (Eds.): HCII 2022, LNCS 13330, pp. 485–499, 2022.
https://doi.org/10.1007/978-3-031-05581-2_34

populations. In developed countries, such as the USA, Europe, and Australia, the combined prevalence of CVD in those over 75 years of age is >50% for conditions, such as coronary heart disease, heart failure, arrhythmias, and stroke [1]. In Canada, 73% of individuals aged 65+ have at least one of ten chronic diseases including hypertension 65.7%; ischemic heart disease 27.0%; diabetes 26.8% and 60% having hypercholesterolemia [2]. Older adults are also at an increased risk of severe COVID-19 [3, 4].

Before the pandemic, the uptake of VCR technologies was slow due to concerns about effectiveness and cost of remote service delivery [1]. Recently, widespread acceptance and rapid adoption of VCR into routine care have been observed in many jurisdictions, including Canada [5, 6]. However, in Canada there is a lack of legislation to ensure equitable delivery of access to virtual care in rural areas [7], while these areas that are more dispersed and less populated could benefit the most from virtual care.

VCR is delivered by virtual mechanisms as a home-based cardiac rehabilitation. This could involve telephone and videoconferencing communication between patients and care providers, e-mail, mail, text messaging solutions, smartphone applications, online platforms, and use of wearable devices [8]. Remote monitoring, decision support and guidelines-recommended clinical algorithms could be applied in the management of cardiovascular risk in patients with no in-person visit required [9].

VCR patient education and care resources are digitized relatively easy, with education and specialist consultation sessions for patients conducted virtually via teleconferencing and document sharing. Other aspects such as supervised exercise and physical activity are more difficult to implement and require use of home cardiac monitoring, mobile and wearable technology. During COVID-19 pandemic public health measures such as social distancing and self-isolation can reduce exposure to the virus for senior adults, however, the resulting lack of timely healthcare access and the increased susceptibility to social isolation and loneliness is associated with poor physical and mental health outcomes [10]. The proper design of VCR services is of utmost importance since the usable design that encourages social interaction and behavioral change can contribute to positive patient outcomes, especially for older patients.

1.2 Technology Acceptance by Older Adults

It has been shown that older adults (65+) are at increasing risk of being digitally marginalized due to lower familiarity with technology, social isolation, and lack of resources, including peers who can provide the needed input [11]. Our recent study on technology acceptance in the context of home health monitoring supports these findings and reveals further insights into older adults' experience with technologies for home health monitoring [12]. Study participants reported many usability problems with home monitoring technology including stress in setting up a tablet for home health monitoring, not having full control of a tablet, difficulties with mobile and wearable device synchronization, and numerous software bugs. Other issues included technology reliability and stability, and lack of immediate technical support. Participants expressed their frustration in not being able to perform simple tasks due to the lack of training and manuals. The study concluded that negative experiences and frustration with technology, if not addressed, could lead to poor user experience with home health monitoring and low technology acceptance by older adults.

The technology acceptance model (TAM) is a widely used theoretical framework that examines how people accept and use a specific technology [13]. Two of the key adoption factors captured by the TAM are usability and perceived usefulness or utility. TAM has been previously used by HCI researchers that studied the factors affecting the adoption of technologies by older adults [14] and health care practitioners' determinants of tele-rehabilitation acceptance [15]. The Unified Theory of Acceptance and Use of Technology (UTAUT) has been also applied to digital healthcare and there is evidence in the literature that suggests that providing adequate support, and promoting trust in the technology can increase the acceptance (e.g., in patient healthcare professional interaction) and thus, potential use of digital health solutions [16].

For example, researchers used TAM model to evaluate older adults' adoption of the early warning wearable cardiac system [17]. The results of the study demonstrated significant relationship between technology anxiety, perceived ease of use, and perceived popularity of technology use among wider population of older adults, e.g., technology coolness factor. Additionally, the studies using the TAM model also demonstrated that in order for seniors to adopt a software system or electronic device such a system must be highly usable, and also offer a recognizable value [11]. This is especially true for software that is not designed to connect older adults with family or friends, which would have very obvious value for older adults, but to provide health and wellness value that could not be as obvious or easily recognizable.

Unfortunately, various technology acceptance models (TAM, UTAUT, and STAM-senior technology acceptance model) have some limitations and fall short in defining which age-related barriers and facilitators influence usability and usefulness of technology, and how they influence technology adoption [18]. The question of how acceptance of technology (i.e., behavioral intention) and actual use behavior are connected has yet to be answered. People do not always act upon their intention and this phenomenon has been described as the "intention-behavior gap" [16]. TAMs are theoretical explanations based on hypothetical scenarios rather than lived experiences of technology use.

In sharp contrast, human-centered design (HCD) focuses on understanding human needs and how design can respond to those needs [19]. The term 'design' is no longer used as a process to create physical products only, but increasingly used as a process that leads to the creation of any type of intervention that changes existing situations into preferred ones, including services, procedures, strategies and policies [19]. As a systemic and more humane approach, HCD could play an important role in dealing with today's care challenges by designing products and services to address current gaps in healthcare based on human needs [19]. To better understand what drives the effectiveness and usage of technologies, the collective perspectives of ends users of technology must be analyzed, including their experiences, needs, and the barriers they face in using digital health solutions [20].

1.3 Perceived Technology Value

As mentioned before, acceptance toward digital interventions by older adults was found to be highly dependent on the perceived value of technology [11, 16]. It was shown that digital interventions can have a positive impact on patients with CVD. However there is a great need for easy to use, personalized, and user-friendly technologies that can benefit patients from all age groups, especially older adults [20]. Some of the motivation factors for using VCR technology components for older adults included technological support for CR and self-management, supportive maintenance of cardiac health, access to peer support groups and specialists, and activity and health status tracking [21]. VCR programs that had the ability to track patients' activities, heart rate, and current health status and showed their progress over time were considered valuable and engaging [20].

Alerts and reminders are generally valued by the patients. For example, text messages can push them to perform exercises, and patients also value alarm reminders for medication management [20]. At the same time, there are some concerns among healthcare providers about the accuracy and reliability of VCR equipment available to patients, and a possible mental toll of home cardiac monitoring using consumer grade devices and not the "gold standard medical equipment," including concerns that some patients could become "e-hypochondriacs" [22] and, alerts and reminders could be upsetting for some patients because they remind them of their sickness [20]. These examples of perceived value (or not) show that the flexible/personalized and collaborative design of the VCR program components is very important in order to improve VCR technology acceptance by patients.

2 Literature Review

Our literature review focused on published research results about various aspects of HCI design for VCR, including usability and technology adoption. The review was conducted for our project under the Aging in Place Program at the National Research Council of Canada. We work in collaboration with health researchers and industry partners and focus on the evaluation and adaptation of assistive technologies for older adults, and on informing policy decisions on early adoption of digital health solutions. The project will develop guidelines and tools for co-creating aging in place technologies and testing virtual applications remotely with older adults, including safe, usable, and affordable solutions in virtual cardiac care.

For this review we reviewed a number of papers published in scientific conferences and journals on the topic of virtual cardiac rehabilitation and remote cardiac monitoring, including papers reporting on home monitoring related to cardiac disease, with publication dates from 2019 to 2021. Table 1 depicts keywords we used to identify papers for our review. We used Google Scholar database to find the research publications, with relevant publications on topics such as design, usability, and technology acceptance listed in Table 2. The highlights of our findings from the literature review and analysis are listed in the sections below.

Table 1. Keywords for Google Scholar

Cardiac; cardiovascular; cardiac rehabilitation; virtual cardiac rehabilitation; cardiac tele-monitoring; cardiac care; digital cardiac rehabilitation; technology acceptance; usability; technology barriers; tele-rehabilitation, m-Health, mobile technology; COVID-19.
Filters: published in the last two years (2020-2021), English language.

Table 2. Research publications reviewed

Author, year, country	Title	Topics	Ref #
*Anttila, 2021, Finland	Patients' experiences of the complex trust-building process within digital cardiac rehabilitation	Cardiac rehabilitation, patient experiences, trust building, technology acceptance	[23]
*Astley, 2021, Australia	Remote cardiac rehabilitation services and the digital divide: implications for elderly populations during the COVID19 pandemic	Cardiac rehabilitation, design considerations, usability	[1]
Babu, 2020, India, USA	COVID-19: a time for alternate models in cardiac rehabilitation to take centre stage	Technology driven cardiac rehabilitation	[25]
Batalik, 2020, Czech Republic	Remotely monitored telerehabilitation for cardiac patients: a review of the current situation	Cardiac rehabilitation, review, technology acceptance, barriers	[26]
Bayoumy, 2021, USA	Smart wearable devices in cardiovascular care: where we are and how to move forward	Wearable devices in cardiovascular care, data security and governance, practical guide for clinicians	[27]
Bhavnani, 2020, USA	Digital Health: opportunities and challenges to develop the next-generation technology-enabled models of cardiovascular care	Cardiovascular care, technology acceptance	[28]
Bond, 2021, USA	Exergaming and virtual reality for health: implications for cardiac rehabilitation	Cardiac rehabilitation, virtual reality, technology acceptance	[29]
Buyting, 2021, Canada	Virtual care with digital technologies for rural and remote Canadians living with cardiovascular disease	Virtual cardiac care, technology acceptance	[7]
Calabrese, 2021, Italy	Exercise training and cardiac rehabilitation in covid-19 patients with cardiovascular complications: state of art	Cardiac rehabilitation, COVID-19 Patients	[30]

(continued)

Table 2. (*continued*)

Author, year, country	Title	Topics	Ref #
Chong, 2021, China	Effectiveness of technology-assisted cardiac rehabilitation: a systematic review and meta-analysis	Cardiac rehabilitation, barriers	[31]
*Ding, 2021, USA	MI-PACE home-based cardiac telerehabilitation program for heart attack survivors: usability study	Cardiac rehabilitation, usability	[32]
*Dohse, 2021, USA	Patient perspective: wearable and digital health tools to support managing our health during the COVID-19 pandemic and beyond	Cardiac care, patient experience, home monitoring, wearables	[33]
Epstein, 2021, USA	Cardiac rehab in the COVID era and beyond: mHealth and other novel opportunities	Cardiac rehabilitation, challenges, barriers	[34]
Falter, 2021, Belgium	Digital health in cardiac rehabilitation and secondary prevention: a search for the ideal tool	Cardiac rehabilitation, sensors, artificial intelligence	[35]
Harky, 2021	Technology and cardiovascular diseases in the era of COVID-19	Cardiac rehabilitation, COVID-19, home monitoring	[36]
Krishnaswami, 2020, USA	Gerontechnology for older adults with cardiovascular diseases	Cardiac rehabilitation, technology acceptance, technology barriers	[24]
Marzolini, 2020, Canada	Cardiac rehabilitation in Canada during COVID-19	Cardiac rehabilitation, COVID-19, barriers	[37]
*Meinhart, 2020, Austria	Mobile technologies to promote physical activity during cardiac rehabilitation: a scoping review	Cardiac rehabilitation, mobile technologies, review, technology acceptance, usability	[21]
Miller, 2020, USA	Home monitoring of cardiac devices in the era of COVID-19	Remote patient monitoring, cardiac management, COVID-19	[38]
Mizuno, 2021, USA	Wearable devices to monitor and reduce the risk of cardiovascular disease: evidence and opportunities	Cardiac rehabilitation, wearable devices, barriers	[39]

(*continued*)

Table 2. (*continued*)

Author, year, country	Title	Topics	Ref #
Moulson, 2020, Canada	Cardiac Rehabilitation During the COVID-19 Era: Guidance on Implementing Virtual Care	Cardiac rehabilitation, barriers	[6]
Nabutovsky, 2021, Israel	Adherence to remote cardiac rehabilitation during the coronavirus pandemic	Remote cardiac rehabilitation, COVID-19	[40]
Nakayama, 2021, Japan	Remote cardiac rehabilitation is a good alternative of outpatient cardiac rehabilitation in the COVID-19 era	Remote cardiac rehabilitation, COVID-19, barriers	[41]
*Nesbitt, 2021, Australia	Co-designing digital cardiac rehabilitation with patients living in rural and remote Australia - the country heart attack prevention project	Digital cardiac rehabilitation, design, user experience	[42]
*Olivier, 2021, USA	Why digital health trials can fail: lessons learned from a randomized trial of health coaching and virtual cardiac rehabilitation	Virtual cardiac rehabilitation, failed digital health trial	[43]
Pecci, 2021, USA	Cardiac rehab in the COVID-19 pandemic	Cardiac rehabilitation, COVID-19, barriers	[44]
Qiu, 2021, Canada	The emerging role of digital health technology in cardiovascular care	Cardiac rehabilitation, digital health, barriers	[8]
Sana, 2021, USA	Wearable devices for ambulatory cardiac monitoring, JACC state-of-the-art review	Cardiac monitoring, devices, barriers	[45]
*Tadas, 2020	Barriers to and facilitators of technology in cardiac rehabilitation and self-management: systematic qualitative grounded theory review	Cardiac rehabilitation, barriers, patient acceptance	[20]
*Thimo, 2021, Switzerland	Patient interest in mHealth as part of cardiac rehabilitation in Switzerland	Cardiac rehabilitation, mHealth, technology acceptance	[46]

Note: Studies that focus on technology usability, patient acceptance and satisfaction are marked with an asterisk (*)

2.1 Common Design Features for VCR Programs During Pandemic

From review of the literature, it is clear that the COVID-19 pandemic has compromised the effective delivery of traditional face-to-face cardiac rehabilitation. This was due to shifting of resources from outpatient care to COVID-urgent priorities and the need to ensure social distancing [1, 6, 44]. Before the pandemic, the uptake of VCR technologies was slow due to concerns about effectiveness and cost of remote service delivery [1]. Since the pandemic, a widespread acceptance and rapid adoption of VCR into routine care have been observed in many jurisdictions, including Canada [5, 6]. A Table 3 below lists common design elements of the VCR process during the pandemic and the patient feedback on the program elements. Not all VCR programs were using all program design elements in Table 3, depending on human and technology resources available. In the next section, we will look at the information available from the literature review on usability and patient feedback on differed parts of VCR programs.

Table 3. Common program design elements for VCR process

Category	Design element
Training support	Initial direct supervision of a specialist in a hospital center, audiovisual electronic presentation with possible chat
Educational support	Educational brochures, booklets e-Learning, smartphone applications for delivering motivational and educational materials to participants, cardiac rehabilitation website
Peer support	Online interaction with a peer group via social networks
Monitoring and coaching	Remote monitoring during home exercise, web-based coaching via a remote connection using web-based software and an activity tracker, real time tele-coaching with physical activity data and communication with patients provided through videoconferences or mobile phones, post-exercise tele-coaching
Communication and interaction modalities	Regular consultations via email/SMS, motivational telephone calls, smartphone applications, real time tele-coaching with physical activity data and communication with patients provided through videoconferences or mobile phones

2.2 Patient Feedback and Usability

Only a few studies among the publications we reviewed focused on technology usability, patient acceptance and satisfaction. These papers are marked by an asterisk (*) in Table 2.

Based on these publications, we identified some commonalities in patient feedback on VCR technology. The most common trends in patient feedback are listed in Table 4 below.

Table 4. Patient feedback on VCR technology

Features and functionalities	Details on the feedback received
Peer group support	Great importance of peer group support, positive importance of face-to-face peer group contact, concerned about isolation in remote rehabilitation without social support [23]
Activity monitoring using mobile and wearable devices and sensors	Technology supports physical activity and lifestyle changes, helps to recognize development, provides immediate feedback on levels of physical activity, allows to measure performance, and motivates to move forward toward achieving goals and further self-management [20, 23, 32, 33] Use of activity tracking technologies requires digital literacy and mostly targets younger user groups [21] Higher dropout rates for the VCR programs could be attributed to the lack of technology acceptance, usability, and user-friendliness of technologies, including activity trackers and mobile devices [21]
Tele- and web-based coaching	The feedback and support from healthcare professionals through a web-based program helps patients seek and utilize information to evaluate their goals and progress [23, 32]
Cardiac rehabilitation website	Co-designing of the website with the patients can improve desired content and features. Improved usability scores can be achieved through further incorporating user feedback into the development of the website [42]
Text messaging	Text messaging can improve medication adherence. Text messaging-only interventions have limited capacity to monitor adherence with small effects [43] Text messages pushed to perform exercises, reminders are needed for medication management. Some patients did not like reminders, as they constantly reminded them of their sickness [20]

(continued)

Table 4. (*continued*)

Features and functionalities	Details on the feedback received
Online and telephone surveys and questionnaires	Limited availability of stable Internet and telephone signals hampers delivery of VCR in rural areas [25] Age-related cognitive impairments limit the applicability of these tools [20]
Personalization and gamification	Personalization and gamification facilitate patient engagement and self-management, care must be taken to avoid overburdening people [20, 29]

3   VCR Technology Acceptance and Barriers

Our literature review revealed that during the COVID-19 pandemic cardiac rehabilitation programs in many jurisdictions, including Canada, have suspended in-person services as a result of large-scale physical distancing recommendations, with up to 50% of all Canadian CR programs ceased [6]. During this time, a widespread acceptance and rapid adoption of VCR into routine care have been observed in many countries, including Canada [1, 5, 6, 30, 34, 36, 37, 41, 44]. According to preliminary research presented at the American Heart Association's Scientific Sessions 2020, remote or virtual cardiovascular or cardiac rehabilitation programs using tele-counselling with specialists provided via telephone or mobile apps and web-based technologies were found to be as effective as on-site programs offered in hospitals [33].

Some of the general challenges listed for VCR program delivery during the pandemic included resource limitations, loss of in-person interactions, difficulties with risk stratification and supervision, and a lack of specific VCR delivery standards that made it difficult to maintain VCR safety, particularly in older and frail cardiovascular patients with comorbid illnesses [6]. Other barriers to adoption included limited access to affordable, effective VCR technologies and a lack of technology literacy that has the potential to exacerbate care delivery gaps in vulnerable populations including the elderly, those of lower socioeconomic status, and those living in rural settings [6]. Additionally, it has been observed that there is a lack of long-term studies to evaluate VCR technology usability, patient acceptance of VCR technology, and sustainability of improved health outcomes [35]. There is also a need to include more gender equality in CR research and implementation, by adopting a participatory VCR design and development methodology, more usability and user experience focus, and including behavioral theories and frameworks in the development of VCR interventions [21].

The literature points to some technology-specific barriers to widespread VCR adoption, including a lack of customization for consumer activity monitoring devices that is cardiac rehabilitation specific. For example, VCR patients reported a concern that interrupted or short walks did not count toward their walking time recorded by activity tracker devices. As we found, Fitbit and other similar activity trackers currently count active minutes only after 10 min of continuous moderate-to-intense activity, which may not apply to older and frailer users, and there is a need to lower the walking time threshold for older adults participating in VCR [32].

Another frequently mentioned technology barrier to address is the accuracy of cardiac monitoring devices used for VCR. Many popular commercial wearable devices in the form of the watch, bracelet, or ring that monitor heart rate can be used to assess cardiorespiratory fitness and allow for remote monitoring of patient safety [34]. For example, the Apple Watch can measure a single-lead ECG and blood oxygen level (SpO2), so does the Fitbit Sense watch, while the Kardia Mobile 6L device can accurately measure 6 lead ECG [22]. The recent study [47] has demonstrated a feasibility of combining serial smartphone single-lead electrocardiograms for the diagnosis of ST-elevation myocardial infarction. These types of mobile devices can notify the patient about heart bradycardia, tachycardia, or irregular rhythms, and Apple Watch is also able to detect when a patient may have fallen and notify emergency contact. According to a recent study, the Apple watch–generated ECGs were 93% to 95% accurate at correctly identifying and distinguishing between different types of heart attacks while among the healthy people, the watch's accuracy was 90% for correctly noting the absence of a heart attack [48]. All these features could be very useful for the purpose of VCR. However the accuracy and diagnostic validity of the above-mentioned devices are still under review by healthcare providers, including VCR service providers.

In general, we found the accuracy of wearables used in VCR programs, such as devices that track exercise activity, sleep, heart beat rate and other health indicators, as compared to the gold standard medical equipment, is not normally tested thoroughly and in many cases demonstrate significant error [26, 27]. The uncertain accuracy of VCR devices could lead to diminished trust toward technology from healthcare practitioners and patients, possibly leading to lower perceived technology value for the users, and serve as a deterrent to a widespread acceptance of VCR technology.

Additionally, the use of activity monitoring mobile devices requires digital literacy [38] and VCR technology is most frequently embraced by and targeted toward younger user groups [39]. The frequently higher dropout rates in the VCR activity monitoring with mobile devices could be attributed to the lack of technology acceptance, usability, and user-friendliness [21]. Therefore, needs and preferences of older adults require special consideration in the design of mobile systems for cardiac rehabilitation. User participation in the design and development of activity monitoring mobile systems for VCR, including technology co-design activities with older adults will help to improve technology acceptance, usability, and user-friendliness [21, 49, 50].

The above-mentioned accuracy shortcomings of VCR technology highlight a need to conduct systematic technology validation studies, including usability evaluations for mobile and wearable equipment for VCR. Remote usability evaluation methods and technologies could be used to study usability of VCR for homebound senior adults. This research area is new and needs urgent research advances to be developed so it could be used for Aging in Place purposes [51].

4 Conclusions

This literature review was conducted for the project on the evaluation and adaptation of assistive technologies for older adults by the National Research Council of Canada under the Aging in Place Program. We work in collaboration with health researchers and industry partners and focus on evaluation and adaptation of assistive technologies for older adults, and on informing policy decisions on early adoption of digital health solutions. Outcomes of the project will include guidelines and tools for co-creating aging in place technologies and evaluating virtual applications remotely with older adults, including safe, usable, and affordable solutions in virtual cardiac care.

Our literature review revealed that while the COVID-19 pandemic led to suspension of in-person cardiac rehabilitation services and rapid adoption of virtual cardiac rehabilitation into routine care, there are numerous barriers for a widespread acceptance of VCR technologies by the patients, especially by older adults. Some of the challenges included resource limitations, loss of in-person interactions, lack of access to technology, and especially lack of specific VCR delivery standards that lead to difficulties in maintaining VCR safety, particularly in older patients with comorbid illnesses.

There is a need to adopt human-centered design approaches targeting older populations in order to improve the usability of home cardiac monitoring devices. Technology acceptance by older patients could be supported by increasing user participation in the design and development of personalized, safe and user-friendly home monitoring systems that better meet their needs. This will require access to new collaborative design and remote evaluation technologies that would support the development of the next generation of VCR programs and services.

References

1. Astley, C.M., et al.: Remote cardiac rehabilitation services and the digital divide: implications for elderly populations during the COVID19 pandemic. Eur. J. Cardiovasc. Nurs. **20**, 521–523 (2021). https://doi.org/10.1093/eurjcn/zvab034
2. Public Health Agency of Canada: Prevalence of Chronic Diseases and Risk Factors among Canadians Aged 65 Years and Older (2020)
3. Shahid, Z., et al.: COVID-19 and older adults: what we know. J. Am. Geriatr. Soc. **68**, 926–929 (2020). https://doi.org/10.1111/jgs.16472
4. Zhou, F., et al.: Clinical course and risk factors for mortality of adult inpatients with COVID-19 in Wuhan, China: a retrospective cohort study. Lancet **395**, 1054–1062 (2020). https://doi.org/10.1016/S0140-6736(20)30566-3
5. Hill, S., Li, K.X., MacDougall, D.: Remote monitoring programs for cardiac conditions in Canada: an environmental scan. Can. J. Heal. Technol. **1**, 1–40 (2021). https://doi.org/10.51731/cjht.2021.44
6. Moulson, N., et al.: Cardiac rehabilitation during the COVID-19 era: guidance on implementing virtual care. Can. J. Cardiol. **36**, 1317–1321 (2020). https://doi.org/10.1016/j.cjca.2020.06.006
7. Buyting, R., et al.: Virtual care with digital technologies for rural Canadians living with cardiovascular disease. CJC Open. (2021). https://doi.org/10.1016/j.cjco.2021.09.027
8. Qiu, Y., et al.: The emerging role of digital health technology in cardiovascular care. Can. J. Cardiol. **37**, 939–942 (2021). https://doi.org/10.1016/j.cjca.2021.04.016
9. Scirica, B.M., et al.: Digital care transformation interim report from the first 5000 patients enrolled in a remote algorithm-based cardiovascular risk management program to improve lipid and hypertension control. Circulation, 507–509 (2021). https://doi.org/10.1161/CIRCULATIONAHA.120.051913

10. Leigh-Hunt, N., et al.: An overview of systematic reviews on the public health consequences of social isolation and loneliness. Publ. Health **152**, 157–171 (2017). https://doi.org/10.1016/j.puhe.2017.07.035
11. Munteanu, C., Axtell, B., Rafih, H., Liaqat, A., Aly, Y.: Designing for older adults: overcoming barriers to a supportive, safe, and healthy retirement. Disruptive Impact FinTech Retire. Syst. 104–126 (2019). https://doi.org/10.1093/oso/9780198845553.003.0007
12. Kondratova, I., Fournier, H., Katsuragawa, K.: review of remote usability methods for aging in place technologies. In: Gao, Q., Zhou, J. (eds.) HCII 2021. LNCS, vol. 12786, pp. 33–47. Springer, Cham (2021). https://doi.org/10.1007/978-3-030-78108-8_3
13. Davis, F.D.: Perceived usefulness, perceived ease of use, and user acceptance of information technology. MIS Q. 319–340 (1989)
14. Neves, B.B., Amaro, F., Fonseca, J.R.S.: Coming of (old) age in the digital age: ICT usage and non-usage among older adults. Sociol. Res. Online **18**, 22–35 (2013)
15. Almojaibel, A.A., et al.: Health care practitioners' determinants of telerehabilitation acceptance. Int. J. Telerehabil. **12**, 43–50 (2020). https://doi.org/10.5195/ijt.2020.6308
16. Philippi, P., et al.: Acceptance towards digital health interventions – model validation and further development of the unified theory of acceptance and use of technology. Internet Interv. **26** (2021). https://doi.org/10.1016/j.invent.2021.100459
17. Tsai, T.H., Lin, W.Y., Chang, Y.S., Chang, P.C., Lee, M.Y.: Technology anxiety and resistance to change behavioral study of a wearable cardiac warming system using an extended TAM for older adults. PLoS ONE **15**, 1–24 (2020). https://doi.org/10.1371/journal.pone.0227270
18. Wildenbos, G.A., Peute, L., Jaspers, M.: Aging barriers influencing mobile health usability for older adults: a literature based framework (MOLD-US). Int. J. Med. Inform. **114**, 66–75 (2018). https://doi.org/10.1016/j.ijmedinf.2018.03.012
19. Melles, M., Albayrak, A., Goossens, R.: Innovating health care: key characteristics of human-centered design. Int. J. Qual. Heal. Care. **33**, 37–44 (2021). https://doi.org/10.1093/intqhc/mzaa127
20. Tadas, S., Coyle, D.: Barriers to and facilitators of technology in cardiac rehabilitation and self-management: systematic qualitative grounded theory review. J. Med. Internet Res. **22**, 1–17 (2020). https://doi.org/10.2196/18025
21. Meinhart, F., Stütz, T., Sareban, M., Kulnik, S.T., Niebauer, J.: Mobile technologies to promote physical activity during cardiac rehabilitation: a scoping review. Sensors (Switzerland) **21**, 1–17 (2021). https://doi.org/10.3390/s21010065
22. Albert, D.: A six-lead heart monitor on your smartphone: an interview with David Albert, **16**, 9–11 (2020)
23. Anttila, M.R., Söderlund, A., Sjögren, T.: Patients' experiences of the complex trust-building process within digital cardiac rehabilitation. PLoS ONE **16**, 1–13 (2021). https://doi.org/10.1371/journal.pone.0247982
24. Creber, M., et al.: Gerotechnology for older adults with cardiovascular diseases: JACC state-of-the-art review, 2019–2021 (2021)
25. Babu, A.S., Arena, R., Ozemek, C., Lavie, C.J.: COVID-19: a time for alternate models in cardiac rehabilitation to take centre stage. Can. J. Cardiol. **36**, 792–794 (2020). https://doi.org/10.1016/j.cjca.2020.04.023
26. Batalik, L., Filakova, K., Batalikova, K., Dosbaba, F.: Remotely monitored telerehabilitation for cardiac patients: a review of the current situation. World J. Clin. Cases **8**, 1818–1831 (2020). https://doi.org/10.12998/wjcc.v8.i10.1818
27. Bayoumy, K., et al.: Smart wearable devices in cardiovascular care: where we are and how to move forward. Nat. Rev. Cardiol. **18**, 581–599 (2021). https://doi.org/10.1038/s41569-021-00522-7

28. Bhavnani, S.P.: Digital health: opportunities and challenges to develop the next-generation technology-enabled models of cardiovascular care. Methodist Debakey Cardiovasc. J. **16**, 296–303 (2020). https://doi.org/10.14797/mdcj-16-4-296

29. Bond, S., Laddu, D.R., Ozemek, C., Lavie, C.J., Arena, R.: Exergaming and virtual reality for health: implications for cardiac rehabilitation. Curr. Probl. Cardiol. **46**, 100472 (2021). https://doi.org/10.1016/j.cpcardiol.2019.100472

30. Calabrese, M., et al.: Exercise training and cardiac rehabilitation in Covid-19 patients with cardiovascular complications: state of art. Life **11**, 1–16 (2021). https://doi.org/10.3390/lif e11030259

31. Chong, M.S., Sit, J.W.H., Karthikesu, K., Chair, S.Y.: Effectiveness of technology-assisted cardiac rehabilitation: a systematic review and meta-analysis. Int. J. Nurs. Stud. 104087 (2021). https://doi.org/10.1016/j.ijnurstu.2021.104087

32. Ding, E.Y., et al.: MI-PACE home-based cardiac telerehabilitation program for heart attack survivors: Usability study. JMIR Hum. Factors. **8**, 1–15 (2021). https://doi.org/10.2196/18130

33. Dohse, H.: Patient perspective: wearable and digital health tools to support managing our health during the COVID-19 pandemic and beyond. Cardiovasc. Digit. Heal. J. **2**, 88–90 (2021). https://doi.org/10.1016/j.cvdhj.2020.12.002

34. Epstein, E., Patel, N., Maysent, K., Taub, P.R.: Cardiac rehab in the COVID era and beyond: mHealth and other novel opportunities. Curr. Cardiol. Rep. **23**(5), 1–8 (2021). https://doi.org/10.1007/s11886-021-01482-7

35. Falter, M., Scherrenberg, M., Dendale, P.: Digital health in cardiac rehabilitation and secondary prevention: a search for the ideal tool. Sensors (Switzerland) **21**, 1–11 (2021). https://doi.org/10.3390/s21010012

36. Harky, A., Adan, A., Mohamed, M., Elmi, A., Theologou, T.: Technology and cardiovascular diseases in the era of COVID-19. J. Card. Surg. **35**, 3551–3554 (2020). https://doi.org/10.1111/jocs.15096

37. Marzolini, S., de Ghisi, G.L.M., Hébert, A.A., Ahden, S., Oh, P.: Cardiac rehabilitation in Canada during COVID-19. CJC Open. **3**, 152–158 (2021). https://doi.org/10.1016/j.cjco.2020.09.021

38. Miller, J.C., Skoll, D., Saxon, L.A.: Home monitoring of cardiac devices in the era of COVID-19. Curr. Cardiol. Rep. **23**(1), 1–9 (2020). https://doi.org/10.1007/s11886-020-01431-w

39. Mizuno, A., Changolkar, S., Patel, M.S.: Wearable devices to monitor and reduce the risk of cardiovascular disease: evidence and opportunities. Annu. Rev. Med. **72**, 459–471 (2021). https://doi.org/10.1146/annurev-med-050919-031534

40. Nabutovsky, I., et al.: Adherence to remote cardiac rehabilitation during the coronavirus pandemic. Eur. J. Prev. Cardiol. **28**, 2021 (2021). https://doi.org/10.1093/eurjpc/zwab061.423

41. Nakayama, A., et al.: Remote cardiac rehabilitation is a good alternative of outpatient cardiac rehabilitation in the COVID-19 era. Environ. Health Prev. Med. **25**, 4–9 (2020). https://doi.org/10.1186/s12199-020-00885-2

42. Nesbitt, K., Beleigoli, A., Du, H., Clark, R., Tirimacco, R.: Co-designing digital cardiac rehabilitation with patients living in rural and remote australia - the country heart attack prevention project. Eur. J. Cardiovasc. Nurs. **20**, 2021 (2021). https://doi.org/10.1093/eurjcn/zvab060.138

43. Olivier, C.B., et al.: Why digital health trials can fail: lessons learned from a randomized trial of health coaching and virtual cardiac rehabilitation. Cardiovasc. Digit. Heal. J. **2**, 101–108 (2021). https://doi.org/10.1016/j.cvdhj.2021.01.003

44. Pecci, C., Ajmal, M.: Cardiac rehab in the COVID-19 pandemic. Am. J. Med. **134**, 559–560 (2021). https://doi.org/10.1016/j.amjmed.2021.01.007

45. Sana, F., Isselbacher, E.M., Singh, J.P., Heist, E.K., Pathik, B., Armoundas, A.A.: Wearable devices for ambulatory cardiac monitoring: JACC state-of-the-art review. J. Am. Coll. Cardiol. **75**, 1582–1592 (2020). https://doi.org/10.1016/j.jacc.2020.01.046

46. Thimo, M., Christian, B., Tabea, G., Judith, P., Prisca, E., Matthias, W.: Patient interest in mHealth as part of cardiac rehabilitation in Switzerland. Swiss Med. Wkly. **151**, 1–6 (2021). https://doi.org/10.4414/smw.2021.20510
47. Muhlestein, J.B., et al.: Feasibility of combining serial smartphone single-lead electrocardiograms for the diagnosis of ST-elevation myocardial. Am. Heart J. **221**, 125–135 (2020). https://doi.org/10.1016/j.ahj.2019.12.016
48. Spaccarotella, C.A.M., et al.: Multichannel electrocardiograms obtained by a smartwatch for the diagnosis of ST-segment changes. JAMA Cardiol. **5**, 1176–1180 (2020)
49. Kleinsmann, M., Sarri, T., Melles, M.: Learning histories as an ethnographic method for designing teamwork in healthcare. CoDesign **16**, 152–170 (2020). https://doi.org/10.1080/15710882.2018.1538380
50. Sumner, J., Chong, L.S., Bundele, A., Wei Lim, Y.: Co-designing technology for aging in place: a systematic review. Gerontologist **61**, E395–E409 (2021). https://doi.org/10.1093/geront/gnaa064
51. Hill, J.R., Brown, J.C., Campbell, N.L., Holden, R.J.: Usability-in-place—remote usability testing methods for homebound older adults: rapid literature review. JMIR Form. Res. **5**, e26181 (2021). https://doi.org/10.2196/26181

Evolution of Applied Variables in the Research on Technology Acceptance of the Elderly

Ruisi Liu[1], Xueai Li[2], and Junjie Chu[1(✉)]

[1] Ocean University of China, Qingdao 266100, China
chujunjie@ouc.edu.cn
[2] Peking University, Beijing 102627, China

Abstract. Since entering the 21st century, the problem of social aging has become increasingly prominent. At the same time, more and more elderly people begin to try to use intelligent technology with the rapid development of science and technology. Many studies have used different models to study the technology acceptance of the elderly. This study reviewed literature on the elderly's acceptance of technologies from 2008 to 2021, and found that the variables in the model change with the development of time and technology. We divided the literature into three main periods and found that the variables in the model gradually changed from focusing on technology to focusing on the social factors, as well as the emotions and feelings of the elderly. The degree of attention to the elderly gradually increased in this process.

Keywords: Elderly · Technology acceptance · TAM

1 Introduction

The global population is aging rapidly. According to the statistics released by the world bank, by 2020, the number of people over the age of 65 has reached 720 million, accounting for 9.3% of the world's total population [1]. It is estimated that by 2100, there will be 2.52 billion people over the age of 65, accounting for about 22.49% of the world's total population [2]. At the same time, China's population over the age of 65 has reached 190 million, accounting for 13.5% of the total population [3]. Obviously, the aging population is becoming more and more serious, and this social phenomenon has also brought many new social problems. Therefore, how to meet the needs of the increasing elderly population has become a challenge for many countries [4].

Nowadays, science and technology have developed rapidly. As the aging problem is becoming increasingly prominent, intelligent products and services also need to gradually adapt to the needs of the elderly and the needs of the new economic environment [5]. However, due to the physiological and psychological characteristics of the elderly, it is difficult for them to integrate into today's digital information society without any help [6]. Therefore, many studies attempt to focus on factors affecting the elderly's acceptance of technology, so as to provide some suggestions for researchers and designers to help the elderly to use innovative technology smoothly. For example, Ma et al. indicated

Q. Gao and J. Zhou (Eds.): HCII 2022, LNCS 13330, pp. 500–520, 2022.
https://doi.org/10.1007/978-3-031-05581-2_35

that facilitating conditions has a significant impact on the use of mobile phones by the elderly, thus that a better environment for the elderly to learn intelligent technologies can be provided, such as carrying out proper training [7].

Several models and theories have been widely utilized in research on user acceptance of new technologies, and researchers usually add some other variables to expand these models according to their research purposes. This study aimed to explore the evolution of variables focused in these studies over time and the development of technology.

2   Background Research

2.1   The Elderly and Their Use of Technology

As illustrated above, the trend of world population aging is intensifying, and the decline in physical condition and cognitive ability are the main reasons that hinder the use of new technologies by the elderly. Iancu et al. indicated that the elderly's acceptance of intelligent technology is relatively low due to the decline [8]. Besides, research found that the decline of cognitive ability, such as memory and information processing speed, will affect the performance of the elderly when using technology products [9]. Because of the lack of assistance from others and the complexity of information technology, it is difficult for the elderly to use new technologies alone, and their anxiety about use will influence their acceptance of new technologies [10].

However, although it may be difficult for the elderly to use technologies, using rationally can help them improve their happiness and quality of life. For example, Li et al. studied the elderly acceptance of wearable devices and pointed out that wearable health detection devices can solve the cognitive ability and action ability barriers of the elderly, which provides medical assistance for the elderly and reduce the cost of physical examinations [11]. Besides, He and Huang indicated that self-confidence and sense of achievement obtained by the elderly in the process of using smartphones and constantly learning to use new programs enhanced their expectation and happiness of life [12].

To sum up, in spite of its difficulty for the elderly to use, intelligent technology can not only provide various conveniences for the elderly, but also help them improve their happiness in daily life. Therefore, understanding factors that affect the elderly's acceptance of intelligent technology has become a common topic for many studies.

2.2   Research Models

A variety of theories and models have been proposed to study technology acceptance, like Theory of Reasoned Action (TRA), Technology Acceptance Model (TAM), Unified Theory of Acceptance and Use of Technology (UTAUT), etc.

TRA was proposed by Fishbein and Ajzen [13], which mainly explains how attitudes affect individual behavior. According to TRA, behavior intention can reflect a person's behavior, which is determined by the person's attitude and subjective norm related to the behavior. The theory holds that any factor can only indirectly affect usage behavior through attitudes and subjective norm. However, this view is based on the assumption that people can completely control their own behavior, but human behavior will also be restricted by external factors in fact [14, 15]. Figure 1 shows the main structure of TRA.

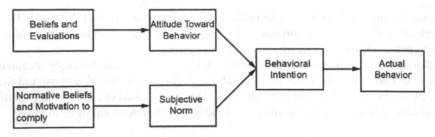

Fig. 1. Theory of Reasoned Action (TRA)

Then, in order to explain the decisive factors in the widespread acceptance of computers, Davis (1989) proposed TAM [16]. The most important constructs in TAM are perceived usefulness and perceived ease of use. Perceived usefulness was defined as the degree to which a person believes that using the particular technology would enhance his/her job performance, and perceived ease of use was defined as the extent to which a person believes that using a technology is free of effort [16]. In addition to these two constructs, the model also includes external variables, attitude toward using, behavioral intention to use, and actual system to use. The main relationships between them are that perceived usefulness and perceived ease of use decide attitude towards using together, and perceived usefulness and attitude have a direct impact on behavior intention. Besides, external variables include user differences, system characteristics, and task characteristics, etc., and their effects are fully mediated by perceived usefulness and perceived ease of use [16]. Figure 2 shows the main structure of TAM.

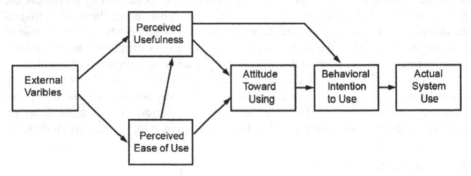

Fig. 2. Technology Acceptance Model (TAM)

Recently, TAM has been widely applied in various technology use contexts such as Augmented reality technology [17, 18], e-book [19, 20], mobile banking [21, 22], smart watch [23, 24], and virtual reality [25, 26].

On the basis of TAM, Venkatesh & Davis developed TAM2 by integrating social influence process and cognitive instrumental process into the original model [28]. In TAM2, subjective norm was considered to have a direct impact on behavioral intention. Compared with TAM, TAM2 explained technology acceptance from more dimensions [28]. Figure 3 showed the structure of TAM2.

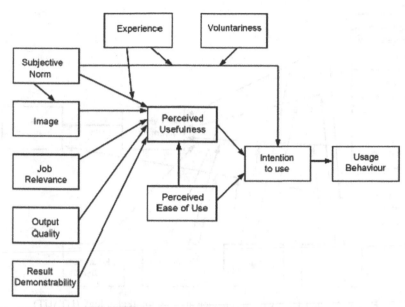

Fig. 3. Technology Acceptance Model 2 (TAM2)

Later, Venkatesh et al. [27] reviewed eight user acceptance models and established UTAUT, which had a stronger predictive power than any of the eight models [27]. UTAUT proposed three direct determinants of behavioral intention (performance expectancy, effort expectancy, and social influence), two direct determinants of use behavior (behavioral intention and facilitating conditions), and four moderators (gender, age, experience, and voluntariness of use). Specifically, the model emphasized "utilitarian value" (external motivation), like performance expectancy and effort expectancy. Due to the ability to integrate different technology acceptance models, UTAUT has made an important contribution to understanding technology acceptance and use [27]. Figure 4 showed the structure of UTAUT.

However, the above models have a common limitation in that they do not consider the complexity of interaction and different tasks in a non-work environment [28]. Therefore, after fully considering the characteristics of consumers and adapting to a specific environment, UTAUT2 has been developed [29]. UTAUT2 adjusted the focus of the "utilitarian value" (external motivation) in the UTAUT to consumer settings, and added three additional dimensions (price value, hedonic motivation, and habits). Figure 5 showed the structure of UTAUT2.

In order to improve the prediction ability of technology acceptance, several studies combined multiple models or added some new variables to meet different research purposes. In the field of technology acceptance for the elderly, Ma et al. combined TAM and UTAUT, and developed a Smartphone Acceptance Model for Chinese Older People (SAMCOP) [7]. Besides, Chen and Chan developed a model on the basis of TAM and UTAUT for the acceptance of aging technologies called the Senior Technology Acceptance Model (STAM), and showed that personal characteristics (like age, education

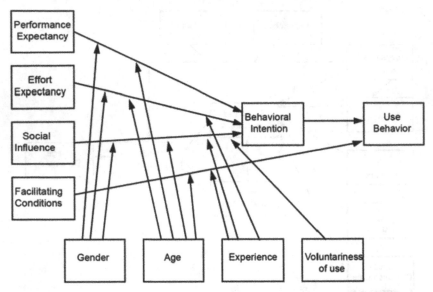

Fig. 4. Unified Theory of Acceptance and Use of Technology (UTAUT)

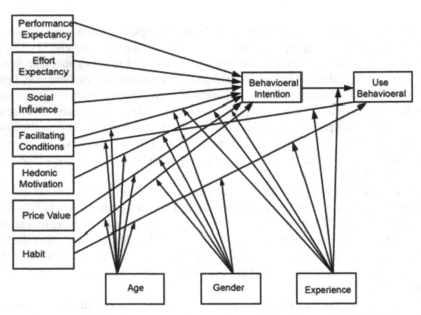

Fig. 5. Unified Theory of Acceptance and Use of Technology 2 (UTAUT2)

level, self-efficacy, anxiety, etc.) and environmental facilitating support (like assistance and guidance) were more helpful to predict the elderly's technology use behavior [9].

3 Method and Findings

In recent years, due to the continuous emergence of new technologies and the increasingly serious phenomenon of the aging society, many studies began to focus on the elderly's acceptance of new technologies. In this study, ACM, Elsevier, Springer, Talor & Francis, and China National Knowledge Infrastructure were used as sources, and (elder or old or senior) and (technology acceptance) were used as keywords. Finally, 33 studies closely related to the technology acceptance of the elderly were selected. The authors, research contents, and results of the studies are shown in the appendix. By sorting out the variables in these studies, we found the changes of research variables in three different periods. Table 1 shows the changes of variables in the literature in these three different periods. The blue part is the variables related to the investigated technology, orange is the variables related to social factors, while green and red represent the variables related to the physiological status of the elderly and the psychological status of the elderly respectively. It can be seen that the concern of the newly added variables for the elderly is gradually increasing.

3.1 Model Used in These Studies

As mentioned above, various acceptance models have their advantages in predicting user acceptance. Meanwhile, research often adapted the original models according to different research purposes. In the selected studies, the majority of applied models are TRA, TAM, TAM2, UTAUT, UTAUT2, and some studies integrated two or three models. Among these models, TAM is the most widely used model, with a total of 22 studies used. The second is the UTAUT, which is used in 8 studies. The numbers of studies using TAM2, TAM3, UTAUT2, STAM, and TRA are 3, 2, 2, and 1.

3.2 Related Variables Change with Technology

In the 33 studies, the models and related variables used vary with the change of technology. These changes were explained in three periods. 2008–2013 is the first period. By summarizing the technologies studied in the literature, we find that the technologies studied in the literature from 2008 to 2013 are relatively niche, including the testing of some design prototypes. From 2014 to 2018, the technologies studied in the literature were more popular and more related to mobile Internet and elderly care. After 2019, the technologies studied in the literature will become more popular, including smart wearable devices and online shopping, which are becoming more and more popular among the elderly in recent years. This may be because since 2014, mobile Internet technology has become popular, and people's lifestyle has also brought great changes.

Table 1. The changes of variables in the literature.

2008-2013	2014-2018	2019-2021
Perceived Risk (PR)	Facilitating conditions (FC)	Trust (TRU)
Perceived physical condition (PPC)	Social Influence (SI)	Perceived Enjoyment (PE),
Perceived Safety (PS) Wii and Game Difficulty (WGD)	Social relationships (Relaion) Subjective Norm (SN)	Eudaimonic Well-Being (EW) Perception, Acceptance and Willingness (PAW)
IT knowledge (IT)	Doctor's Opinion (DOC)	Technology anxiety (TA)
Game Realism (GR)	Health conditions (HC)	Hedonic Motivation (HM)
Output Quality (OQ),	Cognitive ability (CA)	Resistance to Change (RC),
Quality of training materials and manuals	Physical functioning	
Computer Playfulness (CPLAY)	Health Knowledge (HK)	
Compatibility (CP)	Health Care Need (HCN)	
Transfer from using technology in general, Transfer from using similar system, Transfer from learning experiences	Physical condition (PC)	

From the above, we can see that the technology change trend applied by TAM model is from niche to mass, from small coverage to wide coverage, from prototype design to mass production and high maturity products. Therefore, we found that in these literatures, the research variables in TAM gradually changed from paying attention to the availability of technology itself to the impact of social factors on the elderly and the physiological characteristics of the elderly, and then to the emotional experience of the elderly.

Research from 2008 to 2013. There are 10 studies in this period. In these studies, Zaad et al. investigated the elderly's acceptance of ambient intelligence, and results showed that perceived control and subjective norm had the greatest impact on use intention [30]. Besides, Ryu et al. studied the intention of the elderly to participate in video UCC, and results indicated that factors such as prior similar experience, life course events, and computer anxiety will directly or indirectly affect their willingness to use [31]. What's more, Conci et al. demonstrated the important role of perceived safety, self-actualization, and MP support in the acceptance of mobile phones by the elderly [32]. Moreover, a study based on TAM and UTAUT showed that subjective norm has a significant influence on the elderly's use of the Internet [33]. A study of the elderly's acceptance of sharetouch hardware products showed that output quality and result demonstrability have a positive effect on the elderly using the system [34]. To sum up, most of the variables focused in these studies are related to the new technology itself, such as Wii and game difficulty, output quality, etc. Besides, some variables were related to the subjective feelings of the elderly brought by a certain technology, such as computer anxiety, perceived enjoyment, and perceived safety.

Research from 2014 to 2018. There are 14 studies in this period. In these studies, Chen et al. [35] indicated that self-efficacy, technology anxiety, health, and cognitive abilities significantly affected the elderly's acceptance of Gerontechnology. Besides, there are three studies in mobile medicine, which referred to excellent ubiquity, health care need, and health knowledge [36–38]. Doctor's opinion, perceived security, effort expectancy, computer anxiety, resistance to change, and social influence were proved to be the factors that impact the elderly's acceptance. Besides, results of two studies on intelligent pension service [39, 40] showed that the elderly's use of this technology is influenced by perceived cost, perceived security, technology anxiety, and perceived risk. In the two studies on ICT [10, 28], self-satisfaction, social influence, hedonic motivation, and habit were proved to have significant effects on use intention. Additionally, a study on the elder's game intention shown that social interaction, narrative and physical conditions significantly affect the elder's use intention [44].

In this period, social factors and others' opinions have been focused on. Variables such as social influence, social relationships, and doctor's opinions were frequently used.

Research from 2019 to 2021. There are 9 studies in this period. Three of them investigated the acceptance of intelligent wearable devices by the elderly [11, 41, 42]. And results showed that compatibility, perceived social risk, prior experience, and effective quality were important to use intention. Besides, two studies demonstrated that perceived lack of shopping mobility and perceived social isolation will impact online shopping of the elderly [43, 44]. Besides, a study on the use of smartphones by the elderly based on TAM showed that intergenerational technical support will affect the happiness of the elderly [12]. In addition, a study on the acceptance of tablet devices by the elderly proved the impact of trust on use attitude of the elderly [45]. To sum up, the variables focused on in this period are mainly related to the emotional experience of the elderly. Trust, eudaimonic well-being, successful social isolation, affective quality all reflect the importance of the elderly's emotion in the research in this period.

4   Discussion and Conclusions

The problem of world population aging has become more and more serious, which makes researchers gradually consider the use and acceptance of emerging technologies by the elderly.

This study is one of the few that analyzed the evolution of variables in technology acceptance studies in the time dimension. By combing and analyzing literature on the acceptance of intelligent technology by the elderly from 2008 to 2021, the evolution of variables in these studies over time was investigated. Variables in technology acceptance studies changed with time and technology progress, from focusing on the technology itself to the social factors, and then to the psychological feelings of the elderly. The degree of attention to the elderly gradually increased in this process.

Appendix. The Authors, Research Contents, and Results of the Studies.

Authors	Subjects	Technology Studied	Theories/ Models	Constructs	Significant Relationship
Zaad and Allouch (2008) [30]	AU:12 users PU:208 elderly	Ambient Intelligence (AmI)	UCAM (based on TAM)	Perceived Usefulness (PU) Perceived Risk (PR) Perceived Privacy (PP) Perceived Control (PC) Cognitive Attitude (CA) Affective Attitude (AA) Behavioral Intention to use (BI)	AU (actual use): SN→AA, PU, BI, CA CA, PU→BI Potential Users 1: PU, PR, PC→BI SN→CA, PU, PP, PC Potential Users 2:SN→BI, CA, PU, PR, PC PU, PR, PC→BI
Ryu et al. (2009)[31]	290 elderly	Video user-created content service (video UCC)	TAM	Perceived user resource (PUR) Prior similar experience (PSE) Computer anxiety (CA) Perceived physical condition (PPC) Life course events (LCE) Perceived benefit (PB) Compatibility (CP) Perceived ease of participation (PEOP) Perceived enjoyment (PE) Intention to participate Control variables	PUR→CP,PEOP,PE,IP PSE→CP,PB,PE CA→PEOP PPC→IP LCE→PE,IP PB→IP CP→PB, PEOP, PEOP→PB,IP PE→PEOP, IP
Conci et al. (2009) [32]	740 elderly	Mobile Phone	TAM	Self-Actualization (SA) Enjoyment (ENJ) Perceived Safety (PS) Perceived Usefulness (PU) Perceived Ease of Use (PEU) Social Influence (SI) Behavioral Intention (BI) MP Support (SUP) USAGE	PU, PEU, SI, SUP→BI PEU, SI, ENJ, PS,SA→PU SA, ENJ, SUP→PEU SA→ENJ

Study	Sample	Technology/System	Model	Constructs	Results
Theng et al. (2009) [46]	28 elderly	Nintendo Wii(Game player)	TAM	Making Sense (MS), Perceived Benefits (PB), Facilitating Conditions (FAC), Wii and Game Difficulty (WGD), Perceived Usefulness (PU), Perceived Ease of Use (PEOU), Behavioral Intention (BI), Prior Experiences (EXP), Self-Efficacy (SEC), Awareness of Wii (AWA), IT knowledge (IT), Game Realism (GR)	PB, GR→PU WGD, SE→PEOU
Nayak (2010) [47]	592 elderly (Internet non-usage group:292) (Internet users group:300)	Internet	TAM	Gender, Age, Education group, Health group, Usefulness(U), Ease of use (EOU), Relevance (REL), Attitude (ATT), Internet usage (IU)	Study1(hours of Internet usage): ATT, H→IU Study2(using Internet activity): U, ATT, H→IU
Pan and Marsh (2010) [33]	374 elderly (50–81) Model1: 208 Model2: 166	Internet	TAM and UTAUT	Model1: Perceived Usefulness (PU), Perceived Ease of Use (PEU), Subjective Norm (SN), Facilitating conditions(FC), Gender, Age, Internet Use Intension (IUI) Model2: PU, PEU, SN, FC, Gender, Age, Internet Adoption (IA)	Model1:PU, SN, FC→IUI Model2: PU,PEU,SN→IA
Huang and Lee (2013)[48]	400 elderly	Telecare	TAM	Perceived Usefulness (PU), Perceived Ease of Use (PEOU), Attitude (A), Behavioral Intention (BI)	PEOU→PU PU→ATT ATT→BI
Tsai et al. (2012)[34]	52 elderly	Sharetouch system (a user-friendly interface system)	TAM	Intention to Use, (I), Perceived Usefulness (PU), Perceived Ease of Use (PEOU), Enjoyment (ENJ),	PU,PEU, ENJ, OQ, RD→IU

	Sample	Technology	Model	Output Quality (OQ), Result Demonstrability(RD)	Paths
Barnard et al. (2013) [49]	13 elderly	handheld touchscreen	UTAUT and STAM(Senior Technology Acceptance and Adoption Model)	Model1: Perceived self efficacy, Perceived difficulty, Attitude to learning, Intention to learn, Social environment, Experimentation and exploration, Experienced difficulty of learning, Rejection, Acceptance and start of adoption. Model2: Transparency, Affordance, Feedback, Error recovery, Transfer from using technology in general, Transfer from using similar system, Transfer from learning experiences, Quality of training, Quality of training materials and manuals, Support and encouragement from social environment, Rejection, Acceptance and start of adoption	
Kivimäki et al. (2013)[50]	7 elderly (Finland) 4 elderly (Austria)	Ambient COmmunication for Sense Of Presence (AMCOSOP)	TAM3	Perceived Usefulness (PU), Perceived Ease of Use (PEOU), Computer Self Efficacy (CSE), Computer Playfulness (CPLAY), Computer Anxiety (CANX), Perceived Enjoyment (ENJ)	
Chen and Chan (2014)[35]	1012 elderly	Gerontechnology	TAM+UTAUT	Gerontechnology self-efficacy(SE), Gerontechnology anxiety(ANX), Facilitating conditions(FC), Perceived Usefulness(PU), Usage Behavior (UB), Perceived Ease of Use (PEOU), Attitude towards Use (AT)	SE→PU, UB, PEOU; ANX→UB, PEOU; FC→PU, UB, PEOU; PEOU→PU, AT; PU→AT
Niehaves and Plattfaut (2014)[51]	150 elderly	Internet	UTAUT and MATH	Model1: Performance Expectancy (PE), Effort Expectancy (EE), Social Influence (SI), Behavioral Intention(BI). Model2: Performance Expectancy (PE), Effort Expectancy (EE), Social Influence (SI)	Model1:EE, PE,SI→BI; Model2: SI, EDU, EE, PE,FC→BI

Behavioral Intention(BI) Education (EDU) Gender (GEN) Income (INC) Age (AGE)

Reference	Sample	Domain	Model	Variables	Relationships
Chen and Chan (2014)[9]	1012 elderly	Gerontechnology	STAM	Gerontechnology self-efficacy(SE) Gerontechnology anxiety (ANX) Facilitating conditions(FC) Health conditions(HC) Cognitive ability() Social relationships (Relaion) Attitude to life and satisfaction(ALS) Physical functioning Perceived Usefulness (PU) Perceived Ease of Use (PEOU) Usage Behavior (UB) Attitude towards Use (AT)	GSE→PU, UB, PEOU GA→UB, PEOU FC→PU, UB, PEOU,AT HC→UB, PEOU CA→UB SR→PU,UB ALS→UB, PEOU PF→UB, PEOU PEOU→AT,PU PU→AT
Hsiao and Tang (2015)[36]	390 elderly	Mobile health care	MHTAM(mobile healthcare TAM, TRA	Perceived Usefulness (PU) Perceived Ease of Use (PEU) Perceived Ubiquity (PUB) Health Knowledge (HK) Health Care Need (HCN) Attitude (ATT) Subjective Norm (SN) Behavioral Intention (BI)	PEU, PUB, HK, HCN→ATT ATT, SN→BI POEU→PU
Cimperman et al. (2016) [37]	400 elderly	home telehealth services	UTAUT	Doctor's Opinion (DOC), Computer Anxiety (CA), Perceived Security (PS) Perceived Ease of Use(PE) Effort Expectancy(EE) Social Influence(SI) Facilitating Conditions(FC) Behavioral Intention(BI)	DOC.PS,EE→PE CA,PS, →EE PS, FC,EE,PE→BI

Author	Sample	Application	Model	Variables	Relationships
Wang and Sun (2016) [52]	534 elderly	Digital games	ETAM	Perceived Usefulness (PU), Perceived ease of use (PEOU), Narratives (N), Attitude toward play (ATP), Intension to play (BI), Social interaction (SI), Physical condition (PC), Gender (G), Age (A), Experience (E)	N, PU, PC, SI →BI
Ma, Chan and Chen (2016) [7]	120 elderly	smartphone	SAMOP(Smartphone Acceptance Model for Chinese Older People)(based on TAM and UTAUT)	Facilitating conditions(FC), Self-Satisfaction(SS), Cost Tolerance(CT), Perceived Ease of Use(PEOU), Perceived Usefulness(PU), Behavioral Intention(BI), Attitude towards Use(AT)	FC, SS, →PEU; SS→PU; PU→AT; CT→BI; PEU→PU
Qiao (2017)[53]	332 elderly	Digital reading	TAM, TAM2, TAM3	Perceived Usefulness (PU), Perceived Ease of Use (PEOU), Self Efficacy (SE), Attitude (ATT), Behavioral Intention (BI), Social Norm (SN)	SE→PEOU; PU→ATT,BI; PEOU→PU,ATT, SN→ATT,BI; ATT→BI
Judges et al. (2017)[56]	10 elderly	InTouch (a digital communication tool)	TAM2	Perceived Usefulness (PU), Perceived Ease of Use (PEU), Subjective norms(SN), Facilitating conditions(FC)	PU, PEU, SN,FC→BI
Xia (2017)[39]	259 elderly	Smart pension service	TAM	Perceived Usefulness (PU), Perceived Ease of Use (PEOU), Perceived Cost (PC), Perceived Security (PS), Perception Attitude (PA), Perceived Willingness (PA)	PEOU→PU; PEOU, PU, PC, PS→PA; PC, PA→PW

				Variables	Results
Macedo (2017)[28]	278 elderly	ICT	UTAUT2	Performance Expectancy (PE) Effort Expectancy (EE) Behavioural Intention (BI) Use Behaviour (USE) Facilitating Conditions (FC) Social Influence (SI) Hedonic Motivation (HM) Price Value (PV) Habit(HT) Age Gender Experience Education	PE, EE, SI, FC, HM, HT→BI HT, BI→UB
Hoque and Sorwar (2017)[38]	300 elderly	mHealth	UTAUT	Performance Expectancy (PE) Effort Expectancy (EE) Social Influence (SI) Facilitating Conditions (FC) Technology Anxiety (TA) Behavioral Intention (BI) Resistance to Change (RC) Use Behavior (UB)	PE,EE,SI,TA,RC→BI BI→UB
Luo et al. (2018) [40]	680 elderly	Community intelligent pension service	TAM	Technology Anxiety (TA) Perceived Risk (PR) Social Norm (SN) Perceived Ease of Use (PEOU) Perceived Usefulness (PU) Behavioral Intention (BI)	TA→PR, PEOU, PU, BI PR→SN, PEOU, PU PEOU→PU, BI PU→BI
Guner and Acarturk (2018) [10]	Study1:232 elderly Study2:235 younger adults	ICT	TAM	Social Influence(SI) Facilitating Conditions (FC) Anxiety (ANX) Self-Satisfaction(SS) Perceived Usefulness (PU) Perceived Ease of Use (PEOU) Attitude toward Using (ATU) Behavioral Intention (BI)	Study1: SI, FC, ANX→PEOU SS→PU PEOU→PU PU,PEOU→ATU ATU→BI Study2: SI, ANX, SS→PU FC, ANX→PEOU PEOU→ATU,PU ATU→BI

Reference	Sample	System	Model	Variables	Relationships
Li et al. (2019) [11]	146 elderly	Smart wearable systems	SWAM(Smart Wearables acceptance model)	Intention to Use (IU) Perceived Ease of Use (PEOU) Perceived Usefulness (PU) Facilitating Conditions (FC) Compatibility (COM) Social Influence (SI) Perceived Social Risk (PSR) Performance Risk (PR) Self-reported Health Conditions (Health)	PU→ATU FC,COM→PEOU COM, SI, Health, PR, PEOU→PU COM, Health, PU, FC→IU
Ojiako et al. (2019) [45]	203 adults	tablet devices	FTDA(The framework for tablet device adoption)based on TAM	Compatibility (COMP) Perceived Usefulness (PU) Perceived ease of use (PEOU) Primary influence (PI) Secondary influence (SI) Resource facilitating conditions (RFC) Technology facilitating conditions (TFC) Self-efficacy (SE) Attitude (ATT) Subjective Norm (SN) Perceived behavioral control (PBC) Trust (TRU) Intension to Use Tablets Device (INT) Actual use of tablets (AU)	Older group: PBC,ATT→INT COMP, PU, TRU PEOU→ATT Younger group: PBC→INT COMP, TRU→ATT
He and Huang (2020) [12]	330 elderly	smartphone	TAM	Perceived Usefulness (PU) Perceived Ease of Use (PEU) Intergenerational technical support (ITS), Attitude (ATT), Perceived Enjoyment (PE), Behavioral Intention (BI), Actual Use (AU), Eudaimonic Well-Being (EW)	PU, ITS→ATT ITS, ATT→BI ITS, BI→AU ITS, AU→EW PEU→PU

Reference	Sample	Application	Model	Constructs	Results
Soh et al. (2020) [43]	200 elderly(50)	online shopping	UTAUT and IRT	Performance Expectation (PE), Effort Expectation (EE), Social Influence (SI), Facilitating Conditions (FC), Usage Barrier (UB), Value Barrier (VB), Risk Barrier (RB), Tradition Barrier (RB), Image Barrier (IB), Perception, Acceptance and Willingness (PAW)	VB, RB ,TB, UB, SI, FC, PE→PAW
Zhang (2020)[54]	310 elderly	Smart home	TAM	Technology anxiety (TA), Resistance to change (RTC), Perceived Usefulness (PU), Perceived Ease of Use (PEOU), Behavioral intention to use (ITU), Performance risk (PR), Security risk (SR), Financial risk (FR)	RC, TA→PEOU RC, PEOU→PU PU,PEOU, PR, SR, FR→BI
Talukder et al. (2020) [41]	325 elderly	Wearable healthcare technology (WHT)	UTAUT2	Effort Expectancy(EE), Performance Expectancy,(PE), Hedonic Motivation(HM), Technology Anxiety(TA), Facilitating Conditions (FC), Social Influence (SI), Resistance to Change (RC), Functional Congruence (FUC), Self-Actualization (SA), Behavioral Intention to use (BI)	HM, SA, TA, RC, FUC, SI, PE→BI
Lazaro et al. (2020) [42]	76 elderly	Smartwatch	TAM	Prior Experience (PE), Affective Quality (AQ), Technology-Related Anxiety (TRA), Social Support (SS), Accessibility (ACC), Perceived Ease of Use (PEOU), Perceived Usefulness (PU)	AT,ACC→BI SS→AT PE,AQ,TRA→PEOU PEOU→PU PU,SS→AT

				Variables	Relationships
				Attitude (AT) Behavioral Intention (BI)	
Wu and Song (2020) [44]	366 elderly	online shopping continuance intentions	TAM and TPB	Perceived Lack of shopping Mobility (PLM) Perceived Ease of Use (PEU) Perceived Usefulness (PU) Perceived Social Isolation (PSI) Online shopping Attitudes (ATT) Online shopping continuance intensions (INT) Perceived behavioral control (PBC) Social Norm (SN)	PEU,PLM→PSI, PU PEM→PU PU, PEU→ATT PU, ATT→INT PSI→PBC, SN PBC→INT
Zhan and Sun(2021) [55]	885 elderly	Smart pension service	TAM	Perceived Ease of Use (PEOU) Perceived Usefulness (PU) Compatibility (CPB) Testability (TEST) Observability (OB) Complexity (CPL) Comparative Advantage (CA) Attitude (ATT) Intention of using behavior (IUB)	CA, TEST, PEOU, PU→ATT ATT→IUB

References

1. https://ourworldindata.org/grapher/size-of-young-working-elderly-populations?country=~OWID_WRL
2. https://ourworldindata.org/grapher/population-by-age-group-to-2100?country=~OWID_WRL
3. Ning, J.Z.: Report on main data of the Seventh National Census (2021)
4. Mostaghel, R.: Innovation and technology for the elderly: systematic literature review. J. Bus. Res. **69**, 4896–4900 (2016). https://doi.org/10.1016/j.jbusres.2016.04.049
5. Plaza, I., Martín, L., Martin, S., Medrano, C.: Mobile applications in an aging society: status and trends. J. Syst. Softw. **84**, 1977–1988 (2011). https://doi.org/10.1016/j.jss.2011.05.035
6. Klimova, B., Simonova, I., Poulova, P., Truhlarova, Z., Kuca, K.: Older people and their attitude to the use of information and communication technologies – a review study with special focus on the Czech Republic (older people and their attitude to ICT), Educational Gerontology, vol. 42 (2016). https://doi.org/10.1080/03601277.2015.1122447
7. Ma, Q., Chan, A.H., Chen, K.: Personal and other factors affecting acceptance of smartphone technology by older Chinese adults. Appl. Ergon. **54**, 62–71 (2016). https://doi.org/10.1016/j.apergo.2015.11.015
8. Iancu, I., Iancu, B.: Designing mobile technology for elderly. A theoretical overview. Technol. Forecast. Soc. Change **155** (2020). https://doi.org/10.1016/j.techfore.2020.119977
9. Chen, K., Chan, A.H.: Gerontechnology acceptance by elderly Hong Kong Chinese: a senior technology acceptance model (STAM). Ergonomics **57**, 635–652 (2014). https://doi.org/10.1080/00140139.2014.895855
10. Guner, H., Acarturk, C.: The use and acceptance of ICT by senior citizens: a comparison of technology acceptance model (TAM) for elderly and young adults. Univ. Access Inf. Soc. **19**(2), 311–330 (2018). https://doi.org/10.1007/s10209-018-0642-4
11. Li, J., Ma, Q., Chan, A.H., Man, S.S.: Health monitoring through wearable technologies for older adults: smart wearables acceptance model. Appl. Ergon. **75**, 162–169 (2019). https://doi.org/10.1016/j.apergo.2018.10.006
12. He, J., Huang, X.: Smart phone use and well-being of urban elderly: based on intergenerational support theory and technology acceptance model. Chin. J. Journalism Commun. **42**, 49–73 (2020). https://doi.org/10.13495/j.cnki.cjjc.20200409.003
13. Fishbein, M., Ajzen, I.: Belief, Attitude, Intention, and Behavior: An Introduction to Theory and Research. Addison-Wesley Publishing Company, Reading, MA (1975)
14. Bian, P.: Review on technology acceptance model. Res. Libr. Sci. (2012). https://doi.org/10.15941/j.cnki.issn1001-0424.2012.01.022
15. Sun, J., Cheng, Y., Ke, Q.: Advances of research on technology acceptance model. Inf. Sci. **25**, 1121–1127 (2007)
16. Davis, F.D., Bagozzi, R.P., Warshaw, P.R.: User acceptance of computer technology: A Comparison of two theoretical models. Manage. Sci. **35** (1989). 0025–1909/89/3508/0982$01.25
17. Yavuz, M., Çorbacıoğlu, E., Başoğlu, A.N., Daim, T.U., Shaygan, A.: Augmented reality technology adoption: case of a mobile application in Turkey. Technol. Soc. **66** (2021). https://doi.org/10.1016/j.techsoc.2021.101598
18. Do, H.N., Shih, W., Ha, Q.A.: Effects of mobile augmented reality apps on impulse buying behavior: an investigation in the tourism field. Heliyon **6**, e04667. https://doi.org/10.1016/j.heliyon.2020.e04667
19. Jin, C.-H.: Adoption of e-book among college students: the perspective of an integrated TAM. Comput. Hum. Behav. **41**, 471–477 (2014). https://doi.org/10.1016/j.chb.2014.09.056
20. Aharony, N.: The effect of personal and situational factors on LIS students' and professionals' intentions to use e-books. Libr. Inf. Sci. Res. **36**, 106–113 (2014). https://doi.org/10.1016/j.lisr.2014.01.001

21. Hassan, H.E., Wood, V.R.: Does country culture influence consumers' perceptions toward mobile banking? A comparison between Egypt and the United States. Telemat. Inform. **46** (2020). https://doi.org/10.1016/j.tele.2019.101312

22. Ho, J.C., Wu, C.G., Lee, C.S., Pham, T-T.T.: Factors affecting the behavioral intention to adopt mobile banking: an international comparison. Technol. Soc. **63** (2020). https://doi.org/10.1016/j.techsoc.2020.101360

23. Dutot, V., Bhatiasevi, V., Bellallahom, N.: Applying the technology acceptance model in a three-countries study of smartwatch adoption. J. High Technol. Manage. Res **30**, 1–14 (2019). https://doi.org/10.1016/j.hitech.2019.02.001

24. Bölen, M.C.: Exploring the determinants of users' continuance intention in smart-watches. Technol. Soc. **60** (2020). https://doi.org/10.1016/j.techsoc.2019.101209

25. Barrett, A.J., Pack, A., Quaid, E.D.: Understanding learners' acceptance of high-immersion virtual reality systems: insights from confirmatory and exploratory PLS-SEM analyses. Comput. Educ. **169** (2021). https://doi.org/10.1016/j.compedu.2021.104214

26. Schiopu, A.F., Hornoiu, R.I., Padurean, M.A., Nica, A-M.: Virus tinged exploring the facets of virtual reality use in tourism as a result of the COVID-19 pandemic. Telemat. Inform. **69** (2021). https://doi.org/10.1016/j.tele.2021.101575

27. Venkatesh, V., Morris, M.G., Davis, G.B., Davis, F.D.: A theoretical extension of the technology acceptance model: four longitudinal field studies. MIS Q. **27**, 425–478 (2003)

28. Macedo, I.M.: Predicting the acceptance and use of information and communication technology by older adults: an empirical examination of the revised UTAUT2. Comput. Hum. Behav. **75**, 935–948 (2017). https://doi.org/10.1016/j.chb.2017.06.013

29. Venkatesh, V., Thong, J.Y.L., Xu, X: Consumer acceptance and use of information technology: extending the unified theory of acceptance and use of technology. MIS Q. **36**, 157–178 (2012)

30. Zaad, L., Allouch, S.B.: The influence of control on the acceptance of ambient in-telligence by elderly people: an explorative study. Lecture Notes in Computer Science, pp. 58–74 (2008)

31. Ryu, M.-H., Kim, S., Lee, E.: Understanding the factors affecting online elderly user's participation in video UCC services. Comput. Hum. Behav. **25**, 619–632 (2009). https://doi.org/10.1016/j.chb.2008.08.013

32. Conci, M., Pianesi, F., Zancanaro, M.: Useful, Social and Enjoyable: Mobile Phone Adoption by Older People (2009)

33. Pan, S., Jordan-M, M.: Internet use intention and adoption among Chinese older adults: from the expanded technology acceptance model perspective. Comput. Hum. Behav. **26**, 1111–1119 (2010). https://doi.org/10.1016/j.chb.2010.03.015

34. Tsai, T.-H., Chang, H.-T., Chang, Y.-M., Huang, G.-S.: Sharetouch: a system to enrich social network experiences for the elderly. J. Syst. Softw. **85**, 1363–1369 (2012). https://doi.org/10.1016/j.jss.2012.01.023

35. Chen, K., Chan, A.H.S.: Predictors of gerontechnology acceptance by older Hong Kong Chinese. Technovation **34**, 126–135 (2014). https://doi.org/10.1016/j.technovation.2013.09.010

36. Hsiao, C.-H., Tang, K.-Y.: Examining a model of mobile healthcare technology acceptance by the elderly in Taiwan. J. Glob. Inf. Technol. Manag. **18**, 292–311 (2015). https://doi.org/10.1080/1097198x.2015.1108099

37. Cimperman, M., Makovec, B.M., Trkman, P.: Analyzing older users' home tele-health services acceptance behavior-applying an extended UTAUT model. Int. J. Med. Inform. **90**, 22–31 (2016). https://doi.org/10.1016/j.ijmedinf.2016.03.002

38. Hoque, R., Sorwar, G.: Understanding factors influencing the adoption of mHealth by the elderly: an extension of the UTAUT model. Int. J. Med. Inform. **101**, 75–84 (2017). https://doi.org/10.1016/j.ijmedinf.2017.02.002

39. Xia, P.: Construction of Intelligent Health Service Model for Elderly People in Community Based on the Theory of Information Technology Adoption. Zhejiang Chinese Medical University, Degree of Master (2017)

40. Luo, S., et al.: Analysis on demand factors of urban community intelligent elderly care service project based on TAM theory. Chin. J. Health Stat. **35**, 372–379 (2018)
41. Talukder, M.S., Sorwar, G., Bao, Y., Ahmed, J.U., Palash, M.A.S.: Predicting ante-cedents of wearable healthcare technology acceptance by elderly: a combined SEM-Neural Network approach, vol. 150. Technological Forecasting and Social Change (2020). https://doi.org/10.1016/j.techfore.2019.119793
42. Lazaro, M.J.S., Lim, J., Kim, S.H., Yun, M.H.: Wearable technologies: acceptance model for smartwatch adoption among older adults. In: Gao, Q., Zhou, J. (eds.) HCII 2020. LNCS, vol. 12207, pp. 303–315. Springer, Cham (2020). https://doi.org/10.1007/978-3-030-50252-2_23
43. Soh, P.Y., et al.: 2020 Perception, acceptance and willingness of older adults in Malaysia towards online shopping: a study using the UTAUT and IRT models. J. Ambient. Intell. Humaniz. Comput. 1–13https://doi.org/10.1007/s12652-020-01718-4
44. Wu, J., Song, S.: Older adults' online shopping continuance intentions: applying the technology acceptance model and the theory of planned behavior. Int. J. Hum. Comput. Interact. **37**, 938–948 (2020). https://doi.org/10.1080/10447318.2020.1861419
45. Ojiako, U., Choudrie, J., Nwanekezie, U., Chikelue, C.-O.: Adoption and use of tablet devices by older adults: a quantitative study. In: Pappas, I.O., Mikalef, P., Dwivedi, Y.K., Jaccheri, L., Krogstie, J., Mäntymäki, M. (eds.) I3E 2019. LNCS, vol. 11701, pp. 545–558. Springer, Cham (2019). https://doi.org/10.1007/978-3-030-29374-1_44
46. Theng, L.Y., Dahlan, A.B., Akmal, M.L., Myint, T.Z.: An Exploratory Study on Senior Citizens' Perceptions of the Nintendo Wii: The Case of Singapore (2009)
47. Nayak, L.U.S., Priest, L., White, A.P.: An application of the technology acceptance model to the level of Internet usage by older adults. Univ. Access Inf. Soc. **9**, 367–374 (2010). https://doi.org/10.1007/s10209-009-0178-8
48. Huang, J.-C., Lee, Y.-C.: Predicting telecare adoption on senior citizens in institution: application of the technology acceptance model. J. Stat. Manage. Syst. **15**, 81–92 (2012). https://doi.org/10.1080/09720510.2012.10701614
49. Barnard, Y., Bradley, M.D., Hodgson, F., Ashley, D.L.: Learning to use new technologies by older adults: perceived difficulties, experimentation behaviour and usability. Comput. Hum. Behav. **29**, 1715–1724 (2013). https://doi.org/10.1016/j.chb.2013.02.006
50. Kivimäki, T., et al.: User interface for social networking application for the elderly. In: Proceedings of the 6th International Conference on PErvasive Technologies Related to Assistive Environments - PETRA 2013, pp. 1–8 (2013). https://doi.org/10.1145/2504335.2504358
51. Niehaves, B., Plattfaut, R.: Internet adoption by the elderly: employing IS technology acceptance theories for understanding the age-related digital divide. Eur. J. Inf. Syst. **23**, 708–726 (2017). https://doi.org/10.1057/ejis.2013.19
52. Wang, Q.F., Sun, X.: Investigating gameplay intention of the elderly using an Extended Technology Acceptance Model (ETAM). Technol. Forecast. Soc. Chang. **107**, 59–68 (2016). https://doi.org/10.1016/j.techfore.2015.10.024
53. Qiao, Y.: Research on digital reading behavior and acceptance among the elderly. Shanghai Jiao Tong University, De-gree of Master (2017)
54. Zhang, Y.: Research on the influence of aging characteristics and perceived risks on smart home adoption by elderly. Zhejiang Chinese Medical University, Dalian University of Technology, Degree of Master (2020)
55. Zhan, J., Sun, T.: An empirical study on the impact of urban elderly on elderly care services. Theor. Modern. **2**, 117–128 (2021)
56. Judges, A., Laanemets, C., Stern, A., Baecker, M.: "In Touch" with senior: exploring option of a simplified interface for social communication and related social outcomes. Comput. Hum. Behav. **75**, 912–921 (2017). https://dx.doi.org/10.1016/j.chb.2017.07.004

Exploring Older Adults' Adoption of WeChat Pay: A Cognitive Lock-In Perspective

Tianchang Liu[✉] and Xinyue Li

Nanjing University, Nanjing, China
njutcl@smail.nju.edu.cn

Abstract. Mobile payment has become increasingly popular worldwide, especially during the COVID-19 pandemic. However, older adults have more difficulties in adapting to mobile payments than others. To understand the reasons behind this phenomenon, we explore cognitive lock-in and its antecedents in adopting WeChat Pay based on the status quo bias theory. We use the PLS-SEM technique with survey data from Chinese older adults over the age of 50. The results show that the cognitive lock-in of older adults is significantly affected by technology anxiety, habit, regret avoidance, and uncertainty costs. Moreover, older adults' intention to adopt WeChat Pay is positively associated with social influence and self-actualization, while cognitive lock-in is a significant negative determinant. This study can help us better understand the underlying mechanism behind older adults' adoption of mobile payment from a cognitive lock-in perspective. Furthermore, this study steers the discussion about improving older adults' digital literacy and optimizing age-appropriate services for mobile payments.

Keywords: Mobile payment adoption · Cognitive lock-in · Older adults · WeChat Pay · Status quo bias

1 Introduction

Mobile payment, as a representative of financial technology, has developed rapidly and taken over the market with its convenience worldwide, especially after the emergence of the COVID-19 pandemic. According to Worldpay Report 2021, 44.5% of e-commerce transactions were made by digital wallets in 2020 globally, up 6.5% from 2019 [1]. China is the market leader for mobile contactless payments, with 87.3% of the population using such a method [2]. WeChat Pay is a third-party mobile platform, officially launched in 2013, which is based on WeChat, one of the biggest social media in China. Notably, there are quite a few payment applications linked with it, such as WeChat red envelopes and WeChat transfer, which facilitate the penetration of mobile payment in China. It is currently one of the two dominant mobile payment platforms that have been widely adopted in China. The emergence and popularization of WeChat Pay is making China a fast-growing cashless society.

Although mobile payment is not a new technology, plenty of older adults still have difficulty in cognitively adapting to the change from traditional cash to electronic payments, and this not only leads to substantial inconvenience but also hinders their social

Q. Gao and J. Zhou (Eds.): HCII 2022, LNCS 13330, pp. 521–540, 2022.
https://doi.org/10.1007/978-3-031-05581-2_36

integration. Older adults in this study refer to the population over the age of 50, and they are also typified as the silver generation [3]. They have become a larger and more significant group in the contemporary Chinese society. However, there is a digital divide in their information and communications technology (ICT) usage problem. Older adults have lower familiarity with ICT usage, as well as worse sensory and cognitive capabilities [4]. Thus, they experience difficulties in using Internet-related products [5]. In a mobile payment context, they may find it difficult to use the Internet to shop online and participate in certain family activities, such as sending red envelopes. In addition to product flaws, older adults' inherent mindset, including cognitive lock-in, may be a barrier to their use of mobile payments. Therefore, it is essential to explore the reasons for such a fixed mindset and promote older adults' adoption of mobile payments.

In this study, we introduce the cognitive lock-in concept, unearth its antecedents, and explore its effect on older adults' adoption of WeChat Pay. The study contributes to the literature by exploring older adults' adoption of mobile payment from a cognitive lock-in perspective. This study provides suggestions on methods to enhance older adults' user experience and improve their digital literacy.

2 Related Work

A growing number of studies have investigated mobile payment adoption and they can be mainly categorized into five dimensions: determinants, user inclination, innovativeness, technology readiness, catalyst factors, and moderation effect [6]. Although some studies on mobile payment adoption have considered different age groups [7–9], few scholars explore the factors that influence the adoption of mobile payment from the perspective of older adults. Cognition is an important factor in user behavior and there is a relatively strong cognitive lock-in phenomenon in older adults; thus, it is essential to explore the relationship between the two. Furthermore, as a special group, the cognitive lock-in phenomenon of older adults is worth studying; however, few studies have treated it as the core construct.

Cognitive lock-in was first proposed by Arthur [10, 11] when discussing a cognitive path dependence caused by technological innovation, which was highly similar to individual level cognitive inertia defined by Polites [12]. It can significantly predict consumers' deliberate inertia [13]. Notably, cognitive lock-in and cognitive inertia both highlight a state of cognitive reluctance to change. Some scholars posit that transition costs, sunk costs and perceived value [12, 14], uncertainty costs [15], loss aversion, regret avoidance [16, 17], and so on, are determinants of cognitive lock-in. Moreover, the previous literature on cognitive lock-in has focused on different information behaviors or intentions, such as continued use [18], switching [19], and resistance [20]. However, few studies have researched on adoption, especially in the payment scenario.

Overall, factors influencing the resistance to information systems are mainly individual-, system-, and interaction-related, and compared to the other two, studies on individual factors are relatively few [20]. Some studies have examined cognitive lock-in and mobile payment. For instance, Park et al. [21] and Mu and young [22] explored the influence of cognitive lock-in on continuous use intention and switching intention, respectively, and they revealed a significant impact of these phenomena. In our study, cognitive lock-in refers to the phenomenon that even if it has been recognized that mobile payments can engender considerable convenience, older adults still have path dependence to continue to use other traditional payment methods, such as cash and credit card. Older adults are a population with high dispositional resistance to change [23], and they are less enthusiastic and have more anxiety toward adopting new technologies [24, 25]. However, few studies have focused on the cognitive antecedents behind the psychological phenomenon; thus, it is necessary for us to further explore.

Based on the literature above, we propose two research questions as follows:

(1) What are the antecedents of cognitive lock-in in older adults' adoption of WeChat Pay?
(2) What is the relationship between cognitive lock-in and WeChat Pay adoption intention?

3 Research Model and Hypothesis

3.1 Research Model

Status quo bias theory (SQB) is frequently used in to examine cognitive lock-in and inertia [12, 26, 27]. Notably, SQB is mainly used to explain why people do not act on the status quo when facing a new (potentially better) choice and maintain the current state [16]. Samuelson and Zeckhauser claimed that SQB explanations can be divided into three categories: cognitive misperception, rational decision, and psychological commitment [16]. Not all SQB explanations present at the same time in a certain context [12].

In terms of ICT adoption, there are a few previous articles that have explored the determinants of resistance and adoption behavior using SQB, and it has been found that users (a) make rational decisions based on switching and uncertainty costs related to new technology (b) adopt cognitive misperceptions based on perceived value and cognitive inertia, and (c) have a psychological commitment to the current system due to social influence and regret avoidance [12, 28, 29]. We also include habit as a subconscious factor in our model [30].

In this study, we employ cognitive lock-in as the core construct and adoption intention as the dependent variable. Based on the existing literature and research context, we choose perceived value, uncertainty cost, transition costs, social norms, regret avoidance, and habit according to SQB. Additionally, due to our research context of older adults, we will also include technology anxiety and self-actualization to represent their particular personality characteristics. Moreover, gender, age group, length of WeChat use, education level, and health condition are set as control variables [31, 32].

3.2 Research Hypothesis

Cognitive Lock-In. Cognitive lock-in implies that users have higher cognitive momentum caused by several factors, such as regret avoidance and transition cost, to overlook the status quo [27]. Prior studies have explored the cognitive lock-in effect in switching to mobile payment service in Taiwan[33]. In our research, cognitive lock-in entails that because they prefer doing what they have always done for decades, older adults are inclined to stick to the payment methods that they are familiar with and reluctant to use mobile payments. Therefore, we postulate that:

Hypothesis 1: Cognitive lock-in has a negative influence on the adoption of mobile payment by older adults.

Antecedents of Cognitive Lock-In.

Transition Cost and Uncertainty Cost

Transition costs are the tangible costs incurred in adapting to a new alternative, while uncertainty costs are intangible psychological uncertainties or risk perceptions that occur when changing to an unfamiliar situation [14]. Kim and Kankanhalli [14] showed that transition cost and uncertainty cost play a critical role in increasing user resistance. Polites and Karahanna [12] found that high transition costs lead to increased inertia on new system acceptance. In our context, the reasons for transition costs include time, money, effort spent, and unexpected difficulties in learning how WeChat Pay works. Research has also shown that older adults have declining physiological conditions and need more effort to adopt new technologies [18]. Therefore, the transition cost for older adults would be higher, thereby suggesting more inertia. Uncertainty costs are caused by the gap between the limited information and the expectation they have regarding to WeChat Pay and, specifically, they are not well informed about the situation regarding personal information security, financial security, and regulations on this platform. Older adults are more cautious and more likely to avoid the threat they may face after adoption. Thus, we formulate the following hypotheses:

Hypothesis 2: Transition costs have a positive influence on cognitive lock-in by older adults.
Hypothesis 3: Uncertainty costs have a positive influence on cognitive lock-in by older adults.

Regret Avoidance

The main reason for regret avoidance is that the regret caused by action is stronger than that caused by inaction [16]. Previous studies have reported that regret avoidance is a major variable that can increase the resistance to adopt a change [29]. Moreover, regret avoidance is linked with cognitive feelings. Thus, we suggest as follows:

Hypothesis 4: Regret avoidance has a positive influence on cognitive lock-in by older adults.

Habit

Habit is "a type of behavior or action, although not reasoned action. It may nevertheless derive from an action that at one time was reasoned" [34]. Therefore, habits are subconscious, as they are goal-oriented but may occur outside of consciousness. It takes fewer cognitive resources for individuals to exhibit habitual behaviors. Polites and Kankanhalli [12] found that users' habitual use of the current system will significantly and positively affect inertia, thus affecting users' willingness to adopt the system. Regarding the influencing factors of the upgraded system usage, Wang et al. also supported this conclusion [30]. In our study, older adults have used traditional payment for many years, and they have formed a habit that is difficult to change without external forces. Hu and Zhao [35] explored the influencing factors of users' adoption of mobile payment, and the results show that the habit of Internet payment will significantly enhance users' cognitive lock-in. Based on these arguments, it is postulated that:

Hypothesis 5: Habit has a positive influence on cognitive lock-in by older adults.
Technology Anxiety
Technology anxiety and self-actualization have both been identified as aging specific constructs [36]. Previous studies reveal that technology anxiety is a significant inhibitor on older adults' acceptance of mobile health technology, while self-actualization is a significant enabler [23, 36–38].

Technology anxiety refers to users' apprehension when faced with the chance of using new technologies [39][1]. It will have a negative influence on older adults' perception of their ability and reduce their willingness to use a technology [40]. Declining physical and cognitive capabilities may cause older adults to suffer a higher level of anxiety which will further lower their intention to adopt new technology [37].

Hypothesis 6: Technology anxiety has a positive influence on cognitive lock-in.

Perceived Value.
Perceived value evaluates whether the benefits derived are worth the costs incurred in changing from the status quo to the new situation [14]. This construct can be measured based on an SQB principle referred to as loss aversion, which implies that people's perception of the value of loss is stronger than that of gain and larger than it actually is [20]. Prior studies have shown that perceived value is positively associated with transition from web to mobile payment services [41].

In this research, the loss includes time and effort to learn the payment method and the loss of control after using it, while the gain includes performing the payment more quickly, and so on. When the perceived value is lower (higher), older adults are less (more) likely to adopt mobile payments. According to the definitions of cognitive lock-in and cognitive inertia, perceived value will not have a direct impact on it. Therefore, we formulate the following hypothesis:

Hypothesis 7: Perceived value has a negative influence on WeChat Pay adoption intention by older adults.

Self-actualization.
According to Maslow's[42] Hierarchy of Needs, self-actualization is one's internal motivation to achieve everything that one is capable of. According to Erikson's [43] eight stages of life model, a sense of fulfillment becomes a crucial element for the successful adjustment of senior citizens to later life. In our research, learning to use WeChat Pay may present opportunities for older adults to actualize their personal capacity. Therefore, we assume technology anxiety strengthens the cognitive lock-in of older adults. Thus, we propose that:

---

[1] Simonson, M. R., Maurer, M., Montag-Torardi, M., & Whitaker, M. (1987). Development of a standardized test of computer literacy and a computer anxiety index. Journal of Educational Computing Research, 3(2), 231–247. https://doi.org/10.2190/7CHY-5CM0-4D00-6JCG

Hypothesis 8: Self-actualization has a positive influence on the adoption of mobile payment by older adults.

Social Influence.
Social influence implies the influence of people around one's choice and opinion [44]. Previous studies presented that friends, family, and colleagues can all influence an individual's decision to adopt new technologies [45]. Hsieh found that social influence and regret avoidance both hamper consumer's intention to switch from cash payment to medical mobile payment[46]. Thus, it is proposed that:

Hypothesis 9: Social influence has a positive influence on WeChat Pay adoption intention by older adults.

The proposed research model and related hypotheses are shown in Fig. 1.

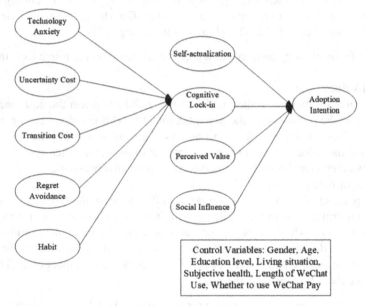

Fig. 1. Research model.

4 Methods

4.1 Measures

To operationalize the research constructs, we use the measurement scales from prior studies and revise the characteristics, as depicted in Table 1. The control variables are derived from Guo et al. [23], Wong et al. [9], Claes et al.[47], and Van et al. [48].

The measures are based on 5-point Likert scales, ranging from 1 (strongly disagree) to 5 (strongly agree) to assess respondents' attitudes on each statement. We employ translation (from English to Chinese) and back-translation (from Chinese to English) techniques to develop the questionnaire.

Table 1. Measurement scale.

Construct	Item	Factor loading	Wording	Reference
Cognitive Lock-in			I [will] continue using my existing method for pay,	Polites and Karahanna (2012) [12]
	CI1	0.956	…even though I know it is not the best way of doing things	
	CI2	0.936	…even though I know it is not the most efficient way of doing things	
	CI3	0.942	…even though I know it is not the most popular way to do things	
Perceived value	PV1	0.809	Considering the time and effort that I have to spend, changing to WeChat Pay is not worthwhile	Kim and Kankanhalli (2009) [14]; Hsieh (2021) [46]
	PV2	0.934	Considering the loss that I incur, changing to WeChat Pay instrument is of good value	
	PV3	0.882	Considering the hassle I will experience, changing to WeChat Pay is not beneficial to me	
Social influence	SI1	0.854	Most of my peers think I should use WeChat Pay	Hsieh (2021) [46]; Kim and Kankanhalli (2009) [46]
	SI2	0.558	Most of my WeChat contacts think that I should use WeChat Pay	
	SI3	0.887	My friends and families think that I should use WeChat Pay for paying my bills	
	SI4	0.923	The opinions of my family, friends, and those who I value are important in my decision to use WeChat Pay	

(continued)

Table 1. (*continued*)

Construct	Item	Factor loading	Wording	Reference
Regret avoidance	RA1	0.924	I think I will be sorry for choosing the WeChat Pay service	Hsieh (2021) [46]
	RA2	0.91	I think I will regret the bad outcomes that are the consequence of using the WeChat Pay service	
Uncertainty costs	UN1	0.878	The confidentiality and security of personal data are not guaranteed when I adopt WeChat Pay	Hsieh (2021) [46]
	UN2	0.88	The present regulations remain unclear regarding who will take responsibility for damages when you adopt WeChat Pay	
	UN3	0.825	Overall, I consider the adoption of WeChat Pay to be risky	
Transition costs	TC1	0.841	Entering the required information to join WeChat Pay is annoying	Hsieh (2021) [46]
	TC2	0.864	It would involve substantial costs to use WeChat Pay services (e.g., internet access, smartphone, and mobile payment charges)	
	TC3	0.784	Learning how to use WeChat Pay would not take much time or effort for me	
Habit	H1	0.737	Whenever I need to pay, I unconsciously use traditional method	Park et al. (2017) [21]
	H2	0.886	It would be difficult to control my tendency to use traditional method when I pay	
	H3	0.911	I do not need to devote a lot of mental effort to deciding that I will use traditional payment method	

(*continued*)

Table 1. (*continued*)

Construct	Item	Factor loading	Wording	Reference
Adoption Intention	AI1	0.911	I would be willing to adopt WeChat Pay	Wong (2021) [9]
	AI2	0.923	I intend to use WeChat Pay in future	
	AI3	0.865	I have a strong desire to interact further with WeChat Pay	
Technology Anxiety	TA1	0.881	I feel apprehensive about using WeChat Pay	Guo et al. (2013) [23]
	TA2	0.866	It scares me to think that I could cause the mobile device to induce bad consequences due to wrong operation	
	TA3	0.908	I hesitate to use technology for fear of making mistakes I cannot correct	
	TA4	0.894	WeChat Pay is somewhat intimidating to me	
Self-actualization	SA1	0.923	Learning to use WeChat Pay gives me the opportunity for personal development	Deng et al. (2014) [37]
	SA2	0.897	Learning to use WeChat Pay increases my feeling of self-fulfillment	
	SA3	0.876	Learning to use WeChat Pay gives me a feeling of accomplishment	

4.2 Data Collection

First, we conduct a pilot survey with 25 representative respondents and revise the questionnaire based on their comments and suggestions. Thereafter, we post the questionnaire on Fengling System (https://www.powercx.com/), which is one of the largest professional data collection platforms in China. A commercial sampling service provided by Fengling System was used to help us reach the target respondents. We obtained 318 questionnaires in this study from January 10 to January 20. Finally, we have 265 valid questionnaires.

4.3 Data Analysis

Partial Least Squares (PLS) was used to test the research model. Notably, PLS is more suitable for theoretical development with empirical data and building a complex model [49]. Furthermore, this type of structural equation model can handle the non-normal distributional sample and a relatively small sample size [50]. We use SmartPLS 3 to examine the measurement and structural models.

5 Results

5.1 Sample Description

Table 2 shows the demographic characteristics of the study. The proportion of males and females in our sample is relatively balanced (male 50.57%; female 49.43%), and their ages are all over 50. Most of the sample respondents are aged between 50 and 60 years old, accounting for approximately 67.93% of the total sample. As for education level, the percentages of Junior college degree/4-year college degree and high school graduate/higher vocational education are, respectively, 58.11% and 26.42%, suggesting an overall high education level of the respondents. The distribution of subjective health status scores is similar to a normal distribution. Less than 10% of the respondents live alone, meaning the majority of them can receive help in daily life from others. Approximately 70% of the respondents have more than 5 years of WeChat usage experience and over 90% of the respondents have used WeChat Pay before, which indicates that they are familiar with ICT and the mobile payment platform.

Table 2. Demographic characteristics (n = 265).

Demographic characteristic		Frequency	Percentage
Gender	Male	134	50.57%
	Female	131	49.43%
Age	50–59	168	67.93%
	60–69	78	24.91%
	70+	19	7.17%
Education level	Primary school graduate	15	6.79%
	Junior high school graduate	8	3.02%
	High school graduate or higher vocational education	70	26.42%
	Junior college degree or 4-year college degree	154	58.11%
	More than 4-year college degree	18	6.79%

(continued)

Table 2. (*continued*)

Demographic characteristic		Frequency	Percentage
Living situation	Home, alone	12	4.53%
	Home, together with husband/wife	167	63.02%
	Home, together with other family members	86	32.45%
Subjective Health Status	10	26	9.81%
	8–9	98	36.98%
	6–7	98	36.98%
	≤5	43	16.22%
Length of WeChat Use	<1 year	10	3.77%
	1–2 year	24	9.06%
	2–4 years	47	17.74%
	5–7 years	69	26.04%
	>7 years	115	43.4%
Whether to use WeChat Pay	Yes	242	91.32%
	No	23	8.68%

5.2 Measurement Model

Table 3 reports the psychometric properties a of all constructs in the proposed research model. First, the internal reliability was assessed by the Cronbach's alpha and composite reliability (CR) values, and all of them are over the recommended value of 0.7 [51], which support strong internal reliability. Second, the convergent validity was assessed by the values of average variance extracted (AVE). The results suggest that all the AVE values are greater than 0.5 [52], and all the item loadings (see Table 1) are above the recommended value of 0.7, which indicates high convergent validity. Third, the discriminant validity was examined by the square root of the AVE, as well as the Heterotrait–Monotrait (HTMT) ratio [53]. The square root of the AVE values for each construct is higher than all of its correlation coefficients with other constructs, as n in Table 3 [49]. All the HTMT values are below the recommended threshold values of 0.85, as in Table 4 ([52], indicating qualified discriminant validity. The aforementioned results present good psychometric properties for all the constructs in our study.

Table 3. Correlations and psychometric characteristics.

	1	2	3	4	5	6	7	8	9	10
1. Perceived value	0.876									
2. Transition cost	0.316	0.830								
3. Uncertainty cost	0.266	0.661	0.861							
4. Regret avoidance	0.282	0.539	0.407	0.917						
5. Social influence	0.128	0.341	0.189	0.183	0.819					
6. Habit	0.178	0.571	0.403	0.487	0.309	0.849				
7. Technology anxiety	0.327	0.733	0.638	0.549	0.394	0.604	0.888			
8. Self-actualization	0.195	0.214	0.19	0.148	0.435	0.108	0.249	0.899		
9. Cognitive lock-in	0.279	0.627	0.545	0.541	0.298	0.625	0.697	0.196	0.945	
10. Adoption intention	0.318	0.530	0.427	0.450	0.455	0.454	0.641	0.404	0.722	0.900
Cronbach's Alpha	0.854	0.776	0.828	0.811	0.832	0.805	0.910	0.882	0.940	0.883
Composite reliability	0.908	0.869	0.896	0.914	0.887	0.887	0.937	0.927	0.961	0.928
Average Variance Extracted (AVE)	0.768	0.689	0.742	0.841	0.670	0.720	0.788	0.808	0.893	0.810

Note(s): Values on the diagonal represent the square roots of the average variance extracted (AVE) for each construct

Table 4. Heterotrait–Monotrait (HTMT) ratios.

	1	2	3	4	5	6	7	8	9	10
1. Perceived value										
2. Transition cost	0.368									
3. Uncertainty cost	0.305	0.829								
4. Regret avoidance	0.329	0.671	0.474							

(*continued*)

Table 4. (*continued*)

	1	2	3	4	5	6	7	8	9	10
5. Social influence	0.146	0.379	0.231	0.231						
6. Habit	0.202	0.481	0.701	0.583	0.344					
7. Technology anxiety	0.354	0.870	0.721	0.638	0.420	0.698				
8. Self-actualization	0.215	0.252	0.215	0.171	0.516	0.118	0.273			
9. Cognitive lock-in	0.285	0.724	0.607	0.617	0.306	0.704	0.753	0.21		
10. Adoption intention	0.344	0.633	0.493	0.532	0.504	0.526	0.716	0.453	0.792	

5.3 Structural Model

We use standard bootstrap in SmartPLS with 5,000 bootstrapping samples to examine the significance. Figure 2 and Table 5 illustrate the structural model results.

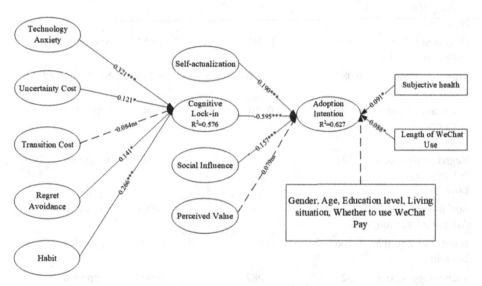

Fig. 2. The results of the structural model. Notes ***p < .001, **p < .01, *p < .05, nsp > .05.

First, we examine the antecedents of cognitive lock-in. Cognitive lock-in is significantly strengthened by technology anxiety ($\beta = 0.321$, $p < 0.001$), habit ($\beta = 0.266$, $p < 0.001$), regret avoidance ($\beta = 0.141$, $p < 0.05$), and uncertainty costs ($\beta = 0.121$, $p < 0.05$) whereas transition cost does not significantly influence cognitive lock-in. Therefore,

the R-squared value indicates that the technology anxiety, habit, regret avoidance, and uncertainty costs can explain 57.6% of the variance in cognitive lock-in. Therefore, H3, H5, H6, and H7 are supported, but H2 is not.

Second, with regard to the determinants of WeChat Pay adoption intention, we found that adoption intention was significantly influenced by cognitive lock-in ($\beta = -0.595$, $p < 0.001$). In addition, self-actualization ($\beta = 0.190$, $p < 0.01$) and social influence ($\beta = 0.157$, $p < 0.001$) have a positive impact on adoption intention while perceived value does not. The R-square value indicates that cognitive lock-in, self-actualization, and social influence explain 62.7% variance of adoption intention. Therefore, H4, H8, and H9 are supported, while H1 is not.

Lastly, among all the seven control variables, only subjective health and length of WeChat use have salient influences on adoption intention with path coefficients of 0.091 and 0.088, respectively ($p < 0.05$).

Table 5. The results of the structural model.

Hypothesis testing	Path coefficient	Standard Deviation	p-value	Hypothesis testing
Cognitive Lock-in -> Adoption Intention	−0.595	0.053	0.000	Supported
Perceived Value -> Adoption Intention	0.079	0.041	0.054	Not Supported
Transition Cost -> Cognitive Lock-in	0.084	0.076	0.266	Not Supported
Uncertainty Cost -> Cognitive Lock-in	0.121	0.061	0.048	Supported
Regret Avoidance -> Cognitive Lock-in	0.141	0.06	0.019	Supported
Social Norm -> Adoption Intention_	0.157	0.049	0.001	Supported
Habit -> Cognitive Lock-in	0.266	0.064	0.000	Supported
Technology Anxiety -> Cognitive Lock-in	0.321	0.087	0.000	Supported
Self-actualization -> Adoption Intention	0.190	0.049	0.000	Supported
Age -> Adoption Intention	0.031	0.042	0.466	

(continued)

Table 5. (*continued*)

Hypothesis testing	Path coefficient	Standard Deviation	p-value	Hypothesis testing
Education Level - > Adoption Intention	0.020	0.053	0.710	
Gender - > Adoption Intention	−0.013	0.040	0.744	
Subjective Health - > Adoption Intention	0.091	0.039	0.020	
Living Condition - > Adoption Intention	0.044	0.038	0.244	
Length of We Chat Use - > Adoption Intention	0.088	0.041	0.032	
Whether to use WeChat Pay - > Adoption Intention	0.047	0.047	0.319	

6 Discussion

6.1 Key Findings

This study employed status quo bias theory to investigate the relationship between cognitive lock-in and WeChat Pay adoption intention as well as the antecedents of cognitive lock-in. The findings indicate that the cognitive lock-in of older adults is significantly strengthened by technology anxiety, habit, regret avoidance, and uncertainty costs. The study also reveals that users' intention to adopt WeChat Pay is positively associated with social influence and self-actualization, while cognitive lock-in is a significant negative determinant.

Among the four antecedents of cognitive lock-in, technology anxiety is the most important ($\beta = 0.321$, $p < 0.001$), which is consistent with the previous literature that technology anxiety is one of the most important barriers in adopting mobile health services in China [30]. According to the research by Tsai, Juin-Ming, et al. [55], technology anxiety negatively impacts the perceptions of compatibility, usefulness, and ease of use, which makes it a subconscious factor for maintaining SQB. Habit, as the second most important factor in our model, is also a subconscious factor. We can assume that the subconscious factor may be more important than the conscious factor in the study of older adults.

Meanwhile, the significance of uncertainty cost reveals that some older adults are not familiar with WeChat Pay and are fearful of losing their privacy or property, which contribute to their cognitive reluctance to change because users' feelings of uncertainty mainly ensue from the fear that the performance of the mobile payment platform may fail to meet expectations. Furthermore, the significance of regret avoidance is possibly due to the telecom fraud they have experienced or heard and the increased convenience, which leads them to spend more money.

Conversely, the insignificant effect of transition cost is a little surprising, given that some prior studies have found it to be significant. (e.g., Heish, 2021; Gong, Xiang, et al. 2020 [41]). We assume that there may be two reasons. One is that the other four antecedents are more vital, and they might be less influential for transition cost, as the transition cost of mobile payment is relatively low compared to other innovative technologies [38]. The other is that the respondents in our sample have generally had access to the Internet for many years, and the cost is steadily reducing.

With regard to the constructs related to adoption intention, social influence has the largest positive effect size, which is aligned with the previous study by Talukder et al. [36]. As we mentioned before, WeChat Pay is dominant in the Chinese mobile payment market and has a good reputation; thus, it is natural for older adults to try and follow the majority, especially those in the same social circle, to prevent social disconnection. It might be a good way to increase the adoption behavior by stimulating users to attract people around them to use WeChat Pay-related functions such as sending red envelopes.

Another enabler we find is self-actualization. The result proves that learning or using ICT might be an opportunity for older adults to achieve a sense of accomplishment or self-actualization. Because of high self-actualization, older adults adopt WeChat Pay to show their learning ability and get a feeling of accomplishment.

However, the impact of perceived value is not significant. This result is in line with Hsieh's [46] study, where perceived net benefit does not significantly influence user' intentions to switch from cash payment to medical mobile payment. The influence of perceived value may be relatively small compared to cognitive lock-in, which is in line with the definition of cognitive lock-in.

6.2 Implications

Theoretically, this study helps us better understand inner mechanisms of older adults' adoption of mobile payment from the perspective of cognitive lock-in based on SQB. First, we explore adoption by older adults from a new perspective of cognitive lock-in, which is a supplement to explain the adoption behavior of older adults. Second, we develop a model of cognitive lock-in in mobile payment, including its antecedents and consequences, which is an extension of cognitive locking itself. We also extended the perspective of SQB by adding habit and technology anxiety as two significant subconscious factors. Third, our research contributes to mobile payment adoption behavior research in older adult groups. This research reveals that in a mobile payment research context, the characteristic of older adults weighs more than ordinary factors. Thus, in future research considering older adults, scholars should pay more attention to the sociocultural characteristic and personalities of older adults.

Practically, our study can help promote older adult-oriented design, relieve the cognitive lock-in, and improve the digital literacy of this group.

First, for WeChat Pay and other mobile payment platforms, this study provides references on optimizing age-appropriate services for mobile payment to further enhance user experience. As Linck et al. [56] argue, perceived security is one of the most important factors for the market breakthrough of mobile payment systems. Low perceived security leads to uncertainty and anxiety. Our research implies that uncertainty cost, regret avoidance, and technology anxiety are significant antecedents of cognitive lock-in. Therefore, to reduce cognitive lock-in by older adults, WeChat Pay and other mobile payment platforms need to pay critical attention toward enhancing the service quality and perfecting the platform security. They should not only design specialized barrier free user interfaces and functions for older adults but also reduce the risk by adding extra authentication regulations and safety confirmation measures into large payment orders.

Second, this study offers suggestions on improving the digital literacy of older adults. As social influence and self-actualization have a significant influence on the WeChat Pay adoption of older adults, WeChat developers can attract more older users by encouraging their families or peers to share the service based on social functions on WeChat. Moreover, intergenerational learning is an effective way to relieve anxiety and enhance confidence [57]. We should encourage children, younger families, caregivers or recruit volunteers to guide, participate, and transfer relevant knowledge and skills to older adults. In addition, product developers as well as communities can provide ICT training courses for older adults through online and offline, which can enhance the sense of self-actualization. Habit is an essential antecedent to their cognitive lock-in. In this case, helpful solutions to change their fixed mindset are still to establish new habits through social influence and reduce the inhibitors including high switching costs (both transition and uncertainty costs), especially for those non-users who have little smartphone usage experience. Once they start using mobile payment, especially during the COVID-19 pandemic, they are likely to continue use it after the pandemic, if they feel satisfied and get accustomed to this technology [58].

6.3 Limitations and Future Research

There are some study limitations which offer implications for future research. First, the data we used are self-reported data collected from the online survey, so older adults' real perceptions may not be fully reflected. The constraints of cross-sectional data also undermined causal relationships. Future studies can use longitudinal data or conduct experimental studies to mitigate these limitations. Second, this research was conducted in China which has a high mobile payment adoption rate, and our respondents have an overall higher education level as well as longer WeChat use experience. These mean that people are more familiar with this technology and have relatively higher digital literacy; thus, it would be interesting to further conduct cross-cultural research with a larger sample size and validate our results.

References

1. The Global Payments Report 2021: https://worldpaymentsreport.com/. Accessed 12 Jan 2021
2. Merchant Savvy Amazing Stats Demonstrating the Unstoppable Rise of Mobile Payments Globally. https://www.merchantsavvy.co.uk/mobile-payment-stats-trends/. Accessed 12 Jan 2021

3. European Commission. Silver economy study: how to stimulate the economy by hundreds of millions of euros per year. https://ec.europa.eu/digital-single-market/en/news/silver-onomy-study-how-stimulate-economy-hundreds-millions-euros-year. Accessed 12 Jan 2021

4. Newell, A.F., Dickinson, A., Smith, M.J., Gregor, P.: Designing a portal for older users: a case study of an industrial/academic collaboration. ACM Trans. Comput.-Hum. Interact. **13**, 347–375 (2006)

5. Choudrie, J., Junior, C.O., McKenna, B., Richter, S.: Understanding and conceptualising the adoption, use and diffusion of mobile banking in older adults: a research agenda and conceptual framework. J. Bus. Res. **88**, 449–465 (2018)

6. Abdullah, Khan, M.N.: Determining mobile payment adoption: a systematic literature search and bibliometric analysis. Cogent Bus. Manage. **8**(1), 1893245 (2021)

7. Esfahani, S.S., Bulent Ozturk, A.: The influence of individual differences on NFC-based mobile payment adoption in the restaurant industry. J. Hosp. Tour. Technol. **10**(2), 219–232 (2019)

8. Li, B., Hanna, S.D., Kim, K.T.: Who uses mobile payments: fintech potential in users and non-users. J. Finan. Couns. Plann. **31**(1), 83–100 (2020)

9. Wong, D., Liu, H., Meng-Lewis, Y., Sun, Y., Zhang, Y.: Gamified money: exploring the effectiveness of gamification in mobile payment adoption among the silver generation in China. Inf. Technol. People **35**(1), 281–315 (2022)

10. Arthur, W.B.: Competing technologies, increasing returns, and lock-in by historical events. Econom. J. **99**(394), 116–131 (1989)

11. Arthur, W.B.: Increasing returns and path dependence in the economy. Econom. Univ. Mich. **37**(2),157–162.4 (1994)

12. Polites, G.L., Karahanna, E.: Shackled to the status quo: the inhibiting effects of incumbent system habit, switching costs, and inertia on new system acceptance. MIS Q. **36**(1), 21–42 (2012)

13. Shi, X., Lin, Z., Liu, J., Hui, Y.K.: Consumer loyalty toward smartphone brands: the determining roles of deliberate inertia and cognitive lock-in. Inf. Manage. **55**(7), 866–876 (2018)

14. Kim, H.W., Kankanhalli, A.: Investigating user resistance to information systems implementation: a status quo bias perspective. MIS Q. **33**(3), 567–582.27 (2009)

15. Hsu, J.S.C.: Understanding the role of satisfaction in the formation of perceived switching value. Decis. Support Syst. **59**, 152–162 (2014)

16. Samuelson, W., Zeckhauser, R.: Status quo bias in decision making. J. Risk Uncertain. **1**(1), 7–59 (1988)

17. Novemsky, N., Kahneman, D.: The boundaries of loss aversion. J. Mark. Res. **42**(2), 119–128 (2005)

18. Talukder, Shamim, M., et al.: Continued use intention of wearable health technologies among the elderly: an enablers and inhibitors perspective. Internet Res. **31**(5),1611–1640 (2014)

19. Liu, Z., et al.: Exploring askers' switching to paid social Q&A services: a perspective on the push-pull-mooring framework. Inf. Process. Manage. **58**(1) 102396 (2021)

20. Li, J., Liu, M., Liu, X.: Why do employees resist knowledge management systems? An empirical study from the status quo bias and inertia perspectives. Comput. Hum. Behav. **65**, 189–200 (2016)

21. Park, M., Jun, J., Park, H.: Understanding mobile payment service continuous use intention: an expectation-confirmation model and inertia. Qual. Innov. Prosper. **21**(3), 78–94 (2017)

22. Mu, H.-L., Lee, Y.-C.: Will proximity mobile payments substitute traditional payments? Examining factors influencing customers' switching intention during the COVID-19 pandemic. Int. J. Bank Mark. Ahead-of-Print (2022)

23. Guo, X., Sun, Y., Wang, N., et al.: The dark side of elderly acceptance of preventive mobile health services in China. Electron Markets. **23**, 49–61 (2013)

24. Nikou, S.: Mobile technology and forgotten consumers: the young-elderly. Int. J. Consum. Stud. **39**(4), 294–304 (2015)
25. Talukder, M.S., Chiong, R., Corbitt, B., Bao, Y.K.: Critical factors influencing the intention to adopt m-government services by the elderly. J. Glob. Inf. Manag. **28**(4), 74–94 (2020)
26. Zauberman, G.: The intertemporal dynamics of consumer lock-in. J. Consum. Res. **30**(3), 405–419 (2003)
27. Li, Z., Cheng, Y.: From free to fee: exploring the antecedents of consumer intention to switch to paid online content. J. Electron. Commer. Res. **15**(4), 281 (2014)
28. Shankar, A., Nigam, A.: Explaining resistance intention towards mobile HRM application: the dark side of technology adoption. Int. J. Manpower. ahead-of-print (2021)
29. Hsieh, P.J., Lin, W.S.: Explaining resistance to system usage in the PharmaCloud: a view of the dual-factor model. Inf. Manage. **55**(1), 51–63 (2018)
30. Wang, Y.-Y., Wang, Y.-S., Lin, T.-C.: Developing and validating a technology upgrade model. Int. J. Inf. Manage. **38**(1), 7–26 (2018)
31. Peek, S.T.M., et al.: Factors influencing acceptance of technology for aging in place: a systematic review. Int. J. Med. Inform. **83**(4), 235–248 (2014)
32. Kavandi, H., Jaana, M.: Factors that affect health information technology adoption by seniors: a systematic review. Health Soc. Care Commun. **28**(6), 1827–1842 (2020)
33. Kuo, R.-Z.: Why do people switch mobile payment service platforms? An empirical study in Taiwan. Technol. Soc. **62**, 101312 (2020)
34. Kahle, B., Kahle, L.R., Beatty, S.E.: The task situation and habit in the attitude-behavior relationship: a social adaptation view. J. Soc. Behav. Personal. **2** (2), 219–232 (1987)
35. Hu, Y., Zhao, L.: Understanding the dual role of habit in cross-channel context: an empirical analysis of mobile payment. Sci. Paper Online. 1–20 (2016)
36. Talukder, Shamim, M., Sorwar, G., Bao, Y., Ahmed, J.U., Palash, M.A.S.: Predicting antecedents of wearable healthcare technology acceptance by elderly: a combined SEM-Neural Network approach. Technol. Forecast. Soc. Change **150**, 119793 (2020)
37. Deng, Z., Mo, X., Liu, S.: Comparison of the middle-aged and older users' adoption of mobile health services in China. Int. J. Med. Informat. **83**(3), 210–224 (2014)
38. Hoque, R., Sorwar, G.: Understanding factors influencing the adoption of mHealth by the elderly: an extension of the UTAUT model. Int. J. Med. Informatics **101**, 75–84 (1987)
39. Simonson, M.R., et al.: Development of a standardized test of computer literacy and a computer anxiety index. J. Educ. Comput. Res. **3**(2), 231–247 (1987)
40. Meuter, M.L., Ostrom, A.L., Bitner, M.J., Roundtree, R.: The influence of technology anxiety on consumer use and experiences with self-service technologies. J. Bus. Res. **56**(11), 899–906 (2003)
41. Gong, X., et al.: Transition from web to mobile payment services: The triple effects of status quo inertia. Int. J. Inf. Manage. **50**, 310–324 (2020)
42. Maslow, A.H.: Motivation and Personality (2nd ed.), Harper & Row, New York (1970)
43. Erikson, E.H., Erikson, J.M., Kivnick, H.: Vital Involvement in Old Age: The Experience of Old Age in Our Time Norton, New York (1986)
44. Venkatesh, V., Morris, M.G., Gordon, B.D., Davis, F.D.: User acceptance of information technology: toward a unified view. MIS Q. **27**(3), 425–478 (2003)
45. Wei, T.T., Marthandan, G., Yee-Loong Chong, A., Ooi, K., Arumugam, S.: What drives Malaysian m-commerce adoption? An empirical analysis. Ind. Manag. Data Syst. **109**(3), 370–388 (2009)
46. Hsieh, P.-J.: Understanding medical consumers' intentions to switch from cash payment to medical mobile payment: a perspective of technology migration. Technol. Forecast. Soc. Chang. **173**, 121074 (2021)

47. Claes, V., et al.: Attitudes and perceptions of adults of 60 years and older towards in-home monitoring of the activities of daily living with contactless sensors: an explorative study. Int. J. Nurs. Stud. **52**(1), 134–148 (2015)
48. Van Houwelingen, C.T.M., et al.: Understanding older people's readiness for receiving telehealth: mixed-method study. J. Med. Internet Res. **20**(4), e8407 (2018)
49. Hair, J.F., Ringle, C.M., Sarstedt, M.: PLS-SEM: indeed a silver bullet. J. Mark. Theory Pract. **19**(2), 139–152 (2011)
50. Khan, G.F., Sarstedt, M., Shiau, W.-L., Hair, J.F., Ringle, C.M., Fritze, M.P.: Methodological research on partial least squares structural equation modeling (PLS-SEM). Internet Res. **29**(3), 407–429 (2019)
51. Fornell, C., Larcker, D.F.: structural equation models with unobservable variables and measurement error: algebra and statistics. J. Mark. Res. **18**, 382–388 (1981)
52. Chin, W.W.: The partial least squares approach for structural equation modeling. In: Marcoulides, G.A. (ed.) Modern methods for business research, Lawrence Erlbaum Associates Publishers, pp. 295–336 (1998)
53. Henseler, J., Ringle, C.M., Sarstedt, M.: A new criterion for assessing discriminant validity in variance-based structural equation modeling. J. Acad. Mark. Sci. **43**(1), 115–135 (2014). https://doi.org/10.1007/s11747-014-0403-8
54. Voorhees, C.M., Brady, M.K., Calantone, R., Ramirez, E.: Discriminant validity testing in marketing: an analysis, causes for concern, and proposed remedies. J. Acad. Mark. Sci. **44**(1), 119–134 (2015). https://doi.org/10.1007/s11747-015-0455-4
55. Tsai, J.-M., et al.: Acceptance and resistance of telehealth: the perspective of dual-factor concepts in technology adoption. Int. J. Inf. Manage. **49**, 34–44 (2019)
56. Linck, K., Pousttchi, K., Wiedemann, D.G.: Security issues in mobile payment from the customer viewpoint. In: Proceedings of the 14th European Conference on information systems (ECIS 2006). Gothenburg, Sweden (2006)
57. Lee, O.E.K., Kim, D.H.: Bridging the digital divide for older adults via intergenerational mentor-Up. Res. Soc. Work Pract. **29**(7), 786–795 (2019)
58. Santosa, A.D., Taufik, N., Prabowo, F.H.E., et al.: Continuance intention of baby boomer and X generation as new users of digital payment during COVID-19 pandemic using UTAUT2. J. Financ. Serv. Mark. **26**, 259–273 (2021)

Attitude to Use Information and Communication Technology in Older Adults Under "Stay Home" to Prevent COVID-19 Infection

Takahiro Miura[1,2](✉), Ryoko Yoshida[3], Ikuko Sugawara[2,4],
Mahiro Fujisaki-Sueda-Sakai[2,5], Kenichiro Ito[6], Ken-ichiro Yabu[2,7],
Tohru Ifukube[2,7], and Hiroko Akiyama[2,8]

[1] Human Augmentation Research Center (HARC), National Institute of Advanced
Industrial Science and Technology (AIST), 6-2-3 Kashiwanoha, Kashiwa, Chiba
277-0882, Japan
miura-t@aist.go.jp
[2] Institute of Gerontology, The University of Tokyo, Tokyo, Japan
[3] Co-Creation Center for Active Aging, Tokyo, Japan
[4] Bunri University of Hospitality, Sayama, Japan
[5] Graduate School of Medicine, Tohoku University, Sendai, Japan
[6] Virtual Reality Educational Research Center,
The University of Tokyo, Tokyo, Japan
[7] Research Center for Advanced Science and Technology (RCAST),
The University of Tokyo, Tokyo, Japan
[8] Institute for Future Initiatives, The University of Tokyo, Tokyo, Japan

Abstract. Owing to the global COVID-19 (coronavirus disease 2019)
pandemic, many people have been forced to adopt a new lifestyle that
makes extensive use of information and communication technology (ICT)
under the slogan "Stay Home." Because older adults have been reported
to be more resistant to information technology, such rapid changes in
their lifestyle would be more difficult for them to accept. However, some
senior citizens have used ICT or have improved their ICT skills since
the COVID-19 pandemic. Analyzing the current situation of older adults
may allow for a detailed analysis of the acceptance process of information
technology. In this article, we aim to clarify the mechanism of acceptance
and use of information technology among older adults in terms of social
conditions, support systems, and the usability and accessibility of interfaces. The results indicated that the transtheoretical model of behavior
change in terms of interest and usage status of ICT/IoT services can be
used to categorize technology acceptance situations.

Keywords: Technology acceptance · Technology resistance ·
COVID-19 · Questionnaire survey · Older adults

© The Author(s), under exclusive license to Springer Nature Switzerland AG 2022
Q. Gao and J. Zhou (Eds.): HCII 2022, LNCS 13330, pp. 541–554, 2022.
https://doi.org/10.1007/978-3-031-05581-2_37

1 Introduction

Japan's aging rate reached 28.7% in 2020 and 29.1% in 2021, and the working population is expected to continue to decline while social security costs are expected to rise [4]. In addition, some of these older people are unaware of how to use information and communication technology (ICT), making it difficult for them to live in an increasingly information-oriented society [10,12,16,23,28,36]. Furthermore, as a result of the global COVID-19 (coronavirus disease 2019) pandemic, many people have been forced to adopt a new lifestyle that makes extensive use of ICT under the slogan "Stay Home" [2,22,34,35]. Because older adults have been reported to be more resistant to information technology, such rapid changes in their lifestyle would be more difficult for them to accept [5,7,13,14,20,33].

However, some senior citizens have been more proficient in the use of ICT than before the COVID-19 pandemic [8,19,27], and there are some learning circles established by older superusers to spread their knowledge on a community basis [31,37]. Furthermore, user interface diversification has recently progressed, and various accessible technologies have been enhanced and prevailed [24,38]. Particularly, recently, since there are an increasing number of health-related technologies with accessible and senior-friendly interfaces, some older people may adopt ICT in their daily lives [9,11,15,17,18,21,29,39,40]. Thus, the barriers for older adults to begin using ICT have been reduced as a result of a combination of social conditions, interfaces and accessibility of information technology, and voluntary support systems, and the situation is thought to be gradually changing to make it easier and easier for them to continue using it. As a result, analyzing the current situation of older adults may allow for a more detailed analysis of the acceptance process of information technology.

Therefore, this study aims to better understand the process of acceptance and use of information technology among older adults in terms of social conditions, support systems, and the usability and accessibility of interfaces. The following are our research questions.

Q1. What are the factors related to the acceptance, resistance, and use of ICT by older adults?
Q2. How can older adults be classified in terms of their attitudes toward the use of ICT?
Q3. What kind of ICTs do older adults start to accept?

2 Method

2.1 Procedure and Questionnaire Items

We conducted a questionnaire survey to ascertain whether the use of information technology had changed as a result of the COVID-19 pandemic in areas where older people volunteered to provide ICT support. A self-administered questionnaire was used to collect responses from 1,177 households in an eastern Japanese

Table 1. Age group of the participants.

Age	<30s	30s	40s	50s	60s	70s	80s
Frequency	2	22	44	52	78	276	172

suburb. Respondents were asked about their socio-demographic characteristics, digital device support needs, use of and intention to use ICT/IoT (Internet of Things) services and their awareness of technology acceptance and resistance in Japanese. We considered 12 items (e.g., smartphones, tablet devices, laptops) for the use and intention to use ICT/IoT services, as shown in Table 2, extracted from the ELSA 50+ Health and Life [1, 30], and participation in online meetings/chats. Participants answered these items with 4-point scale composed of 1. I have been using it before "Stay home," 2. I started using it because of "Stay home," 3. I do not use it, but I am interested in it, and 4. not used and interested. To ensure unidimensionality, we organized the data into three levels based on the start time of use (answers 3. and 4. were considered equal) and three levels based on the interest (answers 1. and 2. were regarded as equal). Because we obtained similar results based on the starting time of use and the interest, this paper will only discuss the results based on the starting time of use.

The questionnaire on technology acceptance and resistance comprised of acceptance-related items include perceived usefulness (PU), perceived ease of use (PEoU), intention to use (IU), facilitating condition (FC), adaptation intention (AI), and subjective norm (SN), and resistance-related items include resistance to change (RC) and technology anxiety (TA), as shown in Table 3. Participants in the questionnaire were asked to rate these items on a 5-point Likert scale: 1. strongly disagree, 2. disagree, 3. neutral, 4. agree, and 5. strongly agree. These items were culled from various studies on technology acceptance and resistance [3,5,6,10,16,23,32].

This study was approved by the ethics committee at The University of Tokyo.

2.2   Dataset and Participants

There were 702 responses (59.6% collection rate). Missing data were omitted for the 90 questions about ICT use and technology acceptance and resistance to the extent that homoscedasticity from the original data distribution was preserved. As a result, when including responses with approximately 25% missing data (N = 646), the equivariance was satisfied for all response items at a significance level of 5%, so we decided to use this data set. There are 350 males and 296 females among the 646 participants. The age group of the participants is shown in Table 1; the majority of the participants were older adults in their 70s and 80s.

2.3   Analysis

First, we ran exploratory and confirmatory factor analyses on two question item sets: intention to use ICT/IoT services and technology acceptance and resistance.

These analyses are intended to see if the factors we initially assumed could be extracted, particularly in terms of technology acceptance and resistance. In this case, we first extracted items for which reliability could be assured using the Kaiser–Mayer–Olkin measures of sampling adequacy, and then used Bartlett's sphericity test to confirm that the observed variables were uncorrelated. After removing the problematic items, we used exploratory factor analysis to extract the factors. At the time, the Kaiser–Guttman criterion, screeprot, parallel analysis, MAP (maximum a posteriori) criterion, and parallel analysis with SMC were used to determine the appropriate number of factors (squared multiple correlation). The factors were then extracted using the maximum likelihood method, and the factor axes were rotated using the promax rotation. Finally, the number of factors extracted by exploratory factor analysis was determined by subjective interpretability and goodness of fit measures such as RMSEA (root mean square error of approximation) and TLI (Tucker–Lewis index). Meanwhile, because of confirmatory factor analysis, we interpret the most appropriate and reasonable factor sets using similar criteria, but we used goodness of fit measures such as RMSEA and TLI, as well as CFI (comparative fit index) and SRMR (standardized root mean square residual).

We used cluster analysis to analyze the respondents' situation after calculating the factor loadings and scores for each response to the obtained factors. We used the k-means method, a non-hierarchical clustering method, to separate the clusters after determining the appropriate number of clusters based on the Gap coefficients. Finally, structural equation modeling was used to create a model of the relationship between changes in ICT usage and the previously mentioned factors. We decided to conduct the analysis using the multiple indicator model at this time. We used the factor scores of the 462 participants with no missing values because factor scores could not be calculated for responses with missing values.

3   Results and Discussion

3.1   The Use and Intention to Use ICT/IoT Services

Figure 1 depicts the use and intent to use ICT/IoT services. In addition to checking the news, maps, and traffic information, most participants used ICT to communicate with family and friends (q2,3, and 12). After staying at home, the most common activity was using online meeting apps (q14), followed by watching movies, TV dramas, and videos, and listening to music and radio programs (q4). Watching over family members and pets (q9) and entertainment (q1) were rarely used by participants.

Table 2 depicts the factor loading matrix of starting time to use applications obtained by exploratory factor analysis. The consistency of the factors extracted by the exploratory and confirmatory factor analyses was also confirmed. We conducted factor analysis for the cases of 1, 3, 4, and 5 factors as a result of the factor numbers criteria. We extracted four factors based on interpretability: 1) information acquisition, 2) entertainment, leisure, and consumption activities,

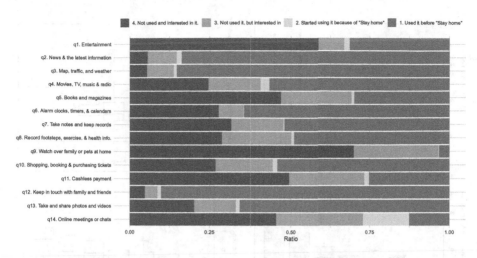

Fig. 1. The use and intention to use ICT/IoT services. Detailed question items are shown in Table 2.

Table 2. Factor loading matrix of starting time to use applications acquired by exploratory factor analysis.

No.	Question	ML1	ML2	ML3	ML4
1)	Enjoy games, puzzles, and other entertainment.				
2)	Get news and the latest information.	0.841			
3)	Look up maps and directions, traffic information, and weather forecasts.	0.941			
4)	Watch movies, TV dramas, and videos, and listen to music and radio programs.		0.661		
5)	Read books and magazines.		0.532		
6)	Use alarm clocks, timers, and calendars.			0.782	
7)	Take notes and keep records as a way to archive information		0.445		
8)	Record footsteps, activity, exercise, and health information			0.494	
9)	Watch over family members or pets at home while away from home		0.454		
10)	Shopping, booking and purchasing tickets, etc.		0.486		
11)	Use cashless payment methods (LINE Pay, PayPay, Apple Pay, etc.)		0.634		
12)	Keep in touch with family and friends				
13)	Take and share photos and videos				0.486
14)	Have online meetings or chats with multiple people (including online drinking parties) with friends or colleagues				0.694
	Interpreted factors	Information acquisition	Entertainment, leisure, and consumption activities	Time, schedule, and activities	Multimedia communication

3) time, schedule, and physical activities, and 4) multimedia communications (RMSEA = .038 < .05, TLI = .968 > .95 in exploratory factor analysis). In confirmatory factor analysis, CFI = .936 > .90, TLI = .911 > .90, RMSEA = .070 < .10, SRMR = .049 < .05 . The factor analysis results revealed little

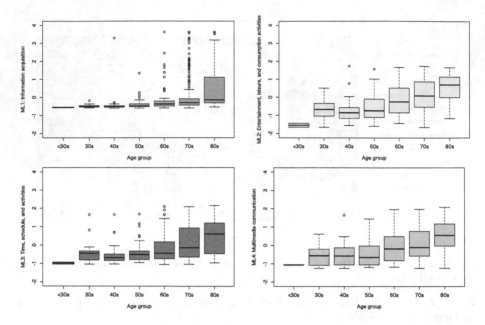

Fig. 2. Factor scores calculated for each age group in four factors extracted by the exploratory factor analysis. In these graphs, the higher the vertical axis value, the less interested the respondents are.

difference between the values reconstructed as the three levels of the starting time of use and the interest. This finding implies that different types of applications begin to be used at different times.

Figure 2 shows the factor scores calculated for each age group and displayed in box plots. In this plot, the higher the vertical axis value, the less interested the respondents are. We discovered that the older the respondents were, the less interested they were in all factors. Factor 1: information acquisition demonstrated a significant difference between participants in their 80s. As the age group grows older, the use of traditional media such as television and newspapers may increase without the use of ICT, and this trend may be especially pronounced in participants in their 80s.

3.2 Factors on Technology Acceptance and Resistance

Table 3 shows the results of the exploratory factor analysis. The consistency of the factors extracted by the exploratory and confirmatory factor analyses was also confirmed. We conducted factor analysis for the cases of 3, 5, 6, and 10 factors as a result of the factor numbers criteria. We extracted the six factors described in the Sect. 2.1 based on the interpretability: perceived ease of use (PEoU), subjective norm (SN), technology anxiety (TA), perceived usefulness (PU), intention to use (IU), and resistance to change (RC) (RMSEA = .036 < .05, TLI = .978 > .95 in exploratory factor analysis). In confirmatory factor

Table 3. Factor loading matrix of technology acceptance and resistance acquired by exploratory factor analysis.

Subscales	Question items	ML1 PEoU	ML4 SN	ML3 TA	ML5 PU	ML2 IU	ML6 RC
Subjective norm (SN)	1) People who influence my behavior think that I should use smartphones and internet services.		0.948				
	2) People who are important to me think that I should use smartphones and internet services.		0.987				
Facilitating condition (FC)	3) I think smartphones and internet services cost is affordable to me.						
	4) I always have a friend or family member who could teach me how to use smartphones and internet services.						
Intention to use (IU)	5) I would take a class of smarphones and internet services.					0.861	
	6) I would explore smarphones and internet services on my own in the class.					0.943	
Adaptation intention (AI)	7) I intend to use smartphones and internet services in the near future						
Resistance to change (RC)	8) I don't want smartphones and internet services to change the way I have lived.						0.818
	9) I don't want smartphones and internet services to change the way I interact with other people.						0.788
Technology anxiety (TA)	10) I feel apprehensive about using smartphones and internet services.			0.764			
	11) It scares me to think that I could cause the smartphones and internet services to induce bad consequences due to wrong operation.			0.941			
	12) I hesitate to use technology for fear of making mistakes I cannot correct.			0.729			
Perceived Usefulness (PU)	13) Smartphones and internet services is useful for information acquisition.				0.902		
	14) Smartphones and internet services is useful for entertainment and leisure.				0.592		
	15) Overall, I find smartphones and internet services to be useful in my life.				0.809		
Perceived Ease of Use (PEoU)	16) Learning to operate smartphones and internet services will be easy for me	0.958					
	17) I can easily become skilful at using smartphones and internet services	1.086					
	18) Overall, smartphones and internet services are easy to use	0.667					

analysis, CFI = .960 > .95, TLI = .944 > .90, RMSEA = .068 < .100, SRMR = .053 < .100. The facilitating condition (FC) and adaptation intention (AI) factors were not extracted.

Figure 3 depicts the path diagram based on the confirmatory factor analysis of technology acceptance and resistance. The correlation coefficients between the factors revealed positive correlations between TA and RC, PU and SN, and TA and IU, as well as negative correlations between TA/RC and PEoU/PU, respectively. Taking these findings into account, it is possible to conclude that those who perceived ICT to be more useful wanted others to use it, whereas those who perceived ICT to be simple to use felt less anxious about it. On the

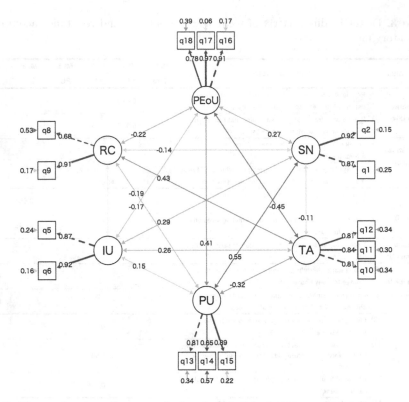

Fig. 3. The exploratory factor analysis calculated factor scores for each age group in six factors about technology acceptance and resistance. The character strings in the circles and rectangle boxes represent the factors and question numbers listed in Table 3.

other hand, as people's fear of technology grew, so did their willingness to use it. This result could have been obtained while staying at home to avoid COVID-19 infection.

3.3   Clusters of Those Who Feel the Acceptance and Resistance to Technology

Table 4 depicts the results of clustering the factor scores of technology acceptance and resistance using the k-means method along with the average factor scores in each cluster. For the sake of Gap statistics and interpretability, the case of seven clusters was used in this analysis. The clusters were analyzed by assigning them to the five stages of Prochaska's transtheoretical model of behavior change [25, 26]. The clusters in Table 4 correspond to the progress of the stages such as maintenance, action, preparation, contemplation, and precontemplation, in order from the top of the table. As a result, classification of ICT usage could be performed to some extent in accordance with the five stages. We could categorize

Table 4. Results of cluster analysis on the factor scores of technology acceptance and resistance shown. Because the directions of acceptance and resistance are positive and negative, respectively, the directions of positive/negative are reversed only for TA (technology anxiety) and RC (resistance to change).

		PEoU	SN	TA	PU	IU	RC	Number of participants	Brief interpretation	Stage on transtheoretical model
Clusters	C1	1.392	1.062	-1.068	0.976	-0.051	-0.466	75	Those who know how to use ICT and want others to use it too.	Action/maintenance (with sense of utility)
	C2	0.936	-0.411	-0.766	0.106	-1.220	-0.431	41	Those who can use ICT but may be reluctant to use it.	Action/maintenance (with sense of fatigue)
	C3	-0.101	0.487	0.164	0.799	0.709	-1.100	51	Those who think ICT is useful and want to use it, but find it difficult.	Preparation
	C4	0.242	0.238	-0.053	-0.020	0.064	0.334	79	Those who are moderate in all of the factors.	-
	C5	-0.668	0.247	0.538	0.036	1.137	0.425	64	Those who think ICT is scary and difficult but want to use it and need support.	Contemplation
	C6	-0.879	-1.823	0.166	-1.333	-1.148	-0.256	45	Those who do not feel the need to learn ICT because it is useless and cumbersome, but are not resistant to it.	Precontemplation (with less disgust)
	C7	-0.726	-0.579	0.977	-0.491	-0.205	0.610	120	Those who feel that ICT is useless and cumbersome and feels resistance to ICT and change their own.	Precontemplation (with strong disgust)

Positive   Negative

Table 5. Age group of participants in each cluster for technology acceptance and resistance shown in Table 4.

		<30s	30s	40s	50s	60s	70s	80s
Clusters	C1	1%	9%	19%	17%	17%	31%	5%
	C2	2%	12%	17%	15%	12%	27%	15%
	C3	0%	2%	16%	14%	10%	39%	20%
	C4	0%	3%	6%	8%	13%	46%	23%
	C5	0%	0%	3%	8%	19%	45%	25%
	C6	0%	0%	4%	0%	0%	42%	53%
	C7	0%	4%	1%	5%	13%	48%	29%

the groups that felt usefulness of ICT and the groups that felt fatigue of ICT use in the action/maintenance (C1/C2) stages based on the average value of each factor score. Furthermore, the contemplation stage (C6/C7) could be divided into two groups: those who are disgusted by ICT and those who are not.

Table 5 depcits the ratio of age groups that comprise each cluster. There were more people in the maintenance/action stage, C1/C2, who were in their 60s or younger than in the other clusters. Clusters C4 to C7, however, had a higher proportion of older people, primarily in their 70s and 80s. It is worth noting, however, that the precontemplation with less disgust in C6 was primarily associated with older adults in their 80s. This finding suggests that many older adults, particularly those in their 80s, may not be resistant to ICT in and of itself, despite difficulties in using and learning ICT.

3.4   Relationship Between the Starting Time to Use Applications and Technology Acceptance and Resistance

Figure 4 depicts the relationship between the factors of technology acceptance and resistance and the factors of starting time to use applications (CFI = .956 > .95, TLI = .944 > .90, RMSEA = .047 < .05, SRMR = .050 < .10). Those that begin with "T_" represent the factors that determine when applications can be used for the first time. In general, all factors influencing the initial time spent using applications were highly and positively related to perceived ease of use (PEoU), perceived usefulness (PU), and subjective norm (SN). However, information acquisition (T_IA), multimedia communication (T_MC), and entertainment, leisure, and cashless payment (T_EL) was negatively and significantly related to technology anxiety (TA). Furthermore, multimedia communication and T_EL were found to be negatively related to resistance to change (RC).

Because T_TS (time, schedule, and activities) had many simple applications and was related to time management, which is essential in everyday life, the influence of RC and TA may be less. Furthermore, because T_IA is a collection of information acquisition methods, it has little impact on lifestyles, etc. Thus, among the negative indicators, it was not strongly related to RC and may have only been related to TA. However, because T_MC and T_EL are functional groups that can influence one's lifestyle, they may be closely related to not only TA but also RC. It is well known that various forms of peer support are effective in dealing with such technology [31,37]. On the other hand, it is difficult to directly improve the RC; however, because the factors of beginning to use applications related to RC are also related to TA, it is possible that the effect of RC can be reduced by moderating TA.

4   Summary and Future Work

We discovered some aspects regarding the use of and attitude toward ICTs under stay-at-home situations based on factor and cluster analyses of the starting time to use ICT/IoT services and technology acceptance/resistance, as well as structural equation modeling of the extracted factors. Our accomplishments are as follows:

A1. The acceptance, resistance, and use of ICT by older adults can be summarized as the factors of perceived ease of use (PEoU), subjective norm (SN), technology anxiety (TA), perceived usefulness (PU), intention to use (IU), and resistance to change (RC). The factors of facilitating condition (FC), and adaptation intention (AI), as initially assumed, was not extracted.

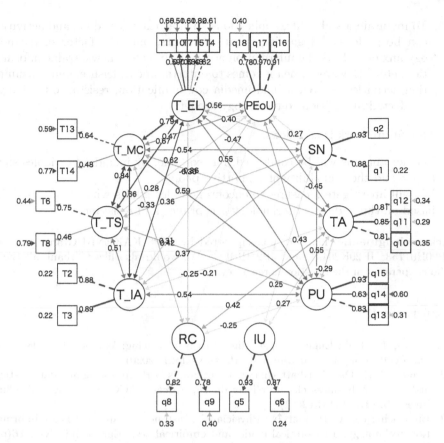

Fig. 4. The relationship between the factors of starting time to use applications and technology acceptance and resistance is depicted in a path diagram. Positive and negative relationships are represented by green and red lines, respectively. The following are the methods for the character strings in the circles: T_EL: Begin using applications for entertainment, leisure, and consumption activities. T_MC: Begin using multimedia communications, T_TS: Begin using time, schedule, and activity-related applications, T_IA: Time to begin using information acquisition applications, PEoU stands for perceived ease of use, SN stands for subjective norm, TA stands for technology anxiety, and PU stands for perceived usefulness. IU stands for intention to use, and RC stands for resistance to change. The strings in rectangle boxes represent question numbers beginning with T, and q represents the question items shown in Table 2 and 3, respectively. (Color figure online)

A2. The transtheoretical model of behavior change in terms of interest and usage status of ICT/IoT services can be used to categorize technology acceptance situations. Furthermore, the presence or absence of a sense of usefulness or fatigue can be used to classify the usage status, and the presence or absence of a sense of disgust can classify the precontemplation status.

A3. To maintain a stable life, applications such as time, schedule, and activities can be preferred. Regarding negative factors, only the factor of technology anxiety affects the information acquisition factor (news, traffic information, etc.). However, when it comes to entertainment, leisure, and consumption activities, as well as multimedia communication, resistance to change is affected in addition to technology anxiety.

Our future work is as follows:

- Further analysis will be conducted, for example, by including variables such as age and the availability of supportive people.
- We will investigate measures to encourage older adults who do not use ICT based on the findings of technology acceptance and resistance.

Acknowledgment. This work was supported by JSPS KAKENHI Grant Numbers JP20H01753, JP20K20494, and JP21H04580. We would also like to thank all those who cooperated in the questionnaire survey.

References

1. Banks, J., et al.: English Longitudinal Study of Ageing: Waves 0–9, 1998–2019. [data collection]. Oxford University Press, Oxford (2020)
2. Bendavid, E., Oh, C., Bhattacharya, J., Ioannidis, J.P.: Assessing mandatory stay-at-home and business closure effects on the spread of COVID-19. Eur. J. Clin. Invest. **51**(4), e13484 (2021)
3. Bhattacherjee, A., Hikmet, N.: Physicians' resistance toward healthcare information technology: a theoretical model and empirical test. Eur. J. Inf. Syst. **16**(6), 725–737 (2007)
4. Cabinet Office, J.: Annual Report on the Ageing Society [Summary] FY2020 (2020). https://www8.cao.go.jp/kourei/english/annualreport/2020/pdf/2020.pdf
5. Chen, K., Chan, A.H.: A review of technology acceptance by older adults. Gerontechnology (2011)
6. Davis, F.D.: Perceived usefulness, perceived ease of use, and user acceptance of information technology. MIS Q. **13**, 319–340 (1989)
7. Di Giacomo, D., Ranieri, J., D'Amico, M., Guerra, F., Passafiume, D.: Psychological barriers to digital living in older adults: computer anxiety as predictive mechanism for technophobia. Behav. Sci. **9**(9), 96 (2019)
8. Dodd, C., Athauda, R., Adam, M.T.: Designing user interfaces for the elderly: a systematic literature review. In: Proceedings of the Australasian Conference on Information Systems (2017). p. 11 pages
9. Duh, H.B.L., Do, E.Y.L., Billinghurst, M., Quek, F., Chen, V.H.H.: Senior-friendly technologies: interaction design for senior users. In: CHI 2010 Extended Abstracts on Human Factors in Computing Systems, pp. 4513–4516 (2010)
10. Guo, X., Sun, Y., Wang, N., Peng, Z., Yan, Z.: The dark side of elderly acceptance of preventive mobile health services in China. Electron. Mark. **23**(1), 49–61 (2013)
11. Hart, T.A., Chaparro, B.S., Halcomb, C.G.: Evaluating websites for older adults: adherence to 'senior-friendly' guidelines and end-user performance. Behav. Inf. Technol. **27**(3), 191–199 (2008)

12. Heart, T., Kalderon, E.: Older adults: are they ready to adopt health-related ICT? Int. J. Med. Informatics **82**(11), e209–e231 (2013)
13. Hoque, R., Sorwar, G.: Understanding factors influencing the adoption of mHealth by the elderly: an extension of the UTAUT model. Int. J. Med. Informatics **101**, 75–84 (2017)
14. Iyer, R., Eastman, J.K.: The elderly and their attitudes toward the internet: the impact on internet use, purchase, and comparison shopping. J. Marketing Theory Pract. **14**(1), 57–67 (2006)
15. Izumi, M., Kikuno, T., Tokuda, Y., Hiyama, A., Miura, T., Hirose, M.: Practical use of a remote movable avatar robot with an immersive interface for seniors. In: Stephanidis, C., Antona, M. (eds.) UAHCI 2014. LNCS, vol. 8515, pp. 648–659. Springer, Cham (2014). https://doi.org/10.1007/978-3-319-07446-7_62
16. Johnston, A.C., Warkentin, M.: Fear appeals and information security behaviors: an empirical study. MIS Q. **34**, 549–566 (2010)
17. Kamesawa, A., et al.: Acceptance and practical use of assistive technologies for frail seniors and caregivers: interview surveys on nursing homes. In: Zhou, J., Salvendy, G. (eds.) ITAP 2018. LNCS, vol. 10926, pp. 70–84. Springer, Cham (2018). https://doi.org/10.1007/978-3-319-92034-4_6
18. Kang, H.G., et al.: In situ monitoring of health in older adults: technologies and issues. J. Am. Geriatr. Soc. **58**(8), 1579–1586 (2010)
19. Kobayashi, M., Hiyama, A., Miura, T., Asakawa, C., Hirose, M., Ifukube, T.: Elderly user evaluation of mobile touchscreen interactions. In: Campos, P., Graham, N., Jorge, J., Nunes, N., Palanque, P., Winckler, M. (eds.) INTERACT 2011. LNCS, vol. 6946, pp. 83–99. Springer, Heidelberg (2011). https://doi.org/10.1007/978-3-642-23774-4_9
20. Lian, J.W., Yen, D.C.: Online shopping drivers and barriers for older adults: age and gender differences. Comput. Hum. Behav. **37**, 133–143 (2014)
21. Miura, T., et al.: Mobile application to record daily life for seniors based on experience sampling method (ESM). In: Stephanidis, C., Antona, M., Gao, Q., Zhou, J. (eds.) HCII 2020. LNCS, vol. 12426, pp. 660–669. Springer, Cham (2020). https://doi.org/10.1007/978-3-030-60149-2_49
22. Nomura, K., et al.: Cross-sectional survey of depressive symptoms and suicide-related ideation at a Japanese national university during the COVID-19 stay-home order. Environ. Health Prev. Med. **26**(1), 1–9 (2021)
23. Oreg, S., et al.: Dispositional resistance to change: measurement equivalence and the link to personal values across 17 nations. J. Appl. Psychol. **93**(4), 935 (2008)
24. Page, T.: Touchscreen mobile devices and older adults: a usability study. Int. J. Hum. Factors Ergon. **3**(1), 65–85 (2014)
25. Prochaska, J.O., DiClemente, C.C.: Stages and processes of self-change of smoking: toward an integrative model of change. J. Consult. Clin. Psychol. **51**(3), 390 (1983)
26. Prochaska, J.O., Marcus, B.H.: The transtheoretical model: applications to exercise (1994)
27. Selwyn, N.: The information aged: a qualitative study of older adults' use of information and communications technology. J. Aging Stud. **18**(4), 369–384 (2004)
28. Selwyn, N., Gorard, S., Furlong, J., Madden, L.: Older adults' use of information and communications technology in everyday life. Ageing Soc. **23**(5), 561–582 (2003)
29. Shirahada, K., Ho, B.Q., Wilson, A.: Online public services usage and the elderly: assessing determinants of technology readiness in Japan and the UK. Technol. Soc. **58**, 101115 (2019)
30. Steptoe, A., Breeze, E., Banks, J., Nazroo, J.: Cohort profile: the English longitudinal study of ageing. Int. J. Epidemiol. **42**(6), 1640–1648 (2013)

31. Takagi, H., Kosugi, A., Ishihara, T., Fukuda, K.: Remote IT education for senior citizens. In: Proceedings of the 11th Web for All Conference, pp. 1–4 (2014)
32. Thatcher, J.B., Perrewe, P.L.: An empirical examination of individual traits as antecedents to computer anxiety and computer self-efficacy. MIS Q. **26**, 381–396 (2002)
33. Tsai, T.H., Lin, W.Y., Chang, Y.S., Chang, P.C., Lee, M.Y.: Technology anxiety and resistance to change behavioral study of a wearable cardiac warming system using an extended TAM for older adults. PLoS ONE **15**(1), e0227270 (2020)
34. Tull, M.T., Edmonds, K.A., Scamaldo, K.M., Richmond, J.R., Rose, J.P., Gratz, K.L.: Psychological outcomes associated with stay-at-home orders and the perceived impact of COVID-19 on daily life. Psychiatry Res. **289**, 113098 (2020)
35. Watanabe, M.: The COVID-19 pandemic in Japan. Surg. Today **50**(8), 787–793 (2020)
36. Weatherall, A., White, J.: A grounded theory analysis of older adults and information technology. Educ. Gerontol. **26**(4), 371–386 (2000)
37. Xie, B.: Information technology education for older adults as a continuing peer-learning process: a Chinese case study. Educ. Gerontol. **33**(5), 429–450 (2007)
38. Xie, B., Charness, N., Fingerman, K., Kaye, J., Kim, M.T., Khurshid, A.: When going digital becomes a necessity: Ensuring older adults' needs for information, services, and social inclusion during COVID-19. J. Aging Soc. Pol. **32**(4–5), 460–470 (2020)
39. Yoshioka, D., et al.: Evaluation of IoT-setting method among senior citizens in Japan. In: Gao, Q., Zhou, J. (eds.) HCII 2021. LNCS, vol. 12786, pp. 278–292. Springer, Cham (2021). https://doi.org/10.1007/978-3-030-78108-8_21
40. Yoshizaki, R., et al.: Design and verification of a smart home management system for making a smart home composable and adjustable by the elderly. In: Proceedings of the HCII 2022. Springer (2022, to Appear)

Internet-Able Older Adults: Text Notifications and Satisfaction with Online Questionnaires

Elizabeth Nichols(✉), Shelley Feuer, Erica Olmsted-Hawala, and Rachel Gliozzi

U.S. Census Bureau, Washington, D.C., USA
elizabeth.may.nichols@census.gov

Abstract. The 2020 Census was the first U.S. census to use an online reporting option as the primary data collection vehicle. The online census questionnaire was available between March and October of 2020. User satisfaction with the online census experience was measured via an online follow-up survey called the 2020 Census User Experience (UX) Survey. A sample of 153,000 web respondents from the 2020 Census were invited to complete the UX survey, and notified with up to three text message invitations. We selected a representative nationwide sample of respondents likely to have had different experiences filling out the Census, such as those who answered the census in March and those who waited until October, or those who answered using a smartphone and those who used a PC. We did not take into consideration the demographics of the respondents when selecting the sample, however, post analysis showed some age related differences in both satisfaction with the online census experience and in responding to the UX survey through a link sent via text message. Older adults who already answered their census online and who likely owned a cell phone were more likely to interact with the text message (either by replying STOP or answering the survey) than either younger users or middle-age users. Older adults were also more satisfied than younger adults. However, satisfaction did not differ between older and middle-aged adults. These findings add to the general research on older adults and technology.

Keywords: SMS · Text · Motivation · Satisfaction · U.S. 2020 Census

1 Introduction

The 2020 Census was the first U.S. census to use an online reporting option as the primary data collection vehicle. The online census questionnaire was available between March and October of 2020, with Census Day being April 1, 2020. Most residential addresses in the U.S. were mailed notifications about answering the census. In these mail pieces, the URL of the online census questionnaire was included along with the authentication code, called the Census ID, specific to that address. The public could report their census information even if they did not have a Census ID, but they would have to enter their address. In May 2020, Census Bureau staff noticed a higher-than-expected use of the online census path where users did not enter a Census ID and these respondents were more likely to exit the census questionnaire before reaching the end

International copyright, 2022, U.S. Department of Commerce, U.S. Government 2022
Q. Gao and J. Zhou (Eds.): HCII 2022, LNCS 13330, pp. 555–566, 2022.
https://doi.org/10.1007/978-3-031-05581-2_38

of it. The former problem could have been due to confusion on the questionnaire's login screen, or problems with the mail material where the authentication code was printed. The latter problem could also have been a usability problem with that questionnaire path. To examine if there were usability issues with the online census questionnaire or the mail materials, staff created and disseminated a short 3-min survey to measure satisfaction with the online census experience called the 2020 Census User Experience (UX) Survey.

Because the UX survey was not originally part of census production planning, and due to restricted mobility during the COVID-19 pandemic, staff needed a convenient way to notify the sample to minimize unanticipated costs and additional staffing needs. Contact via text message appeared to be a viable option, as the Census Bureau requested respondents' phone numbers in the online census in the event of any official business follow-up. The UX survey was the Census Bureau's first experience with text-only notification for an online survey.

While we did not select a sample for the UX survey based on respondent demographic characteristics, this paper repurposes the data to look at age-related differences. One goal is to determine whether older adults who answered their census online would be more or less likely to use text messaging as a communication vehicle to access another online survey. Measuring any limitations associated with notification modes is important to reduce total survey error [1]. The other goal of this analysis is to see whether older adults differed in their satisfaction with the online 2020 Census questionnaire compared to middle-aged and younger adults. As this was the first census to use an internet questionnaire as the primary mode of response, documenting if the online survey was satisfactory for all respondents, regardless of age, was important.

To be in the sampling frame for the UX survey, the respondent had to initiate or complete the online version of the 2020 Census, which included entering a cell phone number as their contact number. There was some concern that the online census questionnaire would pose a burden for older adults as internet access is not as prevalent with that age group [2, 3]. However, older adults traditionally have been considered "good" responders to the census in general, with high response rates. In a study measuring the attitudes and behaviors of the U.S. public, older respondents were more likely to report intent to participate in the census while younger householders were least likely to report they intended to participate in the census [4–6]. These findings suggest that while some older adults will not be able to use the online census questionnaire, for those who have internet access, their likelihood of answering the census online should be higher than younger adults.

To access the UX survey, the census respondent also had to respond to a text message sent to the cell phone number collected by the online census questionnaire. Like internet access, older adults are less likely to text, with differences especially apparent by health and socioeconomic status. Those with fewer physical limitations and higher education levels use technology more [7]. Other studies show that older adults who use text messaging do so successfully to build social relationships [8] and improve health experiences [9, 10]. Given the fact that older adults have been shown to be "good" responders and that these particular older adults are technically savvy since they already completed the 2020 Census online, we predict that there will be age-related differences in engaging with a survey through a text notification. Our hypothesis is that older adults will be more likely to engage with the text message than middle-aged or younger adults. Engagement includes actions such as refusing to participate (engaging with the text by replying STOP) or participating (accessing, initiating, or completing the web survey by selecting the link). We also examine participation as measured by breakoffs while in the survey (this is the difference between those who initiate and complete the survey).

We also wanted to determine whether user satisfaction of the online census questionnaire differed by age. Researchers who have examined the "positivity effect" associated with older adults [11] have observed a shift in behavior and attitude from a negativity bias early in life to a positivity bias in middle and late adulthood [12]. While there is some debate in the literature whether this phenomenon occurs because older adults forget or suppress negative experiences more easily, or because they simply assess those experiences more positively, studies tend to point to the latter [13–16]. In prior Census Bureau research with online mobile web surveys, adults 50 years and older rated their survey experience more positively than adults under 50 [17]. Based on this literature our second hypothesis is that older and middle-aged adults will be more satisfied with their online census experience than younger adults.

2   Methods

Below are highlights of methods relevant to the online follow-up satisfaction survey.

2.1   User Experience Survey Questions

The UX survey took on average three minutes to answer and was programmed in Qualtrics, an off-the-shelf software application for designing web surveys. The first question in the UX survey (Fig. 1) asks for the respondent's satisfaction with their online census questionnaire experience. The UX survey measured respondent satisfaction with the online census questionnaire to examine why census respondents were not using their Census ID. Because respondents who did not use their Census ID were also less likely to click "submit" at the end of the survey, the UX survey also sought to better understand whether something about this path led to increased exiting prior to selecting "submit" at the end of the questionnaire [18].

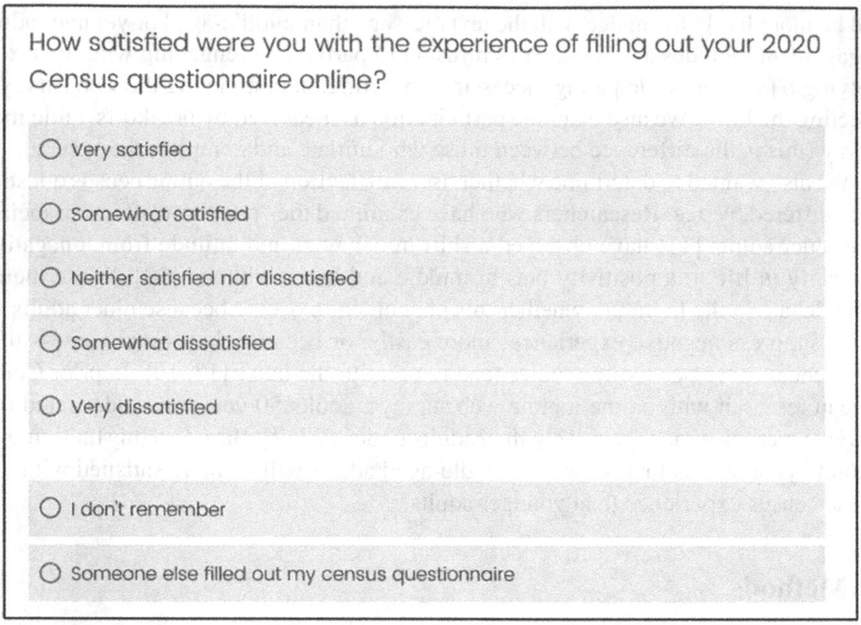

How satisfied were you with the experience of filling out your 2020 Census questionnaire online?

○ Very satisfied

○ Somewhat satisfied

○ Neither satisfied nor dissatisfied

○ Somewhat dissatisfied

○ Very dissatisfied

○ I don't remember

○ Someone else filled out my census questionnaire

Fig. 1. Satisfaction question in the 2020 Census User Experience Survey

2.2 User Experience Survey Sample

We selected a representative nationwide sample of 2020 Census respondents who reported online. This sample consisted of 153,000 phone numbers to receive the User Experience Survey via a web-link in a text notification. These were likely cell phones as we took the phone numbers collected in the online census and matched them to an administrative list of possible cell phone numbers in order to remove landlines before sampling. Online responses from Puerto Rico were also removed as our satisfaction survey was in English only.

We stratified and sorted the sample before sampling. We did not aim to sample particular demographics of respondents, but rather to include 2020 Census online responders who might have had different experiences, such as those who used a mobile phone versus those who used a large device (such as a laptop or PC) to answer the census. We also wanted to oversample those who did not use the Census ID as the authentication code and those who did not fully submit their census during the session (that is, those who had answered a number of the questions in the questionnaire but who had failed to click the "submit" button).

In terms of timing, the "early responders" (those reporting in March through June) were sent the text notification to participate in the UX survey in August. For the later responders, text notifications were sent in one of three additional waves (September, October, or November 2020) based on when they answered the census. Those texts were sent about a month after they had answered the census. Each wave had an 11-day field period from the time the first text was sent until the closeout of that wave.

Fig. 2. Example of the first text notification for the 2020 Census User Experience Survey

2.3 User Experience Survey Notification Method

For this UX survey, we sent up to three texts. Figure 2 is an image of how the first text message looked on a phone. Once respondents finished the UX survey, they did not get the subsequent texts. Recipients could also reply STOP and they would be taken off any subsequent messages.

Texts were sent through the SMS texting capability in Qualtrics. Users saw a five-digit number, like what is shown at the top of Fig. 2, on their phone. The three messages for the three texts underwent expert review and limited pretesting. We sent the texts during the daytime at 12 noon or 6 pm in the respective time zone of the address associated with the phone number. We sent texts during the week and not on the weekend or holidays. We sent the first two texts two or three days apart and then the third text about a week later. See [18] for more details about the text messages.

2.4 Sample for These Analyses

To study age-related differences in the use of text message notifications to access a web survey, we examined three age groupings of respondents: 18–29, 40–51, and 65–76. Those groupings are far apart enough to detect age-related differences and were used in other age-related analysis at the U.S. Census Bureau [19]. Out of the 153,000 in sample for the UX survey, 70,392 fell into one of the three age ranges used in our analysis as shown in Table 1.

Table 1. Recipient age groups used in analyses

Age group	Number	Percent
Younger adults 18–29	22,711	32.3%
Middle-aged adults 40–51	32,589	46.3%
Older adults 65–76	15,092	21.4%
Total	70,392	100.0%

Table 2. Session characteristics sampled and with respondent age

Census characteristics	Percent from original UX sample	Percent with respondent age associated with file and in one of the age brackets
Device used to complete		
Larger device	48.7%	50.8%
Mobile device	51.3%	49.2%
Authentication code		
Census ID used	65.2%	68.4%
Census ID not used	34.8%	31.6%
Submitted census		
Yes	77.6%	86.0%
No	22.4%	14.0%
Date responded		
Early (March–July)	78.3%	79.8%
August	14.3%	12.5%
September	3.8%	4.2%
October	3.6%	3.6%
Total number	153,000	70,392

As stated earlier, the original UX frame was stratified and sorted by characteristics that could impact user satisfaction with the online experience in order to determine why users did not use an authentication code and did not select the submit button. Table 2 includes the breakdown of the original UX survey sample by these different characteristics, and then the breakdown of those characteristics for the 70,392 cases we use in the analyses reported in this paper. The data illustrate that our original percentages differ slightly from the sample we use in this paper. Percentage-wise, our dataset for these age-related analyses includes more larger device users, more users who used the authentication code to access the census, more users who fully submitted the census, and finally more users who reported early to the census.

2.5 Analysis Methods

To address the first hypothesis, we initially conduct a Chi-square test of independence to examine whether the text message usage differs by the three age groups, specifically:

- *Churn rate* (the percent who replied STOP to the text message to remove themselves from receiving future text messages from the Census Bureau);
- *Access rate* (the percent who selected the survey link in the text message – they may or may not have completed any of the survey);
- *Minimum completion rate* (the percent who answered at least the first question in the UX survey, including those who answered or got to the last question in the UX survey);
- *Full completion rate* (the percent who answered or got to the last question in the UX survey); and
- *Breakoff rate* (of those who started the UX survey, the percent who answered at least the first question but who did not finish the UX survey). This is the difference between those who reached minimum survey completion and those who reached full survey completion.

We then use logistic regression models to check for possible confounding factors and examine the same five elements. The independent variable of interest is the age groupings. The older adult age group is the reference group so that we can compare older adults to the young adults and older adults to the middle-aged adults. The models control for other characteristics from Table 2 which might influence responding to the UX survey: the device, use of an authentication code, whether the census was fully submitted, and the date they responded to the census.

For the second hypothesis, first we examine the five-level satisfaction scores (from very satisfied to very dissatisfied) by the three age groupings to see whether there is a relationship between satisfaction and age using a Chi-square test of independence. Then we use a proportional odds model to explore whether there are significant differences in satisfaction by age, again controlling for the same variables mentioned earlier.

In the analysis, we consider significance to be $p = 0.05$ or less.

3   Results

There was a 5.9% access rate and a 15.7% churn rate across all 70,392 recipients, with a small amount of overlap between the two groups. The remainder, 78.6%, did not engage with the texts at all. Most of the people who accessed the survey answered the first question (5.3%). Of the 5.3% who accessed the first question, 16.7% of them broke off before completing the entire UX survey. Overall, satisfaction for the online census questionnaire experience was high; 87.4% reported either being very or somewhat satisfied.

3.1 Hypothesis 1: There Are Age-Related Differences in Engaging with a Text-To-Web Survey

Table 3 includes the percent of each age subgroup who replied STOP to the text, accessed the UX survey link from the text, answered the first question, and finished the survey. The bottom row provides the Chi-square test of independence statistics for each column. Each of the Chi-square statistics are significant so we fail to reject our hypothesis. There is evidence that engaging with the text-to-web survey is dependent on age for these four measures.

Table 3. Text-to-web survey engagement rates by age groups

Age group	Churn rate: Replied STOP to the text message	Access rate: Selected the UX survey link in text message	Minimum completion rate: Responded to the 1st question in UX survey	Full completion rate: Finished UX survey
Younger adults 18–29 (n = 22,711)	11.9%	4.1%	3.5%	2.9%
Middle-aged adults 40–51 (n = 32,589)	15.8%	5.7%	5.2%	4.5%
Older adults 65–76 (n = 15,092)	21.1%	9.4%	8.8%	7.6%
Chi-square statistic (*p < .05; **p < .01)	586.7**	466.2*	501.3**	457.3**

Logistic regression models allow us to examine differences between age subgroups while controlling for fixed effects that might have also influenced participation in the UX survey. For churn, we found that younger adults were less likely to reply STOP than older adults ($\beta = -.33, p < .01$). We found no evidence that middle-aged adults were more or less likely to reply STOP than older adults ($\beta = -.009, p = .5$). On survey access, we found that younger adults and middle-aged adults were both less likely to access the UX survey than older adults ($\beta = -.4, p < .01$ and $\beta = -.06, p < .01$, respectively). This same pattern held for answering the first question in the survey. However, for fully completing the survey, while young adults were less likely to fully complete the UX survey than older adults ($\beta = -.04, p < .01$), there was only marginal evidence that middle-aged adults were less likely to fully complete the survey compared to older adults ($\beta = -.04, p = .06$).

We separate breakoffs from the other engagement elements in Table 3 because for breakoffs, we subset the data to examine only those who answered the first question in the survey. Table 4 includes the percent of each age subgroup who broke off before completing the entire UX survey with the Chi-square test of independence statistic. In the table we see the pattern of younger adults having the highest breakoff rate followed by middle-aged adults and then older adults. However, the Chi-square was not significant for age groupings by breakoffs. Thus, we conclude the tendency to break off is independent of age. When controlling for the other factors in the logistic model, we confirm this finding. That is, we did not find evidence that age groupings differ in their breakoff rates (Wald $\chi^2(2) = 1.5, p = .5$). Younger adults were no more or less likely to breakoff within the UX survey than older adults ($\beta = -.05, p = .5$), and the same held for middle-aged adults. They too were no more or less likely to breakoff compared to older adults ($\beta = -.03\ p = .6$).

Table 4. Respondent age groups by breakoffs

Age group	User experience survey breakoff
Younger adults 18–29 (n = 797)	16.3%
Middle-aged adults 40–51 (n = 1,702)	14.6%
Older adults 65–76 (n = 1,330)	13.3%
Chi-square statistic	3.6 (n.s)

3.2 Hypothesis 2: Older Adults and Middle-Aged Adults Will Be More Satisfied with Their Online Census Questionnaire Experience Than Younger Adults.

Table 5 contains the satisfaction results for the three age groupings: younger adults, middle-aged adults, and older adults. The Chi-square statistic was significant ($\chi^2(8) = 99.0, p < .01$) meaning satisfaction differed by age group.

The proportional odds model found age to be associated with satisfaction when controlling for the other fixed effects. Younger adults were more likely to report lower satisfaction than older adults (with coefficient $\beta = -0.3849, p < 0.01$), but middle-aged adults and older adults did not differ in satisfaction ratings (with coefficient $\beta = 0.0037, p = 0.5$). This provides evidence in favor of Hypothesis 2.

Table 5. Satisfaction by age groups

Age group	Very satisfied	Somewhat satisfied	Neutral	Somewhat dissatisfied	Very dissatisfied
Younger adults 18–29 (n = 728)	64.2%	17.5%	11.7%	2.8%	4.0%
Middle-aged adults 40–51 (n = 1,655)	75.2%	12.2%	8.1%	2.2%	2.2%
Older adults 65–76 (n = 1,309)	82.4%	8.3%	5.7%	2.0%	1.6%

4 Discussion

The purpose of this research was two-fold: to learn more about older adults' use of text messages for survey notification and to explore whether these older adults had a satisfactory experience using the 2020 Census online questionnaire, or whether there were age-related differences in satisfaction. While the 65 and older population in the U.S. generally has the lowest rate of internet access, still more than 60% of them have internet access and many of them used it to complete the 2020 Census online.

Most of the U.S. was notified about the online census through letters and postcards mailed through the U.S. Postal Service. In a follow-up survey measuring user satisfaction, the Census Bureau was able to study how text-notification for an online survey would work for the public. We defined engaging with the text messages as either selecting the survey link and answering some or all of the survey, or replying STOP to end the text message notifications. For older adults (defined in our experiment as those 65–79 years old) who answered the census online and who had a cell phone, we found that they were more engaged with the text messages than either younger adults (18–29 years old) or middle-aged adults (40–56 years old). Based on these data, we conclude that text message is a viable communication tool for older adults who are already online and who have a cell phone.

It is impossible, however, to disentangle whether using text message to notify older adults of other survey opportunities would result in the same level of engagement had the survey not been for census follow-up purposes. Past research has shown that older adults are aware of the census and its importance. These factors likely contribute to the high rate of self-report among this age group. Nevertheless, knowing that it is possible for older adults to engage with text messages for survey purposes is useful for other survey research activities. Also, once engaged in the online survey, older adults are not more or less likely to break off before completing than the other age groups studied.

In this experiment we examined satisfaction with the online census questionnaire experience. Similar to prior research findings [17], we continue to find that older adults report higher satisfaction with their survey experience compared to younger adults. However, so were the middle-aged adults (40–56 years old). As suggested in the literature, older adults exhibit a "positivity effect" which could help explain these findings.

5   Conclusions

This research set out to examine the use of text messaging for survey notification and to gather more data on how satisfaction of survey experiences differs by age, specifically if we could replicate a previous result that older adults tend to rate survey experiences as more satisfactory than younger adults. For older adults who are able to answer online questionnaires, like the census, and who have cell phones, text notifications about an online survey can be as effective as it would be for other age groups. We also found a greater satisfaction for those 40 years and older compared to those 18 to 29 years old, which may be explained by the general "positivity effect" found in middle aged and older adults. Greater satisfaction might also be explained by differences in household composition between younger adults and middle-aged and older adults. Future research should address whether controlling for covariates such as the household size and relationships within the household affects the differences in satisfaction by respondent age. Finally, the data used in this analysis continue to show how engaged older adults are with the U.S. Census.

6   Limitations and Implications for Future Research

Our research on older adults is limited to the group who uses the Internet and who has a cell phone to receive text messages. Other older adults who do not have these characteristics might behave differently.

Acknowledgements. We thank Shaun Genter, Paul Beatty, and Joanne Pascale for reviews of the paper, and Matthew Virgile for the statistical review.

References

1. Groves, R.M., Lyberg, L.: Total survey error: past, present, and future. Public Opin. Q. **74**(5), 849–879 (2010). https://doi.org/10.1093/poq/nfq065
2. Cohn, D.: Four-in-ten who haven't yet fill out U.S. census say they wouldn't answer the door for a census worker. Pew Research Center, 28 July 2020. https://www.pewresearch.org/fact-tank/2020/07/28/four-in-ten-who-havent-yet-filled-out-u-s-census-say-they-wouldnt-answer-the-door-for-a-census-worker/. Accessed 14 Dec 2021

3. Rodriguez, R.: Older Adults and the 2020 Census: A Colorado Story. National Council for Aging, 30 January 2020. https://www.ncoa.org/article/older-adults-and-the-2020-census-a-colorado-story. Accessed 14 Dec 2021

4. García Trejo, Y.A., Walejko, G.: Decennial census knowledge and participation among groups with low 2010 census mail response. Presented at the American Political Science Association, Boston, Massachusetts (2018)

5. Bates, N., García Trejo, Y.A., Vines, M.: Are sexual minorities hard-to-survey? Insights from the 2020 census barriers, attitudes, and motivators study (CBAMS) survey. J. Off. Stat. 35(4), 709–729 (2019)

6. McGeeney, K., et al.: 2020 Census barriers, attitudes, and motivators study survey report. U.S. Census Bureau, 24 January 2019. https://www2.census.gov/programs-surveys/decennial/2020/program-management/final-analysis-reports/2020-report-cbams-study-survey.pdf

7. Gell, N.M., Rosenberg, D.E., Demiris, G., LaCroix, A.Z., Patel, K.V.: Patterns of technology use among older adults with and without disabilities. Gerontologist 55(3), 412–421 (2015). https://doi.org/10.1093/geront/gnt166

8. Waycott, J., et al.: Older adults as digital content producers. In: CHI 2013: Proceedings of the SIGCHI Conference on Human Factors in Computing Systems, pp. 39–48, April 2013. https://doi.org/10.1145/2470654.2470662

9. Kim, B.H., Glanz, K.: Text Messaging to motivate walking in older African Americans: a randomized controlled trial. Am. J. Prev. Med. 44(1), 71–75 (2013). https://doi.org/10.1016/j.amepre.2012.09.050

10. Fortuna, K.L., et al.: Text message ex-changes between older adults with serious mental illness and older certified peer specialists in a smartphone-supported self-management intervention. Psychiatr. Rehabil. J. 42(1), 57–63 (2019). https://doi.org/10.1037/prj0000305

11. Kennedy, Q., Mather, M., Carstensen, L.L.: The role of motivation in the age-related positivity effect in autobiographical memory. Psychol. Sci. 15, 208–214 (2004)

12. Carstensen, L.L.: Integrating cognitive and emotion paradigms to address the paradox of aging. Cogn. Emot. 33(1), 119–125 (2018)

13. Reed, A.E., Chan, L., Mikels, J.A.: Meta-analysis of the age-related positivity effect: age differences in preferences for positive over negative information. Psychol. Aging 29(1), 1–15 (2014)

14. Sasse, L.K., Gamer, M., Büchel, C., Brassen, S.: Selective control of attention supports the positivity effect in aging. PLoS One 9(8), e104180 (2014)

15. Mikels, J.A., Larkin, G.R., Reuter-Lorenz, P.A., Carstensen, L.L.: Divergent trajectories in the aging mind: changes in working memory for affective versus visual information with age. Psychol. Aging 20(4), 542–553 (2005)

16. Mammarella, N., Di Domenico, A., Palumbo, R., Fairfield, B.: When green is positive and red is negative: aging and the influence of color on emotional memories. Psychol. Aging 31(8), 914–926 (2016)

17. Gao, Q., Zhou, J. (eds.): HCII 2020. LNCS, vol. 12207. Springer, Cham (2020). https://doi.org/10.1007/978-3-030-50252-2

18. Nichols, E., Olmsted-Hawala, E., Feuer, S.: 2020 Census User Experience Survey Report. U.S. Census Bureau (2021). https://www2.census.gov/adrm/CBSM/rsm2021-03.pdf

19. Olmsted-Hawala, E., Romano Bergstrom, J.C., Rogers, W.A.: Age-related differences in search strategy and performance when using a data-rich web site. In: Stephanidis, C., Antona, M. (eds.) UAHCI 2013. LNCS, vol. 8010, pp. 201–210. Springer, Heidelberg (2013). https://doi.org/10.1007/978-3-642-39191-0_23

Older Icelanders' Experience of Barriers to Health Information: Association with Age, Sex, and Education

Ágústa Pálsdóttir(✉)

Information Science, University of Iceland, Oddi v/Sæmundargötu, 101, Reykjavík, Iceland
agustap@hi.is

Abstract. The aim of the study is to examine the perceived barriers to health information among people at the age 60 years or older in Iceland. The following questions were asked: 1) What barriers do older adults experience in relation to information about healthy living? 2) How do the perceived barriers relate to their age group, sex, and education? The data was gathered by a telephone survey using a random sample of 300 people aged 60 years or older, the response rate was 42%. Information barriers were measured by a total of 10 questions. The participants were divided into two groups, people who are aged 60–67 years and those who are 68 years and older, and the interaction of age and education on the experience of barriers examined for each group. The results indicate that the participants experience of barriers were primarily related to beliefs about the availability of information, the ability to seek and find it, and the capability to interpret and understand information. Deciding what information can be trusted was not considered to be a hindrance. The experience of barriers varied by age and education, with people in the older age group being less likely to be confronted with hindrances than people in the younger group. In addition, in both age groups people with university education experienced higher barriers than people with secondary or primary education. The results and possible explanations are discussed in the article.

Keywords: Age · Education · Health information barriers · Older adults

1 Introduction

In an information landscape that is getting ever more complex, the resources and the capacity required to gain access to and assess the contents and functions of health information have become increasingly more important. The current paper will examine how people at the age 60 years and older experience barriers to health information.

The term health literacy is significant in this context. The World Health Organization has defined health literacy as "the cognitive and social skills which determine the motivation and ability of individuals to gain access to, understand and use information in ways which promote and maintain good health" (p. 264) [1]. Health literacy is, furthermore, closely related to a joint definition by UNESCO and IFLA (International Federation of

Q. Gao and J. Zhou (Eds.): HCII 2022, LNCS 13330, pp. 567–583, 2022.
https://doi.org/10.1007/978-3-031-05581-2_39

Library and Information Association) of media and information literacy, which allows individuals to "...access, retrieve, understand, evaluate and use, create, as well as share information and media content in all formats..." [2]. Thus, competency in media and information literacy is important as a tool for lifelong learning, which provides people with better opportunities to make informed health decisions. Various factors, however, may act as barriers that older adults perceive as limiting their possibilities to add to their knowledge and understanding of the interrelated aspects of health and lifestyle.

In the past years, the emphasis has been on the digitalization of health information and the challenges that senior citizens deal with in that respect, e.g., weak physical condition [3], problems with the visual and auditory presentation of information [4–6], and changes in peoples motor ability [4, 7]. Nevertheless, there has been a substantial growth in older adults' use of digital sources [8]. It has also been pointed out that by taking the needs of older people into account when information technology is designed, for example with suitable interface design and touch screen solutions [9], some of the obstacles that they are faced with might be minimized.

Lack of confidence in information sources has, furthermore, been identified as a hindrance. Particularly health information on the internet may be regarded as less reliable than information from other sources or channels [10–14]. Moreover, there are indications that people prefer to get support from health professionals to identify reliable health information [15].

The same applies to beliefs about the lack of utility of information in different kind of sources [12, 16]. Thus, the relevance of digital information is important, and if older people consider it to be high, they are more motivated and prone to make more effort at seeking it [17]. Finding an information source, however, as well as knowing what kind of information is to be found in it, can be problematic [18, 19]. There are, for example, indications that information about various health matters, provided by professionals through a health system, is rarely being sought [20]. In addition, health information has sometimes been described as complex and difficult to understanding [15, 21].

Furthermore, the increase in false health information has been described as a complex issue that may create serious health risk, whether it is misinformation, which are not put forward with the intention to deceive the receiver, or disinformation, which are published or presented for the purpose of deception [22, 23]. International organizations have warned that false information, recently termed as "Infodemic" [24], can cause serious harm during an international epidemic such as COVID-19 [25, 26]. An identification of ways to conteract the situation has emphasized the importance of supporting people's media and information literacy [27, 28].

Aim and Research Questions. It is a crucial issue that older adults have a possibility to improve their knowledge about healthy behaviour. Otherwise they will not be able to make informed choices that promote their health and wellbeing. Yet, there is still a number of unanswered questions about the information barriers that they may be confronted with. The aim of the current study is to examine the perceived barriers to health information among people at the age 60 years or older in Iceland. People aged 60 or over are, however, not a homogeneous group but can consist of many different social groups with different backgrounds and it is necessary to take this into account.

The paper will seek answers to the following questions: 1) What barriers do older adults experience in relation to information about healthy living? 2) How do the perceived barriers relate to their age group, sex, and education? By identifying these barriers, the professionals who are responsible for health promotion are given the opportunity to diminish, or preferably eliminate, them. Subsequently, people's access to health information and their capacity to use it effectively to improve their way of living can be enhanced.

2   Methods

2.1   Data Collection

This is a quantitative study using data that were gathered by a telephone survey from November 2018 to January 2019. The sample consisted of 300 people aged 60 years and older from the whole country, randomly selected from the National Register of Persons in Iceland.

It is traditional to use retirement age to define "elderly" in Western countries [29]. In Iceland. elderly is defined by law as people who have reached the age of 67 [30], when it is usual for people to retire. This has, however, been criticized for not taking into consideration the heterogeneity of older adults [31]. It has been pointed out that people's chronological age is less important than determinants, like their physical, cognitive, and social capabilities [32]. In accordance with the viewpoints, that there is no clearly defined age when people become senior citizens, the associations for senior citizens in Iceland admit those who have reached the age of 60 to become members [33]. In view of this, it was decided that people who have reached the age of 60 should be included in the study, and that those who are at the age 60 to 67 years, a group who is approaching retirement, should be compared with people aged 68 years or older, who have already reached the retirement age.

The total response rate was 42%. Because of the response rate, the data were weighed by gender, age, place of residence and education, so that it corresponds with the distribution in the population. Table 1 shows the number of participants before and after the data was weighed.

Table 1. Number of participants within the sample before and after weighing the data

	Before weighing the data	After weighing the data
60–67 years old	51	66
68 years and older	75	96

2.2   Measurements and Data Analysis

The measurement consisted of socio-demographic variables as well as variables that measure information barriers:

1. Socio-demographic information included traditional background variables. Based on previous analysis the variables sex and education are used in the current study. Education was measured as the highest level of education completed. Three levels were distinguished: 1) primary education includes those who have finished compulsory education; 2) secondary education includes those who have completed vocational training or secondary school; 3) university education.
2. Age groups. To assess how the experience of information barriers may relate to age, the participants were divided into two groups, those who are aged 60 to 67 years and those who are 68 years and older.
3. Information hindrances were measured by a total of 10 questions, which are all in the form of statements that refer to challenges in relation to people's attitudes and cognitive aspects. The statements were developed from the concept of media and information literacy and the discussion of information barriers above. They were categorized into four groups: Two of them refer to beliefs about the availability of information, three refer to beliefs about the ability to seek and find information, two refer to beliefs about the capability to interpret and understand information, and three refer to trust in information. Each statement had a 5-point response scale (1 = Strongly disagree – 2 = Disagree – 3 = Neither agree nor disagree – 4 = Agree – 5 = Strongly agree).

All analysis is based on weighed data. For each age group, ANOVA (one-way) was performed to examine difference across educational groups and t-tests to examine differences by sex, Tuckey test was used to examine if the differences were statistically significant. Differences between participants who are 60–67 years old and those who are 68 years or older were assessed by comparing the mean values for the age groups.

3 Results

The chapter starts with presentation of results about the participants beliefs about the availability of information.

The results in Fig. 1 show that in both age groups, mean values for the statement "Information that I may need do not exist" are above median (3, neither agree nor disagree), for both men and women, as well as for all educational groups.

Despite some differences by sex, it was not significant, neither in the younger group it (p = 0,133) nor in the older group (p = 0,165). There is, however, a significant difference by education in the younger group (p = 0,039), as well as the older group (p = 0,019). People with university education were more likely to agree with the statement than the other two educational groups (Fig. 1).

A comparison of the age groups shows that, women, and people with primary education in the younger group were more likely to agree with the statement than those in the older group, but apart from this the values for the groups are similar (Fig. 1).

Figure 2 shows that in the younger group, mean values for the statement "Information exists but I do not have access to it" are above 3 (neither agree nor disagree), except for people with secondary education. In the older group, values for all groups, except people with university education, are below 3.

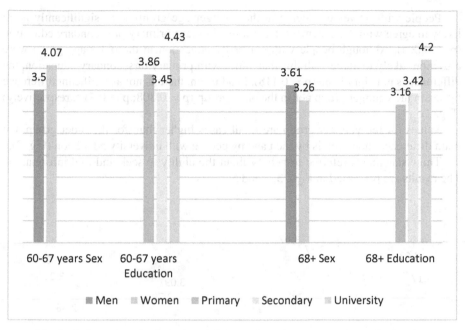

Fig. 1. Information that I may need do not exist – Age groups, sex, and education

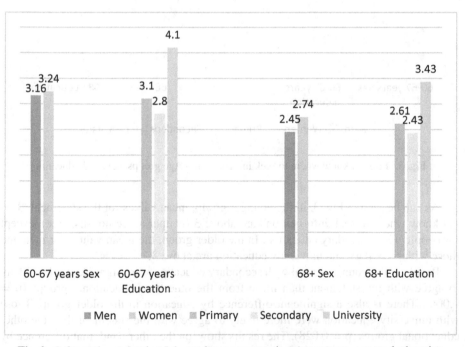

Fig. 2. Information exists but I do not have access to it – Age groups, sex, and education

People with university degree in the younger age group were significantly more likely to agree with the statement than those who have primary or secondary education (p = 0,004). Although people with university education in the older age group were also more likely to agree with this than those with primary or secondary education, the difference is not significant (p = 0,118). In addition, there is not a significant difference by sex in the younger group nor in the older group (p = 0,808; p = 0,313, respectively) (Fig. 2).

Values for the younger group are in all cases higher than for the older group, the main difference, however, is by men and by people with university education (Fig. 2).

Three statements referred to beliefs about the ability to seek and find information. The results are presented in Figs. 3, 4 and 5.

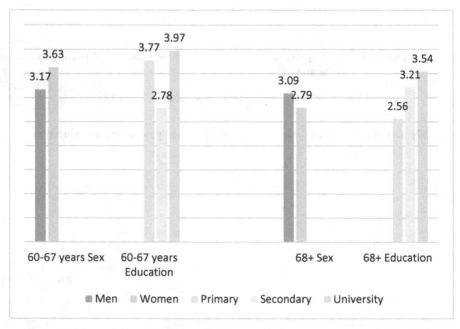

Fig. 3. I do not know where to seek information – Age groups, sex, and education

As can be seen in Fig. 3, in the younger group, mean values for the statement "I do not know where to seek information" are above 3 (neither agree nor disagree), except for people with secondary education. In the older group, the mean values for men and those with secondary and university education are above 3.

People in the younger group with secondary education were significantly less likely to agree with the statement than those from the other two educational groups (p = 0,006). There is also a significant difference by education in the older group. Those with university education were more likely to agree with the statement than the other educational groups (p = 0,028). The results show, on the other hand, that difference by sex is not significant, neither in the younger age group (p = 0,204) nor in the older group (p = 0,292) (Fig. 3).

The values for the younger group are higher than for the older group, except for people with secondary education. The main difference across the age groups is for people with primary education and women (Fig. 3).

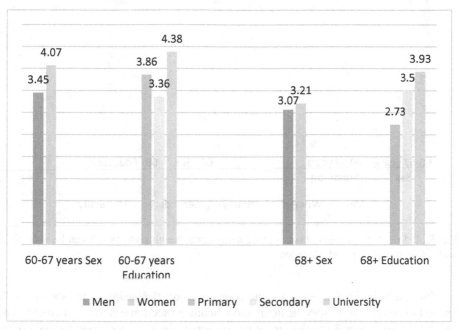

Fig. 4. It is difficult to find information with useful advice about health protection – Age groups, sex, and education

Figure 4 shows that the means for the statement "It is difficult to find information with useful advice about health protection" are above 3 (neither agree nor disagree) in the younger group. The same applies to the older group, except for people with primary education where the mean is below 3.

There is a significant difference by education. In the younger group, those who have university education were most likely to agree that "it is difficult to find information with useful advice about health protection", while people with secondary education were least likely to do so (p = 0,045). In the older group, those with university education were also most likely to agree with the statement but those who have primary education were least likely to agree with it (p = 0,002). Although there is some difference by sex in the younger group, with women being more likely to agree with the statement than men, it is not statistically significant (p = 0,11). In the older group there is only a slight difference by sex, and it is not significant (p = 0,622) (Fig. 4).

A comparison of the age groups shows that the mean values are higher for the younger group, except for people with secondary education where the means of those who belong the older group are slightly higher. The main difference across the age groups is between primary education and women (Fig. 4).

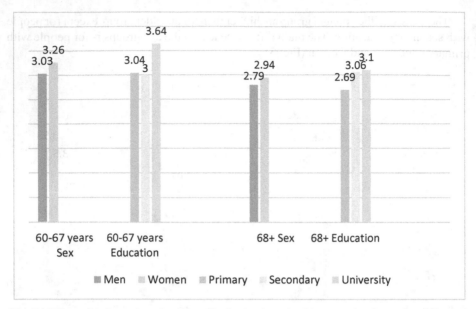

Fig. 5. If I need information about specific items about health protection it can be difficult to find – Age groups, sex, and education

The results in Fig. 5 show that in the younger group, the means for the statement "If I need information about specific items about health protection it can be difficult to find" are in all cases above 3 (neither agree nor disagree). In the older group the means are above 3 for people with secondary and university education, but below for those with primary education and for both men and women.

Difference by sex, is not significant, neither for the younger group (p = 0,443), nor the older group (p = 0,591). Although people with university education were more likely to agree with the statement than those in the other two educational groups, the difference is not significant (p = 0,198). Differences by education in the older group were smaller and not significant (p = 0,385) (Fig. 5).

The means for the younger group are somewhat higher than for the older group, apart from people with secondary education, where there is only a very slight difference. The main difference across the age groups is between those with university education (Fig. 5).

Two statements referred to beliefs about the capability to interpret and understand information, the results are presented in Figs. 6, 7.

Figure 6 shows that the means for the statement "There is too few information in Icelandic" are above 3 (neither agree nor disagree), except for men in the older group.

Men in the older age group were significantly less likely to agree with the statement than women (p = 0,001). Although there was some difference across men and women in the younger group it is not significant (p = 0,069). Furthermore, there is not a significant difference by education, neither in the younger group nor in the older group (p = 0,238; p = 0,664, respectively) (Fig. 6).

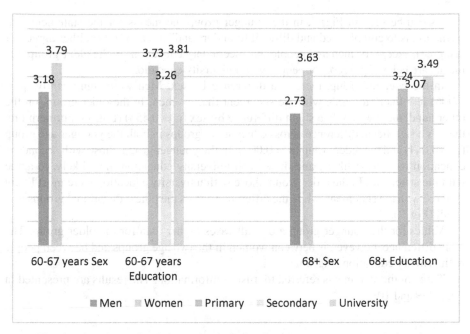

Fig. 6. There is too few information in Icelandic – Age groups, sex, and education

Values for the younger group are in all cases higher than for the older group, although the difference by women and people with secondary education is small (Fig. 6).

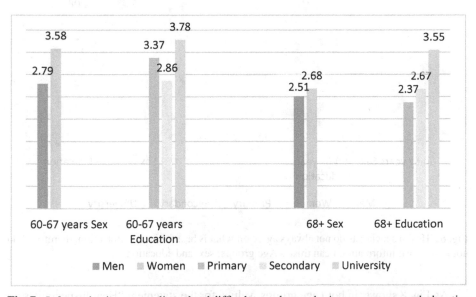

Fig. 7. Information is too complicated and difficult to understand – Age groups, sex, and education

As can be seen in Fig. 7, in the younger group the means for the statement "Information is to complicated and difficult to understand" are above 3 (neither agree nor disagree), except for men and people with secondary education. In the older group, the means are below 3, except for people with university education.

In the younger group, there is a difference by sex. Men were significantly (p = 0,006) less likely to agree with the statement than women. In the older group, on the other hand, there was only a slight difference by sex (p = 0,455) (Fig. 7). Furthermore, there is a significant difference across educational groups in both the younger age group (p = 0,041) and the older group (p = 0,007). In the younger group, those with secondary education were least likely, and those with university education most likely, to agree with the statement. In the older group, those with university education were most likely to agree with the statement, while the difference across the other educational groups was small (Fig. 7).

Values for the younger group are in all cases higher than for the older group. The main difference, however, is between women in the two age groups and between people with primary education (Fig. 7).

Three of the statements referred to trust in information. The results are presented in Figs. 8, 9 and 10.

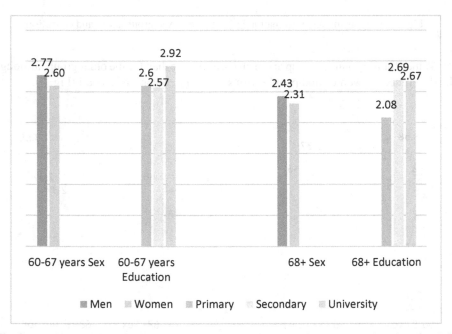

Fig. 8. Health specialists do not always agree on what is best for health protection, therefore I do not know what information I can trust – Age groups, sex, and education

As Fig. 8 shows, in both age groups, values for the statement "Health specialists do not always agree on what is best for health protection, therefore I do not know what information I can trust" are below median (3, neither agree nor disagree), for both men and women, as well as for all educational groups.

There is only a slight difference, and not significant, by sex in both the younger group (p = 0,569) and the older group (p = 0,642). In addition, results about differences across educational groups are not significant for the younger group (p = 0,628) and the older group (p = 0,066) (Fig. 8).

The means for the younger group are somewhat higher than in the older group, except for people with secondary education, where those in the older group are slightly higher (Fig. 8).

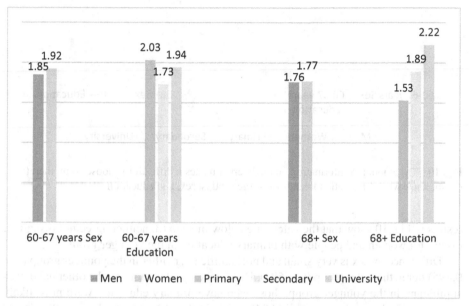

Fig. 9. The media often publishes information from people whose qualifications I don't know, therefore it's difficult to know the reliable and quality of it – Age groups, sex, and education

Figure 9 shows that the values for the statement "The media often publishes information from people whose qualifications I don't know, therefore it's difficult to know the reliable and quality of it" are below 3 (neither agree nor disagree) for all groups.

There is no significant difference by sex, neither in the younger group (p = 0,666) nor the older group (p = 0,95). In the younger group there is not a significant difference by education (p = 0,95). There is, however, a significant difference in the older group (p = 0,009), people with university education were most likely to agree with this and those with primary education least likely (Fig. 9).

The means for the younger group are somewhat higher than in the older group, except for people with university education, where those in the older group are slightly higher (Fig. 9).

When presented with the statement "The amount of information on the internet makes it difficult to choose from, therefore I do not know what information I can trust", the

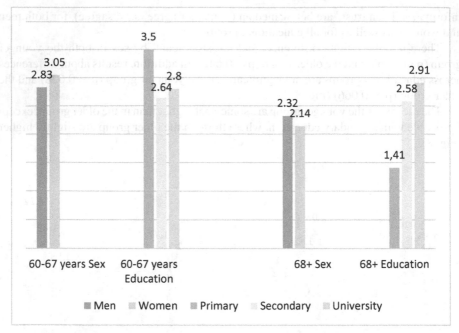

Fig. 10. The amount of information on the internet makes it difficult to choose from, therefore I do not know what information I can trust – Age groups, sex, and education

results in Fig. 10 show that the values are below median (3, neither agree nor disagree), except for women and people with primary education in the younger group.

Difference by sex is very small and not significant, neither in the younger group (p = 0,495) nor in the older group (p = 582). Difference by education, on the other hand, was significant. In the younger group, those who have primary education were most likely to agree with the statement (p = 0,024), while in the older group, those with primary education were least likely to do so (p = 0,0001) (Fig. 10).

The means for the younger group are higher than the older group, except for people with university education where the older group is slightly higher. The main difference is between those who have primary education, the means of people in the younger group are considerably higher than for those in the older group (Fig. 10).

4 Discussion

As a key to older adults' health and wellbeing it is important to promote their possibilities to be actively involved in health promotional interventions through life-long learning. This cannot be achieved while they are confronted with hindrances to information. The study results provide some insight to the barriers that older adults are confronted with. On a scale of 1 to 5, values over 3 (neither agree nor disagree) represented barriers, while values below 3 do not. Because the results were analyzed by both sex and education it was decided that although a value was below 3 for one of the socio-demographic groups, it should still be considered a barrier. Likewise, if a value was above 3 for only one group it was not considered a barrier.

The participants' experience of hindrances varied by their age group. Of the 10 statements presented in the study, six were found to represent information barriers for the younger group (Figs. 1, 2, 3, 4, 5 and 6), while for people who are 68 years or older, only three of them did so (Figs. 1, 4, 6). These statement all fall in the groups referring to beliefs about the availability of information, the ability to seek and find information, and the capability to interpret and understand information.

Likewise, the age groups experiences of what did not stand for barriers varied. For the older group four statements did not stand for barriers, that is the ones referring to trust in information, as well as the one stating that information is to complicated and difficult to understand (Figs. 7, 8, 9 and 10). For the younger group, two of the statements referring to trust in information did not stand for barriers (Figs. 8 and 9).

Thus, the study results indicate that older people were less likely to be confronted with hindrances in relation to health information than those who are younger. In addition, participants in both age groups did not consider it problematic to decide what information can be trusted, although the older group believed more strongly in this that the younger group. It is, however, important to keep in mind that data for the study were obtained before the outbreak of the COVID-19 epidemic. People may have different opinions and beliefs regarding health information today than they did before, particularly in terms of trust in information.

A closer examination, where the age group were tested against education and sex, revealed certain trends about the participants experience of information barriers. A significant difference was found by sex for only two statements. In the younger group, men were less likely to find information to be complicated and difficult to understand than women, and in the older group women were more likely to believe that there is too few information in Icelandic than men.

Education, on the other hand, was found to interact significantly with age for seven of the statements (Figs. 1, 2, 3, 4, 7, 9 and 10). The main result here is that participants with university education experienced higher barriers than those in the other two educational groups. These results were comparable for the age groups, in the younger group this was found for five statements and in the older group for six statements.

At first sight, this finding may appear contradictory, as it seems more logical for those who have higher education to experience lower information barriers than people who are less educated. The key elements of health literacy and of media and information literacy is that people possess the motivation and the personal skills that allow them to acquire health information and draw knowledge from it, for their own advantage [1, 2]. Previous research has reported that people who are more educated are also more likely to engage in health information seeking than those who are less educated [15, 34–36]. In addition, the need to pay more attention to motivation, especially how interest in a topic may act as a driving force that inspires people to seek health information, has been stressed in several studies [37–39]. Thus, more educated older adults might also be more motivated and likely to seek information about healthy living and, as a result of this, it is possible that they are more aware of information barriers than those who are less educated. Although this is merely speculations that serve to seek an explanation, the findings of the study are interesting and give reasons to look further into the connection between the perceived information barriers and the skills of media and health information literacy that people possess.

The overall study is limited by a total response rate of 42%. Even though his may be considered satisfactory in a survey it raises the question whether or not those who answered the survey are giving a biased picture of those who did not respond. In order to compensate for this bias the data were weighed by gender, age, place of residence and education, so that it corresponds with the distribution in the population. Thus, the findings may provide valuable knowledge about the barriers that older adults living in Iceland experience in relation to health information.

5   Conclusion, Limitations and Policy Implications

As a key to older adults' health and wellbeing, it is important to promote their possibilities to be actively involved in health promotional interventions, through life-long learning. For that, they must be enabled to acquire the information and understanding that is necessary to maintain, and preferably to renew, their knowledge of healthy behavior. The study examined what barriers older adults experienced in relation to information about healthy living and how it related to their age group, sex, and education. Answers were sought to the following research questions: 1) What barriers do older adults experience in relation to information about healthy living? 2) How do the perceived barriers relate to their age group, sex, and education?

Taken together, the results indicate that the participants experience of barriers were primarily related to their beliefs about the availability of it, the ability to seek and find it, and the capability to interpret and understand information. Furthermore, deciding what information can be trusted was not considered to be a hindrance. Their experience of hindrances varied by their age and education, and to some extent their sex. The results indicate that people at the age 68 years or older were less likely to be confronted with hindrances than people aged 60 to 67 years. In addition, in both age groups people with university education were found to experienced higher barriers than people with secondary or primary education. It must, however, be stressed that these findings need to be taken with caution, as it is possible that groups that previous results have shown that seek information more often, such as those who are more educated, may also be the ones more likely to be aware of information barriers. Furthermore, the data for the study was collected before the outbreak of the COVID-19 epidemic. Although the study participants seem to be confident about their capabilities at critically evaluate health information, it may be that older adults evaluate information differently today because of the health threat that it has caused. Thus, there is a need to study the topic further, particularly if and how COVID-19 has changed the information landscape and peoples' beliefs about health information.

The overall study is limited by a total response rate of 42%. Even though his may be considered satisfactory in a survey it raises the question whether or not those who answered the survey are giving a biased picture of those who did not respond. In order to compensate for this bias the data were weighed by gender, age, place of residence and education, so that it corresponds with the distribution in the population. Thus, the findings may provide valuable knowledge about the barriers that older adults living in Iceland experience in relation to health information.

The policy implications of the findings are that health authorities and professionals need to work together to find ways to stimulate older adults' media and health information literacy. By identifying the hindrances that older people are confronted with, the professionals who are responsible for health promotion are given the opportunity to diminish, or preferably eliminate, them. Subsequently, people's access to health information, and their capacity to evaluate and use it effectively to improve their way of living, can be enhanced.

Acknowledgments. The research project was supported by the University of Iceland Research Fund.

References

1. Nutbeam, D.: Health promotion glossary. Health Promot. Int. **13**, 349–364 (1998)
2. UNESCO: Media and Information Literacy (2014). http://www.uis.unesco.org/Communication/Pages/information-literacy.aspx
3. Pew Research Centre: Older adults and technology use (2014). http://www.pewinternet.org/2014/04/03/older-adults-and-technology-use/?utm_expid=53098246-2.Lly4CFSVQG2lphsg-KopIg.0
4. Loos, E.F., Romano Bergstrom, J.: Older adults. In: Romano Bergstrom, J., Schall, A.J. (eds.) Eye Tracking in User Experience Design, pp. 313–329. Elsevier, Amsterdam (2014)
5. Rosales, A., Fernández-Ardèvol, M.: Smartphone usage diversity among older people. In: Sayago, S. (ed.) Perspectives on Human-Computer Interaction Research with Older People. HIS, pp. 51–66. Springer, Cham (2019). https://doi.org/10.1007/978-3-030-06076-3_4
6. World Health Organization: Global Age Friendly Cities: A Guide. WHO, Geneva (2007). http://www.who.int/ageing/publications/Global_age_friendly_cities_Guide_English.pdf
7. Hoogendam, Y.Y., et al.: Older age relates to worsening of fine motor skills: a population-based study of middle-aged and elderly persons. Front. Aging Neurosci. **6**, 259 (2014). http://www.ncbi.nlm.nih.gov/pmc/articles/PMC4174769/
8. Dumitru, E.-A., Ivan, L., Loos, E.F.: Why it is easier to slay a dragon than to kill a myth about older people's smartphone use. In: Gao, Q., Zhou, J. (eds.) HCII 2022. LNCS, vol. 13330, pp. xx–yy. Springer, Cham (2022)
9. Piper, A.M., Campbell, R., Hollan, J.D.: Exploring the accessibility and appeal of surface computing for older adult health care support. In: Mynatt, E., Schoner, D., Fitzpatrick, G., Hudson, S., Edwards, K., Rodden, T. (eds.), CHI 2010: Proceedings of the 28th International Conference on Human Factors in Computing Systems, Atlanda, GA, USA, 10–15 April 2010, pp. 907–916. ACM, New York (2010)
10. Hesse, B.W., et al.: Trust and sources of health information the impact of the internet and its implications for health care providers: findings from the first health information national trends survey. JAMA Intern. Med. **165**(22), 2618–2624 (2005)
11. Eriksson-Backa, K.: Finnish 'silver surfers' and online health information. In: Eriksson-Backa, K., Luoma, A., Krook, E. (eds.) WIS 2012. CCIS, vol. 313, pp. 138–149. Springer, Heidelberg (2012). https://doi.org/10.1007/978-3-642-32850-3_13
12. Pálsdóttir, Á.: Icelanders' and trust in the internet as a source of health and lifestyle information. Inf. Res. **16**(1) (2011). paper 470. http://InformationR.net/ir/16-1/paper470.html

13. Soederberg Miller, L.M., Bell, R.A.: Online health information seeking: the influence of age, information trustworthiness, and search challenges. J. Aging Health **24**(3), 525–541 (2012)
14. Pálsdóttir, Á.: Senior citizens, media and information literacy and health information. In: Kurbanoğlu, S., Boustany, J., Špiranec, S., Grassian, E., Mizrachi, D., Roy, L. (eds.) ECIL 2015. CCIS, vol. 552, pp. 233–240. Springer, Cham (2015). https://doi.org/10.1007/978-3-319-28197-1_24
15. Lee, K., Hoti, K., Hughes, J.D., Emmerton, L.: Dr Google is here to stay but health care professionals are still valued: an analysis of health care consumers' internet navigation support preferences. J. Med. Internet Res. **9**(6), e210 (2017). https://doi.org/10.2196/jmir.7489
16. Mettlin, C., Cummings, M.: Communication and behavior change for cancer control. Prog. Clin. Biol. Res. **83**, 135–148 (1982)
17. Loos, E.: Senior citizens: digital imigrants in their own country? Observatorio **6**(1), 1–23 (2012)
18. Dunne, J.E.: Information seeking and use by battered women: a "person-in-progressive-situations" approach. Libr. Inf. Sci. Res. **24**(4), 343–355 (2002)
19. Davies, J., et al.: Identifying male college students' perceived health needs, barriers to seeking help, and recommendations to help men adopt healthier lifestyles. J. Am. Coll. Health **48**(6), 250–267 (2000)
20. Pálsdóttir, Á.: The use of new information and communication technology for health information among older Icelanders. In: Gao, Q., Zhou, J. (eds.) HCII 2020. LNCS, vol. 12208, pp. 354–364. Springer, Cham (2020). https://doi.org/10.1007/978-3-030-50249-2_26
21. McKenzie, P.J.: Communication barriers and information-seeking counterstrategies in accounts of practitioner-patient encounters. Libr. Inf. Sci. Res. **24**, 31–47 (2002)
22. Ratzan, S.C., Sommariva, S., Rauh, L.: Enhancing global health communication during a crisis: lessons from the COVID-19 pandemic. Public Health Res. Pract. **30**(2), e3022010 (2020). https://doi.org/10.17061/phrp3022010
23. Vosoughi, S., Roy, D., Aral, S.: The spread of true and false news online. Science **359**(6380), 1146–1151 (2018). https://doi.org/10.1126/science.aap9559
24. World Health Organization: Infodemic. https://www.who.int/health-topics/infodemic#tab=tab_1
25. Dramé, D.: The health crisis: fertile ground for disinformation. UNESCO Courier **3**, 24–26 (2020). https://en.unesco.org/courier/2020-3/health-crisis-fertile-ground-disinformation
26. Stop Corona Fake News. https://www.stopcoronafakenews.com/en/
27. WHO. Fighting misinformation in the time of CoVID-19, one click at the time (2020a). https://www.who.int/news-room/feature-stories/detail/fighting-misinformation-in-the-time-of-covid-19-one-click-at-a-time
28. WHO. Novel Coronavirus (2019-nCoV). Situation Report – 18 (2020b). https://www.who.int/docs/default-
29. Thane, P.: History and the sociology of ageing. Soc. Hist. Med. **2**(1), 93–96 (1989)
30. Lög um málefni aldraðra nr. 125/1999 [Act on the affairs of the elderly]
31. Berger, K.S.: The Developing Person Through the Lifespan, 3rd edn. Worth Publishers, New York (1994)
32. Ries, W., Pöthiga, D.: Chronological and biological age. Exp. Gerontol. **19**(3), 211–216 (1984)
33. Landsamband eldri borgara. http://leb.is/. Association for senior citizens
34. Eriksson-Backa, K.: In sickness and in health: how information and knowledge are related to health behaviour. Åbo Akademis Förlag - Åbo Akademi University Press, Åbo (2003)
35. O'Keefe, G.J., Boyd, H.H., Brown, M.R.: Who learns preventive health care information from where: cross-channel and repertoire comparisons. Health Commun. **10**(1), 25–36 (1998)
36. Reagan, J.: The "repertoire" of information sources. J. Broadcast. **40**(1), 112–121 (1996)

37. Pálsdóttir, Á.: Information behaviour, health self-efficacy beliefs and health behaviour in Icelanders' everyday life. Inf. Res. **13**(1) (2008). paper 334. http://InformationR.net/ir/13-1/paper334.html
38. Eriksson-Backa, K., Ek, S., Niemelä, R., et al.: Health information literacy in everyday life: a study of Finns aged 65–79 years. Health Inform. J. **8**(2), 83–94 (2012)
39. Gaziano, C.: Forecast 2000: widening knowledge gaps. Journal. Mass Commun. Q. **74**(2), 237–264 (1997)

Internet Use of Older Caregivers and Their Sociodemographic Characteristics

Javiera Rosell[1,2](✉) (iD), Josefa Guerra[3], and Felipe Bustamante[4]

[1] Instituto Milenio para la Investigación del Cuidado (MICARE), Santiago, Chile
jerosell@uc.cl

[2] Escuela de Psicología, Pontificia Universidad Católica de Chile, Santiago, Chile

[3] Observatorio del Envejecimiento para un Chile con Futuro, Pontificia Universidad Católica de Chile, Santiago, Chile
josefa.guerra@uc.cl

[4] Escuela de Medicina, Pontificia Universidad Católica de Chile, Santiago, Chile
fnbustam@uc.cl

Abstract. People over 60 years have found themselves caring for other dependent older adults in many countries. This situation is an especially relevant topic in Latin America, where the lack of care systems affects the lives of caregivers. Research has shown that the Internet is a helpful tool in providing information and methods to minimize the negative consequences of caregiving but also, age is negatively related to its use. Thus, using the national representative Chilean Sociodemographic Characterization Survey (2017), we performed weighted descriptive analysis and weighted logistic regressions of five types of Internet use related to information seeking, communication, and entertainment, in association with sociodemographic characteristics. We included sociodemographic variables such as age, gender, education level, marital status, and the number of people living within the household among a subsample of older caregivers. Education level was a significant and positive predictor of all types of Internet use among caregivers, while age decreased the probability of using the Internet. Gender was only associated with communication through social networks, where females were more likely to report this type of use. This information helps develop interventions to overcome the barriers of age and educational level, allowing the most vulnerable older caregivers to access the benefits of technology use.

Keywords: Caregivers · Older adults · Internet use

1 Introduction

Population aging has led to an increase in the number of caregivers over 60 years of age who are compelled to take care of other people in a situation of dependency. In addition, it is known that the probability of requiring care from others increases with age as the prevalence of diseases is higher. Thus, people over 60 years have found themselves caring for others.

The aging of caregivers is especially relevant in Latin America, where there is still no high-quality care system, and family members are obliged to take responsibility. For example, in the case of Chile, there is still no national care plan, and the cost of a long-stay residence or in-home professional support cannot always be afforded by families if required. Thus, care is typically provided by the family members themselves, who are generally women [1].

According to the Sociodemographic Characterization Survey of Chile [2], 47.3% of people over 60 years with functional dependence have an older caregiver, and the average age of caregivers is 60.1 years, with a range between 20 and 91 years [3].

On the other hand, extensive literature shows the impact of caregiving on caregivers' psychological well-being. The number of caregiving hours has been associated with greater depressive symptomatology [4], anxious symptoms [5] and lower cognitive functioning [6]. A Chilean study revealed that anxious and depressive symptomatology explained 25% of the variance in the quality of life of caregivers of people living with dementia [7]. This context arises the concept of caregiver burden, understood as a negative indicator of caregiving on the well-being of caregivers [8]. The caregiver burden affects the caregiver, but also the person being cared for [8], decreasing the quality of life of both people.

Studies focused on older caregivers concur in reporting negative life changes after taking on caregiving tasks, including decreased leisure activities, financial difficulties, and increased loneliness and isolation [9].

Additionally, the experience of older caregivers can be more challenging due to their health difficulties [10]. Namely, some caregivers report having complex health situations such as Parkinson's, cancer, or a history of heart attacks [11]. Moreover, older people report more difficulties asking for help than younger caregivers [9, 12].

Confronted with this scenario, some people can face this new reality through effective coping strategies. In contrast, others experience high frustration levels, accounting for the diversity of the impact of care [11].

This context shows the relevance of exploring the reality of caregivers over 60 years, considering the particularities that this group has in contrast to other age groups.

1.1 Older Caregivers and Internet Use

The resources available for caregiving are essential to decrease the possible negative consequences [8]. The Internet is considered a helpful tool in providing information and methods to minimize the negative consequences of caregiving [13]. For example, it could reduce isolation and loneliness reported by older caregivers [9].

A study in Greece reported that 84.1% of caregivers of people with dementia used the Internet, and 47.5% used it to receive online services associated with dementia care [14]. However, this was linked to sociodemographic characteristics, being younger and more educated caregivers most likely to use the Internet to search for information about dementia and caregiving [15]. In contrast, a study in the United States found that caregivers of people with dementia use the Internet less frequently than the general population, and only 59% reported using the Internet to search for health information. In this case, educational level was also associated with greater Internet use.

In addition, higher caregiver stress impacted higher Internet use [15, 16]. A Portuguese study coincides with lower Internet use in caregivers of people with dementia and highlights different uses. While information-seeking is frequent, finding emotional support is infrequent [13].

In this context, the Internet is considered a resource that provides knowledge and support, increasing the levels of participation [17]. As a result, even some research teams began to design interventions focused on caregivers. These programs have the advantage of being flexible in time, less expensive, and personalized [17]. They also have greater accessibility, for example, by reaching rural areas. Moreover, online interventions prevent the caregiver from leaving the person they care for too long or from not attending the program because they have no one to replace them [18]. Thus, online-based intervention can be adapted to the reality and demands of caregivers, allowing them access from their homes [18]. In this way, the Internet provides opportunities for support resources that contribute to reducing the burden [19], decreasing anxious and depressive symptomatology [20, 21], as well as increasing self-efficacy [22] and the feeling of being more prepared for the task [23].

Beyond interventions through the Internet, it also allows an everyday use, gaining access to multiple resources in a variety of categories, such as news, health information, videos, music, books, articles, etc. Namely, the Internet can be a source of information and support during demanding circumstances such as informal care [17]. Thus, Internet use can be transformed into a coping strategy in the face of possible negative consequences of caregiving (e.g., decreased leisure and entertainment activities) [11, 17].

However, some caregivers reported long caregiving hours and do not have the time or energy to use the Internet for information and support, which highlight the need for initiatives that give a rest to the caregiver, allowing the availability of time for Internet use [15] and the maintenance of their social life and personal goals [24].

In Chile, 16.2% of the population is over 60 years, reaching 2,850,171 people [25]. Among this age group, 31.5% use the Internet [2]. Also, smartphone use by older people increased from 45.9% in 2019 to 54.8% at the beginning of the pandemic (2020) [26]. Of internet users, over 60.79% report doing so at least once a day [27]. Additionally, 50% of people over 60 years declared having Internet at home [28] and smartphone ownership increased by 38.9% between 2013 and 2019. However, no disaggregated analysis considers whether the person is a caregiver.

Currently, there is limited evidence on the Internet use of informal caregivers over 60 years (e.g., Reinwand's study [17]). This lack of information is even more evident in Latin America. Thus, it is necessary to explore this topic in a cultural context where the population has aged rapidly, and caregiving is most often performed by untrained family members [1].

Furthermore, previous literature shows benefits of technology use on psychological well-being in older people, such as reduced depressive symptomatology [29, 30], decreased loneliness [31, 32], and increased life satisfaction [33] and connectedness [34, 35].

The present study aims to describe the types of Internet use in informal caregivers over 60 years old. In addition, the relationship of sociodemographic variables (e.g., age, gender, educational level, and the number of people living in the household) with the different types of Internet use were analyzed. Thus, the questions we seek to answer are: what sociodemographic variables impact Internet use in caregivers over 60 years old? Are there differences in the types of Internet use depending on the sociodemographic variables of caregivers over 60 years old?

Hopefully, this information will contribute the development of public policies and initiatives for the digital inclusion of older people, especially caregivers.

2 Methodology

2.1 Sample and Procedures

This study used data from the National Socioeconomic Characterization Survey (CASEN) [2]. This survey has national representativeness and collects information from wide age ranges, including older people. It is conducted every three years and allows analysis with a weighted and expanded sample, where the last complete survey was during 2017.

Due to the covid pandemic, there was a shorter survey version during 2020. For this reason, we used the CASEN 2017, which includes information about dependency, caregivers, and Internet use.

The CASEN used a stratified probability sampling and collected information about all residents within the household. This survey is representative of the Chilean population.

2.2 Measures

Caregiving Role. The CASEN asked about who provides care within the household. However, the person that is characterized in detail is the respondent. Therefore, the question does not allow us to know the Internet use of the caregiver. Because of this, we selected the question about reasons for not having a paid job and the alternatives (1) "I have no one to leave an older adult" or (2) "I have no one to leave a family member." This question was used to filter persons that cannot have paid work because of their role in caring for a family member. Thus, it was assumed that all those people are informal caregivers who do not receive formal payment for their work. It is important to note that we excluded people who reported to care their grandchildren.

Internet Use. Different types of Internet use were measured through four dichotomous (yes or no) questions. For instance, use the Internet to seek information (through search engines, digital media, or social networks), communicate through social networks, and entertainment (Table 2). Also, a measurement of general Internet use was carried out creating a new variable considering if the person uses or not the Internet independently of the type of use.

Sociodemographic   Characteristics. Age   (continuous   variable),   gender (i.e., female/male), educational level (i.e., primary or secondary education, technical or training school-college, and bachelor's degree or postgraduate degree), marital status (i.e., single, divorced, widowed, and living with a partner or married), and the number of people living within the household were considered for the analysis (dichotomized in living alone or with someone else).

2.3 Data Analysis

We conducted all the analysis with a weighted and expanded sample of all caregivers over 60 years. Firstly, data were described using frequency tables.

Five logistic regressions were carried out, including different types of Internet use and general Internet use as outcome variables, and sociodemographic characteristics as predictors. For this, age was considered a continuous variable. Education level, gender, marital status, and people living within the household were included as categorical variables as described in Sect. 2.2.

All data were analyzed using the survey package in R Studio [36].

3 Results

3.1 Sample Characteristics

The mean age of the sample is 66.09, with a range of 60 to 96 years. Most of the participants were female (88.01%) and had primary or secondary education (77.96%). Regarding marital status, 60.63% of the participants were married, 19.37% were single, 12.42% were divorced, and 7.57% were widowed. Additionally, most participants lived with more than one person (97.98%), while only 2.02% lived alone. Detailed demographics by Internet Use are summarized in Table 1.

The mean age of caregivers that use the Internet is 65. Female caregivers make more extensive use of the Internet than males, mainly when used for entertainment and communication through social networks. In addition, caregivers with higher education use more Internet functions than those with primary/secondary education and technical training education, except for getting information through digital media or social networks. Whereas married, divorced, and single caregivers have a broad Internet usage, widowed participants use it substantially less, remaining below 16.88%. Lastly, caregivers who live with more than one person have greater general Internet use and seek information with a search engine, while those who live alone use the Internet mainly for entertainment, to communicate, and get information through social networks. All these characteristics are representative of Chile's caregiving population.

3.2 Logistic Regressions

Table 2 shows the results of our five logistic regression models of Internet use related to general Internet use, Internet use for information seeking, Internet use for communication, and Internet use for entertainment.

The variables most often associated with Internet use were age and education level. As the age increased, caregivers were slightly less likely to use the Internet, and caregivers with a bachelor's or postgraduate degree were more likely to use the Internet than those with primary or secondary education.

Age and education level were statistically significant for general Internet use (model 1). A one-year increase in the caregiver's age decreased the probability of general Internet use by 7% (OR = 0.93). Caregivers with technical or training education were 5.84 times more likely to use the Internet than caregivers with primary or secondary education.

Table 1. Frequency table of sociodemographic characteristics and types of Internet use (expanded sample)

	Total population n (%)	General internet use n (%)	Internet use for information seeking using a search engine n (%)	Internet use for getting information through digital media or social networks n (%)	Internet use for communicating through social networks n (%)	Internet use for entertainment n (%)
Age	66.09	64.95	64.61	64.47	64.81	64.79
Gender						
Male	3061 (11.85)	646 (21.1)	418 (13.66)	626 (20.45)	352 (11.50)	262 (8.56)
Female	22761 (88.14)	7516 (33.02)	6733 (29.58)	4574 (20.10)	6115 (26.87)	4651 (20.43)
Education level						
Primary/secondary education	20131 (77.96)	5076 (25.21)	4470 (22.2)	3035 (15.08)	3667 (18.22)	3079 (15.29)
Technical/training education	2394 (9.27)	1294 (54.05)	889 (37.13)	1004 (41.94)	1146 (47.87)	541 (22.6)
Bachelor's degree/postgraduate degree	3297 (12.77)	1792 (54.35)	1792 (54.35)	1161 (35.21)	1654 (50.17)	1293 (39.22)
Marital Status						
Married or living with a partner	15657 (60.63)	5403 (34.51)	4725 (30.18)	3010 (19.22)	4217 (26.93)	3327 (21.25)
Divorced	3207 (12.42)	1095 (34.14)	1038 (32.37)	998 (31.12)	860 (26.82)	736 (22.95)
Widowed	1955 (7.57)	330 (16.88)	319 (16.32)	231 (11.82)	224 (11.46)	128 (6.55)
Single	5003 (19.37)	1334 (26.66)	1069 (21.37)	961 (19.21)	1166 (23.31)	722 (14.43)
Number of people living at the household						
Alone	10184 (39.44)	136 (26.1)	136 (26.1)	137 (26.1)	138 (26.1)	139 (26.1)
More than two people	15638 (60.56)	8026 (31.72)	7015 (27.73)	5064 (20.02)	6331 (25.02)	4777 (18.88)

In the case of caregivers with a bachelor's degree or a postgraduate degree, they were 4.36 times more likely to use the Internet than caregivers with primary or secondary education.

Age and education levels were significantly associated with Internet use for information seeking using a search engine (Model 2a). A one-year increase in the caregiver's age decreased the probability of Internet use for information seeking by 9% (OR = 0.91). Also, information seeking was positively associated with education level. Caregivers with technical or training education were 3.25 times more likely to use the Internet for information seeking than those with primary or secondary education. Caregivers with a bachelor's or a postgraduate degree were 5.50 times more likely to use the Internet for information seeking than those with primary or secondary education. Similar results were found when the outcome variable was Internet use for getting information through digital media (model 2b).

The use of the Internet for communicating through social networks (model 2c) was the only type of usage where gender was significant. Female caregivers were 4.20 times more likely to use the Internet for communicating through social networks than male ones. Furthermore, education level was positively associated with communicating through social networks. Caregivers with technical or training education were 8.38 times more likely to use the Internet for Communicating through social networks than those with primary or secondary education. Caregivers with a bachelor's degree or a postgraduate degree were 5.97 times more likely to use the Internet for communicating through social networks than those with primary or secondary education.

Only bachelor's or postgraduate degree education was significant for Internet use for entertainment (model 2d). In this case, caregivers with higher educational levels were 4.30 times more likely to use the Internet for entertainment than those with primary or secondary education.

In addition, marital status and the number of people living within the household were not significantly associated with any type of Internet use.

4   Discussion

This study explored the sociodemographic characteristics of older caregivers and their influence on different types of Internet use. 31.6% of older caregivers were identified as Internet users. This data revealed a difference of 1.1% between the general use of the Internet in the older population (30.50%) and older caregivers.

In this context, the education level had the greater impact on general Internet use after controlling by age, gender, marital status, and the number of persons living in the household. Caregivers that reported more education levels also reported higher Internet use.

Regarding specific types of use, the education level was also related to more Internet use for information seeking (through search engines and social networks), communicating (through email and social networks), and entertainment. Also, all types of Internet use, excluding communicating through social networks and entertainment use, were negatively related to age. Those with higher age also presented a lower probability of using the Internet for those activities. These findings are in line with one of the few studies on everyday Internet use and caregivers, which found that younger and more educated caregivers are more likely to use the Internet to search for health-related information, especially about characteristics of dementia and tips for caregiving [15]. While Kim's study was conducted in North America, our results show that the same sociodemographic variables are linked to Internet use in caregivers in Latin America. However, as mentioned above, being a caregiver reduces the probability of Internet use [8, 16].

The task of caregiving involves several challenges, and older caregivers are confronted at the same time with their age-related changes [10]. Thus, older caregivers need effective coping mechanisms to face this reality and find a balance between their own life and the caregiving task that could lead to a feeling of lack of realization [24]. The Internet could be helpful for this purpose since it offers information and tools that could

Table 2. Logistic regression for internet use for older caregivers

Variable	General Internet use		Internet use for information seeking using a search engine		Internet use for getting information through digital media or social networks		Internet use for communicating through social networks		Internet use for entertainment	
	Model 1		Model 2a		Model 2b		Model 2d		Model 2e	
	OR	95% CI	OR	95% CI	OR	95% CI	OR	95% CI	OR	95%
Age	0.93*	0.85, 1.01	0.91*	0.84, 0.99	0.91*	0.85, 0.99	0.93	0.86, 1.00	0.93	0.86, 1.02
Gender (ref: male)										
Female	2.12	0.49, 12.57	2.52	0.73, 8.73	1.02	0.28, 3.42	4.20*	1.10, 16.10	2.65	0.69, 10.22
Education level (ref: primary or secondary education)										
Technical/Training Education	5.84***	1.35, 28.91	3.25*	1.30, 8.14	4.93**	1.68, 14.46	8.38***	2.77, 25.38	2.49	0.83, 7.44
Bachelor's degree postgraduate	4.36**	1.29, 15.74	5.50**	1.76, 17.20	3.58*	1.31, 9.17	5.97**	1.90, 18.76	4.30*	1.36, 13.64
Marital status (ref: married or living with a partner)										
Divorced	0.57	0.14, 2.10	0.66	0.26, 1.68	1.18	0.45, 3.07	0.51	0.16, 1.62	0.70	0.23, 2.12
Widowed	0.27	0.02, 1.66	0.38	0.09, 1.64	0.42	0.09, 2.05	0.20	0.03, 1.34	0.21	0.03, 1.69
Single	0.54	0.15, 1.69	0.50	0.19, 1.34	0.71	0.22, 2.23	0.67	0.24, 1.90	0.52	0.19, 1.43
Number of people at the household (ref: living alone)										
2 or more people within the household	0.57	0.02, 52.80	0.44	0.05, 4.17	0.45	0.04, 4.93	0.34	0.04, 3.29	0.23	0.03, 2.02
Nagelkerke's r-squared	0.12		0.12		0.09		0.14		0.08	

Note. * p < .05, ** p < .01, *** p < .001

minimize the negative consequences of caregiving [13]. Accordingly, a North American study revealed that stressed caregivers use the Internet more [8, 16], suggesting Internet use as a coping strategy.

Communication through social networks also showed a positive association with being female. These conclusions are consistent with previous literature that claims a higher use of social networks by older women [38].

At this point, it is important to note that being a caregiver does not happen randomly in the population [39, 40]. In general, females and lower educational levels are more likely to be caregivers [41]. Thus, they are exposed to greater vulnerability than the general population [42, 43].

Internet use for entertainment was only associated with education level. Particularly those who hold a bachelor's or postgraduate degree are more likely to use the Internet for this purpose. Previous research concluded that Internet use for entertainment acts as a coping mechanism in adverse contexts, for example, the COVID-19 pandemic [44]. Also, a pre-pandemic study state that leisure use was the only one related to better psychological well-being in older people [33]. Considering the possible negative health outcomes of caregiving [45], Internet use for leisure and entertainment could be a relevant tool to enhance the well-being of older caregivers. However, it is crucial to consider that some caregivers have neither energy nor time for leisure and entertainment [15], so this must be combined with programs that support the caregiver's availability for these types of activities.

Likewise, caregivers could feel a loss of freedom combined with a reduction of leisure and entertainment activities [9]. Regardless of that, some evidence suggested a higher frequency for online gaming in older caregivers, which coincides with the theory of Internet use for leisure and entertainment as a coping strategy that allows the reduction of stress [17].

5   Conclusion, Limitations, and Implications for Future Research

The use of the Internet has great potential to promote the well-being of older adults, especially those engaged in caregiving tasks. The present study investigated the sociodemographic characteristics linked to different types of Internet use in older caregivers. We answered the research questions: what sociodemographic variables impact Internet use in caregivers over 60 years old? Are there differences in the types of Internet use depending on the sociodemographic variables of caregivers over 60 years old?

We found that educational level is one of the most relevant variables for Internet use, with those with a higher education level being more frequent Internet users. In addition, age was negatively associated with most types of Internet use; therefore, the older the caregiver, the lower the probability of using the Internet. In general, this situation is similar in almost all types of uses measured, except entertainment, where age has no significant association, and use for communicating through social networks, where gender was significant.

This information is relevant for developing interventions that strengthen the Internet use of most vulnerable older caregivers. This focus will allow overcoming the barriers imposed by educational level and, in some cases, age and associated factors.

These findings need to be interpreted considering some limitations. Even though the data is representative of the country's population, there was no detailed information about the characteristics of the person being cared for (e.g., relationship with the caregiver or kind of pathology). Previous evidence concluded that the severity of dependence and type of pathology (e.g., dementia) are related to the impact of caregiving [11]. Therefore, it is relevant to explore the relationship between Internet use and caregiving considering this information.

Moreover, being a partner could influence the caregiver's health because they share similar risk factors, lifestyles, and access to health services [46]. Additionally, some older caregivers do not recognize their role because they feel that it is a task they must perform to help their partner [47].

Future research needs to explore the link between Internet use and caregivers' well-being, especially mental health. Previous evidence showed that loneliness and isolation are common in caregivers, particularly the older ones [9], which, in turn, reduces their quality of life [48]. In a caregiving situation, the Internet could be important to strengthen the social connection of caregivers. Also, considering that females are more likely to be caregivers and use more social networks for communication, some interventions that aim to reduce caregiver burden could consider this information to enhance its benefit.

Acknowledgments. This work was funded by the ANID Millennium Science Initiative Program – ICS2019_024.

References

1. Torrado Ramos, A.M., Sánchez Pérez, L., Somonte López, R., Cabrera Marsden, A.M., Henríquez Pino Santos, P.C., Lorenzo Pérez, O.: Envejecimiento poblacional: una mirada desde los programas y políticas públicas de América Latina, Europa y Asia. Revista Novedades en Población **10**, 18–29 (2014)
2. Ministerio de Desarrollo Social de Chile: Encuesta de Caracterización Socioeconómica Nacional. Adultos Mayores. Síntesis de Resultados (2017)
3. Slachevsky, A., et al.: The CUIDEME Study: determinants of burden in chilean primary caregivers of patients with dementia. J. Alzheimers Dis. **35**(2), 297–306 (2013). https://doi.org/10.3233/jad-122086
4. Loi, S.M., et al.: Factors associated with depression in older carers. Int. J. Geriatr. Psychiatry **31**(3), 294–301 (2016). https://doi.org/10.1002/gps.4323
5. Duarte, E.S.R., Silveira, L.V.A., Citero, V.A., Jacinto, A.F.: Common mental disorder among family carers of demented older people in Brazil. Dement Neuropsychol. **12**(4), 402–407 (2018). https://doi.org/10.1590/1980-57642018dn12-040010
6. Pavarini, S.C.I., et al.: Factors associated with cognitive performance in elderly caregivers. Arq. Neuropsiquiatr. **76**(10), 685–691 (2018). https://doi.org/10.1590/0004-282X20180101
7. Miranda-Castillo, C.: Predictors of quality of life in Chilean family caregivers of people with dementia. Alzheimer's Dementia **16**(S7) (2020). https://doi.org/10.1002/alz.041987
8. Kim, H., Chang, M., Rose, K., Kim, S.: Predictors of caregiver burden in caregivers of individuals with dementia. J. Adv. Nurs. **68**(4), 846–855 (2012). https://doi.org/10.1111/j.1365-2648.2011.05787.x
9. Greenwood, N., Pound, C., Brearley, S., Smith, R.: A qualitative study of older informal carers' experiences and perceptions of their caring role. Maturitas **124**, 1–7 (2019). https://doi.org/10.1016/j.maturitas.2019.03.006
10. Greenwood, N., Pound, C., Smith, R., Brearley, S.: Experiences and support needs of older carers: a focus group study of perceptions from the voluntary and statutory sectors. Maturitas **123**, 40–44 (2019). https://doi.org/10.1016/j.maturitas.2019.02.003
11. Oliveira, D., Vass, C., Aubeeluck, A.: Quality of life on the views of older family carers of people with dementia. Dementia (London) **18**(3), 990–1009 (2019). https://doi.org/10.1177/1471301217700741

12. Milne, A., Larkin, M.: What matters to older careers: evidence from practice-related research. Innov. Aging **1**(suppl_1), 1109–1109 (2017). https://doi.org/10.1093/geroni/igx004.4063

13. Teles, S., Paúl, C., Ferreira, A.M.: Internet use among informal caregivers of people with dementia: results of an online survey. In: García-Alonso, J., Fonseca, C. (eds.) IWoG. CCIS, vol. 1185, pp. 44–55. Springer, Cham (2020). https://doi.org/10.1007/978-3-030-41494-8_5

14. Efthymiou, A., Papastavrou, E., Middleton, N., Markatou, A., Sakka, P.: How caregivers of people with dementia search for dementia-specific information on the internet: survey study. JMIR Aging **3**(1), e15480 (2020). https://doi.org/10.2196/15480

15. Kim, H.: Understanding internet use among dementia caregivers: results of secondary data analysis using the US caregiver survey data. Interact. J. Med. Res. **4**(1), e1 (2015). https://doi.org/10.2196/ijmr.3127

16. Kim, H., Rose, K.M., Netemeyer, R.G., Merwin, E.I., Williams, I.C.: A secondary data analysis of Internet use in caregivers of persons with dementia. Nurs. Open **1**(1), 15–22 (2014). https://doi.org/10.1002/nop2.2

17. Reinwand, D.A., Crutzen, R., Zank, S.: Online activities among elder informal caregivers: results from a cross-sectional study. Digit. Health **4**, 2055207618779715 (2018). https://doi.org/10.1177/2055207618779715

18. Parra-Vidales, E., Soto-Pérez, F., Perea-Bartolomé, M.V., Franco-Martín, M.A., Muñoz-Sánchez, J.L.: Online interventions for caregivers of people with dementia: a systematic review. Actas Esp. Psiquiatr. **45**(3), 116–126 (2017)

19. Guay, C., et al.: Components and outcomes of internet-based interventions for caregivers of older adults: systematic review. J. Med. Internet Res. **19**(9), e313 (2017). https://doi.org/10.2196/jmir.7896

20. Blom, M.M., Zarit, S.H., Groot Zwaaftink, R.B., Cuijpers, P., Pot, A.M.: Effectiveness of an Internet intervention for family caregivers of people with dementia: results of a randomized controlled trial. PLoS ONE **10**(2), e0116622 (2015). https://doi.org/10.1371/journal.pone.0116622

21. Duceppe, A., Camateros, C., VÈzina, J.: Internet interventions for family caregivers of people with neurocognitive disorder - a literature review. In: ICT4AWE (2018)

22. McKechnie, V., Barker, C., Stott, J.: Effectiveness of computer-mediated interventions for informal carers of people with dementia-a systematic review. Int. Psychogeriatr. **26**(10), 1619–1637 (2014). https://doi.org/10.1017/S1041610214001045

23. Davies, N., et al.: The key aspects of online support that older family carers of people with dementia want at the end of life: a qualitative study. Aging Ment. Health **24**(10), 1654–1661 (2020). https://doi.org/10.1080/13607863.2019.1642299

24. Oliveira, D., Sousa, L., Aubeeluck, A.: What would most help improve the quality of life of older family carers of people with dementia? A qualitative study of carers' views. Dementia (London) **19**(4), 939–950 (2020). https://doi.org/10.1177/1471301218791906

25. Ministerio de Salud de Chile & Servicio Nacional del Adulto Mayor: Envejecimiento Positivo en Chile. In. (n.d.)

26. Herrera, M.S., et al.: A longitudinal study monitoring the quality of life in a national cohort of older adults in Chile before and during the COVID-19 outbreak. BMC Geriatr. **21**(1), 143 (2021). https://doi.org/10.1186/s12877-021-02110-3

27. Subsecretaría de Telecomunicaciones: IX Encuesta Accesos y Usos de Internet (2017)

28. Pontificia Universidad Católica de Chile, Caja Los Andes: Chile y sus mayores: Resultados de la V Encuesta Nacional Calidad de Vida en la Vejez (2020)

29. Jun, H.J., Kim, M.Y.: What accounts for the relationship between internet use and suicidal ideation of Korean older adults? A mediation analysis. J. Gerontol. B Psychol. Sci. Soc. Sci. **72**(5), 846–855 (2017). https://doi.org/10.1093/geronb/gbw163

30. Wang, Y., Zhang, H., Feng, T., Wang, H.: Does internet use affect levels of depression among older adults in China? A propensity score matching approach. BMC Public Health **19**(1), 1474 (2019). https://doi.org/10.1186/s12889-019-7832-8

31. Chang, P.F., Choi, Y.H., Bazarova, N.N., Lockenhoff, C.E.: Age differences in online social networking: extending socioemotional selectivity theory to social network sites. J. Broadcast. Electron. Media **59**(2), 221–239 (2015). https://doi.org/10.1080/08838151.2015.1029126

32. Heo, J., Chun, S., Lee, S., Lee, K.H., Kim, J.: Internet use and well-being in older adults. Cyberpsychol. Behav. Soc. Netw. **18**(5), 268–272 (2015). https://doi.org/10.1089/cyber.2014.0549

33. Lifshitz, R., Nimrod, G., Bachner, Y.G.: Internet use and well-being in later life: a functional approach. Aging Ment. Health **22**(1), 85–91 (2018). https://doi.org/10.1080/13607863.2016.1232370

34. Forsman, A.K., Nordmyr, J.: Psychosocial links between internet use and mental health in later life: a systematic review of quantitative and qualitative evidence. J. Appl. Gerontol. **36**(12), 1471–1518 (2017). https://doi.org/10.1177/0733464815595509

35. Berg, T., Winterton, R., Petersen, M., Warburton, J.: "Although we're isolated, we're not really isolated": the value of information and communication technology for older people in rural Australia. Australas. J. Ageing **36**(4), 313–317 (2017). https://doi.org/10.1111/ajag.12449

36. Lumley, T.: Survey: analysis of complex survey samples. R package version 4.0 (2020)

37. Villalobos Dintrans, P.: Informal caregivers in Chile: the equity dimension of an invisible burden. Health Policy Plan. **34**(10), 792–799 (2019). https://doi.org/10.1093/heapol/czz120

38. Mohta, R., Halder, S.: Elderly population and new age technology. J. Psychosoc. Res. **15**(1), 151–158 (2020). https://doi.org/10.32381/JPR.2020.15.01.12

39. Fernández, M.B., Herrera, M.S.: El efecto del cuidado informal en la salud de los cuidadores familiares de personas mayores dependientes en Chile. Rev. Med. Chil. **148**, 30–36 (2020)

40. von Kanel, R., et al.: Refining caregiver vulnerability for clinical practice: determinants of self-rated health in spousal dementia caregivers. BMC Geriatr. **19**(1), 18 (2019). https://doi.org/10.1186/s12877-019-1033-2

41. de Zwart, P.L., Bakx, P., van Doorslaer, E.K.A.: Will you still need me, will you still feed me when I'm 64? The health impact of caregiving to one's spouse. Health Econ. **26**(Suppl), 127–138 (2017). https://doi.org/10.1002/hec.3542

42. Amankwaa, B.: Informal Caregiver stress. ABNF J. **28**(4), 92–95 (2017)

43. Santos-Orlandi, A.A.d., et al.: Profile of older adults caring for other older adults in contexts of high social vulnerability. Escola Anna Nery - Revista de Enfermagem **21**(1) (2017). https://doi.org/10.5935/1414-8145.20170013

44. Nimrod, G.: Changes in internet use when coping with stress: older adults during the COVID-19 pandemic. Am. J. Geriatr. Psychiatry **28**(10), 1020–1024 (2020). https://doi.org/10.1016/j.jagp.2020.07.010

45. Capistrant, B.D.: Caregiving for older adults and the caregivers' health: an epidemiologic review. Curr. Epidemiol. Rep. **3**(1), 72–80 (2016). https://doi.org/10.1007/s40471-016-0064-x

46. Pinquart, M., Sorensen, S.: Differences between caregivers and noncaregivers in psychological health and physical health: a meta-analysis. Psychol. Aging **18**(2), 250–267 (2003). https://doi.org/10.1037/0882-7974.18.2.250

47. Adelman, R.D., Tmanova, L.L., Delgado, D., Dion, S., Lachs, M.S.: Caregiver burden: a clinical review. JAMA **311**(10), 1052–1060 (2014). https://doi.org/10.1001/jama.2014.304

48. Ekwall, A.K., Sivberg, B., Hallberg, I.R.: Loneliness as a predictor of quality of life among older caregivers. J. Adv. Nurs. **49**(1), 23–32 (2005). https://doi.org/10.1111/j.1365-2648.2004.03260.x

Non-use of Digital Services Among Older Adults During the Second Wave of COVID-19 Pandemic in Finland: Population-Based Survey Study

Petra Saukkonen(✉) ⒾD, Emma Kainiemi ⒾD, Lotta Virtanen ⒾD,
Anu-Marja Kaihlanen ⒾD, Seppo Koskinen ⒾD, Päivi Sainio ⒾD, Päivikki Koponen ⒾD,
Sari Kehusmaa, and Tarja Heponiemi ⒾD

Finnish Institute for Health and Welfare, P.O. Box 30, 00271 Helsinki, Finland
petra.saukkonen@thl.fi

Abstract. This study aimed to examine the associations of sociodemographic factors and factors related to physical, mental, cognitive, and social functioning with the non-use of digital services among older adults during the second wave of the COVID-19 pandemic. Nationally representative data from Finland were collected between October 2020 and January 2021. The present study included 1524 respondents (response rate 68.2%, 56.6% female) aged between 70 and 100. The analyses were conducted with multivariable logistic regression. Almost half of the respondents did not use digital services independently. Those who needed assistance due to functional limitations, had insufficient energy in everyday life, perceived that their memory or ability to learn was impaired, had three or more members in the household, and lived in rural region had greater odds of being non-users of digital services than their counterparts. Thus, challenges to cope independently in everyday life, cognitive impairment, and rural living seemed to expose older adults to risk for exclusion from digital services. Factors may be interconnected, further weakening the inclusion of older people in society. It seems that adapting to rapid digital development and face-to-face service delivery constraints during the pandemic may have been particularly challenging for these vulnerable individuals. To ensure wider use of digital services, the natural decline in functioning with age should be noted, and older adults should be included in the development of digital services. Accessible support and traditional face-to-face services must be secured.

Keywords: Older adults · Digital divide · Digital exclusion · Digital services · Internet use · COVID-19

1 Introduction

The global COVID-19 pandemic has led to a remarkable surge in the provision of digital services, and technological advances have been increasingly used to promote and enable societal services [1]. Older adults have experienced the strictest COVID-19 restrictions to maintain social distance and minimize the risk of infection [2], as they are at an

---

The original version of this chapter was revised: an error in Table 1, "Characteristics of the respondents according to non-use of digital services" on page 602 has been corrected. The correction to this chapter is available at https://doi.org/10.1007/978-3-031-05581-2_46

Q. Gao and J. Zhou (Eds.): HCII 2022, LNCS 13330, pp. 596–613, 2022.
https://doi.org/10.1007/978-3-031-05581-2_41

increased risk for severe health outcomes and mortality due to the virus [3]. Restrictions have been found to increase loneliness and social isolation among older adults, which in turn might lead to deterioration of mental and physical health [4]. Older adults' quality of life [5], health and well-being have also been negatively affected by the COVID-19 quarantine [6]. Digital services provide numerous opportunities for people of all ages to communicate, access information, and engage in recreational activities [7, 8]. Technology is also increasingly used in healthcare for service delivery, self-monitoring, health information sharing, and peer support [9]. Internet use appears to contribute to older adults' well-being and sense of empowerment by affecting their interpersonal interactions, cognitive functioning and contributing to their experience of control and independence [10]. Technology use also appears to improve the older adults' quality of life [11] by augmenting their ability to perform a variety of tasks, access information, and remain independent longer [9]. In addition, higher levels of social support, less loneliness [7, 12], and less depression [7, 11] have been observed as benefits of Internet use among older adults. However, in order to benefit from digital services, one must be able to use them [13].

Older adults have been shown to have lower access and usage of digital technologies [13–15] and be less likely to learn [16] and adopt information technologies than younger generations [17, 18]. Often, the most vulnerable individuals who would benefit the most from the use of digital solutions have less access to these technologies [2]. Unfortunately, the age-related digital divide continues to prevent these benefits from being achieved [11, 19].

The concept of the digital divide was defined by Castells [20] as inequalities in access and use of information and communication technology (ICT). Access may refer in a narrow sense to physical access or in a broader sense to motivation, physical requirements, skills, and usage [21]. The digital divide can be considered to encompass at least three levels [22]; 1) infrastructural access, such as Internet connection (first-level digital divide) [22], 2) differences in skills and usage patterns (second-level digital divide) [23], and 3) inequalities in Internet use outcomes (third-level digital divide) [22, 24]. Furthermore, Helsper's [25] corresponding fields model suggests that digital and social exclusion influence each other, and the resources individuals have offline influence their ability to use online digital solutions. Therefore, sociodemographic factors and factors related to physical, mental, cognitive, and social functioning have potential effects on the digital divide. It is important to examine older adults as socially situated, psychophysical human beings, with the emphasis on the relationship to their environment [26].

Previous research has reported the association of demographic and socioeconomic factors with the Internet use among older adults [27]. Lower educational level [11] and poor financial status have been found to increase the likelihood of not using digital devices and services [16, 27]. Moreover, disabilities or reduced functional abilities may hinder Internet use among older adults [16]. Cognitive abilities have been reported to be particularly important for older adults' Internet use [8] because impairments that affect daily activities and social interactions are most likely to occur later in life [27]. In addition, older adults with a wider social network have been found to use the Internet more likely than those with a more limited network [11]. Previous research has also shown that living alone can decrease older adults' access to computer-based technologies [16].

However, above-mentioned earlier studies have been conducted prior to the COVID -19 era and therefore have limited applicability to the changed situation caused by the pandemic. The COVID -19 pandemic has had a significant negative impact on the daily lives of even the healthiest and most active people [6] and the rapid application of digital services has increased the risk of digital divide for the vulnerable group of older adults [1]. Therefore, it is necessary to obtain up-to-date information in a highly digitalized society, such as Finland, about the factors associated with the non-use of the digital services among older adults.

This study aimed to examine which factors are associated with older adults' non-use of digital services. More specifically, we examined the associations of sociodemographic factors (urbanicity, financial situation) and factors related to physical, mental, cognitive, and social functioning (functional disability, need of assistance, energy in everyday life, psychological distress, memory, ability to learn new things, household size, loneliness) with the non-use of digital services among older adults during the second wave of the COVID-19 pandemic in Finland. By examining these factors together, we were able to identify the various causes of digital exclusion among older adults. Our findings may provide information that will help identify older adults who are most at risk of being excluded from services due to increasing digitalization of services. The information gained from this study can be used in the development of digital services and targeting support to promote digital inclusion and equality for older adults in society.

2   Methods

2.1   Study Sample and Data Collection

This study was a cross-sectional study whose nationally representative data on older adults were collected between October 2020 and January 2021 as a part of the FinHealth 2017 Follow-up Study conducted by the Finnish Institute for Health and Welfare [28]. The sample was drawn from the Finnish Population Information System by two-stage stratified cluster sampling. The sampling method for original FinHealth 2017 data gathering has been reported elsewhere [29]. The invitation to participate in 2020 was sent to all those who were invited in 2017 with some exceptions (e.g., those who had moved abroad or died). Altogether 2233 participants aged 70 years and older were invited to respond to the survey. Of those, 1524 older adults aged from 70 to 100 years responded (response rate 68.2%, 56.6% female). Participation in the study was possible electronically (33% of respondents), by completing a postal questionnaire (62%), or by participating in a telephone interview (5%). The questionnaires were available in Finnish, Swedish, and English. Ethics approval was obtained from the Ethics Committee II of the Helsinki and Uusimaa hospital region (HUS/2391/2020).

2.2   Context

Finland is a Nordic country with approximately 5.5 million inhabitants [30]. At the end of 2020, almost 20% of the population were aged 65–84 years and approximately 3%

were 85 years or older [31]. The rapid growth of the aging population lays Finland as one of the fastest aging societies in Europe [32]. The population density of Finland was 18.2 inhabitants per square kilometer in 2021, referring to a relatively sparse population. Differences in population density are large as the population is heavily concentrated in the southern parts of the country as well as in the largest urban areas [33]. Finland has uniformly high standard broadband coverage and high-speed Internet connections are widely available. Altogether 98 percent of the Finnish households in the capital region and 88 percent in rural areas had an Internet connection in 2021 [34].

Finland is one of the leading countries in digitalization [35]. In 2019, Finland enacted a law on the provision of digital services to promote their availability, quality, information security, and equal opportunities in the use [36]. There are currently more than a hundred public digital services available to private customers, such as services in the areas of social security, tax administration, health care, transport, and housing [37].

Nearly all adults in Finland used the Internet in 2021, but the utilization rate decreased with age [38]. The Internet was used daily by 78% of those aged 65–74 and 42% of those aged 75–89, but in both age groups, usage was approximately 20 percentage points higher than in 2019 [38, 39]. Number of online shoppers increased only among those over 65, as the majority of younger people already bought goods and services online [38]. In 2021, the use of the Internet increased also for communication among older adults compared to the previous year [38]. Video calls and social media use were more prevalent among 75–89-year-olds [38].

2.3 Measurements

Dependent Variable. Non-use of digital services referred to that the respondent did not use digital services independently. The non-use of digital services was assessed by asking whether the respondent used the Internet for electronic transactions or services (e.g., online banking, Social Insurance Institution KELA, tax office, ticket sales, local public services, online shops). The response options were 1) yes, 2) I need assistance, or someone else does it on my behalf, and 3) never. For the analyses, the measure was binary coded: 0 = yes, uses the Internet independently (response option 1) and 1 = does not use the Internet independently (response options 2–3).

Independent Variables. Independent variables included sociodemographic factors and factors related to physical, mental, cognitive, and social functioning.

Sociodemographic Factors. The age and gender of the respondents were received from the national Population Information System. Age was categorized in intervals of five years: 70–74, 75–79, and 80–84. In addition, respondents aged 85 years or older formed one group.

Education was assessed by asking for the highest educational degree. The variable was categorized as 1) primary level (response options elementary school, basic education, or lower secondary education), 2) secondary level (vocational school or equivalent, upper secondary education, or high school), and 3) higher level (non-university lower education, Bachelor's Degree, and Master's Degree).

Urbanicity was based on the municipality number. Municipalities were classified into four regional categories: 1) urban, 2) semi-urban, 3) rural heartland, and 4) sparsely populated rural. The variable was coded as a dichotomous variable: 0 = urban or semi-urban (response options 1–2) and 1 = rural (response options 3–4).

Financial situation was determined by the question: "Do you have enough money to meet your needs?" with five response alternatives: 1) not at all, 2) a little, 3) moderately, 4) mostly and 5) completely. The variable was coded as a dichotomous variable: 0 = reasonably or adequately (response options 3–5) and 1 = not at all or a little (response options 1–2).

Factors Related to Physical, Mental, and Cognitive Functioning. Functional disability was assessed with The Global Activity Limitation Indicator (GALI) [40]. GALI has been used as a measure of disability in many European surveys [41] and has shown good validity and reliability [42]. The first part of the two-part GALI asked, "Are you limited in the activities you normally do because of a health problem? Would you say you are…?" with three response alternatives 1) severely limited, 2) limited but not severely, or 3) not limited at all. If the respondent indicated being limited, the question continued: "Have you been limited for at least the past 6 months?" with response alternatives 1) yes or 2) no. Those who had any limitations (first question, response options 1 and 2) that had existed for at least 6 months (second question, response option 1) are classified as having longstanding activity limitation [41]. The variable was coded as 0 = no functional disability and 1 = functional disability.

The need for assistance was asked with the question "Do you need and do you get help for your everyday activities due to your impaired functional capacity?" with five response alternatives: 1) I do not need help and do not get it, 2) I would need help but do not get it, 3) I get help, but not enough, 4) I get enough help and 5) I get more help than I need. For analysis, the variable was coded as a dichotomous variable to describe the need for help in daily life due to functional limitations: 0 = no need for help (response option 1) and 1 = needs help (response options 2–5).

Sufficient energy in everyday life was assessed asking whether the respondent had enough energy for everyday life. The response options were: 1) not at all, 2) little, 3) moderately, 4) almost enough and 5) completely enough. The variable was coded as a dichotomous variable: 0 = somewhat or enough (response options 3–5) and 1 = not at all or little (response options 1–2). The question is one of the eight EuroHIS-8 indicators of quality of life [43] and is used in this study only to map the energy perceived by older adults as sufficient for daily living.

Current psychological distress was assessed with the Mental Health Inventory (MHI-5) [44], derived from the SF-36 scale [45]. The MHI-5 includes five questions: "How much of the time during the past 4 weeks: Have you 1) been a very nervous person? 2) felt so down in the dumps that nothing could cheer you up? 3) felt calm and peaceful? 4) felt downhearted and blue? 5) been a happy person? All items have a 6-point scale, ranging from "all of the time" to "none of the time". In calculating the total score, the answers to two items (the third and the fifth) were reversed and the raw scores were converted to a scale ranging from zero to 100. The cut-off value for current psychological distress was a total score of 52 or less [44]. Based on this value, a dichotomized variable was formed: 0 = no psychological distress and 1 = psychological distress.

Memory functioning and the ability to learn new things were assessed with the question "How would you estimate your present memory and learning capabilities?" Respondents rated their abilities in these functions with the questions a) "How well does your memory work?" and b) "Are you able to acquire new information and learn?". Response options were 1) very well, 2) well, 3) adequately, 4) poorly and 5) very poorly. Both variables were coded as dichotomous variables: 0 = well (response options 1–2) and 1 = impaired (adequately or poorly; response options 3–5).

Factors Related to Social Functioning. Household size was measured with the question, "How many members are there presently in your household (yourself included)?" The variable was categorized as follows: 1) one, 2) two, and 3) three or more members.

Loneliness was assessed with the question "Do you ever feel lonely?" with five response options: 1) never, 2) very rarely, 3) sometimes, 4) fairly often and 5) all the time. The variable was coded as a dichotomous variable: 0 = at most occasionally (response options 1–3) and 1 = fairly often or constantly (response options 4–5).

2.4 Statistical Analysis

Multivariable logistic regression analyses were used to examine the relationships between the independent variables and the dependent variable. Analyses were conducted in two steps. First, we examined the independent effect of each variable adjusted for age, gender, and education in Model A. Age, gender, and education were only used as adjustments, as these factors have already been extensively studied. Second, we examined further the multivariable associations in a fully adjusted model that included all the examined variables to determine the relative importance of each variable when the effects of all other variables were controlled for (Model B). We included all adjustment variables in Model B because previous research has shown that the selected independent variables may influence Internet use among older adults. Inverse Probability Weighting (IPW) was used to correct for possible nonresponse bias [46]. Therefore, methods appropriate for weighted data were used: Complex Samples Logistic regression and Complex Samples Descriptives or Frequencies for descriptive statistics. Due to non-response for some items, the number of observations in the analyses varied. Analyses were performed using the SPSS 27 statistical package.

3 Results

3.1 Characteristics of the Study Population

The characteristics of the respondents are shown in Table 1. Nearly half of the respondents (46.8%) did not use digital services independently. This proportion included respondents who used digital services with assistance (weighted count 207/1449, 14.3%). The weighted mean age of the respondents was 78.4 years (SE = 0.20). More than half of the respondents were females, and the majority lived in urban or semi-urban areas. Almost half of the respondents had primary education. More than half of the respondents had a disability that had lasted for longer than 6 months. However, less than a quarter of the respondents required assistance with daily living. Less than one in ten experienced psychological distress, and even fewer reported insufficient energy in everyday life. Well over a third estimated that their memory was impaired, and an even larger proportion felt that their ability to learn new things was impaired. Less than half of the respondents lived alone, and one-tenth experienced at least frequent feelings of loneliness.

3.2 Non-use of Digital Services Among Older Adults

The results of the complex samples logistic regression analyses regarding non-use of digital services can be seen in Table 2. Respondents with a need for assistance, insufficient energy in everyday life, impaired memory, impaired ability to learn new things, and three or more members in the household had greater odds of not using digital services independently compared to their counterparts according to the results of Model A. In the fully adjusted Model B, all the detected associations remained significant. In addition, urbanicity was associated with the non-use in the fully adjusted model.

The independent variables in the fully adjusted model (Model B) explained 36.8% (Nagelkerke R2) of the variance in the non-use of digital services. Respondents who needed assistance in everyday activities had almost two times greater odds of being non-users of digital services compared to respondents who did not need help with daily living. Those who did not have enough energy in everyday life had 2.7 times greater odds of not using digital services than respondents who had at least adequate amount of energy. Memory impairment was associated with greater odds of not using digital services independently. Respondents who felt that their ability to learn was impaired had nearly two times greater odds of not using digital services compared to respondents who felt that they learned new things well. Older adults who had three or more members in their household had 3.6 times greater odds of not using digital services than those who lived alone. Rural living area was associated with greater odds of not using digital services independently.

Table 1. Characteristics of the respondents according to non-use of digital services

	All (n = 1524) n[a] (%)	Non-users (n = 678) n[a] (%)	Users (n = 771) n[a] (%)	p[b]
Sociodemographic background				
Age				<.001
70–74	607 (39.8)	184 (27.1)	407 (52.8)	
75–79	375 (24.6)	150 (22.2)	215 (27.9)	
80–84	277 (18.2)	159 (23.5)	103 (13.4)	
85–100	265 (17.4)	184 (27.2)	45 (5.9)	

(continued)

Table 1. (*continued*)

	All (n = 1524) n[a] (%)	Non-users (n = 678) n[a] (%)	Users (n = 771) n[a] (%)	p[b]
Gender				.007
Female	879 (57.7)	415 (61.2)	413 (53.5)	
Male	645 (42.3)	263 (38.8)	358 (46.5)	
Education				<.001
Primary	646 (43.6)	386 (58.8)	221 (28.9)	
Secondary	376 (25.3)	185 (28.2)	178 (23.3)	
High	460 (31.1)	85 (13.0)	366 (47.8)	
Urbanicity				<.001
Urban or semi-urban	1142 (74.9)	477 (70.4)	620 (80.4)	
Rural	382 (25.1)	200 (29.6)	151 (19.6)	
Income in relation to needs				.001
Reasonably or adequately	1329 (94.9)	572 (92.7)	724 (96.6)	
Not at all or little	72 (5.1)	45 (7.3)	25 (3.4)	
Physical, mental, and cognitive functioning				
Functional disability				<.001
No	738 (48.4)	277 (40.8)	426 (55.2)	
Yes	786 (51.6)	401 (59.2)	345 (44.8)	
Need of assistance				<.001
No	1110 (76.4)	410 (62.5)	675 (88.6)	
Yes	343 (23.6)	246 (37.5)	87 (11.4)	
Sufficient energy				<.001
Reasonably or adequately	1307 (93.2)	543 (88.0)	732 (97.4)	
Not at all or little	95 (6.8)	74 (12.0)	20 (2.6)	
Psychological distress				.051
No	1202 (91.8)	509 (90,0)	673 (93.3)	
Yes	107 (8.2)	57 (10.0)	48 (6.7)	

(*continued*)

Table 1. (*continued*)

	All (n = 1524) n^a (%)	Non-users (n = 678) n^a (%)	Users (n = 771) n^a (%)	p^b
Memory functioning				<.001
Well	883 (60.3)	306 (45.5)	563 (73.3)	
Impaired	581 (39.7)	366 (54.5)	205 (26.7)	
Learning new things				<.001
Well	633 (43.4)	179 (26.7)	445 (58.1)	
Impaired	826 (56.6)	492 (73.3)	322 (41.9)	
Social functioning				
Household size, members				<.001
One	657 (43.1)	334 (49.2)	266 (34.5)	
Two	824 (54.1)	315 (46.5)	493 (64.0)	
Three or more	43 (2.8)	29 (4.3)	12 (1.5)	
Loneliness				.004
At most occasionally	1308 (89.8)	579 (87.3)	706 (91.8)	
Fairly often or constantly	149 (10.2)	84 (12.7)	63 (8.2)	

[a]Weighted population size estimate
[b]Chi-square

Table 2. The results of the logistic regression analyses for non-use of digital services[a]. Odds Ratios (OR) and their 95% Confidence Intervals (95% CI) (n = 1228[b])

	Model A[c]			Model B[d]		
	OR	95% CI	p	OR	95% CI	p
Sociodemographic background						
Urbanicity			0.080			.023
Urban or semi-urban	1			1		
Rural	1.37	0.96–1.95		1.51	1.06–2.15	
Income in relation to needs			0.390			.968
Reasonably or adequately	1			1		
Not at all or little	1.31	0.71–2.41		0.99	0.54–1.82	

(*continued*)

Table 2. (*continued*)

	Model A[c]			Model B[d]		
	OR	95% CI	p	OR	95% CI	p
Physical, mental, and cognitive functioning						
Functional disability			0.066			.944
No	1			1		
Yes	1.29	0.98–1.69		1.01	0.72–1.43	
Need for assistance			<0.001			.002
No	1			1		
Yes	2.35	1.70–3.26		1.81	1.23–2.66	
Sufficient energy			<0.001			.008
Somewhat or enough	1			1		
Not at all or little	3.19	1.71–5.94		2.69	1.30–5.58	
Psychological distress			0.813			.120
No	1			1		
Yes	1.07	0.61–1.90		0.60	0.31–1.14	
Memory functioning			<0.001			.024
Well	1			1		
Impaired	2.32	1.79–3.01		1.45	1.05–1.99	
Learning new things			<0.001			<.001
Well	1			1		
Impaired	2.43	1.86–3.19		1.91	1.38–2.66	
Social functioning						
Household size, members			0.002			.027
One	1			1		
Two	0.85	0.67–1.08		0.96	0.70–1.30	
Three or more	2.93	1.43–5.99		3.63	1.38–9.59	
Loneliness			0.262			.498
At most occasionally	1			1		
Fairly often or constantly	1.26	0.84–1.87		0.84	0.51–1.39	

[a]Inverse Probability Weighting (IPW) corrected
[b]Number of unweighted cases in model B
[c]Model A included the main effect of variable adjusted for age, gender, and education
[d]Model B included all examined variables adjusted for age, gender, and education

4 Discussion

The strong digitalization of society and the increased shift of transactions to the Internet, fueled by the COVID-19 pandemic, pose a challenge to equal access to services. In addition, as the population ages, it is increasingly important to understand and address the digital divide among older adults. This study aimed to examine the association between sociodemographic factors and factors related to physical, mental, cognitive, and social functioning with the non-use of digital services among older adults during the second wave of the COVID-19 pandemic. Based on our results, nearly half of those aged 70 years and older did not use digital services independently. Factors that predispose older adults to digital exclusion included need for assistance in everyday activities, insufficient energy in everyday life, impaired memory, impaired ability to learn new things, having three or more members in the household, and rural living area.

According to our results, the need for assistance due to impaired functional ability was associated with non-use of digital services. Respondents who needed assistance in everyday activities were almost twice more likely to be non-users of digital services compared to respondents who did not need help with daily living. However, functional disability was not associated with non-use of digital services. Our findings suggest that functional disability impairs independent use of digital services when abilities have declined to the point that external assistance for everyday functions is required. Previous studies have suggested that poorer health is associated with lower computer, Internet [47–49] and patient portal use [50]. Keränen et al. [51] discovered that the frail older adults used less ICT compared to their non-frail counterparts. The use of technology has the potential to enhance older adult's quality of life by improving their ability to perform tasks and remain independent for longer [8]. However, our findings raise concerns about whether older adults with limited functioning benefit from digital services.

Older adults who experienced insufficient energy in everyday life were over two times more likely to be non-users of digital services compared to those with at least adequate amount of energy. Experiencing insufficient energy in everyday life might be the result of several factors that weaken the overall feeling of vitality. According to Gruet et al. [52], fatigue is a common, non-specific symptom associated with many health conditions. It can be classified as mental, referring to the cognitive or perceptual aspects of fatigue, or physical, referring to the performance of the motor system [52]. Fatigue or lack of energy in everyday life may thus deprive older adults' motivation and resources to learn to use new digital services.

We found that older adults who perceived that their memory was impaired were 1.5 times more likely to be non-users of digital services than those experiencing well-functioning memory. This is congruent with a previous finding showing cognitive impairments as barriers to the use of personal health records [53]. According to a previous study by Gusman-Parra et al. [54], people with dementia or mild cognitive impairment frequently used smartphones and tablets, but they had only limited use of certain applications or softwares to support memory. The cognitive abilities of older adults who use the Internet daily have been shown to be better than the abilities of non-frequent users [14]. In addition, the use of various forms of digital technology is believed to stimulate cognitive abilities such as executive function, memory, and reasoning [55, 56]. However, more evidence is needed on whether the Internet use contributes to maintaining good cognitive function [57–59]. Digital services could potentially support people with cognitive problems to live independently, support their functioning, and improve collaboration between older adults, their loved ones, and care providers.

Our results showed that respondents who experienced impairments in their ability to learn were almost two times more likely not to use digital services compared to those experiencing that they learned new things well. Increased age is generally associated with a decline in processing and reasoning, which are fundamental elements for learning [8]. In the study by Kaihlanen et al. [60], older adults expressed their willingness to receive digital support because insufficient digital skills hindered or even prevented their use of digital services. However, due to the COVID-19 pandemic, the opportunities for receiving digital support were limited as many services providing support were cancelled or switched to online [60].

Based on our result, older adults who had three or more members in their household were over three times more likely not to use digital services than those who lived alone. However, there was no statistically significant difference between those living alone and those whose household also included another member. Previous findings have highlighted the importance of social participation and the presence of a partner for using the Internet [13, 22, 48, 61]. As the population ages, there are more older people living alone who may be at risk of social isolation which may have an adverse impact on their health and wellbeing [62]. According to Friemel [63], family and friends are the most important sources for learning Internet use among older adults [63]. Non-professional support from a close person has been shown to increase the range of digital devices and services available to older adults [64]. Our findings may suggest that in multigenerational families, other family members use digital services on behalf of older family members. A previous study by Bunyan and Collins [65] found that households with younger people were more digitally engaged. In addition, social networks have been shown to motivate older adults to use digital services independently [63]. Based on our results, we cannot say whether these older adults living with more than two family members are however engaged in digital society even if they do not use digital services independently.

Loneliness, also a factor related to social functioning, was not significantly associated with the non-use of digital services in our results. However, previous research has reported that older adults mitigated their increased loneliness during the COVID-19 pandemic by using new online services to maintain social relationships [66]. Even before the pandemic, it was argued that Internet use is an important tool for older adults with functional limitations to restore and maintain social relationships [12]. Older adults who interact via the Internet have also been found to have a lower risk for social isolation and loneliness [62]. Previous research has reported that older adults suffering from loneliness more often indicated a lack of access to online services as a reason for disengagement than a lack of interest [67]. Based on our findings, no conclusions can be drawn about the extent to which digital services are inaccessible to older adults who suffer from loneliness.

According to our findings, older adults living in rural areas were more likely not to use digital services than those living in urban or semi-urban areas. This association was not significant in Model A, but became significant when the effects of all other factors were controlled for in Model B. Furthermore, the unadjusted main effect was significant.

Berner et al. [61] have also previously reported lower Internet usage among older adults in Swedish rural areas. Global differences in Internet access and connection speeds between urban and rural areas are well stated before [68]. The standard broadband coverage is uniformly high and high-speed Internet connections are widely available in Finland, although there are some rural parts, especially in the Northern Finland, with poor connections. The aging of the population combined with urbanization in an already sparsely populated country like Finland creates imbalances in the needs for services, revenue, and resources [30]. Despite the extensive research suggesting that online technologies have the potential to improve service delivery in rural areas, our findings support previously expressed concerns that older adults in rural areas may not benefit equally from digital services [69, 70].

Financial situation was not associated with the independent use of digital services among older adults according to the results of our study. However, previous research has shown an association between lower income and lower Internet use [27, 63]. Expenses related to technology may hinder the older adult's use of digital services [16, 60]. It should be noted that we asked older adults whether they had enough money to meet their needs. Needs and adequacy can be defined differently according to individual experiences. The technology needed to use digital services may not be a high priority for some older adults. In addition, public libraries provide free access to computers and the Internet for all Finnish residents. However, the COVID-19 pandemic forced libraries to temporarily close, leaving some people without access to digital services. The distance to the library can also be a challenge, especially for older adults living in rural areas with limited functional abilities.

Strengths and Limitations. We used a national population-based sample with a relatively good participation rate and register-based individual-level data to adjust for non-participation. This allowed us to better generalize our results to the entire population of older adults in Finland. In addition to the option of responding by mail or web-based, respondents also had the option of answering the survey by telephone interview, allowing those older adults who have difficulty answering paper questionnaires or web-based surveys to participate. However, the non-use of digital services by older adults is presumably an even broader phenomenon than captured by our study, since poor functioning may have limited the participation to this survey. This study was conducted during the second wave of COVID -19 when the provision and use of digital services had increased and restrictions were set due to the pandemic. Presumably, avoiding face-to-face encounters motivated older adults to use digital services. However, the restriction measures in Finland were not quite as strict as in many other countries.

Our study has some limitations that should be considered when interpreting our results. First, the results are based on self-report, which may lead to problems related to general method variance and the inflation of the strength of associations. Second, the non-use of digital services referred to respondents who did not use digital services independently. Thus, the non-users also included respondents who used digital services with assistance. In addition, non-users may include persons on whose behalf a relative has used digital services, as transactions on behalf might not be perceived as assisted use in some responses. Therefore, caution is warranted when arguing the importance of support and guidance based on our findings. However, assisted use of digital services among older adults in our study was relatively low (14.3%). Third, although many factors in our fully adjusted model were controlled, possibility of residual bias remains. In addition, several factors with possible influence on the Internet use were not examined in our study, such as access to digital tools or the Internet. In addition, comparing different studies of older adults' non-use of digital services is difficult due to differences in age categories [27] and adjustments in analyses. Fourth, because cross-sectional survey data were used, no causal conclusions can be drawn from the results. Finally, Finland is one of the pioneers of digitalization with a high standard of living [71]. Therefore, caution should be exercised when generalizing our findings to countries with a different ICT infrastructure or socioeconomic status among the population of older adults.

5 Conclusion

Challenges to cope independently in everyday life, cognitive impairment, and rural living seem to expose older adults to the risk for exclusion from digital services. Factors related to older adults' digital exclusion and functional capacity may be interrelated, and perpetuate in other areas of life, further weakening older adults' inclusion in society. Adapting to rapid digital development and limitations in the face-to-face service provision due to the COVID -19 pandemic may have been particularly challenging for these vulnerable individuals.

Overall, this study highlights the importance of recognizing the individual needs and perspectives of older adults from diverse backgrounds and environments. The potentially growing need for services due to aging, in addition to the proliferation of digital services, underline the importance of personal support equally in rural and urban areas. Age-related cognitive and functional challenges should be considered in the development of digital tools, services, and support. Therefore, older adults should be involved throughout the development processes [2]. With the natural decline of functional capacity in older age, the use of digital services may become more difficult or even impossible, suggesting that the availability of traditional face-to-face services and support for digital service usage should be ensured. Further research should be conducted to examine the impact of COVID-19 on the third level digital divide among older adults, particularly in the critical service areas such as health and social care.

Acknowledgements. This study was supported by the Strategic Research Council (SRC) at the Academy of Finland (project 327145) and THL coordinated funding for COVID-19 research which is included in the supplementary budget of the Finnish government. The authors would like to express their great gratitude to older adults who responded to the questionnaire.

References

1. Renu, N.: Technological advancement in the era of COVID-19. SAGE Open Med. **9**, 20503121211000912 (2021)
2. Cosco, T.D., Fortuna, K., Wister, A., Riadi, I., Wagner, K., Sixsmith, A.: COVID-19, social isolation, and mental health among older adults: a digital catch-22. J. Med. Internet Res. **23**, e21864 (2021)
3. Shahid, Z., et al.: COVID-19 and older adults: what we know. J. Am. Geriatr. Soc. **68**, 926–929 (2020)
4. Wu, B.: Social isolation and loneliness among older adults in the context of COVID-19: a global challenge. Glob. Health Res. Policy **5**, 27 (2020)
5. Siette, J., et al.: The impact of COVID-19 on the quality of life of older adults receiving community-based aged care. Australas. J. Ageing **40**, 84–89 (2021)
6. Colucci, E., et al.: COVID-19 lockdowns' effects on the quality of life, perceived health and well-being of healthy elderly individuals: a longitudinal comparison of pre-lockdown and lockdown states of well-being. Arch. Gerontol. Geriatr. **99**, 104606 (2022)
7. Erickson, J., Johnson, G.M.: Internet use and psychological wellness during late adulthood. Can. J. Aging **30**, 197–209 (2011)
8. Czaja, S.J., Lee, C.C.: The impact of aging on access to technology. Univers. Access Inf. Soc. **5**, 341–349 (2007)
9. Czaja, S.J., et al.: Factors predicting the use of technology: findings from the center for research and education on aging and technology enhancement (CREATE). Psychol. Aging **21**, 333–352 (2006)
10. Shapira, N., Barak, A., Gal, I.: Promoting older adults' well-being through Internet training and use. Aging Ment. Health **11**, 477–484 (2007)
11. Quittschalle, J., et al.: Internet use in old age: results of a German population-representative survey. J. Med. Internet Res. **22**, e15543 (2020)
12. Heo, J., Chun, S., Lee, S., Lee, K.H., Kim, J.: Internet use and well-being in older adults. Cyberpsychol. Behav. Soc. Netw. **18**, 268–272 (2015)
13. Heponiemi, T., Jormanainen, V., Leemann, L., Manderbacka, K., Aalto, A.-M., Hyppönen, H.: Digital divide in perceived benefits of online health care and social welfare services: national cross-sectional survey study. J. Med. Internet Res. **22**, e17616 (2020)
14. Wu, Y.-H., Lewis, M., Rigaud, A.-S.: Cognitive function and digital device use in older adults attending a memory clinic. Gerontol. Geriatr. Med. **5**, 2333721419844886 (2019)
15. Kumar, D., Hemmige, V., Kallen, M.A., Giordano, T.P., Arya, M.: Mobile phones may not bridge the digital divide: a look at mobile phone literacy in an underserved patient population. Cureus **11**, e4104 (2019)
16. Lee, B., Chen, Y., Hewitt, L.: Age differences in constraints encountered by seniors in their use of computers and the internet. Comput. Hum. Behav. **27**, 1231–1237 (2011)
17. Niehaves, B., Plattfaut, R.: Internet adoption by the elderly: employing IS technology acceptance theories for understanding the age-related digital divide. Eur. J. Inf. Syst. **23**, 708–726 (2014)
18. Renaud, K., Biljon, J.: Predicting technology acceptance and adoption by the elderly: a qualitative study. Presented at the ACM International Conference Proceeding Series (2008)
19. Din, H.N., McDaniels-Davidson, C., Nodora, J., Madanat, H.: Profiles of a health information-seeking population and the current digital divide: cross-sectional analysis of the 2015–2016 California health interview survey. J. Med. Internet Res. **21**, e11931 (2019)
20. Castells, M.: The Internet Galaxy: Reflections on the Internet, Business, and Society. Oxford University Press, Oxford (2002)

21. van Dijk, J.A.G.M.: Digital divide research, achievements and shortcomings. Poetics **34**, 221–235 (2006)
22. van Deursen, A.J.A.M., Helsper, E.J.: The third-level digital divide: who benefits most from being online? In: Communication and Information Technologies Annual, pp. 29–52. Emerald Group Publishing Limited (2015)
23. Hargittai, E.: Second-level digital divide: differences in people's online skills. First Monday **7**(4) (2002)
24. Wei, K.-K., Teo, H.-H., Chan, H.C., Tan, B.C.Y.: Conceptualizing and testing a social cognitive model of the digital divide. Inf. Syst. Res. **22**, 170–187 (2011)
25. Helsper, E.J.: A corresponding fields model for the links between social and digital exclusion. Commun. Theory **22**, 403–426 (2012)
26. Tretter, F., Löffler-Stastka, H.: The human ecological perspective and biopsychosocial medicine. Int. J. Environ. Res. Public Health **16**, 4230 (2019)
27. Hunsaker, A., Hargittai, E.: A review of Internet use among older adults. New Media Soc. **20**, 3937–3954 (2018)
28. Finnish Institute for Health and Welfare: The FinHealth 2017 Follow-up Study (2021). https://thl.fi/en/web/thlfi-en/research-and-development/research-and-projects/national-fin health-study/the-finhealth-2017-follow-up-study. Accessed 24 Feb 2022
29. Borodulin, K., Sääksjärvi, K.: FinHealth 2017 Study: Methods (2019). Finnish Institute for Health and Welfare. Report 17/2019. Helsinki, Finland
30. Fina, S., Heider, B., Mattila, M., Rautiainen, P., Sihvola, M.-W., Vatanen, K.: Unequal Finland: Regional socio-economic disparities in Finland (2021). http://library.fes.de/pdf-files/bueros/stockholm/17739.pdf
31. Official Statistics of Finland (OSF): Population structure. http://www.stat.fi/til/vaerak/index_en.html. Accessed 24 Feb 2022
32. Pirhonen, J., Lolich, L., Tuominen, K., Jolanki, O., Timonen, V.: "These devices have not been made for older people's needs" – older adults' perceptions of digital technologies in Finland and Ireland. Technol. Soc. **62**, 101287 (2020)
33. Association of Finnish Municipalities: Kuntien pinta-alat ja asukastiheydet. [Municipal areas and population densities. https://www.kuntaliitto.fi/tilastot-ja-julkaisut/kaupunkien-ja-kun tien-lukumaarat-ja-vaestotiedot/kuntien-pinta-alat-ja-asukastiheydet. Accessed 24 Feb 2022
34. Statista: Finland: households with internet by region. https://www.statista.com/statistics/543 959/internet-connection-availability-in-households-by-region-in-finland/. Accessed 24 Feb 2022
35. European Commission: DESI I Shaping Europe's digital future (2021). https://digital-strategy.ec.europa.eu/en/policies/desi
36. Ministry of finance: Act on the Provision of Digital Services 306/2019. https://www.finlex.fi/fi/laki/smur/2019/20190306. Accessed 24 Feb 2022
37. European Commission: Digital Public Administration factsheets – 2020 Finland (2020). https://joinup.ec.europa.eu/sites/default/files/inline-files/Digital_Public_Administr ation_Factsheets_Finland_vFINAL.pdf
38. Official Statistics of Finland (OSF): Use of information and communications technology by individuals (2021). https://www.stat.fi/til/sutivi/2021/sutivi_2021_2021-11-30_tie_001_en.html. Accessed 24 Feb 2022
39. Official Statistics of Finland (OSF): Väestön tieto- ja viestintätekniikan käyttö. [Use of information and communications technology by individuals] (2019). https://www.stat.fi/til/sutivi/2019/sutivi_2019_2019-11-07_kat_001_fi.html. Accessed 24 Feb 2022
40. Bogaert, P., Van Oyen, H., Beluche, I., Cambois, E., Robine, J.-M.: The use of the global activity limitation indicator and healthy life years by member states and the European Commission. Arch. Public Health **76**, 30 (2018)

41. Sainio, P.: Global activity limitation indicator. In: Borodulin, K., Sääksjärvi, K. (eds.) Fin-Health 2017 Study: Methods (2019). Finnish Institute for Health and Welfare. Report 17/2019. Helsinki, Finland

42. Van Oyen, H., Bogaert, P., Yokota, R.T.C., Berger, N.: Measuring disability: a systematic review of the validity and reliability of the Global Activity Limitations Indicator (GALI). Arch. Public Health **76**, 25 (2018)

43. Schmidt, S., Mühlan, H., Power, M.: The EUROHIS-QOL 8-item index: psychometric results of a cross-cultural field study. Eur. J. Public Health **16**, 420–428 (2006)

44. Suvisaari, J., Partonen, T., Solin, P.: Mental health. In: Borodulin, K., Sääksjärvi, K. (eds.) FinHealth 2017 Study: Methods (2019). Finnish Institute for Health and Welfare. Report 17/2019. Helsinki, Finland

45. McHorney, C.A., Ware, J.E. Jr.: Construction and validation of an alternate form general mental health scale for the Medical Outcomes Study Short-Form 36-Item Health Survey. Med. Care **33**, 15–28 (1995)

46. Seaman, S.R., White, I.R.: Review of inverse probability weighting for dealing with missing data. Stat. Methods Med. Res. **22**, 278–295 (2013)

47. Tavares, A.I.: Self-assessed health among older people in Europe and internet use. Int. J. Med. Inf. **141**, 104240 (2020)

48. Cresci, M.K., Yarandi, H.N., Morrell, R.W.: The digital divide and urban older adults. Comput. Inform. Nurs. **28**, 88–94 (2010)

49. Gracia, E., Herrero, J.: Internet use and self-rated health among older people: a national survey. J. Med. Internet Res. **11**, e49 (2009)

50. Gordon, N.P., Hornbrook, M.C.: Differences in access to and preferences for using patient portals and other eHealth technologies based on race, ethnicity, and age: a database and survey study of seniors in a large health plan. J. Med. Internet Res. **18**, e50 (2016)

51. Keränen, N.S., et al.: Use of information and communication technologies among older people with and without frailty: a population-based survey. J. Med. Internet Res. **19**, e29 (2017)

52. Gruet, M., Temesi, J., Rupp, T., Levy, P., Millet, G.Y., Verges, S.: Stimulation of the motor cortex and corticospinal tract to assess human muscle fatigue. Neuroscience **231**, 384–399 (2013)

53. Lober, W., et al.: Barriers to the use of a personal health record by an elderly population. AMIA. Annu. Symp. Proc. **2006**, 514–518 (2006)

54. Guzman-Parra, J., et al.: Attitudes and use of information and communication technologies in older adults with mild cognitive impairment or early stages of dementia and their caregivers: cross-sectional study. J. Med. Internet Res. **22**, e17253 (2020)

55. Small, G.W., et al.: Brain health consequences of digital technology use. Dialogues Clin. Neurosci. **22**, 179–187 (2020)

56. Vaportzis, E., Martin, M., Gow, A.J.: A Tablet for healthy ageing: the effect of a tablet computer training intervention on cognitive abilities in older adults. Am. J. Geriatr. Psychiatry **25**, 841–851 (2017)

57. Chan, M.Y., Haber, S., Drew, L.M., Park, D.C.: Training older adults to use tablet computers: does it enhance cognitive function? Gerontologist **56**, 475–484 (2016)

58. Choi, E.Y., Wisniewski, K.M., Zelinski, E.M.: Information and communication technology use in older adults: a unidirectional or bi-directional association with cognitive function? Comput. Hum. Behav. **121**, 106813 (2021)

59. Slegers, K., van Boxtel, M., Jolles, J.: Effects of computer training and internet usage on cognitive abilities in older adults: a randomized controlled study. Aging Clin. Exp. Res. **21**, 43–54 (2009)

60. Kaihlanen, A.M, et al.: Towards digital health equity - a qualitative study of the challenges experienced by vulnerable groups in using digital health services in the COVID-19 era. BMC Health Serv. Res. **22**, 188 (2022)

61. Berner, J., et al.: Factors influencing Internet usage in older adults (65 years and above) living in rural and urban Sweden. Health Inform. J. **21**, 237–249 (2015)
62. Findlay, R.A.: Interventions to reduce social isolation amongst older people: where is the evidence? Ageing Soc. **23**, 647–658 (2003)
63. Friemel, T.N.: The digital divide has grown old: determinants of a digital divide among seniors. New Media Soc. **18**, 313–331 (2016)
64. Hänninen, R., Pajula, L., Korpela, V., Taipale, S.: Individual and shared digital repertoires – older adults managing digital services. Inf. Commun. Soc. 1–16 (2021)
65. Bunyan, S., Collins, A.: Digital exclusion despite digital accessibility: empirical evidence from an English city. Tijdschrift voor Economische und Social Geografie **104**, 588–603 (2013)
66. Kaihlanen, A., et al.: Haavoittuvat ryhmät etäpalvelujen käyttäjinä: kokemuksia COVID-19-epidemian ajalta. Finnish Institute for Health and Welfare, Helsinki (2021)
67. Helsper, E.J., Reisdorf, B.C.: A quantitative examination of explanations for reasons for internet nonuse. Cyberpsychol. Behav. Soc. Netw. **16**, 94–99 (2012)
68. International Telecommunication Union (ITU): Household Internet access in urban areas twice as high as in rural areas. https://www.itu.int:443/en/mediacentre/Pages/pr27-2020-facts-figures-urban-areas-higher-internet-access-than-rural.aspx. Accessed 24 Feb 2022
69. Newman, L.A., Biedrzycki, K., Baum, F.: Digital technology access and use among socially and economically disadvantaged groups in South Australia. J. Community Inform. **6**(2) (2010)
70. Warburton, J., Cowan, S., Winterton, R., Hodgkins, S.: Building social inclusion for rural older people using information and communication technologies: perspectives of rural practitioners. Aust. Soc. Work. **67**, 479–494 (2014)
71. Ylipulli, J., Luusua, A.: Smart cities with a Nordic twist? Public sector digitalization in Finnish data-rich cities. Telemat. Inform. **55**, 101457 (2020)

Adoption of a COVID-19 Contact Tracing App Among Older Internet Users in Finland

Sakari Taipale[1,2](✉) ⓘ and Tomi Oinas[1] ⓘ

[1] University of Jyvaskyla, 40014 Jyvaskyla, Finland
sakari.taipale@jyu.fi
[2] University of Ljubljana, 1000 Ljubljana, Slovenia

Abstract. The outbreak of the COVID-19 pandemic created an unequal need for limiting physical contacts and tracing possible exposures to a novel coronavirus. Smartphone-based contact tracing applications (CTAs) were presented as a vehicle for stopping virus transmission chains and supporting the work of contact tracing teams. In this study, older adults' adoption of a CTA was studied using socioeconomic background factors, satisfaction with health, and the measure of digital activity as predictors. The data were drawn from a larger questionnaire survey targeted at older internet users. A subsample of older Finnish internet users ($N = 723$) was analyzed using a logistic regression model. Results showed that older internet users had widely adopted the Finnish CTA called *Koronavilkku* irrespective of demographic background factors, level of education, and self-assessed satisfaction with health. Besides high income and retirement status, digital activity measured through the breadth of mobile phone features used and the use of an online symptom checker increased the likelihood of having the CTA installed on a smartphone. The results of the study lend themselves to be used for future epidemics and other occasions that require a real-time and/or retrospective tracing of people and their physical encounters.

Keywords: Contact tracing app · COVID-19 · Internet · Older adults · Online symptom checker · Smartphone

1 Introduction

The outbreak of the COVID-19 pandemic in early 2020 created an unequal need for limiting physical contacts and tracing possible exposures to a novel coronavirus all over the world [1, 2]. From very early on, the oldest people, especially those with various health conditions, were found to be at a higher risk for a serious infection [3–6]. Therefore, both recommendations for self-isolation and statutory measures to limit moving and face-to-face contact were pronouncedly targeted at older citizens. For instance, the Finnish government released the instructions in March 2020, according to which "people over the age of 70 are obliged to separate from contacts with other people where possible" [7].

Despite certain privacy concerns, smartphone-based contact tracing applications (CTAs) were presented in many countries as a vehicle for stopping virus transmission

Q. Gao and J. Zhou (Eds.): HCII 2022, LNCS 13330, pp. 614–624, 2022.
https://doi.org/10.1007/978-3-031-05581-2_42

chains and supporting the work of contact tracing teams soon after the outbreak of the pandemic [8]. Voiced privacy concerns were mainly related to the various ways in which tracing apps manage, store, and transmit personal data. The "decentralized" solutions kept user data on the device itself, while "centralized" solutions transmitted data to a central repository [9]. While the former solution provoked somewhat less privacy concerns than the latter, in general CTAs were perceived as an intrusive technology that compromised the sovereignty of an individual [9].

Whereas privacy concerns may have hindered the adoption of CTAs, smartphone ownership was an absolute precondition for adoption. Hence, CTA adoption could not be taken for granted, especially among the oldest population. For example, in Finland, 75% of adults aged 65–74 and only 34% of those aged 75–89 had a smartphone equipped with a 3G or 4G connection and touchscreen for their personal use in 2020 [10]. The limited prevalence of smartphones as well as a sizable variation in digital skills and in ways of using smartphones [11, 12] may have affected older adults' use of COVID-19 CTAs in particular ways.

This paper aims to investigate older adults' adoption of a COVID-19 CTA in Finland using socioeconomic background factors, satisfaction with health, and measures of digital activity as key predictors. All respondents included in the sample are internet users, constituting a highly select group of older adults (aged 62–92). First, this study explores (RQ1) what socioeconomic and well-being factors are related to the use of COVID-19 CTAs. Second, it is investigated whether (RQ2a) the breadth of mobile phone features used and (RQ2b) the use of an online symptom checker—two measures of digital activity—are associated with the adoption of CTA. To obtain answers to these questions, a subsample of questionnaire survey data ($N = 723$) collected in November 2020 is analyzed using a logistics regression model.

The rest of the paper is organized as follows. The paper begins with a short overview of what is already known about the willingness to adopt and actual use of COVID-19 CTAs in different countries. After this, the Finnish COVID-19 CTA called *Koronavilkku* is introduced. The data, measures, and methods are presented before the results section. In the discussion and conclusions, the significance of retirement status, income, and overall digital activity for the use of CTAs is highlighted, and the implications for further research and practices are discussed.

2 Previous Literature on COVID-19 Contact Tracing Apps

In less than two years from the launch of the first COVID-19 CTAs in Asian countries, such as China, South Korea, and Singapore [13], many studies have been published about citizens' intentions and willingness to adopt these applications [1, 2, 14]. More recently, a study has also been conducted on the actual usage of CTAs [15]. So far, most of the studies have focused on entire adult populations [14–16], and some studies have addressed specific subpopulations like health care students [17]. Older adults have not yet attracted special attention in CTA studies, although they are both at a higher risk for serious COVID-19 infection and often less likely to adopt new technology than younger age groups. Despite this lack of research on older age cohorts, the earlier studies on CTAs provide much useful information about potential predictors of older adults' CTA adoption.

As regards age, a Dutch study found that the predicted adoption rate of a COVID-19 CTA was significantly lower for the oldest respondents (aged 75 or more, 45.6%) than for the youngest age bracket (aged 15–34, 79.4%) [2]. In a five-country study including respondents from France, Germany, Italy, the United Kingdom, and the United States, it was reported that the acceptability of CTAs was considerably high in all age groups, yet it slightly decreased with the increasing age of respondents [1]. Likewise, in a study from the United States, it was found that the oldest respondents were slightly less willing to adopt a CTA than younger respondents [14]. In contrast to others, a study dealing with the use of COVID-19 CTAs in Switzerland found no relationship between age and application use [15].

To date, no gender differences have been found regarding the acceptability or use of COVID-19 CTAs. Altmann et al. [1] showed that the acceptability of these apps did not vary by gender in their five-country study. Similarly, von Wyl et al. [15] reported no gender differences in Switzerland. Regarding education, prior findings have shown equally consistent results. Both a Dutch study [2] and a U.S. study [4] reported that the more educated people were, the more willing they were to adopt COVID-19 CTAs. Prior studies have paid relatively little attention to family-related factors. One of the few studies found that neither partnership status nor having children was associated with the use of COVID-19 CTAs in Switzerland [15].

Previous research has reported mixed findings regarding the predictive power of economic factors. In Switzerland, it was found that higher household income was associated with the use of COVID-19 CTAs [15], while another study from the United States detected no household income effect [14]. Due to major differences in countries' economic structures, taxation models, and welfare systems, these inconsistencies in findings are not surprising. Similarly, there are also notable differences in population density and degree of urbanization. Nevertheless, previous studies have provided only limited information about the connections between these factors and CTA use. In the United States, a study found that the urban residency of respondents was not associated with CTA use [14]. Other types of regional information were provided by a Swiss study. In Switzerland, people residing in French-speaking or Italian-speaking regions were associated with a lower CTA adoption than those living in German-speaking regions [15].

In addition to sociodemographic and economic factors, the connection between health status and CTA use has attracted some attention in previous research. In the Netherlands, a study revealed a connection between a worsened perception of general health and the preference to adopt a CTA [2]. The same study also found a positive relationship between some specific health issues, such as lung disease, kidney disease, and a compromised immune system, and the preference of having a CTA. Similarly, it was reported in a five-country study that respondents with one or more comorbidities were more likely to support the use of a CTA than those with no comorbidities [1]. In the United States, a study showed that the respondents who belonged to a high-risk group due to a certain health condition were 1.5 times likelier to adopt a CTA than the respondents without medical conditions [14]. To sum up, there is solid evidence that health conditions constituting a higher risk for infection increase the willingness to use and actual use of COVID-19 CTAs in various country contexts.

Lastly, previous studies have indicated that overall digital activity is associated with the use of COVID-19 CTAs. For example, both the higher frequency of mobile phone use [1] and internet use [15] were related to an increase in the likelihood of adopting and using CTAs. Similarly, higher internet skills were found to be associated with the willingness to install CTAs on a smartphone in the United States [14]. In contrast, the main reasons for the nonuse of COVID-19 CTAs in Switzerland were the perceived lack of usefulness (37%), not having a suitable smartphone or operating system (23%), and privacy concerns (22%) [15]. In the same study, it was concluded that the older respondents were, the more often they reported "not the right phone" as a reason for nonuse [15].

3   COVID-19 Contact Tracing App in Finland

In Finland, the COVID-19 CTA called *Koronavilkku* was developed by the Finnish Institute for Health and Welfare (THL). It was developed to assist in finding out if its user had been exposed to the coronavirus and should therefore self-isolate oneself and contact the health care services for a possible COVID-19 test. In the case of a positive test result, a person could share this information anonymously with those who had been in proximity with him/her. In terms of data privacy, *Koronavilkku* is based on a decentralized protocol. The app sends a randomly generated anonymous code to other apps in close proximity, and these codes are locally stored on mobile phones only.

The *Koronavilkku* app was rolled out on August 31, 2020, and it was promoted with nationwide advertising campaigns. The app was free to download from the Google Play Store and Apple's App Store. The oldest supported operating system for Android phones was 6.0 and for Apple iOS13.5, which was possible to install on iPhone 6s and subsequent models. The app required a Bluetooth connection to function.

When the survey data used in this study were collected in November 2021, THL reported that the *Koronavilkku* app had been downloaded over 2.5 million times in a country of 5.5 million inhabitants. According to an opinion survey commissioned by THL [18], 90% of Finns had at least heard about it in late 2020. Of the surveyed people under the age of 25, 71% had downloaded the app, while the adoption rate was the lowest among adults aged between 45 and 54.

4   Data and Method

4.1   Survey Data

For this study, the data were drawn from the third wave of the Aging + Communication + Technology (ACT) cross-national longitudinal survey collected in November 2020. The countries involved in the survey study were Austria, Canada, Israel, Finland, the Netherlands, Romania, and Spain. The initial target population of the survey was older internet users aged 60 or above in 2016 (Wave 1). Respondents were recruited from the respondent panels of commercial research agencies. Questionnaires were administered and filled out online in every country except Romania [19]. The third-wave data set includes 4,445 respondents in total. After completing the main survey questionnaire, a couple of additional questions concerning the use of COVID-19-related digital services were presented to Finnish respondents. These questions dealt with the use of the *Koronavilkku* CTA and the use of the *Omaolo* online service developed to facilitate self-assessment of various symptoms, including those of COVID-19, and service needs. As the COVID-19-related questions were only collected from Finland and in the latest wave of the survey, the analysis of this study was restricted to the subsample of older Finnish internet users ($N = 723$).

4.2 Measures

Descriptive statistics of the dependent and independent variables are presented in Table 1. As the dependent variable, the study used the question, "Do you have *Koronavilkku* installed on your mobile phone?" Independent variables, selected following the above-presented literature review, consisted of demographic measures (gender, age, family status, urban/rural residency, the Nomenclature of Territorial Units for Statistics (NUTS) region), socioeconomic variables (education, income, retirement status), self-assessed satisfaction with health, and two measures of digital activity—the breadth of mobile phone features used and the use of the *Omaolo* online symptom checker.

4.3 Statistical Procedures

A binary logistic regression model was applied to find out how different background factors and the two measures of digital activity—the breadth of mobile phone features used and the use of online symptom checker—are associated with the use of the COVID-19 CTA. McFadden's Pseudo R^2 was used as a goodness-of-fit indicator.

5 Results

Table 1 shows that almost two-thirds of our respondents had the *Koronavilkku* CTA installed on their smartphone, and less than a fifth had experience in using the *Omaolo* online symptom checker at the time of the data collection in late 2020. Respondents' self-perceived health was at a good level on average. A vast majority of respondents reported their health satisfaction being either at a high or at a medium level.

All results concerning the research questions are presented in Table 2. Regarding RQ1, the analysis revealed no associations between basic demographic measures (gender, age, family status, urban/rural residency, NUTS region) and COVID-19 CTA use. Similarly, education and self-reported health satisfaction turned out to be insignificant predictors. On the contrary, employment status and self-reported income (relative to a national average) were strongly associated with the adoption of the *Koronavilkku* CTA. More precisely, the retired respondents had the CTA downloaded on their phones more likely than the nonretired (i.e., the employed, unemployed, volunteer workers). Respondents with an average or above-average income had, in turn, the app more commonly installed on their phones than those who reported having an income lower than a national average.

Table 1. Descriptive statistics.

Variable	N	%
COVID-19 contact tracing app		
No	291	40.2
Yes	432	59.8
Gender		
Female	349	48.3
Male	374	51.7
Age		
64–69	345	47.7
70–75	242	33.5
76–92	136	18.8
Family status		
No spouse, no children	121	16.9
No spouse, with children	128	17.9
Spouse, no children	258	36.0
Spouse, with children	209	29.2
Rural/urban residency		
City or suburb	326	45.5
Town	262	36.5
Countryside	129	18.0
NUTS[a] regions		
Helsinki-Uusimaa (Capital region)	193	26.7
Southern Finland	166	23.0
Western Finland	187	25.9
Northern and Eastern Finland	177	24.5
Education		
Primary	101	14.1
Secondary	326	45.7
Tertiary	287	40.2
Income		
Below average	296	46.3
Average	115	18.0
Above average	228	35.7

(*continued*)

Table 1. (*continued*)

Variable	N	%
Retirement status		
Other	55	7.6
Retired	668	92.4
Satisfaction with health		
Low	46	6.4
Med	297	41.4
High	374	52.2
Breadth of mobile phone features used		
Narrow	238	32.9
Medium	306	42.3
Broad	179	24.8
Online symptom checker use		
No	582	82.7
Yes	122	17.3

[a]The Nomenclature of Territorial Units for Statistics (NUTS)

In response to RQ2a, it was found that the breadth of mobile phone features used was strongly associated with the adoption of the *Koronavilkku* CTA among the studied population. The wider the array of mobile phone features used, the higher the likelihood of having the CTA installed on the phone. Regarding RQ2b, the results showed that the use of the *Omaolo* online symptom checker was associated with the use of the CTA. Respondents who had used the online symptom checker were 2.8 times likelier to have the *Koronavilkku* CTA installed on their mobile phone than those with no experience in using it.

Table 2. Predictors of COVID-19 tracing app use (binary logistic regression).

Variable	Odds ratio	SE	t-value	p-value
Gender (ref. female)	1			
Male	1.004	.204	0.02	.984
Age group (ref. 64–69)	1			
70–75	.835	.184	−0.82	.412

(*continued*)

Table 2. (*continued*)

Variable	Odds ratio	SE	*t*-value	*p*-value
76–92	.703	.177	−1.40	.162
Family status (ref. no spouse, no children)	1			
No spouse, with children	.968	.299	−0.10	.916
Spouse, no children	1.124	.309	0.42	.671
Spouse, with children	1.211	.345	0.67	.502
Education (ref. primary level)	1			
Secondary	.615	.175	−1.70	.088
Tertiary	.642	.201	−1.42	.157
Satisfaction with health: (ref. low)				
Med	.741	.288	−0.77	.439
High	.933	.367	−0.18	.859
Monthly personal income (ref. below average)	1			
Average	1.944	.509	2.54	.011
Above average	2.278	.561	3.34	.001
Rural/urban residency (ref. city or suburb)	1			
Town	1.144	.247	0.62	.534
Countryside	.773	.206	−0.97	.333
NUTS (ref. Helsinki-Uusimaa (capital region))	1			
Southern Finland	.898	.245	−0.39	.695
Western Finland	1.214	.319	0.74	.460
Northern and Eastern Finland	1.498	.403	1.50	.133
Retirement status (ref. other)	1			
Retired	2.958	1.022	3.14	.002
Breadth of mobile phone features used (ref. narrow)	1			
Medium	2.603	.542	4.59	<.001
Broad	5.271	1.398	6.27	<.001
Online symptom checker use (ref. no)	1			
Yes	2.752	.745	3.74	< .001
Constant	.235	.142	−2.39	.017
McFadden's Pseudo R^2	0.132			
N	614			

6 Discussion and Conclusions

The results of the study show that older internet users had widely adopted the COVID-19 tracing app irrespective of demographic background factors, level of education, and self-reported satisfaction with health. These results align well with previous studies that have found no gender effects [1, 15] or variation in the adoption of CTAs according to family status or marital status [15]. However, the results depart from the earlier findings regarding age and education. Unlike previous studies [1, 2], this study did not support the negative association between the use of COVID-19 CTAs and age. Similarly, this study did not find evidence for a connection between education and the adoption of CTA [cf. 2, 14]. These less anticipated findings may be interpreted as acknowledging the characteristics of the target population. Older internet users are more likely to be highly educated and experienced users of CTAs than their agemates not using the internet and thus not included in our data.

Strong associations between socioeconomic factors and the adoption of COVID-19 CTAs were found in the analysis. First, retired respondents were significantly more likely to use the CTA than other respondents who were mostly full-time or part-time workers. Since virtually all the respondents had reached their minimum retirement age, it can be presumed that employed respondents comprise a relatively healthy subgroup of individuals. In fact, it is unlikely that the employed respondents would have serious health conditions as they have continued to work beyond the age of 64. For the same reason, they may not consider themselves at an equivalent risk of getting a serious infection compared with their retired agemates and had therefore not installed a COVID-19 CTA on their phones.

More surprisingly, the study found that the respondents with a below-than-average income were less likely to use the COVID-19 CTA than the respondents with higher incomes. Although this finding is in line with some previous findings [15], it can be considered at least partly counterintuitive as the CTA is completely free to download. A possible explanation for this finding lies in mobile phones and their operating systems. Without further evidence, it can only be hypothesized that the respondents with a low income may have possessed older phone models that cannot run the *Koronavilkku* CTA requiring a Bluetooth connection and a relatively new version of iOS or Android operating system.

Based on the results of this study, the subjective measure of health satisfaction is not associated with the adoption of the COVID-19 CTA among the studied population of older Finnish internet users. This finding complements the previous knowledge, according to which both specific heath conditions constituting a high risk for a severe infection and self-perceived general health [1, 2, 14] are positively associated with CTA use. This divergent finding indicates that subjective measures of health satisfaction do not inevitably correlate with diagnosed health conditions and may not similarly increase people's awareness of risks related to COVID-19 infection.

Lastly, RQ2a and RQ2b dealt with the associations between two measures of digital activity—the breadth of mobile phone features used and the use of the *Omaolo* online symptom checker—and the adoption of the *Koronavilkku* CTA. Both measures were strongly and positively associated with having the CTA installed on a mobile phone. In this respect, the results are consistent with the previous studies that applied other measures of digital activity, such as the frequency of mobile phone use [1] and of internet use [15]. Regarding the online symptom checker, it is worth mentioning that it was developed before the COVID-19 pandemic to self-check the symptoms of other common health conditions. Hence, some respondents may have been familiar with and even used it before the pandemic. Prior knowledge of e-health applications like *Omaolo* may have lowered the threshold for adopting the *Koronavilkku* app. To conclude, the results of the study imply that apart from higher income and retirement status, digital activity in general increases the likelihood of CTA adoption among older internet users.

7 Limitation and Future Research

This study has certain limitations that arise from its sample and measures. As the survey was originally developed to study older people's media use, the sample was only indicative of older internet users. Additional measures on COVID-19 CTA use and online checker use were only added to the Finnish version of the questionnaire. Hence, it was not possible to make country comparisons. The data set also included some obvious limitations regarding potential independent variables. It did not involve measures of digital skills or detailed information about respondents' personal techno-biography, which could have served as good predictors of CTA adoption. Similarly, the data did not contain information about respondents' diagnosed health conditions, which have been successfully applied as independent variables in some prior studies [2]. Moreover, it is likely that older adults' social connectedness and lifestyles are related to their perceived need for and willingness to adopt a CTA. If a person's lifestyle is home-centered and in-person encounters with others are rare, the need for a CTA is certainly perceived as relatively small. These types of measures would be important to include in future models to also cover motivational factors behind the adoption of CTAs.

As new pandemics may break out at any time, it is crucial to understand what factors influence their adoption rates. The effectiveness of CTAs is largely dependent on the overall adoption rate, which should be as high as possible. Although the effectiveness of CTAs in breaking and tracking infection chains has been questioned, a recent systematic review shows that CTAs can be a valuable addition to the work of manual tracing teams [20]. The results of this and similar studies also lend themselves to other possible applications of CTAs on occasions where real-time and/or retrospective tracing of people and their physical encounters are required. In the future, portable CTAs may turn out to be useful in other types of emergencies, such as natural disasters or bioterrorism. It is hence important to pay attention to their acceptability and reliability in the future.

Acknowledgments. This study was funded by the Strategic Research Council at the Academy of Finland (grants 327145 and 327149 for the DigiIN project) and the Academy of Finland for the Centre of Excellence in Research on Ageing and Care (grants 312367 and 336671).

References

1. Altmann, S., et al.: Acceptability of app-based contact tracing for COVID-19: cross-country survey study. JMIR Mhealth Uhealth **8**(8), e19857 (2020)

2. Jonker, M., de Bekker-Grob, E., Veldwijk, J., Goossens, L., Bour, S., Rutten-Van Mölken, M.: COVID-19 contact tracing apps: predicted uptake in the Netherlands based on a discrete choice experiment. JMIR Mhealth Uhealth 8(10), e20741 (2020)
3. Bidzan-Bluma, I., et al.: A Polish and German population study of quality of life, well-being, and life satisfaction in older adults during the COVID-19 pandemic. Front. Psych. 11, 585813 (2020)
4. Campos-Castillo, C.: Gender divides in engagement with COVID-19 information on the internet among US older adults. J. Gerontol. Ser. B 76(3), e104–e110 (2021)
5. Zhou, F., et al.: Clinical course and risk factors for mortality of adult inpatients with COVID-19 in Wuhan, China: a retrospective cohort study. Lancet 395(10229), 1054–1062 (2020)
6. Xie, B., Charness, N., Fingerman, K., Kaye, J., Kim, M.T., Khurshid, A.: When going digital becomes a necessity: ensuring older adults' needs for information, services, and social inclusion during COVID-19. J. Aging Soc. Policy 32(4–5), 460–470 (2020)
7. STM: Uusi koronavirus—COVID-19 Toimintaohjeita yli 70-vuotiaille. https://aineistop ankki.thl.fi/l/wFdKSXz2Jdg7. Accessed 4 Jan 2022
8. Abeler, J., Bäcker, M., Buermeyer, U., Zillessen, H.: COVID-19 contact tracing and data protection can go together. JMIR Mhealth Uhealth 8(4), e19359 (2020)
9. Savona, M.: The saga of the COVID-19 contact tracing apps: lessons for data governance. In: SPRU Working Paper Series SWPS 2020–10 (June), University of Sussex. https://www.sus sex.ac.uk/webteam/gateway/file.php?name=2020-10-swps-savona.pdf&site=25. Accessed 4 Jan 2022
10. Official Statistics of Finland: Use of information and communications technology by individuals. https://www.stat.fi/til/sutivi/2020/sutivi_2020_2020-11-10_tau_013_fi. Accessed 4 Jan 2022
11. Hänninen, R., Pajula, L., Korpela, V., Taipale, S.: Individual and shared digital repertoires—older adults managing digital services. Inf. Commun. Soc. 1–16 (2021)
12. Hänninen, R., Taipale, S., Luostari, R.: Exploring heterogeneous ICT use among older adults: the warm experts' perspective. New Media Soc. 23(6), 1584–1601 (2021)
13. Du, L., Raposo, V.L., Wang, M.: COVID-19 contact tracing apps: a technologic Tower of Babel and the gap for international pandemic control. JMIR Mhealth Uhealth 8(11), e23194 (2020)
14. Hargittai, E., Redmiles, E.M., Vitak, J., Zimmer, M.: Americans' willingness to adopt a COVID-19 tracking app. First Monday 25(11) (2020)
15. von Wyl, V., et al.: Drivers of acceptance of COVID-19 proximity tracing apps in Switzerland: panel survey analysis. JMIR Publ. Health Surveill. 7(1), e25701 (2021)
16. Lin, J., Carter, L., Liu, D.: Privacy concerns and digital government: exploring citizen willingness to adopt the COVIDSafe app. Eur. J. Inf. Syst. 1–14. (2021)
17. Montagni, I., Roussel, N., Thiébaut, R., Tzourio, C.: Health care students' knowledge of and attitudes, beliefs, and practices toward the French COVID-19 app: cross-sectional questionnaire study. J. Med. Internet Res. 23(3), e26399 (2021)
18. THL: Koronavilkku has been downloaded more than 2.5 million times—widespread use increases the app's effectiveness. https://thl.fi/en/web/thlfi-en/-/koronavilkku-has-been-dow nloaded-more-than-2.5-million-times-widespread-use-increases-the-app-s-effectiveness. Accessed 4 Jan 2022
19. Ivan, L., Schiau, I.: Older audiences and digital media: focus on Romania. Manag. Dyn. Knowl. Econ. 6(3), 423–447 (2018)
20. Jenniskens, K., et al.: Effectiveness of contact tracing apps for SARS-CoV-2: a rapid systematic review. BMJ Open 11(7), e050519 (2021)

Prediction and Analysis of Acceptance of the Elderly for Bus Interior Space Layout Based on Visual Search

Hao Yang[1], Quanxin Jin[1], Xinrui Zhang[1], Yueran Wang[2], and Ying Zhao[3(✉)]

[1] North China University of Technology, Beijing, China
[2] Tianjin Academy of Fine Arts, Tianjin, China
[3] Beijing Institute of Graphic Communication, Beijing, China
wuyue8656@163.com

Abstract. The mobility of bus space is strong and there are many facilities and functional areas in the bus, which makes interior design works difficult. Visual search can reflect the adaptability of passengers to a certain space to some extent. However, this ability of the elderly is significantly different from that of the young group. Therefore, an interior layout suitable for older passengers should make up for the lack of information in their process of visual search. This paper summarized 48 bus interior layouts and established the correlation model between the acceptability of the elderly and their eye movement characteristics including fixation, saccade and pupil diameter when observing these layouts. On this basis, the visual search law of the elderly was found and the important areas were located. By means of this method, the priority of the key functional areas to guide the vision of the elderly was figured out. The study found that for old people, the initial recognition degree of the rear seat area was higher, and there were more meaningful clues in the middle right part. The conclusions provided a reference for determining the position of visual symbols which were used to guide the line of sight and designing an elderly-oriented layout in buses.

Keywords: Bus interior · Elderly passengers · Visual search · Eye movement · Acceptability · Seat arrangement

1 Introduction

The establishment of new standards for bus comfort, safety and environmental protection in the new era provides passengers with a better commuting environment and comfortable experience. Although the subway has gradually become the first choice for young passengers such as office workers in big cities, the bus is still the main means of transportation for the elderly in medium and long distance travel. However, the concept of universal design, which has been constantly raised, still does not take into account the perceptual and physical characteristics of elderly passengers well, especially in the number of seats, seat density, seat direction, aisle width and the imperfection of barrier free facilities. With the progress of social development, passengers pay more attention

© The Author(s), under exclusive license to Springer Nature Switzerland AG 2022
Q. Gao and J. Zhou (Eds.): HCII 2022, LNCS 13330, pp. 625–640, 2022.
https://doi.org/10.1007/978-3-031-05581-2_43

to the safety and space experience brought by the layout of seats and handholds when taking public transport. Consumer groups with different professional backgrounds and ages have differences in preference, which puts forward higher requirements for the optimal design of bus interior space. It can be considered that in the future bus ride process, people will no longer perceive multiple information sources dispersedly, but the overall information space.

Compared with the functional travel for the purpose of going to school or work, the travel of the elderly is mainly to meet the needs of daily life. The elderly usually avoid the rush hours in the morning and evening, so the space in the bus is relatively ample. In this case, the layout of facilities in the bus plays an important role in guiding visual attention and keeping the body stable, so as to avoid the elderly passengers feeling blocked in movement or difficult to stand. An ideal aging-oriented layout should conform to the visual search law of the elderly, so that they can judge the problems that may be encountered in the process of maintaining physical stability and movement at a glance.

Researchers found that with the increase of age, people's visual search ability showed a downward trend [1]. The ability of the elderly is significantly different from that of the young group. This study took buses in Beijing as examples, analyzed the visual attention law of the elderly induced by interior space of buses, and located important functional areas. In this way, the role of each functional area in guiding the vision of the elderly was proposed. The purpose is to optimize the interior layout design of existing buses and improve the convenience and safety of elderly passengers.

2 Literature Review

In recent years, remarkable achievements have been made in the modeling of bus interior layout and passenger characteristics. For example, Agent-based simulation could evaluate the performance of different bus layout designs from the perspective of passengers [2], so as to help bus manufacturers design more attractive interior layout. The study summarized eight types of passenger personas, and passengers' preferences and characteristics had been realized through a calibrated decision-making algorithm. The research method was advanced.

There are significant differences between older and younger passengers in boarding and alighting time, handhold use, seat position preference and posture stability maintaining [3]. For the elderly passengers, low floor buses are safer. The barrier-free accessibility of its interior facilities is reflected in the door position, seat configuration and large front wheel housing, which jointly affect getting on and off the bus and internal movement of passengers. Relevant study had shown that the specific design conditions of low floor buses could significantly influence the preferences of walking aid users [4]. However, passengers using wheeled mobile devices still faced safety problems and low efficiency in boarding, alighting and internal circulation in low floor buses, and high passenger load had adverse effects across three types of interior layouts [5].

At present, there are many studies on injuries of passengers in public transport. For example, a study used modeling of MADYMO Hybrid III 50% Dummy to explore the factors related to passenger injury in crash accidents, including the direction of sitting passengers and the spacing of seats [6]. Such method can also be used to improve the safety of elderly passengers. As for the design issues which might bring about injury, Solah et al. [7] studied the problems of doors, seats, handrail and steps, and proposed design principles for reducing injury of occupants, especially the elderly passengers.

In terms of bus ride human-machine system, Pityn et al. [8] analyzed the windshield glare produced by the illuminants inside the bus primarily set for improving the safety of passengers. The study gave a quantitative reference for optimizing the driver conditions and evaluating design components in public transport. Yang [9] researched the physiological problems of joint stiffness and insufficient muscle strength of lower limbs of the elderly, and put forward the design scheme of passenger leaning facility according to the research conclusions.

In the era of intelligent public transport, the in-vehicle information system is becoming more and more important to passengers. Researchers designed an embedded device to inform passengers that they had arrived at the destination through both auditory channel (speakers) and visual channel (LCD screens) [10], which was of great value to the elderly and illiterates. As the information media become abundant, the research on human response time and adaptability gets more difficult. Eye-tracking is a useful research method. A study for the elderly users showed that it was feasible to analyze the dialogue boxes, graphical user interface and touch screen operations of the vehicle information system through eye movement on color, icons and characters, and the visual feature model and relevant design tactics of old people could be obtained [11]. The conclusion also provided theoretical guidance and technical support for bus interior study.

3 Method

3.1 Eye Movement Analysis

The diversity of bus interior facilities improves the ride experience, but also increases the information burden of passengers and distracts attention. In addition to searching for seats and handholds to avoid stumbling, it is also necessary for the passengers to pay attention to visual interfaces such as bus stop posters, LED rolling display screens and LCD advertising screens. This requires the layout of the facilities can meet the visual search law of the elderly. Visual search refers to the task that people scan visual images to find important information. Tinelli et al. [12] pointed out that visual search meant users could determine targets in an interference environment based on rapid visual processing and accurate control of eye movement. To study the visual search of elderly passengers for interior layout and facilities, which can be reflected through eye movement to a certain extent, has guiding significance for designing interior human-machine system in line with the cognitive load of the elderly.

Visual processing of the elderly is quite different from that of the young. Some studies have found that the elderly cannot adjust attention processing according to the situation, and the flexibility declines. When goals are highlighted, the elderly are more vulnerable to distractions [13–15]. Therefore, for the analysis of elderly-oriented layout of buses, it is necessary to understand and refer to the visual search law of the elderly. Visual search has two main functions: firstly, to determine the spatial layout of object surface in an environmental scene; secondly, to identify objects.

By the comparison of sub items of the data from different area of interest (AOI), the general visual search law of people can be summarized. Correspondingly, this study analyzed the eye movement characteristics of the elderly when gazing at bus interior images. Generally, the more the total fixation times (FT) in the target area, the lower the search efficiency. More FT of an AOI shows that the region is more important for the observer and can attract more attention. At the same time, it also reflects the region is a key part for design. Besides, longer fixation duration (FD) of an AOI means the area is more difficult for the passenger to extract information or the target is more attractive. For elderly-oriented buses, the seat unit planning should be helpful to reduce the elderly's fear for extreme open space and standing in the bus. Therefore, we used eye movement law to reflect the attentional situation of elderly passengers to different functional areas and the difficulty to plan their movement path. In addition, the first fixation duration (FFD) is the lasting time of the first fixation spent on an object or a region, which is usually used to express the initial recognition degree of the target stimulus. The shorter the FFD of the target, the more it can attract the attention. For the research on the spatial layout of bus interior, eye movement is useful to judge which areas are more in line with the visual search law of elderly passengers.

Due to the need to study the information hidden in the process of regional shifting of the elderly's fixation, saccade is meaningful to be taken into consideration. Saccade is the eye movement that makes an individual quickly move his sight line to the position of interest when exploring a visual environment. For the interior layout with the highest acceptance, we analyzed the subjects' saccade amplitude (SA). The greater the SA, the more meaningful clues in the new location, which reflects that the area attracts the attention of the elderly to a certain extent, and should be paid more attention in design works.

Moreover, researches showed that for simple tasks, the pupil diameter (PD) would present an increasing trend with the augment of cognitive load [16]. Therefore, in the image observation task of this study, we also collected the average PD of both eyes as one of the input layer indicators of the prediction model for acceptance degree.

3.2 Stimulus Materials

Existing research found that visual acceptability and emotion could be helpful for people to discriminate between different instrument panels by means of observing pictures [17]. Although the immersion degree of pictures is not high enough, they can still reflect the users' experience and preference [18]. In this study, we took the pictures that could comprehensively show the layout of interior space as the eye-tracking stimulation materials, analyzed the eye movement characteristics of the elderly in the process of bus observation and recognition, summarized the laws and provide reference basis for elderly-oriented design.

In the bus interior, there are more than ten features, such as seat distribution, handhold distribution, handhold density, handhold shape, auxiliary armrest position, leaning facility position, wheelchair area configuration, etc. And each feature has a variety of changes. In order to locate the key design opportunities, we selected the most typical four features (front seat distribution, middle seat distribution, rear seat distribution and wheelchair area location). Cabin parameters and interior photos and videos of buses in Beijing were collected from authoritative websites as the reference for drawing stimulation materials. The sources included the official website of Beijing Public Transport (http://www.bjbus.com/home/index.php), Buspedia (https://buspedia.top/) and Chinabuses (https://www.chinabuses.com/), as well as the official websites of companies providing buses for Beijing, such as Youngmanbus Co., Ltd, Yutong Bus Co.,Ltd., and Sunlongbus Co., Ltd. A total of 87 bus model images were collected, basically covering all types of single-deck and single-cabin models used in operating lines on Beijing roads.

After classifying the interiors of the 87 bus models, excluding special buses, customized buses and special cases, the four features of the remaining samples were summarized into specific categories. The category number of each feature is shown in Table 1:

Table 1. Specific categories of the main interior features

	A: Front seat distribution	B: Middle seat distribution	C: Rear seat distribution	D: Wheelchair area
Category	A1. Two columns of seats are arranged horizontally on both sides and face each other	B1. Two columns of seats are arranged vertically and horizontally respectively	C1. The middle two rows of seats face each other	D1. There is a wheelchair area in the space
	A2. One column of seats are arranged vertically	B2. Two columns of seats are both arranged horizontally	C2. All seats face the same direction	D2. No wheelchair area
	A3. Two columns of seats are arranged vertically on both sides and for each column, the two seats are back-to-back	B3. Two columns of seats are both arranged vertically	–	–
	A4. No seat in this area	–	–	–

By combining different categories of the four features, a total of $4 * 3 * 2 * 2 = 48$ interior layouts can be obtained, which is the eye movement stimulation material of this study. Referring to the idea of Delphi method, six experts in the field of shared travel and vehicle design were invited to score the color matching and handhold quantity of the 87 samples. After scoring, the staff will make statistics and sort, and feedback the results to the experts, so that they can compare their specific opinions with others, modify their judgments and then score for the second round. By this means, in the third round a unanimous conclusion has been basically reached. The quantity of handholds and color scheme with the highest scores were selected for applying in the stimulating materials, which were 3D modeled by the software Rhinoceros and rendered out by Keyshot.

In order to make the pictures clear and highlight the layout features, the production of the picture follows three principles: (1) Ignoring the color particularity of special seats for the old, young, disabled and pregnant, all seats are uniformly set to blue. (2) Do not separate the seat surface into several pieces with color blocks. The whole seat is blue (R:96; G:134; B:196), and the armrest is yellow (R:252; G:234; B:56). The 48 stimulating materials are shown in Fig. 1:

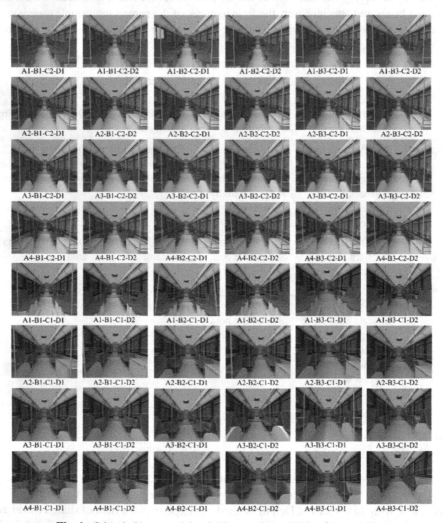

Fig. 1. Stimulating materials of this experiment (Color figure online)

3.3 Experimental Process

We applied a desktop telemetry type eye-tracker (SMI Co. Ltd., German) to collect the elderly's eye movement. The sampling rate was set to 60 Hz. Each picture was played on the screen for eight seconds, and the time interval was five seconds. The AOI editor in the software BeGaze was used to edit polygonal AOIs, as shown in Fig. 2.

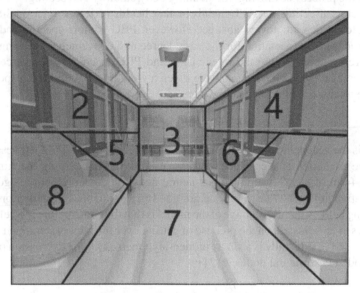

Fig. 2. AOIs of one of the stimuli

33 elderly people aged 65–81 were invited to participate in the experiment, including 19 males and 17 females. The experimental task is to observe the bus layout pictures. Based on their own riding experience, the subjects should observe each functional area on the picture according to their natural observation habits after getting on a bus. The subjects were required to observe and memorize the interior details as comprehensively as possible, and were told that there was a subsequent feature memory test for the 48 layouts after the experiment, to enhance the subjects' attention to the layout.

After completing the eye movement experiment task, the subjects were asked to fill in a questionnaire and describe the biggest difficulty encountered in the process of taking a bus.

3.4 Acceptability and Extreme Learning Machine

The elderly-oriented design emphasizes the importance of taking the elderly as the foundation. Therefore, it is needed to underline the expression of individual wishes of elderly users. For the acceptability analysis of bus layout, we referred to the Technology Acceptance Model (TAM). Although the model is oriented to information system and technologies, it can play a role in researches of elderly care needs [19]. The model proposed two main determinants: perceived usefulness (PU) and perceived ease of use (PEU). Starting from the above two concepts, this study used Likert scale with 7-level to quantify the acceptance of the elderly. Subjective evaluation can reflect the comprehensive experience of users in a human-machine system [18, 20]. The specific connotation of the two indicators was explained to the subjects during data collection, which is the extent to which a certain bus interior layout will make the elderly feel useful or easy to control in the process of moving, maintaining body stability and seating.

The factors affecting users' PU mainly include health anxiety, service quality, privacy security, etc., which are always abstract. However, PEU is more specific and intuitive, which is the users' expectation for the ease degree and convenience of using a system [19]. Therefore, considering the roles of PU and PEU in bus interior perception, the original scores of the two concepts were given a weight of 0.4 and 0.6 respectively to obtain the total score of acceptance, which is:

$$Y = 0.4 * Z_1 + 0.6 * Z_2 \tag{1}$$

where Y is the acceptance score, Z_1 and Z_2 are the scores of PU and PEU respectively.

For the prediction of acceptance score, we used Extreme Learning Machine (ELM). ELM is a form of feedforward artificial neural network. As a prediction algorithm, its generalization ability and learning rate are good [21], suitable for prediction works in engineering field. A main advantage of the model is that the constructure is brief, with few parameters to be adjusted, on the premise of getting over the fault of iterating repeatedly. The ELM used in this study is a single hidden-layer network. The expression of an ELM with L hidden layer neural nodes is [21]:

$$\sum_{i=1}^{L} \beta_i g(w_i x_i + b_i) = o_j \tag{2}$$

where β_i means the weight linking the hidden layer and the output layer, g(*) refers to the activation function being selected, w_i indicates the weight connecting nodes of the input layer and hidden layer, and b_i is the hidden layer bias.

During the ELM training, w_i and b_i are determined by random generation. In order to calculate the output result of the network, the weight (β_i) is the only parameter that needs to be figured out [22]. The model was trained and saved by the training set, and then the testing set was used to verify the prediction performance. In this study, the Sine function was selected as the activation function. The model was established by taking FD, FT and PD in the nine AOIs of the subjects under 48 layouts as the input data (a matrix with 48 rows and 27 columns), and the average acceptance score of each layout as the output data (a column vector with 48 rows). 36 rows of data were randomly picked out as the training set, and the leftover 12 rows were the testing set.

4   Results

4.1   General Trend of the 48 Types of Layouts

Set the quantity range of hidden layer nodes of the ELM model as 1–100, and build models respectively. The Sine function was used as the activation function to train the models. Each model was trained 50 times and the error variation curve was generated. When the quantity of hidden layer nodes got 55, the error started to converge. Thus, the quantity was determined to be 55. The model with a mean relative error (MRE) of less than 10% would be accepted, or else the model would be trained again. The finally obtained prediction outcome of the acceptance score is illustrated in Fig. 3.

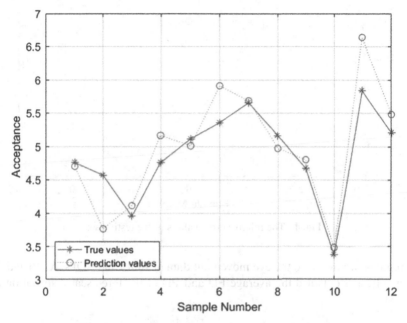

Fig. 3. The prediction result of acceptance by ELM

The performance criteria of the final model are shown in Table 2. The results indicated that the model could accurately predict the elderly's acceptance for different bus layouts.

Table 2. The performance criteria of the ELM model

	MRE	MAE	MSE	R^2
Model	0.061	0.303	0.163	0.817

Figure 4 presents the relative error values of the testing set, in which it can be seen that the relative errors of most testing samples are less than 10%, and only one exceeds 15%. This confirms that the elderly's visual search characteristics are indeed related to their acceptance.

The seats in the carriage are generally arranged in three regions: the left (linear arrangement), the right (also linear arrangement) and the rear (U-shaped arrangement). In order to reflect the differences brought by the visual search of the elderly in these

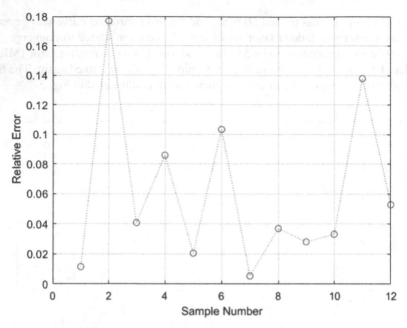

Fig. 4. The relative error values of the testing set

three regions, we averaged the eye movement data of AOI5 and AOI8, AOI6 and AOI9 respectively, and obtained the average FD and PD of the three seat distribution areas (Table 3).

Table 3. FD and PD of the three seat distribution areas (n = 48)

	Left seat area	Right seat area	Rear seat area	Levene Statistic (sig.)	F value (sig.)
FD (s)	0.475	0.509	0.51	0.013 (0.987)	11.595 (0.000)
PD (mm)	3.544	3.626	3.762	0.007 (0.993)	15.337 (0.000)

The Analysis of Variance (ANOVA) results showed that the differences among the three areas were significant ($p < 0.001$). The average FD of the rear part was the longest, followed by that of the right side. However, after making post hoc multiple comparison (by LSD method), it was found that the difference between the two parts was not significant ($p = 0.924$). And the average FD values of the two parts were both significantly longer than that of the left region. In addition, for the average PD, LSD test showed that the difference between each pair of the three regions was significant. Among them, the average PD of the rear region was the largest, which reflected the visual search or information extraction in this region was relatively difficult and the cognitive load was higher. It might be because the seats in this area were densely arranged and the object was big when near and small when far, which was not conducive to the visual search of the elderly. FD and PD in the left part were both the smallest, reflecting the characteristics of visual search of the elderly. Therefore, in elderly-oriented design works, it is more necessary to improve the perceived ease of use in the rear and right areas to compensate for the difficulties encountered by elderly passengers in visual search.

4.2 Analysis of the Case with the Highest Acceptance Score

According to the acceptance score, the spatial layout with the highest user acceptance (mean = 6.024) among the 48 stimulation materials was figured out. Focusing on this layout (Fig. 5), we further analyzed the laws of the first fixation and saccade to find the most important AOI.

Fig. 5. The spatial layout with the highest user acceptance (with features composed of A1, B1, C2 and D1 as illustrated in Table 1)

Figure 6 showed the distribution in each AOI of the first fixation. It can be seen from the figure that for this layout, the first fixation of the 33 subjects occurred in AOI3 mostly, followed by AOI6 and AOI5, and rarely in other AOIs. To some extent, it indicated that the above three AOIs could attract more attention of the elderly, and played an important role in the visual search in the bus.

The location distribution of the first fixation verified the results in Table 3 to a certain degree. Therefore, it is meaningful to ulteriorly analyze SA in these three AOIs and judge the extent to which a certain AOI can attract the elderly. In this study, we selected large SA above 9° for statistics. The ANOVA results of FFD and SA of the three AOIs are shown in Table 4:

Levene's statistical results indicated that both FFD and SA met the homogeneity of variances (p > 0.05). The ANOVA result showed that among the three AOIs, FFD of

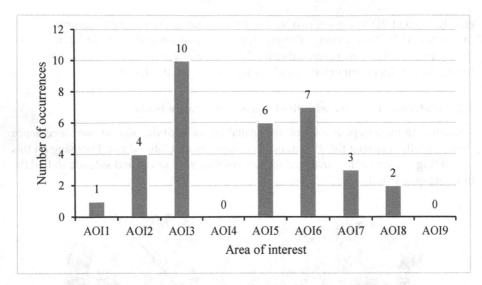

Fig. 6. The distribution in each AOI of the first fixation (n = 33)

Table 4. The ANOVA results of FFD and SA of the main AOIs (n = 33)

	AOI3	AOI5	AOI6	Levene Statistic (sig.)	F value (sig.)
FFD (s)	0.378 ± 0.063	0.452 ± 0.052	0.41 ± 0.071	1.235 (0.295)	11.817 (0.000)
SA (°)	11.802 ± 0.949	10.058 ± 1.125	13.072 ± 1.333	0.738 (0.481)	57.5 (0.000)

AOI3 was the shortest, reflecting the initial recognition degree of the target stimuli in the rear seat area was higher for the elderly. SA of AOI6 was the largest, indicating more meaningful clues existed in this region.

The above law showed that in order to compensate for the lack of information in the visual search process of the elderly and assist the elderly in planning moving routes, priority should be given to strengthening the layout design of AOI6 and AOI3. Among the two areas, there is a common factor in AOI6, which is the wheelchair area. This area breaks the original layout of the seats and forms a semi-independent space, which may be the main reason for the large average SA of AOI6.

5 Discussion

The elderly often travel off peak, which can reduce the pressure of urban public transport and avoid some dangers to a certain extent. However, the relatively low passenger density is also more likely to expose the inconvenience to the elderly caused by improper layout. Therefore, it is needed to improve the elderly-oriented level in buses. However, this kind of reconstructions are difficult. The mobility of bus space is strong, and there are many facilities and functional areas. It is hard to grasp which area is more important for the elderly passengers and find breakthrough points on the layout by using traditional design evaluation methods. Breaking the existing arrangement rashly may be unacceptable to people. However, if designers only fine-tune on the basis of the existing pattern, such as merely removing several seats, the problems faced by the elderly can barely be solved. This needs designers to find out the priority order of the functional areas in guiding visual search of old people, and on this basis, reconstruct the layout.

Eye movement indirectly feeds back users' brain thinking rules and helps to assess cognition objectively [23]. This study analyzed the eye movement characteristics that reflected the law of attention change, including fixation, saccade and pupil diameter in each AOI in a bus. These characteristics were used to predict the acceptance level of the elderly to the layout design of an interior space, and provide a reference basis for elderly-oriented designs. The ELM network indicated that the visual search of old people when observing a bus interior was related to their acceptance. Among the nine AOIs, elderly passengers paid more attention to the middle right part and the rear region, while other areas were less important for their visual search. Therefore, in the elderly-oriented design works of public transport facilities, it is rational to give more consideration to the optimization of these areas, or guide the visual search route of elderly passengers through designs of color blocks, lights or other symbols.

Visual search can reflect the adaptability of passengers to a certain space design to some extent. After getting on the bus, the elderly need to keep their body stable and move smoothly. In this process, they will constantly adjust their visual search and make judgments. However, the efficiency of visual search decreases significantly with age [1]. The decline of visual search ability of the elderly may be caused by the descent of capability of visual attention distribution, because visual search is essentially a selective attention problem. For example, studies found that the elderly could not adjust attention processing according to situation, and the flexibility declined. When goals were high-lighted, older people were more vulnerable to distractions [13–15]. In this study, it was also found that the middle right and rear regions, which were not easy to be observed clearly from the perspective of getting on from the front door, intensively reflected some laws in eye movement. Therefore, a design suitable for the elderly should compensate for the deficiency of the elderly in visual search.

For example, the preliminary design scheme shown in Fig. 7 strengthens the visual guidance of the middle right and rear parts with a unified color strip which is darker green (R:178; G:220; B:165). A light bar is set above the wheelchair area and emphasizes the particularity of the area. The rear seats are placed in a U-shaped arrangement, leaving a central area free for passengers to use the space flexibly. The seat density is reduced and some leaning facilities are provided as compensation. When there are few people, the facilities can be folded down and expanded into small seats. The leaning posture reduces the personal occupied area and is more conducive to the elderly with leg or waist pain to stand up [9]. This layout helps to compensate the elderly for their lower attention distribution ability and extract relevant information quickly and accurately. The seats are hung on the walls on both sides of the bus and has no chair legs, so it is not easy to cause passengers to stumble during movement. Through the small armrests on the back of the seats, the elderly are easier to correct their standing posture at any time. In next phase of research, we will collect the visual search rules of the elderly for a series of completed design schemes to verify the rationality.

Fig. 7. One of the preliminary schemes of elderly-oriented interior layout

6 Limitation

Compared with young people, it is harder for the elderly to accept the experimental equipment such as computers and the eye-tracker. Therefore, there were some difficulties during the training and calibration works, which might cause the data not accurate enough and reduce the generalization ability of the prediction model. In addition, because existing researches had confirmed that the visual search of the elderly was significantly different from that of the young, this study did not make a comparison between the elderly group and the young group, but only analyzed the visual search law of the elderly. In the future, it will be compared with that of the young, so as to make the designs more specific.

Another limitation comes from the stimuli which are static. Therefore, the blurry parts of the pictures, such as the wheelchair area and rear part, might confuse the elderly. The display effect is not as good as in the real bus, in which people's vision field will change and the visibility can be higher with the body swing. In the next research, it is proposed to use virtual reality interactive animation to present the layout schemes.

7 Conclusion

(1) The eye movement characteristics of the elderly when observing a bus interior could be applied to practice of predicting their acceptance by means of ELM. The prediction performance of the model was good (MRE = 0.061, R^2 = 0.817).

(2) The average FD in the rear region was the longest, followed by the middle right, and was significantly longer than that in the left region (p < 0.001). In addition, the average PD of the rear region was the largest, which reflected the difficulty in visual search or information extraction, indicating the cognitive load of the elderly was high.

(3) Based on the spatial layout with the highest acceptance of the elderly (mean = 6.024), further analysis was made. It was found that AOI3, AOI5 and AOI6 played

a more important role in the visual search of the elderly. Among them, FFD of AOI3 was the shortest, reflecting the initial recognition degree of the target stimuli in the rear seat area was higher for the elderly. SA of AOI6 was the largest, indicating that there are more meaningful clues in this region. These laws provided a reference for designing the bus interior suitable for old people and determining the position of visual symbols to guide their sight line.

Acknowledgement. This research was funded by Beijing Urban Governance Research Project, grant number 21CSZL09; Scientific Research Program of Beijing Education Commission, grant number KM202010009003; and 2022 National Innovation and Entrepreneurship Training Program for College Students–Study on the design for travel and life care of the mildly disabled elderly.

References

1. Potter, L.M., et al.: Aging and performance on an everyday-based visual search task. Acta Physiol. (Oxf) **140**(3), 208–217 (2012)
2. Schelenz, T., et al.: Application of agent based simulation for evaluating a bus layout design from passengers' perspective. Transp. Res. C Emerg. Technol. **43**, 222–229 (2014)
3. Aceves-Gonzalez, C., May, A., Cook, S.: An observational comparison of the older and younger bus passenger experience in a developing world city. Ergonomics **59**(6), 840–850 (2016)
4. D'Souza, C., et al.: Low-floor bus design preferences of walking aid users during simulated boarding and alighting. Work **41**(6), 4951–4956 (2012)
5. D'Souza, C., et al.: Effects of transit bus interior configuration on performance of wheeled mobility users during simulated boarding and disembarking. Appl. Ergon. **62**, 94–106 (2017)
6. Wang, W.B.: Influence factors of railway vehicle interior impact injury. Appl. Mech. Mater. **79**, 227–231 (2011)
7. Solah, M.S., et al.: Assessment of bus interior design in Malaysia. Adv. Eng. Forum **10**, 367–372 (2013)
8. Pityn, P., Clouse-Jensen, S.: Windshield glare from bus interiors: potential impact on city transit drivers at night. SAE Int. J. Transp. Safety **7**(2), 153–161 (2019)
9. Yang, H.: Bus leaning facility design for senior people based on user demands. Packag. Eng. **39**(2), 32–36 (2018)
10. Saravanan, M., Soundarya, S.: Smart system for preventing passenger destination missing in bus. J. Phys. Conf. Ser. **1717**(1), 012016 (2021)
11. Li, Y.-J., Zhu, H.: Research on interactive design of vehicle information interface for old people based on visual characteristics. In: Stephanidis, C. (ed.) HCI 2018. CCIS, vol. 851, pp. 167–174. Springer, Cham (2018). https://doi.org/10.1007/978-3-319-92279-9_23
12. Tinelli, F., et al.: Greater sparing of visual search abilities in children after congenital rather than acquired focal brain damage. Neurorehabil. Neural Repair **25**(8), 721–728 (2011)
13. Spreng, R.N., et al.: Attenuated anticorrelation between the default and dorsal attention networks with aging: evidence from task and rest. Neurobiol. Aging **45**, 149–160 (2016)
14. Madden, D.J., et al.: Age mediation of frontoparietal activation during visual feature search. Neuroimage **102**, 262–274 (2014)
15. Monge, Z.A., et al.: Functional modular architecture underlying attentional control in aging. Neuroimage **155**, 257–270 (2017)

16. Li, J.B., Xu, B.H.: Synthetic assessment of cognitive load in human-machine interaction proces. Acta Psychol. Sin. **41**(1), 35–43 (2009)
17. Herbeth, N., Blumenthal, D.: Product appraisal dimensions impact emotional responses and visual acceptability of instrument panels. Food Qual. Prefer. **29**(1), 53–64 (2013)
18. Yang, H., Zhao, Y., Wang, Y.: Identifying modeling forms of instrument panel system in intelligent shared cars: a study for perceptual preference and in-vehicle behaviors. Environ. Sci. Pollut. Res. **27**(1), 1009–1023 (2019). https://doi.org/10.1007/s11356-019-07001-0
19. Chen, H.X., Wang, L.: Frame analysis on the aging oriented of intelligent care for the disabled elderly-based on technology acceptance model. Health Econ. Res. **38**(11), 40–42 (2021)
20. Yang, H., Wang, Y., Jia, R.: Dimensional evolution of intelligent cars human-machine interface considering take-over performance and drivers' perception on urban roads. Complexity **2020**, 6519236 (2020)
21. He, K.D., et al.: Application of EEMD multi-scale entropy and ELM in feature extraction of vibration signal of hydropower unit. China Rural Water Hydropower (5), 176–182+187 (2021)
22. Chen, X., et al.: Electricity price forecasting with extreme learning machine and bootstrapping. IEEE Trans. Power Syst. **27**(4), 2055–2062 (2012)
23. Yang, H., et al.: Exploring relationships between design features and system usability of intelligent car human–machine interface. Robot. Auton. Syst. **143**, 103829 (2021)

Age and Gender Differences in Mobile Game Acceptance Amongst Older Adults

Rita W. L. Yu[✉], Alan H. S. Chan, and T. H. Ko

Department of Advanced Design and Systems Engineering, City University of Hong Kong,
Kowloon, Hong Kong
{winglamyu7-c,tsunhonko2-c}@my.cityu.edu.hk,
alan.chan@cityu.edu.hk

Abstract. This study aimed to explore age and gender differences in older adults' mobile game acceptance. Factors affecting older adults' game attitudes towards playing mobile games were examined using qualitative research methods. A structured questionnaire was utilised with 60 adults (30 females and 30 males) aged 50 and above. Five external factors influencing older adults' acceptance of mobile games were examined using the technology acceptance model (TAM): challenge, quality of game interface, genre, self-satisfaction and social interaction. Challenge represents the perceived difficulty of older adults in mobile games. Quality of game interface refers to how well an interface is designed for older adults to interact with the game. Genre denotes gameplay contents and characteristics of mobile games. Self-satisfaction refers to the degree of satisfaction that older adults acquire from their achievements in mobile games. Lastly, social interaction is related to older adults' interaction with others, such as friends or family members.

Correlation analysis and multiple and hierarchical regressions were used to verify the relationships amongst the factors and TAM constructs. Results supported the proposition that perceived ease of use and perceived usefulness of mobile games positively affect older adults' attitudes towards playing mobile games. This study also demonstrated that quality of game interface, self-satisfaction, social interaction, perceived usefulness, perceived ease of use and attitude towards playing mobile games are negatively moderated by age. Surprisingly, older males were more positively associated with challenge than older females, and older females were more positively associated with social interaction than older males. Findings are beneficial for understanding the factors that influence mobile game acceptance by older adults.

Keywords: Acceptance · Attitude · Mobile games · Older adults · Qualitative research

1 Introduction

In 2019, the number of people aged 60 years or above globally was 1.02 billion (United Nations 2019). This number will increase to 1.4 billion by 2030 and 2.1 billion by 2050 (World Health Organization 2021). Predominantly consumed by younger adults and the

© The Author(s), under exclusive license to Springer Nature Switzerland AG 2022
Q. Gao and J. Zhou (Eds.): HCII 2022, LNCS 13330, pp. 641–657, 2022.
https://doi.org/10.1007/978-3-031-05581-2_44

youth in the past decade, mobile games in recent years are developed to be entertaining, challenging and capable of providing cognitive, physical and socioemotional benefits for older gamers (Lee et al. 2021).

For mobile games, older adults are a player group with distinct playing behavior characteristics, such as game preference (Yu et al. 2021). Multiple age-related changes in older adults, such as declining cognition and motor functions, affect their ability to play games (Yu and Chan 2021). Therefore, these changes may influence older adults' willingness to play mobile games. However, much is to be learned about the acceptance and attitude of older players towards mobile games and how individual demographic differences, such as age and gender, would influence their future involvement in mobile games.

Age has been found to be one of the factors causing differences in video game acceptance. Although people aged between 60 and 70 years may have preserved their functionalities, people older than this age range may profoundly experience the burdens of aging (Toril et al. 2014). Older populations tend to have minimal experience and often have negative attitudes towards playing video games (Przybylski 2014). Ferguson (2015) found that older adults with negative thoughts towards video games could be predicted by their negative attitudes towards youngsters. Negative attitudes of older adults on the younger generation can be caused by the link between violence and video games (Ferguson et al. 2017).

Evidence suggests that gender differences in gaming behaviour, such as game preference and time devoted to games, vary across the life course (Gómez-Gonzalvo et al. 2020). Amongst the youth, boys have been shown to play video games longer than girls (Huang et al. 2017). Furthermore, boys prefer action, shooting and racing games, whereas girls like social, puzzle and arcade games. Gender differences also affect adults' (18–64 years) gaming platform preference (i.e., computer, console and mobile devices) and motivations to play games (Lopez-Fernandez et al. 2019). Female adults have a higher preference for mobile gaming platforms than male adults. Moreover, competition has a higher impact on males' motivation for gaming than that of females. Older adults' ($\geq$ 65 years) game preference can be predicted by their gender. Older females favour puzzle games, whereas older males prefer strategy-board games (Yu et al. 2021). Although age and gender differences in gaming behaviour vary across the life span, research on how these differences affect the acceptance of mobile games amongst older players has remained scarce.

The objectives of this study are as follows: (1) apply technology acceptance model (TAM) constructs and test their validities in the mobile game application; (2) examine the effects of age and gender on older adults' attitudes towards participating in mobile games and (3) investigate the role of external factors in predicting mobile game acceptance amongst older adults.

2 TAM Constructs and Hypothesis Development

2.1 TAM Constructs

This study adopts TAM to investigate age- and gender-related differences in attitude and perception of older adults to play mobile games. TAM has been adopted to investigate the acceptance and usage of technological products and services (Davis 1989). This model has also been used to examine older adults' technology (Chen and Chan 2014) and game adoption, such as virtual reality (Roberts et al. 2019), video shooting games (Yu et al. 2020) and exergames (Chen et al. 2018). In TAM, attitude towards using (AT) technology is based on two key variables: perceived usefulness (PU) and perceived ease of use (PEOU). PU is defined as the degree to which people believe that using a particular system would enhance their job performance, whilst PEOU is defined as the degree to which people believe that using a particular system would be effortless (Davis 1989). Causal linkages from PEOU to PU, PU to AT and PEOU to AT have been repeatedly validated (Man et al. 2020; Man et al. 2021; Wong et al. 2021). Therefore, the following hypotheses related to TAM constructs are suggested:

H1a. PEOU is positively associated with PU of mobile games.
H1b. PEOU is positively associated with AT mobile games.
H1c. PU is positively associated with the AT mobile games.

Age-related declines in physical and cognitive functions, such as motor skills and hand–eye coordination, may cause delays in playing video games (Yu and Chan 2021). Therefore, older adults' perception of mobile games is likely to be moderated by age. The relationships between age and TAM constructs are hypothesised as follows:

H2a. Age is negatively associated with PEOU of mobile games.
H2b. Age is negatively associated with PU of mobile games.
H2c. Age is negatively associated with AT mobile games.
H2d. The relationship between PEOU and PU of mobile games is moderated by age.
H2e. The relationship between PEOU and AT playing mobile games is moderated by age.
H2f. The relationship between PU and AT mobile games is moderated by age.

2.2 Potential Moderators

This study investigates the perceptual and attitudinal factors that could influence older adults' participation in mobile games. Bandura's (2001) social cognitive theory addresses technology learning as interaction amongst personal, environmental and behavioural factors. Personal factors explain older adults' technology confidence, self-efficacy, desire to learn new games and benefits of mobile games (Jin et al. 2019). Environmental factors refer to social connections, such as support from friends and family members (Jin et al. 2019). Behavioural factors explain older adults' skills and resources for tasks that could influence their behavioural intentions towards adopting technology (Wu and Song 2021).

Personal factor
Self-satisfaction
Motivation is key for older adults to maintain the frequency and intensity of playing mobile games. The specific form relevant to the motivation to play mobile games is self-satisfaction, which is the degree of satisfaction that older adults acquire from their achievements in games (Pacheco et al. 2020). Self-satisfaction is a significant predictor

of PU and PEOU in the context of using smartphones (Ma et al. 2016) and information and communication technologies (Guner and Acarturk 2020). Thus, self-satisfaction is expected to be one of the factors positively influencing older adults' participation in mobile games.

Age and gender differences have been found to affect the self-satisfaction of gamers. For age differences, older adults often think they are considerably old to learn new technology and have low self-efficacy in its use (Chung et al. 2010). The older population has more technology anxiety than younger generations, leading the former to show less satisfaction from mobile games. However, older adults have been found to feel confident in using technology when they gain skills, thereby enabling them to use the technology with minimal anxiety and considerable self-satisfaction (Stanziano 2016). For gender differences, males are found to value a sense of accomplishment and emphasise winning the competition in video games. By contrast, females are found to value self-satisfaction, access to knowledge and enrichment (Casile et al. 2021). Therefore, the following hypotheses are proposed:

H3a. Self-satisfaction is positively associated with PEOU of mobile games.
H3b. Self-satisfaction is positively associated with PU of mobile games.
H3c. Age is negatively associated with self-satisfaction.
H3d. Older females are more positively associated with self-satisfaction than older males.

Environmental Factors
Environmental factors, including social connection via electronic devices and support of family members and friends, have been used to understand and analyse how older adults learn technology (Jin et al. 2019). The quality of game interface and social interaction are the environmental factors relevant to older adults' mobile game behaviours (Lee et al. 2019).

Quality of Game Interface
Game interfaces are designed for players to interact with games and aim to motivate and engage gamers to play games frequently (Lee et al. 2019). The quality of game interface affects players' gaming experience. Petrovčič et al. (2018) confirm that the perceived usability of smartphones is limited by the level of adaptation of the interface and design of devices. Marston (2013) suggests that the game interface design for senior gamers should offer simple and intuitive interaction and consider the ease of player-interface interaction. Therefore, older adults' acceptance of mobile games is expected to be positively associated with the quality of game interfaces.

Age and gender differences have been found to affect the interaction between gamers and game interface. For age differences in interface interaction, age-related declines in physical and cognitive functions are expected to affect mobile game acceptance by older adults. Older adults demonstrate poorer performance on tasks requiring motor control and coordination than younger adults, thereby significantly affecting the former's ability to interact with games (Yu and Chan 2021). For gender differences in interface interaction, the influencing relationship between video game experience and the ability to interact with games through a game interface has been investigated. Males are found to have more gaming experience, thereby resulting in the former becoming more proficient in controlling the game interface than the latter (Martens and Antonenko 2012). Therefore, the following hypotheses are proposed:

H4a. Quality of game interface is positively associated with PEOU of mobile games.
H4b. Quality of game interface is positively associated with PU of mobile games.
H4c. Age is negatively associated with the quality of game interface.
H4d. Older males are more positively associated with quality of game interface than older females.

Social Interaction
Mobile games relatively contribute to the social interaction of older adults. Social influence improves interpersonal relationships and gamers' attitudes towards entertainment (Lin and Chuang 2019). Chen et al. (2018) find that the impact of social interaction on intention to play and usage behaviour is significant in exergames for older adults. Furthermore, results of clinical studies have shown that increased social interaction is associated with the improved cognitive performance of older adults (Dodge et al. 2015).

Studies have shown that video games positively impact the social interaction of players amongst different age groups. Adolescents playing video games with others may provide them with the needed social interactions and support from friends (Ohannessian 2018). Younger adults often guide and motivate older adults to use technology that may facilitate family cohesion and strengthen relationships (Taipale 2019). Moreover, older adults leverage technology to connect, communicate and participate in online formats, such as digital gaming, to connect with their adult children and grandchildren (Freeman et al. 2020). For gender differences, older females are more likely to play with family members and friends than older males (Zhang and Kaufman 2016). Moreover, female gamers are more likely to have met with game friends in real life than male gamers (Zhang and Kaufman 2016). The following hypotheses are proposed on the bases of the previous studies:

H5a. Social interaction is positively associated with PEOU of mobile games.
H5b. Social interaction is positively associated with PU of mobile games.
H5c. Age is positively associated with social interaction.
H5d. Older females are more positively associated with social interaction than older males.

Behavioural Factors
Individual skills and resources for tasks could influence individuals' behavioural intentions towards technology adoption (Wu and Song 2021). Challenge and genre are behavioural factors relevant to mobile game behaviours.

Challenge
Challenge is defined by the difficulty level of the main task, which can be adjusted by game designers, such as varying the number of enemies and level of artificial intelligence (Tornqvist and Tichon 2021). Older adults have been found to enjoy challenging and

narratively rich games because they perceive challenging games as potentially beneficial for cognitive functioning (Boot et al. 2018; Lee et al. 2021). These results imply that challenges in games play an important role in shaping mobile game acceptance by older adults.

Age differences should also be considered when attempting to understand the relationship between challenge and attitude of older adults towards mobile gaming. Mobile games should appropriately challenge gamers with various skill levels and enable them to participate by offering different play levels (McLaughlin et al. 2012). Younger adults admitted that they like to play games (with older adults) that are easy to learn and control, enabling all players of different ages and skill levels to enjoy such games (Osmanovic and Pecchioni 2016). For gender differences, male bias in game design leads to female gamers overcoming more significant challenges than male players (De Schutter 2011). For example, some of the most popular games are action or adventure games, favoring the interest of male gamers and discouraging female gamers from playing these games (Lucas and Sherry 2004). Therefore, female gamers play less frequently than male gamers, and prefer games that offer challenges that better suit their skills and interests (De Schutter 2011). The following hypotheses are suggested on the bases of the preceding results:

H6a. Challenge is positively associated with PU of mobile games.
H6b. Age is negatively associated with challenge.
H6c. Older males are more positively associated with challenge than older females.

Genre
Different perceptual, cognitive and physical functions demanded by different game genres affect mobile game acceptance by older adults with age-related cognitive declines (Yu and Chan 2021). Game genre determines the willingness of older adults to play video games by influencing the ease of interaction and levels of cognitive demand (Chesham et al. 2017). Moreover, older adults have been found to perceive video games as a useful intervention if they believe playing specific genres improve their cognitive abilities (Talaei-Khoei and Daniel 2018).

Age-related cognitive, perceptual and motor changes are important considerations in developing mobile games for older adults (Fisk et al. 2020). For example, age-related declines in fine motor control and hand–eye coordination change the way older adults interact with games (Ijaz et al. 2019). These changes enable older adults to select slow-paced genres, such as card, puzzle and virtual board games, over other game genres owing to their familiarity and simplicity (Salmon et al. 2017). Gender differences have also been found to differ across genres. Male gamers prefer multi-player online games, whilst social network games cater to female gamers (Wohn et al. 2020). These results imply that age and gender differences in genre selection may be key factors influencing senior gamers' acceptance of mobile games. Therefore, the following hypotheses are suggested:

H7a. Genre is positively associated with PU of mobile games.
H7b. Genre is positively associated with PEOU of mobile games.

H7c. Genre selection is moderated by age.
H7d. Genre selection is moderated by gender.

3 Method

3.1 Participants and Measurement

The participants of this study were 60 Chinese adults in Hong Kong (30 females and 30 males) aged between 50 to 82 years. The respondents were identified and approached in public areas, such as parks and libraries, in Hong Kong. A consent form was signed by all participants to ensure that they completely understood the study objectives, process and their right to withdraw at any time.

A survey questionnaire was designed to collect information on mobile game acceptance by older adults. The questionnaire consisted of two parts. Apart from demographic information, questions on three TAM constructs (i.e., PEOU, PU, AT) and five external variables (i.e., quality of game interface, self-satisfaction, social interaction, challenge and genre) were included. All items, except demographic characteristics, were measured with questions in Table 1 using a 5-point Likert scale (1 = strongly disagree, 5 = strongly agree). Each survey was conducted in Cantonese and lasted approximately 30 min.

Table 1. Questionnaire items for TAM constructs and external variables

Factors	Items
Attitude towards using (AT)	'I think playing mobile games is a good idea'
	'I like to play mobile games'
	'I think mobile games are addictive'
Perceived usefulness (PU)	'I think playing mobile games can improve my quality of life'
	'I think playing mobile games can exercise my brain'
	'I think I can gain benefits from mobile games'
Perceived ease of use (PEOU)	'I think learning how to play mobile games is easy'
	'I think playing mobile games is easy'
	'I think playing mobile games is skilful'
Social interaction (SI)	'I think playing mobile games with other people is better than playing alone'
	'I think mobile games that can be played with other people are attractive to me'
	'I think that playing VSGs encourages me to integrate with my friends/family members'
Self-satisfaction (SS)	'I think playing mobile games would give me a sense of accomplishment'

(continued)

Table 1. (*continued*)

Factors	Items
	'I think playing mobile games makes me happy'
	'I think playing mobile games makes me feel more relaxed'
Quality of game interface (GI)	'I like mobile games with good graphic quality'
	'I like mobile games with a user-friendly interface'
	'I like mobile games with visual effects'
Genre (GE)	'I like playing casual mobile games'
	'I like playing games that I am familiar with'
	'I like playing exciting mobile games'
Challenge (CH)	'I like playing challenging mobile games'
	'I think mobile games that are too difficult to play are boring'
	'I like playing mobile games that are easy to get started with'

3.2 Data Analysis

Hypotheses were tested using correlation and hierarchical regression analyses. The explanatory power of gender over external variables and TAM constructs (PEOU, PU and AT) were analysed by dividing gender into two groups (i.e., male and female) in the correlation analysis.

Hierarchical regression was conducted in three steps. Firstly, four external factors (i.e., self-satisfaction, quality of game interface, social interaction and genre) and PU were entered for PEOU. Secondly, the same external variables with the addition of challenge and PEOU were entered for PU. Thirdly, age was added to determine if it has any moderating effect on external variables and PU. Fourthly, cross-product (interaction) of age and PEOU were entered. For AT, PEOU and PU were entered firstly. Age was added in the next step. Lastly, interactions between age and PEOU and PU were included in the analysis to determine if they have any explanatory power over AT.

4 Results

4.1 Descriptive Statistics

A total of 60 respondents with mobile gaming experience participated in this study. Ages (i.e., between 50 and 59 years: 25%; between 60 and 69 years: 25%; between 70 and 79 years: 25%; 80 years and above: 25%) and gender (30 males and 30 females) of the participants were evenly distributed. The majority of the participants were retired (55%), obtained secondary education (61.7%) and of middle economic status (60%). Detailed demographic information is shown in Table 2.

Table 2. Demographic information ($N = 60$)

Items			Frequency	Percentage (%)
Age	50–59	Male	7	11.7
		Female	8	13.3
	60–69	Male	8	13.3
		Female	7	11.7
	70–79	Male	8	13.3
		Female	7	11.7
	Over 80	Male	7	11.7
		Female	8	13.3
Education	Primary		15	25.0
	Secondary		37	61.7
	Post-secondary		8	13.3
Work status	Full-time work		22	36.7
	Part-time work		5	8.3
	Retired		33	55.0
Economic status	Poor		14	23.3
	General		36	60.0
	Rich		10	16.7

4.2 Hypothesis Testing

Table 3 shows the results of zero-order correlations amongst external variables, TAM constructs and age. The results show that age was negatively associated with PEOU ($r = -.541, p < .01$), PU ($r = -.380, p < .01$), AT ($r = -.276, p < .05$), social interaction ($r = -.342, p < .01$), self-satisfaction ($r = -.265, p < .05$) and quality of game interface ($r = -.433, p < .01$). Therefore, H2a, H2b, H2c, H3c and H4c are supported by correlation analysis. Correlation between age and other variables were not statistically significant.

Table 3. Zero-order correlations amongst external variables, TAM constructs and age

Variables	1	2	3	4	5	6	7	8	9	10	11
1. Age	1										
2. PEOU	−.541**	1									
3. PU	−.380**	.703**	1								
4. AT	−.276*	.792**	.692**	1							

(*continued*)

Table 3. (*continued*)

Variables	1	2	3	4	5	6	7	8	9	10	11
5. Social interaction	$-.342^{**}$	$.522^{**}$	$.500^{**}$	$.631^{**}$	1						
6. Self-satisfaction	$-.265^{*}$	$.705^{**}$	$.713^{**}$	$.716^{**}$	$.541^{**}$	1					
7. Quality of game interface	$-.433^{**}$	$.664^{**}$	$.538^{**}$	$.665^{**}$	$.578^{**}$	$.578^{**}$	1				
8. Genre	.085	.146	$.378^{**}$	$.280^{*}$	.198	$.477^{**}$	.006	1			
9. Challenge	.010	.072	$.292^{*}$	.208	.179	$.280^{*}$	.025	$.737^{**}$	1		
10. Age x PEOU	$-.039$	$-.079$	.192	.024	.170	.167	.142	.225	.089	1	
11. Age x PU	.046	.201	$.314^{*}$	.215	.214	.205	$.343^{**}$	.169	.034	$.687^{**}$	1

$^{*}p < .05$ (2-tailed)
$^{**}p < .01$ (2-tailed)

Table 4. Correlation between external variables and TAM constructs by gender.

Variables	Gender	1	2	3	4	5	6	7	8
1. PEOU	F	1							
	M	1							
2. PU	F	.663**	1						
	M	.745**	1						
3. AT	F	.826**	.637**	1					
	M	.758**	.746**	1					
4. Social interaction	F	.638**	.362*	.690**	1				
	M	.418*	.599**	.584**	1				
5. Self-satisfaction	F	.807**	.689**	.647**	.509**	1			
	M	.596**	.769**	.805**	.603**	1			
6. Quality of game interface	F	.672**	.455*	.675**	.688**	.522**	1		
	M	.653**	.616**	.653**	.478**	.651**	1		
7. Genre	F	.112	.331	.117	$-.122$	.394*	$-.138$	1	
	M	.200	.428*	.456*	.517**	.585**	0.168	1	
8. Challenge	F	$-.072$	.209	$-.098$	$-.274$	.170	$-.212$	.760**	1
	M	$-.203$	.352	.490**	.552**	.403*	0.253	.724**	1

$^{*} p < .05$ (2-tailed)
$^{**}p < .01$ (2-tailed)

Table 4 shows that gender was positively associated with social interaction, self-satisfaction and quality of game interface. AT of older females was more positively associated with social interaction (r = .690, p < .01) and quality of game interface (r

= .675, p < .01) than older males. Moreover, AT of older males was more positively associated with self-satisfaction (r = .805, p < .01) than older females. Therefore, H5d is supported by correlation analysis. Interestingly, correlation between genre and challenge was positive in both groups of older males (r = .724, p < .01) and older females (r = .760, p < .01). The relationship between AT and genre of older females was positive but not statistically significant.

Table 5 shows the results of the hierarchical regression analyses. Self-satisfaction (β = .384, p < .01) and PU (β = .354, p < .01) were positively associated with the dependent variable PEOU. Thus, H3a is supported. As indicated in the second block of the hierarchical regression, only PEOU (β = .410, p < .01) was positively associated with the dependent variable of PU. Hence, H1a is supported. Moreover, the effect of age on PU was not significant. Interaction between age and PEOU did not significantly affect PU. Therefore, H2d is not supported.

As shown in the third block of the hierarchical regression, PEOU (β = .435, p < .01) was positively associated with AT. Therefore, H1b is supported. The results also indicated that interaction between age and PEOU and between age and PU did not significantly affect AT. Therefore, H2e and H2f are not supported. Moreover, social interaction (β = .192, p < .05) was positively associated with AT. The summary of hypothesis tests is shown in Table 6.

Table 5. Hierarchical regression for the TAM constructs

Steps	Independent variables	Dependent variables								
		PEOU			PU			AT		
		R2	ΔR^2	β	R^2	ΔR^2	β	R^2	ΔR^2	β
1	Social interaction			.040			.058			.192*
	Self-satisfaction			.384**			.277			.112
	Quality of game interface			.230			.069			.146
	Genre			−.180			.102			.063
	Challenge						.098			.032
	PEOU						.410**			.435**
	PU				.354**						.099
		0.667	0.636		0.619	0.576			0.736	0.700	
2	Social interaction						.033			.218*
	Self-satisfaction						.260			.059
	Quality of game interface						.019			.178

(*continued*)

Table 5. (*continued*)

Steps	Independent variables	PEOU			PU			AT		
		R2	ΔR^2	β	R^2	ΔR^2	β	R^2	ΔR^2	β
	Genre						.058			.026
	Challenge						.124			.053
	PEOU						.463**			.537**
	PU									.137
	Age						−.039			.231**
	Age x PEOU						.151			−.034
					0.640	0.584		0.771	0.735	
3	Social interaction									.211*
	Self-satisfaction									−.008
	Quality of game interface									.219
	Genre									.043
	Challenge									.044
	PEOU									.618**
	PU									.152
	Age									.288**
	Age x PEOU									.079
	Age x PU									−.152
								0.780	0.735	

* $p < .05$ (2-tailed)
** $p < .01$ (2-tailed)

Table 6. Summary of hypothesis tests

Hypothesis	Support
H1a. PEOU -> PU (positively)	Supported
H1b. PEOU -> AT (positively)	Supported
H1c. PU -> AT (positively)	Not supported
H2a. Age -> PEOU (negatively)	Supported
H2b. Age -> PU (negatively)	Supported
H2c. Age -> AT (negatively)	Supported

(*continued*)

Table 6. (*continued*)

Hypothesis	Support
H2d. Age moderates the relationship between PEOU and PU	Not supported
H2e. Age moderates the relationship between PEOU and AT	Not supported
H2f. Age moderates the relationship between PU and AT	Not supported
H3a. Self-satisfaction -> PEOU (positively)	Supported
H3b. Self-satisfaction -> PU (positively)	Not supported
H3c. Age -> Self-satisfaction (negatively)	Supported
H3d. Older females will be more positively associated with self-satisfaction than older males	Not Supported
H4a. Quality of game interface -> PEOU (positively)	Not supported
H4b. Quality of game interface -> PU (positively)	Not supported
H4c. Age- > Quality of game interface (negatively)	Supported
H4d. Older males will be more positively associated with quality of game interface than older females	Not Supported
H5a. Social interaction -> PEOU (positively)	Not supported
H5b. Social interaction -> PU (positively)	Not supported
H5c. Age -> social interaction (positively)	Not Supported
H5d. Older females will more positively associated with social interaction than older males	Supported
H6a. Challenge -> PU (positively)	Not supported
H6b. Age -> Challenge (negatively)	Not supported
H6c. Older males will be more positively associated with challenge than older females	Not Supported
H7a. Genre -> PU (positively)	Not supported
H7b. Genre -> PEOU (positively)	Not supported
H7c. Amongst older adults, genre selection is moderated by age	Not supported
H7d. Amongst older adults, genre selection is moderated by gender	Not supported

5 Discussion and Conclusion

This study adopted the TAM model in the context of mobile games acceptance and attempted to extend it with external factors and moderators of age and gender. The results partially supported the propositions of TAM and moderating effects of age and gender differences on external variables.

For the first objective of this study (i.e., validation of TAM constructs with respect to mobile game application), this research found that PEOU was a predictor of the attitude of older adults towards playing mobile games. Particularly, acceptance of mobile games is related to older adults' perception of the games' ease of use. Older adults accept and play games if they believe that mobile games are easy to play. However, the effect of PU on AT was not significant. This result indicates that the health benefits of playing mobile games may not be a facilitating factor for motivating older adults to accept mobile games.

For the second objective (i.e., investigation of age and gender differences in perceptions of mobile games), findings of this study show that age was positively correlated with PEOU, PU and AT. Specifically, positive correlations between age and TAM constructs show significant generational gaps amongst older adults. Moreover, negative correlations amongst age, self-satisfaction and quality of game interface imply that older adults continue to have problems enjoying mobile games. This situation may be caused by a lack of achievements acquired in games or poor interface design. These results align with those of previous studies, in which self-satisfaction and quality of game interface are critical factors in motivating and engaging older adults to play games (Jin et al. 2019; Lee et al. 2019). As hypothesised, the current study found some relationships between gender and external factors. The correlation between older females and social interaction was found to be more positive than that of older males. In deciding whether or not to play mobile games, older females were more influenced by the social aspect of mobile games than older males. Furthermore, a positive correlation between challenge and genre in the older female and male groups suggest that older adults perceived challenges in games as associated with the game genre. This result aligns with those of previous studies, in which different genres contain considerably varying elements that stimulate older players' cognition in different ways and produce variable effects and challenges (McCord et al. 2020).

For the last objective, moderating effects were only found for the correlation between social interaction and AT and the path of self-satisfaction to PEOU. Attitudes of older adults towards mobile gameplays were considerably influenced by the social benefits of mobile games. Similarly, perception of the ease of use of mobile games amongst older adults was influenced by self-satisfaction. Older adults are likely to engage in mobile games if they think they are able to earn achievements throughout the games.

The findings of this study indicate the importance of considering the effects of age and gender in influencing older adults' attitudes towards playing mobile games. The results also illuminate the underlying correlations between external variables and TAM constructs, thereby providing novel insights into the factors contributing to mobile game acceptance amongst older males and females. Lastly, the findings of this study also extend the prior research on older adults' acceptance of mobile games by linking the effects of age and gender on external factors to TAM constructs and empirically validating their correlations.

References

Bandura, A.: Social cognitive theory of mass communication. Media Psychol. **3**(3), 265–299 (2001)

Boot, W.R., et al.: Exploring older adults' video game use in the PRISM computer system. Innovat. Aging **2**(1), igy009 (2018)

Casile, M., Gerard, J.G., Soto-Ferrari, M.: Gender differences in self-efficacy, acceptance, and satisfaction in business simulations. Int. J. Manage. Educ. **19**(2), 100473 (2021)

Chen, C.K., et al.: Acceptance of different design exergames in elders. PLoS ONE **13**(7), e0200185 (2018)

Chen, K., Chan, A.H.S.: Gerontechnology acceptance by elderly Hong Kong Chinese: a senior technology acceptance model (STAM). Ergonomics **57**(5), 635–652 (2014)

Chesham, A., Wyss, P., Müri, R.M., Mosimann, U.P., Nef, T.: What older people like to play: genre preferences and acceptance of casual games. JMIR Serious Games **5**(2), e8 (2017)

Chung, J.E., Park, N., Wang, H., Fulk, J., McLaughlin, M.: Age differences in perceptions of online community participation among non-users: an extension of the Technology Acceptance Model. Comput. Hum. Behav. **26**(6), 1674–1684 (2010)

Davis, F.D.: Perceived usefulness, perceived ease of use, and user acceptance of information technology. MIS Quart. **13**, 319–340 (1989)

De Schutter, B.: Never too old to play: the appeal of digital games to an older audience. Games Cult. **6**(2), 155–170 (2011)

Dodge, H.H., et al.: Web-enabled conversational interactions as a method to improve cognitive functions: results of a 6-week randomized controlled trial. Alzheimer's Dementia Transl. Res. Clin. Intervent. **1**(1), 1–12 (2015)

Ferguson, C.J.: Clinicians' attitudes toward video games vary as a function of age, gender and negative beliefs about youth: a sociology of media research approach. Comput. Hum. Behav. **52**, 379–386 (2015)

Ferguson, C.J., Nielsen, R.K., Maguire, R.: Do older adults hate video games until they play them? A Proof-of-Concept study. Curr. Psychol. **36**(4), 919–926 (2017)

Fisk, A.D., Czaja, S.J., Rogers, W.A., Charness, N., Sharit, J.: Designing for Older Adults: Principles and Creative Human Factors Approaches. CRC Press, Boca Raton (2020)

Freeman, S., et al.: Intergenerational effects on the impacts of technology use in later life: insights from an international, multi-site study. Int. J. Environ. Res. Public Health **17**(16), 5711 (2020)

GómezGonzalvo, F., Molina, P., DevísDevís, J.: Which are the patterns of video game use in Spanish school adolescents? Gender as a key factor. Entertainment Comput. **34**, 100366 (2020)

Guner, H., Acarturk, C.: The use and acceptance of ICT by senior citizens: a comparison of technology acceptance model (TAM) for elderly and young adults. Univ. Access Inf. Soc. **19**(2), 311–330 (2018). https://doi.org/10.1007/s10209-018-0642-4

Huang, V., Young, M., Fiocco, A.J.: The association between video game play and cognitive function: does gaming platform matter? Cyberpsychol. Behav. Soc. Netw. **20**(11), 689–694 (2017)

Ijaz, K., Ahmadpour, N., Naismith, S.L., Calvo, R.A.: An immersive virtual reality platform for assessing spatial navigation memory in predementia screening: feasibility and usability study. JMIR Mental Health **6**(9), e13887 (2019)

Jin, B., Kim, J., Baumgartner, L.M.: Informal learning of older adults in using mobile devices: a review of the literature. Adult Educ. Q. **69**(2), 120–141 (2019)

Lee, L.N., Kim, M.J., Hwang, W.J.: Potential of augmented reality and virtual reality technologies to promote wellbeing in older adults. Appl. Sci. **9**(17), 3556 (2019)

Lee, S., Oh, H., Shi, C.K., Doh, Y.Y.: mobile game design guide to improve gaming experience for the middle-aged and older adult population: user-centered design approach. JMIR Serious Games **9**(2), e24449 (2021)

Lee, S., Shi, C.K., Doh, Y.Y.: The relationship between co-playing and socioemotional status among older-adult game players. Entertainment Comput. **38**, 100414 (2021)

Lin, C.T., Chuang, S.S.: A study of digital learning for older adults. J. Adult Dev. **26**(2), 149–160 (2019)

Lopez-Fernandez, O., Williams, A.J., Griffiths, M.D., Kuss, D.J.: Female gaming, gaming addiction, and the role of women within gaming culture: a narrative literature review. Front. Psych. **10**, 454 (2019)

Lucas, K., Sherry, J.L.: Sex differences in video game play: a communication-based explanation. Commun. Res. **31**(5), 499–523 (2004)

Ma, Q., Chan, A.H., Chen, K.: Personal and other factors affecting acceptance of smartphone technology by older Chinese adults. Appl. Ergon. **54**, 62–71 (2016)

Man, S.S., Alabdulkarim, S., Chan, A.H.S., Zhang, T.: The acceptance of personal protective equipment among Hong Kong construction workers: an integration of technology acceptance model and theory of planned behavior with risk perception and safety climate. J. Safety Res. **79**, 329–340 (2021)

Man, S.S., Xiong, W., Chang, F., Chan, A.H.S.: Critical factors influencing acceptance of automated vehicles by Hong Kong drivers. IEEE Access **8**, 109845–109856 (2020)

Marston, H.R.: Design recommendations for digital game design within an ageing society. Educ. Gerontol. **39**(2), 103–118 (2013)

Martens, J., Antonenko, P.D.: Narrowing gender-based performance gaps in virtual environment navigation. Comput. Hum. Behav. **28**(3), 809–819 (2012)

McCord, A., Cocks, B., Barreiros, A.R., Bizo, L.A.: Short video game play improves executive function in the oldest old living in residential care. Comput. Hum. Behav. **108**, 106337 (2020)

McLaughlin, A., Gandy, M., Allaire, J., Whitlock, L.: Putting fun into video games for older adults. Ergonom. Des. **20**(2), 13–22 (2012)

Ohannessian, C.M.: Video game play and anxiety during late adolescence: the moderating effects of gender and social context. J. Affect. Disord. **226**, 216–219 (2018)

Osmanovic, S., Pecchioni, L.: Beyond entertainment: motivations and outcomes of video game playing by older adults and their younger family members. Games Cult. **11**(1–2), 130–149 (2016)

Pacheco, T.B.F., de Medeiros, C.S.P., de Oliveira, V.H.B., Vieira, E.R., De Cavalcanti, F.A.C.: Effectiveness of exergames for improving mobility and balance in older adults: a systematic review and meta-analysis. Syst. Rev. **9**(1), 1–14 (2020)

Petrovčič, A., Rogelj, A., Dolničar, V.: Smart but not adapted enough: heuristic evaluation of smartphone launchers with an adapted interface and assistive technologies for older adults. Comput. Hum. Behav. **79**, 123–136 (2018)

Przybylski, A.K.: Who believes electronic games cause real world aggression? Cyberpsychol. Behav. Soc. Netw. **17**(4), 228–234 (2014)

Roberts, A.R., De Schutter, B., Franks, K., Radina, M.E.: Older adults' experiences with audiovisual virtual reality: perceived usefulness and other factors influencing technology acceptance. Clin. Gerontol. **42**(1), 27–33 (2019)

Salmon, J.P., Dolan, S.M., Drake, R.S., Wilson, G.C., Klein, R.M., Eskes, G.A.: A survey of video game preferences in adults: building better games for older adults. Entertainment Comput. **21**, 45–64 (2017)

Stanziano, S.: Information seeking behavior of older adults. Ser. Libr. **71**(3–4), 221–230 (2016)

Taipale, S.: Intergenerational Connections in Digital Families. Springer, Cham (2019). https://doi.org/10.1007/978-3-030-11947-8

Talaei-Khoei, A., Daniel, J.: How younger elderly realize usefulness of cognitive training video games to maintain their independent living. Int. J. Inf. Manage. **42**, 1–12 (2018)

Toril, P., Reales, J.M., Ballesteros, S.: Video game training enhances cognition of older adults: a meta-analytic study. Psychol. Aging **29**(3), 706 (2014)

Tornqvist, D., Tichon, J.: Motivated to lose? Evaluating challenge and player motivations in games. Behav. Inf. Technology **40**(1), 63–84 (2021)

United Nations, Department of Economic and Social Affairs, Population Division: World Population Prospects (2019). https://population.un.org/wpp/

Wohn, D., Ratan, R., Cherchiglia, L.: Gender and genre differences in multiplayer gaming motivations. In: Fang, X. (ed.) HCII 2020. LNCS, vol. 12211, pp. 233–248. Springer, Cham (2020). https://doi.org/10.1007/978-3-030-50164-8_16

Wong, T.K.M., Man, S.S., Chan, A.H.S.: Exploring the acceptance of PPE by construction workers: an extension of the technology acceptance model with safety management practices and safety consciousness. Saf. Sci. **139**, 105239 (2021)

World Health Organization. Ageing and Health (2021). https://www.who.int/news-room/fact-she ets/detail/ageing-and-health/

Wu, J., Song, S.: Older adults' online shopping continuance intentions: Applying the technology acceptance model and the theory of planned behavior. Int. J. Hum.-Comput. Interact. **37**(10), 938–948 (2021)

Yu, R.W.L., Yuen, W.H., Peng, L., Chan, A.H.S.: Acceptance level of older Chinese people towards video shooting games. In: Gao, Q., Zhou, J. (eds.) HCII 2020. LNCS, vol. 12208, pp. 707–718. Springer, Cham (2020). https://doi.org/10.1007/978-3-030-50249-2_50

Yu, R.W.L., Chan, A.H.S.: Meta-analysis of the effects of game types and devices on older adults-video game interaction: implications for video game training on cognition. Appl. Ergon. **96**, 103477 (2021)

Yu, R.W.L., Ho, T.H., Chan, A.H.S.: Factors affecting mobile game genre preference for Chinese older adults in Hong Kong. In: Kalra, J., Lightner, N.J., Taiar, R. (eds.) AHFE 2021. LNNS, vol. 263, pp. 394–401. Springer, Cham (2021). https://doi.org/10.1007/978-3-030-80744-3_49

Zhang, F., Kaufman, D.: Older adults' social interactions in massively multiplayer online role-playing games (MMORPGs). Games Cult. **11**(1–2), 150–169 (2016)

Older Adults' Actual Use and Adoption Intention of Smart Health Care Technologies in Hong Kong

Jiaxin Zhang[1], Hailiang Wang[1], Brian Y. H. Lee[1], Marco Y. C. Pang[2], and Yan Luximon[1(✉)]

[1] School of Design, The Hong Kong Polytechnic University, Hung Hom, Hong Kong SAR, China
yan.luximon@polyu.edu.hk
[2] Department of Rehabilitation Sciences, The Hong Kong Polytechnic University, Hung Hom, Hong Kong SAR, China

Abstract. Smart health care technologies (SHCTs) can assist older adults to manage their health and acquire convenient medical and caring services, which can support older adults to live healthy and independent lives. Currently, there are various kinds of SHCTs, such as smart wearable devices, smart health monitors, health care applications, and nursing and assistive robots. Nevertheless, due to the decrease of physical and cognitive capabilities, older adults may encounter many difficulties and problems when applying different types of SHCTs, which could affect their willingness to adopt SHCTs. However, there is still unclear about Hong Kong older adults' actual use and intention adoption of different types of SHCTs, as well as the possible factors relevant to adoption. Therefore, this study attempted to investigate Hong Kong older adults' actual use and adoption intention of different kinds of SHCTs, and explore the possible factors of SHCTs adoption. We employed a structured interview to approach the actual use and adoption intention of four types of SHCTs and recruited eight Hong Kong older adults from a local community. The data analysis revealed the most popular and the least used types of SHCTs. The reasons for adopting SHCTs and possible factors of adoption intention toward each kind of SHCTs were discussed.

Keywords: Smart health care technology · Older adults · Actual use of technology · Adoption intention · Interview study

1 Introduction

By 2021, there was about 15.7% of the population above 65 years in Hong Kong [1]. It is predicted that about 31.9% of people will be aged 65 and above in Hong Kong by 2038 [2]. The aging process is often associated with frailty. Accordingly, demand for health care is increasing, which could put a heavy burden on society. Applying smart health care technologies (SHCTs) is one of the solutions to address the growing needs of older adults for health care supports and services [3, 4]. Currently, various kinds of smart health care technologies (e.g. smart wearable devices, smart health care monitors, applications for medical consultations and health management, and nursing and assistive robots) have been developed. Even though SHCTs were initially created for a general population rather than older adults, these technologies have the potential to assist older adults with maintaining independence, managing health conditions, and improving well-being. To facilitate the adoption of SHCTs, scholars and practitioners have attempted to adapt these technologies to meet older adults' cognitive capabilities by improving the usability of SHCTs and proposed various models to predict older adults' adoption intentions towards smart technologies [3, 5–8]. Although previous research has allowed suggestions and directions for developing SHCTs, the actual use and adoption intention of SHCTs by Hong Kong older adults are still unclear. Additionally, prior studies mainly focused on one kind of SHCTs, such as wearable devices only [8], or home health monitoring only [9]. There is a lack of a holistic picture of older adults' actual use and adoption intentions towards SHCTs. Therefore, this study attempted to investigate Hong Kong older adults' actual use and adoption intention towards the SHCTs by approaching the research questions: What kinds of SHCTs are older adults from a local community actually using and why they used SHCTs? To what extent are older adults from a local community willing to adopt SHCTs? Are demographic features, health conditions, quality of life, and cognitive capabilities related to older adults' adoption intention towards SHCTs?

To get a deep insight into the actual use and adoption intention of SHCTs, we employed a structured interview with 8 older adults recruited from a Hong Kong elderly center located in a local community. Descriptive statistics were employed to explore the reasons for actually use and the possible factors that related to the adoption intention of SHCTs.

2 Method

2.1 Participants

We targeted Hong Kong older adults aged above 60 years old and without neurological diseases. Eight participants were recruited from an elderly center of a local community in Hong Kong.

2.2 Smart Health Care Technologies (SHCTs)

We investigated older adults' actual use and adoption intention of four types of SHCTs, namely smart wearable devices (SWDs), smart health monitors (SHMs), health care applications (HCAs), and nursing and assistive robots (NARs). To be specific, SWDs refer to wearable devices embedded with sensors to provide wireless real-time monitoring and assistance [6, 8]. SWDs, such as smartwatches, smart cardio tachometers, and smart garments allow users with basic clock functions, to record their physical signals (e.g. heart rate, blood pressure, body temperature), to track their daily activity (e.g. steps, body movement, sleeping hours, walking distance, location) [6, 8]. SHMs indicate health monitor devices that support users' self-management of chronic disease (e.g. hypertension, diabetes, obesity) or health conditions by measuring and recording physical indicators [7]. These devices usually work cooperating with smartphone applications or systems which help to visualize the health conditions, predict the healthy trend, and inform medical-related behaviors (e.g. take medicine, seek medical consultations). Different from SWDs, SHMs provide in-situ monitors or functions. Currently, smart glucometers, blood pressure monitors, electronic pillboxes, smart weighting machines, and the HKT eSmartHealth health station are SHMs that widely used for health management in Hong Kong. HCAs are the applications that provide health-related services in an online platform or system. Mobile medical booking applications, mobile medical consultations applications, and fitness applications are HCAs that help users to access convenient and effective health services [10–12]. NARs are the robots that provide nursing-care, emotional and physical therapy, communication, and emergent assistance [13–15]. Various kinds of NARs are available in the markets, such as animal-like robots (i.e. Paro), machine-like robots (i.e. Temi), and human-like robots (i.e. Nexi) [15, 16]. To ensure that our participants could clearly understand the definition of each type of SHCTs, we explained the functions and showed the products of each category of SHCTs to our participants during the interview. To be specific, we selected the products of SHCTs which were commonly used in the local community to enhance the understanding of SHCTs functions, including the care-on-call smart watch, smart cardio tachometer, smart blood pressure monitor, smart glucometer, HKT eSmartHealth health station, Ha Go health management application, alihealth application, keep application (for physical training), the human-like nursing robot, and the machine-like assistive robot.

2.3 Interview Design

The interview questions consisted of three parts. Firstly, we inquired about demographic information of participants, including age, gender, education, economic condition, and living environment. Since our study aimed to investigate the use of SHCTs, participants' health status, sensation, and capability could be the motivators of actual use and adoption intention of SHCTs. Therefore, we asked about chronic diseases, quality of life, sensation, and cognitive capabilities in the second part. Specifically, the quality of life was rated using the EQ-5D-5L scale [17], which comprises a five-level self-evaluation in five dimensions, namely mobility, self-care, usual activities, pain/discomfort, and anxiety/depression, as well as an evaluation of overall health on the day of the interview completion. Participants described their health by rating 1 to 5 to represent the level of the problem that ranges from no problem to extremely problems in each dimension and scored how good their overall health is from 0 (the worst health condition) to 100 (the best health condition). The sensation and cognitive capability of our participants were evaluated with 6 dimensions, namely hearing, vision, memory, learning ability, concentration, and thinking ability adapted from Chen and Chan (2014) with a 7-point Likert scale ranging from 1 (extremely bad) to 7 (extremely good). In the third part of the questionnaire, we investigated participants' actual use and adoption intention toward each category of SHCTs. The adoption intention was measured with the question "To what extent are you willing to adopt this kind of SHCTs" with a 7-point Likert scale ranging from 1 (extremely unwilling to) to 7 (extremely willing to).

The interview study was conducted in a face-to-face setting in a local elderly center. Each interview was last for around 60 min. At the beginning of each interview, the interviewer explained the purpose, the procedure, and the use of the data of this study to the participants. After the participant agreed to take part in the study and signed the consent form, the interviewer would read the Part 1 and Part 2 questions to the participants. Then, participants responded to the questions. Before inquiring about the actual use and adoption intention towards SHCTs in Part 3, the interviewer would show figures and explain the definitions and functions of SHCTs in each category. The participants would point out the specific types of SHCTs that they had used and indicate their adoption intention. The interviews were audio-recorded and the audio data was transcript into text for data analysis.

3 Results and Discussion

3.1 Demographic Characteristics

Table 1 showed the demographic characteristics of the participants. Eight participants, with 5 females and 3 males, were in an age range between 69 and 80 years old. Out of 8 participants, 50% of them had received middle school education and the other of them received primary school or below education. All of them reported a general level (4 points) of economic condition on the 7-point Likert scale. Three participants were living alone, while 5 of them were living with their partners or family members. All participants lived in the apartment, and most of them (62.5%) thought that the living space of their apartments was suitable.

Table 1. Demographic characteristics

		Frequency	Percentage (%)
Gender	Male	3	37.50
	Female	5	62.50
Age	65–74	5	62.50
	74–85	3	37.50
Education	Primary School and under	4	50.00
	Middle school	4	50.00
Economic condition	Very poor	0	0.00
	Poor	0	0.00
	Slightly poor	0	0.00
	General	8	100.00
	Slightly rich	0	0.00

(*continued*)

Table 1. (*continued*)

		Frequency	Percentage (%)
	Rich	0	0.00
	Very rich	0	0.00
Living situation	Living alone	3	37.50
	Living with families	5	62.50
Living space	Crowded	1	12.50
	Suitable	5	62.50
	Spacious	2	25.00
Number of types of chronic disease	0 type	3	37.50
	2 types	3	37.50
	3 types	2	25.00

3.2 Health Conditions

Regarding the chronic disease condition (see Tables 1 and 2), 37.5% of participants lived with two types of chronic disease, 25.0% of them lived with three types of chronic disease, and 37.5% of them did not suffer from any chronic disease. Hypertension was the most frequently reported chronic disease, with 62.5% of participants under this condition. Hyperlipidemia, hypercholesterolemia, osteoporosis, joint/lumbar/leg pain, hyperuricemia, gastropathy, and emotional illness accounted for 12.5% of chronic disease conditions, respectively. Although 67.5% of participants were under at least two types of chronic diseases condition, all of them were able to take care of themselves.

Table 2. Chronic diseases conditions of older adults in this study

Participant No	Chronic disease conditions
1	None
2	None
3	None
4	Hypertension, osteoporosis, emotional illness
5	Hypertension, hyperlipidemia
6	Hypertension, hypercholesterolemia
7	Hypertension, hyperuricemia, gastropathy
8	Hypertension, Joint pain

Regarding the quality of life, most of our participants maintained healthy physical conditions and had slight mental problems (see Table 3). Seven of our participants suggested that they had no problem in mobility and one participant reported slight problems in mobility because she was suffering knee-joint pain (Participant No. 8). None of them have any problem with self-care and usual activity. 50% of them had slight pain and discomfort. However, 62.5% of participants reported a slightly anxious or depression (with a 2-point score). Participants reported their subjective health conditions on the day of conducting the interview with a range from 60 to 90 (with a mean of 80.63).

Table 3. Quality of life

		Mean	Standard Deviation
Quality of life	Mobility[a]	1.13	0.35
	Self-care[a]	1.00	0.00
	Usual activity[a]	1.00	0.00
	Pain/discomfort[a]	1.63	0.52
	Anxiety/depression[a]	1.75	0.46
	Subjective health[b]	80.63	9.80

[a]The score of mobility, self-care, usual activity, pain/discomfort, and anxiety/depression ranged from 1 (no problem) to 5 (extremely problem)
[b]The score of subjective health ranged from 0 (the worst health condition) to 100 (the best health condition).

3.3 Sensation and Cognitive Capability

Table 4. Sensation and cognition capability

		Mean	Standard Deviation
Sensation	Hearing	5.13	1.25
	Vision	4.88	1.25
Cognitive ability	Memory	4.63	1.19
	Learning ability	5.00	1.31
	Concentration	5.25	1.04
	Thinking ability	5.25	1.16

[*] Each item was measured with 7-point Likert scale from 1 (extremely bad) to 7 (extremely good).

Table 4 describes the sensation and cognitive capability of participants. Our participants exhibited a somewhat good level of sensation and cognitive capability. Six participants rated their hearing above the somewhat good level (with a score of above 5), one participant reported that he/she had a general level of hearing, and another participant thought that he/she had a slightly bad hearing. Regarding vision, five participants believed that they had a somewhat good level of vision (with a score of above 5), two participants thought that they had a general level of vision, and one participant reported a slightly bad level of vision. For cognitive ability, the most serious problem was reported with memory in comparison with other cognitive abilities, with 50% of participants scoring less than 4 points in memory. Learning ability was also a concern for one participant, who rated his/her learning ability as slightly bad. However, for concentration and thinking ability, most of our participants believed that they had at least somewhat good levels (with a score of above 5) of these two abilities, accounting for 75% and 62.5% respectively.

3.4 Actual Use and Adoption Intention

Table 5. Actual use and adoption intention of SHCTs

	Actual use		Adoption intention	
	Frequency	Percentage (%)	Mean	Standard Deviation
SWDs	3	37.50	4.88	1.89
SHMs	8	100.00	6.63	0.74
HCAs	6	75.00	5.25	1.85
NARs	0	0.00	5.00	2.31
Overall SHCTs	/	/	5.38	1.60

In general, 62.5% of participants showed a willingness to adopt SHCTs (with a score of above 5), while 37.5% of participants suggested that they were unwilling to adopt SHCTs (with a score of below 4). As shown in Table 5, participants showed the highest willingness to adopt SHMs, while the lowest willingness to apply SWDs. The reasons for the actual use of SHCTs and the possible relationships between demographic features, health condition, quality of life, sensation, cognitive capabilities, and older adults' adoption intention were discussed in the following part.

Smart Wearable Devices (SWDs). Three participants reported that they had worn or were wearing SWDs. Among these three participants, two of them reported that they were using the Xiaomi wristband, while another one did not specify the brand. The Xiaomi wristband can help to record the heart rate and the daily activities, which could help to monitor the health status (Participant No. 3). The main reasons for using SWDs were due to the curiosity towards SHCTs (Participant No. 2 and Participant No. 6), the concerns about health status (Participant No. 3), and the participation of research (Participant No. 2).

We investigated the possible predictors of SWDs. It was noted that gender, living situation, and subjective health could be important predictors of adoption intention

Table 6. The mean values of different groups of older adults' adoption intention towards each category of SHCTs

		Frequency	Mean values of adoption intention				
			SWDs	SHMs	HCAs	NARs	Overall in SHCTs
Gender	Male	3	5.33	6.33	6.50	5.67	6.33
	Female	5	4.60	6.80	4.50	4.50	4.80
Age	65–74	5	5.00	6.80	5.50	5.40	5.40
	75–84	3	4.67	6.33	4.83	4.00	5.40
Education	Primary School and under	4	4.50	6.75	4.50	4.33	5.25
	Middle school	4	5.25	6.50	6.00	5.50	5.50
Living situation	Living alone	3	6.00	6.33	5.50	4.00	6.00
	Living with families	5	4.20	6.80	5.10	5.40	5.00
Number of types of chronic disease	0 type	3	5.33	6.33	6.17	5.00	6.33
	2–3 types	5	4.60	6.80	4.70	5.00	4.80
Score of subjective health	60–80	4	4.25	6.25	4.38	4.00	4.75
	81–100	4	5.50	7.00	6.13	6.33	6.00
Score of sensation and cognitive capability	Below 30	4	4.75	6.25	5.13	3.67	5.50
	Above 30 (including 30)	4	5.00	7.00	5.38	6.00	5.25

towards SHCTs, as there was at least 1 point in the mean value of the difference in adoption intention between the groups (see Table 6). We deduced that older adults who live alone might be more likely to adopt SWDs. The reason could be due to the need for the functions of health monitor and risks recognition provided by SWDs to maintain a safe and independent life [18]. Additionally, older adults in better health conditions demonstrated a greater adoption intention towards SWDs than those under worse health conditions. This could be because the adoption intention towards SWD reflected older adults' consciousness towards health. SWDs can help to monitor physical conditions. If older adults care about their health status and make efforts to maintain their health, they are more like to have a better health conditions, and reverse.

Smart Health Monitors (SHMs). All participants had used the HKT eSmartHealth health station, which was a type of SHMs that placed in the elderly center. Based on the interview, this health station allowed older adults to measure blood pressure, blood oxygen, weight, height, and temperature. Additionally, the health data collected by the health station would be uploaded to the cloud service for health management. Older adults could check their physical indicators and health records via an application that worked cooperating with the health station. All participants responded that they used the health station because they cared about health and would like to know more about their health status (Participants No. 1 to No. 8). In the meanwhile, the promotion and training courses provided by the elderly centers were also critical to facilitating the use of the health station (Participants No. 7 and No. 8). Most of the participants reported a very strong willingness to adopt the HKT eSmartHealth health station (n = 5; mean = 7.00), and the other two participants also exhibited a positive attitude towards the adoption (mean = 5.50). However, it seemed that the differences in demographic characteristics, health status, and sensation and cognitive capability may not influence older adults' adoption intention towards SHMs. This could be because most older adults were able to operate the health stations by themselves, as the elderly center provided the training program to promote the use of the health station. Therefore, the differences in age, education, living situation, and sensation and cognitive capability groups did not show an impact on the adoption intention in this study.

Health Care Applications (HCAs). For HCAs, 75% of participants had adopted smartphone applications (e.g. eSamrtHealth, eHealth, Ha Go, and the step-counting applications) which provided health management functions. However, none of them had applied HCAs that allowed medical consultation services or training guides for fitness. Similar to SWDs and SHMs, the concern for health was a critical motivator for actually adopting HCAs (Participants No. 1 to No. 3). Additionally, the elderly center encouraged the older adults to adopt HCAs by allowing training (Participants No. 2 and No. 4). This was another main reason why our participants had applied HCAs. Also, participants (Participants No. 3 and No. 4) thought that HCAs provided convenient access to their medical records and online medical booking, and these were why they decided to use HCAs. In general, 62.5% of participants exhibited a positive attitude (scored more than 5 points) towards the adoption of HCAs, but 37.5% of participants reported a negative attitude (scored less than 3 points). According to Table 6, gender, education level, and health conditions could be the possible indicators of the adoption intention of HCAs. Prior research had revealed that education level affects older adults' adoption of smartphone applications [19], and males might be more positive to adopt the m-health [20]. This explained why the mean values in the male group and middle school group were above 1.5 point higher than female groups and primary school and under groups, respectively. Similar with SWDs, we found older adults with better health conditions showed a stronger willingness to adopt HCAs. We deduced that healthier older adults might be more health-conscious, and therefore they exhibited a higher intention to manage their health.

Nursing and Assistive Robots (NARs). Although none of our participants had actually used NARs, surprisingly 62.5% of participants exhibited a willingness to applied NARs in their lives (mean = 6.20). Two participants said that they were extremely unwilling (with a score of 1) and slightly unwilling (with a score of 3) to adopt NARs.

One participant did not report his/her adoption intention of NARs, because his/her had never seen this type of product. To be specific, gender, age, education level, living situation, subjective health, and sensation and cognitive capability could be important factors related to older adults' adoption intention towards NARs, based on the mean values shown in Table 6. Currently, NARs were still really new smart health care products in the HK market, as none of the participants had ever used or seen them (Participants No.1 to No.8). The descriptive analysis suggested that older adults who were male, aged below 75, had a higher education level, living with families, have a better health condition, or better sensation and cognitive capabilities demonstrated a stronger willingness to adopt NARs. However, older adults living with families exhibited a higher adoption intention towards NARs than those who live alone. This might be because older adults living with families were more likely to acquire support when using innovative smart technology. Therefore, they demonstrated a stronger willingness to use NARs than those who lived alone. Future studies could further explore and validate the factors that influence older adults' adoption intention towards the really new SHCTs.

4 Conclusion

This study attempted to approach the actual use and adoption intention of four types SHCTs by interviewing eight Hong Kong older adults from a local community. The results indicated that SHMs were the most popular SHCTs among older adults, with 100% of participants having used them. In the meanwhile, participants also shown the strongest adoption intention towards SHMs in comparison with other types of SHCTs. Although three participants had used SWDs, the adoption intention towards SWDs was the lowest among the four types of SHCTs. To be specific, the adoption intention of SWDs could be related to gender, living situation, and subjective health; the adoption intention of HCAs might be affected by gender, educational level, chronic diseases, and subjective health; and the adoption intention of NARs could be influenced by gender, age, educational level, living situation, and sensation and cognitive capabilities. Due to the training program provided by the elderly centers, the adoption intention of SHMs (i.e. the HKT eSmartHealth health station) was high and might not be affected by the differences of demographic characteristics, health conditions, and sensation and cognitive capabilities. However, since this research was a preliminary interview study, the sample size was small. Future studies are needed to validate the factors in relation to the actual use and adoption intention of different types of SHCTs.

Acknowledgement. The work described in this paper was supported by grants from the Hong Kong Polytechnic University (School of Design Collaborative Research Funding Project No. P0035058, Postdoc Matching Fund Scheme Project No. P0036676, and Departmental Supporting Fund Project No. P0038546).

References

1. Elderly Commission: Report on healthy ageing executive summary (2021)
2. Wong, K., Yeung, M.: Population ageing trend of Hong Kong (2019)
3. Golant, S.M.: A theoretical model to explain the smart technology adoption behaviors of elder consumers (Elderadopt). J. Aging Stud. **42**, 56–73 (2017). https://doi.org/10.1016/j.jaging. 2017.07.003
4. Liu, L., Stroulia, E., Nikolaidis, I., Miguel-Cruz, A., Rios Rincon, A.: Smart homes and home health monitoring technologies for older adults: a systematic review. Int. J. Med. Inform. **91**, 44–59 (2016). https://doi.org/10.1016/j.ijmedinf.2016.04.007
5. Chen, K., Chan, A.H.S.: Gerontechnology acceptance by elderly Hong Kong Chinese: a senior technology acceptance model (STAM) (2014).https://doi.org/10.1080/00140139.2014. 895855
6. Fang, Y.M., Chang, C.C.: Users' psychological perception and perceived readability of wearable devices for elderly people. Behav. Inf. Technol. **35**, 225–232 (2016). https://doi.org/10. 1080/0144929X.2015.1114145
7. Harris, M.T., Rogers, W.A.: Developing a Healthcare Technology Acceptance Model (H-TAM) for older adults with hypertension. Ageing Soc. 1–21 (2021). https://doi.org/10.1017/ S0144686X21001069
8. Li, J., Ma, Q., Chan, A.H., Man, S.S.: Health monitoring through wearable technologies for older adults: Smart wearables acceptance model. Appl. Ergon. **75**, 162–169 (2019). https:// doi.org/10.1016/j.apergo.2018.10.006
9. Zhang, X., Liu, S., Wang, L., Zhang, Y., Wang, J.: Mobile health service adoption in China: integration of theory of planned behavior, protection motivation theory and personal health differences. Online Inf. Rev. **44**, 1–23 (2020). https://doi.org/10.1108/OIR-11-2016-0339
10. Nunes, A., Limpo, T., Castro, S.L.: Acceptance of mobile health applications: examining key determinants and moderators. Front. Psychol. **10**, 1–9 (2019). https://doi.org/10.3389/fpsyg. 2019.02791
11. Zhang, J., Li, Q., Luximon, Y.: Building trust in mobile medical consultations: the roles of privacy concerns, personality traits, and social cues. In: Gao, Q., Zhou, J. (eds.) HCII 2021. LNCS, vol. 12786, pp. 293–304. Springer, Cham (2021). https://doi.org/10.1007/978-3-030-78108-8_22
12. Zhang, J., Luximon, Y., Li, Q.: Seeking medical advice in mobile applications: How social cue design and privacy concerns influence trust and behavioral intention in impersonal patient–physician interactions. Comput. Human Behav. **130**, 107178 (2022). https://doi.org/10.1016/ j.chb.2021.107178
13. Mukai, T., et al.: Development of a nursing-care assistant robot RIBA that can lift a human in its arms. IEEE/RSJ 2010 International Conference on Intelligent Robotics System IROS 2010 – Conference on Proceedings, pp. 5996–6001 (2010). https://doi.org/10.1109/IROS. 2010.5651735
14. Shibata, T., Wada, K.: Robot therapy: a new approach for mental healthcare of the elderly - a mini-review. Gerontology **57**, 378–386 (2011). https://doi.org/10.1159/000319015
15. Bemelmans, R., Gelderblom, G.J., Jonker, P., de Witte, L.: Socially assistive robots in elderly care: a systematic review into effects and effectiveness. J. Am. Med. Dir. Assoc. **13**, 114-120.e1 (2012). https://doi.org/10.1016/j.jamda.2010.10.002
16. Pino, M., Boulay, M., Jouen, F., Rigaud, A.S.: "Are we ready for robots that care for us?" Attitudes and opinions of older adults toward socially assistive robots. Front. Aging Neurosci. **7**, 1–15 (2015). https://doi.org/10.3389/fnagi.2015.00141
17. EuroQol Research Fundation: EQ-5D-5L User Guide (2019)

18. Dermody, G., Fritz, R., Glass, C., Dunham, M., Whitehead, L.: Factors influencing community-dwelling older adults' readiness to adopt smart home technology: a qualitative exploratory study. J. Adv. Nurs. **77**, 4847–4861 (2021). https://doi.org/10.1111/jan.14996

19. Li, Q., Luximon, Y.: Understanding older adults' post-adoption usage behavior and perceptions of mobile technology. Int. J. Des. **12**, 93–110 (2018)

20. Zhang, X., Guo, X., Lai, K.H., Guo, F., Li, C.: Understanding gender differences in m-health adoption: a modified theory of reasoned action model. Telemed. e-Health. **20**, 39–46 (2014). https://doi.org/10.1089/tmj.2013.0092

Correction to: Non-use of Digital Services Among Older Adults During the Second Wave of COVID-19 Pandemic in Finland: Population-Based Survey Study

Petra Saukkonen(iD), Emma Kainiemi(iD), Lotta Virtanen(iD),
Anu-Marja Kaihlanen(iD), Seppo Koskinen(iD), Päivi Sainio(iD),
Päivikki Koponen(iD), Sari Kehusmaa, and Tarja Heponiemi(iD)

Correction to:
Chapter "Non-use of Digital Services Among Older Adults During the Second Wave of COVID-19 Pandemic in Finland: Population-Based Survey Study" in: Q. Gao and J. Zhou (Eds.): *Human Aspects of IT for the Aged Population. Design, Interaction and Technology Acceptance*, LNCS 13330, https://doi.org/10.1007/978-3-031-05581-2_41

In an older version of this paper, the category names (user and non-user) in Table 1, "Characteristics of the respondents according to non-use of digital services" on page 602, were incorrect. This has been corrected.

The updated version of this chapter can be found at
https://doi.org/10.1007/978-3-031-05581-2_41

Author Index

Printed in the United States
by Baker & Taylor Publisher Services